Anthropology of
Humor and
Laughter

Edited by Ewa Wasilewska
University of Utah

San Diego, CA

Bassim Hamadeh, CEO and Publisher
Michael Simpson, Vice President of Acquisitions
Jamie Giganti, Managing Editor
Jess Busch, Graphic Design Supervisor
Jessica Knott, Project Editor
Luiz Ferreira, Licensing Associate

First published in the United States of America in 2013 by Cognella, Inc.

Trademark Notice: Product or corporate names may be trademarks or registered trademarks, and are used only for identification and explanation without intent to infringe.

Printed in the United States of America

ISBN: 978-1-60927-404-7 (pb) / 978-1-60927-405-4 (br)

www.cognella.com 800.200.3908

Contents

CHAPTER 1: TOWARD DEFINITION OF HUMOR ...
PAST, PRESENT, AND FUTURE OF HUMOR RESEARCH

CHAPTER 2: TOWARD DEFINITION OF LAUGHTER ...
LAUGHING DOGS, PANTING CHIMPANZEES, AND PLEASURE-DRIVEN RATS

CHAPTER 3: TOWARD LAUGHTER BENEFITS ...
LE CHAT BOTTÉ (PUSS IN BOOTS) LAUGHS THE BEST

Dedication

To all people, young and old, who suffer from seizure disorders
and those loved ones who care for them and about them...
Don't ever give up!

Preface

If somebody had told me years ago that one day I would be considered an "expert" on laughter and humor, I would have laughed. This has been a long and unexpected journey from archaeology through cultural anthropology to brain and mind research. It has taken me from the deserts of the Middle East through the steppes of Central Asia to a brain trauma unit at the University of Utah Hospital, where I decided that my life is worth living as long as I can laugh. Watching my own seizures on a monitor whose connecting wires were glued to my head with glue that would give Krazy Glue a run for its money, I realized that feeling sorry for myself could be replaced with a lot of laughter (and talking; yes, I can talk… a lot!), frequently disrupting even the worst of the seizures. This was the day I took my interest in laughter and humor to the next level. This was more than a scientific curiosity, this was personal. Consequently, this book is dedicated to all people who suffer from seizure disorders, the condition that afflicts at least 0.5% of the human population but doesn't get much publicity and fundraising support because its symptoms are plain ugly and frightening, while the treatment is only slightly better and not always very effective. The social stigma associated with these disorders is almost impossible to overcome and knowing that in some societies (mostly in the past) I could have been considered a "chosen one" communicating with the supernatural, usually evil, is not of much help. While I no longer need to be afraid of being burned at the stake, explaining to others that some very famous people like Alexander the Great, Julius Caesar, Joan of Arc (not the luckiest one), Napoleon, Lord Byron, Pius IX, Fyodor Dostoyevsky, Vincent van Gogh, and Vladimir Lenin (just to name a few and boast about good company) suffered from this "pathophysiology" but managed to reach their potential and more, is not a very easy task. So possessed or not, I try to do my share of laughing through hard times and joking all the time.

Back to the book… this a hybrid of something old, something new, and something to treat one's blue(s). The "old" refers to the articles/chapters of distinguished scholars, writers, journalists, and commentators, reprinted here for the benefit of the students and readers in general who have an interest in the studies of humor and/or laughter but not much time to explore all their intricacies. This book doesn't pretend to be as comprehensive and in-depth as Mahadev Apte's *Humor and Laughter: An Anthropological Approach*, the most "sacred text" for all students of humor, scientists and enthusiasts alike. Unfortunately, this "bible" of anthropological research on humor was published in 1985 and is presently out of print. While it will never be dated, Apte's work has been expanded with the research of other scholars, who have been using a variety of novel approaches, and frequently focusing on less-than-traditional issues and examples. Globalization has made humor less culture-specific and more accessible than ever before—making it easier to study through modern technological advances but, at the same time, more challenging to understand and discuss. Cosmopolitan communication of humor sometimes oscillates around Western values (the "L.A. Effect," i.e., cultural convergence), at other times causes polarization of national cultures (the "Taliban Effect"), but most of the time meshes all together fusing all national cultures (the "Bangalore Effect").

The "new" refers to my former students' and my own work. I understand that some of my colleagues may feel offended that I have ignored their contributions but… I wanted to have a fresh look and less conventional approach to the topics in which both Martina Volfova (and her co-author, Mercedes Douglass) and John Simpson excelled in my classes. Students' approaches are often more personal, allowing an audience to explore what they have been taking for granted. Giving such students a chance to share their research and ideas with a much wider audience than their peers and instructor only encourages them to join their mentors in the proverbial search for truth.

As for my own work … Some of my interpretations may appear to be somewhat controversial, others unfinished, as they are just proposals of new directions in the study of laughter and humor. However, they are all intended to stir up more dialogue and exploration into the less-known or even unknown aspects of human and animal minds and emotions, as well as of "mechanical," neurological processes leading to the reasoning necessary for the creation of a complex pseudo-reality expressed through humorous "truth."

And, finally, this book is also aimed at those who just want to laugh. Thus, it includes numerous jokes that are often of unknown origin since the Internet is an entity in itself characterized by a rather loose understanding of copyrights. Nevertheless, they are not less appreciated than signed works and I am indebted to their anonymous authors or collectors.

Denise Morgan took a challenge to adapt some pictures for this publication and my former student, Jason Graf, made me laugh with his contribution (my favorite rat ever [not a reference to the student]!). I truly appreciate their sense of humor and hard work.

My most heartfelt gratitude goes to Andy Gowans, my love and my rock, who has never doubted me but questioned medical sciences (and, at times, laws of physics as applicable to my situation), encouraging me to "research" and "experiment" on my own brain. Here, I must thank the producers and writers of *The Big Bang Theory, The Colbert Report, and The Daily Show with Jon Stewart*, for making some of these experiments possible (Sheldon Cooper [Jim Parsons], Steven Colbert, and Jon Stewart—you are my heroes) and providing me with a lot of material to consider when thinking about new hypotheses and evaluating the old ones. Dr. Fumisuke Matsuo has been taking care of me as a patient but also as his less-brilliant student of neurological mysteries of the brain. "Thank you, Sir, and please, don't retire unless we have answers that we seek." There is no way this book would ever be finished without Dr. Silvia Smith, my friend, ad hoc editor of the text, and an assistant on call in the crunchiest of times. I am definitely in her debt. I must thank my best friends, Linda Adams and Elaine Weiss, who have "suffered" through the creative process of this book, listening and challenging me all the time; even worse—they had to keep me focused and laugh at all of my jokes! My thanks must be extended to all of my close friends who are too numerous to mention here, but they are not forgotten. Finally, to all my students who have taken my class on "Anthropology of Humor and Laughter"—thank you for being my inspiration (even if some of your papers should have been eaten by a dog) and your support whenever I needed it. And, no—I won't ever let you text me although, one day, I may join Facebook. "Bazinga!"

—Ewa Wasilewska
Department of Anthropology
University of Utah
Salt Lake City, Utah

Disclaimer

The following disclaimer has been prepared in cooperation with Eric K. Johnson of Smart, Scholfield, Shorter & Lunceford at Salt Lake City, Utah, whose assistance I sought before offering my first class on *Anthropology of Humor and Laughter* at the University of Utah. Some of my colleagues and friends thought that I was overcautious but … We are living in a very litigious society where a few hundred dollars' fee for filing a lawsuit may cost thousands of dollars in securing a "victory" at the end. The original text proposed by Eric that included an Academic Informed Consent Form to be signed by students was little bit too much and none of us wanted to set precedence in academia. The final draft is short and sufficient for all courses I teach and adaptable to this book:

> Some of the writings, lectures, films, or presentations in this course may include material that conflicts with the core beliefs of some students. Please review the syllabus carefully to see if the course is one that you are committed to taking.

> Some of the writings in this book may include material that conflicts with the core beliefs of some readers. Please review the content carefully to see if this book is one that you are committed to reading.

However, my favorite draft of the class disclaimer was a transitional one cited here for… what else… humorous purposes.

To the Student from the Instructor

It is understood that the principles of academic freedom permit topics of all types, including those with offensive content, to be part of courses, lectures, and other academic pursuits. Much of humor is inherently offensive. Indeed, it is the offensive aspect that often makes for the humorous nature of a particular setting.

The materials in this course consist of offensive content that is used or displayed in an educational setting for educational purposes. This course will present students with objects, pictures, videotapes, audio recordings, computer communications, literature, and lectures that are potentially—even certainly—offensive. Offense or the potential for offense is innate to humor. I cannot teach this course fully or effectively without exposing students to much offensive material.

The risks of taking this course include damage to property, personal and/or bodily injury or death, or any other imaginable or unimaginable damage. You are responsible for protecting yourself and you take this course at your own risk.

The [University of Utah] adheres to the principles and traditions of academic freedom, and recognizes that these freedoms take into consideration [the University of Utah's] desire to notify students and their parents or guardians (when the student is a minor or otherwise not an emancipated adult) of the choice of whether or not to be exposed to offensive material and even potentially offensive material.

This course surely contains one or more elements that can and certainly will offend you. This course cannot be all things to all people, nor does it aspire to be. Accordingly, for your protection:

- If you have no tolerance for being offended, you must not take this course.
- If you have little tolerance for being offended, you must not take this course.
- If you wish to avoid being offended, you should avoid this course.
- If you are unsure as to whether or not you may be offended in taking this course, I suggest that you err on the side of caution and not take this course;
- And if, despite these disclaimers, disclosures, and warnings, you take this course and become offended in the course of study, please withdraw from this course immediately for your sake and the sake of everyone and everything else involved in the course, as changing the content of this course after it commences would be no easier or more ludicrous than having a French professor change course to some other language on the basis that you subsequently discovered you struggle with comprehension or pronunciation, or having a Criminal Justice professor eliminate references to and the discussion of assault or murder because the topics upset you.

The content won't change but your mood might, so enjoy reading this book and keep on laughing!

Introduction

Dr. Ewa Wasilewska
Department of Anthropology
University of Utah

"The human race has but one really affective weapon, and that is laughter."
—Mark Twain (1835–1910)
An American humorist, writer, and lecturer.

Humor and laughter (or laughter and humor?)… Neither one is a laughing matter, but are they serious enough to require their own field of studies? Or should scholars who study them be banished to the academic purgatory since wasting one's Ph.D. on a triviality of a seizure-like activity (laughter) or elephant jokes doesn't fit into an image of a serious scientist? Or should we all just keep on laughing and stop dissecting humor like a frog before we kill it?

There are no simple answers because neither laughter nor humor has received proper attention from the scientific world until recently with the creation of such fields as gelotology and paleohumorology. These studies are based on many (but partial) theories of humor, some of which have been proposed hundreds of years ago and retold/reexamined as well as adjusted since then. Most scholars who have worked on humor approached this topic from a psychological point of view, or simply recorded humor-related information as part of ethnographies of various societies in the hope that more data could yield a greater understanding of this pervasive phenomenon. Consequently, humor has been either dissected as a part of human emotions, or discussed with culture-specific examples, which have been subsequently applied to other cultures in comparative studies. Both approaches have been very useful, but their limited scope complicates the discussion of humor as an independent phenomenon whose principles can be applicable through time and space. This has changed with a publication of *Humor and Laughter: An Anthropological Approach* by Mahadev L. Apte in 1985. In the "Preface" to his book, Apte explained his reasons for writing this "bible" of humor in the following words:

> … my own growing interest in the phenomena of humor, my discovery that much research on humor in the social sciences has been carried out by psychologists and lacked a cross-cultural perspective, and my realization in the course of my reading that the anthropological literature included no single comprehensive treatment of the subject (Apte 1985: 9).

Apte's work remains the most important book on humor in spite of many more books and articles that have sprouted as a result of his "comprehensive treatment of the subject." He has accomplished his main goal of stimulating "more anthropological interest in humor" and, *de facto*, established humor as an interdisciplinary field of studies. After all, anthropology as a discipline is the study of human and animal "everything" expanding exponentially, combining data, methods, and theories of many other disciplines. The only shortcoming of Apte's book is the lack of discussion of laughter as a separate phenomenon—a topic that had to wait for its "discoverer," Robert R. Provine, for another twenty-five (25) years to get scholarly attention with his publication of *Laughter: A Scientific Investigation* (2000)[1].

The main hindrance in the studies of laughter and humor is twofold: limited data regarding laughter and almost unlimited data regarding humor. Bringing those two together is a challenge as, inevitably, one must go outside of his/her comfort zone to address both topics sufficiently to do them any justice. This requires an understanding of many topics and familiarity of a researcher with the fields that he or she has never suspected to study, and thus is not really well prepared for. I consider myself lucky that my formal education includes history, archaeology, anthropology, and languages, as well as fieldwork in many regions of Eurasia, from Europe through the Middle East and Central Asia to the Western frontiers of China. However, I have struggled through the mysteries of the brain, as anything starting with "neuro-" was so new to me. Furthermore, my interest in the mechanics and functionality of a human body was very limited. To use anthropological terms, mine was an *emic* approach, since I could easily describe my behavior, disorders, and illnesses, but to explain them any further I relied on trained specialists who are medically and culturally "neutral" (*etic*). Once I decided to study both laughter and humor, I had to venture into new territories. I have learned a lot, or rather enough, to discern valuable information regarding laughter and propose future avenues for its research, but I am still lacking expertise that would provide many answers sought.

Unfortunately, such a handicap is common among most, if not all, scholars studying humor and laughter. There is no Ph.D. in Humor and Laughter Studies, at least not yet. Without it, any attempt on comprehensive treatment of both will always have its shortcomings. However, this doesn't mean that we should give up and limit our research only to our strengths in fear of weaknesses overpowering the value of a more general work. There is no encyclopedia of humor and laughter that covers all their aspects in an adequate manner, but there are very good publications and anthologies directing one's attention to specific topics (e.g., Fry 1963; Legman 1968 and 1975; Chapman and Foot 1976; McGhee 1979; McGhee and Goldstein 1983; Koller 1988; Davies 1990; Wyer and Collins II 1992; Berger 1993; Veatch 1998; Latta 1999; Nilsen and Nilsen 2000; Spalding 2001; Billig 2005; Gervais and Wilson 2005; Martin 2006; Ferguson and Ford 2008; Morreall 2009; Kozintsev and Martin 2010). The approach presented in this book is somewhat different as it is more general, tackling a variety of issues through a combination of general introduction and more specialized articles/chapters serving as either more in-depth explanations, examples of practical applications, or a more specialized issue-oriented research. While the majority of humor discussed here is contemporary and oriented toward a North American audience, the effort was made to use as many universal examples of humor as possible from the contexts that are easily accessible through the Internet. Some categories of humor, e.g., political humor[2], have only been referenced as their examples might be already dated by the time of publication, or have been discussed as a part of

---

1 This does not mean that there were no other publications before this date either by Provine or by others (see bibliography). However, Provine has made this topic the subject in itself, gaining attention from both scientists and laypersons.

2 *God is a Republican and Santa Claus is a Democrat.*

God is an elderly or, at any rate, middle-aged male, a stern fellow, patriarchal rather than paternal and a great believer in rules and regulations. He holds men strictly accountable for their actions. He has little apparent concern for the material well-being of the disadvantaged. He is politically connected, socially powerful, and holds the mortgage on literally everything in the world. God is difficult. God is unsentimental. It is very hard to get into God's heavenly country club.

a larger group. Literary works, comedic in their character, are not included here since they are best examined by literary critics, rather than by anthropologists interested in humor and laughter. However, the main strength or weakness of this book is that it postulates viewing humor and laughter as an X-factor necessary for physical existence of humans and possibly even for other animals.

SECTION 1
TOWARD DEFINITION OF HUMOR:
Past, Present, and Future of Humor Research.

"Humor is just another defense against the universe."
—Mel Brooks (1926–)
An American film director, producer, screenwriter, comedian, and actor.

N one of the humor theories has been universally accepted because the definition of humor is an elusive one and, as many other difficult-to-define concepts, is more "felt" than "measured." The elusiveness of the humor definition can be compared to impreciseness of elucidation of another concept to which humor is related: that of religion. Since humor in religion and about religions is discussed below, the focus here is only on definition of humor as compared to a myth, one of the main components of any definition of religion (e.g., Durkheim 1954, 1972; Wallace 1966). However, it is not only about the clarification of meaning, which is necessary to define any concept; it is also about its physical presence as one of our senses without which our quality of life is diminished. Moreover, when viewed in connection with laughter, which is a physiological reaction, it may even signal the end of life as we know it. This proposition may seem somewhat radical but… one must remember that death can be, and is medically defined as, a permanent and irreversible cessation of brain activity. While the focus of numerous discussions about when life ends and death begins is on cognitive functions performed in and by the cerebral cortex, the most ancient and basic part of the brain is the subcortex (lower brain) that regulates vital "biological" functions of our bodies, i.e., is responsible for basic survival needs/instincts/functions including eating, drinking, mating, breathing, etc. It is argued here that humor, either its most "primitive" or complex form, is an indication of functionality of the brain cortex, while laughter is one of the vital functions "controlled" by the subcortex[3]. Consequently, damage to one results in malfunctioning of the other, thus potentially leading to death[4].

Santa Claus is another matter. He's cute. He's non-threatening. He's always cheerful. And he loves animals. He may know who's been naughty and who's been nice, but never does anything about it. He gives everyone everything they want without thought of quid pro quo. He works hard for charities, and he's famously generous to the poor. Santa Claus is preferable to God in every way but one: There is no such thing as Santa Claus (O'Rourke 1991: xx).

3   I agree with Kozintsev and Martin (2010) that there is only one kind of laughter. The division proposed by Keltner and Bonanno (1997) and strongly "defended" by Gervais and Wilson (2005) into so-called Duchenne laughter and non-Duchenne laughter is not only superficial but simply incorrect because laughter is different from smiling. See more discussion in Section 2 of this Introduction and Chapter 2.

4   The Uniform Death Determination Act of 1980 refers to recognition of human death as follows: "Part (1) codifies the existing common law basis for determining death—total failure of the cardiorespiratory system. Part (2) extends the common law to include the new procedures for determination of death based upon irreversible loss of all brain functions.

As Latta has noted "Humor is a genuine mystery… "since"…[D]espite centuries and indeed millennia of effort, however, no one has succeeded in determining just what it is at bottom" (1999: 3). He is correct; many have tried but seem to ultimately fail in defining humor as new theories and/or objections to old ones have been continuously proposed, polished, and stirred. More than "100 theories," and this term is being used here very loosely, have been identified by different scholars (e.g., Schmidt and Williams 1971; Lyttle 2003) and many of them have been a topic of numerous reviews since the day of their publication. As these studies are all important to specialized studies of humor, I will list them here using the most concise summary found in a Ph.D. dissertation of Jim Lyttle partially published on Internet at http://myweb.brooklyn.liu.edu/jlyttle/Humor/Theory.htm:

> One very influential review is that of Patricia Keith-Spiegel (1972), who created a typology of eight categories. The first category consisted of biological theories (e.g., Darwin, 1872), which suggest that humor is an adaptive disposition. The second category consisted of superiority theories (e.g., Hobbes, 1968 [1996]), which suggest that people laugh at others to whom they feel superior. The third category consisted of incongruity theories (e.g., Kant, 1951 [1987]), which suggest that humor consists of incongruous events and situations. The fourth category consisted of surprise theories (e.g., Descartes, 1649 [1985]), which suggest that humor requires suddenness and therefore weakens with repeated exposure. The fifth category consisted of ambivalence theories (e.g., Joubert, 1980), which suggest that humor is the result of opposing emotions or ideas within an appreciator. The sixth category consisted of release theories (e.g., Spencer, 1860 [1966]), which suggest that humor is experienced when people are relieved from strain or stress. The seventh category consisted of configuration theories (e.g., Maier, 1932), which suggest that humor depends directly on the resolution of incongruities. The eighth category consisted of psychoanalytic theories (e.g., Freud, 1928), which suggest that humor results from economies of psychic energy that has been built up by and for repression (Lyttle: 2003).

Lyttle then continued to syncretize them into a more manageable number of categories as based on function "(biological, psychoanalytic or relief, and ambivalence theories)," stimuli "(incongruity, surprise, and configuration theories)" and response to humor "(superiority, and the newer cognitive theories")." With so many theories of humor that need to be categorized, re-categorized, syncretized, de-syncretized, grouped, re-grouped, constructed, de-constructed, argued, etc., how then can I justify my opening statement that "neither laughter nor humor has received proper attention from the scientific world?" The answer is very simple—somehow, many theories seem to have lost the focus of the theorized issue, humor. Amazingly, there are articles and books written about humor without one "funny" example. In the process of dissecting a proverbial frog, it seems that the frog disappeared and its imprint has become a subject of the autopsy. While humor might be some or all the things claimed by different authors, there is only one thing that we can be sure about—humor is funny and we laugh at it because we enjoy and appreciate its content,

The overwhelming majority of cases will continue to be determined according to part (1). When artificial means of support preclude a determination under part (1), the Act recognizes that death can be determined by the alternative procedures.
Under part (2), the entire brain must cease to function, irreversibly. The 'entire brain' includes the brain stem, as well as the neocortex. The concept of 'entire brain' distinguishes determination of death under this Act from 'neocortical death' or 'persistent vegetative state.' These are not deemed valid medical or legal bases for determining death" (Uniform Law Commission. The National Conference of Commissioners on Uniform State Laws http://www.nccusl.org/Act.aspx?title=Determination%20of%20Death%20Act

structure, delivery, and context. It is inherent in human (might be even in non-human animal) nature, not an "artificial" construct like religion, which humans have "created" in order to survive, co-operate, and adapt to their changing environment. Humor is simply "there" in our nature and must be there for a reason as it is strongly connected with laughter, a physiological response to it. This means that trying to define humor by arguing whether superiority, surprise, relaxation or lack of thereof, incongruity, congruency, relief, stress, aggression, etc., are the main or even only components of humor is more or less an exercise in futility. It would produce a lot of dissertations and a myriad of acrimonious articles that may provide us with better tools and methodologies to analyze humor, but it won't define the core of its existence. While its existence can be proven, its non-existence cannot be argued for as even the so-called humorless people enjoy humor and those whose cognitive abilities have been impaired by brain damage may still enjoy a slapstick type of comedy. Humor ceases to exist when the whole body stops functioning and laughter can no longer occur as its result due to the physical deterioration of the entire system, which makes humor possible in the first place. Thus, Descartes' statement *"Je pense donc je suis"* (*Discourse on Method* 1637; here 1985) made famous in Latin as *cogito ergo sum* ("I think, therefore I am [exist]"), can be adjusted from a "humor and humorous" point of view to *rideo ergo sum*—"I laugh, therefore I exist."

Credo ergo sum, "I believe, therefore I exist," is applicable to the human practice of religion that involves the presence of two components: myth and ritual. While humor is used in religious rituals or can be considered a ritual in itself (a stretch, but still possible), myths are a humorous or humorless version of truthiness[5] on which humor is based. Consequently, humor can be defined as a myth if one applies Strensky's definition of myth to humor as being,

> Everything and nothing at the same time. It is the true story or a false one, revelation or decep-
> tion, sacred or vulgar, real or fictional, symbol or tool, archetype or stereotype. It is either
> strongly structured and logical or emotional and pre-logical, traditional and primitive or part
> of contemporary ideology. Myth is about the gods, but often also the ancestors and sometimes
> certain men… Such confusion indicates graphically enough that there is no such "thing" as myth
> (1987: 1).

However, myths exist and so does humor. While myths focus on more divine, spiritual, and unknown elements of the human universe explained through archetypes, humor is mundane, based on real or perceived knowledge often displayed through stereotypes. Congruity between sacred and profane is sought through myths, while incongruity in humor deconstructs perceived reality[6]. Their structure and logic are both affective as they are creating cohesiveness among a group through sharing a message whose truthfulness or fallacy is acceptable to its members. While both address, in different degrees, what is

---

5   Defined by Stephen Colbert as "truth that comes from the gut, not books" (*The Colbert Report*, October 2005), "truthiness" has been officially elected as the 16th annual Word of the Year by the American Dialect Society and defined as "the quality of preferring concepts or facts one wishes to be true, rather than concepts or facts known to be true" (American Dialect Society, January 6, 2006). On its way to the top, it knocked out the competition including such words as "podcast," "intelligent design" and the President Bush's phrase "heck of the job." www.americandialect.org/Words_of_the_Year_2005.pdf

6   While I agree with Latta (1998) that humor might be defined by our response, i.e., in his proposed Theory L, by relaxation that is the result of laughter induced by humor (a physiological reaction discussed later in this book), I also believe that incongruity of humor cannot be ignored regardless of whether it is resolved or not. His theory as well as Berlyne's earlier proposal (1969) belongs to the so-called cognitive theories category in which humor as a stimulus is not really important—the physical response is (Berlyne, a state of arousal; Latta, relaxation and pleasure).

sacred in a society, vulgarity is not uncommon in their expression. There are no topics too irrelevant to be an object of their attention, though settings can be both fictional and rooted in reality. After all, they are just stories of different lengths that are created to do one thing and one thing only—to make a point (or points).

Myths and humor are both an important part of human history as well as of our everyday activities, whether on a conscious or subconscious level. The use of humor is much more frequent than that of myths, as humorous situations are often created spontaneously in response to a variety of human emotions, behaviors, and physically restrained or freely floating environments, regardless of one's beliefs and ideological systems followed. Most of our humor comes not from movies, YouTube, cartoons, stand-up comedians, or even jokes exchanged in public and private fora; rather, it comes from interactions with each other and even from disappointments and failures that are so plentiful in our daily lives[7]. Humor seems to be inherent in human nature in its unstructured and emotional form, which can in turn morph into structured and logical social practices whenever desired. While the latter requires a complex cognitive processing[8] involving the same parts of the brain as those used in solving complicated mathematical formulas, the former is more responsive[9] and intuitive, resulting in laughter over which we have no or little control as it is produced in our subcortex where basic moods and motivations are "stored."

It is the structured humor that has drawn the attention of many scholars who tried to explain its role in human societies. From ancient thinkers to modern scientists, the focus has been on humor as some sort of an adaptive strategy allowing humans to express their deepest desires, transform socially unacceptable behaviors into tolerable communication tools, and to assert one's perceived superiority over others, even if only for a moment. Thus, most theories of humor oscillate about its "usefulness" in creating and resolving incongruities, in reflecting affectivity and/or expression of sexual and aggressive impulses, and in establishing, maintaining, and reinforcing social integration or social seclusion, even isolation. The most inclusive of all theories might be evolutionary theories that have sprouted in the last twenty years or so, pointing out to adaptive qualities of humor and laughter, although the latter seems to be more of a biological issue than of social adaptation.

The present and the future of humor research, as well as of "topics potentially salient to the evolution of humor" are presented here, as the first chapter, through an excellent article entitled, *The First Joke: Exploring the Evolutionary Origins of Humor,* written by Joseph Polimeni and Jeffrey P. Reiss and originally published in *Evolutionary Psychology* (2006). Many of these topics, among the others, are addressed in this

---

7   For example, when in Syria in 2008, my driver and I were regularly followed by the not-so-secret Syrian police (*mukhabarat*) when traveling in non-tourist areas. Regardless of their motives (protection or an attempt to catch a dangerous "spy" like me), they were on our tail almost continuously. However, one day it seemed that inadvertently we "lost" them only to receive a phone call, "Please, slow down. Our car is too old to keep up with you!"

8   *Question: What is the truest definition of Globalization? Answer: Princess Diana's death.*
Question: How come? Answer: An English princess with an Egyptian boyfriend crashes in a French tunnel, driving a German car with a Dutch engine, driven by a Belgian who was drunk on Scottish whiskey, followed closely by Italian paparazzi on Japanese motorcycles, treated by an American doctor, using Brazilian medicines! And this is sent to you by an American, using Bill Gates' technology, which he enjoyed stealing from the Japanese. And you are probably reading this on one of the IBM clones that use Taiwanese-made chips, and Korean-made monitors, assembled by Bangladeshi workers in a Singapore plant, transported by trucks driven by Indians, hijacked by Indonesians, unloaded by Sicilian longshoremen, trucked by Mexican illegal aliens, and finally sold to you. That, my friend, is Globalization! Finally, an explanation in English.

9   During my lonely travels through the Middle East, Central Asia, or China, I often hire a driver to share adventures with me, which I try to describe briefly when sending email updates to my friends whenever possible. One of my comments from Iran in 2004 regarding my driver read as follows: "Honestly, I have no idea why at the beginning of my trip all my drivers want to marry me but at the end all are looking for a place to bury me." My friends are still laughing about this line—presumably because they know the answer.

book, although not in the order listed by Polimeni and Reiss. This article was selected because of its least bias and its briefness (less than a couple of volumes) in summarizing past and present research and in proposing new avenues for the study of humor as based on evolutionary theories. Additionally, it points our attention to the possible importance of humor in understanding human behavior from a simple play through language to religion and even a group size. Hence, it plays straight into my belief that humor is innate and, in combination with laughter, humor acts like an X-factor of the human body. Its (humor and/or laughter) malfunction signal a physical disorder and its non-functioning can be equated with death of the whole system.

SECTION 2
TOWARD DEFINITION OF LAUGHTER:
Laughing Dogs, Panting Chimpanzees, and Pleasure-Driven Rats.

"If we may believe our logicians, man is distinguished from all other creatures by the faculty of laughter. He has a heart capable of mirth, and naturally disposed to it."
—*Joseph Addison (1672–1719)*
An English essayist, poet, and dramatist.

One of the most common misconceptions is equating humor with laughter. In all probability laughter predates humor, although it is a visual and auditory expression of its appreciation. However, laughter is an uncontrollable physiological reaction[10], independent of humor, as it may occur in response to or triggered by such strong emotions as pleasure/happiness, anger, embarrassment, and even fear. While humor is a complex cognitive process, laughter is a much "simpler" activity that can be activated, with little or no cognition at all, in the subcortical parts of our brain. Laughter can also be induced "mechanically" by tickling and probably by manipulating/touching the so-called center of laughter, which is believed to be located in the left superior frontal gyrus (a part of frontal lobe) (Fried et al. 1998) or in some other areas of the brain[11]. Consequently, since laughter's neural circuits (sort of a terminal) seem to be located in the most ancient parts of the brain (subcortex), there is a strong possibility that all mammals (at least) have an ability to laugh, although their laughter is not necessary vocalized and thus may remain unrecognized.

The most visible physical manifestation of human laughter is its sound/acoustics, or rather a series of sounds ("ha-ha," "ho-ho," or "he-he"). This obvious connection of laughter with vocalization is even reflected in the onomatopoeic[12] etymology of the English verb "to laugh" from the Old English *hliehhan*, which can in turn be traced back to the Proto-Germanic *hlahjanan* derived from the reconstructed Proto-Indo-European *klek-, *kleg-, *klak-, *klag- ("to shout"). However, there is a strong possibility that

---

10 The so-called involuntary/emotional laughter in contrast to "natural" laughter induced, for example, by humor. This does not mean, however, that there are different types of laughter; what is different are stimuli, cognitive or not.

11 Whether there is one or more "centers" or just a network of systems responsible for eliciting laughter remains to be seen.

12 Words formed from sounds associated with them.

vocalized laughter is actually the most "recent"[13] form of laughter, preceded by some other form of non-vocalized or non-audible laughter-like-activity seen, for example, in rats and dogs. The neurological and physiological characteristics and origination of laughter are the topic of the second chapter focusing on the origin of laughter, its "location," and processing as an important part of human physiology. It also further explores the possibility that laughter is not limited to humans as it plays an important, if not vital, role in the proper functioning of a whole system. Panksepp postulates the once almost-inconceivable idea[14] of the affective nature of animal minds, even in "low" ones such as rats, and rejects neural reductionism. The notion that affective experiences might be responsible for behavioral choices not only in humans but also in other animals is, in my opinion, more than plausible because, as Panksepp pointed out,

> There is little doubt among neurogeneticists, neuroanatomists, neurochemists and neurophysiologists that basic neurophysiological mechanisms are remarkably similar in all mammals and that many of the functional controls can be traced much further down in phylogeny (2007: 236).

The conventional resistance of the academic world toward anthropomorphizing animal behavior, i.e., considering it also an affective one, rather than merely instinctive (reinforcement theory), might be at least partially caused by the lack of a general agreement on research methodologies that can empirically show the existence of emotions and their importance in animals. As one of the reviewers of Panksepp's original article reportedly stated, "Even if this phenomenon is true, you [Panksepp] would never be able to convince your colleagues" (2007: 234). So, rats (and other animals) may indeed laugh, but some scholars may never get a "joke," because laughter, in all probability, is more than an expression of emotions but also a means of communication preceding the origin of speech.

SECTION 3
TOWARD LAUGHTER BENEFITS ...
Le Chat Botté (Puss in Boots) Laughs the Best.

"Laughter—An interior convulsion, producing a distortion of the features and accompanied by inarticulate noises. It is infectious and, though intermittent, incurable."
—Ambrose Bierce (1842–1914)
An American newspaperman and short-story writer.

Vocalized or not, laughter is like "modeling head to toe,"[15] i.e., it involves the whole body as laughing is an involuntary[16], respiratory–emotional behavior, with its center (sort of a push-button) being

---

13   To be counted in millions of years.

14   More and more scholars begin recognizing the affective nature of animals other than humans (see Chapter 2).

15   Tyra Banks' advice to young wanna-be models on her popular show *America's Next Top Model*.

16   It must be noted here that, as explained in the chapter itself, laughter elicited by humor is somewhat less involuntary because it involves cognitive and emotional processing of information leading to its final outcome in the form of laughter or any other emotion as based on other variables.

located in the region of the supplementary motor area (SMA), which has long been suspected to be associated with the initiation of speech and movement. Thus, one should not be surprised that benefits of laughter seem to extend beyond the feelings of pleasure (the limbic system) to actual physical benefits assuring well-functioning of a whole body.

Perceived physical benefits of laughter are commonly extended to humor since these two behaviors are closely connected. Consequently, gelotology, the science of laughter born in 1960s, focuses on the effects that laughter has on the human body and psyche through its induction by the means of humor. Although gelotology didn't start as a search for purely medical benefits of laughter (Krois et al. 2007: 200), it soon became such with the work of the renowned psychiatrist William F. Fry (e.g., 1966; 1994). The appeal of laughter as a natural healer was broadly popularized by the publication of the *Anatomy of an Illness* article by Norman Cousins in 1976 (followed by the book in 1979), which narrates his story of curing himself from a painful degenerative disease (a form of arthritis known as *ankylosing spondylitis*) with mega-doses of vitamin C and comedy shows. He reported that, among other things, "ten minutes of solid belly laughter would give [him] two hours of pain-free sleep" (1989: 126). This has led to the development of several therapies that use humor-induced laughter to help patients suffering from a variety of ailments. Unfortunately, the success of such therapies like laughter meditation, laughter yoga[17], holy laughter, etc., is difficult to measure since many of such therapies take place outside of any medical settings and are led by enthusiasts, rather than by scientists. The exploitation and commercialization of laughter and humor as "the best medicine" that can free you of any problems, improve your work performance, make you look younger and more desirable, etc., have been inimical to serious research on these topics. The possibility that laughter is an adaptive strategy to promote the healthy maintenance of the human body (laughter as "natural" healer) is explored in Chapter 3 of this book. However, one must be warned here that even, or especially, Robert R. Provine[18], a leader in evolutionary approach to laughter, scolds enthusiasts of "Laughing Your Way to Health," stating that "laughter no more evolved to make us feel good or improve our health than walking evolved to promote cardiovascular fitness" (2000: 189–191). While this statement might be difficult to challenge, I believe that there is a basic fallacy involved in the statement itself. Provine is correct in maintaining that walking did not "evolve[d] to promote cardiovascular fitness," but since he is not proposing any specific function for the existence of laughter, one cannot eliminate the possibility that it evolved to assist with general maintenance of a body, perhaps even promoting its self-healing. If this is the case, the role of laughter in humans (and perhaps other creatures) might be similar to feline purring, whose frequencies seem to correspond to a self-repairing of the system. Once again then, humans may laugh, but cats may get a joke.

17   One of the leading yoga research organizations is SVYASA in Bangalore, India, that conducts research on the effects of yoga (including laughter yoga) on almost everything (or rather everyone).

18   Most of the references to Provine's work are made to his book; its publication in 2000 followed a number of articles in which Provine had been developing his ideas regarding laughter (see bibliography).

SECTION 4
TOWARD AGGRESSION AND OFFENSIVENESS:
Sticks and Stones May Break My Bones But Words Will Never Hurt Me.

"Against the assault of laughter nothing can stand."
—Mark Twain (1835–1910)
An American humorist, writer, and lecturer.

Fascination with gelotology has pushed paleohumorology and humorology into the background as any theory of humor and its practice explores the darkest side of humor—its offensiveness.

All humor is offensive. There is no such a beast as innocent humor because there is always someone who might be "hurt" by its content or setting. Fortunately, in most cases, the response to the offensiveness of humor is not violent and rarely legally pursued (cats, dogs, elephants and the like don't sue, at least not yet[19]). However, this doesn't mean that humor is harmless, whether at the individual or societal level. Humor promotes cohesiveness among various groups as easily as it destroys it, propagating divisiveness along boundaries that otherwise remain unexpressed due to numerous factors of which political correctness and rules of social "etiquette," for example in the United States, are most common. Humor is a tool with an infinite potential to reflect and shape social values and attitudes, although most humorous situations, as coming from our daily routines and due to the repetitive nature of jokes, are not intended (i.e., not on a conscious level) to carry a scholarly overanalyzed hidden, or not-so-hidden, message. Do popular mother-in-law[20] jokes help us to release hidden aggression toward them without physically harming them? Or do they reinforce hostile attitudes toward them by creating/maintaining a culture in which acting on such attitudes is acceptable because, after all, these jokes are so hilarious that they cannot be "so bad"? What about structured humor of stand-up comedians who have built their careers on exposing societal incongruities although, at the same time, they are a part of a group that they ridicule and offend? Stephen Colbert is my very favorite comedian and a "practicing Catholic"[21] whose numerous skits involve making fun of Christianity (and religions in general) by exposing the incongruities

---

19   *A cat dies and goes to Heaven. God meets him at the gate and says, "You've been a good cat all of these years. Anything you desire is yours, all you have to do is ask."*

The cats says, "Well, I lived all my life with a poor family on a farm and had to sleep on hardwood floors." God says, "Say no more." And instantly, a fluffy pillow appears. A few days later, six mice are killed in a tragic accident and they go to Heaven. God meets them at the gate with the same offer that He made the cat. The mice said, "All our lives we've had to run. We've been chased by cats, dogs, and even women with brooms. If we could only have a pair of roller skates, we wouldn't have to run anymore." God says, "Say no more." And instantly, each mouse is fitted with a beautiful pair of tiny roller skates.

About a week later, God decides to check and see how the cat is doing. The cat is sound asleep on his new pillow. God gently wakes him and asks, "How are you doing? Are you happy here?"

The cat yawns and stretches and says, "Oh, I've never been happier in my life. And those Meals on Wheels you've been sending over are the best!"

20   *George went on a vacation to the Middle East with most of his family, including his mother-in-law. During their vacation, and while they were visiting Jerusalem, George's mother-in-law died. With the death certificate in hand, George went to the American Consulate Office to make arrangements to send the body back to the States for proper burial. The Consul, after hearing of the death of the mother-in-law, told George, "My friend, the sending of a body back to the States for burial is very, very expensive. It could cost as much as 5,000 dollars." The Consul continued, "In most of these cases, the person responsible for the remains normally decides to bury the body here. This would only cost 150 dollars." George thinks for some time, and answers the Consul, "I don't care how much it will cost to send the body back. That's what I want to do." The Consul, after hearing this says, "You must have loved your mother-in-law very much, considering the difference in price between 5,000 and 150 dollars." "No, it's not that," says George. "You see, I know of a case many, many years ago of a person who was buried here in Jerusalem, and on the third day he was resurrected. Consequently, I do not want to take that chance!"*

21   A humorous (incongruous) designation by itself as a non-practicing Catholic is simply an oxymoron. What is left of Catholicism (or any other religion), if its rituals, moral codes, etc., are not practiced and a story of Adam and Eve loses its validity in view of scientific evidence?

of religious beliefs. Take, for example, his monologues "Yahweh or No Way" from 2011 in which he refers to God as a "gaffe machine" whose approval rating of 52% is low in America because "the public is always tough on any prominent figure who has a child out of wedlock." He is notorious for making fun of "God's logic as written in the Bible, every word of which is true, and we know every word is true because the Bible says that the Bible is true…" *(Islam versus Christianity: Which Is Right?).* This also applies to religious functionaries, rituals, and believers who ascribe to any faith. There seems to be nothing too sacred for him to address on *The Colbert Report* (lose the "t's" when pronouncing) or on his website "Colbert Nation." Colbert's characterization of the Christian God and his followers is no doubt offensive to some Christians, but does it reinforce anti-religious attitudes contributing to the godless society so much feared by many of our politicians? Or is this harmless fun at the expense of one's religion without having a major impact on social dynamics?

All humor is offensive, but is it equal? Tucker Max, a blogger, writer, producer, and Internet phenomenon has millions of followers, especially among young college students. On his website, TuckerMax.com, he introduces himself as

> My name is Tucker Max, and I am an asshole.
> I get excessively drunk at inappropriate times, disregard social norms, indulge every whim, ignore the consequences of my actions, mock idiots and posers, sleep with more women than is safe or reasonable, and just generally act like a raging dickhead.
> But, I do contribute to humanity in one very important way. I share my adventures with the world. They are known as… The Tucker Max stories http://www.tuckermax.com

His stories, full of vulgarities, are narratives of his "adventures," more often than not involving excessive drinking and easy hook-ups. Never a member of a fraternity, Tucker Max is considered to be one of the founders of a new genre, *fratire*, that "represents the non-mainstream literary reaction to the feminization of masculinity" or, simply, "nothing more than men writing about being men in an honest and authentic way" (Tucker Max, *Pass the Beer: In Defense of "Fratire.* http://www.tuckermax.com/other/pass-the-beer-in-defense-of-fratire/ His views on feminism might be considered controversial and his understanding of masculinity, by his own admission, is still in its formative stage. However, his humor has already been the subject of a few lawsuits and he's been pronounced "a poster child for […] vulgarity" by Judge Stewart R. Dalzell of the United States District Court for the Eastern District of Pennsylvania (http://brian.carnell. com/articles/2006/dimeo-v-max/). His critics point out that he promotes "a culture of rape" and "blurs the lines between offensiveness and humor" creating "a culture that can reinforce misogynistic attitudes" (for example, Miller and Ekin 2010). However, Tucker Max is a supporter of women's rights, and agrees "with the basic tenet of feminism—that women are legally and morally equal to men and should have every opportunity that men do" (http://www.tuckermax.com/other/pass-the-beer-in-defense-of-fratire/).

What Colbert and Tucker Max have in common is the potential of high offensiveness in their humor. While Colbert's comments about religion may seem to be less offensive due to their relatively low degree of vulgarity and only subtle references to sex, they could be perceived as much stronger material because it "attacks" what is sacred; for example, in the U.S., Christian religion. He is making fun of God in the country whose level of religiosity is comparable to some Middle Eastern countries like Lebanon (between 65% and 70%) and definitely the highest among all so-called industrialized countries. However, with the exception of a few zealots, Colbert's humor is a mainstream humor, widely accepted and even encouraged. On the other hand, Tucker Max's humor, although it evokes laughter in over a million people in the U.S., is considered to cross the line between "offensiveness and humor." This is not due to its vulgarity, but rather to the sensitivity of the topic, as he often focuses on women, who some argue should require special protection from misogynistic attacks. The irony is that, at the same time, women are considered perfectly capable of taking care of themselves, and Tucker Max's sexual conquests might as well be their sexual conquests since they do have a choice on whether or not they want to hook up with a self-proclaimed jerk. The differences between these two types of humor, religious and sexual/aggression, are discussed in appropriate chapters of this book; here the key word, *offensiveness*, is an inherent part of humor: it exists outside of humor but humor cannot exist without offensiveness. Thus, the fourth chapter of this book focuses on the offensiveness of humor and on basic elements and functions on which different theories of humor are based that make humor such an effective tool in communicating everything and nothing at the same time. This chapter also argues that while offensiveness is in the eye of the beholder, the so-called hate humor crosses a proverbial line as it can be defined in terms of instigation of physical violence and direct interference with a human life.

SECTION 5
TOWARD VERBAL EXPRESSIONS ... You Speak Funny.

"If every word I said could make you laugh, I'd talk forever..."
—The Beach Boys
An American rock band. From "Forever" lyrics, written by Dennis Wilson

Human communications include language, a highly sophisticated network of symbolic connections whose effectiveness relies on a very complex network of relationships within the human brain, especially of the cortex. Since humans are the only animals seemingly using language[22] for

---

22   It must be clarified here that vocalized communication is not foreign to other animals but the question of whether or not this vocalized communication can actually be compared to human speech and therefore language is a subject of ongoing research (e.g., Hocket 1963). While there seems to be little doubt as to the intentional character of at least some vocalized "messages," these appear to be rather limited in their scope relating to survival needs only. However, the existence of "language" (and I use this term very loosely) in its non-vocalized, "gesture" form leading to its full vocalization with humans has been suggested for the members of the Hominoidea superfamily, i.e., apes and humans (by various scholars, e.g., Corballis 2002, Byrne 2006; Pollick and de Waal 2007) as a part of the so-called multimodal animal

communication, so far it is impossible to understand the so-called brain linguistic system as based on animal models[23]. However, the beauty of studying language and the brain is that the understanding of the brain pathways involved in processing linguistic information is also responsible for our understanding of brain structure (the neural network), and vice versa (Lamb 1999). Language itself sort of "exhausts" our brain resources since not only a speaker is creating a very complex symbolic product but, at the same time, he or she must evaluate comprehension and appreciation of this product by another party. Once humor is added to the already busy network of interconnected neurons involved in the linguistic processing, an additional network of symbolic connections is imposed, leading to the desired outcome, i.e., laughter as cognitively induced seizure-like activity ("modeling from head to toe"). The superimposing of separate—but connected—networks of symbols is further complicated by the main characteristic of humor: its incongruity[24]. Consequently, the so-called switching scripts, or

---

communication. The so-called gestural flexibility hypothesis suggests that gestures might "have acquired symbolic meaning in early hominins" (Pollick and de Wall 2007: 8187) since they are less connected with specific emotions than facial expressions and vocalizations are and require more of the cortical control of the brain. Furthermore, "gestures seem subject to modification, conventionalization, and social transmission" (ibid: 8188) in a similar way as a language is.

23   For more discussion on language and speech in connection with laughter, see Chapter 2 of this book.

24   Example of the so-called Bushisms (President George W. Bush's "struggles" with English):

"Neither in French nor in English nor in Mexican."—declining to answer reporters' questions at the Summit of the Americas, Quebec City, Canada, April 21, 2001

"Rarely is the question asked: Is our children learning?"—Florence, S.C., Jan. 11, 2000

"You teach a child to read, and he or her will be able to pass a literacy test."—Townsend, Tenn., Feb. 21, 2001

"Too many good docs are getting out of the business. Too many OB/GYNs aren't able to practice their love with women all across the country."—Poplar Bluff, Mo., Sept. 6, 2004

"There's a huge trust. I see it all the time when people come up to me and say, 'I don't want you to let me down again.'"—Boston, Oct. 3, 2000

frames, due to humor-introduced incongruities requires re-interpretation of an underlying "normal" script[25] within its social framework as an additional "interference" that entails an executive center of the brain to "kick in." This complexity of the language-based humor may suggest that, as Polimeni and Reiss have already noted, "humor may arguably be humankind's most complex cognitive attribute" (2006, p. 348). Furthermore, if one accepts verbal (and its offshoot, textual) humor as a sort of linguistic tickling, then it is quite plausible that this cognitive tickling might be an equivalent (or close to it) of physical tickling and of social grooming among primates. After all, these activities activate the limbic system where the pleasure center, associated with laughter, among other things, is located. As the enjoyment linked with these activities increases, so does communication and social bonding among both humans and non-human primates. This connection between social grooming and laughter and/or language as a "replacement" for grooming among humans has been previously postulated by different scholars (e.g., Dunbar 1993; Aiello and Dunbar 1993; Dunbar 1998; Barret, Dunbar, and Lycett 2002; Polimeni and Reiss 2006). Although the verbal humor might not have facilitated the development of language as Polimeni and Reiss suggest (2006), it has definitely expanded our options for making either friends or enemies and, consequently, regulating and "manipulating" interactions with other individuals. Thus, the importance of language in humor[26] and language play are the topics of the fifth chapter addressed by my former graduate student, Martina Volfova (presently at Northern Arizona University, Flagstaff, AZ) and her colleague, also a graduate student, Mercedes Douglass (the University of California, Los Angeles).

SECTION 6
TOWARD CONFLICT RESOLUTION …
Thank you for Insulting.

"You are not angry with people when you laugh at them. Humor teaches tolerance."
W. Somerset Maugham (1874–1965).
An English novelist and playwright.

The complex network of symbolic associations necessary for humor creation and processing must be activated and conceptualized in order to produce a humorous result. This implies intent of the humor creator to generate a story, whether true or false, real or fictional, or based on archetypes and/ or stereotypes[27]. While this is true when humor is to be created as a conscious effort (e.g., comedians, writers, cartoonists, et al.), most humorous situations are not created but re-created or re-transmitted (structured humor) or arise spontaneously. The phenomenon known as a "joking relationship" is a

---

25   For fundamentals of linguistic theories of humor see works of Victor Raskin (*Semantic Script Theory of Humor* [SSTH]) and Salvatore Attardo (General Theory of Verbal Humor [GTVH]) as listed in the bibliography. An excellent summary of theories and future venues for the research on this topic are reviewed by Geert Brône and Kurt Feyaerts in their paper "The Cognitive Linguistics of Incongruity Resolution: Marked Reference-Point Structures in Humor," presented at the session on "Cognitive Linguistic Approaches to Humor," held at the 8th International Cognitive Linguistics Conference (Logroño 2003).

26   The focus is on performance, intersubjectivity, and multivocality.

27   One must remember that these two terms, archetype and stereotype, are not mutually exclusive.

combination of all the above "humor-creation scenarios" as it is both created and re-created/re-transmitted involving spontaneity within its institutionalized framework. First observed among small-scale, pre-literate societies whose structural ties can be relatively easily discerned due to their group size, the "joking relationship" has been originally perceived as a form of alliance also referred to as a *"parenté à plaisanteries"* (Mauss 1926). While the original focus was on studying these relationships within the kinship context, i.e., as highly structured and formalistic[28], this type of relationship soon became a subject of research in the non-kin context from small-scale to large-scale industrialized societies. The "alliance" explanation of the joking relationships stressing symmetry and reciprocity (e.g., Lowie 1947 [1920], Mauss 1926), the act of exchange itself (e.g., Lévi-Strauss 1972), their transcendental/mythic origins (e.g., Griaule 1948, *"l'alliance cathartique"* [cathartic alliance]) has been competing with Radcliffe-Brown's notion of social solidarity where "the [joking] relationship is one of permitted disrespect" (1940: 196) providing "the means of establishing and maintaining social equilibrium" (1949: 135). The debate on "joking relationship," its terminology, meaning, functions, manifestations, affectivity or lack of thereof, cognition or repetitive (structured or non-structured) spontaneity, etc., may never result in a definable conceptualization because the concept itself is a construct of modern scholars, which encompasses nothing and everything at the same time; thus, is both culture- and individual-related. Modern operational definitions, unless culture-specific, are so broad that they basically describe humor itself in the most observable form and function. For example, Apte defined

> …the joking relationship as a patterned playful behavior that occurs between two individuals who recognize special kinship or other types of social bonds between them; it displays reciprocal or nonreciprocal verbal of action-based humor including joking, teasing, banter, ridicule, insult, horseplay, and other similar manifestations, usually in the presence of audience (1985: 30–31).

All humor, structured or non-structured, involves at least two individuals who are establishing or maintaining some sort of a social bond, whether required or voluntary. The continuation of this bond depends on the permissible or forbidden degree of offensiveness supported by cognitive comprehension and/or recognition of both the humor content and the participants involved. Permissibility of offensiveness use (in humor or otherwise) is regulated in all societies by behavioral rules of conduct expressed through time/space/actors, specific customs, rules of etiquette, political correctness, hierarchy, etc. Joking relationships are actually a modern construct that is applicable to any humorous situation chosen for discussion by any scholar as long as it is not a required and institutionalized behavior, regardless of the size of a group. Consequently, the "joking relationship," as a distinct concept within the framework of humor, should be used when referring to kin-based joking relationships, including interclan, intervillage, and intertribal ones, and to specific situations in other cultures when the context calls for symmetrical or asymmetrical humor-based disrespect (purposeful offensiveness toward one or more parties). Furthermore, as joking relationships encompass a variety of humorous activities indiscriminately referred to by preferred terms used in their description[29], there is not much difference among the activities themselves. What is different

---

28   This original focus reflects the interest in development of universal theories by pioneers of anthropology as summarized, for example, by Apte (1985) and Jones (2007). For the purpose of this book, the history of anthropological theory regarding kinship and joking relationship is limited in its scope.

29   For example, Apte maintains that "'Joking activity' has been used as a synonym for such other terms as 'teasing,' 'swearing,' 'taunting,' 'making fun of (another),' 'banter,' 'horseplay,' 'vulgar or obscene remarks,' 'playful insults,' 'sexual innuendos,' 'petting,' 'heavy petting,'

and context-dependent are the participants and "motivations" behind joking situations since, although different rules of avoidance behavior exist in all societies, their strictness is exercised on different levels. Thus, having a joking relationship toward potential marriage partners is expected in many kinship-based societies "where cross-cousin marriage is either prescribed or preferred" (Apte 1985: 39) but so is the roasting of a President of the United States during the White House Correspondents' Dinner held since 1920s. The asymmetrical joking relationship between a featured speaker/comedian and a president allows for an almost unrestrained expression of dissatisfaction with the ruling establishment, criticism of some or all aspects of domestic and foreign policy, and for channeling both personal and/or group animosity and resentment toward the hapless individual. Using this asymmetrical, institutionalized, and required joking relationship for social and political correction/control has never been more evident than in 2006, when Stephen Colbert delivered his sixteen-minute speech and seven-minute "audition video" to the audience of over 2,500 guests. "He was stunning and they [the audience] were stunned," someone—who was reportedly not a fan of Colbert[30]—from the blog *Daily Kos* wrote (Sternbergh 2006). The applause did not come from the audience, which was full of supporters of President Bush and the media (some of whom left their dinners barely touched as they stormed out of the posh Hilton Washington Hotel [the Hinckley Hilton]), but rather from millions of Internet viewers who were empowered by Colbert's "truthiness" in action. The main target of "permitted disrespect," President Bush, sat through the whole speech visibly uncomfortable but obligated to bear the insults[31] sanctified by the joking relationship. At the end he shook hands with Colbert, and his lovely wife, Laura Bush, even complimented the insufferable comedian with the "well done" utterance. Well done, indeed... The First Couple silently suffered through witty remarks of Colbert's character, based on such TV personalities as Bill O'Reilly or Sean Hannity, regardless of whether they were personal[32] or not[33]. However, the same cannot be said about the media that did not have an obligatory joking relationship with the roaster. Colbert's attack on the press[34] did not help him with the evaluation of his joking performance by the media lambasting him for *unfunniness* and poor taste, turning otherwise a cheerful occasion to a funeral-like silence (*The Death of The Room*). The mainstream media tried their best to avoid any references to his "abuse" of the joking relationship, which led to the accusations of the "Colbert Blackout." The press, in general, was not amused, nor were they willing to respond "in kind," i.e., in joking manner. As a matter of fact, no response at the time seemed to be a better option than any response at all. Colbert failed to establish a joking relationship of any kind with most of the reporters covering this annual event.

However, his network of asymmetrical and non-institutionalized (voluntary) joking relationships has expanded profusely. Within a few days millions in the U.S. and abroad turned to the Internet to view his speech. The Colbert Nation was born of the viewers who, through Colbert's character, have established asymmetrical "joking relationships" with a variety of political, religious, social, etc., figures,

---

'rough horseplay,' 'fondling,' and 'practical jokes'" (1985, pp. 35–36).

30   One of my students described Colbert with regard to this roast as "lowly fake political pundit."

31   There are numerous transcripts of Colbert's speech on the Internet. The most complete one seems to be posted at http://www.dai-lykos.com/story/2006/04/30/206303/-Re-Improved-Colbert-transcript-%28now-with-complete-text-of-Colbert-Thomas-video!%29)

32   For example, "We're not brainiacs on the nerd patrol."

33   For example, "So the White House has personnel changes. Then you write, 'Oh, they're just rearranging the deck chairs on the Titanic.' First of all, that is a terrible metaphor. This administration is not sinking. This administration is soaring. If anything, they are rearranging the deck chairs on the Hindenburg!"

34   For example, "Over the last five years you people were so good—over tax cuts, WMD intelligence, the effect of global warming. We Americans didn't want to know, and you had the courtesy not to try to find out. Those were good times, as far as we knew."

"institutionalizing" Colbert in the process to the point that, jokingly speaking, he has become not only a political phenomenon but the "force" to be reckoned with. After all, Stephen Colbert topped presidential candidate Jon Huntsman in the South Carolina Republican primary of January 21, 2012, by 1% (Colbert, 5%; Huntsman, 4%), according to a Public Policy Polling survey conducted among 1,112 likely Republican voters. And he didn't even run for the office!

As stated above, "traditional" joking relationships are institutionalized and occur in small-scale societies, both kin and non-kin based. Thus, in order to understand them, the student of humor is given an opportunity here to study them "in action." In his article, *Special Affinities and Conflict Resolution: West African Social Institutions and Mediation*, Mark Davidheiser examines joking relationships among the Mandinka of southwestern Gambia, and describes them as a very effective institution in reconciling feuding parties, transforming and/or ending conflicts, and resolving any societal problems. He points out differences in Gambian and American approaches to conflict resolution, which stem from different conceptualizations of conflict and mediation when forgiveness plays a much more important role than a "win-win" strategy in the Western world.

The second article, *Notes On Some Joking Relationships Between Hui and Han Villages in Henan*, by Elisabeth Allès, addresses the role of non-kin joking relationships in controlling violence between the Chinese Muslims (the Hui) and the Han, who share a limited geographical area where peaceful co-existence (commercial links) is vital to the survival of these religiously divided groups. The importance of this article is not only in a selection of the area known more for conflict than its resolution, but also because Allès has tried to identify the origin of this "unusual" alliance in China and discussed it in the context of much more comprehensive and popular studies of joking relationships in Africa. The uneasy relationship between the Hui and Han is also reflected in ethnic jokes about both groups in China. The Hui, as a minority among the Han population of China, have been a frequent topic of jokes and insults related to their most visible difference from others—the avoidance of pigs as prescribed by Islam. Constant references to the Hui as "sons of pigs," "pig worshippers," etc., have been exploited in many situations, including humorous ones that, at times, carried over to actions that could easily be considered at least "tasteless." Atwill provides an example of "a shocking demonstration of this [against the Hui] bias in nineteenth-century Yunan ... [as] the street running past one of Kumming's oldest mosques was called Zhuji Jie (Pig-gathering Road)" (42). The Hui are among many examples of minorities around the world whose "strange ways" make them outsiders in so-called mainstream cultures and, consequently, they are perceived to be "troublemakers," often blamed for each and every societal, political, economic, etc., shortcoming or misfortune.

SECTION 7
TOWARD ETHNICITY ...
My Culture or Yours?

"One horse-laugh is worth ten thousand syllogisms. It is not only more effective; it is also vastly more intelligent."
—*Henry Louis Mencken (1880–1956)*
An American journalist, satirist, and social critic.

E thnic humor is one of the most popular categories of humor as its target can be anyone and everyone who is perceived to be a part of any "social group." The problem with ethnic humor is the definition of ethnicity itself. For the purpose of discussing ethnic humor, Apte used a definition of an ethnic group as proposed by the International Encyclopedia of Social Sciences, which states, "[a]n ethnic group is a distinct category of the population in a larger society whose culture is usually different from its own. The members of such a group are, or feel themselves, or are thought to be, bound together by common ties of race or nationality or culture" (1985: 112). While this is quite a workable definition, the reality is that almost all of its parts can easily be contested. Concepts of race, nationality, and culture are themselves among the most elusive notions to delineate in fewer than one hundred (100) pages for anyone who wants to cover "just" general aspects of these terms. While each group is always a part of some larger group, in humor studies, this concept is often applied to minorities perceived as "inferior" social groups (e.g., Boskin 1985: 81), with respect to a larger group defined through its spatial boundaries whether physical (e.g., the United States of America, China) or otherwise (e.g., major linguistic groups). However, such groups don't have to be perceived as minorities per se, since many ethnic groups are defined just by their distinctiveness from others based on any number of possible attributes. These attributes may include, but are not limited to, such common elements as origin (e.g., national, linguistic, geographical, genealogical), culture (by any chosen definition), race or physical characteristics (as subjective as these phenotypes might be), language, religion, political associations, gender, and "consciousness of mind" (I'm still not sure what this means). Consequently, ethnicity is a matter of identity as both self-defined and "imposed" by others. Furthermore, perception of ethnicity is also a fluid one as Isajiw pointed out so succinctly in 1974 and thereafter by saying,

> Identification of others in turn usually stimulates self-identification and may condition new forms of social organization. Hence, ethnicity is a matter of a double boundary, a boundary from within, maintained by the socialization process, and a boundary from without established by the process of intergroup relations (1993: 6 [as based on his previous published work from 1974]).

The concept of fluidity or "shifting" (e.g., Lowe 1986) boundaries within ethnic groups is especially important when ethnic humor is concerned, because of the continuous nature of the process of redefining oneself in the process of creating, transmitting, and responding to humorous situations rooted in ethnicity.

Ethnic humor is considered to be among the most offensive types of humor due to its extensive use of stereotypes. While many scholars often point out that stereotypes are not necessary negative[35] and are different from prejudice, the common perception is that as funny as they might be, they are usually harmful to groups who are a butt of such jokes. There are many well-meaning people who would like to eradicate ethnic humor from our lives in the name of equality and, especially in the U.S., political correctness, using arguments similar to the following introduction to a popular website http://www. stereotypeandsociety.typepad.com:

> In a complex and dangerous world, the allure of the simple is addictive. But the habits of type-casting can offer us little wisdom. We must educate ourselves to understand these habits, and to demand public discussion that is based on knowledge, understanding, and a belief in the possibility of egalitarian community. Without this, democracy cannot exist. Join Typecasting authors, Stuart and Elizabeth Ewen, in an ongoing discussion of the influence of stereotypes, past and present, and strategies for combating divisive ways of seeing.

A renowned scholar of ethnic humor, Christie Davies[36] has quite a simple counterargument to all dreamers who believe that it is possible to control ethnic humor through either governmental means or education: "To become angry about jokes and to seek to censor them because they impinge on sensitive issues is about as sensible as smashing a thermometer because it reveals how hot it is" (1990: 9). There is no doubt that ethnic jokes not only might be offensive, but even emotionally painful to certain people or to certain groups[37]. However, more often than not, neither a transmitter nor a recipient of an ethnic joke means any harm, and, for better or worse, many people don't fully understand the stereotypes that they help to spread or reinforce. This is because they have neither personal experience with such a group nor even general (forget about factual) knowledge about the group upon which to base an opinion. They simply have no prejudice against the group in question, period[38]. Instead, there is a sort of short-lasting funny image based on "truthiness" or even just a "feeling" that something is to be laughed about/at because the way "truthiness" is presented.

P.J. O'Rourke is a master of stereotyping and of wit in his journalistic reports and books. While undoubtedly many readers of his work might be offended by characterizations of their countries, groups, professions, politics, etc., the images painted with his words are not only funny but also very powerful, especially for those who share similar experiences and knowledge of the peoples, cultures, and events described. They can also serve as great educational material to discuss stereotypes, truthiness, and truth

---

35   For example, "Stereotypes should properly be regarded as concept-systems, with positive as well as negative functions, having the same general kinds of properties as other concepts, and serving to organize experience as do other concepts" (Vinacke 1957).

36   He is a British professor of sociology whose book on "Ethnic Humor Around the World" is a best-of collection of modern ethnic jokes and their analyses. He refers to such jokes as "a means by which the joke-tellers ascribe human deficiencies to other ethnic groups in an excessive or ludicrous fashion" as they "express and for the time being resolve the uncertain situations [of uncertainty and ambivalence] that gave rise to them by mocking excess and corresponding failure…" (1990: 307).

37   Ethnic humor is considered to be among the most aggressive of all humors. According to Apte this is because "…attitudes of ingroup adulation and outgroup hate, stereotyping, and prejudice, must all be considered to be concomitants of ethnocentrism. Treating or thinking of other cultures and people as inferior, for example, is one way of strengthening self-image. Prejudice reinforces ethnocentrism, just as negation of cultural values of other people nurtures self-esteem and feelings of superiority" (1985: 142).

38   However, it must be noted here that lack of knowledge does not equal lack of prejudice. This is particularly visible with all facets of the so-called hate humor, which is discussed in Chapter 4.

in an open forum. This is the reason that O'Rourke's *The Innocents Abroad, Updated* is included here. To appreciate a variety of O'Rourke's stereotypes, the reader must have not only a good general background in peoples and cultures of the world, but also—especially for younger generations—access to Google so they can "get" such references as "the Spirit of Free Enterprise," "Liverpool United," and being back to a "place of unemployment on Monday"; and these are just for stereotyping the British. Inspired by Mark Twain's travelogue to Europe and the Middle East, O'Rourke's vision of the world in 1980s is as entertaining and as witty as—though much, much shorter than—Twain's bestselling original[39]. In some ways it is also timeless, showing that stereotypes live for a very, very long time although their humorous descriptions might be toned down as the result of increasing or decreasing sensitivity toward specific ethnic groups[40]. *The Innocents Abroad, Updated* is a part of the book *Holidays in Hell,* which consists of various articles by O'Rourke who has

been working as a foreign correspondent for the past few years, although "working" isn't the right word and "foreign correspondent" is too dignified a title. What [he has] really been is a Trouble Tourist—going to see insurrections, stupidities, political crises, civil disturbances and other human folly because... because it's fun (1988: 1).

---

39   Mark Twain's original book, *The Innocents Abroad, or the New Pilgrims' Progress: Being Some Account of the Steamship Quaker City's Pleasure Excursion to Europe and the Holy Land, with Descriptions of Countries, Nations, Incidents and Adventures, as They Appeared to the Author,* published in 1869, was an edited version of his original letters from this trip. These letters were often not very kind toward either the people or places he visited so he toned them down and adapted "his writing to his new readers 'by purifying his expression, by deleting or modifying coarse passages, and by altering his remarks in order to avoid the charge of blasphemy'" (McKeithan 1958: xiv).

40   Some of Twain's original descriptions of different ethnic groups would be probably edited out today. He was quite harsh when depicting his fellow human beings and not very appreciative of some cultural icons of humankind (for example, his description, too long to cite, of Da Vinci's "Last Supper" is simply superb, finishing with the comment that "...Maybe the originals [of the great artists] were handsome when they were new, but they have got over it now," McKeithan 1958: 58). Jews in Tangier "... are an inconceivably rusty-looking set now and consequently must have in the days of the Old Testament—and how they ever came to be the chosen people of the Lord is a mystery which will stagger me from this day forth till I perish" (McKeithan 1958: 33). "The good Catholic Porthughee [at Horta] crossed himself and prayed God to shield him from all blasphemous desire to know more than his father did before him... The people lie, and cheat the stranger, and are desperately ignorant, and have hardly any reverence for their dead. The latter trait shows how little better they are than the donkeys they eat and sleep [with]" (McKeithan 1958: 17). Most of the modern Frenchmen would not appreciate a note sent by Twain's fellow traveler regarding their American-perceived French (European in general) aversion to cleanliness and composed in a rather peculiar combination of languages: "*Monsieur le* Landlord—Sir: *Pourquoi* don't you *mettez* some *savon* [soap] in your dang bed-chambers? *Est-ce que vous pensez* I am going to steal it? ... Savon is necessary *de la vie* to anybody but a Frenchman, *et je l'aurai hors de cet hôtel* or bust. You hear me. A *prés cet avis, vous trouverez à intérêt* to go slow, anyways *sur le savon* question. *Allons,* Brown." (McKeithan 1958: 56).

Is O'Rourke's stereotyping of almost everyone and everything offensive? Yes. Is he prejudiced toward the whole world? No. He, as many other people, uses humorous stereotypes for a variety of reasons, with none of them being divisiveness.

> Finally, people are all exactly alike. There's no such thing as a race and barely such a thing as an ethnic group. If we were dogs, we'd be the same breed. George Bush and an Australian aborigine have fewer differences than a Lhasa Apso and a toy fox terrier. A Japanese raised in Riyadh would be an Arab. A Zulu raised in New Rochelle would be an orthodontist. I wish I could say I found this out by spending arctic nights on ice floes with Inuit elders and by sitting with tribal medicine men over fires made of human bones in Madagascar. But, actually, I found it out by sleeping around. People are all the same, though their circumstances differ terribly. Trouble doesn't come from Slopes, Kikes, Niggers, Spics or White Capitalist Pigs; it comes from the heart (1988: 4).

O'Rourke uses humorous stereotyping without prejudice neither as a "sword" nor as a "shield" (an expression used, for example, by Nilsen and Nilsen 2000). Rather, he uses them as the most effective communication tool to introduce the reader to events, locations, and people, which and whom he covers as a journalist, exposing in the process absurdities of wars, conflicts, self-inflicted human tragedies, governments, and stereotypes themselves.

> The Belfast pictures in *Time* magazine, the rubble-and-barbed wire, litter-and-graffiti Belfast, is, in fact, a patch of highly photogenic impoverishment no more than a mile long and half a mile wide. It's as though *Architectural Digest* came to a house and only took pictures of the teenager's bedroom. The rubble is from slum clearance, not bombs (though which is worse may be argued by critics of the modern welfare state). And the barbed wire is on top of the "Peace Wall," a kind of sociological toddler gate erected by the British to keep the ragamuffin Protestant homicidal maniacs of Shankhill Road away from the tatterdemalion Catholic murderers in Falls Road two blocks over. The graffiti and litter are real (1993: 26).

Irish himself, O'Rourke ironically points out the absurdity of conflict and violence between the Irish and the English as being "justifiable" because they are "so ancient and honorable." He compares them to any other groups involved in any (sometimes loosely defined) ethnic conflicts such as,

> the Shi'ites in Lebanon, the peasants in El Salvador, the blacks in America, the Jews in Palestine, the Palestinians in Israel (and everybody everywhere, if you read your history)—enough barbarism has been visited on the Irish [and other ethnic groups] to excuse all barbarities by the Irish [and any other ethnic groups] barbarians (ibid: 32–33).

These noble and ethnic conflicts are often reflected in ethnic humor through the use of stereotypes portraying one or more groups as losers (Gruner's "winners and losers theory"—1997), regardless of whether they are a minority or not. They provide "the balance in an unbalanced world" as Davies has pointed out (1990: 308).

An English man and an Irish man are driving head on, at night, on a twisty, dark road. Both are driving too fast for the conditions and collide on a sharp bend in the road. To the amazement of both, they are unscathed, though their cars are both destroyed. In celebration of their luck, both agree to put aside their dislike for the other from that moment on. At this point, the Englishman goes to the boot and fetches a 12-year-old bottle of whiskey. He hands the bottle to the Irish man, who exclaims, "May the Irish and the English live together forever, in peace, and harmony." The Irish man then tips the bottle and gulps half of the bottle down. Still flabbergasted over the whole thing, he goes to hand the bottle to the Englishman, who replies: "No thanks, I'll just wait till the Police get here!"

The English, i.e., "the oppressor," are stereotyped as cool, calculative, and canny and the winner over a well-meaning—but stupid—and always helpless-in-face-of-a-drink Irish. However, replace the Irish with a Catholic priest, the English with a Jewish rabbi and whiskey with kosher wine and suddenly the "oppressor" is the "stupid one" outsmarted by the "minority" winner. This joke includes two recurring themes in ethnic humor: of stupidity/ignorance/ineptness and of canniness/craftiness/calculativeness that, according to Davies, are "far more widespread, numerous and more durable than any others" (1990: 10). While "stupidity" jokes seem to be easily switchable[41], the "canniness" ones are reserved for a limited number of groups with Jews, in all probability, being the leader of the pack. Indeed, Davies' table (2.1; 1990: 11–12) lists Jews as representing "canniness" in fifteen (15) geographical regions out of twenty-seven (27) listed. None of any other ethnic groups is so widely associated with any of the typical content (stupidity or canniness) of ethnic jokes, i.e., so "international." This popularity and Davies' noted geographical distribution can be explained by the Jewish diaspora, and by their contribution to the development of modern industrialized societies of the so-called Western tradition. None of the Middle Eastern, Far Eastern, and African (exception: South Africa) countries appear to regard Jews as being particularly canny in the majority of printed jokes that were the subject of Davies' study. This could have been the result of a relatively very small number of Jewish communities in these areas, as well as severe intermittent hostilities toward Jews in the Middle East. In the latter case, showing Jews as being canny might not be the trait to be perpetuated among the surrounding Islamic populations, as canniness "implies cleverness and rationality" (Davies 1990: 15), i.e., superiority traits that are not to be recognized and acknowledged in the area with such a long history of the conflict[42].

---

41   This point is argued by Davies in response to Joey Adams' famous statement … (ethnic jokes "can apply to any minority"). Davies believes that Adams' statement is true but only in theory (Davies 1990: 40).

42   While such jokes are not so popular in the Middle East, they are among the funniest, for example in the United States, when two groups are compared in political jokes. See, for example, this old joke:

Sharon sits down with Arafat at the beginning of negotiation regarding the resolution of the conflict. Sharon requests that he be allowed to begin with a story. Arafat replies, "Of course."

Sharon begins his story. "Years before the Israelites came to the Promised Land and settled here, Moses led them for 40 years through the desert. The Israelites began complaining that they were thirsty and, lo and behold, a miracle occurred and a stream appeared before them. They drank their fill and then decided to take advantage of the stream to do some bathing—including Moses. When Moses came out of the water, he found that all his clothing was missing. 'Who took my clothes?' Moses asked those around him. 'It was the Palestinians,' replied the Israelites."

"Wait a minute," objected Arafat immediately, "there were no Palestinians during the time of Moses!" "All right," replies Sharon, "Now that we've got that settled, let's begin our negotiations."

"We hold the Jews in horror, and we insist that all which has been written by them, and collected by us, bears the stamp of Divinity. There never was so palpable a contradiction."
—*François-Marie Arouet de Voltaire (1694–1778)*
A French writer, philosopher, and historian.

The subject of Jewish humor has been discussed by numerous scholars and commented on by thousands of enthusiasts (e.g., Landmann 1962; Wisse 1971; Ben-Amos 1973; Novak and Waldoks 1981; Brandes 1983; Oring 1983; Boskin and Dorinson 1985; Ziv 1988; Radday and Brenner 1990; Friedman 1998; Cohen 1999; Epstein 2002; Brook 2003; Halkin 2006; Weinstein 2008; Harris 2009; Weis 2009; Gillota 2010). While it is usually classified as ethnic humor, one must remember that being Jewish is a religious affiliation, so much of Jewish humor can also be classified as humor about religions. While many jokes about Jewish religion have been narrated by non-Jews, there are many hermetic[43] jokes, whose meaning is often lost due to a lack of understanding of Judaism and its practices. Such jokes are mostly funny for Jews themselves who have been trying to decide about their own religious identity ranging from the Orthodox (the oldest and most conservative) through Conservative, Reform (most popular in America, a liberal form that started in the late 1800s in Germany), Reconstructionist, and finally Humanistic Judaism (the last two are relatively new movements). This internal struggle over what being Jewish actually means has been reflected by the so-called periods of "fighting satire" and "loving satire" (the 18th and 19th centuries) and continues today with constant adaptation to social, political, and technological advancements[44].

The Jewish identity, Myhill's so-called national church (2006), was formed at the beginning of the first millennium B.C. but has been preserved throughout the diaspora after their Yahweh-given homeland was lost. Since the loss of this "homeland" has been believed to be the punishment from God for a non-Jewish way of life, and is to be regained only through purity of faith, the Jews in diaspora focused on preservation of all original commands, language, customs, etc. Continuously reminded about their uniqueness as "children of Israel," "chosen people," etc., Jews enhanced their repertoire of rituals, etc., in order to assure the Jewish purity. While the "homeland" Jews were perceived as becoming more attached to the land than to the religion, mixing up with non-Jewish population of the area (e.g., Ezra, Nehemiah[45]), the exilic Jews were reinforcing the concept of Jewish identity as based on social separatism, endogamy, and centrality of ancestry, among others. The uniqueness of the Jewish history, most of which occurred in

---

43   Hermetic jokes are "highly specialized," i.e., somewhat specialized knowledge is required in order to understand and enjoy the joke. For example:
Before perestroika we were all dogs, wearing muzzles, chained to a two-meter leash, with the food just out of reach. After perestroika the chain was longer, the food dish further away, but we can bark as much as we want.

44   *A suburban family bought a new Mercedes, and wanted a rabbi to bless it. They called the Orthodox Rabbi. "Rabbi, would you make a bracha over our Mercedes?" "How can I do that?" he replied. "I don't even know what a Mercedes is." Next they called a Conservative Rabbi. "Rabbi, would you make a bracha over our Mercedes?" "I'm sorry," he answered, "I'm not sure whether I can or cannot." Finally, they called a Reform Rabbi. "Rabbi, would you make a bracha over our Mercedes?" "Sure," he answered, "But what is a bracha?"*

45   Ezra is believed to lead a high number of Jewish exiles from Babylonia to Jerusalem at the beginning of the 5th c. B.C. under the rule of the Persian king, Artaxerxes. His dreams of the purity of his homeland and his Jewish counterparts were simply shattered when arriving to Jerusalem where Jewish men gladly married non-Jewish women, thus disobeying Moses' laws. He was joined by Nehemiah (sent by the same Persian king to rebuild the walls of Jerusalem) and, together, they reinforced the Jewish identity by "renewing" the covenant and separating themselves from the all others. Interestingly enough, Ezra (Uzair) is considered to be one of the lesser prophets of Islam, although he is not mentioned in the Qur'an. This recognition is not shared by all Muslims, but it doesn't stop anyone from visiting Ezra's traditional tomb at El Uzair, near Basra (Iraq). Somewhat forgotten and gathering dust, his coffin is still an object of veneration, although none of the local Arabs could have explained to me who Ezra was.

not-so-hospitable "host" countries, has led to a clearly defined double boundary—both from within and from outside (see Isajiw above)—of the ethnicity. The Jewish struggle for physical, spiritual, social, and economic survival has been reflected in Jewish humor, thus demonstrating a variety of coping strategies and defensive mechanisms, allowing the people to make the best of the living at the bottom of the social ladder, while continuously trying to better themselves. Amidst all tragedies, the Jews have always had one advantage over the others—something that might be called "an expedited training of the brain." Jewish children, most born in foreign lands, traditionally have had to master at least three languages at an early age: Yiddish[46] (or Ladino[47]) as an everyday language of local Jewish communities; Hebrew as the language of the sacred texts (the *Torah* and *Talmud*); and the language of the "host" country. The children, especially boys, have always been treasured, protected, and highly nurtured[48]. At the age of four most boys and even girls have had to learn "Jewish reasoning," i.e., how to examine, evaluate, argue, clarify, etc., various issues on both abstract and concrete levels to provide as concise and simple an answer as possible to very complex problems leading to the famous Jewish "logic[49]." "The religious tradition and the study of the Bible and the Talmud"[50] were the main intellectual occupations of the Jews in Diaspora. "Humor and satire are generally antagonistic approaches to accepted values.... However, because humorous relief was needed, some liberties were admitted and even encouraged" (Ziv 1988: 116). Out of necessity Jews

---

46   The Yiddish language (Jewish) is a combination of German, Hebrew, Slavic, and Romance languages that have been used by the Ashkenazi Jews of Europe. Many Yiddish words have become a part of vocabulary in languages of the countries where the Jewish population was relatively significant. For example, every Pole knows all of the following expressions:

Bobehla: "little grandmother" (sweet)

Chutzpah: to have guts, gall

Kibitz: joking around

Mishmash: total disorder, disorderly mix, confusion

Schmooz: a heartfelt visit

Schlemiel: clumsy or inept, rather pitiful individual. One of the best examples of modern schlemiel is Larry David's character in "Curb Your Enthusiasm" so well discussed by Gillota (2010).

Shiksa: a young, usually pretty, gentile girl / young woman whose behavior is not really quite appropriate; a temptress especially for Jewish men.

Shlimazl: fall guy with really a lot of bad luck.

47   Ladino is a Judeo-Spanish (Judezomo) "equivalent" of Yiddish, which has been popularized after the expulsion of Jews from Spain in 1492. Today this language is rarely used.

48   In a recent round-table discussion group, the question was asked of the Ministerial Panel, "At what point does life begin?" The Catholic priest spoke first and said, "At conception, of course!" The Presbyterian minister said, "No, no, it certainly begins at birth." The United minister tried to buffer the obvious argument point and suggested, "Perhaps you're both wrong, and it's a compromise in that the fetus is not functional with a heartbeat until the third month." They had to prod the Jewish Rabbi for his answer, and he finally leaned forward to his mike and spoke softly "All of my friends here are wrong. Life begins when the last child leaves home and the dog they left behind dies!"

49   *In nineteenth-century Russia a young Jew was told he is to be conscripted into the army. So he asked an old Jew for advice. "There is nothing to worry about," says the old man. "Just go to the army and things will turn out well." "How can you be so sure?" asks the young man. "Well when you have joined the army, there are two possibilities—either you will be sent to a combat group, or you won't. If not, then there is nothing to worry about. If you are sent to a combat group, then there are two possibilities—either the group will be sent into combat, or it won't. If not, then there is nothing to worry about. If your group is sent into combat, then there are two possibilities—either you will be wounded or you won't. If not, then there is nothing to worry about. If you are wounded, then there are two possibilities—either your wound will be mortal or it won't. If not, then there is nothing to worry about. If your wound is mortal, then there are two possibilities—either you will go to hell or you will go to heaven. If you go to heaven, then there is nothing to worry about. If you go to hell, then there are two possibilities—either they take bribes or they don't. If they take bribes, there is nothing to worry about. Of course they take bribes."*

50   Both the *Torah* (*Old Testament*) and *Talmud* are often mentioned as the earliest written evidence of Jewish humor (e.g., Radday and Brenner: 1990). While a laughing Sarah is not too unusual—any woman over 100 years old might be more than amused when hearing about her pregnancy (forget about pregnancy...think "sex")—a laughing monotheistic god of the Talmud (e.g., Friedman 1998) is seemingly an unheard-of phenomenon in monotheistic religions. For some reasons the divine sense of humor seems to disappear with the polytheistic deities of the Middle East who have enjoyed both good liquor and a joke.

had to "invent" jobs in the host countries since they were pushed out of traditional Christian (and Islamic) occupations such as farming, herding, or crafts. Thus, almost every time when given an opportunity, the Jewish people have exceeded in the fields that require high and creative functionality of the brain[51], be it banking (or finance in general), medical sciences, physics, law, trade, or entertainment[52]. Long before my esteemed colleagues at the University of Utah, Gregory Cochran, Jason Hardy, and Henry Harpending published their controversial paper[53] on the superiority of the Ashkenazi Jews, "verbal and mathematical intelligence" being "a product of natural selection, stemming from their occupation of an unusual social niche" (2005: 27), creators of Jewish humor consistently have pointed out to the very same attributes. But, who are they?

Most of the scholars analyzing Jewish humor agree that overwhelming majority of Jewish humor is created by Jews for Jewish people[54] who are aware of their own stereotypical attributes, of incongruities of their customs and traditions, as well as of the irony of being "the chosen people[55]." After all, the above higher intelligence in verbal and mathematical fields translates really well into evolutionary adaptiveness of humor[56] favoring the survival of the group. Furthermore, Jewish comedians traditionally have dominated American comedy as Nilsen and Nilsen pointed out in their power point presentation on Jewish humor referring to the 1978 study of Samuel Janus "which found that although Jews constituted only 3 percent of the U.S. population, 80 percent of the nation's professional comedians were Jewish[57]."

---

51   "My son," says Yetta, "is a physicist." "My son," says Sadie, "is a president of an insurance company." "My son," says Becky, "is the head of a law firm and president of the Law Society." "My son," says Hannah, "is a rabbi." "A rabbi? What kind of career is that for a Jewish boy?"

52   According to the National Jewish Population Survey (2000–01) released in October 2002, "the Jewish population is very well educated [as a quarter (24%) of Jewish adults 18 years of age and older have received a graduate degree, and 55% have earned at least a bachelor's degree... The current comparable numbers for non-Jews are 5% and 28%... [And] the majority of employed Jews (59%) work in management, business and professional/technical positions, compared to fewer non-Jews (46%). The plurality of Jews are in professional/technical positions (41%), noticeably more than in the case among non-Jews (30%)." The rest... they must be comedians!

53   Although their article entitled *Natural History of Ashkenazi Intelligence* in the *Journal of Biosocial Science* of 2005 has had mixed reviews from both the scientific community and the general audience, it is really hard to deny their evidence and conclusions. So, are Jews truly "God's chosen people?" Not so fast, the Ashkenazim high IQ comes at high price—a number of diseases such as Tay-Sachs, Bloom's syndrome, Fanconi anemia, Gaucher's disease, and mutations in the BRCA1 and BRCA2 genes are associated with the same selective pressure that made them so smart. Yahweh has definitely some explaining to do.

54   One bit of evidence of this perception is that Jewish jokes when told "by non-Jews, rarely came off well" (Brandes 1983: 234) as even friendly gentiles could not master proper linguistic level (vocabulary, accent, phonetic transpositions, etc.) necessary for the full enjoyment and appreciation of a humorous story especially in the New World of "preoccupation with changing speech patterns over several generations" (Brandes 1983: 234).

55   In the *Fiddler on the Roof*, a musical and a movie (1971), which are based on Sholem Aleichem's stories, "Tevye, the Dairyman in Russia," asks God, "I know, I know. We are your chosen people. But, once in a while, can't you choose someone else?" Aleichem's original line from "Teyve the Dairyman" is "Thou hath chosen us from all other nations... Why did you have to pick on the Jews?" "Sholem Aleichem" ("How do you do?") is a humorous pen name of Solomon Naumovich Rabinovich (1859–1916) born in Pereyeslan, now in the Ukraine, formerly in Russia.

56   The so-called sense of humor seems to be an indicator of intelligence (e.g., Howrigan and MacDonald 2008).

57   This number has been referred to on many websites with references to different original sources. The total Jewish world population in 2010 was 13,428,300 as reported by the Berman Institute: "more than 80 percent of world Jews currently live in two countries, the United States and Israel, and 95 percent are concentrated in the ten largest communities" (Dashefsky, DellaPergola, Sheskin 2010: 7). There were 5,275,000 Jews in the U.S. (ibid. 19) in 2010, but, unfortunately, the same report didn't provide any data regarding their professions although definitely they were "urban related" since more "than half (52.5 percent) of world Jewry lived in only five metropolitan areas. These areas—including the main cities and vast urbanized territories around them—were Tel Aviv, New York, Jerusalem, Los Angeles, and Haifa" (ibid. 20). This number constitutes 17.1% of the total U.S. population—one could only wish that the number of Jewish comedians would have grown proportionately!

Currently, this number appears to be smaller, not because Jewish comedians became less funny but because more comedians of other groups have joined the crowd. American comedy is still dominated by Jewish comedians, and such comedians as Albert Brooks, Billy Crystal, Paul Reiser, Ben Stiller, Jon Stewart, Jerry Seinfeld, Joan Rivers, Sarah Silverman, Adam Sandler, Paul Rudd, Sacha Baron Cohen, and Jack Black might be even more popular than American icons of Jewish comedy such as George Burns, Jerry Lewis, Lenny Bruce, Mel Brooks, Woody Allen, and Larry David. Thus, periodical cries that "Jewish humor is dead!" are not really justifiable (e.g., Harris 2009; Weiss 2009), at least as long as this humor is connected with comedians of Jewish background. However, the question must be raised on whether or not these comedians truly represent what is considered to be the Jewish humor, "anthropologically speaking." After all, modern Jewish comedians think about themselves as comedians only, who see very little "Jewish" about their work. For example, both Woody Allen and Larry David seemed to act rather surprised when their movie, *Whatever Works*, (2009) was pronounced the "last" Jewish-American comedy.

> "Right," Allen says politely. "You know, it's funny. I have a blind spot there. Because I wouldn't see what I do as Jewish humor. I would see it as funny if you think it's funny, or not if you don't. But I never think of it as Jewish in any way. Now, as I say, this is a blind spot. Because you and other people might feel differently."
>
> "I get the same thing," says David, laughing. "People, you know, Jews, they come up to me, they go, 'I'm a Jew—I get it.' 'I'm a *landsman*—love your show!' Jews want to be the only ones who like it! They think it's for them. It's not just for them. And I don't think that way either" (Harris: 2009).

Does one need to be a Jew to create and/or appreciate Jewish humor? The Marx Brothers (Chico, Harpo, Gummo, Zeppo, and Groucho) were the Yorkville Jews, although only Groucho seemed to play on his Jewishness, but still, as Weiss asked, "When Groucho took a pratfall, was it any more Jewish than when Chaplin did?" (2009). The *Seinfeld* sitcom, an American-Jewish comedy of the late 1980 and 1990s is supposedly Jewish to its core as its main characters, Jerry Seinfeld, George Costanza (Jason Alexander), and Cosmo Kramer (Michael Richards) embody all aspects of Jewishness and its stereotypes, and with Elaine Benes (Julia Louis-Dreyfus) bringing into the picture a *"shiksa"* factor (not a blonde but still a *shiksa*). In one of its most famous episodes, *The Yada Yada*,[58] Jerry is upset that his dentist, Dr. Tim Whatley, has converted to Judaism just "for the jokes." "Don't you see what Whatley is after? Total joke-telling immunity. He's

---

58   This episode, the nineteenth of the eighth season (1997), was nominated for an Emmy.

already got the two big religions [Catholicism and Judaism] covered. If he ever gets Polish citizenship[59], there'll be no stopping him[60]." This, of course, plays into the perception that only Jews tell/create Jewish humor[61], as based on the quintessential contradiction of two opposite notions: self-disparagement and superiority with its foundation in suffering "whether…over the oppression of a people or a bad piece of whitefish" (Harris 2009). This idea has been promoted by many scholars and non-scholars[62] alike since Sigmund Freud but… is it true or is this just a myth? Dan Ben-Amos examines this issue in an article, *The "Myth" of Jewish Humor*, published in *Western Folklore* in 1973. Highly critical of the notion that Jewish humor[63] is self-deprecatory, he points out "that these stories are neither anti-Semitic nor are they a case of self-mockery. By introducing accent into their anecdotes, the narrators do not laugh at themselves altogether, but rather ridicule a social group within the Jewish community from which they would like to differentiate themselves" (1973: 125). If this is the case, then Jewish humor is not really different from any other humor as it too focuses on "the very boundaries of the joke-tellers' identity, on ambiguous people who are not quite separate yet not quite members of the joke-teller's group" (Davies 1990: 312). So, why then is it so much funnier and more discussed than any other humor? Ben-Amos doesn't really provide an

---

59   For young people who don't know and those who might not remember, Polish jokes have been the most popular stupidity jokes in the United States for decades. Today, their popularity seems to be replaced by jokes about another ethnic group, Mexicans, who are experiencing similar struggles in the process of assimilation in and with the so-called American culture.

60   According to Seinfeld's theory, I should be more unbearable than Dr. Whatley because I am Polish, raised Catholic, a woman, and a blonde! Just to make a few topics of the most popular jokes in the U.S.…

61   To be fair to Seinfeld, he presented the "ownership" of the Jewish humor here the same way as of other ethnic groups, be it Catholic or Polish, i.e., only members of the same group are "allowed" to make jokes about themselves and enjoy them. Obviously, this is not reality. I don't know many Poles or Catholics who would be as cavalier about self-disparaging humor as many Jews are.

62   Dr. Whatley even commented that, "…this is our sense of humor that's sustained us as a people for three thousand years." The irony is that the convert seems to know more about the Jewish history than a "true" Jew, Seinfeld, who corrects him, "five thousand years." Unfortunately, this correction is yet another myth: there is no mention of Israel and/or the Jews before the reign of the Egyptian pharaoh, Merneptah. He was a son of Rameses II, under whose rule the Hebrews supposedly were led out of Egypt by Moses. This traditional "dating" is based on a mention of Rameses in the Old Testament. The problem is that there were eleven rulers with this name and under none of them such an event is ever recorded. The assignation of the most famous of them, Rameses II, to the Exodus was perpetuated by Hollywood, i.e., the first *Ten Commandments* movie directed by Cecil B. DeMille in 1923. The story itself is as believable as this popular joke: *A boy was sitting on a park bench with one hand resting on an open Bible. He was loudly exclaiming his praise to God. "Hallelujah! Hallelujah! God is great!" he yelled without worrying whether anyone heard him or not.*

Shortly after, along came a man who had recently completed some studies at a local university. Feeling himself very enlightened in the ways of truth and very eager to show this enlightenment, he asked the boy about the source of his joy.

"Hey" asked the boy in return with a bright laugh, "Don't you have any idea of what God is able to do? I just read that God opened up the waves of the Red Sea and led the whole nation of Israel right through the middle."

The enlightened man laughed lightly, sat down next to the boy and began to try to open his eyes to the "realities" of the miracles of the Bible. "That can all be very easily explained. Modern scholarship has shown that the Red Sea in that area was only 10 inches deep at that time. It was no problem for the Israelites to wade across."

The boy was stumped. His eyes wandered from the man back to the Bible lying open in his lap. The man, content that he had enlightened a poor, naive young person to the finer points of scientific insight, turned to go. Scarcely had he taken two steps when the boy began to rejoice and praise louder than before. The man turned to ask the reason for this resumed jubilation.

"Wow!" Exclaimed the boy happily, "God is greater than I thought! Not only did he lead the whole nation of Israel through the Red Sea, but he topped it off by drowning the whole Egyptian army in 10 inches of water!"

63   Some may even question if there is such a phenomenon as Jewish humor. Oring, for example, refers to Jewish humor more as conceptualization than a phenomenon. He points out (all in capital letters) that, "The conception of Jewish Humor Derives from a conceptualization of Jewish history as a history of suffering, rejection, and despair. Given this history, the Jews should have nothing to laugh about at all. That they do laugh and jest can only signal the existence of a special relationship between the Jews and humor and suggests that the humor of the Jews must in some way be distinctive from other humors which are not born of despair" (1983: 266–267).

answer, but since he represents a minority in the studies of Jewish humor, this article is included here to provide the student with as many diversified points of view as possible.

Regardless of whether Jews or others created "traditional" Jewish humor[64], modern humor of Jewish comedians in the United States might also be classified as "New York metropolitan humor," as Lenny Bruce summarized it in one of his famous quotes "to me, if you live in New York or any other big city, you're Jewish." This metropolitan character of Jewish humor is a result of a very high concentration of Jews in "trendy" cities of the world, especially in the U.S., in both New York and Los Angeles. Consequently, some critics point out that, for example, popular TV shows such as *The Nanny* (1993–1999), *Friends* (1994–2004), *Dharma and Greg* (1997–2002), *Will & Grace* (1998–2006), and even *Seinfeld* (1989–1998), which include strong Jewish characters, are not explicit enough to allow their ethnic identity being classified as [purely] Jewish (e.g., Brook 2003; Gillota 2010). Arguably the most popular sitcom on American TV in the last few years has been *The Big Bang Theory*, and it too includes references to Jewish stereotypes: the one of a genius, as most of the famous theorists in the history of science recited in the sitcom are Jewish, and the one of a typical *schlemiel*. The first one has reached its *apogaeum* in the episode in which the main character, Sheldon Cooper, acquires a very high number of cats to whom he gives "cute Jewish names," as commented by his mother, a devout Evangelical Christian from Texas. The *schlemiel* is Howard Wolowitz, a Jewish aerospace engineer (oops… a wrong career for a Jewish boy, especially because is supported only by a Master's degree [see above])[65], with an overbearing mother, selective appreciation of Jewish traditions, and a victim of failures of his own doing. However, the only "true" Jewish comedy of the small screen in America is undoubtedly *Curb Your Enthusiasm* (2010 till present) as its Jewishness "is invoked in ways that invite even the neophyte viewer to recognize its Jewish content" (Byers and Krieger 2006: 283). This comedy is much more than just a collection of funny

episodes—it is a reflection of what it means to be Jewish in today's world, regardless of the "degree" of Jewishness. The brilliance of Larry David, a co-creator of "Seinfeld," who plays himself in *Curb Your Enthusiasm*, doesn't come from his ability as a writer or an actor but from his heart and true confusion about one's identity in the contemporary world. By blending traditional aspects of a Jewish *schlemiel* with a modern perception of a successful assimilation into the melting pot of the immigrant culture of America, he exposes incongruities of the desire and reality in and of creating a homogeneous society. His personal struggle, rooted in his Jewish ancestry, to "fit" in with "the others" is a struggle of any minority in the U.S. and of any other multicultural societies defined either through physical or virtual boundaries[66].

---

64   It must be mentioned here that Jewish humor can be traced back to as far as to the Old Testament (e.g., Ziv 1988), through European history especially from the 18th century, and finally to its more recent form of American-Jewish humor (e.g., Landmann 1962; Cray 1964; Brandes 1983).

65   Q: *What's the difference between a Jewish mother and a Rottweiler? A: A Rottweiler eventually lets it go.*

66   However, one must always remember that Jews in America are different from other groups because they are "white minority" as Gladstone, a commentator on a popular website www.cracked.com, funnily pointed out in his article "3 Reasons There are so Many Jews in Comedy" (July 6, 2011): "[Jews in America] can live comfortably, practice freely and bowl adequately. But being a Jew in America is like

In one of the episodes of the third season of *Curb Your Enthusiasm*, Larry "assumes" his "black identity" ("I am your nigger, absolutely") in response to Krazee-Eyez Killa, an African-American artist's comment to Larry: "You my dog. You my nigger." This is a classic example of switching scripts/frames in humor but more meaningful here than in many other ethnic jokes as it brings together two ethnic groups whose histories and cultural experiences are so profound in creating their distinct forms of humor. While both groups can be described, using O'Rourke's words, as "involuntary tourists" (1988: 7), at least Jews had a "choice" in their destinations, Africans didn't. Their misfortunes brought them to a new nation whose identity they have helped to create through both hard work and entertainment rooted in their cultures. American Jews built it from the top through dominating both Wall Street and Hollywood; African-Americans built it from the bottom through sweat and tears of plantations owned by everyone but them and through providing "foundation" for minstrelsy. *The Jazz Singer*, the first full-length American musical film of 1927, might be considered

a symbolic convergence point of these cultures and their experiences as the "racial cross-dressing." At the end of the movie, a Jewish immigrant, both in real life and in the film, Al Jolson (Asa Yoelson)[67]/Jackie Rabinowitz sings the famous "My Mammy" song to Sara Rabinowitz, his movie-mom, proud of her son, now a fully "born" American under a new name of Jack Robin. His new American identity is stressed not only by his career and name but also by the blackface in which he performs. Two pieces of Americana, the Jewish and African cultures, the cantor and the minstrel, came together in the song directed to a mother. Whose mother? The Jewish one who wouldn't ever let her son go, or the African one, who had limited time to care for her offspring as she was raising her master's white children? This is the question asked by Rogin (and others) in his book, *Blackface, White Noise: Jewish Immigrants in the Hollywood Melting Pot*:

> How could blacking up and then wiping off burnt cork be a rite of passage from immigrant to American? To whose mother is the man born in the Old World Pale of Jewish Settlement really singing? "My Mammy" forces us to consider these questions by condensing into a single figure the structures of white supremacist racial integration that built the United States: black labor in the realm of production, interracial nurture and sex (the latter as both a private practice and a unifying public prohibition) in the realm of reproduction, and blackface minstrelsy in the realm of culture (1996: 5).

---

using left-handed scissors: You [A Jew] can make it work, but it just doesn't feel right. This is Jesusland. Always has been, always will be. So, perhaps what makes Jews so funny is not Judaism, but Christianity—and the American Jew's constant immersion in it. Don't believe me? Who could blame you? It's easy to accept that Jesus healed the sick, raised the dead and walked on water, but believing he begat the funniest fuckers on the planet would take a true leap of faith."

67   Jolson's career and the movie itself have been analyzed by numerous authors (e.g., Carringer 1979; Rogin 1996; Bradley 2004; Harrison-Kahan 2010) as they are among the most important events of American cinematography and culture.

As the topic here is humor, we must then concentrate on the so-called Negro humor whose range has been underappreciated until publication of *The Book of Negro Humor* in 1966 by Langston Hughes. This collection of humorous poems, stories, and anecdotes mostly collected from Harlem and presented within the context of all other works of Hughes, one of the most prolific American writers of the 20th century, may be the most important book connecting the traditional Negro humor with modern Black humor (humor by black comedians) rooted in slaves' mocking their masters (e.g., the John-Master stories; Boskin and Dorinson 1985). Being born and raised in Poland where there is no racial diversity as there is rarely a black person to see, seemingly there has not been any need for discussion of racial diversity[68]. However, Polish primary schools have promoted, hopefully unwittingly, racism by using this particular poem, *Murzynek Bambo* ("A Negro [named] Bambo) written for children by one of the most famous Polish writers, Julian Tuwim (1864–1953). It rhymes and really sounds so sweet in Polish that after so many years I still remember it without much help from the Internet. Below is an original text in Polish with my very rough and definitely not poetic translation in English:

---

68   The overwhelming majority of Poles has known Blacks only from American movies (not a very good introduction) and as occasional tourists or exchange students. According to Maslikowski (2009) there are around 3,000 to 4,000 Africans living in Poland today, mostly in Warsaw, and approximately 60,000 studied in Poland between 1958 and 1980 (she cites these numbers after Pawel Sredzinski). I remember being called a whore, hooker, and many more "colorful" names when my black colleague, a student from Sudan, helped me to the train in Warsaw when I was on my way to visit my parents in Gdansk for Christmas in 1981. Why? Because we hugged! This was way too much in a very hugging and kissing Polish society.

Murzynek Bambo w Afryce mieszka,
A Little Negro boy, Bambo, lives in Africa

Czarną ma skórę ten nasz koleżka.
This friend of ours has a black skin.

Uczy się pilnie przez całe ranki
He studies diligently all morning,

Ze swej murzyńskiej pierwszej czytanki.
from his first Negro ABC book.

A gdy do domu ze szkoły wraca,
And when he comes back home from school,

Psoci, figluje—to jego praca.
He's naughty and boisterous—this is his work.

Aż mama krzyczy: "Bambo, łobuzie!"
So his mother yells: "Bambo, you little scoundrel!"

A Bambo czarną nadyma buzię.
And Bambo frowns his black face.

Mama powiada: "Napij się mleka,"
Mother says, "Drink a glass of milk,"

A on na drzewo mamie ucieka.
but he runs away and climbs a tree.

Mama powiada: "Chodź do kąpieli,"
Mother says, "Come and take a bath,"

A on się boi, że się wybieli.
but he's scared that he will turn white.

Lecz mama kocha swojego synka,
But mother loves her little son,

Bo dobry chłopak z tego Murzynka.
because this little Negro boy is a good boy.

Szkoda, że Bambo czarny, wesoły,
Too bad that Bambo, black and cheerful,

Nie chodzi razem z nami do szkoły.
doesn't go to school with us.

Millions of Polish children have been reciting this poem for years. Only a very few of them have ever questioned its clearly racist (at least to me) content when they grew up. Neither the poem nor the term used, *Murzynek* ("a little Negro boy"; recently more often translated as "a little black boy"), is considered offensive, even today. There is a Polish cake named *Murzynek* and many Polish dogs and cats are "proudly" carrying the same name as long as they are black. The "Bambo" poem clearly demonstrates to Poles that all white Polish people are quite inclusive, as the terms used are of endearment directed toward a good, little, non-civilized savage. This image is so strong that even a Polish "Foreign Minister Radoslaw Sikorski is on record as having joked to colleagues that U.S. President Barack Obama had a Polish connection because 'his grandfather ate a Polish missionary!'" (Maslikowski 2009)

At the time when I recited this poem as a little girl and even got an award for its emotional interpretation, I was quite proud of myself for having so much empathy for all "little Negroes" of the planet. By the time I immigrated to the Unites States in the 1980s, my "knowledge" about African-Americans was a cross between the "Bambo" love and the fear of all black people, as their portrayal in the American movies was so violent. I was terrified to walk the streets of Philadelphia and remember a great relief when moving to Utah, the state where the percentage of black population is barely higher than in my native country[69]—even today. I've gotten over the fear but not because "[I'm not racist.] Some of my Facebook friends are black" (a popular T-shirt on the Internet; and, no, I don't have a Facebook page). As an anthropologist I have studied numerous African cultures, and as a first-generation Polish-American immigrant, I have studied the history of my new homeland. Thus, I can say that I understand the history of black people in the U.S., have compassion for horrible hardships they have experienced, viewed and read

---

69   According to the U.S. Census of 2010 (http://2010.census.gov/2010census/) 1.1% of Utahns (Utahan) defined themselves as black or African-American, i.e. as "a person having origins in any of the black racial groups of Africa. The black racial category includes people who marked the "black, African Am., or Negro" checkbox. It also includes respondents who reported entries such as African-American; Sub-Saharan African entries, such as Kenyan and Nigerian; and Afro-Caribbean entries, such as Haitian and Jamaican (a definition used for the purpose of this census)."

a lot about minstrel shows, and truly enjoy modern black humor (i.e., as presented by black comedians), but ... at the same time, my approach is more that of an outsider, lacking a strong emotional attachment, whose importance in fully comprehending offensiveness of the Negro/Black humor is stressed, for example, by Thomas Veatch (1998). Thus, in order to give the topic its proper attention and compassion, I asked one of my students, John Simpson, to prepare a chapter for this book included as *Negro Humor: The Power of Racial Stereotypes. A Student's View*. Yes, he is a white male but he has experienced racial inequality in the U.S. through an interracial marriage at a time when such marriages were still a rarity. I remember him sitting in my class with teary eyes and a lot of anger when young students, almost all white, tried to discuss the origin and history of Negro humor and its transition to the Black humor of modern days, continuously focusing on the success of such comedians as David Chappelle and Chris Rock. His original short essay on this topic made me stop and think again about how much I really know or rather understand about Negro humor.

> *"Observe it, the vulgar often laugh, but never smile, whereas well-bred people often smile, and seldom or never laugh. A witty thing never excited laughter, it pleases only the mind and never distorts the countenance."*
> —*Lord Chesterfield (1694–1773)*
> *A British statesman.*

"There is nothing like Negro humor. It is loud, profane, juicy, wondrous, scabrous, willful, tricky, and sometimes delivered in coded language" (Haygood 2001). As enjoyable as its loudness is in theatrical/cinematographic/stage settings, the loudness in general is perceived in modern Western societies as a sign of a less-refined/-educated and "inferior" people. The association of "noise" with the dark skin color of the African people has been used as "evidence" for their racial inferiority by many racists, both in the past and the present[70]. While this notion is simply preposterous in view of our current knowledge of human biology, it must be mentioned here because laughter is noise. As such, it attracts others ("mirror laughter" discussed elsewhere) for better or worse. However, a loud noise also frightens others when safety is a concern. It is a deterrent as it has been shown by many studies to scare both people and other animals, especially if such a noise is unfamiliar. Net hunters in Africa still use loud noises to drive animals toward their nets (Haviland et al. 2010: 215). All members of this society usually participate in these noise-making activities, including women and children. These "loud practices" have not been limited to Africa but have been abandoned in other areas, in all probability, with the transition to different and more rewarding subsistence strategies. Gradually, the excessive noise in everyday interactions has been eliminated, as it is considered a sign of poor manners[71]. As the transition from hunting-gathering practices to other modes of subsistence has taken place only very recently in many African societies, the loudness is still very welcomed and needed "activity." Thus, it is not surprising that it has carried on to all forms of

---

70   Although I am not known for my political correctness, I believe it is not necessary here to list a number of people whose well outdated "ideas" are still appealing to a, hopefully, small percentage of modern Americans. Just a quick search on the Internet is more than enough for students interested in this topic to gather the "data." Obviously, none of such authors has ever heard about DNA. The classification of humans as based on phenotypes (physical traits such as skin pigmentation, head and nose shapes, hair, etc.), which has developed as a scientific theory in the seventeenth century, a theory already rooted in racism, is simply faulty, as phenotypes are determined by genotypes. Such differences are, biologically speaking, insignificant in view of the fact that the genetic difference between any two people of the world is only 0.2%; of which only 6% is a variation that can be assigned to racial categories. The rest is a just a variation within any race.

71   However, noise-making devices are still used in modern cultures both for hunting and as a deterrent to keep all sorts of creatures away.

African arts and as such has survived in modern America finding its expressions in humor, among other things.

African-rooted rhythms are syncopated in their nature and can be recognized in all African music performances, regardless of whether it is drumming, foot stomping, or hand clapping. When American slaves were not allowed to use drums, as Whites were afraid that secret messages might be transmitted through loud drumming, slave songs were enhanced with an increased use of hand clapping and foot stomping. This has added to the perception of very expressive nature of Africans and became a soul of minstrelsy, a combination of everything known to entertain masses. Thomas Dartmouth "Daddy" Rice (1808–1860) was the first "official" white performer[72] who incorporated elements of African slaves' forms of entertainment into his act as Jim Crow. The tremendous success of his song-and-dance routine led to the establishment of many minstrel groups, whose performances became standard in their format. White Americans in blackface (courtesy of burnt cork) dominated minstrelsy, but Black minstrels started to join numerous troupes in the 1840s but didn't really change its character[73].

Like Whites, the Blacks too darkened their faces and played up to already established stereotypes. The Whites, on the other hand, remained unaware of the fact that what they were laughing at was often not of African origin, but rather the slaves' interpretation of the Whites and their perception of the perception created by Black slaves of their masters. The famous "cakewalk," for example, was an elaborated form of the plantation slaves' exaggerated imitation of their masters' walk! Defenders of minstrel shows always referred to their seemingly benign character, since plantation slaves were presented as happy and carefree creatures (e.g., a popular song of 1848, *A Darkie's Life Is Always Gay*). Unfortunately, "happiness and naïveté" played into the common belief of inferiority of Africans, not only because of denigrating images, but also because of perpetuating an "obligation" to civilize them for their own good. After all, in the view of many Whites, the slavery was a Christian act of mercy as good Christians were not really profiting from it but, instead, were spending their resources on providing their slaves with fine things of life like clothing, shelter, and, of course, food. Furthermore, minstrel shows, blackface, and all stereotypes presented in a form of entertainment were seemingly instrumental in providing a "proof" to scientific theories propagating "truthiness" of racial distinctions. This view wasn't in fact damaging to Biblical ideals of "equality," as we all are "children" of Adam and Eve (e.g., Leahy 2011). Minstrels themselves mocked the common origin of all races as, for example, in this monologue full of malapropisms that were to supposedly reflect the Negro dialect:

Adem and Eve was bofe brack men, and so was Cane and Abel. Now I s'pose it seems to strike yer understanding how de fust white man cum. Why, I let you know. Den you see when Cane kill his brudder, de massa come and say, "Cane, whar's your brudder Abel?" Cane say, "I don't know, massa." But the nigger node all the time. Massa not git mad and cum agin; speak mighty

---

72 Leahy, in his Ph.D., refers to different sources that traced back this genre to as early as 1769 (2011).

73 As Boskin and Dorinson noted "the black artist had to participate in self-caricature" in order to survive (1985: 93). Interestingly, they pointed to the importance of the minstrel humor for the whites: "The white performer who put on his blackface minstrel mask was performing a rite of exorcism. He was operating a safe valve for repressed emotions. The black persona he portrayed—indolent, inept, indulgent—embodied the anti-self and objectified between social norms and man's instincts. Imparting a sense of freedom and inviting a return to childhood, minstrelsy answered deep psychic needs for white audiences, 'the mammy for security and comfort... the Negro male for ridicule and jest.' For blacks themselves, this ridicule forged psychic chains: a bag for Uncle Ben, a box for Aunt Jemima, a cabin in the sky for Uncle Tom, a pancake restaurant chain for Sambo, and a joke for Rastus" (1985: 92–93).

dis time. "Cane, whar's your brudder Abel, yu nigger?" Cane not git frightened and he turn white; and di de way de furst white man cum upon dis eartht! And if it had not been for dat dar nigger Cane we'd nebber been trubbled wid de white trash 'pon de face ob dis yer circumular globe (*Minstrel Gags*, 144 as cited by Leahy 2011).

The minstrel shows started to lose their popularity in the late 1800s but they were "revived" in cinematography and lasted until the late 1970s (e.g., the BBC TV *The Black and White Minstrel Show* starring the George Mitchell Minstrels). Does this mean that the minstrel show is dead? Who knows? The term itself has started to be used in reference to shows that mock any minority group in the U.S., regardless of whether it is a musical (e.g., *The Book of Mormon*) or an imaginary dialogue associated, for example, with the "geeky subculture" (*The Big Bang Theory*[74]).

The origin, transformation, and adaptiveness of Jewish and Negro humor are unique in and of themselves, but in conjunction they have created an extraordinary piece of Americana. Consequently, Jewish and African-American comedians currently dominate humor in the U.S.A., since both types of humor have been essential for formulating the American identity. Furthermore, it seems that they are becoming very similar, as Jewish humor changes from its very verbal, clever, intellectual origins into its more physical form (e.g., Sacha Cohen). Likewise, the Negro humor is toning down its loudness and physical focus into more conceptual and cognitive expressions (e.g., Chris Rock[75]). The result is a wide-acceptance and enjoyment of both, increasing cohesion of the American multicultural society (always a "melting pot") while, at the same time, preserving the uniqueness of individual, cultural identities.

"When you laugh, be sure to laugh at what people do and not at what people are."
Unknown Source

Jewish and Negro humors are strongly embedded in the American culture, and rarely switchable with any other ethnicities. While, at times, other ethnic humors are treated as "unique" in terms of reference to, for example, history and experiences of a specific ethnic group, their content is often very "standard" when they are told and/or acted out by outsiders in the U.S. or in other countries. Within the same ethnic environment, such humor becomes more epiphinal, especially because it is performed in a native language with its peculiarities often non-translatable in other languages. Many examples for humor that often "get lost in translation" are provided by Laurian and Nilsen 1989; Davies 1990; Delabistita 1997; Charo 2006; Raskin 2008; Chiaro 2010a and 2010b; among others. The following two examples are often cited when translatability of humor is in question.

FRENCH (e.g., Lauriand and Nilsen 1989: 6; Chiaro 2008: 575–576):

Q.: *Qu'est-ce qui a cinq cent pattes et qui ne peut pas marcher?*
A.: *La moitié d'une mille-pattes.*

---

74 An "Uncle Tron" geeky protagonist is described in the urban dictionary as "a stereotypical presentation of a member of a traditionally nerdy or geeky subculture that is meant to both represent [and] appeal to that subculture. It is more often than not presented in a way that would be outrageously offensive to any other subculture or minority group that society has deemed it politically incorrect to make fun of, e.g., blacks, Jews, or women." http://www.urbandictionary.com

75 "You know that the world is going crazy when the best rapper is a White guy, the best golfer is a Black guy, the tallest guy in the NBA is Chinese, the Swiss hold the America's Cup, France is accusing the U.S. of arrogance, [and] Germany doesn't want to go to war" (Chris Rock).

In translation:

> Q.: What has five hundred legs and cannot walk?
> A.: Half a centipede.

The "funniest" part of this joke is lost in translation because a French centipede actually refers to "thousand-feet" (*"mille-pattes"*). Thus, we have an appropriate reference but not the same humor. Of course, as with most of the jokes, the "centipede joke" is based on truthiness as the number of legs usually varies between twenty (20) and three hundred (300).

ITALIAN (e.g., Chiaro 2008: 583):

> Q.: *Che cosa scrivono sul fondo delle lattine di Coca-Cola che si trovano nei distributori di bibite nelle caserme dei carabinieri?*
> A.: *Aprire dall'altro lato.*

In translation to English about Irish:

> Q: What do they write on the bottom of Guinness bottles in Ireland?
> A.: Open at other end.

In translation to American-English:

> Q: What does it say on the bottom of a Coke bottle in Poland?
> A: Open at other end.

In translation to Polish about Russian stupidity:

> Q: *Co jest napisane na dnie butelki z Coca-Cola produkowanej w Rosji?*
> A: *Otwierać z drugiej strony.*

Same joke, different ethnic groups. The Italian version doesn't focus on an ethnic group but on a profession, i.e., the *carabinieri* (not-so-smart police force)[76]. The English one "attacks" Irish because they are a butt of many stupidity jokes in Great Britain with a long history of conflict over land and religion. The American-English version goes after Poles as they have been at the bottom of the immigration ladder in the U.S.A., at least until a new wave of Mexican immigrants has pushed them up (or down?) in the "stupidity hierarchy." Interestingly enough, neither Italians nor Irish in America are targeted by the same

---

76 The *carabinieri* are supposedly associated with the South (Dr. Silvia Smith does not believe this is correct—personal communication) and most popular targets of Italian jokes although, in real life, they are preferred to the police (*polizia*). Italians also have many regional stereotypes but none of them is considered really "stupid," although they have many quirks as the rhymed Italian "poem" about North Eastern Italy indicates,

joke, as they are considered slightly smarter than Poles[77]. In Poland, this joke switches the "victim" to Russians as they are not only considered to be stupid, uncivilized, and pretenders to a proud title of being a "European," but also quite hated by many Poles who have blamed Russia ("the neighbor from hell") for almost every calamity in Polish history[78]. The Irish national drink, Guinness, is used as a bottled beverage, while Coca-Cola took its place in more international versions regardless of whether there is a national drink (vodka in Russia) or not (Italy). While Poles and Russians drink mostly bottled Coke (cans used to be more expensive), Italians prefer a canned one, so instead of a bottle, a can is used. This international joke about stupidity gets its point across in translation but its funniness varies depending on emotional attachment (naïve but still likeable *carabinieri* versus mortal enemy—Russians) of a joke-teller and the audience.

The national humor can be considered a variation of an ethnic humor. However, such humor doesn't focus on ethnicity per se as its targets are numerous and without traceable origin, their content might be hermetic, and their enjoyment limited to "offenders." Many national humors focus on politics, whether of the past or of the present, and rarely make fun of the ethnic group itself, i.e., here a nationality is an entity. There are, of course, some exceptions but they are rare. It is rather difficult to meet a Pole who would agree, jokingly or not, that one of the national characteristics assigned to Poles by outsiders is belief in "the Polish conviction that life is fundamentally miserable and meaningless, meant to be endured rather than enjoyed" (Weber 2003). This "endurance" is the result of a tumultuous history of Poland leading to the notion that Poles saved "the world" (i.e., Europe) on more than one occasion at the expense of their own greatness. Consequently, the irony of the other "chosen people," as Poles occasionally refer to themselves,

Veneziani gran signori	[People from] Venice are noble
Padovani gran dottori	[People from] Padua are educated
Vicentini mangiagatti	[People from] Vicenza eat cats
Veronesi tutti matti	[People from] Verona are all mad
Udinesi castellani	[People from] Udine build castles
Con il nome di furlani	And call themselves Friulani
Trevisani pane e trippe	[People from] Treviso eat bread and tripe
Rovigotti bacco e pippe	[People from] Rovigo drink and smoke
Ne volete di più tristi?	You want to know the meanest?
Bergamaschi bruciacristi	[People from] Bergamo who burn Christ.

77   *There is a box of candy on a table. Beside it are Santa Claus, the Easter Bunny, a dumb Italian, and a smart Polack. Who gets the candy? The dumb Italian—because the others are charitable and there's no such thing as a smart Polack.*

78   The following joke cleverly summarizes Polish attitude toward Russians.

One day an old Pole, living in Warsaw, has his last light bulb burn out. To get a new one he'll have to stand in line for two hours at the store (and they'll probably be out by the time he gets there), so he goes up to his attic and starts rummaging around for an old oil lamp he vaguely remembers seeing. He finds the old brass lamp in the bottom of a trunk that has seen better days. He starts to polish it and (poof!) a genie appears in a cloud of smoke.

"Hoho, Mortal!" says the genie, stretching and yawning, "For releasing me I will grant you three wishes."

The old man thinks for a moment, and says, "I want Genghis Khan resurrected. I want him to re-unite his Mongol hordes, march to the Polish border, and then decide he doesn't want the place and march back home."

"No sooner said than done!" thunders the genie. "Your second wish?"

"Ok. I want Genghis Khan resurrected. I want him to re-unite his Mongol hordes, march to the Polish border, and then decide he doesn't want the place and march back home."

"Hmmm. Well, all right. Your third wish?"

"I want Genghis Khan resurrected. I want him to re-unite his—"

"OK. Ok. OK. Right. What's this business about Genghis Khan marching to Poland and turning around again?"

The old man smiles. "He has to pass through Russia six times."

is not celebrated in a humorous fashion. The other "chosen people," the Irish, whose humor[79] origins, are comparable to Jewish humor as it "developed out of pain and tragedy that resulted in a diaspora" (Nilsen 1996: xv), have a similar problem since their pride interferes with the perception of others that Irish are simply stupid, drunks, and speak "funny" ("Irish being Irish"). However, as they have not been saving the world as Poles have, their humor about themselves is more critical, lighter, and in good nature being born "out of the oral tradition (the telling of jokes and stories in Irish pubs)" (Nilsen 1996: xv). Such a tradition is foreign to Poles, whose outlook on life is usually fatalistic but always full of melodrama, creating more heroes than jesters or tricksters.

While discussion of national humors, including many regional and local ones, is far beyond the scope of this book[80], it must be noted here that some ethnic stereotypes about different nations are much more effective (i.e., funnier) than others. The images are so appealing and hilarious that a respondent doesn't even care about the truthiness, as he/she doesn't have any point of reference at all. The following ethnic joke makes my students roll with laughter although their knowledge of some ethnic groups mentioned here is very limited or non-existent and, in some severe cases of under-education, they cannot find even a proper continent to locate some of the countries mentioned below[81].

Desert Island
There were thirty people stranded on a deserted island:
Two Italian men and one Italian woman.
Two French men and one French woman.
Two German men and one German woman.
Two Greek men and one Greek woman.
Two English men and one English woman.
Two Bulgarian men and one Bulgarian woman.
Two Romanian men and one Romanian woman.
Two Japanese men and one Japanese woman.
Two American men and one American woman.

---

79   The uniqueness of Irish culture as rooted in bilingualism, biculturalism (Gaelic/Celtic and English) and comic tradition dated back to the 9th century or so is a "Touchstone of Irish Studies" (Cahalan 2004).

80   There are many resources to study national humors on both the Internet and in print. They include, for example, works of Dundes 1987; Ziv 1988; Laurian and Nilsen 1989; Ruch 1991; Delabistita1997; Nilsen and Nilsen 2000; Chiaro 2005; Davies 2005; Raskin 2008 and these Internet websites as listed by Nilsen in one of his ppt. presentations:

International and cross-cultural humor: Danish humor resources (Josef Weitemeyer): www.humor.dk

International Society for Humor Studies (Martin Lampert): www.humorstudies.org

International Studies in Humor Research (Willibald Ruch):

http://www.uni-duesseldorf.de/WWW/MathNat/Ruch/SecretaryPage.html

81   A similar statement can be made about the following joke, which requires a basic knowledge of world affairs:

Last month, a survey was conducted by the U.N. worldwide. The only question asked was: Would you please give your honest opinion about solutions to the food shortage in the rest of the world?" The survey was a HUGE failure:

• In Africa they do not know what "food" means.
• In Western Europe they do not know what "shortage" means.
• In Eastern Europe they do not know what "opinion" means.
• In the Middle East they do not know what "solution" means.
• In South America they do not know what "please" means.
• In Asia they do not know what "honest" means.
• And in the U.S.A. they do not know what "the rest of the world" means!

Two Irish men and one Irish woman.

After a month the following had happened:

One Italian man had killed the other Italian man over the Italian woman.

The two French men were living happily together with the French woman in ménage à trois.

The two German men have a strict weekly schedule of alternate visits with the German woman.

The two Greek men are sleeping with each other and the Greek woman is doing all the cleaning and cooking.

The two English men are waiting for someone to introduce them to the English woman.

The two Bulgarian men took one long look at the ocean, another long look at the Bulgarian woman, and started swimming.

The three Romanians spend their time begging of the other 27 and flashing their gold teeth.

The two Japanese men have faxed Tokyo and are awaiting instructions.

The two American men are contemplating suicide because the American woman keeps complaining about her body, the true nature of feminism, how she can do everything they can do, the necessity of fulfillment, the division of household chores, how sand and palm trees make her look fat, how her last boyfriend respected her opinion and treated her nicer than they do, and how her relationship with her mother is improving.

The two Irish men have divided the island into North and South and set up a distillery. They do not remember if sex is in the picture because it gets sort of foggy after the first few liters of coconut whiskey, but they are satisfied because at least the English aren't having any fun.

Why do they laugh then? There are probably multiple reasons, from the mirror laughter (see Chapter 2) to the pure pressure because they are in a class about humor and this is assumed to be funny[82]. Most of them are laughing because they understand a few most common stereotypes (Italian, French, German, English, Japanese, and American) to which they have been exposed personally or through various media. Some are laughing because of references to Greeks and Irish whose history or cultural aspects they have been studying in the past so they are able to recognize and appreciate the truthiness of the statement. However, the Romanian and Bulgarian stereotypes are not getting through because their "message" is foreign to many American students. They are funny because they are in the context of other ethnic groups' hypothetical behavior and visual images are powerful enough to invoke laughter but not any critical processing. The problem thus emerges that as harmless, enjoyable, and laughable this joke is with regard to ethnic groups already known or recognized, it also initiates a negative image of both Bulgarians and Romanians. Thus, an innocent (or as innocent as a joke can be) joke reinforces or rather creates a perception on which such a group might be judged in the future. However, as Brigham has already theorized in the past (1971), stereotypes don't seem necessarily to influence (at least not to any significant degree) an attitude toward a stereotyped ethnic (or other) group, since even a creator or a joke-teller himself/herself considers them unjustified generalizations. In other words, although it has been expected that "ethnic stereotypes may serve as significant determinants of behaviors toward ethnic group members" (Brigham 1971: 35), there is not much measurable evidence that it actually does. The common stereotypes are repeated as long as

---

82   It has been documented that expectations are important when assessing the funniness of a humorous situation (e.g., Wimer and Beins 2008), i.e., if one expects to be amused by a joke, etc., usually such a joke is rated higher on a "humometer" in comparison to those who have no such expectations.

verbal and visual images are appealing, i.e., funny, even if the basis for their truthiness is known to be non-existent or very weak. If these images are positive, then an ethnic group may easily accept them and "live up" to expectations perpetuating truthiness even further[83]. If they are negative, their offensiveness might be "fought" against by a targeted group with jokes of their own against an offender as any factual explanation of truthiness in the context of humor exchange won't work. For example, the French won't mind a reference to *a ménage à trois* as it portrays them as passionate and adventurous lovers, but there is no French who would tolerate any humorous references to the Second World War and French politics during this time (and at other times too). Certainly, the following group of "question and answer" jokes won't be appreciated by the French, would be absolutely enjoyable to many other Europeans who detest the French-perceived cultural superiority[84], and laughed at in America, as cowardness and promiscuity are human attributes frowned upon in general.

Q.: How do you say "Give me liberty or give me death!" in French?
A. I give up.

Q.: How many Frenchmen does it take to defend Paris?
A.: Nobody knows. It's never been tried.

Q.: What do you call 100,000 Frenchmen with their hands up?
A.: The French Army.

Q.: Why was the Channel built under the English Channel?
A.: So the French government could to flee to London.

Q.: Did you hear about the new French tanks?
A.: They have 5 gears…4 in reverse, and one forward gear just in case they're attacked from behind!

Q.: Why do they have trees in Paris?
A.: So the Germans can march in the shade instead of the sun.

Q.: Why is good to be French?
A.: You can surrender at the beginning of the war, and U.S. will win it for you.

Q.: What is the first thing you are taught when joining the French army?
A.: To say "I surrender" in German.

---

83   *Five Jews changed the way we see the world:*
Moses: "The Law is everything."
Jesus: "Love is everything."
Marx: "Money is everything."
Freud: "Sex is everything."
Einstein: "Everything is relative."
84   *How many Frenchmen does it take to change a light bulb? One. He holds the bulb and all of Europe revolves around him.*

Q.: Why was Jesus not born in France?
A.: Because they couldn't find three wise men or a virgin.

The French cultural contribution, from arts through architecture, cuisine to fashion, to Western civilization is undeniable. However, *la supériorité française* is just a perception, especially with the development of modern technology and post-war "superiority" of America as both a political leader and a cultural trendsetter (New York and Los Angeles vs. Paris), and as such is resented by the most of ethnic groups in both Europe and the U.S. This resentment is easily expressed through humor as it doesn't require any proof, just enough truthiness to assert one's own superiority. In Davies' words "[This] is a sense in which all ethnic jokes mocking another group are assertions of the joke-tellers' perceptions of themselves and their own merits—the 'others' are comically stupid/cowardly/canny; we are not" (1990: 312).

This "sword and shield" aspect of ethnic humor reinforces then both positive and negative stereotypes especially when they are compared and contrasted in one joke.

An elderly man was walking through the French countryside, admiring the beautiful spring day, when over a hedgerow he spotted a young couple making love in a field. Getting over his initial shock he said to himself, "Ah, young love... ze spring time, ze air, ze flowers... C'est magnifique!" and continued to watch, remembering good times. Suddenly, he drew in a gasp and said, "Mais... Sacre bleu! Ze woman—she is dead!" and he hurried along as fast as he could to the town to tell Jean, the police chief. He came, out of breath, to the police station and shouted, "Jean... Jean zere is zis man, zis woman ... naked in farmer Gaston's field making love." The police chief smiled and said; "Come, come, Henri you are not so old; remember ze young love, ze spring time, ze air, ze flowers? Ah, l'amour! Zis is okay." "Mais non! You do not understand... ze woman, she is dead!" Hearing this, Jean leapt up from his seat, rushed out of the station, jumped on his bike, pedaled down to the field, confirmed Henri's story, and pedaled all the way back non-stop to call the doctor: "Pierre, Pierre, ... this is Jean, I was in Gaston's field. Zere is a young couple naked 'aving sex." To which Pierre replied, "Jean, I am a man of science. You must remember, it is spring, ze air, ze flowers... Ah, l'amour! Zis is very natural." Jean, still out of breath, grasped in reply, "NON, you do not understand... ze woman, she is dead!" Hearing this, Pierre exclaimed, "Mon dieu!" grabbed his black medicine bag, stuffed in his thermometer, stethoscope, and other tools. He jumped in the car and drove like a madman down to Gaston's field. After carefully examining the participants, he drove calmly back to Henri and Jean, who were waiting at the station. He got there, went inside, smiled patiently, and said, "Ah, mes amis, do not worry. Ze woman, she is not dead; she is British."

Clearly, the French are the winners here when the British are the losers if we are to apply Gruner's terminology (1997). The setting and use of French words/phrases only emphasizes a romantic, sexual, and spontaneous nature of the French in contrast to stuffiness, seriousness, and doubtful sexuality of the Brits. Such jokes are even more powerful when both positive and negative stereotypes of one or more ethnic groups are bundled together in one consistent story. This combination may be "deadly" by dragging down one superior group to the level of the inferior one like in this popular joke:

> Q.: What is the right career for a son of a Polish-Jewish marriage?
> A.: A janitor in a medical school.

However, such a combination may also be quite enjoyable since the positive equalizes the negative.

> Heaven is the place where the cooks are French, the police are English, the mechanics are German, the lovers are Italian, and everything is organized by the Swiss.
> Hell is where the cooks are English, the police are German, the mechanics are French, the lovers are Swiss, and everything is organized by the Italians (Nilsen and Nilsen 2000: 162).

There are no losers nor are there winners in the above joke, as all five nationalities are treated equally. Their perceived superiority in certain fields is acknowledged, and their perceived "shortcomings" are treated humorously, i.e., lightly. The audience and a joke-teller are satisfied regardless of whether they are a part of the above group or an outsider who can bask himself/herself in a comfortable feeling of mediocrity.

Much of ethnic/national humor has a political character, which is more profound during times of uncertainty and directed against real or perceived oppressors and/or competitors for real or imaginary power.

> Thus, political humor functions to scrutinize power politics lest its excesses become intolerable or unacceptable. This "watchdog" function carries with it the need to socially correct abuses of powers and, consequently, to move agencies in directions more acceptable to those affected by the exercise of political powers (Koller 1988: 216).

The essence of these politically charged humorous situations is often lost on those who are not a part of daily events, even if they are keen observers from afar. Many times the audience doesn't have necessary information to appreciate complexity of a joke and, although its content can be explained, the meaning escapes as its emotional value, especially in totalitarian societies, cannot be conveyed[85]. Only a few of international conflicts have global, cosmopolitan appeal, as the politics are associated with the wide recognition of ethnicity or the event is very current and affects majority of the world. This can be seen with popularity of jokes about Israel and the rest of the Middle East (especially the Arab World).

---

85   *Not long after the Six-Day War in the Middle East, a class was meeting in the Soviet Union, a class in the Russian War College. The problem under discussion that day was how the Soviet Union might fight a war against China. Some of the students were distressed and puzzled, and one of them said, "How could we possibly fight a war against China? We could put at most, what, 150 or 200 million soldiers in the field? The enemy would have an army of nearly a billion. It would be hopeless." "Not necessarily," said the teacher, a distinguished Soviet commander. "It is entirely possible for the smaller army to win. Just notice what happened not long ago in the Middle East. Israel can field an army of at most 2 or 3 million soldiers, while the combined Arab armies number 100 million, and yet Israel won that war." "Yes," objected the student, "but where can we find 3 million Jews?"*
This particular joke can easily be explained using historical references. However, what makes this joke so powerful for people like me who were raised in a communist system and had to attend military courses to graduate from college are references to "the Russian War College" and "a distinguished Soviet commander." Not only are these phrases oxymoronic to me, but I can also visualize such a commander—I had to suffer through his "training" when he barely could speak, having been mummified in Russian vodka.

Ethnic/national/political jokes are usually very fluid, dated, and outdated too, so they are excluded from this book, although they play a very important role in shaping and re-shaping views of the masses[86] (e.g., Koller 1988). The success of *The Daily Show with Jon Stewart*[87] and *The Colbert Report* on the Comedy Central channel in the U.S. speaks for itself because many Americans are learning to ignore "serious" news on other channels in favor of Internet sources and comedy in general. Mimicking personality-driven American media networks dominated by commentary upon commentary with a very little amount of news, Stewart's show has become a satirical and journalistic phenomenon being nominated for and/or winning numerous awards in both fields. Its spin-off, *The Colbert Report*, has been built almost entirely on a fake TV personality of *The Daily Show's* former correspondent, Stephen Colbert, and is probably *The Daily Show's* the most affable competitor for these awards. *The Daily Show* was proclaimed one of All-Time 100 TV Shows by *Time* magazine in 2007. Poniewozik's justification for this particular selection explains an appeal of such an unholy matrimony between politics and satire (both offensive) in the following words:

> Jon Stewart's nightly fake-newscast has become a bold, truth-telling Onion of the air for a cynical, disaffected, not-as-ill-informed-as-you-might-think audience. And while we journalists often characterize the show as being about politics, it's really about us: the show has nailed the reflexive media impulse to rationalize conventional wisdom, to sensationalize, and to reduce everything important to a branded phrase and a dandy graphic. ("Mess O'Potamia," e.g., for the war in Iraq.) Stewart and company have found the B.S. detector that stenographic media outlets seem to have thrown in the trash, cleaned it off, souped it up, and cranked up its sensitivity to 11 (Poniewozik 2007; http://entertainment.time.com/2007/09/06/the-100-best-tv-shows-of-all-time/slide/the-daily-show-2/#the-daily-show-2#ixzz1tC3E9jls)

The Daily Show with Jon Stewart has a tremendous appeal especially to younger generations who get their TV news from Comedy Central instead of FOX, CNN, or MSNBC.

> According to the May [2011] Nielson ratings, *The Daily Show with Jon Stewart* beat the entire Fox News network in terms of total viewers. Stewart averaged 2.3 million viewers, while the Fox News prime time and day time line up averaged 1.85 million viewers. ...Jon Stewart is the biggest threat to Fox News' future out there. He is literally teaching his audience, which is bigger than FNC's, how to see through the partisan propaganda that Rupert Murdoch has based his network on. Stewart is educating an entire generation of viewers on how to watch cable news, or more specifically how not to watch Fox News (http://www.bilerico.com/2011/06/daily_show_ratings_beat_all_of_fox_news.php).

---

86 Political humor in totalitarian societies is a very risky business but a very enjoyable one because it offers hope and the feeling that one is not helpless and can "fight" the government in his or her own way. However, ridiculing the government or a tyrant likely earns a humorist at least a term in jail. At times, the fear of a dictator is so strong that people are even afraid to mention his name in public. I saw this happening in 1999 in Iraq, when Iraqis were freely joking and commenting about President Clinton's affair with Monica Lewinsky; however, when I asked them an innocent question about Saddam Hussein's family, they simply ran away from me. For more information about socio-political functions of humor, see, for example, Nilsen 1990.

87 Jon Stewart (Jonathan Stuart Leibowitz) is yet another American comedian of Jewish origin.

The numbers don't lie, although some statements made in the "war" between Jon Stewart and Fox media might be more on the side of truthiness than that of truthfulness. For example, on the June 19, 2011 edition of *Fox News Sunday*, Jon Stewart asked Chris Wallace "Who are the most consistently misinformed media viewers?" and answered himself, "The most consistently misinformed? Fox, Fox viewers, consistently, every poll." PolitiFact.com checked this claim only to find out that

> Fox isn't the lowest [on the low-informed list], and other general-interest media outlets—such as network news shows, network morning shows and even the other cable news networks—often score similarly low. Meanwhile, particular Fox shows—such as *The O'Reilly Factor* and Sean Hannity's show—actually score consistently well, occasionally even outpacing Stewart's own audience (http://www.politifact.com/truth-o-meter/statements/2011/jun/20/jon-stewart/jon-stewart-says-those-who-watch-fox-news-are-most/).

Since the accuracy of TV media[88] in reporting news is not a topic of this book, it seems sufficient to say that political humor is consistently gaining its ground in shaping political views of generations raised on cable TV and the Internet. *The Daily Show* is becoming the leading news "agency" while FOX (#1 out of the "Big Three"), CNN, and MSNBC are competing for "serious" viewers. Whether or not the "humor news" will improve the U.S. (and other countries') national and international policies is yet to be seen.

There is no doubt that ethnic humor is aggressive. However, it can also affirm and celebrate ethnic unity, pride, and absorption into a larger and dominant group (e.g., LaFave and Mennell 1976; Fish 1980; Boskin and Dorinson 1985; Leveen 1996). Once absorbed, the disparaged group can "turn the tables" on others and deflect attention from their own stereotypical images to new groups who are in a similar position as they once were in multicultural and multilinguistic societies (e.g., replacement of Polish jokes with similar Mexican ones[89]). Ethnic humor also mediates conflicts by negotiating in- and out-groups' emotions arising from a perceived status quo that, in turn, may lead to changes in the existing state of affairs. It builds alliances by finding something in common to laugh at in other groups or dismantles them by focusing on peculiarities, which makes further cooperation highly unlikely. The role of humor in mediation and/or negotiation of cultural and societal values is also quite visible in the next category of humor: humor and religion.

---

88 Public Policy Polling provides press releases in January of each year on viewers' ratings of all TV news. The 2011 release (TV News Poll 2011) indicates that the most trusted TV news comes from PBS, followed by FOX news, which held the honor the year before.

89 The growing popularity of Mexican stupidity jokes at the "cost" of Polish jokes reflects immigration policy of and economic reality in the U.S. today, following the pattern explained by Davies, "Those peoples who are the butt of jokes about stupidity tend to dwell on the backward periphery of a given society and to be (or to have been in the past) unskilled immigrants moving to new industrial centers" (1990: 314–315). However, one must remember that ethnic jokes tend to preserve their cultural and situational uniqueness, as in the following jokes:
Why does a Mexican refry their beans? Have you seen a Mexican do anything right the first time?
Why does a Mexican eat tamales for Christmas? So they have something to unwrap!
What are the first three words in the Mexican national anthem? "Attention K-Mart shoppers."
What kind of cans are there in Mexico? Mexicans.
What are the first three words in every Mexican cookbook? "Steal a chicken."
Why doesn't Mexico have an Olympic team? Because every Mexican who can run, jump, and swim is already across the border!

SECTION 8
TOWARD RELIGION … My Religion, Not Yours.

"God is a comedian, playing to an audience too afraid to laugh."
—*François-Marie Arouet de Voltaire (1694–1778)*
A French writer, philosopher, and historian.

T he first problem that emerges with this topic is terminology. "Humor and religion" is a very general description but so far the only one that actually covers all aspects of the use of humor with regard to religion. The term "religious humor" used by some scholars (e.g., Koller 1988) is too narrow because technically it covers only humor in religion, i.e., as prescribed, allowed, or even encouraged by religion. While it might include an alleged use of humor by religious figures such as Moses and Jesus or even God himself (e.g., in Judaism, Christianity, and Islam), the problem is that most of the time (if not all the time) humor assigned to the "founders" of various religions, whether they are divine, semi-divine, or messengers of a deity or deities, is assumed, construed, and/or imposed by its interpreters. Such interpretations are very subjective, especially because they refer to "hearsay" from various individuals whose existence is believed but not proven and, consequently, their authorship is doubtful. Whether such "records" are oral, aural, or even textual is irrelevant, as they all are a part of literary traditions that are subject to different type of analyses and criticism within a group itself or outside of it. Furthermore, even historical records of the use of humor by prominent figures in any religion does not qualify such jokes or humorous situations as "religious humor[90]" because its connection is with an individual and his or her "sense of humor[91]," but not with the religion per se; i.e., it is not required to be a part of religious practices. Finally, humor about religion is not a matter of religious conviction, regardless of whether a teller is of the same faith or of a competing one. Humor, in fact, focuses on mocking its believers and practices[92], and rarely on questioning the existence of supernatural/s, although his/her/their perception might be the subject of a joke. Consequently, the line between humor about religion and ethnic humor is often quite blurry, as some ethnic groups are "ethnic" because of their religion (e.g., Jews),

90   Koller uses this term when he analyzes humor within Judaism, Roman Catholicism, and Protestantism (1988). Unfortunately, his approach is non-discriminatory so his references to Jewish humor are not really focused on religion but on Jewish humor in general, and Christian humor is limited to recordings of some humorous situation ascribed to religious personalities and functionaries.

91   Measuring a sense of humor is not a very easy task and some even doubt that such a task can be accomplished. The term "humometer" that I like to use has been "invented" by Sheldon Cooper, a character on the TV show, *The Big Bang Theory*. It doesn't exist but there is a scientific way to do it by using Thorson and Powell's Multidimensional Sense of Humor Scale (MSHS) (1993a; 1993b). Its objectivity can be questioned as it is still based on self-evaluation and most of us believe ourselves to have more than an average sense of humor (e.g., Allport 1961; Lefcourt and Martin, 1986; Beins and O'Toole 2010). On the other hand, the self-evaluation of the sense of humor seems to be quite accurate in the research conducted by Beins and O'Toole: "the correlation between the humor production factor of the MSHS and the self rating of funniness was .765, which would account for over 58% of the variance in that relation. This figure is very high for measurements of such a complex psychological construct" (2010: 282).

92   It is interesting to note Alston and Platt's study of religious cartoons from *The New Yorker* magazine between 1930 and 1968 (1969). They recorded visible trends in "target" changes over the years pointing out, for example, that "the clergy had declined as a target since 1950–1953, when almost three-fourths (71%) of religious cartoons were anticlerical" (1969: 221). Their analysis indicates, quite convincingly, that societal changes with regard to attitudes toward religion are well reflected in humor and, in this particular case of studies, "secularization has influenced definitions of what is humorous" (1969: 222). This is one of not-so-common examples of how the importance of humor can be measured both qualitatively and quantitatively.

while others' humor-prone national identity is a combination of language, geographical boundaries, and religious unity (e.g., Irish, Poles, Italians).

In order to understand "humor and religion" as a category of humor one must first concentrate on finding a suitable definition for religion. There are almost as many definitions of religion as there are scholars (e.g., Durkheim 1964 and 1972; Eliade 1958 and1959; Wallace 1966; Malefijt 1968; Geertz 1972; Lessa and Vogt 1972; Pickering 1984; Stark and Bainbridge 1987; Wasilewska 1991 and 2000) who have discussed this topic because this concept is continuously redefined to address various elements of this fundamental human[93] notion, presumably existing from the beginning of humankind in each and every culture. Furthermore, the term "religion" is in common use on a daily basis, recognized "instinctively" and conceptualized as based on a personal background, education, and preference. For example, when qualifying a system of beliefs as a religion or as a cult, most people are not concerned with any scientific reasoning/validation/definition of religion; rather, they classify religious systems based on one's set of moral values, and often very limited knowledge, issuing a judgment, not an objective classification. Religions and "sects" that are not considered to be mainstream are misunderstood and threatening, and/or have little of general approval, are then becoming, terminologically speaking, "cults" regardless of their structure and even number of followers. The conflict may then arise over such a classification, which can be "resolved" through different means, from humor to violence. The Church of Jesus Christ of Latter-Day Saints (LDS or "affectionately" known as Mormons) has been struggling with its image for years, as the term "cult" is consistently affixed to this organization, in spite of having over fourteen (14) million followers worldwide. The choice of "weapon" against them is humor[94] but mostly at a local level, as the majority of Americans know very little about Mormon beliefs[95]. The Taliban has proclaimed the Hazara, a mysterious Persian-speaking group of people (descendants of Genghiz Khan?[96]) who live in central Afghanistan and Pakistan and practice the Shi'a version of Islam, to be "cultists" and infidels—a reason good enough to try exterminating them[97]. Very few people would use the term "religion" when referring to any system of belief involving a worship of Satan ("satanic cult" versus "satanic" religion).

When defining "religion" for discussion of humor and religion, one must take into consideration its two different forms: humor *in* religion and humor *about* religion. The first concept focuses on physical manifestations and practices involved in religious rituals that "require" humor, while the second refers to the issue of identity in a similar fashion as different ethnicities are described.

---

93   As long as there is no evidence that other animals have a similar notion, we fit their "religious feelings" into our belief system like in this very common joke:

The difference between cats and dogs:

The dog looks at you and thinks to himself,

"You feed me, you shelter me, you love me. YOU must be GOD!"

The cat looks at you and thinks to himself,

"You feed me, you shelter me, you love me. I must be GOD!"

94   A good source of Mormon jokes can be found at http://www.mormonzone.com/jokeindex.aspx

95   For example, outsiders are fascinated by a practice of plural marriages (polygyny) among the Mormons, not knowing that it was outlawed in 1890.

96   The Hazara's oral tradition of their connection with the Mongols seems to be confirmed genetically by polymorphism on the Y chromosome, which was traced to possibly Genghiz Khan and his offspring, and appears in the highest frequency among the Hazara men of Pakistan (Zerjal et al. 2003). One might note that another ruler of the steppe, Manas of Kyrgystan, might fit a scenario proposed by Zerjal and others, but historical evidence regarding his existence and his empire's expansion in the 9th century is limited.

97   At least 8,000 Hazara men and boys were singled out and executed by the Taliban at Mazar-I Sharif in 1998. Many women and girls were allegedly kidnapped and raped. A few more incidents have been reported since then, but on a lesser scale.

The most basic interpretation of the meaning of religion is connected with the origin of the word itself as it is presumed to have its roots in the Latin combination of *legare* (to rebind/reconnect) and *religio* (to restrain/hold). Thus, religion is a construct that connects/reconnects all separate parts of one's life into one logical whole for the purpose of directing/controlling one's behavior, motivations, etc. There is no reference to the presence of supernatural/s in the basic meaning of the term itself, so *religion* is also applicable to philosophical movements like Buddhism. Such reference was not needed because the modern concept of religion focusing on identity (my "religion, not yours") was not present. The ruling religions up to the fourth century A.D.[98] were polytheistic, and there is no record in any ancient language recorded in writing (e.g., Sumerian, Akkadian, Hittite, Egyptian) that the notion of "religion" focusing on supernatural/s and one's personal relationship and identity based on it existed. The closest concept in the later part of the first millennium B.C. was the Hebrew *yir at shamayim*, "fear of Heaven" (Hallo 1996: 212), which, by itself, was not applicable to the existing systems of beliefs in the Middle East and in the Mediterranean region (Wasilewska 2000: 23–24). It seems that the modern concept of religion has emerged with the so-called monotheistic religions[99], as they don't allow for the presence of other deities. Simply, in order for one god to be a true god, all the others must be gone; i.e., their existence denied. This was not a problem in polytheistic societies where a number of deities were fluid and there was never a need to "kill" other gods as long as yours were perceived to be more powerful. Furthermore, polytheistic deities/beings are usually more approachable[100], personal, and can be swayed one way or another with offerings, sacrifices, and prayers. In other words, the assumption is that they can be "bribed" as they are quite "human"—but only better; i.e., more powerful, eternal, and wiser. In such polytheistic societies there is always room for humor, whether accidental or ritually prescribed. After all, Sumerian deities created humans just to work for them because gods themselves, by their own admission, were too lazy to work. The second "wave" of human creation happened when deities were drunk (CUI, "creation under influence") celebrating their first "wave" of human creation (*Enki and Ninmah: The Creation of Humankind*; see, for example, Kramer and Maier 1989; Wasilewska 2000). They played with their humans using trickery to strip them of their one and only chance to become immortal as in the case of Adapa, Etana, and Gilgamesh. Appropriately, they laughed in the process as Anu did at Adapa when he refused to accept the "food and water of life" (immortality), blindly following an "advice" of another god, Ea (Enki),

> Anu looked at him [Adapa]
> He has laughed at him.
> "Come, Adapa, why did you not eat nor drink?
> Hence you cannot live!
> Alas, poor humanity!" (Izre-el 1992: 218)

---

98   The statement refers to "ruling" religions—none of the forms of perceived monotheism was a ruling religious ideology on international scale, not even Judaism.

99   None of the monotheistic religions, which emerged in the Middle East, i.e., Judaism, Christianity, and Islam, are truly monotheistic. At best, they all can be called henotheistic, i.e., recognizing one "high-god" but are ambivalent with regard to other possible beings. They are not to be worshipped but their existence is not denied (e.g., angels, Satan, etc. For the transition from the polytheistic beliefs of the Middle East to monotheistic traditions based on the Old Testament see, for example, Wasilewska 2000).

100   Pre-Biblical deities of the Middle East have been known for their overindulgence, hangovers, love-making (not necessarily to a spouse only), and having fun (e.g., Wasilewska 2000).

So, the best we got out of this deal was insomnia and, because of his "obedience," Adapa was "rewarded" with all diseases of humankind (Heidel 1951; Kramer and Maier 1989; Wasilewska 2000).

The idea of a drunken god is unthinkable in the so-called monotheistic religions, so post-creation celebration was replaced in the Old Testament with a day of rest[101]; likewise, the number of "crazy" celebrations has been significantly limited. The concept of sin and rewards has been "invented" and/or reorganized. Stark and Bainbridge used such a concept for their definition of religion proposed as a general optimality model, which stresses that "Humans seek what they perceive to be rewards and avoid what they perceive to be costs" (Stark and Bainbridge 1987: 27). Their line of inquiry, reported in the form of axioms, propositions, and definitions, led them to the statements that some of the desired rewards are limited in supply, some might not exist, and their distribution is unequal among persons and groups in any society[102]. Due to this inequality in distribution, some individuals or groups may acquire greater resources than others, and with them more power, which is defined by Stark and Bainbridge as "the degree of control over one's exchange ratio" (1987: 33). Since this power is usually used to confer still more power, eventually some of the most desired rewards become relatively unavailable to others. In addition, some rewards are so rare that they seem not to exist. Thus, "in the absence of a desired reward, explanations often will be accepted which posit attainment of the reward in the distant future or in some other non-verifiable context" (Stark and Bainbridge 1987: 35). In other words, compensators—substitutes for desired rewards—must be offered as rewards for human efforts, and must be taken on faith. This concept of compensators "is the key to the theory of religion"[103] (1987: 36) and is quite practical but not always applicable. What about if there is no such thing as an after-life[104]? How are you going to collect on such rewards or to be punished for your shortcomings?

Much more "flexible" definition of religion is provided by Geertz (1972). According to him religion is

(1) a system of symbols which acts to
(2) establish powerful, pervasive, and long-lasting moods and motivations in men by
(3) formulating conceptions of a general order of existence and
(4) clothing these conceptions with such an aura of factuality that
(5) the moods and motivations seem uniquely realistic (Geertz 1972: 168).

This definition is quite helpful in analyzing humor and religion because it is based on three components that are also characteristic of humor: system of symbols, moods and motivations, and, finally, a perception of reality (truthiness).

---

101 A brilliant switch but… for skeptics like me it has raised yet another question: rest from what?

102 The discussion of Stark and Bainbridge's theory of human action is limited here only to the most important points relevant for the topic of humor and religion.

103 In fact, religion as presented by them is a system of compensators based on supernatural assumptions, since "the most general compensators can be supported only by supernatural explanations" (Stark and Bainbridge 1987: 39). Within the framework of this definition Stark and Bainbridge explained all religious behavior known to them.

104 For example, in ancient Mesopotamia all beings were believed to end up exactly in the same place, *Kur*, after their deaths. This was not a reward but rather a storage room for no-longer-useful servants (see, for example, Wasilewska 2000).

"I believe that imagination is stronger than knowledge—myth is more potent than history—dreams are more powerful than facts—hope always triumphs over experience—laughter is the cure for grief—love is stronger than death."
—Robert Fulghum (b. 1937)
An American author.

Humor in religion is often difficult to understand/explain because it involves at least three different systems of symbols (language, religion, and culture-specific humorous references) that work together at the same time, and must be processed through the brain without overloading its cognitive ability and without negative affect. In other words, it must be simple enough to be translatable between three already complex systems of neurons, while switching three scripts back and forth at the same time. Any offensiveness that is to be produced by such humor must be controllable and within the parameters of what is considered to be Geertz' "aura of factuality," confirming the perceived order of existence. Since humor is profane and religion is sacred[105], their combination must have a certain balance that does not threaten the existing order, but rather complements and enhances it to ensure social cohesion and support. Humor must be set within an explicit or implicit context of ritualistic behavior, which must be reversible because the order cannot be destroyed. Consequently, humor is often used in the so-called rituals of rebellion (e.g., Gluckman 1954; Norbeck 1963; Schröter 2004) that often include or imitate violent or otherwise socially unacceptable behavior. These rituals are believed to relieve whatever tension underlies community interrelationships and to "act out" suppressed feelings and/or hostilities in order to preserve a society as a whole. They have a liberating factor similar to liberating properties of humor. Freud considered jokes an outcome of *superego* (a learned and controlling part of human psyche [a system of values]) releasing control over *ego* (a sort of reality "dispenser" of unstructured basic drives of *id*) to express our repressed sexual and aggressive propensities (hostilities) in a socially appropriate manner creating a joyful experience in the process (1905 [1960]; 1916; 1928). Humor then, rebellious in its nature (Freud 1928), is used in religious rituals to express what is suppressed through regular worship, and forbidden or frowned upon in daily life. It allows acting out inappropriateness to remind all why order must be preserved and provides a sanctioned venue to do so. Furthermore, we must remember that humor, separately or in combination with religion, is a powerful political weapon that may lead to socio-political changes. Consequently, some rituals of rebellion that include humor might be more social/political than ceremonial in their character (e.g., Schröter 2004), as they do express social conditions in which they are formed. Mary Douglas explicitly states this condition as her hypothesis

> …that a joke is seen and allowed when it offers a symbolic pattern of a social pattern occurring at the same time. As I [Douglas] see it, all jokes are expressive of the social situations in which they occur. The one social condition necessary for a joke to be enjoyed is that the social group in which it is received should develop the formal characteristics of a "told" joke: that is, a dominant pattern of relations is challenged by another. If there is no joke in the social structure, no other joking can appear (1975: 98).

---

105   However, they are similar since they are both, "…omnipresent, pervasive and yet unobtrusive at the level of individual consciousness in the ways in which it affects the rest of human behavior" (Apte 1985: 151).

For her, a joke "as a symbol of social, physical and mental experience" has a formula of a rite but in contrast to a rite, which "imposes order and harmony," jokes "denigrate and devalue" what is valued in a society, and thus must be classified as an anti-rite. The situation changes "when joking is used in a ritual [because then] it should be approached nonetheless as a rite. Like any other rite, the joke rite is first and foremost a set of symbols" (1975: 101–103). This interpretation of joking in ritual adds the fourth dimension to humor in religion. No longer a "joke is just a joke" with its own set of symbols, but as a rite in itself, it assumes another set of symbols that may enhance or obscure an understanding and/or a meaning of a ritual in progress. Consequently, an interpretation of humor in religion is quite a challenge for anyone, either an insider or an outsider. The ritual itself might not be then what it appears to be, i.e., for example, a ritual of rebellion, but the one of pollution as

> African joking institutions combine the following elements: first, a crude scatology; second, a range of specific relationships; and third, certain ritual occasions (namely funerals and purifications) expressed scatologically. The subject is therefore closely related to ritual pollution in general (Douglas 1975: 92).

Jokers/jokes assume the role of ritual purifiers, and return order and harmony to a society by regaining control over chaos. Consequently, humor in religion breaks a boundary between sacred and profane in order to re-establish and return them to their formal purity. This can be seen, for example, with the *Purim*, pre-Lent carnivals, the Feast of Fools, American Halloween, and the Mexican Day of the Dead. These are the times when what is normally forbidden is suddenly allowed and, even if it doesn't have the official blessing of religious functionaries of a religion under whose umbrella these "rituals" are conducted/performed, they are still an undeniable part of it. All the celebrations mentioned above are the result of meshing traditions of different faiths, leading to the survival of the former ones in an adjusted and accepted/tolerated form of a new religion (for different examples see, for example, Segal 1998). Thus, the Jewish *Purim* based on *The Book of Esther* might be traced to the Babylonian celebrations (e.g., Rubenstein 1992); Christian carnivals and the famous (or infamous) Feast of Fools go back to pagan traditions of Roman Saturnalia and even before (e.g., Gilhus 1990; see Harris 2011 for a new interpretation); the Mexican Day of the Dead is a continuation of the Aztec celebration of the dead (e.g., Norget 2006); and American Halloween is a leftover of Celtic rituals (e.g., Rogers 2002). In order to provide the reader with a wider range of the use of humor in religion and more in-depth discussion, Apte's chapter under the same title is included in this book.

> *"Whoever undertakes to set himself up as a judge of Truth and Knowledge is shipwrecked by the laughter of the gods."*
> —*Albert Einstein (1879–1955)*
> *A German-born American physicist and a Nobel Prize winner for physics in 1921.*

While monotheistic religions of the Middle Eastern progeny include humor in some of their rituals, they seem to be much more serious than their polytheistic predecessors. The reason is that they are based on a system of rewards and compensators, referred to by Stark and Bainbridge (1987), not because religion in general is not compatible with humor or, at best, they can be considered "estranged bedfellows" (a term used by Capps 2006b). Compatibility of religion and humor has been a subject of different studies (for a good review, see Capps 2006b), which continuously point out to "the mistrust of religion toward humor" (Capps 2006b: 437). However, all compatibility research of which I am aware has been done in reference to the monotheistic Christian religion, which operates on very different principles from polytheistic religions.

Polytheistic predecessors of the Middle Eastern monotheistic religions didn't really have a system of rewards and compensators similar to the ones based on the *Old Testament*[106] or the *Bible* in general. Deities were powerful but also self-centered, and often couldn't care less about humans, whom they created to work for them. They had their own "jobs" and parties to attend so there was very little time to keep scores on human behavior. Thus, the Final Judgment either didn't happen and everyone was sent to the same place, which served as a landfill site for all the dead whose usefulness expired with their death (e.g., *Kur* in Mesopotamia); or the responsibility of convincing gods to enjoy the After-Life was put on the shoulders of believers themselves who, through their confessions and construction of elaborate tombs, were given a chance to spend a limited "eternity" in the conditions that they had created for themselves (e.g., Egypt)[107]. Since the interaction among gods and goddesses was human-like in nature, humor was a part of their lives too. With the monotheistic religions such an interaction is not supposed to exist because, technically speaking, there is nobody to interact with[108]. Thus, the only way god can express "his sense of humor[109]" is through his actions in establishing and maintaining the universe or through his interaction with humans. There are many works attempting to show that the *Bible* and Jesus Christ are not devoid of humor (e.g., Webster 1960; Trueblood 1964; Vos 1967; Kissinger 1979; Borowitz 1980; Koller 1988; Ziv 1988; Radday and Brenner 1990; Adams 1997; Friedman 1998)[110]. However, it seems that humor was "forced" on these religious scriptures by scholars themselves[111]. Since the *Bible* and other associated religious texts are authored by a high number of human authors[112] of different backgrounds, attributing this humor to god himself is rather "demeaning" to the god. Being the best at everything, the only god

---

106   The concept of "sin" is a biblical invention as someone had to be blamed for all miseries of the world because the only god was/is all about goodness, justice, and mercy. This is very different from polytheistic traditions of the Middle East in which deities themselves were fallible, so their expectations of humans were not that high. Moral perfection was desired but not expected, and earthly rewards were more dependent on the divine caprice than on the virtues of humankind.

107   Even then ancient Egyptians were guaranteed nothing. If their bodies were destroyed either accidentally or through an act of malice, their after-life was gone too (for more information see, for example, Wasilewska 2000).

108   This statement is correct only from a point of view of a believer because there is plenty of evidence that none of the so-called monotheistic religions is actually truly monotheistic (see, for example, Wasilewska 2000). There are references to the presence of higher number of divine beings in the Old Testament such as "the sons of God" (Gen. 6:1-4; Job 1:6, 2:1, 38:7), "the host of heaven" (1 Kings 22:19), "angels" (Gen. 19:1; Ps. 103:20) and a definite statement of God himself, "let us make man in OUR image" (Gen. 1:26).

109   And only if we assume that he has one, which, of course, must be appreciated by humans.

110   This doesn't mean that there are no publications denying a sense of humor to Jesus Chris, etc. My "favorite" one (and obviously of Capps, 2006b, too) is an over-hundred-year-old article by Harris (1908) showing that Jesus Chris was truly a humorless individual as based on the New Testament. However, the arguments for a somber nature of Jesus are quite humorous in themselves. They include: 1. He was a Jew and "the Jew is not humorous," and "the Hebrew nation has never produced a great humorist" (too bad he didn't study Voltaire); 2. "The spiritual temper does not readily combine with humor"; 3. Intensity of the religious temperament is "the very anti-thesis of humor"; 4. Integrity and unity of Jewish people is "fatal to humor," which dwells on diversity; 5. Jesus was both feminine and masculine; 6. He was a primitive type; 7. He was divine so nothing to laugh about, etc. There are other gems in this article such as a straightforward statement that women "are defective in the sense of humor" (462) because in contrast to men they are always "physically negative and spiritually positive" (463).

111   One cannot ignore the issue of translatability of humor. We don't have an original of the Old Testament in Hebrew.

112   The *Pentateuch* (the Christian *Old Testament*) alone is a compilation of four different sources: Yahwistic (J), Elohistic (E), Deuteronomic (D), and Priestly (P), all dating from the very beginning of the first millennium to the sixth or the fifth century B.C. (e.g., Wasilewska 2000).

should be expected to meet the highest standards of comedic performance (just kidding). Regardless, operating on the premise that humor should be found in the *Bible*[113] and other holy scriptures leads to too many over-interpretations. Defending an allegedly divine sense of humor is simply impossible because the rendition that we have is of human origin and rather humorless: there are no joking relationships that can really be discerned. Blaming it on the so-called cultural conditioning (here: rather a hermetic nature of a joke) because "we may fail to recognize humor when we encounter it in the *Bible*, while another passage, which was not at all funny to its author, may amuse us. Even a report of laughter carries no assurance that it is a response to something funny" (Nieting 1983: 168) is rather a scientific cop-out. The reality seems to be more prosaic... monotheistic religions have less room for humor and more for piety, while a pantheon of deities almost seems to guarantee human-like interactions that inherently include humor. This does not mean that humor cannot be found in the holy scriptures, but it is usually very limited and mostly hermetic. Thus, the research on humor in monotheistic religions should be directed more toward permissibility of humor, rather than toward proving or disproving whether or not the divine had/has a sense of humor.

This is what Georges Tamer did with his analysis of humor in the *Qur'an*, a chapter entitled *The Qur'an and Humor* included here but originally published as a part of the *Humor in der arabischen Kultur/Humor in Arabic Culture* book edited by him in 2009. The *Qur'an* differs from the earlier scriptures of Judaism and Christianity not only because it is truly believed to be the [direct] word of Allah[114] as a "book," but also because it is an eyewitness account through Prophet Muhammad as Allah's messenger. Revelations were received within a relatively short period of time of 22/23 years and written down almost immediately after the Prophet's death in 632. The text has not been changed, altered, or otherwise manipulated since the third Caliph, Uthman (~579–656), preserved it as a standard text in the Qurayish dialect (all other copies were destroyed; the so-called Uthmanic recension[115]). In contrast, the *Old Testament* is a compilation of different sources, both earlier texts and/or oral traditions, that were put in its "final" form some time in the post-Exilic period (i.e., late 6th c. B.C. or the beginning of the 5th c. B.C.) after hundreds of years of combining them. While both the *Old Testament* and the *Qur'an* can be considered to be "minority reports" at the time of their compilation/revelation/writing, they have become the foundation of identity for millions of people who now constitute the majority of the world. The Bible has been translated and used in many languages, often losing its original meaning in translation, as any translation is a matter of interpretation. The *Qur'an*, on the other hand, is considered to be an infallible word of Allah that can only be revealed/studied in the original "edition" of the 7th century Arabic. The *Qur'an*, consisting of one hundred fourteen (114) *suras* (chapters) with each one of them staring with the *Bismillah*, "in the name of Allah, compassionate, all merciful," is divided into thirty parts (*juz*) allowing a believer for daily readings/recitations "designed" to serve as a manual for every aspect of life[116]. Consequently, the *Qur'an* has established permissibility of humor to the point that even Qur'anic verses can be a subject of parodies and humor in general. However, "The *Qur'an* can shape humor, but

---

113   *To most Christians, the Bible is like a software license. Nobody actually reads it. They just scroll down to the bottom and click "I Agree."*

114   Actually, the translation of "Allah" as "god" should be avoided since this is an imposition of Christian views on another religion. Allah is not necessarily a male, but rather an entity whose names and attributes include both male and female characteristics.

115   This move plus other controversial decisions cost him his life as he was assassinated in the year 656 by rebellious forces from Kufa and Egypt.

116   The *Qur'an* then serves as a manual for prayer; as an ethical and religious code; as a source for practical knowledge as well as spiritual guidelines and religious wisdom; and finally as a basic law governing an Islamic society.

it is not allowed to be made an object of humor. This restriction equally applies to making fun of God, Muhammad [117] and other prophets. These themes are in Islam taboo for humorists" (Tamer 2009: 28). These restrictions are not really too severe. Many people of other faiths have similar ones, albeit not written down. Furthermore, once again, humor about religions is usually focused on believers, practices, and religious functionaries only. However, many Muslim websites, and those who use them, propagate the idea that there are more rules on the use of humor in Islam. They base their findings on the *Hadiths* (oral narratives of the *Sunnah*, i.e., "path [way, manner] of life" attributed to Prophet Muhammad). The most common listing includes eleven (11) such rules (after http://amuslimsistermaria200327.wordpress.com/2009/09/14/15-rules-in-islam-on-joking/[118]):

1. UNDERLINE MAKE SURE you don't make fun of any aspect of Islam:

   Jokes should not involve verses from the Qur'aan, hadith, or any of fundamentals of Islam. Unfortunately, some people tell jokes about the verses of the Qur'aan, Prophets, angels, or they make fun of the Hijaab[119], the beard, etc. This is the most dangerous as it can make a person a Kaafir[120], EVEN IF YOU ARE ONLY JOKING.

   Sheikh Al-'Uthaymeen said: "One who mocks Allah, His verses, His signs or His Messengers is a disbeliever because this action nullifies belief."

   Rasulullah (SAW) said: "A slave (of Allah) would utter a word, without paying attention to it, which would result in him going down into the Hellfire further than the distance between the east and the west." (Muslim)

   So the sister in the Niqaab[121] is NOT A NINJAA and the brother who shortens his pants or lengthens his beard is NOT A NERD!

   Allah says:
   "If you ask them, they declare: 'We were only talking idly and joking.' Say: 'Was it at Allah, and His verses and His Messenger that you were mocking?' Make no excuse; you disbelieved after you had believed." (Surah al-Tawbah 9: 65–66)

2. NEVER joke about something that is HARAAM[122]:

---

117 The repercussion that may follow breaking such a rule, especially by non-Muslims, is discussed elsewhere in this book.
118 The full English part of the text is included here to maintain an objectivity of the presentation. No changes have been made in any shape or form, including spelling.
119 A traditional head covering for Muslim women and, in more general terms, modesty in dressing for all Muslims.
120 An infidel.
121 A veil. Part of *hijaab*.
122 "Forbidden [by religion]." This is one of the most "useful" phrases for people like me who work in the Middle East. Every time I don't want to do something, eat something, etc., I can use this phrase as it is applicable to all religions and, with some luck and even with more laughter from my Muslim company, I can get away with it. Granted, in some cases I had to "invent" a sect of the Catholic religion (as a Pole I am a Catholic by definition) that, for example, would allow me to drink wine but not arak (I hate anise), but this was done in good spirit (pun intended) and acceptable to both sides, each recognizing is as a "white lie."

Some people, especially the youth living in the western society tend to take the things that are Haraam too lightly and something to joke about. For example, they make jokes about a person being GAY or being "high," having committed zinaa[123], etc.

Subhaan Allah[124]! We forget that these are things among the worst in the sight of Allah and bring on Allah's wrath and curse and are certainly NOT things to joke about.

3. SAY only that which is true:
    Rasulullah (SAW[125]) used to joke but he would only speak the truth.

    Someone asked Rasulullah (SAW)): "Do you joke with us?" Rasulullah (SAW) replied: "I do, but I only say that which is true." (Al-Bukhari, Tirmidhi)
    If it involves lying and making up stories, then it is not allowed.

    Rasulullah (SAW) said, "Woe to the one who speaks and tells a lie in order to make the people laugh at it. Woe to him. Then again, woe to him." (Al-Tirmidhi)

4. Don't make jokes to make "FUN" of people:
    Be careful that your joking does not hurt anybody's feelings or harms them in any way. So don't make those snide remarks or wink behind their backs. Allah says:

    "O you who believe! Let not a group ridicule another group, it may be that the latter are better than the former. Nor let (some) women scoff at other women, it may be that the latter are better than the former. Nor defame one another, nor insult one another by nicknames. How bad is it to insult one's brother after having Faith." (Surah Hujuraat 49: 11)

5. Don't laugh if someone slips or falls or is afflicted with something:
    Rasulullah (SAW) said, "Do not express malicious joy towards your brother's misfortune, for Allah may have mercy on him and you may be stricken by the thing you made fun of." (Al-Tirmidhi)

6. Never scare anybody while joking or otherwise:
    Rasulullah (SAW) said: "It is not permissible for a Muslim to frighten another Muslim." (Abu Dawud).

7. Joking should not involve backbiting:
    Don't ever joke about others when they are not there, even if you "think" they wouldn't mind, as it would involve backbiting.

---

123   Sexual intercourse between two people who are not married.
124   "Praise be to Allah."
125   "*Sallallahu alaihi wasallam.*" This phrase is usually translated in English as "peace be upon him" (PBUH), although the Arabic language makes distinctions between this term and other similar phrases as well as in the practical applications of such salutations among the Sunni and the Shi'a.

"(Backbiting is) your mentioning about your brother something that he dislikes." (Muslim)

8. <u>Beware of excessive laughing and joking:</u>
    Don't be like the one who jokes ALL the time. The amount of joking should be like the amount of salt in one's food, as too much laughing and joking makes the heart hard, distracts one from the remembrance of Allah and makes you lose respect.

    Rasulullah (SAW) said: "Do not laugh too much, for laughing too much deadens the heart." (Sahih al-Jaami)

    'Umar ibn al-Khattaab (RA[126]) said: "Whoever laughs too much or jokes too much loses respect, and whoever persists in doing something will be known for it."

9. <u>Choose appropriate time and place for your jokes:</u>
    Some people don't appreciate the time or place for joking and do so indiscriminately. There is a time and place for everything. For example, what might be amusing at a picnic or at the dinner table might not be so amusing in the middle of a Halaqah[127]. Sufyaan ibn 'Uyaynah said, "..... It (joking) is Sunnah, but only for those who know how to do it and do it at the appropriate time."

10. <u>Use appropriate language:</u>
    Some people resort to immoral or obscene language when joking around, even though under 'normal' circumstances they would not even think of using such words. Rasulullah (SAW) said: "The Muslim does not slander, curse, speak obscenely or speak rudely." (Al-Tirmidhi)

11. <u>Acknowledge people's status:</u>
    Some people may joke with everyone indiscriminately, but scholars and the elderly have special positions and rights, so you have to be aware of the character of the person with whom you are dealing. You should also not joke with people whom you do not know or who won't understand, or it may lead to unpleasantness.

    'Umar ibn 'Abd al-'Azeez said: "Fear joking, for it is folly and generates grudges."

    Thus, we see that Islam is not against jokes. Good humor is part of Islam and Islam does not go against this because it is typically a part of human nature. A Muslim should develop a positive and optimistic personality, and not a gloomy and pessimistic one that is negative towards life. However, moderation is the key, and it is what distinguishes Muslims from others. We should not go overboard in our jokes and humor, (or in anything else, for that matter) and if we follow the Sunnah of Rasulullah (SAW), and his guidance, we will certainly not get lost.

---

126 "*Radhiallahu 'anhu.*" This phrase usually translated to English as "may Allah be pleased with him."
127 "Circle"—referring to a religious gathering where usually people sit in a circle.

"O you who believe! Be patient, and excel in patience, and remain steadfast and fear Allah, that you may be successful." (Surah Al-Imran 3: 200).

Based on these rules alone, one would think that Muslims are the most humorless people in the world because they are not allowed to joke about anything, including such trivial things as "pork" (*haraam*) or a falling model on a catwalk (#5). This cannot be any further from the truth. They are like anyone else and use humor among themselves and with outsiders. Marzolph recorded "about 5,600 jocular texts" in his research arriving at the conclusion that

"Medieval Islamic society was quite liberal inasfar as a dogmatic interpretation of the basic tenets of Islam is concerned—this being an evaluation confirmed by the large number of jokes about drinking, illicit sexual relations and social conduct otherwise contradicting the religious rules" (2000: 486–487)[128].

He also pointed out that approximately 3% of them "deal with or mention the Qoran[129]" (2000: 486). However, they don't make fun of the Qur'an per se but use it to make a funny point. One of the most commonly cited "old" jokes is the Islamized version of a Greek joke (Marzolph 2000: 478):

Ibrahim b. al-Hasib was stupid (*ahmaq*). He owned a donkey, and whenever the people at night provided their steeds with a nosebag, he would take his donkey's nosebag, recite above it the qoranic verse: "Say: He is God, One." (Q 112: 1). Then he would attach the empty bag to the animal while remarking: "May God curse anybody who thinks that a measure (*kaylaga*) of barley is better than the verse "Say: He is God, One." He continued to do so until his donkey died, whereupon he exclaimed: "By God, I never would have thought that the verse "Say: He is God, One" kills donkeys! By God, I am sure it is even more lethal for humans, so I will not recite it again as long as I live!"

The Quranic verses are not only used in jokes but are also enjoyed as a sort of divination even in officially conservative Iran. I have seen many "stands" in regard to the Quranic verses and quotations from famous people of Islamic tradition offering a parakeet to pick up your fortune for a little bit of money! This pleasure, oftentimes, was administered by *mullahs*[130] themselves. There are quite a few Muslim comedians who are thriving in the Middle East and in the Western world (Islam and Comedy 2011). Given the present sensitivity surrounding Islam and Islamic culture in the West, their job is not an easy one. Given the "11 rules," which they are supposed to follow, this job should be impossible to even attempt. However, the Islamic tradition is full of an excellent humor, including everyone's favorite character, Nasreddin Hoca (Mullah Nasruddin), who not only is claimed by every Islamic nation but whose stories are recorded by the thousands!

128   For modern jokes, cartoons, etc., see, for example, Mahfouz (2010).
129   There are many different spellings of the Qur'an and the choice of which one to use usually depends on a scholarly preference.
130   From Arabic "*mawla*"—a male cleric who is believed to be proficient in the Qur'an and Hadiths as well as in the basics of Islamic law (Sharia) due to his education in a religious school (*madrasa*) or, at times, somewhat self-proclaimed. In Iran, mullahs who wear a black turban are considered to be descendants of Prophet Muhammad (PBUH), while a white turban is an indication of a religious standing only.

Once, the people of the city invited Mullah Nasruddin to deliver a speech. When he got on the *minbar* (pulpit), he found the audience was not very enthusiastic, so he asked, "Do you know what I am going to say?" The audience replied "NO," so he announced "I have no desire to speak to people who don't even know what I will be talking about" and he left. The people felt embarrassed and called him back again the next day. This time when he asked the same question, the people replied "YES" So Mullah Nasruddin said, "Well, since you already know what I am going to say, I won't waste any more of your time" and he left. Now the people were really perplexed. They decided to try one more time and once again invited the Mullah to speak the following week. Once again he asked the same question: "Do you know what I am going to say?" Now the people were prepared and so half of them answered, "YES" while the other half replied "NO." So Mullah Nasruddin said "The half who know what I am going to say, tell it to the other half" and he left!

Thus, the question arises, why then have such rules not been followed by so many good Muslims? The answer is rather simple—these rules are not really "rules." They are based on the *Hadiths* that are not considered infallible as the *Qur'an* is. They are not the words of Allah. There are many thousands[131] of them and often they are contradictory to each other as well as to the Qur'an itself. Many of them even record jokes made by Prophet Muhammad. The most quoted one is a story of an old woman who came to him,

> … and said: "O Messenger of Allah, pray to Allah (Subhanahu Wa Ta'ala) that I will enter Paradise." Holy Prophet Muhammed (SAW) said jokingly, "O Mother of so-and-so, no old women will enter Paradise." The old woman went away crying, after hearing from Holy Prophet Muhammed (SAW). Then Holy Prophet Muhammed (SAW) sent one of his companions to tell her that, she will enter Paradise by becoming a young lady, because the Paradise is for only young people."

The bottom line is the only *Sunnah* ("path") to follow in Islam is Allah's *Sunnah* of the *Qur'an*. Prophet Muhammad is not equal to Allah. As a human being, the only knowledge that he had was granted to him by Allah so he should be followed only as a Messenger, not necessarily as a person, since humans are not perfect. There are even *Hadiths* (from Ali Saeed Al-Khudry and Zayid ibn Thabit) reporting that the Prophet himself forbade writing down anything about him for this very reason[132]. Consequently, there are *Hadiths* on *Hadiths*. They are always open to interpretation so relying only on them is not advisable in Islam because they are not the word of Allah. The source of all and true knowledge for Muslims is the *Qur'an* only.

"One man's religion is another man's belly laugh."
—Robert Anson Heinlein (1907–1988)
An American science fiction writer.

---

131 The exact number is difficult to establish for different reasons so it is probably safe to say that any number between 5,000 and 10,000 seems to be "reasonable."

132 It was narrated from Abu Sa'eed al-Khudri that the Messenger of Allah (peace and blessings of Allah be upon him) said: "Do not write anything from me; whoever has written anything from me other than the Qur'an, let him erase it and narrate from me, for there is nothing wrong with that" (Narrated by Muslim, al-Zuhd wa'l-Raqaa'iq, 5326).

The seriousness of monotheistic religions, the conviction that "theirs" is the only "true" religion, and differences in practices make them an easy target of humor. Humor about religions is very popular, although its degree of possible offensiveness is very high. In the United States, religion is "fair game" as long as its sacred values are not being mocked. Thus, "comparative studies" of different religions are among most successful and least offensive jokes about religion as all beliefs appear to be treated equally. This includes a series of the so-called light bulb jokes.

1. How many charismatics does it take to change a light bulb?
Only one since his/her hands are in the air anyway.
2. How many Calvinists does it take to change a light bulb?
None. God has predestined when the lights will be on. Or...
Calvinists do not change light bulbs. They simply read the instructions out loud and pray the light bulb will decide to change itself.
3. How many Baptists does it take to change a light bulb?
 CHANGE???????
4. No. Really, how many Baptists does it take to change a light bulb?
At least fifteen. One to change the light bulb, and three committees to approve the change and decide who brings the potato salad.
5. How many Neo-Evangelicals does it take to change a light bulb?
No one knows. They can't tell the difference between light and darkness.
6. How many Church of Christ does it take to change a light bulb?
Six men. One to authorize the change; two to look up the scriptures to see if it's something Jesus or Paul would approve of; and three to keep the women in submission, i.e., keeping them from giving advice, instructions, or usurping authority over the men.
7. How many Pentecostals does it take to change a light bulb?
Ten. One to change the bulb and nine to pray against the spirit of darkness.
8. How many Tele-Evangelists does it take to change a light bulb?
One. But for the message of light to continue, send in your donation today.
9. How many fundamentalists or independent Baptists does it take to change a light bulb?
Only one because any more would be compromise and ecumenical standards of light would slip.
10. How many liberals does it take to change a light bulb?
At least ten, as they need to hold a debate on whether or not the light bulb exists. Even if they can agree upon the existence of the light bulb they still may not change it to keep from alienating those who might use other forms of light.
11. How many Anglicans or Catholics does it take to change a light bulb?
None. They always use candles.

Comparisons of a high number of religions are often accomplished with one-liners and might be enhanced with no-so-sacred words contrasting the seriousness or sacrality of the beliefs with the profanity of daily life:

Taoism: Sh*t happens.

Agnosticism: I don't know if sh*t happens.

Confucianism: Confucius say, "Sh*t happens."

Calvinism: Sh*t happens because you don't work hard enough.

Buddhism: If sh*t happens, it really isn't sh*t.

Seventh-Day Adventist: No sh*t on Saturdays.

Zen: What is the sound of sh*t happening?

Hedonism: There is nothing like a good sh*t happening.

Hinduism: This sh*t happened before.

Mormonism: This sh*t is going to happen again.

Islam: If sh*t happens, it is the will of Allah.

Moonies: Only happy sh*t really happens.

Stoicism: This sh*t is good for me.

Protestantism: Let the sh*t happen to someone else.

Catholicism: Sh*t happens because you deserve it.

Hare Krishna: Sh*t happens, rama rama.

Judaism: Why does this sh*t always happen to US?

Zoroastrianism: Sh*t happens half the time.

Christian Science: Sh*t is in your mind.

Atheism: No sh*t.

Existentialism: What is sh*t, anyway?

Rastafarianism: Let's smoke this sh*t.

Psychic: Erase this sh*t.

Jehovah's Witness: Knock knock, sh*t happens.

TV Evangelism: Send more sh*t and smile.

New Age: You are completely sh*t free here and now.

Integral Bunch: Include and transcend this sh*t.

Jedi Knights: May the sh*t be with you!

These one-liners are obviously more than oversimplifications of religious systems in question but, at the same time, they tend to focus on what is perceived to be "the otherness" of any particular religion, its distinguishing feature that is considered to be humorous. The result is laughter even if one's religion is included because the other religions seem to be even more "ridiculous." However, the best comparative jokes are those that include references to bits and pieces of factual information, exposing the perceiver's self-proclaimed righteousness as an absurdity. The master of this type of humor is Stephen Colbert whose skit with Steven Carell ("Even Stevphen"), "Islam vs. Christianity. Which Is Right?" on Comedy Central (http://www.thedailyshow.com/watch/thu-may-29-2003/even-stevphen---islam-vs--christianity) is not only a "classic in my book," but also a type of humorous entertainment that can easily be used for educational purposes in more ways than one. Each line of the exchange between a "Muslim" (Steve Carell) and a "Christian" (Stephen Colbert) can serve as an invitation to the discussion on truthiness and truthfulness of statements made, rationality of beliefs, and circularity of religious arguments.

Steve Carell:
"There is no God but Allah and Mohammed is his Prophet..."

Stephen Colbert:

"This debate is about religion. Let's discuss it rationally…"

Stephen Colbert (cont.):

"If you were god would you manifest your divine glory to a shepherd in a cave in Saudi Arabia in the 7th century or, as the son of the carpenter, in the manger of Judea in the year zero?"

Steve Carell:

"Stephen, what part of 'There is no God but Allah and Muhammad is his Prophet' don't you understand? Look, let's assume for the sake of argument that your god is the one true god. That would mean Allah is not the one true god, which we know he is. Don't you see your logic eats itself?"

Stephen Colbert:

"First of all, it's not my logic, Steve, it's God's logic as written in the Bible, every word of which is true. And we know every word is true because the Bible says that the Bible is true and, if you remember from earlier in this sentence, every word of the Bible is true. Now, are you following me here or are you some kind of a mindless zealot?"

Steve Carell:

"You know, there is one way of settling this…"

Stephen Colbert:

"Crusade…"

Steve Carell:

"All right, there are two ways of settling this…" (and so on… leading to an extremely humorous ending involving Jon Stewart)….

Jon Stewart:

"Guys… I'm sorry but I'm starting to think that this religious thing, we're not going to settle in three minutes so… if we just wrap it and find some common ground it would be great so…"

Steve Carell:

"Maybe the Jew is right?"

Stephen Colbert:

"Yeah… maybe, maybe so… you know …which is funny because I normally don't care for Jews."

Steve Carell:

"We don't either…"

Stephen Colbert:

"Really?"

Steve Carell:

"We seem to find them kind of scheming…"

Stephen Colbert:

"We're very big on that too…"

Steve Carell:

"Really?"

Stephen Colbert:

"Yes."

Steve Carell:

"We are not so different after all!"

The brilliance of this skit is in showing not only obvious similarities in reasoning about superiority of one faith over the other, but also in an extremely brief history of the conflict[133] with a possible "solution" of directing one's dislike of the other to the third party. However, the heart of this exchange is definitely the line "This debate is about religion. Let's discuss it rationally...," is absurd, as any religion is based on belief, not on facts.

Different religions are targets of humor for different reasons. It is interesting to note that Polish, Irish, Italian, and Mexican jokes that are among the most popular targets of stupidity jokes in the United States have more than one common denominator. However, the one that makes me chuckle is that these are all ethnicities with a very strong Roman Catholic population. One may wonder then, whether mostly Protestant America is making a "statement" about thousands of years of blindly following a Pope, as the only god representative on earth, pointing out in the process the stubbornness of the Vatican to adjust to modern reality[134]? Not that the rest of Christian denominations are much more adaptable to change—of course, there are always exceptions. Regardless, Christianity rules in the U.S., contributing to and even creating a humorous environment that is exploited by professional and non-professional comedians.

This is what Gladstone termed *The Comedic Effect of Christianity* (on July 6, 2011). Christianity is a missionary religion trying to capture or save as many lost souls as possible. The race for these souls is not only with those of other faiths who may or may not have missionary and/or conversional aspirations[135] too, but

---

133 "Piety and belief are powerful things, and few forces in nature can stand against one who is true to his faith, his god/goddess, and the deal made in exchange for the soul. However, it is also true that gods tend to side with the heaviest artillery, so be prepared to change sides at the drop of a hat." (Sorry, I couldn't find the original source of this quote).

134 *The Pope arrives in heaven, where St. Peter awaits him. St. Peter asks who he is.*
The Pope:"I am the pope."
St. Peter:"Who? There's no such name in my book."
The Pope:"I'm the representative of God on Earth."
St. Peter:"Does God have a representative? He didn't tell me ..."
The Pope:"But I am the leader of the Catholic Church ..."
St. Peter:"The Catholic Church ... Never heard of it ...Wait, I'll check with the boss."
St. Peter walks away through Heaven's Gate to talk with God.
St. Peter:"There's a dude standing outside who claims he's your representative on earth."
God:"I don't have a representative on earth, not that I know of ...Wait, I'll ask Jesus."(Yells for Jesus)
Jesus:"Yes father, what's up?"
God and St. Peter explain the situation.
Jesus:"Wait, I'll go outside and have a little chat with that fellow."
Ten minutes pass and Jesus reenters the room laughing out loud. After a few minutes St. Peter asks Jesus why he's laughing.
Jesus:"Remember that fishing club I started 2000 years ago? It still exists!"

135 Out of six leading religions and/or religious movements in the world with ten million or more followers, Christianity is the only true missionary religion; Islam, Buddhism, Sikhism, and Hinduism are sort of ambiguous in this respect as their missionary efforts are of different character; and Judaism is a by invitation-only religion.

also within itself. With over 34,000 different Christian orders/sects/groups in the world (http://www.religioustolerance.org/worldrel.htm), there is plenty of material to focus on in order to assert one's own "truth" and point out "mistakes" of others. Thus, Catholics are considered "brainwashed," always afraid of being judged[136], carrying with them the proverbial Catholic guilt, and gullible, as they believe that sharing their sins with a priest will lead them to salvation[137]. Protestants of different denominations are laughed at for their willingness to change their churches[138], enjoying too much social contact[139] and being rich[140]. Mormons are believed to be righteous[141], naïve[142], and not fun, as any earthly vices are forbidden[143].

In contrast to Islam, jokes about Jesus Christ are allowed, although not all Christians enjoy them. However, Jesus Christ (occasionally lovingly referred to as J.C.[144]) was mocked, beaten, and finally

---

136   Little Tommy was having trouble in math, so his mother enrolled him in a Catholic school, thinking the discipline would help him. When Tommy came home with an A on his first report card, his mother was thrilled "Tommy, how did you do it!'"Well," he replied, "when I got to school and I saw the guy nailed to the plus sign, I knew they were serious about math."

137   Two five year-olds, one Jewish, the other Catholic, are playing in a sandpit. Sean says to David, "Our priest knows more about things than your rabbi!" To which David replies, "Of course he does, you tell him everything."

138   A protestant gets in a plane crash and ends up stuck on a deserted island. Years go by, and finally someone else gets stuck on the same island with him. The protestant says: "Let me show you around." Pointing to a small hut, he says: "That's where I live." The visitor then notices two other huts nearby. "What are those huts for?" The protestant replies: "Well this one is where I go to church, and that other one is where I USED to go to church."

139   A line of people was formed up at the Pearly Gates, waiting to enter. St. Peter was checking their names off a clipboard. The next man stepped up and said, "Peter, I'm Jewish, can I still get in?" St. Peter said, "Why, of course. We have a reciprocity agreement. Let me just check your records here... Uh oh. You know that BLT sandwich you had last week? The 'B' is for bacon, and bacon is pork, and you know you're not allowed to eat pork. Sorry, come back later." The next man stepped up. "St. Peter, I'm Roman Catholic, surely you'll let me in." St. Peter says, "Why, of course. Let me just check the documentation here... Hmmmm—you know that Big Mac you ate last Friday. It's Lent, you know—no meat on Friday. You'll have to come back later." The next man steps up. "I'm Episcopalian, I can get in right away, can't I?" St. Peter says, "Naturally! Let me just check this over... Uh oh. That vestry dinner last week? You ate your salad with the fish fork."

140   A man in Topeka, Kansas, decided to write a book about churches around the country. He started by flying to San Francisco and worked east from there. Going to a very large church, he began taking photographs and notes. He spotted a golden telephone on the vestibule wall and was intrigued with a sign that read: "$10,000 a minute." Seeking out the Pastor he asked about the phone and the sign. The Pastor answered that the golden phone was, in fact, a direct line to Heaven and if he paid the price he could talk directly to God. The man thanked the Pastor and continued on his way. As he continued to visit churches in Seattle, San Diego, Greensboro, Tampa, Chicago, and all around the United States, he found more phones with the same sign with the same answer from each Pastor. Finally, he arrived in Texas. Upon entering a church in Dallas, behold, he saw the usual golden telephone. But THIS time, the sign read: "Calls: 35 cents." Fascinated, he asked to talk to the Pastor. "Reverend, I have been in cities all across the country and in each church I have found this golden telephone. I have been told it is a direct line to Heaven and that I could talk to God, but, in the other churches the cost was $10,000 a minute. Your sign reads 35 cents. Why?" The Pastor, smiling benignly, replied, "Son, you're in Texas now... it's a local call."

141   St. Peter conducts a group of people on a tour through heaven and shows them where the different churches are located. As they pass one room, St. Peter says, "Shhh! Quiet! Those are the Mormons; they think they're the only ones here."

142   A three-year-old boy and a little Catholic girl once sneaked away to a pond behind the boy's house and stripped to the buff to go swimming, the boy looked at his naked companion and exclaimed, "Gosh, I didn't know there was such a difference between Mormons and Catholics!"

143   A young girl was sent away to BYU [a private Mormon university in Provo, Utah] by her parents and at the end of the first semester, she came back home telling her parents that she had to drop out of school because she was pregnant. Her parents were astonished that their daughter with such a fine Mormon upbringing could have this happen to her. They immediately asked her if the boy didn't intend to do the right thing and marry her. To which the girl replied, "Oh, Mother, I couldn't marry him! He smokes!"

144   A new priest at his first mass was so nervous he could hardly speak. After mass, he asked the monsignor how he had done. The monsignor replied, "When I am worried about getting nervous on the pulpit, I put a glass of vodka next to the water glass. If I start to get nervous, I take a sip." So the next Sunday, he took the monsignor's advice. At the beginning of the sermon, he got nervous and took a drink. He proceeded to talk up a storm. Upon returning to his office, he found the following note on his door. 1) Sip the vodka, don't gulp. 2) There are 10 Commandments, not 12. 3) There are 12 Disciples, not 10. 4) Jesus was consecrated, not constipated. 5) Jacob wagered his donkey, he did not bet his ass. 6) We do not refer to Jesus Christ as the late J. C. 7) The Father, Son, and Holy Ghost are not referred to as Daddy, Junior, and Spook. 8) David slew Goliath, he did not kick the shit out him. 9) When David was hit by a rock and knocked off his donkey, don't say he was stoned off his ass. 10) We do not refer to the cross as the "Big T." 11) When Jesus broke the bread at the Last Supper, he said, "Take this and eat it, for it is my body." He did not say, "Eat me." 12) The Virgin Mary is not referred to as "Mary with the Cherry." 13) Recommended grace before a meal is not "Rub-A-Dub-Dub, thanks for the grub, yeah God." 14) Next Sunday there will be a taffy-pulling contest at St. Peter's, not a peter-pulling contest at St. Taffy's.

crucified for human sins, so he is believed to encounter the worst possible humiliation already—nothing else could "hurt" him more. Since he can take a joke, so can his followers.

What Was Jesus?

My black friend had three arguments that Jesus was Black:

1. He called everyone "brother."
2. He liked Gospel.
3. He couldn't get a fair trial.

My Jewish friend had three arguments that Jesus was Jewish:

1. He went into His Father's business.
2. He lived at home until he was 30.
3. He was sure His Mother was a virgin and His mother was sure He was God.

My Italian friend gave his three arguments that Jesus was Italian:

1. He talked with his hands.
2. He had wine with every meal.
3. He used olive oil.

My California friends had three arguments that Jesus was a Californian:

1. He never cut his hair.
2. He walked around barefoot all the time.
3. He started a new religion.

My Irish friend then gave his three arguments that Jesus was Irish:

1. He never got married.
2. He was always telling stories.
3. He loved green pastures.

But my lady friend had most compelling evidence that Jesus was a woman:

1. He fed a crowd at a moment's notice when there was no food.
2. He kept trying to get a message across to a bunch of men who just didn't get it.
3. And even when he was dead, he had to get up because there was more work to do.

While the above joke is a humorous "narrative" of Jesus Christ's life and, due to its theme, is classified as humor in religion, this story is also an example of ethnic and gender humor. It employs common stereotypes with references to five (groups) and finishes out with the reversal of genders as a punch line. Thus, the level of funniness on "humometer" is increased through merging three different categories of humor.

Combination of religion, politics, and/or sex might be, humorously speaking, "lethal" as it opens even more layers of joke interpretation. It can be rather subtle with reference to sex, but nevertheless blasphemous to religious beliefs [145] or quite vulgar but still "innocent" in terms of religion[146].

The reaction to such a humor depends on which shift is considered to be of more damaging, if at all, to the moral values of a joke recipient. Thus, the next section is about gender, sex, and sexual humor to demonstrate that transition from the sacred to the profane can easily be made with any joke. However, before this transition can be made, one must be reminded what it means to be a Christian—of course, in humorous terms.

How to become a "good" Christian in twenty easy steps.

1. Confess to all your friends, associates, and church leaders that you love Jesus and intend to become His slave and that you will devote your life to Him. It doesn't matter whether you believe it or not, just saying it will put you in a Christian mode.

2. Join a church, get baptized, and attribute your conversion to the priest or minister. Gaze reverently into his eyes as he pontificates about the nature of God. Sighing every once in a while or wiping a tear will guarantee their devotion. If you join a revival church, fall to the floor, shake your body, put up both hands, and yell: JAYsus-ah! NEVER bring up the topic of sexual molestation to your priest, no matter how many boys or girls he may have poked.

3. Every Sunday, make sure you put a large sum of **MONEY** into the church's **MONEY** basket. Make sure that everyone in the congregation sees you giving **MONEY**.

4. When talking with your priest and religious friends, occasionally confuse something that they said with something that Jesus said. This will impress them and they will think more highly of you.

5. Read the Bible, but ignore the atrocities and concentrate only on what seems "good" to you. For instance, discard the parts where God kills firstborns, pregnant women, et al., and only keep verses such as "God is love." It's like taking a sugar-coated bitter pill, but it will *appear* good and that's what counts here.

6. Learn a few basic Hebrew words and whenever you're in a religious discussion, mention them in the context of their original meaning and comparing them to the English version.

---

145 *President Clinton and the Pope died on the same day, and due to an administrative foul-up, Clinton was sent to heaven and the Pope gets sent to hell. The Pope explained the situation to the devil, he checked out all of the paperwork, and the error was acknowledged. The Pope was told, however, that it would take about 24 hours to fix the problem and correct the error. The next day, the Pope was called in and the devil said his good-byes as he went off to heaven. On his way up, he met Clinton who was on his way down, and they stopped to chat.*
Pope: "Sorry about the mix up."
President Clinton: "No problem."
Pope: "Well, I'm really excited about going to heaven."
President Clinton: "Why's that? It's not that great."
Pope: "All my life I've wanted to meet the Virgin Mary."
President Clinton: "Sorry, Your Holiness, You're a day late."
146 *In Sunday school, Sister Mary asked the class: "What part of the body goes to heaven first?" In the back of the class, nasty Billy waved his hand frantically, but Sister Mary, suspecting a wrong answer, turned to another child. "Yes, Susan?" "The heart goes to heaven first because that's where God's love lives." "Excellent," said Sister Mary, "and you, Charlotte?" "The soul, Sister Mary, because that's the part that lives beyond death." "Very good, Charlotte," said the Sister, as she noticed Billy's hand still waving in desperation. "OK, Billy, what do you think?" "It's the feet that go first, Sister, the feet." "That's a strange answer Billy. Why the feet?" Billy answered, "Because I saw my mom with her feet up in the air, shouting, 'God, I'm coming, I'm coming!'"*

This will impress others of your Biblical knowledge, even if you don't know squat about theology.

7. Rely on faith and believe in the Bible superstitions, regardless of how silly they may seem. Yes, even the talking donkey, unicorns, and the strolling-on-water part. Even if you don't believe in them, just pretend that you do; no one will be able to tell the difference.

8. Abandon all reason and critical thinking. This is imperative. You cannot become a good Christian if you question the Bible with reason or skepticism.

9. Smile a lot to everyone you see. Say you love them even when you hate their guts. You must pretend, at all costs, to love your worst enemies even if it kills them in the end.

10. Attempt to convert your unbelieving friends. Make an ass out of yourself to the point of getting them angry. Make sure you always keep smiling and tell them how much you love them. This will escalate their anger and leave you fully satisfied. If they persist, claim that they are in league with the Devil and only faith in Jesus can release them (make sure you keep smiling).

11. If anyone presents reasonable arguments against Christianity, simply go into denial. Say that their tempting only makes your faith grow stronger. Never submit to them.

12. If your antagonists quote a verse from the Bible that contradicts your position, simply say that they're taking that verse out of context. The out-of-context ploy will get you out of many difficult situations and will make it seem that you actually understand the correct context when in fact you don't.

13. Pray. Make sure you pray, not just in church, but in public parks, schools, libraries, and when visiting friends and relatives. Praying out loud is a sure way to convince others of your Christianity.

14. Advertise your Christianity. Examples: wear religious symbols such as a cross; always have a Bible handy; put fish symbols on your car; put a baby Jesus on the front lawn; put a plastic Jesus in your car. Cross yourself a lot.

15. Wear conservative clothes. For the best effect: Men should wear white shirts and dark pants. Suits should be baby blue. Women should wear long dresses and veils. The hairstyle should be frumpish. Old ladies should dye their hair blue. NEVER attempt to look sexy. Never tattoo your body with religious symbols. Women should never expose their breasts. Men should NEVER expose their genitals.

16. Get married and raise a family. The bigger the better. If you cannot conceive, adopt. Profess family values. If you cheat on your spouse, never make it known to them. Never get a divorce, regardless of how miserable you both feel.

17. When making love to your spouse, make it known that it's for Christ (and I don't mean yelling out Jesus' name). Think of Jesus when you come. After sex, instead of smoking a cigarette, discuss the works of the virgin Jesus.

18. If any power threatens your Christianity, make sure your political stance aims to destroy that threat (always through love, of course.) If the threat comes from a foreign country, support the military to crush the enemy (always through love, of course). If the threat comes from within your country, support legislation to change the constitution so that your Christian position will prevail.

19. If you're fortunate to achieve political power, use your religious beliefs to direct your actions. It doesn't matter how many enemies you slaughter or what freedoms are lost; as long as your justification is based on the Bible, you will become a Christian of history.

20. The most important of all: Give your possessions away (charity). The Bible says give all you have to anyone who asks (Luke 6:30). May I suggest that for practice, give me all your money. I'm officially asking that you to please give me ALL your MONEY. Warning: If you do not do this, you are disobeying a direct Jesus request. However, if you do obey this command, it will guarantee you a Christian position and you will garner my greatest esteem and respect for you.

If you follow the above examples (especially step 20), you will become an authentic Christian.

SECTION 9
TOWARD GENDER, SEXUALITY, AND SEXUAL INEQUALITY ...
"Sex and the City"

"Really, sex and laughter do go very well together, and I wondered—and I still do—which is more important."
—Hermione Gingold (1897–1987)
A Canadian actress.

The issue of gender and humor is very broad. It includes all humor focusing on biological differences between sexes, psychological and social gender, all social and cultural constructs associated with both gender and sex, as well as sex and gender roles[147] in a given society. This kind of humor is about relations among and between genders[148], perceptions of who/what they should be and how they are[149],

---

147 These two concepts, sex and gender, are listed here separately because social roles are not always determined according to biological differentiation of sexes, but can be a matter of a gender construct/perception. For example, *hijra* of India and Pakistan are physiological men (a few exceptions of intersex variations) whose identity is female. Consequently, the role they play in their societies is neither male nor female (sometime referred to as the third sex).

148 *A woman rubbed a bottle and out popped a genie. The amazed woman asked if she got three wishes.*

The genie said, "Nope, sorry, three-wish genies are a story-book myth. I'm a one-wish genie. So...what'll it be?"

The woman did not hesitate. She said, "I want peace in the Middle East. See this map? I want these countries to stop fighting with each other and I want all the Arabs to love the Jews and Americans and vice versa. It will bring about world peace and harmony."

The genie looked at the map and exclaimed, "Lady, be reasonable. These countries have been at war for thousands of years. I'm out of shape after being in a bottle for five hundred years... I'm good, but not THAT good! I don't think it can be done. Make another wish and please be reasonable."

The woman thought for a minute and said, "Well, I've never been able to find the right man. You know—one who's considerate and fun, likes to cook and help with the house cleaning, loves to dance, is great in bed, and gets along with my family, doesn't watch sports all the time, and is faithful. That is what I wish for...a good man."

The genie let out a sigh and said, "Let me see the fucking map again!"

149 *Postmarital sex:*

1. The first is Smurf Sex. This happens during the honeymoon period; you both keep doing it until you're blue in the face.

2. The second is Kitchen Sex. This is at the beginning of the marriage; you'll have sex anywhere, anytime, even in the kitchen.

3. The third kind is Bedroom Sex. You've calmed down a bit, perhaps have kids, so you gotta do it in the bedroom.

mutual attitudes, physical interaction[150], or lack of thereof. It reflects what they are and helps to shape them for the future, being, at times, a much more influential factor than any other societal tools[151]. Humor helps to construct and deconstruct gender allowing men and women to "constitute themselves as masculine men and feminine women" (Crawford 2003: 1427[152]). Consequently, this is a category of humor that may include almost each and every joke with references to any sex or gender perception, identity, and/or activity[153]. This is probably the most common form of humor whether institutionalized (e.g., joking relationships) or spontaneous. Humor of this category can be extremely offensive or perceived as such because it often involves sex and/or sexism. Both topics are of rather sensitive natures in modern societies[154]. While sex is a natural part of animal kingdom[155], it is still considered to be a "vocational and visual" taboo in modern societies, including the United States, when it comes to different media. European commercials involving even non-explicit sex or strong sexual innuendos are banned in the United States, and so are movies with nudity on regular TV channels. However, violence and aggression are served in unlimited quantities everywhere, from video games to movies—something that is considered very unusual in the eyes of the rest of the world. So sex is bad, aggression is fine. Sexism, which "works" both ways[156] since it is a prejudice or even hatred against one's sex/gender (either

---

4. *The fourth kind is Hallway Sex. This is the phase in which you pass each other in the hallway and say, "Screw you!"*

5. *There is also a fifth kind of sex: Courtroom Sex. This is when you get divorced and your wife screws you in front of everyone in the courtroom.*

150 *The bride tells her husband, "Honey, you know I'm a virgin and I don't know anything about sex. Can you explain it to me first?""OK, Sweetheart. Putting it simply, we will call your private place 'the prison' and call my private thing 'the prisoner.' So what we do is: put the prisoner in the prison." And then they made love for the first time. Afterwards, the guy is lying face up on the bed, smiling with satisfaction. Nudging him, his bride giggles, "Honey the prisoner seems to have escaped." Turning on his side, he smiles. "Then we will have to re-imprison him." After the second time, the guy reaches for his cigarettes but the girl, thoroughly enjoying the new experience of making love, gives him a suggestive smile, "Honey, the prisoner is out again!" The man rises to the occasion, but with the unsteady legs of a recently born foal. Afterwards, he lies back on the bed, totally exhausted. She nudges him and says, "Honey, the prisoner escaped again." Limply turning his head, he YELLS at her, "Hey, it's not a life sentence, OKAY!"*

151 *Is it possible that Sex and the City actually has done more for the perception of a modern woman as being independent, etc...?*

152 Crawford has defined humor as "a mode or discourse and a strategy for social interaction" while gender is defined in the social context as "a system of meanings that influences access to power, status and material resources" (2003).

153 *A farmer went out one day and bought a brand new stud rooster for his chicken coop. The new rooster struts over to the old rooster and says, "OK old timer, time for you to retire." The old rooster replies, "Come on, surely you cannot handle ALL of these hens. Look what it has done to me. Can't you just let me have the two old hens over in the corner?" The young rooster says, "Beat it! You are washed up and I am taking over..." The old rooster says, "I tell you what, young stud. I will race you around the farmhouse. Whoever wins gets exclusive domain over the entire chicken coop." The young rooster laughs. "You know you don't stand a chance, old man. So, just to be fair, I will give you a head start." The old rooster takes off running. About 15 seconds later the young rooster takes off running after him. They round the front porch of the farmhouse and the young rooster has closed the gap. He is only about five feet behind the old rooster and gaining fast. The farmer, meanwhile, is sitting in his usual spot on the front porch when he sees the roosters go running by. He grabs his shotgun and—BOOM—he blows the young rooster to bits. The farmer sadly shakes his head and says, "Damn... third gay rooster I bought this month."*

Moral of this story?

1) You don't get old being a fool!

2) Age, skill, and treachery will always overcome youth and arrogance!

3) Don't mess with OLDTIMERS!

154 There is no doubt that religion is often a big factor in shaping views on sex as a physiological and physical construct as well as on assigned gender roles, which in turn form psychological, social, and cultural attitudes toward each other. Consequently, sensitivity to any subject involving sex is the result of a combination religious, cultural, and social "values" that vary from one society to another and are too complex to be addressed here even in their most general form.

155 *Sex is hereditary. If your parents never had it, chances are you won't, either.*

156 **What men would do if they had a vagina for a day:**

10. Immediately go shopping for zucchini and cucumbers.

9. Squat over a hand-held mirror for an hour and a half.

8. See if they could finally do the splits.

7. See if it's truly possible to launch a ping pong ball twenty feet.

biological or otherwise), has been traditionally directed against women[157]. Modern western societies are becoming increasingly more sensitive to this issue but this doesn't lower the number of sexist jokes at the expense of either sex, although it might have increased the number of male-victim jokes[158]. Humor, as it is based on stereotypes and truthiness[159], is a contributor in propagating or changing them. It is also one of the most effective tools to negotiate one's temporary or permanent identity[160], either by a joke teller or a joke recipient, especially when used in conversations of and between men and women (e.g., Hay 2000). As Koller has pointed out,

> For those who do promote sexual humor, there are several advantages. They have found that humor can defuse emotionally charged subjects such as sex and sexuality because they are not "serious"; they can symbolically break the rules against improprieties but not actually break

---

6. Cross their legs without rearranging their crotch.

5. Get picked up in a bar in less than ten minutes ... BEFORE closing time.

4. Have consecutive multiple orgasms and still be ready for more without sleeping first.

3. Go to the gynecologist for a pelvic exam and ask to have it recorded on video.

2. Sit on the edge of the bed and pray for breasts, too.

1. Finally find that damned G-spot.

What women would do if they had a penis for a day:

10. Get ahead faster in corporate America.

9. Get a blowjob.

8. Find out what is so fascinating about beating the meat.

7. Pee standing up while talking to other men at a urinal.

6. Determine WHY you can't hit the bowl consistently.

5. Find out what it's like to be on the other end of a surging orgasm.

4. Touch yourself in public without thought as to how improper it may seem.

3. Jump up and down naked with an erection to see if it feels as funny as it looks.

2. Understand the scientific reason for the light refraction that occurs between a man's eyes and the ruler situated next to his member, which causes two inches to be added to the final measurement.

1. Repeat number 9...

157   A little boy goes up to his father and asks: "Dad, what's the difference between hypothetical and reality?" The father replies: "Well son, I could give you the book definitions, but I feel it could be best to show you by example. Go upstairs and ask your mother if she'd have sex with the mailman for $500,000." The boy goes and asks his mother: "Mom, would you have sex with the mailman for $500,000?" The mother replies: "Hell yes I would!" The little boy returns to his father: "Dad, she said 'Hell yes I would!'" The father then says: "Okay, now go and ask your older sister if she'd have sex with her principal for $500,000." The boy asks his sister: "Would you have sex with your principal for $500,000?" The sister replies: "Hell yes I would!" He returns to his father: "Dad, she said 'Hell yes I would!'"
The father answers: "Okay son, here's the deal: Hypothetically, we're millionaires, but in reality, we're just living with a couple of whores."

158   A man escapes from prison where he has been for 15 years. He breaks into a house to look for money and guns and finds a young couple in bed. He orders the guy out of bed and ties him to a chair, while tying the girl to the bed he gets on top of her, kisses her neck, then gets up and goes into the bathroom. While he's in there, the husband tells his wife: "Listen, this guy's an escaped convict, look at his clothes! He probably spent lots of time in jail and hasn't seen a woman in years. I saw how he kissed your neck. If he wants sex, don't resist, don't complain, do whatever he tells you. Satisfy him no matter how much he nauseates you. This guy is probably very dangerous. If he gets angry, he'll kill us. Be strong, honey. I love you." To which his wife responds: "He wasn't kissing my neck. He was whispering in my ear. He told me he was gay, thought you were cute, and asked me if we had any Vaseline. I told him it was in the bathroom. Be strong, honey. I love you too!!"

159   The wise never marry. And when they marry, they become otherwise.

160   A professor of mathematics sent a fax to his wife. It read: "Dear wife, You must realize that you are 54 years old and I have certain needs which you are no longer able to satisfy. I am otherwise happy with you as a wife, and I sincerely hope you will not be hurt or offended to learn that by the time you receive this letter, I will be at the Grand Hotel with my 18-year-old teaching assistant. I'll be home before midnight. - Your Husband"
When he arrived at the hotel, there was a faxed letter waiting for him that read as follows: "Dear Husband. You too are 54 years old, and by the time you receive this, I will be at the Breakwater Hotel with the 18-year-old pool boy. Being the brilliant mathematician that you are, you can easily appreciate the fact that 18 goes into 54 a lot more times than 54 goes into 18. Don't wait up."

them; and they can demonstrate their emancipation or liberation from sexual taboos without necessarily requiring it of others (1988: 112–113).

Thus, it creates, to use Geertz' term from his definition of religion, "an aura of factuality," which fosters an environment that is either desirable (assuming positive) or hostile (assuming negative).

Traditionally, humor has been a field ruled by men, at least in the public sphere (e.g., Apte 1985). At the risk of stating the obvious, whoever is in control of humor is also in control of his/her audience on any scale, and in any particular timeframe, regardless of how limited it might be. Most societies have been ruled/governed/led by men. So far, nobody has been able to prove (archaeologically, historically, or otherwise) the existence of a pure matriarchy[161] (e.g., Eller 2001), defined as simplistically as possible to be "a society where women rule over men" (an opposite to patriarchy). There are, however, societies in which women have played dominant role in both public and private spheres from ancient Amazons[162] to modern Tuaregs of Africa and the Mosuo in China[163]. It would be very interesting research to compare the use of humor by men and women in such societies to discover if there is a discernible correlation between power and gender utilization of humor. Since, to my knowledge, such research has not been conducted, I would like to posit here the interesting possibility that humor and laughter are instrumental in acquiring, exercising, displaying, using, and abusing power in interpersonal relationships and in public life. This is nothing too extraordinary, as many scholars of humor pointed out, to such a quality of humor but... the difference here is the introduction of laughter to this equation and treating it as a physiological equivalent to cognitive humor in establishing, maintaining, and controlling emotional and social relationships. In other words, both have equally important roles in gender interaction leading to real or perceived power. However, while men assert this power through humor, women assume their control through laughter.

The marginalization of women in humor, whether institutionalized or spontaneous, has been demonstrated by many scholars in the past. Helga Kotthoff discusses both the reasons and the research that has been done on this topic in her article, *Gender and Humor: The State of Art,* (2006) in the Special Issue of Journal of Pragmatics on Gender and Humor (Vol. 38: 1). She points out that this marginalization is the result of "four dimensions of joking as specially sensitive to gender: status, aggressiveness, social alignment, and sexuality" (2006: 4). While women are becoming more and more visible on the humor scene, i.e., there are many more professional female comedians now than ever before. Likewise, females are less "timid" with their use of humor in daily life, there still seems to be an invisible line in explicit perception of offensiveness, especially with regard to gender, sex, and sexual humor portraying female victims. However, one should ask the question of whether or not what is perceived is actually what is happening. I believe not. This perception is just conditioned by traditional values of our Western society (and probably of others) as expressed through Kotthoff's four dimensions of joking, i.e., observable and even measurable gender differences in offensiveness, resulting from gender, sex, and sexual humor, are a processed product, not an original, emotional and cognitive recognition and response.

---

161   Also presented under such terms as gynecocracy, gynaecocracy, gynocracy, gyneocracy, and gynarchy. Just the sheer number of such terms is indicative of the contentious character of the definition itself and what it represents, especially to gynocentrists.

162   This doesn't mean that their existence has ever been proven. So far, the source of knowledge about the Amazons is a TV show, *Xena, the Warrior Princess.*

163   As a woman I am somewhat torn between objectivity of scientific data and subjective desire to idolize a society rules by women but... I always must remind myself that if these mythical matriarchies were so great, just, productive, etc., how could it be that "lazy" and "inferior" men could have taken them over and held power for such a long time?

From Provine's research we have learned that "females are the leading laughers, but males are the best laugh getters" (2000: 28)[164]. Female laughter appears to be not only more frequent but also friendlier than male laughter. The acoustic variability of laughter seems to indicate that laughter is a strategy and changes in its sounding are "designed" to "manipulate" a receiver or a situation to the best outcome of a laughter giver by inducing desired affects in others (Bachorowski and Owren 2001). This could suggest that women are more instinctive and emotional in their responses than men because in order to "force" someone to laugh (a desirable but "manipulated" and thus controlled outcome), one must perform a cognitive activity of creating or recreating a humorous situation. Since women have been culturally and socially conditioned "to be passive and receptive, rather than active and initiating" (Coser 1960: 85), men are to be initiators of and in interpersonal relations[165]. Humor in conversational settings is then to be initiated by men as "ladylike" behavior is an antithesis of humor (e.g., Walker 1988). Depending on a woman's responses, it may continue or it can be interrupted. If a woman laughs at a joke (or a humorous situation in general), this is a signal that a degree of intimacy (not necessarily based on sex) has been achieved. If she doesn't, the awkwardness follows and a new set of choices for further actions must be made. It is interesting to note that according to many different dating websites, women always seek men who make them laugh, while men look for women with a sense of humor[166]. McGee and Shevlin's research (2009) has confirmed that "targets" with a good sense of humor were perceived to be more attractive and suitable than those with an average or below-average humor. The difference was especially visible in the case of men for whom women with a good sense of humor rated significantly higher in their attractiveness. Grammer and Eibl-Eibesfeldt (1990) have established that women look for men who make them laugh and men seem to be attracted to a female's number of voiced laughs (ritualized vocalization). Since it has been noticed on numerous occasions that humor plays a very important role in selection of a mate[167] by attracting his or her attention[168] (e.g., Buss 1988), I have been running a sort of personal "experiment" observing young couples on their dates. One can easily see if a woman is not that "much into her date" when she is simply faking her laughter ("been there, done that") since, at least in some social situations, "the necessary stimulus for laughter is not a joke, but another person" (Provine 2004: 215). She might be polite and her partner might be funny, i.e., has a great sense of humor and a lot of jokes ready to tell, but she is processing the humorous situation

---

164   This one may explain while women usually live longer than men regardless of whether they can be "accused" of having a sense of humor or not. Farfetched? Not necessarily, as the third chapter of this book suggests.

165   Being raised and "indoctrinated" in Poland, especially by my grandmother who had only the highest standards of women's behavior applicable to the 19th century society in mind, I was taught, among other things, to "make men stand up when you sit, make them listen when you speak, but never ever initiate any contact with them." As liberated and independent I believe myself to be, to this day I have never asked any man for a date. However, I "broke" my grandmother's rules and occasionally opened a door myself even if a man was present. I also stopped teaching men how to walk upstairs and downstairs in a company of women. I had no choice in the U.S. If I didn't break my grandma's rules, I would be still waiting for my first ride from an American airport and be limited to elevators only (a whole set of other rules).

166   I am not aware of any specific research that addresses this issue, so this statement is based on what I have seen and learned from my Internet-dating friends and students. Of course, this one is off limits for me, as it means an initiation of contact.

167   However, one must remember that preference does not necessarily translate to "actual mating behavior" (e.g., McGhee and Shevlin 2009).

168   Even rats seem to be attracted to each other through their laughter. However, there is no evidence so far that they are "telling" any jokes.

differently than a man does. First of all, she may actually find his jokes funny[169], but she is able to control her response because males and females process humor differently. According to Azim et al.,

> Males and females share an extensive humor-response strategy as indicated by recruitment of similar brain regions: both activate the temporal-occipital junction and juxtaposition, and the inferior frontal gyrus, likely to be involved in language processing. Females, however, activate the left prefrontal cortex more than males, suggesting a greater degree of executive processing and language-based decoding. Females also exhibit greater activation of mesolimbic regions, including the nucleus accumbens, implying greater reward network response and possibly less reward expectations (2005: 16496).

In lay terms, it appears that both sexes have the same recognition of funniness or lack of thereof, but humor appreciation and reaction depend on how this humor is being processed. For men, it seems to be a rather "simple" path; for women, this path has its "turns." Having a stronger activation of the left prefrontal cortex translates to "a greater use of executive functions involved in coherence, potentially using working memory, mental shifting, verbal abstraction, self-directed attention, and irrelevance screening" (ibid: 16500). Females' "greater activation of mesolimbic regions" means that after all this "hard work," women enjoy humor more (higher reward) than men. Azim et al. suggest "females may expect the reward less, resulting in a larger reward prediction error when the 'punch line' arrives" (ibid: 16500). Consequently, women seem to be more "calculative" in their response to humor. Both coherence and affect may play a role in their response. The former allows women to decide whether it is "appropriate" to laugh after analyzing a humorous situation, previous experiences, environments, social conditioning, etc.; the latter evaluates whether it is "worth it." Does the latter include evaluation of a male's worthiness (if we keep referring to the dating example) not only in terms of his appearance and chemistry but also in terms of his social standing, earning potential, etc.[170]? At this point it is just a speculation but it is fascinating that Azim et al.'s research suggests that women laugh more not because they are amused more but because they expect less[171]!

---

169   Martin and Gray's experimental investigation seems to confirm that men and women find a humorous material comparably funny when there is no group interaction and their spontaneous laughter is enhanced with the use of audience laughter (1996).

170   ***Ten Husbands, Still a Virgin***

A lawyer married a woman who had divorced ten husbands. On their wedding night, she told her new husband, "Please be gentle, I'm still a virgin.""What?" said the puzzled groom. "How can that be if you've been married ten times?"

"Well, Husband #1 was a sales representative: he kept telling me how great it was going to be.

Husband #2 was in software services: he was never really sure how it was supposed to function, but he said he'd look into it and get back to me.

Husband #3 was from field services: he said everything checked out diagnostically but he just couldn't get the system up.

Husband #4 was in telemarketing: even though he knew he had the order, he didn't know when he would be able to deliver.

Husband #5 was an engineer: he understood the basic process but wanted three years to research, implement, and design a new state-of-the-art method.

Husband #6 was from finance and administration: he thought he knew how, but he wasn't sure whether it was his job or not.

Husband #7 was in marketing: although he had a nice product, he was never sure how to position it.

Husband #8 was a psychologist: all he ever did was talk about it.

Husband #9 was a gynecologist: all he did was look at it.

Husband #10 was a stamp collector: all he ever did was... God! I miss him!

But now that I've married you, I'm really excited!""Good," said the new husband, "but, why?""You're a lawyer. This time I know I'm gonna get screwed!"

171   Do they? (Just kidding...)

A group of girlfriends is on vacation when they see a five-story hotel with a sign that reads: "For Women Only." Since they are without their boyfriends and husbands, they decide to go in. The bouncer, a very attractive guy, explains to them how it works. "We have five floors. Go up floor by floor, and once you find

The "calculativeness" of the female brain in humor responses and appreciation may explain situations in which women would refrain from the use of laughter and humor exchange, as they consider some environments inappropriate for such activity. For example, it has been noted that professional women, with otherwise an excellent sense of humor expressed in informal situations, would restrain themselves from both humor and laughter during professional meetings (e.g., Coser 1960; Kotthoff 1988; 2006). Whatever is the reason for such a behavior, and there are a few well-argued hypotheses (Coser 1960, Kramarae 1981; Nilsen and Nilsen 1987; Kotthoff 2006), it is quite surprising that women are able to exercise that much control.

As the reaction to humor is both cognitive and affective, i.e., intellectual and emotional, different research and experiments have been performed in order to understand the mutual relationship between humor and emotions (see, e.g., Prerost 1995; Gruner 1997 and their numerous references). Basically, the question is not only what kind of emotions humor can trigger, but also if the state of emotions in which one finds himself/herself affects recognition and appreciation of humor. While the results are quite confusing at times (e.g., see, for a review, Prerost 1995a and b), it seems that there is "a link between anger/frustration/aggression and aggressive humor" (Gruner 1997: 111). However, what is even more interesting is Gruner's suggestion that sexual humor releases aggression (1997: 107–112)! One study to which Gruner refers in his chapter is of great importance for this section. He discusses an experiment at Western Illinois University (Prerost 1975) focused on rating humor by both male and female students, both when in a normal emotional state and when they were deliberately angered. Humor was divided into three categories: "neutral," "aggressive," and "sexual." Students were asked to rate different categories from the least funny to the funniest. When in a normal state of emotions, male students rated the "sexual" humor the funniest and the "neutral" humor as the least funny. Female students rated it exactly opposite. However, when angered, both sexes rated the "sexual" humor the highest while "neutral" humor was at the bottom. For Gruner, such ratings indicate that aggression is best "released" through sexual humor[172], confirming a strong link between aggressiveness and increased sexuality in both genders. Prerost explained this link as these "two arousal states of sex and aggression may have similar components and internal emotional clues. Sexual and aggressive humor may have similar components of messages, relating both to the aggressive mood" (1975: 287). Consequently, aggression arousal can be released by both sexual and aggressive humor[173] (not by neutral) with preference, at least in this

what you are looking for, you can stay there. It's easy to decide since each floor has a sign telling you what's inside." So they start going up and on the first floor the sign reads: "All the men on this floor are short and plain." The friends laugh and without hesitation move on to the next floor. The sign on the second floor reads: "All the men here are short and handsome." Still, this isn't good enough, so the friends continue on up. They reach the third floor and the sign reads: "All the men here are tall and plain." They still want to do better, and so, knowing there are still two floors left, they continued on up. On the fourth floor, the sign is perfect: "All the men here are tall and handsome." The women get all excited and are going in when they realize that there is still one floor left. Wondering what they are missing, they head on up to the fifth floor. There they find a sign that reads: "There are no men here. This floor was built only to prove that there is no way to please a woman."

172   Baron also reported that exploitative sexual humor significantly reduced aggression in males toward their "original" target. He further hypothesized that female response should be similar to men's (his experiment involved only forty-eight male students), as they were found in previous experiments to respond similarly not only to different forms of humor but also to "mild forms of erotica" (Baron 1978). His ideas have been questioned by Prerost, for example in 1995b.

173   In yet another experiment, Prerost and Brewer pointed out that not all aggressive humor released aggressions because "humor appreciation may have the capacity to reduce aggressive feelings, but only special types of humor related to aggression are effective. Neither non-aggressive nor 'unsafe' aggressive threatening humor produced any reduction in mood" (1977: 230). This means that the content of humor is also, if not more, important in order to achieve a desirable result (the need for "a cognitive determination of humor content in relation to one's mood state" 1977: 231).

experiment, for sexual humor[174]. The reversal of rating by women is of equal importance. As we all know emotions[175] often cloud our judgment. When angered, women in Prerost's experiment seemed to "lose control" over a typical processing of humor and, like men, responded directly to the funniness (content) of a humorous situation. Does this mean that the brain path of humor processing has changed and the female brain has taken a "shortcut"? If so, does it mean that social selection[176] (here: thousands of years of an imposed "ladylike" behavior) is responsible for different processing of humor in a human brain by males and females? Definitely, more research is needed.

However, "a battle" or "a war of sexes," whether reviewed as a part of a game theory with its mathematical formulas regarding decision-making strategy or just a laical observation, seems to be a "fact of life." Humor can be a "deadly weapon." Although aggressive and sexual humor seemed to release aggression, Berkowitz reported in his research that aggressive humor increased aggression in his female subjects, which then carried on (or was directed) toward an available target (1970). At first, it seems that the results of these two experiments are in conflict with each other but, in fact, they do not contradict each other. Females (as well as males) can be angered through aggressive humor, which then changes the state of their emotional arousal from neutral to aggressive (angry). When the release of this aggression is not available through humor, women "forget" their role-expectant behavior and act not-ladylike.

Further empirical investigations of Prerost (1983) have raised yet another question: when is sexual humor appreciated the most? The results were not too surprising since they confirmed an enhanced appreciation of humorous sexual material with both female and male subjects who have positive/enjoyable sexual experience and expression. He pointed out to "the converging pattern of male and female reactions to sexual stimuli" (1983: 27) that has been also seen in Wilson and Molleston's experiment revealing that the highest rating of four kinds of humor[177] was given to sexual-non-exploitative humor[178] by both genders (1981). The difference in appreciation of humorous material with sexist content (presumably focusing on female victims) between men and women was apparent, except for "the high frequency and enjoyment females" who might have been exhibiting "cross-sex attitudes as they strive to break traditional sex-role restraints on sexual behavior and opinions" (1983: 27). The change in expressive attitudes toward sex,

174   The later research reported by Prerost in 1995b has clarified the situation somewhat more. The findings relating to the release of aggressive moods are true for individuals with high levels of sexual desire. Both genders "were able to utilize the appreciation of both sexual and aggressive content humor to dissipate the angry feelings" (1995b: 50). Low-desire individuals neither enjoyed sexual humor nor were able to use it for lowering their angry mood. Low-desire men appreciated aggressive humor more.

175   The best article to date discussing "A socio-relational framework of sex differences in the expression of emotion" was published by Jacob Miguel Vigil in 2009.

176   I am not aware if similar studies were conducted with regard to humor processing by transgender and homosexual people. Thus type of research would be very helpful to clarify whether such differences in humor processing are purely biological or not.

177   Sexual-exploitative; sexual-non-exploitative; nonsexual-hostile; nonsexual-nonhostile.

178   The sixth grade science teacher, Mrs. Parks, asked her class, "Which human body part increases to ten times its size when stimulated?

No one answered until little Mary stood up angry, and said, "You should not be asking sixth graders a question like that! I am going to tell my parents, and they will go and tell the principal, who will then fire you!" With a sneer on her face, she then sat back down.

Mrs. Parks ignored her and asked the question again, "Which body part increases ten times its size when stimulated?" Little Mary's mouth fell open; then she said to those around her, "Boy, is she gonna get in big trouble!"

The teacher continued to ignore her and said to the class, "Anybody?" Finally, Billy stood up, looked around nervously, and said, "The body part that increases ten times its size when stimulated is the pupil of the eye." Mrs. Parks said, "Very good, Billy," and then turned to Mary and continued, "As for you, young lady, I have three things to say:

1. You have a dirty mind,

2. You didn't read your homework, and

3. One day you are going to be very, very disappointed!"

sexual stimuli, and sexual humor—including sexist humor—was already visible at the time of the study. It seems that sexual desire plays a very important role in an appreciation of sexual and sexist humor in both sexes and in turn it alleviates hostile emotions/moods (Prerost 1995a). Those who have it, "get it." Those who don't, don't. However, men of low sexual desire still found sexist humor funny but did not have much appreciation for sexual humor. In all probability, their focus in such situations was more on aggression (victimization) than on sex.

Experimental investigations are very important in providing an insight into evaluations of humor. However, interpretations might be subjective leading to conclusions that are highly unlikely. As the focus of such investigations is on sexual, sexist, and aggressive/hostile humor, the danger of misinterpretation and too far-drawn conclusions may lead to over-censoring of humorous material. The following is an abstract of an article that I found rather disturbing in its premise and its final implications.

> The current study tested Freud's (1905/1960) theory that sexist humor may be associated with hostility toward women and extended previous research showing a link between hostile humor and aggression. College students (N=399: approximately 92% white, 5% African American, and 3% other minorities) rated 10 sexist jokes on their perceived funniness. Results showed that the enjoyment of sexist humor was positively correlated with rape-related attitudes and beliefs, the self-reported likelihood of forcing sex, and psychological, physical, and sexual aggression in men. For women, the enjoyment of sexist humor was only positively correlated with Adversarial Sexual Beliefs and Acceptance of Interpersonal Violence. Women also found the jokes to be less enjoyable, less acceptable, and more offensive than the men, but they were not significantly less likely to tell the jokes (Ryan and Kanjorski 1998: 743).

While the article claims to test Freud's hypotheses, the not-so-hidden premise is actually a statement by Richlin, who maintained that, "cultures where rape is a joke are cultures that foster rape" (1992: xxviii). This statement is reinforced in a paraphrased form at the end of the article as "cultures where women and their sexuality are a joke may be cultures that foster rape" (Ryan and Kanjorski 1998: 753). The "remedy" proposed is "expressing intolerance for sexist humor and rape-supportive beliefs" (ibid. 754). There are many objections that I, both as a woman and a scholar, may raise with regard to this article, or rather to its premises and conclusions, but here I focus on a few only.

First of all, sexist humor is not only about victimization of women, but also about victimization of men. None of the ten (10) sexist jokes[179] used for rating had a male victim. Obviously then men enjoyed them more than women. Professor Barney Beins' Psychology of Humor Research Team has proven on numerous occasions[180] that each sex prefers humor about the other (e.g., Beins et al.: 2005; Donkor et al. 2006; Gordon et al. 2009; Wells et al. 2009; Carella and Beins 2010). However, if one were to follow Prerost's research (1995a), women of low sexual desire may find humor that victimizes men not very entertaining, as it is connected more with aggression than with sex. It appears that female-victim jokes are considered more offensive and/or less preferred today (Donkor et al. 2006; Wells et al. 2009;

---

179   I am also quite surprised at the misspelling of the vice president's name in the Saddam Hussein joke—it is Quayle, not Quail! Unless, of course, there is a deeper meaning in this rather shallow joke that would make a quail a symbol of sexism. Or, as a blonde and a "bad" woman, I am missing something.

180   For more of the presentations please see "Research Team Presentations" at http://www.ithaca.edu/beins/rt/present.htm

Gordon et al. 2009) than in the past (e.g., Losco and Epstein 1975). This seems to be confirmed by Beins' and others' research, which showed that modern women regard male-victim jokes as being "extremely low in offensiveness" (Carella and Beins 2010). The female-victim jokes are still considered to be funnier than male-victim jokes (Barbie versus Ken syndrome?) for both groups with men enjoying them more than females. However, women are no longer "shrinking violets," as they are more accepting toward the so-called benevolent sexist statements,[181] and are quite opposed to the so-called hostile sexism (Emas and Beins 2010).

> When women were primed, their level of BS predicted whether their rating of offensiveness both of female-victimizing (FV) jokes and of male-victimizing (MV) jokes, but not when they were not primed. This result suggests that women may not respond to the offensive potential of jokes unless they are primed to do so (Emas and Beins 2010).

There is no such difference with men; whether primed or not, they rated funniness and offensiveness the same way. Back to the article… not only the choice of jokes was biased, but also the subjects were primed through the use of attitude measures such as Rape Myth Acceptance, Acceptance for Interpersonal Violence, Adversarial Sexuality, and Hostility toward Women. Ryan and Kanjorski even implied that [only] women "who have relatively more hostile beliefs about women may enjoy sexist and hostile humor about women more than those who don't" (1998: 753). This alone is a misogynistic statement propagating a stereotypical division of women into "good ones" who don't enjoy sexist humor and "bad ones" who do (the old virgin/whore dichotomy or dumb/promiscuous response to sexual/sexist humor).

The premise itself is simply false. There is nothing too sacred for humor and its offensiveness comes in many "shapes and colors[182]." However, joking about something doesn't mean doing something. "Dead baby" jokes[183], as distasteful as they might be, don't foster infanticide or abortion in the U.S., much like humor about religion doesn't lead to crusades or *jihads*. Along the same line, mother-in-law jokes don't cause animosity in individual families unless these jokes are repeatedly introduced in direct conversations about/with the involved parties. Singling out sexual and sexist jokes or humor in general as being something very "special" and different from the rest is not confirmed by any unbiased research, as all jokes are found similar in their structure but different in content (e.g., Gruner 1997).

Finally, the researchers themselves reported that women were as likely as men to retell the jokes. So, both "good" women and "bad" women didn't find them offensive "enough" to become intolerant of them and thus preventing fostering the "culture of rape" as it should be their duty. In summary, I consider such

---

181   Benevolent sexism is described as "more positive attitudes that are seen as restrictive toward women" while hostile sexism is "an antipathy toward women" (Emas and Beins).

182   There are many jokes that only a very few people would find enjoyable because of their content. The following two jokes are among them:

A man goes into a pharmacy. He says to the druggist: "I need some birth control for my eleven-year-old daughter." "Is your little girl sexually active?" asks the druggist. "Nah, she just lays there like her mother."

A young boy is playing in the street when a man asks him if he would like some sweets. The boy says "yes please," so the man asks him to follow him so that he can get him some. A bit later they're walking through the woods and it's starting to get dark. The little boy says, "Mister, it's getting dark, I'm starting to get scared." The man says, "How do you think I feel? I have to walk back by myself…"

They reflect socially unacceptable behaviors but their existence doesn't promote such the behavior.

183   The following is one of the least tasteless "dead baby" jokes:

What's funnier than a dead baby? A dead baby in a clown costume!

biased experimental investigations not only to be detrimental to "fostering" equality among the sexes but also damaging to the scholarly quality of humor research.

Both men and women process humor differently but this doesn't mean that they don't enjoy humor characteristics as incongruity and superiority set in the standard structure of the jokes the same way, even if these jokes are hostile/aggressive, sexual and sexist. When primed or in a social setting that requires ladylike behavior, people's responses seem to be based on social pressure/expectations, not on funniness of a humorous situation.

If women are "wired" to be more "calculative" in their responses to humorous situations than men, does this also mean that their humor is more deliberate? So far I was not able to find answers directly addressing this question but… Do women even create humor? I have referred previously to Harris' statement that women are "physically negative and spiritually positive" (1908: 463), and consequently don't have a sense of humor. However, he is not the only one who denies women their contribution into humor "production." Somehow, even some humor researchers seem to equate the "art" of joke-telling with one's sense of humor.

> It is axiomatic in the middle-class American society that first, women can't tell jokes—they are bound to ruin the punchline, they mix up the order of things and so on. Moreover, they don't "get" jokes. In short, women have no sense of humor (Lakoff 1975: 56).

As recently as in 2005, Morreall (e.g., 2009) confirmed to the *New York Times'* reporter that, "women can't remember jokes. That's because they don't give a damn. Their humor is observational humor about the people around that they care about. Women virtually never do that old-style stuff." (St. John 2005: 2). While giving women credit to be ahead of their times in the "humorology evolution," he still has played to the stereotype of non-joking women. Regardless, the common perception seems to be that most[184] women don't tell jokes, either because they don't have a sense humor, don't remember them, or because it is still socially unacceptable for women to initiate a humorous conversation[185]. Obviously, those who ascribe to such ideas have never watched *Sex and the City*, a TV comedy-drama (1998–2004; 94 episodes) based on the book by Candace Bushnell, created by Darren Star, and produced by HBO. This cultural phenomenon has instigated many discussions about modern women and their changing attitudes in the battle of sexes (e.g., Jermyn 2009). As Bing discusses in her article, *Liberated Jokes: Sexual Humor in All-Female Groups*, (2007) reprinted here, none of the above is true. According to some researchers, not only do women tell jokes, but they also enjoy sexual humor even more than men do (e.g., Lundell 1993). The "world" simply doesn't know about it because most of the researched humor was created, written, told, shared, and analyzed by men. Even today, many young women don't feel like they are free of any social restrains to fully enjoy and/or create all humor, not necessarily just the "dirty" kind, in mixed company. However, when in the company of other women, they explore all "taboo" topics to the fullest extent. There are no boundaries and many sexual jokes are not only sexual but also sexist. In this sense, liberated sexual jokes are women's "swords" aimed at social norms to which they have been forced to

---

184   Women comedians are no longer a rarity in the U.S. and many other countries.

185   "Clinton lied. A man might forget where he parks or where he lives, but he never forgets oral sex, no matter how bad it is." This quote is ascribed to Barbara Bush, a former First Lady, a wonderful wife, mother, and grandmother whose ladylike behavior has never been in doubt but her ability to tell jokes is!

confirm for such a long period of time. Female victimization in male jokes has been "answered" with male victimization in female jokes. The difference is that modern women have learned to deal with and even enjoy sexist humor created by men, while men are struggling with the role reversal (see experimental investigations above).

Sensitivity about sexual, sexist, and gender humor places these jokes in the funniest category because it combines a variety of emotions of which laughter is an expression. Mirthful laughter from cognitive enjoyment of humor content blends in with the laughter brought on by embarrassment, nervousness, anger, and even fear. While a joke-teller establishes his/her authority through "demanding" laughter from the joke recipient (a submissive party), both are participating in a game, which might be, but doesn't have to be, a reflection of sexual attraction between two parties. Either way, such jokes always receive attention and reaction from the audience and this is what laughter commands. However, sensitivity alone wouldn't make sexual, sexist, and gender humor funny if not for its content and frequent mixture with other themes (e.g., politics and sex[186]).

Sexual humor is usually divided into two categories: "clean" and "dirty." The line between them seems to be rather blurry, as its evaluation depends on emotional attachment (Veatch's system of moral values), and is also somewhat fluid as it may change with age, social circumstance, etc. Sexual jokes are often also sexist because they usually victimize either gender. Responders might be offended not because of the "sexuality" of a humorous situation but because of other elements that might be associated with it: for example, vulgarity, descriptive visuality (e.g., sexual organs and "indecent exposure"), and parties involved (e.g., incest; animals, etc). The evaluation of sexual humor is closely connected with socialization and its constant reinforcement (e.g., Koller 1988). Legman, a controversial independent scholar with a life's worth of TV drama[187], has postulated a long time ago that "clean" and "dirty" jokes are not necessary that "clean" or that "dirty," offering a sort of the third category of "clean dirty jokes[188]."

---

186   *Lessons in sex and politics.*

A son asks his father, "What can you tell me about politics? I have to learn about it for school tomorrow." The father thought some and said, "OK, son, the best way I can describe politics is to use an analogy. Let's say that I'm a capitalist because I'm the breadwinner. Your mother will be the government because she controls everything, our maid will be the working class because she works for us, you will be the people because you answer to us, and your baby brother will be the future. Does that help any?"

The little boy said, "Well, Dad, I don't know, but I'll think about what you said." Later that night, after everyone had gone to bed, the little boy was awakened by his baby brother's crying. Upon further investigation, he found a dirty diaper. So, he went down the hall to his parent's bedroom and found his father's side of the bed empty and his mother wouldn't wake up. Then he saw a light on in the guest room down the hall, and when he reached the door, he saw through the crack that his father was in bed with the maid. The son then turned and went back to bed.

The next morning, he said to his father at the breakfast table, "Dad, I think I understand politics much better now.""Excellent, my boy," he answered, "What have you learned?" The little boy thought for a minute and said, "I learned that capitalism is screwing the working class, government is sound asleep ignoring the people, and the future's full of crap."

187   Whether or not he invented the famous phrase "make love, not war," Legman definitely lived accordingly (for more about Legman, see, for example, Dudar 1984; Brottman 2002).

188   The following are quotes from famous people that can be categorized as "clean" to "clean dirty" jokes, depending on one's sensibility to the topic. However, they are more about gender roles than about sex.

"You know 'that look' women get when they want sex? Me neither."(Steve Martin)

"Having sex is like playing bridge. If you don't have a good partner, you'd better have a good hand."(Woody Allen)

"Bisexuality immediately doubles your chances for a date on Saturday night."(Rodney Dangerfield)

"There are a number of mechanical devices which increase sexual arousal, particularly in women. Chief among these is the Mercedes-Benz 380SL."(Lynn Lavner)

"Leaving sex to the feminists is like letting your dog vacation at the taxidermist."(Matt Barry)

"Women might be able to fake orgasms. But men can fake whole relationships."(Sharon Stone)

"My mother never saw the irony in calling me a son-of-a-bitch."(Jack Nicholson)

"Women need a reason to have sex. Men just need a place."(Billy Crystal)

Regardless of terminology involved, Legman has produced two volumes of sexual jokes and their analysis (1968; 1975), which would make a lot of people blush (and it has). His work has become more respectable as the time has passed. He was definitely the most dedicated scholar of sexual humor and almost obsessive with categorizing it. Gruner commented on it in the following words:

Legman's taxonomy allows for fifteen major groupings of dirty jokes by subject matter: Children [189], Fools [190], Animals [191], The Male Approach [192], the Sadistic Concept [193], Women [194], Premarital Sexual Acts [195], Marriage [196], Adultery [197], Homosexuality [198], Prostitution

---

"*According to a new survey, women say they feel more comfortable undressing in front of men than they do undressing in front of other women. They say that women are too judgmental, where, of course, men are just grateful.*" (Robert De Niro)

"*There's very little advice in men's magazines, because men think, I know what I'm doing. Just show me somebody naked.*" (Jerry Seinfeld)

"*See, the problem is that God gives men a brain and a penis, and only enough blood to run one at a time.*" (Robin Williams)

189   For example (penis-envy):

A little girl is being bathed with her little brother. She points to his penis and begins to cry. "I want one of those!" "If you're a good little girl," says her mother, "you'll get one later." "Yes," says her father, "and if you're a bad little girl you'll get lots of them" (Legman 1968: 55).

190   For example (nincompoops):

Two farm boys working in the field are picked up by two city girls in a roadster who show them how to use condoms, "to prevent disease," before having intercourse. Two weeks later. "Zeke, have you got a disease?" "No, I ain't got a disease." "Neither have I. Let's take these damn things off" (Legman 1968: 120).

191   For example (animals):

A male and female rabbit are hiding in a thicket from a pack of wolves. "Shall we make a run for it, or outnumber them?" (Legman 1968: 193).

192   For example (cash on delivery):

A preacher tells a man who does a great deal of cursing that every time he does so he should hand a dollar to the nearest stranger, and that will cure him soon enough. The man stubs his toe leaving, and silently hands a dollar to a woman just entering the church. "O.K.," she whispers, "but can you wait till after the services?" (Legman 1968: 251).

193   For example (the penis):

A girl driving across the desert runs out of gas. An Indian gives her a ride, seated behind him on his pony. Every few minutes as they ride he gives a wild whooping yell that echoes across the desert. Finally he deposits her at a gas station and goes off with a last "Woo-whoo!" "What were you doing?" the station attendant asks the girl. "Nothing," she says. "I was just sitting behind him holding onto the saddle-horn." Attendant: "Lady! Indians ride bare-back!" (Legman 1968: 288–289).

194   For example (parrying propositions):

A woman asks a man for his seat on a crowded bus, saying that she is pregnant. He gives her his seat grudgingly, but remarks that she does not look very "filled out." "Oh," she explains, "It only happened half an hour ago." (Legman 1968: 344).

195   For example (:

Girl, to the boy who is petting her: "Oh, I feel so silly." Boy: "Well reach in here and you'll feel nuts." (Legman 1968: 402).

196   For example (mutual mismatching):

The young husband is standing naked before the mirror in the wedding suite admiring himself. "Two inches more and I'd be king," he says proudly. "Yes," says the bride, "and two inches less and you'd be queen." (Legman 1968: 536).

197   For example (adultery by the husband):

A man comes home from a lodge dinner and tells his wife, "The funniest thing happened. The lodge president said he'd give a new hat to any man who'd get up and say he'd been faithful to his wife since the day they were married. And not a single man got up." Wife: "Very funny. Where's your new hat?" (Legman 1968: 704–705).

198   For example (homosexual recognitions):

Oscar Wilde is in a Paris whorehouse. Madam: "A lovely French girl, Monsieur? From Marseilles. Very salacious. True Latin temperament..." "No, thank you. I'm tired of French girls." "A lovely Swedish girl. Only fifteen years old. Very blonde. Wonderful specialties." "No, I'm tired of Swedish girls. Do you happen to have a nice, fat-bottomed boy?" "Monsieur! I shall call a gendarme!" "Don't bother. Really, I'm tired of gendarmes too." (Legman 1975: 81).

[199], Disease and Disgust [200], Castration [201], Dysphemism and Cursing and Insults [202], and Scatology [203]. These categories he subdivides into another 178 specific types. One might wonder at the great diversity that one man can find in dirty jokes! (1997: 115).

Legman has also addressed perceived national preferences regarding sexual humor such as of the English (doubtful sexuality) or of German and Dutch (feces). While some of his evaluations have been questioned, his work of over two thousand (2,000) jokes is the point of reference of all scholars who even attempt addressing such a complex and "dangerous" topic.

The most innocent jokes of sexual, sexist, and gender category are those told from a perspective of a child. The Internet is saturated with a variety of quotes from children, so I have selected a few pertinent for the end of this section:

Sexist:
Q.: How Do You Decide Whom To Marry?
A: You got to find somebody who likes the same stuff. Like, if you like sports, she should like it that you like sports, and she should keep the chips and dip coming.
(Alan, age 10)

Q.: What Do Most People Do On A Date?
A.: Dates are for having fun, and people should use them to get to know each other. Even boys have something to say if you listen long enough.
(Lynnette, age 8)

Q.: Is It Better To Be Single or Married?
A.: It's better for girls to be single but not for boys. Boys need someone to clean up after them.
(Anita, age 9)

---

199   For example (priestess and prostitute):
A hiker at a youth hostel hears they do things very well there, and that you even get a woman at the end of every evening. He has a good meal and goes to his room, and hasn't been there long when a girl comes in without knocking and begins to undress. "Do you need a piece?" she asks. "Oh, do I ever!" he replies enthusiastically. "Long time since you had a piece?" "I've lost count!" "By the way," she adds, "are you married or unmarried?" He (off his guard): "Married." She begins to dress again. "No go," she says; "I'm here to serve the needy, not the greedy." (Legman 1975: 193).

200   For example (the fear of touch):
A man goes to the doctor with a suspicious red ring around his penis. The doctor merely hands him an alcohol-soaked piece of cotton and says, "Wipe off the lipstick, you fool!" (Legman 1975: 309).

201   For example (castration by women):
A man is berated by the state-troopers for not having strapped on his girlfriend's seat belt before the accident in which she was thrown through the windshield and killed, while he is still alive behind the steering wheel. "So what?" he says bitterly, "go take a look at what she's got in her hand!" (Legman 1975: 438).

202   For example (fuck):
A soldier is telling about a date he went on with a friend while on leave. "It's the first fucken furlough they gave us in six fucken months. I put my fucken uniform in a fucken locker at the 'Y,' and we went out and had a hell of a fucken time. We picked up two fucken broads in some fucken beer-joint and took 'em to a fucken hotel and laid 'em out on the fucken bed, and had sexual intercourse." (Legman 1975: 698).

203   For example (farting):
A girl is playing the piano for her boyfriend in the parlor after a heavy country dinner of beans. Whenever she feels a fart coming on, she hammers out "The Storm" on the piano. When she asks later, "Shall I play 'The Storm' again?" he replies, "Go ahead! But for Gawd's sake, Melinda, leave out that part where the lightning strikes the shithouse!" (Legman 1975: 861).

Fatalistic:

Q.: How Do You Decide Whom To Marry?

A.: No person really decides before they grow up whom they're going to marry. God decides it all way before, and you get to find out later who you're stuck with.

(Kirsten, age 10)

Pragmatic/Observational:

Q.: When Is It Okay To Kiss Someone?

A.: When they're rich.

(Pam, age 7)

Q.: What Is the Right Age to Get Married?

A.: No age is good to get married at. You got to be a fool to get married.

(Freddie, age 6)

Q: How Can a Stranger Tell If Two People Are Married?

You might have to guess, based on whether they seem to be yelling at the same kids.

(Derrick, age 8)

Q.: What Do Your Think Your Mom and Dad Have In Common?

A.: Both don't want any more kids.

(Lori, age 8)

Q.: How Would the World Be Different If People Didn't Get Married?

A.: There sure would be a lot of kids to explain, wouldn't there?

(Kelvin, age 8)

SECTION 10
TOWARD THE END ...
A Long Way To Go.

The most wasted of all days is that on which one has not laughed.
—Nicolas Chamfort (1741–1794)
A French writer.

Studying laughter and humor is not an easy task as this is a truly multidisciplinary, multicultural, and multi-everything topic. However, it is also, in my view, the most rewarding scientific discipline that I can think of—not only is your brain well exercised, but so is the rest of your body and your soul (assuming that there is one). While research on humor may seem to be exhausted in view of thousands of books and articles, and hundreds of theories, research on laughter has just barely started, opening new avenues for humor analysis. The more we understand about both subjects (laughter and humor), the more we can enhance all aspects of our lives so the future may look brighter. There is no better communication tool than humor and no more satisfying affect than a mirthful laughter. They are part of us for a reason, which we have yet to discover. In the meantime, the evolution of laughter and humor can be summarized by,

VENIMUS, VIDIMUS, RISIMUS!
(We came, we saw, we laughed!)

BIBLIOGRAPHY

"11 Rules in Islam on Joking." The Muslimah website at http://amuslimsistermaria200327.wordpress.com/2009/09/14/15-rules-in-islam-on-joking/

Adams, D. (1997) *The Prostitute in the Family Tree: Discovering Humor and Irony in the Bible.* Louisville: Westminster John Knox Press.

Aiello, L.C. and R.I.M. Dunbar (1993) "Neocortex Size, Group Size and the Evolution of Language." *Current Anthropology,* 34: 184–193.

Allès, E. (2003) "Notes on Some Joking Relationships Between Hui and Han Villages in Henan." *China Perspectives* [online] 49, September–October. French Centre for Research on Contemporary China.

Allport, G.H. (1961) *Pattern and Growth in Personality.* New York: Holt, Rinehart, and Winston.

Alston, J. P. and L.A. Platt (1969) "Religious Humor: A Longitudinal Content Analysis of Cartoons." *Sociological Analysis,* 30 (4): 217–222.

Apte, M. (1985) *Humor and Laughter. An Anthropological Approach.* Ithaca and London: Cornell University Press.

Attardo, S. (1994) *Linguistic Theories of Humor.* (Series: *Humor Research* 1). Berlin/New York: Mouton de Gruyter.

Attardo, S. (1997) "The Semantic Foundations of Cognitive Theories of Humor." *HUMOR: International Journal of Humor Research* 10 (4): 395–420.

Attardo, S. (2000) "Irony as Relevant Appropriateness." *Journal of Pragmatics,* 32: 793–826.

Attardo, S. (2001) *Humorous Texts: A Semantic and Pragmatic Analysis.* (Series: *Humor Research* 6). Berlin/New York: Mouton de Gruyter.

Attardo, S. and V. Raskin (1991) "Script Theory Revisited: Joke Similarity and Joke Representational Model. *HUMOR: International Journal of Humor Research,* 4 (3/4): 293–347.

Attardo, S., Hempelmann, C.F., and S. Di Maio (2002) "Script Oppositions and Logical Mechanisms: Modeling Incongruities and Their Resolutions." *HUMOR: International Journal of Humor Research,* 15 (1): 3–46.

Atwill, D.G. (2005) *The Chinese Sultanate: Islam, Ethnicity, and the Panthay Rebellion in Southwest China 1856–1873.* Stanford University Press.

Azim, E., Mobbs, D. Booil J., Vinod M., and A.L. Reiss (2005) "Sex Difference in Brain Activation Elicited by Humor." *Proceedings of the National Academy of Sciences of the United States of America,* 102 (45): 16496–16501.

Bachorowski, J-A. and M.J. Owren (2001) "Not All Laughs Are Alike: Voiced but Not Unvoiced Laughter Readily Elicits Positive Affect." *Psychological Science* 12 (3): 252–257.

Baron, R.A. (1978) "Aggression-Inhibiting Influence of Sexual Humor." *Journal of Personality and Social Psychology,* 36 (2): 189–197.

Barret, L., Dunbar R., and J. Lycett (2002) *Human Evolutionary Psychology.* Princeton: Princeton University Press.

Beins, B.C. and S.M. O'Toole (2010) "Searching for the Sense of Humor: Stereotypes of Ourselves and Others." *Europe's Journal of Psychology.* 6 (3): 267–287.

Beins, B.C., Agnitti J., Baldwin V., Yarmosky S., Bubel A., MacNaughton K., and N. Pashka (2005) *How Expectations Affect Perceptions of Offensive Humor.* Poster presented at the annual convention of the New England Psychological Association. New Haven, CT.

Ben-Amos, D. (1973) "The 'Myth' of Jewish Humor." *Western Folklore,* 32(2): 112–131.

Berger, A. Asa (1966) "Authority in the Comics." *Transaction,* 4 (December): 22–26.

Berger, A. Asa (1993) *An Anatomy of Humor.* Transaction.

Bergson, H. (1911) *Laughter: An Essay on the Meaning of the Comic.* New York: Macmillan.

Berkowitz, L. (1970) "Aggressive Humor as a Stimulus to Aggressive Responses." *Journal of Personality and Social Psychology,* 16 (4): 710–717.

Berlyne, D. (1969) "Laughter, Humor and Play." *The Handbook of Social Psychology.* Lindzey, Gardner and Aronson, Elliot, eds. Reading, MA: Addison-Wesley Pub. Co. pp: 795–852.

Billig, M. (2005) *Laughter and Ridicule: Toward a Social Critique of Humour.* London, Thousand Oaks, New Delhi: Sage Publications.

Bing, J. (2007) "Liberated Jokes: Sexual Humor in All-Female Groups." *HUMOR: International Journal of Humor Research,* 20 (4): 337–366.

Borowitz, E. (1980) *Contemporary Christologies.* New York: Paulist Press.

Boskin, J. and J. Dorinson (1985) "Ethnic Humor: Subversion and Survival." *American Quarterly.* 37(1). Special Issue: American Humor (Spring): 81–97.

Bradley, E.M. (2004). *The First Hollywood Musicals: A Critical Filmography of 171 Features, 1927 Through 1932.* Jefferson, NC: McFarland.

Brandes, S. (1983) "Jewish-American Dialect Jokes and Jewish-American Identity." *Jewish Social Studies,* 45 (3/4): 233–240.

Brigham, J.C. (1971) "Ethnic Stereotypes." *Psychological Bulletin,* 76 (1): 15–38.

Brook, V. (2003) *Something Ain't Kosher Here: The Rise of the "Jewish" Sitcom.* New Brunswick: Rutgers University Press.

Brook, V. (2006) *You Should See Yourself: Jewish Identity in Postmodern Culture.* New Brunswick: Rutgers University Press.

Brottman, M. (2002) "The Scholar Who Found a Life's Work in Dirty Jokes." *The Chronicle of Higher Education,* 12: 14.

Brône, G. and K. Feyaerts (2003) "The Cognitive Linguistics of Incongruity Resolution: Marked Reference-Point Structures in Humor." A paper presented at the session on *"Cognitive Linguistic Approaches to Humor"* held at the 8th International Cognitive Linguistics Conference in Logroño.

Buchler, I.R. and H.A. Selby (1968) *Kinship and Social Organization: An Introduction to Theory and Method.* New York: Macmillan.

Buss, D.M. (1988) "The Evolution of Human Intrasexual Competition: Tactics of Mate Attraction." *Journal of Personality and Social Psychology,* 54: 616–628.

Byers, M. and R. Krieger (2006) "Something Old Is New Again: Postmodern Jewishness in *Curb Your Enthusiasm, Arrested Development,* and the *O.C.*" *You Should See Yourself: Jewish Identity in Postmodern Culture.* Ed. Vincent Brook. New Brunswick: Rutgers University Press: 277–297.

Byrne, R.W. (2006) "Parsing Behaviour. A Mundane Origin for an Extraordinary Ability?" *The Roots of Human Sociality: Culture, Cognition, and Interaction.* S. Levinson and N. Enfield, eds. New York: Berg. pp 478–505.

Cahalan, J.M. (2004) "Mercier's Irish Comic Tradition as a Touchstone of Irish Studies." *New Hibernia Review.* 8(4) Geimhreadh/ Winter: 139–145.

Capps, D. (2006a) "The Psychological Benefits of Humor." *Pastoral Psychology.* 54 (5): 393–411.

Capps, D. (2006b) "Religion and Humor: Estranged Bedfellows." *Pastoral Psychology.* 54 (5): 413–438.

Carella, K., Bernard M., and C. Beiss (2010, March) *Expectations of Offensiveness in Humor: A Reverse Priming Effect.* Poster presented at the annual convention of the Eastern Psychological Association, Brooklyn, NY.

Carringer, R.L. (1979) *The Jazz Singer.* Madison: University of Wisconsin Press.

Chapman A.J. and H. Foot, eds. (1976) *Humor and Laughter: Theory, Research and Applications.* London: John Wiley and Sons.

Chiaro, D. ed. (2005) "Humor and Translation." Special issue of *HUMOR: International Journal of Humor Research,* 18 (2) 135–234.

Chiaro, D. (2008) "Verbally Expressed Humor and Translation." *Primer of Humor Research.* Raskin, V., ed. New York, NY: Mouton de Gruyter. pp 569–608.

Chiaro, D, ed. (2010 a) *Translation, Humour and the Media: Translation and Humour.* Continuum Advances in Translation.

Chiario, D., ed. (2010b) *Translation, Humour and Literature: Translation and Humour* Continuum Advances in Translation.

Clark, G.A. (2006) "Some Observations on 'The Neanderthals: A Social Synthesis.'" *Cambridge Archaeological Journal,* 16 (3) 349–51.

Cochran, G., Hardy J., and H. Harpending (2005) Natural History of Ashkenazi Intelligence. *Journal of Biosocial Science,* 00: 1–35.

Cohen, T. (1999) *Jokes. Philosophical Thoughts on Joking Matters.* The University of Chicago Press.

Corballis, M.C. (2002) *From Hand to Mouth: The Origins of Language.* Princeton: Princeton University Press.

Cormier, H. (1977) *The Humor of Jesus.* New York: Alba House.

Coser, R. L. (1960) Laughter Among Colleagues. *Psychiatry,* 23: 81–95.

Cousins, N. (1979) *The Anatomy of an Illness as Perceived by the Patient.* New York: E.P. Dutton.

Cousins, N. (1989) *Head First: The Biology of Hope.* New York: Norton.

Crawford, M. (2003) "Gender and Humor Social Context." *Journal of Pragmatics,* 35: 1413–1430.

Cray, E. (1964) "The Rabbi Trickster." *Journal of American Folklore,* 77: 331–45.

Daily Show Ratings Beat All of Fox News (2011). Filed By Bill Browning on June 06. http://www.bilerico.com/2011/06/ daily_show_ratings_beat_all_of_fox_news.php

Darwin, C. ([1872] 1996) *The Expression of the Emotions in Man and Animals.* New York. D. Appleton.

Dashefsky, A., DellaPergola, S. and I. Sheskin, eds. (2010) World Jewish Population, 2010. *Current Jewish Population Reports* 2. Berman Institute North American Jewish Data Bank in cooperation with Jewish Federations of North America and the Association for the Social Scientific Study of Jewry.

Davidheiser, M. (2005) "Special Affinities and Conflict Resolution: West African Social Institutions and Mediation." *Beyond Tractability.* Eds. G. Burgess and H. Burgess. Conflict Research Consortium, University of Colorado, Boulder. Posted: December 2005 <http://www.beyondintractability.org/essay/joking_kinship/>.

Davies, C. (1990) *Ethnic Humor Around the World: A Comparative Analysis.* Bloomington, IN: Indiana University Press.

Davies, C. (2005) "European Ethnic Scripts and the Translation and Switching of Jokes." Chiaro, Delia, ed.: Special issue of *HUMOR: International Journal of Humor Research* 18.2. Pp.147–160.

Delabistita, Dirk, ed. (1997) *Traductio: Essays on Punning and Translation.* Manchester, England: St. Jerome/Presses Universitaire de Namur.

Descartes, René (1985) "The Philosophical Writings of Descartes." 3 volumes. Trans. John Cottingham, Robert Stoothoff, and Dugald Murdoch. Cambridge and New York: Cambridge University Press.

Donkor, K., Hull, J., Laport, M., Nagengast, K., O'Connor, A., and B.C. Beins (2006) *The Effects of Priming on Humor Responses.* Presentation at the Eastern Colleges Science Conference, Philadelphia, PA.

Douglas, M. (1975) Jokes. *Implicit Meanings. Essays in Anthropology.* Routledge and Kegan Paul: 90–114.

Dudar, H. (1984) "Love and Death (and Schmutz): G. Legman's Second Thoughts." *Village Voice* (May): 41–43.

Dunbar, R. (1993) "The Co-Evolution of Neocortical Size, Group Size and Language in Humans." *Behavioral and Brain Sciences,* 16: 681–775.

Dunbar, R. (1998) *Grooming, Gossip, and the Evolution of Language.* Harvard University Press.

Dundes, A. (1987) *Cracking Jokes: Studies of Sick Humor Cycles and Stereotypes.* Berkeley, CA: Ten Speed Press.

Durkheim, E. (1954) *The Elementary Forms of the Religious Life.* London: George Allen and Linwin Ltd.

Durkheim, E. (1972) "The Elementary Forms of the Religious Life." *Reader in Comparative Religion. An Anthropological Approach.* W. A. Lessa, and E. Z. Vogt, eds. Third Edition. New York: Harper and Row. pp. 28–36.

Eliade, M. (1958) *Patterns in Comparative Religion.* London and New York: Sheed and Ward.

Eliade, M. (1959) *The Sacred and the Profane. The Nature of Religion.* New York: Harper and Row.

Eller, C. (2001) *The Myth of Matriarchal Prehistory: Why an Invented Past Won't Give Women a Future.* Boston: Beacon Press.

Emas, A.B. and C. Bernard (2010) *Sexism and Priming for Offensiveness in Humor.* Poster presented at the annual convention of the Eastern Psychological Association, Brooklyn, NY.

Epstein, L.J. (2002) *The Haunted Smile: The Story of Jewish Comedians America.* Public Affairs.

Ferguson, M.A. and T.E. Ford (2008) "Disparagement Humor: A Theoretical and Empirical Review of Psychoanalytic, Superiority, and Social Identity Theories." *Humor* 21(3): 283–312.

Fish, L. (1980) "Is the Pope Polish? Some Notes on the Polack Joke in Translation." *Journal of American Folklore,* 93: 450–454.

Fisher, P., Ai A.L., Aydin N., Dieter F., and S.A. Haslam (2010) "The Relationship Between Religious Identity and Preferred Coping Strategies: An Examination of the Relative Importance of Interpersonal and Intrapersonal Coping in Muslim and Christian Faiths." *Review of General Psychology,* 14 (4): 365–381.

Freud, S. (1928) "Humor." *The International Journal of Psycho-Analysis,* 9: 1–6.

Freud, S. and J. Strachey tr., ed. (1960) *Jokes and Their Relation to the Unconscious.* New York: Norton. (Original work published in 1905.)

Freud, S. (1916) *Wit And Its Relations to Unconscious.* New York: Moffat, Yard and Company.

Fried, I., Wilson C.L., MacDonald K.A., and E.J. Behnke (1998) "Electric Current Stimulates Laughter." *Nature,* 391: 650.

Friedman, H.H. (1998) "He Who Sits in Heaven Shall Laugh: Divine Humor in Talmudic Literature." *Thalia: Studies in Literary Humor,* March: 36–50.

Fry, W. Jr. (1963) *Sweet Madness: A Study of Humor.* Palo Alto, CA: Pacific Books.

Fry, W.F. (1994) "The Biology of Humor." *HUMOR: International Journal of Humor Research,* 7: 111–126.

Geertz, C.C. (1972) "Religion as a Cultural System." *Reader in Comparative Religion. An Anthropological Approach.* W. A. Lessa and E. Z. Vogt, eds. Third Edition. New York: Harper and Row. pp. 167–178. Reprint from 1965.

Gervais, M. and D.S. Wilson (2005) "The Evolution and Functions of Laughter and Humor: A Synthetic Approach." *The Quarterly Review of Biology.* 80 (4): 395–430.

Gillota, D. (2010) "Negotiating Jewishness: *Curb Your Enthusiasm* and the Schlemiel Tradition." *Journal of Popular Film and Television,* 38-4: 152–161.

Gilman, S.L. (2008) "Are Jews Smarter Than Everyone Else?" *The Looking Glass* 6 (1): 41–47.

Gladstone (2011) *3 Reasons There Are So Many Jews in Comedy.* On www.cracked.com July 6, 2011.

Gluckman, M. (1954) *Rituals of Rebellion in South-East Africa.* Manchester, England: Manchester University Press.

Goldstein J.H. and P.E. McGhee, eds. (1972) *The Psychology of Humor.* New York: Academic Press.

Gordon, E.D., Emas A.B., Nutter G.A., Rugg J.C., McCarthy C.A., O'Reilly D.M., and Beins B.C. (2009) *Why Did the Man Cross the Road? Sexist Attitudes and Gender-Based Humor.* Poster presentation at the annual convention of the Eastern Psychological Association, Pittsburgh, PA.

Grammer, K. and I. Eibl-Eibesfeldt (1990) "The Ritualisation of Laughter." *Natürlichkeit der Sprache und der Kultur: Acta Colloquii,* ed. W. A. Koch. Brockmeyer: 192–214.

Griaule, M. (1948) "L'Alliance Cathartique." *Africa: Journal of the International African Institute,* 18 (4): 242–258.

Gruner, C.R. (1997) *The Game of Humor.* Transaction.

Halkin, H. (2006) "Why Jews Laugh at Themselves." *Commentary.* 121 (4): 47–58.

Hallo, W.W. (1996) *Origins: The Ancient Near Eastern Background of Some Modern Institutions.* Leiden, New York, and Cologne: Brill.

Harris, H. (1908) "The Absence of Humor in Jesus." *Methodist Quarterly Review,* 57: 460–467.

Harris, M. (2009) "Twilight of the Tummlers." *New York Magazine.* http://nymag.com/print/?/movies/features/56930/index1.html

Harris, M. (2011) *Sacred Folly: A New History of the Feast of Fools.* Cornell University Press.

Harrison-Kahan, L. (2010). *The White Negress: Literature, Minstrelsy, and the Black-Jewish Imaginary.* Piscataway, NJ: Rutgers University Press.

Haviland, W., Walrath A.D., Harald E., Prins L., and B. McBride (2010) *Evolution and Prehistory: The Human Challenge.* Wadsworth.

Hay, J. (2000) "Functions of Humor in the Conversations of Men and Women." *Journal of Pragmatics,* 32: 709–742.

Haygood, W. (2001) "Why Negro Humor Is so Black." *The American Prospect,* 11 (26). http://prospect.org/article/why-negro-humor-so-black

Heidel, A. (1951) *The Babylonian Genesis: The Story of Creation.* Chicago: The University of Chicago Press.

Hobbes, T. (1996) *Leviathan.* Cambridge: Cambridge University Press.

Hockett, C.F. (1963) "The Problem of Universals in Language." *Universals of Language.* J.H. Greenberg, ed. Cambridge: MIT: 1–22.

Holmes, J. (2006) "Sharing a Laugh: Pragmatic Aspects of Humor and Gender in the Workplace." *Journal of Pragmatics,* 38 (1): 26–50.

Howrigan, D.P. and K.B. MacDonald (2008) "Humor as a Mental Fitness Indicator." *Evolutionary Psychology,* 6: 625–666.

Hughes, L., ed. (1958) *The Book of Negro Humor.* Dodd Mead.

Isajiw, W.W. (1974) "Definition of Ethnicity." *Ethnicity* 1, 111–124.

Isajiw, Wsevolod W. (1992). "Definitions and Dimensions of Ethnicity: A Theoretical Framework." Paper presented at "Joint Canada-United States Conference on the Measurement of Ethnicity," Ottawa, Ontario, Canada, April 2, 1992. Published in *Challenges of Measuring an Ethnic World: Science, Politics and Reality: Proceedings of the Joint Canada-United States Conference on the Measurement of Ethnicity April 1–3, 1992,* Gustave J. Goldmann, Statistics Canada (CS91-515E) and the U.S. Census Bureau of the Census, eds. Washington, D.C.: U.S. Government Printing Office; pp. 407–27, 1993.

Islam and Comedy. "Two Mullahs Went into a Bar…" (2011) *The Economist,* Nov. 26. http://www.economist.com/node/21540233

"Even Stevphen." Christianity vs Islam? Which Is Right? *Comedy Central.* (http://www.thedailyshow.com/watch/thu-may-29-2003/even-stevphen---islam-vs--christianity)

Izre'el, S. (1992) "The Study of Oral Poetry: Reflections of a Neophyte." *Mesopotamian Epic Literature: Oral or Aural?* M.E. Vogelzang and H.L.J. Vanstiphout (eds.). The Edwin Mellen Press.

Jermyn, D. (2009) *Sex and The City.* TV Milestones Series. Wayne State University Press.

Jon Stewart says those who watch Fox News are the"most consistently misinformed media viewers" (2011) http://www.politifact.com/ truth-o-meter/statements/2011/jun/20/jon-stewart/jon-stewart-says-those-who-watch-fox-news-are-most/

Jones, R.A. (2007) "'You Eat Beans!': Kin-Based Joking Relationships, Obligations, and Identity in Urban Mali." *Honors Projects. Macalester College*, Paper 2. http://digitalcommons.macalester.edu/anth_honors/2

Kant, I. (1987) *Critique of Judgment*. Trans. Werner S. Pluhar. Indianapolis: Hackett.

Kao, G. (1975) *ChineseWit and Humor*. New York: Sterling.

Keith-Spiegel P. (1972) "Early Conceptions of Humour: Varieties and Issues." *The Psychology of Humor*. J.H. Goldstein and McGhee, P.E., eds. NewYork: Academic Press. pp. 3–39.

Keltner D. and G.A. Bonanno (1997) "A Study of Laughter and Dissociation: Distinct Correlates of Laughter and Smiling During Bereavement." *Journal of Personality and Social Psychology*, 73: 687–702.

Kissinger, W. (1979) *The Parables of Jesus: A History of Interpretation and Bibliography*. Metuchen, New Jersey: Scarecrow Press.

Koller, M.R. (1988) *Humor and Society. Exploration in the Sociology of Humor*. Houston: Cap and Gown Press.

Kotthoff, H. (1988 [1996]) "Vom Lächeln der Mona Lisa zum Lächen der Hyänen." Kotthoff, H. (Ed.), *Das Gelächter der Geschlechter*. Universitätsverlag, Konstanz: 121–165.

Kotthoff, H. (2006) Editorial. Introduction. *Journal of Pragmatics*, 38 (1): 1–3. Special Issue: Gender and Humor.

Kotthoff, H. (2006) "Gender and Humor: The State of the Art." *Journal of Pragmatics*, 38 (1): 4–25.

Kozintsev, A. and R. Martin (2010) *The Mirror of Laughter*. Transaction.

Kramarae, C. (1981) *Women and Men Speaking*. Newbury House.

Kramer, S.N. and Maier, J. (1989) *Myths of Enki, the Crafty God*. New York and Oxford: Oxford University Press.

Krois, J.M. (2007) *Embodiment in Cognition and Culture*. John Benjamins.

Kruger, J. and D. Dunning (1999) "Unskilled and Unaware of It: How Difficulties in Recognizing One's Own Incompetence Lead to Inflated Self-Assessments." *Journal of Personality and Social Psychology*, 77: 1121–1134.

Kuhlman, T.L. (1985) "A Study of Salience and Motivational Theories of Humor." *Journal of Personality and Social Psychology*, 49: 281–286.

LaFave, L., and R. Mennell (1976) "Does Ethnic Humor Serve Prejudice?" *Journal of Communication*, 26.

Lakoff, R. (1975) *Language andWoman's Place*. New York: Harper and Row.

Lamb, S.M. (1999) *Pathways of the Brain: The Neurocognitive Basis of Language*. Amsterdam and Philadelphia: John Benjamins. (Current Issues in Linguistic Theory, Number 170).

Landmann, S. (1962) "On Jewish Humor." *Jewish Journal of Sociology*, 4:195–198.

Latta, R.L. (1999) *The Basic Humor Process. A Cognitive-Shift Theory and the Case Against Incongruity*. Berlin and New York: Mouton de Gruyter.

Laurian, A.-M. and Don L.F. Nilsen, eds. (1989) "Humor et Traduction/Humor and Translation." Special Issue of Meta: *Journal des Traductors/Journal of Translators*, 34.1.

Leahy, M. H. (2011) *The Mockery of Nature: Blackface Minstrel Humor and Race Science in Nineteenth-Century America*. Ph.D. dissertation. August. Purdue University.

Leveen, L. (1996) "Only When I Laugh: Textual Dynamics of Ethnic Humor." *MELUS*, 21 (4): 29–55.

Lefcourt, H.M., and R.A. Martin (1986) *Humor and Life Stress: Antidote to Adversity*. New York: Springer/Verlag.

Legman, G. (1968) *Rationale of the Dirty Joke: An Analysis of Sexual Humor*. First Series. New York: Grove.

Legman, G. (1975) *Rationale of the Dirty Joke: An Analysis of Sexual Humor*. Second Series. Wharton, NJ: Breaking Point.

Lessa, W.A. and E.Z. Vogt, eds. (1972) *Reader in Comparative Religion: An Anthropological Approach*. Third Edition. New York: Harper and Row.

Lévi-Strauss, C. (1972) *The Savage Mind*. London: Weidenfelt and Nicolson.

Liebertz, C. (2005) "A Healthy Laugh: Got Problems? A Little Humor Will Help You Get Past Them—and Could Even Ward Off Illness." *Scientific American,* 21.

Losco, J., and S. Epstein (1975) "Humor Preference as a Subtle Measure of Attitudes Toward the Same and the Opposite Sex." *Journal of Personality,* 43(2): 321–325.

Lowe, J. (1986) "Theories of Ethnic Humor: How to Enter, Laughing." *American Quarterly,* 38 (3): 439–460.

Lowie, R.H. (1947 [1920]) *Primitive Society.* New York: Liveright.

Lyttle, Jim (2003) *Theories of Humor.* Ph.D. dissertation. http://myweb.brooklyn.liu.edu/jlyttle/Humor/Theory.htm

Mahfouz, T. (2010) *Arab Culture, 1: Exploring the Arabic-Speaking World Through Cartoons, Satire, and Humor.* Lulu.com.

Maier, N.R.F. (1932) "A Gestalt Theory of Humour." *British Journal of Psychology General Section,* 23: 69–74.

Malefijt, A.M. de Waal (1968) *Religion and Culture.* New York: Macmillan.

Martin G.N. and C.D. Gray (1996) "The Effects of Audience Laughter on Men's and Women's Responses to Humor." *The Journal of Social Psychology,* 136 (2): 221–231.

Martin, R.A. (2006) *The Psychology of Humor: An Integrative Approach.* Academic Press.

Marzolph, U. (2000) "The Qoran and Jocular Literature." *Arabica,* T. 47, Fasc. 3, Les usages du Coran. Présupposés et Méthodes: Formgebrauchdes Korans. Voraussetzungen und Methoden. pp. 478–487.

Maslikowski, D. (2009) "Africans in Poland Gradually Sinking Roots." TopNews.in. October 29. http://www.topnews.in/africans-poland-gradually-sinking-roots-2226490

Mauss, M. (1926) "Parentés à Plaisanteries." *Annuaire de l'École Pratique des Hautes Ètudes, Section des Sciences Religieuses, Paris, 1928. Texte d'une communication présentée à l'Intistut Français d'Anthropologie en 1926.*

McGee, E. and M. Shevlin (2009) "Effect of Humor on Interpersonal Attraction and Mate Selection." *The Journal of Psychology,* 143 (1): 67–77.

McGhee, P.E. (1979) *Humor: Origins and Development.* San Francisco: W.H. Freeman and Co.

McGhee, P.E. and J.H. Goldstein (1983) *The Handbook of Humor Research.* New York: Springer-Verlag.

McKeithan, D.M., ed. (1958) *Traveling with the Innocents Abroad. Mark Twain's Original Reports from Europe and the Holy Land.* Norman: University of Oklahoma Press.

Mercier, V. (1962) *The Irish Comic Tradition.* Oxford: Clarendon Press.

Miller, J. and N. Eakin (2010) "Rethinking Humor: Tucker Max and Gender-Based Humor Creates a Culture that Can Reinforce Misogynistic Attitudes." *Cavalier Daily,* Sept. 24. http://www.cavalierdaily.com/2010/09/24/rethinking-humor/

Morreall, J. (2009) *Comic Relief: A Comprehensive Philosophy of Humor.* Wiley-Blackwell.

National Jewish Population Survey (2000–01). October 2002. The United Jewish Communities. www.jewishvirtuallibrary.org/jsource/US-Israel/ujcpop.html

Nieting, L. (1983) "Humor in the New Testament." *Dialog,* 22: 168–170.

Nilsen, D.L.F. (1990) "The Social Functions of Political Humor." *The Journal of Popular Culture.* 24 (3): 35–47.

Nilsen, D.L.F. (1996) *Humor in Irish Literature.* Westport, CT: Greenwood.

Nilsen, D.L.F. (1997) "The Religion of Humor in Irish Literature." *Humor: International Journal of Humor Research.* 10 (4).

Nilsen, D.L.F. and A. Nilsen (1987) "Humor, Language, and Sex Roles in American Culture." *International Journal of the Sociology of Language,* 65: 67–78.

Nilsen, A.P., and D.L.F. Nilsen (2000) *Encyclopedia of 20th Century American Humor.* Westport, CT: Greenwood.

Norbeck, E. (1963) "African Rituals of Conflict." *American Anthropologist,* 65: 1254–1279.

Norget, K. (2006) *Days of Death, Days of Life: Ritual in the Popular Culture of Oaxaca.* New York: Columbia UP.

Novak, W. and M. Waldoks (1981) *The Big Book of Jewish Humor.* New York: Harper and Row.

Oring, E. (1983) "The People of the Joke: On Conceptualization of a Jewish Humor." *Western Folklore,* 42:4: 261–271.

O'Rourke, P.J (1988) *Holidays in Hell.* New York: Grove Press.

O'Rourke, P.J. (1991) *Parliament of Whores. A Lone Humorist Attempts to Explain the Entire U.S. Government.* New York: The Atlantic Monthly Press.

O'Rourke, P.J. (1993) *Give War a Chance: Eyewitness Accounts of Mankind's Struggle Against Tyranny, Justice and Alcohol-Free Beer.* Vintage.

Pickering, W.S.F. (1984) *Durkheim's Sociology of Religion.* London: Routledge and Kegan Paul.

Polimeni, J., and J.P. Reiss (2006) "The First Joke: Exploring the Evolutionary Origins of Humor." *Evolutionary Psychology,* (4): 347–366.

Pollick, A.S., and F.B.M. de Waal (2007) "Ape Gestures and Language Evolution." *Proceedings of the National Academy of Sciences of the United States of America,* 104 (19): 8184–8189.

Poniewozik, J. (2006) "Stephen Colbert and the Death of 'the Room.'" *Time. Uncategorized.* May 3. http://entertainment.time. com/2006/05/03/stephen_colbert_and_the_death/

Poniewozik, J. (2007) "All-TIME 100 TV Shows." *Time Magazine.* September 6. http://entertainment.time.com/2007/09/06/the-100-best-tv-shows-of-all-time/slide/the-daily-show-2/#the-daily-show-2

Prerost, F.J. (1975) "The Indication of Sexual and Aggressive Similarities Through Humor Appreciation." *Journal of Psychology 91:* 283–288.

Prerost, F.J. (1976) "Reduction of Aggression as a Function of Related Content of Humor." *Psychological Report,* 38: 771–777.

Prerost, F.J. (1983) "Changing Patterns in the Response to Humorous Sexual Stimuli: Sex Roles and Expression of Sexuality." *Social Behavior and Personality,* 11 (1): 23–28.

Prerost, Frank J. (1995a) "Humor Preferences Among Angered Males and Females: Associations with Humor Content and Sexual Desire." *Psychological Report,* 77: 227–234.

Prerost, F.J. (1995b) "Sexual Desire and the Dissipation of Anger Arousal Through Humor Appreciation; Gender and Content Issues." *Social Behavior and Personality,* 23 (1): 45–52.

Prerost, F.J. and R.E. Brewer (1977) "Humor Content Preferences and the Relief of Experimentally Aroused Aggression." *The Journal of Social Psychology,* 103: 225–231.

Provine, R.R. (1991) "Laughter: A Stereotyped Human Vocalization." *Ethology,* 89: 115–124.

Provine, R.R. (1992) "Contagious Laughter: Laughter Is a Sufficient Stimulus for Laughs and Smiles." *Bulletin of the Psychonomic Society,* 30: 1–4.

Provine R.R. (1993) "Laughter Punctuates Speech: Linguistic, Social, and Gender Contexts of Laughter." *Ethology,* 95: 291–298.

Provine, R.R. (1996) "Laughter." *American Scientist,* 84: 38–45.

Provine, R.R. (2000) *Laughter: A Scientific Investigation.* New York: Penguin Books.

Provine, R.R. (2004) "Laughing, Tickling, and the Evolution of Speech and Self." *Current Directions in Psychological Science,* 13: 215–218.

Radcliffe-Brown, A.R. (1940) "On Joking Relationships." *Africa: Journal of the International African Institute,* 13 (3):195–210.

Radcliffe-Brown, A.R. (1949) "A Further Note on Joking Relationships." *Africa: Journal of the International African Institute,* 19 (2):133–140.

Radday, Y.T., and A. Brenner, eds. (1990) "On *Humor and the Comic in the Hebrew Bible.*" JSOT Supplement Series 92; Bible and Literature Series 23. Sheffield: Almond Press.

Raskin, V. (1985) *Semantic Mechanisms of Humor.* Dordrecht/Boston/Lancaster: D. Reidel.

Raskin, V., ed. (2008) *Primer of Humor Research.* New York, NY: Mouton de Gruyter.

Richlin, A. (1992) *The Garden of Priapus: Sexuality and Aggression in Roman Humor.* (rev. ed.) New York: Oxford University Press.

Rogers, N. (2002) *Halloween: From Pagan Ritual to Party Night.* Oxford University Press.

Rogin, M. (1996) *Blackface, White Noise. Jewish Immigrants in the Hollywood Melting Pot.* University of California Press.

Rubenstein, J. (1992) "Purim, Liminality, and Communitas." *AJS Review,* 17 (2): 247–277.

Ruch, W., Ott, C., Accoce, J., and Françoise Bariaud (1991) "Cross-National Comparisons of Humor Categories: France and Germany." *HUMOR: International Journal of Humor Research,* 4 (3–4): 391–414.

Ryan, K.M., and J. Kanjorski (1998) "The Enjoyment of Sexist Humor, Rape Attitudes, and Relationship Aggression in College Students." *Sex Roles,* 38 (9/10): 743–756.

Schmidt, N.E., and D.I. Williams (1971) "The Evolution of Theories of Humor." *Journal of Behavioral Science, 1,* 95–106.

Schröter, Susanne (2004) "Rituals of Rebellion: A Theory Reconsidered." In: Kreinath, Jens/Constance Hartung/Annette Deschner, Hg.: *The Dynamics of Changing Rituals: The Transformation of Religious Rituals within Their Social and Cultural Context.* (Toronto Studies in Religion: 29). New York: Peter Lang, S. Pp. 41–58.

Segal, R.A., ed. (1998) *The Myth and Ritual Theory: An Anthology.* Wiley-Blackwell.

Spalding, H.D. (2001) *Encyclopedia of Jewish Humor: From Biblical Times to the Modern Age.* Jonathan David.

Spencer, H. (1966) "The Physiology of Laughter." *The Work of Herbert Spencer,* 14: 452–466. Osnabruck: Otto Zeller.

St. John, W. (2005) "Seriously, the Joke Is Dead." *New York Times.* May 22. http://www.nytimes.com/2005/05/22/fashion/sundaystyles/22joke.html?pagewanted=all

Stark, R. and W.S. Bainbridge (1987) *A Theory of Religion.* New York: Peter Lang.

Sternbergh, A. (2006) Stephen Colbert Has America by the Ballots. *New York Magazine.* 2006-10-16. http://nymag.com/news/politics/22322/index3.html

Strensky, I. (1987) *Four Theories of Myth in Twentieth-Century History: Cassirer, Eliade, Lévi-Strauss and Malinowski.* Iowa City, IA: University of Iowa Press.

Tamer, G., ed. (2009) *Humor in der Arabischen Kultur/Humor in Arabic Culture.* Berlin, New York: Walter De Gruyter.

Tamer, G. (2006) "The Qur'an and Humor." Tamer, George, ed. (2009) *Humor in der Arabischen Kultur/Humor in Arabic Culture.* Berlin, New York: Walter De Gruyter.

Thorson, J.A., and F.C. Powell. (1993a). "Development and Validation of a Multidimensional Sense of Humor Scale." *Journal of Clinical Psychology, 49*: 13–23.

Thorson, J.A., and Powell, F.C. (1993b). "Relationships of Death Anxiety and Sense of Humor." *Psychological Reports, 72*: 1364–1366.

The Uniform Death Determination Act (1980). The Uniform Law Commission. The National Conference of Commissioners on Uniform State Laws. http://uniformlaws.org/ActSummary.aspx?title=Determination of Death Act

Trueblood, E. (1964) *The Humor of Christ: A Bold Challenge to the Traditional Stereotype of a Somber, Gloomy Christ.* San Francisco: Harper and Row.

Twain, Mark (2003): *The Innocents Abroad, or the New Pilgrims' Progress.* Modern Library Edition. Original edition: 1869; Hartford: American Publishing Company. The full title: *The Innocents Abroad, or the New Pilgrims' Progress; Being Some Account of the Steamship Quaker City's Pleasure Excursion to Europe and the Holy Land, with Descriptions of Countries, Nations, Incidents and Adventures, as They Appeared to the Author.*

Veatch, T.C. (1998) "A Theory of Humor." *HUMOR: Tthe International Journal of Humor Research.* 11: 161–215.

Vigil, J.M. (2009) "A Socio-Relational Framework of Sex Differences in the Expression of Emotion." *Behavioral and Brain Sciences,* 32 (5): 375–428.

Vinacke, W. Edgar (1957) "Stereotypes as Social Concepts." *Journal of Social Psychology,* 46: 229–43.

Vos, N. (1967) *For God's Sake, Laugh!* Richmond, VA: John Knox.

Walker, N. (1988) "A Very Serious Thing: Women's Humor in American Culture." Minnesota: University of Minnesota Press.

Wallace, A.F.C. (1966) *Religion. An Anthropological View.* New York: Random House.

Waller, M. Bridget K., Bard A., Vick S.-J., and M.C. Smith Pasqualini (2007) "Perceived Differences Between Chimpanzee (Pan Troglodytes) and Human (*Homo sapiens*) Facial Expressions Are Related to Emotional Interpretation." *Journal of Comparative Psychology,* Vo. 121(4): 398–404.

Wasilewska, E. (1991) *The Search for the Sacred: The Archaeology of Religion and the Interpretation of Color Symbolism in Prehistoric Societies.* Ph.D. dissertation. Department of Anthropology, University of Utah.

Wasilewska, E. (2000) *Creation Stories of the Middle East.* London and Philadelphia: Jessica Kingsley.

Weber, B. (2003) "Lessons from a Meatheaded Uncle Spawn an Identity Crisis." *New York Times.* March 19. http://theater. nytimes.com/mem/theater/treview.html?pagewanted=printandres=940ceedb1531f93aa25750c0a9659c8b63

Webster, G. (1960) *Laughter in the Bible.* St. Louis: Bethany Press.

Weinstein, S. (2008) *Shtick Shift: Jewish Humor in the 21st Century.* Fort Lee: Barricade Books.

Weiss, A. (2009) "The End of Jewish Humor." *Forward.com.* http://forward.com/articles/107058/the-end-of-jewish-humor/

Wells, N.M., D'Annunzio S.S., Harris T.M., Robbins J.B., Doyle H.E., Pfadt-Trilling A.M., and Beins B.C. (2009) *A Guy Walks into a Bar: Sense of Humor and Reactions to Offensive Jokes.* Poster presentation at the annual convention of the Eastern Psychological Association, Pittsburgh, PA.

Wilson, D.W. and J.L. Molleston (1981) "Effects of Sex and Type of Humor on Humor Appreciation." *Journal of Personality Assessment,* 45 (1): 90–96.

Wimer, D.J., and B.C. Beins. (2008) "Expectations and Perceived Humor." *Humor: International Journal of Humor Studies,* 21(3): 347–363.

Winick, C. (1961) "Space Jokes as Indications of Attitudes Toward Space." *Journal of Social Issues,* 17 (April): 43–49.

Wisse, R.R. (1971) *The Schlemiel As A Modern Hero.* University of Chicago.

Wyer, R.S. and J.E. Collins II (1992) *A Theory of Humor Elicitation. Psychological Review,* 99 (4): 663–688.

Zerjal, T., Y. Xue, G. Bertorelle, R.S. Wells, W. Bao, S. Zhu, R. Qamar, Q. Ayub, A. Mohyuddin, S. Fu, Pu Li, N. Yuldasheva, R. Ruzibakiev, J. Xu, Q. Shu, R. Du, H. Yang, M.E. Hurles, E. Robinson, T. Gerelsaikhan, B. Dashnyam, S. Qasim Mehdi, and C. Tyler-Smith (2003) "The Genetic Legacy of the Mongols." *American Journal of Human Genetics,* March 72 (3): 717–721.

Ziv, A. (1988) *National Styles of Humor.* Greenwood Press.

Chapter 1

TOWARD DEFINITION OF HUMOR ...
Past, Present, and Future of Humor Research

The First Joke

Exploring the Evolutionary Origins of Humor

by Joseph Polimeni,
Department of Psychiatry, University of Manitoba,
771 Bannatyne Avenue Winnipeg, Manitoba, Canada, R3E 3N4, JPolimeni@shaw.ca

Jeffrey P. Reiss,
Department of Psychiatry, University of Manitoba,
771 Bannatyne Avenue Winnipeg, Manitoba, Canada, R3E 3N4, JPReiss@cc.umanitoba.ca

Abstract: Humor is a complex cognitive function which often leads to laughter. Contemporary humor theorists have begun to formulate hypotheses outlining the possible innate cognitive structures underlying humor. Humor's conspicuous presence in the behavioral repertoire of humankind invites adaptive explanations. This article explores the possible adaptive features of humor and ponders its evolutionary path through hominid history. Current humor theories and previous evolutionary ideas on humor are reviewed. In addition, scientific fields germane to the evolutionary study of humor are examined: animal models, genetics, children's humor, humor in pathological conditions, neurobiology, humor in traditional societies and cognitive archeology. Candidate selection pressures and associated evolutionary mechanisms are considered. The authors conclude that several evolutionary-related topics such as the origins of language, cognition underlying spiritual feelings, hominid group size, and primate teasing could have special relevance to the origins of humor.

Keywords: humor, evolution, laughter, teasing, language, group size.

Introduction

E volutionary forces will have shaped, or at least not selected against, any phenotype that has an appreciable connection to genotype and has existed over a number of generations. T. Dobzhansky, the pre-eminent geneticist, emphasized this point in his famous aphorism, "Nothing in biology makes sense, except in the light of evolution" (as cited in Mayr, 2001, p. 39). The ability to generate and perceive humor is a biological process—a cognitive phenotypic trait—almost certainly dependent on a corresponding genetically-based neurological substrate. Humor has certainly been around for thousands of years and possibly even a few million years. This article will systematically and briefly review topics that could be germane to the evolutionary origins of humor.

Humor and laughter are closely related; however, they are not synonymous. Humor is the underlying cognitive process that frequently, but not necessarily, leads to laughter. Laughter is a seizure-like activity that can be elicited by experiencing a humorous cognitive stimulus but also other stimuli such as tickling. Thus, one can laugh without a humorous stimulus and similarly one can experience humor without laughter.

The basic ability to perceive humor seems "instinctive" and, thus, likely reliant on genetic machinations. Humor is complex; arguably too complicated to learn without an assemblage of specific neural pathways or an associated cognitive module. Whether something is funny or not is often dependent on nuanced verbal phrasing in combination with a full appreciation of prevailing social dynamics. In fact, humor's inherent opacity yields itself to be purposely used occasionally when ambiguous communication is particularly desired. Humor is ubiquitous and universal, further implicating a genetic substrate. To our knowledge, no culture exists that is unfamiliar with humor. It appears that all healthy individuals reliably comprehend obvious attempts at humor.

Humor has been part of the behavioral repertoire of modern *Homo sapiens* for thousands of years. Ancient Greek texts contain descriptions of "professional" jesters and jokebooks (Bremmer, 1997, pp. 11–18). One of the earliest historical figures to be firmly associated with humor and laughter was the Greek philosopher Democritus. Known as the "laughing philosopher," he not only had a reputation for his mirthful disposition but perhaps also for his tendency to "[laugh] at the stupidity of his fellow citizens" (Bremmer, 1997, p. 17).

Using two pieces of available evidence, a minimum figure for the age of humor can be proposed. First, humorous conversation has been observed by the pioneering anthropologists in first contact with Australian aboriginals (Chewings, 1936; Schulze, 1891). Second, it appears that Australian aboriginals have been essentially genetically isolated for at least 35,000 years (O'Connell and Allen, 1998). If genetic factors dictate the fundamental ability to perceive or produce humor (and barring convergent evolution), then 35,000 years may reflect a minimum age for humor in *Homo sapiens*.

There are several reasons to suppose humor and laughter could be evolutionarily adaptive. As previously mentioned, the complexity of humor implicates an established genetic substrate that in turn could suggest evolutionary adaptiveness. Given that even a simple joke can utilize language skills, theory-of-mind, symbolism, abstract thinking, and social perception, humor may arguably be humankind's most complex cognitive attribute. Despite its ostensible complexity, humor is also paradoxically reflexive—people typically laugh without consciously appreciating all the causal factors. Other human behavioral reflexes such as the corneal reflex or startle response clearly reflect behavioral adaptations. In fact, laughter may perhaps represent an ethological *fixed action pattern*. Supporting this notion are several accounts of runaway pathological laughter originating in various neurological brain insults (Black, 1982; Dabby et al., 2004; McCullagh et al., 1999; Okuda, Chyung, Chin and Waubant, 2005). One could perhaps frame humor in reductionistic ethological terms: exposure to a humorous stimulus induces laughter—a loud multi-second seizure-like signal—that generates a positive emotional state in conspecifics and facilitates further social activity.

Something evolutionarily positive seems to be occurring around humor and laughter—another reason to invite adaptationist thinking. Foremost, laughter is pleasurable and, consequently, a reinforceable behavior. Perhaps, the most overarching use of humorous communication is to help navigate contentious social situations. In addition, humor is widely utilized during courtship (Weisfeld, 1993). Outside the social domain, humor may have modest physiological benefits such as boosting immunity (Bennet, Zeller, Rosenburg, and McCann, 2003, Martin, 2001).

It has been forwarded that there are certain evolutionary costs to humor and laughter—disadvantages that prompt the expectation of countervailing evolutionary advantages. Appreciable physiological energy is spent during vigorous laughter (McGhee, 1983). Almost every culture spends appreciable time communicating in a humorous context. Laughter is noisy and could even attract the attention of predators (Weisfeld, 1993).

If humor and laughter are, in fact, evolutionarily advantageous, a myriad of questions must accordingly follow. How does humor specifically enhance fitness? Which vehicle of selection (individual, kin, or group) most benefits? Invoking the principle of gradualism, how would early or intermediate forms of humor be configured? Which cognitive attributes had to be in place before humor evolved (i.e. language, theory-of-mind)? Have any contemporary cognitive functions been exapted from the neural mechanics of humor?

This article cannot definitively answer all these questions. However, we do intend to methodically explore important areas that could reveal further clues to humor's enigmatic evolutionary history. The first section will review contemporary humor theories including previous evolutionary ideas on humor. The second section will explore a number of topics which could be related to the evolution of humor, 1) animal models, 2) genetics, 3) children's humor, 4) humor in pathological conditions, 5) neurobiology, 6) humor in traditional societies, and 7) cognitive archeology. In addition, the reader is directed to two other reviews, emphasizing different aspects of humor and laughter's evolutionary history (Vaid, 1999; Weisfeld, 1993).

Humor Theories

Because of the multilayered nature of humor, no single humor theory has been completely satisfactory and thus clinched universal acceptance. Plato perhaps expounded the earliest recorded speculations on the subject, although according to Provine (2000, pp. 12–13), he appears to have discussed the effects of laughter rather than humor per se. Aristotle commented on the social effects of laughter (Provine, 2000, pp. 13–14) although evidence exists that one of his lost manuscripts may have "concentrated on humor" (Bremmer and Roodenburg, 1997, p. 4).

Similar to the familiar story about the blind men, each figuring their own unique representation of an elephant, every humor theory seems to reflect a partial truth. Three essential themes, however, are repeatedly observed in the majority of humor theories: 1) humor reflects a set of incongruous conceptualizations, 2) humor involves repressed sexual or aggressive feelings, and 3) humor elevates social status by demonstrating superiority or saving face. These ideas reflect separate cognitive domains and therefore are not necessarily mutually exclusive. Incongruency theories, for example, emphasize the underlying cognitive structure of humor, while the latter two ideas relate putative social purposes to humor. Evolutionary humor theories have emphasized the possible adaptive characteristics of humor and laughter.

1) Incongruity Theories of Humor

Notions that humor involves incongruity can be seen in the writings of Immanuel Kant (LaFollette and Shanks, 1993), Norman Maier (Vaid, 1999), Arthur Schopenhaur (Provine, 2000) and Arthur Koestler (1964). Suls was perhaps the first to formalize the incongruity model of humor by unequivocally demarcating the congruous and incongruous components of humor in his two-stage model (Suls, 1972) According to Suls, solving an incongruity by applying an alternative formulation to the discrepancy forms the basis of humor.

Building on Raskin's (1985) linguistic–semantic theory of verbal humor, T. C. Veatch (1998) has perhaps formulated the most precise and encompassing humor theory. Veatch utilizes the established idea that humor contains two incongruous elements; however in Veatch's formulation, one element is socially normal while the other constitutes a violation of the "subjective moral order." Veatch defines this moral order as the "rich cognitive and emotional system of opinions about the proper order of the social and natural world" (p. 168). Using one of the series of "Mommy, Mommy" jokes as an example:

Mommy, Mommy! What is a delinquent child?
Shut up and pass me the crowbar.

The inferred setting is a young child asking his mother an innocent question about a topic the child presumably knows nothing about. The social violation is embedded in mother's incongruous reply—mothers are supposed to disapprove rather than encourage egregious antisocial behavior. The congruency is that it is also natural, to a small extent, to teach your children some non-altruistic strategies in order to more effectively compete with others. Humor is complex and dependent on a myriad of subjective associations. Consequently, its specific makeup is open to subjective interpretation. In this joke, there is arguably a secondary layer of incongruency and an associated resolution. Despite asking, "What is a delinquent child?" it becomes clear that an act of delinquency is precisely what the child is doing. People are supposed to know the essential features of their character and when they don't—that is incongruous. However, children can be exempt from this stringent expectation due to their immaturity and this detail could be the associated resolving element.

There are other factors to consider when determining the funniness of any situation such as how surprised one is by a punch line or the mood of the respective participants. Laughter facilitates laughter in others (Chapman, 1976) and therefore could conceivably cue and enhance humor perception. Also, it has been hypothesized that an optimum state of arousal exists to enjoy humor (Apter and Smith, 1997; Rothbart, 1977). Notwithstanding the lack of clarity around the construct of psychological arousal, entrenched boredom or extreme fear seem to limit laughter.

2) Humor and Laughter Originating in Repressed Expression of Sexual or Aggressive Feelings

The aggressive quality of jokes has been cleverly captured in Mel Brook's amusing characterization of humor, "Tragedy is when I cut my finger. Comedy is when you fall into an open manhole and die." Freud (1905/1963) viewed humor as a release of excessive sexual or aggressive tension. Framed within his views of the unconscious mind, humor and laughter release the psychic tension related to inhibiting unconscious sexual or aggressive impulses. Expressing laughter is considered anxiety-reducing, pleasurable and healthy. Subsequent researchers have studied various aspects of humor within this framework

(Ziv and Gadish, 1990). Although numerous jokes do, in fact, have a hostile edge, many others seem to lack prominent aggressive themes (although it is acknowledged that depending on social context, covert or low level aggression could conceivably be interpreted in any humorous comment).

3) The use of Humor to demonstrate superiority and elevate social status

Several humor thinkers have emphasized how humor is often utilized to demonstrate superiority or elevate social status. Weisfeld (1993) provides several examples such as the Greenland Inuit who "traditionally resolved disputes by engaging in public contests of ridiculing each other" (p. 154). Thomas Hobbes (1651/1981) in Leviathan was the first to clearly articulate this idea, characterizing laughter as an extension of "sudden glory." Critics point out that most jokes do little to boost feelings of superiority.

4) Evolutionary Theories of Humor

In *Expressions of the Emotions in Man and Animals,* Darwin (1872/1920, p. 196) conjectured, "Laughter seems primarily to be the expression of mere joy or happiness." By comparing the behavioral aspects of laughter in "savages," "imbeciles," and apes, Darwin thus implied some evolutionary advantage. He did not address the concept of humor.

Alexander (1986) was one of the first to methodically analyze humor and laughter within an evolutionary context. Advancing an idea clearly rooted in Hobbes' superiority theory, Alexander figured humor led to greater reproductive success by enhancing one's social standing through ostracizing others. Ostracism steers "conflicts and confluences of interest" ultimately altering access to resources. Humor is considered one method of social ostracism. Thus, according to Alexander, the major benefits of telling jokes are varied and include 1) raising one's own status, 2) lowering the status of certain individuals and 3) raising the status of designated listeners and thereby enhancing camaraderie or social unity.

Weisfeld (1993) proposed a general humor theory suggesting humor provides valuable social information to others while laughter provokes pleasurable feelings that positively reinforce the humorist. In return, the humorist gets forthcoming reciprocation by putting an ally in a favorable disposition. It is an interesting hypothesis although difficult to critique given that the mechanics of mammalian cooperation are exceedingly complex and yet unsolved (Wilson, 1975/2000).

Ramachandran's (1998) "false alarm theory" suggests "the main purpose of laughter is for the individual to alert others in the social group that the anomaly detected by that individual is of trivial consequence". The immediate social group would be close relatives who are likely to share similar genes. Ramachandran further speculates that the cognitive perspective necessary to distinguish between trivial and serious could have somehow evolved into a cognitive framework that classifies congruous and incongruous components of humor.

Noticing that both laughter and social grooming release endogenous opiates, Barrett, Dunbar and Lycett (2002) have speculated that the enjoyment associated with humor eventually replaced the pleasure associated with social grooming in primates. In each case, the feelings of gratification positively reinforce each respective behavior. These ideas are based on the hypothesis that language eventually replaced social grooming as the principal social bonding device between hominids (Dunbar, 1993; Aiello and Dunbar, 1993). In this context, humor and laughter would have facilitated the development of language by maintaining a pleasurable association to conversation.

W. E. Jung (2003) suggests that the fundamental evolutionary purpose of humor and laughter was to facilitate cooperation between people. According to Jung, the ability to attribute mental states to others (theory-of-mind) is humor's most essential feature. His "Inner Eye" theory proposes that "laughter is a signal that facilitates cooperation by transfer of information on the laugher's empathy with attributed mental states and his sympathy levels for others" (p. 245) Ultimately, a laughing response signals that one is both ready and able to cooperate.

Topics Potentially Salient to the Evolution of Humor

1) Animal Models

Perhaps the most primitive ethological behaviour linked to humor and laughter has been contemplated by Van Hooff (1972). He proposed that the possible phylogenetic roots of smiling could reside in the "bared-teeth display" seen in many mammals while laughter could be related to the "relaxed open-mouth display" observed in primates and often associated with playful activities. Panksepp and Burgdorf (2003) have detected a 50 kHz chirp in young rats during social interactions resembling play, and wonder if this positive affective vocalization could be related to human laughter. Certain vocalizations in dogs may also demonstrate parallels to conventional laughter (Simonet, Murphy and Lance, 2001).

When tickled, the higher primates (humans, chimpanzees, gorillas and orangutans) all display a laughter-like behaviour (Caron, 2002; Fry, 1994). Fry dates the "rudimentary elements of contemporary humor" to 6.5 million years ago—a figure representing the last common ancestor of Homo sapiens and chimpanzees. However, it appears that Fry inadvertently misses the last common ancestor of humans and orangutans, which is approximately 14 millions old (Dawkins, 2004). This means that the rudimentary origins of laughter could be at least 14 million years old.

Some primate researchers have been struck by the pervasiveness of teasing-like behaviours in captive apes—particularly chimpanzees (Butovskaya and Kozintsev, 1996; De Waal, 1996, p. 114; Gamble, 2001). In contrast, it appears that Goodall (1986) witnessed much less playful teasing behaviour in the wild. Nonetheless, a spectrum of interactions from aggressive confrontations to teasing is apparent in the behavioural repertoire of chimpanzees. Teasing seems more commonly initiated by youngsters in the form of play. For example, young chimpanzees may throw dirt, hit with sticks or jump on their elders (De Waal, 1996, p. 114). Often, the older chimpanzees will react in a playful manner such as tickling the youngster or engage in a mock chase. De Waal figures that teasing, "serves to gather information about the social environment, and to investigate authority" (p. 114). Butovskaya and Kozintsev frame such teasing as "quasi–aggression". Although the authors are not explicit, the implication seems to be that teasing is a novel mammalian behaviour falling between aggression and peacefulness. The need to readily integrate these two mutually exclusive behavioural states could perhaps have led to the congruous and incongruous elements of humor.

Unlike any other animal, only humans seem to fully possess the cognitive machinations necessary for humor. The use of rich complex symbols within the framework of a universal syntactical structure, in combination with a high-powered working memory invariably leads to intricate conceptualizations. This ability—to quickly manipulate multifaceted symbols in the service of even more intricate conceptualizations—may be an essential distinguishing feature of Homo sapiens (Deacon, 1997). Leaving aside the disputed accounts of the occasional primate combining two words when using sign language, apes undeniably have trouble integrating two juxtaposed conceptualizations (Roberts, 1998).

2) Genetics

The genetics of multifaceted behaviors is just beginning to be systematically investigated. For example, a few twin studies have attempted to parse the relative genetic versus environmental contributions related to humor appreciation (Cherkas et al, 2000; Lichtenstein et al, 2003; Wilson, 1977). These studies have measured personal preferences to various forms of humor rather than humor competence per se. One study found a potential genetic effect for appreciating aggressive jokes (Wilson, 1977).

In the future, various epidemiological characteristics of humor could conceivably point to candidate genes involved in humor perception or production. For example, there may be gender differences in the predilection to laugh, which could implicate sex chromosomes. According to Provine (2000, pp. 27–28) women laugh 126% more than men during conversations with each other. In this particular case, cultural factors such as contemporary gender imbalances in social status are probably more important than genetic differences (it has been observed that persons in higher positions of authority seem to laugh less than those in lower positions).

In a similar vein, bipolar disorder patients (previously known as manic-depressives) clearly have a greater propensity to initiate and enjoy humor during manic episodes (although this too awaits systematic study). Candidate susceptibility genes are being actively investigated for all major psychiatric conditions, however, as of yet, no conclusive chromosomal regions have yet been associated with bipolar disorder. Results from future bipolar genetic studies could conceivably produce a list of genes potentially involved with humor comprehension or production.

3) Children's Humor

Because ontogeny can sometimes recapitulate phylogeny, the maturation of humor in children could perhaps have some evolutionary relevance. It is certainly conceivable that the various stages of humor development seen in children mimics humor's evolutionary path. In the 1970's, a number of pioneering studies on children's humor were conducted; however, the pace of research has appeared to slacken— perhaps, because these early attempts produced few firm conclusions to build further research upon.

Smiling and laughter occur within the first year of life and are undoubtedly triggered by stimuli separate from the conventional processes associated with adult humor. Laughter in infants could, however, represent an embryonic form of fully developed humor. Using the widest possible definition of humor, Shultz (1976/1996, pp. 11–36) linked four primitive forms of "humor"—smiling in infancy, peek-a-boo, tickling and chase games—to formal incongruity models of humor. Extending Piaget's ideas on the subject, Shultz viewed infant smiling as a pleasurable response to perceived mastery over a situation. Mastery, which brings pleasure, reflects resolution of a previous uncertain and incongruous situation.

The Peek-a-boo game also has possible analogues with conventional humor. Object permanence forms around 6–12 months and when it is well formed in infants, no explicit anxiety is caused by having items temporarily out-of-view. According to Schultz, it is during this transition en route to object permanence that uncertainty exists during peek-a-boo. Seeing mother's face, for example, solves the incongruency and elicits smiling.

Tickling, chase games, and other forms of play have an intuitive appeal for all children. Darwin (1872/1920) first recognized that the areas most vulnerable to tickling such as the neck, abdomen and soles of the feet are perhaps equally the most vulnerable areas to predator attack. Koestler (1964) framed tickling as a "mock attack" and therefore evolutionary adaptive. According to Shultz, the re-creation of a predatory attack inherently possesses incongruous and congruous parts. Tickling and chase games fall within a certain window of arousal similar to humor (an actual attack would be too arousing and therefore scary and no attack is not arousing at all). Laughter accompanies the reduction in arousal.

By about 7 or 8 years old, children's humor approaches that of an adult although it understandably lacks the same richness. In a series of experiments with children 6, 8, 10, and 12 years, 6 year-olds understood the incongruities in a story but failed to recognize the resolvable elements (Schultz, 1976/1996). Children aged 8 and older appreciated both elements. The timing coincides with the usual advent of concrete operational thought in children. Similarly, theory-of-mind researchers have shown that children under age 6 have a particular difficult time distinguishing lies from jokes (Winner, Brownell, Happe, Blum, and Pincus, 1998).

There have been few cross-cultural studies involving children's humor. Apte's (1985) surveillance of the anthropological literature gleaned two patterns: 1) children mimicking adults in a comical manner may be universal and 2) humor involving ridicule is always more common in children compared to adults.

4) Humor in Pathological Conditions

Because the consequences of brain damage can help connect brain anatomy to function, any deficit in humor perception associated with specific neuropathology has the potential to be illuminating. It is well known that brain damage, particularly in the frontal lobes, causes deficits of humor appreciation. The precise cerebral areas most closely associated with humor deficits will be reviewed in the next section. The neurological condition most often associated with changes in humor and laughter is epilepsy. For many years, an "epileptic personality" has been described with "humorlessness," a common associated feature (Kaplan and Saddock, 1985). Recent studies have confirmed previous clinical observations—specifically, patients with frontal lobe epilepsy demonstrate deficits in humor appreciation (Farrant et al, 2005). Gelastic seizures, also known as laughter epilepsy, are most commonly associated with hypothalamic hamartomata (benign hypothalamic malformations consisting of heterotopic nervous tissue) but can also arise from the frontal or temporal lobes (Pearce, 2004).

Among psychiatric conditions, only schizophrenia has been systematically shown to be accompanied by humor perception deficits (Corcoran, Cahill, and Frith, 1997; Polimeni and Reiss, 2006). Anecdotal observations of humorlessness in severe obsessive–compulsive disorder have not been methodically investigated.

To our knowledge, humor perception in clinical depression has also not been systematically explored although clinical observation suggests no appreciable deficits. Anyone who has grieved recognizes that although we may be less inclined to laugh, our ability to perceive humor is more or less preserved.

The best documented case of a laughing epidemic originated in Tanzanian schoolchildren in 1962 (Rankin and Philip, 1963). Over two hundred adolescents and young adults were overcome by recurrent bouts of hysterical laughter and crying over a period of a few months. Although no initiating factor was ever discovered, this incident exemplifies the social and contagious aspects of laughter.

5) Neurobiology

An outline of the brain areas responsible for humor appreciation is beginning to emerge (Wild, Rodden, Grodd, and Ruch, 2003). Delineation of the neural pathways responsible for humor could have evolutionary significance, especially if the phylogenic history of the human brain could be precisely retraced. The elucidation of the neurobiology of humor has benefited from two approaches: 1) observing the effects of various brain lesions on humor perception and 2) functional magnetic resonance imaging (fMRI) studies which monitor brain activity in normal subjects while perceiving humor.

Thirty years ago, Gardner, Ling, Flamm, and Silverman (1975) demonstrated humor deficits in both left and right hemispheric damaged subjects. However, subtle distinctions between subjects may not have been possible since all sixty subjects were inpatients and therefore likely to have had considerable cognitive impairment. A study by Dagge and Hartje (1985) using a continuum of simple to complex cartoons showed that patients with right-sided lesions fared worse than left-sided patients and both groups inferior to controls.

Perhaps the most comprehensive study to date utilizing brain lesioned individuals in order to localize humor centers was conducted by Shammi and Stuss (1999). They administered various humor tests to 21 right-handed individuals with focal brain damage documented by CT or MRI, and compared them to 10 controls. In addition, they administered a general battery of cognitive tests. They concluded that right frontal lobe lesions (particularly Brodman areas 8, 9, 10) most disrupted humor appreciation. However, it was not clear whether subjects with right-sided lesions demonstrated greater general impairment (because the results of the accompanying cognitive battery were not available). Furthermore, only five subjects possessed impairment from singular frontal lesions (R = 3, L = 2). Of note, deficits in working memory, mental shifting and verbal abstraction significantly correlated with poor humor appreciation for all subjects. This study exposes one of the most formidable problems in humor cognitive research—that the integrity of humor perception is subservient to numerous cognitive skills such as working memory, long-term memory, executive functions, emotional expression and language skills.

Three functional magnetic resonance imaging (fMRI) experiments involving humor in unimpaired participants have been published to date. fMRI is an especially appealing new technology because it allows non-invasive measurement of localized brain activity during various cognitive–behavioral tasks. However, fMRI is characterized by low signal-to-noise ratios and other potential confounding variables, which can easily produce inconsistent results between various research groups.

Using event-related fMRI, Goel and Dolan (2001) observed differences in neural activations between semantic and phonological jokes—the former preferentially activating bilateral temporal lobes while the latter predominantly accessing a left hemispheric network centered around speech production regions. Activation in the medial ventral prefrontal cortex (MVPFC) bilaterally correlated with how funny a joke was rated. The authors suggest their results indicate "the affective appreciation of humor involves access to a central reward system in the MVPFC" (p. 238).

Moran, Wig, Adams, Janata, and Kelley (2004) monitored humor detection versus humor appreciation using *The Simpsons* and *Seinfeld* comedies in an event-related fMRI experiment. They found significant activations in the left posterior middle temporal gyrus and left inferior frontal gyrus, with additional activations in the bilateral anterior temporal cortex, left inferior temporal gyrus, right posterior middle temporal gyrus and right cerebellum. Of note, the authors point out that the left inferior frontal cortex has been previously associated with "reconciling ambiguous semantic content with stored knowledge" (p. 1058).

Mobbs, Greicius, Abdel-Azim, Menon, and Reiss (2003) event related fMRI study used captioned funny cartoons versus non funny ones and showed that humorous content primarily activated, the left temporal-occipital junction, left inferior frontal gyrus, left temporal pole, left supplementary motor area, left dorsal anterior cingulate and bilateral subcortical structures including ventral striatum, nucleus accumbens, ventral tegmentum area and amygdale, which are key components of the mesolimbic dopaminergic reward system. The authors point out a similar pattern is commonly observed in "monetary and video-game reward tasks" (p. 1043).

Consolidating the results of all neuroanatomical humor perception studies reveals two general patterns: 1) the integrity of humor may rely more heavily on right-hemispheric structures (although recent fMRI results are not entirely in accordance with the brain lesion studies pointing towards greater right-side involvement) and 2) the prefrontal cortex seems intimately involved (the involvement of the temporal lobes is probably related to the language component of humor). The natural question that follows is what can these two tentative conclusions tell us about the evolution of humor in human beings?

The right hemisphere appears to be preferentially involved in the "interpretation of emotional material presented linguistically" or more broadly, the "expression and comprehension of emotion" (Edwards-Lee and Saul, 1999, pp. 310–311). In addition, the right hemisphere may be more instrumental in maintaining "global attention to the environment" (Edwards-Lee and Saul, 1999, p. 306). Both characteristics could be essential to humor appreciation and may explain why right-sided lesions seem to disrupt humor perception more than left-sided pathology. Cerebral asymmetry is most pronounced in humans compared to any other animal and this may perhaps be due to the need to accommodate language (Banyas, 1999. p. 97; Deacon, 1997, p. 309). The possible evolutionary relationship between language and humor will be addressed in a subsequent section.

The prefrontal cortex is a part of the brain consistently associated with higher cognitive functions. Attentional tasks, executive functions, cognitive flexibility and incorporation of emotional behavior are higher cognitive functions generally affiliated with the prefrontal cortex (Fuster, 1997, p. 251; Grady, 1999, p. 197). Semantic memory retrieval, episodic memory, working memory and theory of mind are more specific cognitive skills also repeatedly linked to prefrontal cortical structures (Grady, 1999, pp. 203–205). Additionally, the subcortical dopaminergic reward system projects to the prefrontal cortex (Schultz, 2000).

The prefrontal cortex appears to be a distinguishing cerebral feature in the evolution of man. In primates, the prefrontal cortex consists of 3 major regions (but only 2 regions in other mammals) (Streidter, 2005, p. 307). The "lateral prefrontal region, namely area 10 is almost twice as large (percentagewise) in humans as in other apes" (Striedter, 2005, p. 329). It is therefore not surprising that such a seemingly complex mental activity like humor would be anatomically affiliated with the prefrontal cortex.

6) Humor in Traditional Societies

Modern culture has a remarkable ability to transform adaptive behaviors so completely that it makes it difficult to comprehend why certain behavioral propensities exist at all. Listening to music alone through headphones for hours couldn't possibly be adaptive; however, witnessing a ceremony of song and dance in preparation for tribal warfare puts an entirely different perspective on the potential evolutionary functions of music. Similarly, can the use of humor in traditional societies provide any insight to the possible evolutionary purposes of humor?

Despite language and cultural barriers, humor in traditional societies is generally comprehensible to visiting anthropologists (Schiefenhövel, 1984). For example, Wulf Schiefenhövel, who spent a number of years in the highlands of West New Guinea, had no significant trouble comprehending humor in the Eipo (personal communication, March, 2005). This seems to be the prevailing perspective whenever anthropologists comment on humor in traditional societies (Turnbull, 1961/1968).

Two humor phenomena especially standout in the anthropological literature: joking relationships and clowns. Since the turn of the century, various anthropologists have noted certain kinships ties are accompanied by greater joviality and humor. Despite the lack of a satisfactory operational definition, Mahedev Apte's (1985) synthesis of joking relationships, nevertheless, reveals several interesting patterns. First, joking relationships in preliterate societies are most commonly observed between extended relatives. Nuclear families do not typically communicate extensively in this manner. Siblings-in-law and cousins, particularly of the opposite sex, seem to most readily demonstrate humor in their conversations. Second, there are definite customary expectations associated with some joking relationships. The most common expectation is that the participants not take offense. Third, a variety of topics are typically involved in joking relationships although sexual humor between sibling-in-laws of opposite sex is commonly witnessed. Reducing potential conflict and aggression is the usual explanation for this type of communication.

Tribal clowns, from several different continents, are described in a variety of cultures. Turnbull noted, for example, that each Mbuti band seemed to have an unofficially designated clown. "His function is to act as a buff between disputants, deflecting the more serious disputes away from their original sources, absolving other individuals of blame by accepting it himself" (Turnbull, 1965, p. 183). The tribal clown, typically male, can also have a more formalized position, particularly in native North American tribes. Apte (1985) refers to them as "ritual clowns" and some descriptions cross over with shamanism. Since shamanistic experiences can resemble psychotic symptoms, one naturally wonders whether this reflects underlying mania in the individual. Ritual clowns have been known to act in an exaggerated feminine manner, spoof neighboring tribes, mock formal religious ceremonies and utter sexual or obscene humor (Apte, 1985).

In an attempt to methodically assess humor in traditional societies, our group had three independent raters judge 95 humorous situations from ten hunting and gathering societies. Using the eHRAF (Human Relation Area Files) database, we searched ethnographic texts for 30 words (laugh, joke, humor, funny, tease, giggle, etc …) that could perhaps reveal humorous situations. The eHRAF Collection of Ethnography is an online cross-cultural database containing over 350,000 pages of information about many world-wide cultures, including numerous accounts of the first Western contact with a number of hunting and gathering societies. The ethnographic search was confined to ten hunting and gathering cultures (Bororo, Mbuti, Aranda, Assiniboine, Copper Inuit, Trobrianders, Tlinglit, Chukchee, Kapauka and Yanomamo) chosen because of the authors' familiarity with literature related to these cultures. For a humorous account to be included, at least one native participant had to laugh or acknowledge the humorous situation. Accounts that were incomprehensible (uncommon) or humorous situations directly involving the ethnographer were excluded. For each humorous account, we explored nine possible functions of humor: 1) expressing superiority, 2) indirect expression of anger, 3) indirect expression of sexual feelings, 4) desire for approval or diverting attention from a misdeed (saving face), 5) signaling affiliation to a specific subset of individuals, 6) enhancing group cohesiveness or settling differences in a positive manner, 7) signaling to others that a discrepancy or anomaly is trivial (Ramachandran, 1998), 8) expressing an idea that is simultaneously normal but also violates a social or moral expectation (Veatch, 1998), and 9) play. Inter-rater reliability was poor (52% with random chance being 33%) and, therefore, no firm conclusions could be drawn. This substandard data exemplifies how difficult it is to analyze something as indistinct and ambiguous as humor.

Reviewing the 95 humorous situations led us to the same broad conclusions as previous anthropologists—that humor in traditional societies grossly appears similar to our own. Examples involved such varied situations as laughter at the antics of children, lewd comments, sexual jokes, teasing, mocking others who were too serious or in positions of authority, spousal jibes, slapstick maneuvers, uncomfortable laughter to save face, and humor to quell conflicts within a tribe. One particularly unsettling example of humor involved the brutal but perhaps necessary Inuit custom of occasionally sacrificing one twin infant to save the other. Resembling the Freudian concept of reaction formation, "One woman laughed over a baby girl she had killed two or three years before, and said that it had provided the foxes with a good meal" (Jenness, 1886/1969, p. 166).

7) Cognitive Archeology

a) Humor and Language

There is no way to know with certainty when humor evolved relative to language although it would appear that at least sophisticated humor must have succeeded language. The credible range for the origins of language lands between a few hundred thousand years to about 2–4 million years ago. The authors tend to side with those linguists who date the origins of language to coincide with the first appreciable increase of brain size about 2 million years ago (Deacon, 1997). For example, one Homo habilis brain cast (2.4–1.5 MYA) shows a bulge which seems to represent Broca's area (Banyas, 1999, pp. 9599). The precise syntactical evolution of protolanguages are, for now, indeterminate.

In our view, larger brains seem to be fundamentally related to language because the majority of higher cognitive functions appear to have been "designed" specifically to support language functions. Working memory, long-term memory, executive functions and rich associative thinking make significant demands on neural networks and are simultaneously integral to language function. Capacity for theory-of-mind and other enhanced social abilities may also necessitate significant cerebral computing power. Other plausible but less convincing candidates responsible for the initial enlargement of ancient human brains are visual-spatial skills (to hunt) and fine motor control of hands (tool use, hunting).

One does not need words to convey humor; however, conversation greatly enhances the opportunity for humorous expression. Consequently, humor usually utilizes a string of complex symbols (words). If incongruency based humor theories are on the right track, the vast majority of humor shared between people must involve, at minimum, several intricate symbols (words) and two concepts (incongruous and congruous). Disparate words can be similar but never truly identical in meaning. Each word has its own unique fingerprint of manifold connotations (associations) which slightly changes its meaning. Remove one subtle connotation and you can significantly lessen the humor of any given statement—this explains why comedians choose their words carefully and why so many jokes cannot withstand translation. At the risk of stating the obvious, at the very least, the full expression of humor in contemporary humans is fundamentally contingent on language.

"A concept or category is said to have been learned when an organism responds to a group of stimuli in the same way because these stimuli have common properties" (Roberts, 1998, p. 356). Within this definition, even pigeons have demonstrated rudimentary concept recognition. Using American Sign Language, the famous chimpanzee, Washoe, seems to have "invented" 2 or 3 word combinations to describe singular objects such as "water bird" after spotting a swan and "candy fruit" after tasting watermelon (Roberts, 1998). An alternative explanation would be that Washoe was just describing various aspects of her experience without any significant sense of the relationship between the two ideas. In any case, Washoe's sporadic and simple juxtaposition of 2 or 3 word combinations would probably reflect an upper limit of a chimpanzee's ability to instantly manipulate more than one abstract concept.

In a recent article, Hauser, Chomsky and Techumseh Fitch (2002) hypothesize that syntactical recursion is a defining feature of Homo sapiens. In simple terms, linguistic recursion is the ability to construct a phrase within a phrase indefinitely (only limited by the constraints of memory) to create an almost limitless number of ideas. Again, using incongruency based humor theories as our framework, there could be similarities between syntactical recursion (the ability to form a concept within a concept) and humor's apparent juxtaposition of a congruous and incongruous idea. If recursion is a truly special cognitive ability, it could have conceivably been co-opted by other evolving cognitive traits, like humor.

b) Milestones in Human Evolution

In addition to language, are there any other milestones in human evolution that must have either come before or after the advent of humorous thinking? The complexity of various tool technologies (Oldowan, Mousterian, Acheulean and Upper Paleolithic) has improved through human evolution. However, the enhanced appreciation for causality or visual spatial skills presumably necessary for more sophisticated tool development (Geary, 2005; Povinelli, 2000) does not readily lend itself to be compared with humor skills. The betterment of social intelligence through such "cognitive modules" as theory-of-mind or cheater-detection would also seem integral to humor development; however, the evolutionary timing of various social skills is, as of yet, undetermined.

There is increasing evidence that a new level of symbolic thought was achieved around 50,000 years ago. A figurine integrating the head of a lion with the legs of a person dated around 32,000 years old is among the earliest evidence for symbolic art (Mithen, 1996). Placing importance on items that integrate complementing facets (human legs and lion head) from two disparate categories (lion and person) does bear a certain resemblance to the postulated integration of the congruent and incongruent aspects of humor.

Evidence for spirituality also begins around this time through archeological depictions resembling contemporary shamanistic art. Because of the presumed fluidity in thinking involved, the cognitive innovation behind spirituality could also somehow be related to humor. Interestingly, Pascal Boyer's (2001) theory on the cognitive mechanics of spirituality bears a striking resemblance to Veatch's hypothesized cognitive structure of humor. Boyer's theory says that all magico–religious thinking consists of a direct violation of an ontological category—the five most basic ontological categories are person, animal, plant, tool and natural object. For example, a zombie or ghost is a spiritual idea because being dead is a direct violation of an essential quality related to being a person. In contrast, a person with five arms may be unusual but the concept would not be a spiritual thought because it does not violate the essence of a living person. Boyer's theory broadly applies to all forms of spirituality and magico–religious thinking, including shamanistic spirituality, magic rituals and modern religions.

Humor can perhaps be framed as an incongruent social concept "violating" the essence of a congruent social concept. Recall, that in Veatch's humor theory, acting in a socially bizarre or "incongruent" manner is not enough to be funny—the incongruency must violate the "subjective moral order". Therefore, the term "incongruent" so often used in humor literature may be analogous to Boyer's term "violation" and Veatch's "subjective moral order" may be akin to an ontological category.

If humor and spirituality are related, which trait is phylogenetically older? Assuming animal models for humor have some merit, spirituality could be an exaptation succeeding humor. The similarities between humor and spirituality are certainly intriguing and worthy of further analysis.

c) Humor and Group Size

Dunbar (1993) has put forward a theory that, in primates, neocortical size is proportional to group size and that language ultimately replaced grooming as the primary social bond (Aeillo and Dunbar, 1993). Furthermore, laughter could have been the affirming social "bonding agent" which replaced the positive reinforcing experience of physical touch (Barrett, Dunbar and Lycett, 2002, p. 346). Dunbar could well be on the right track since there appears to be a richer rationalization behind his proposition.

Nicely captured in Frans De Waal's (1982) phrase "chimpanzee politics," primate life is characterized by constant negotiations between empathic and aggressive tendencies. Grooming engenders pleasurable feelings that countervail aggressive tendencies. But with language replacing grooming, what mitigates aggressive tendencies between lesser-related individuals? Humor seems to inject positive feelings while hierarchal competition and other minor social quarrels are being worked out. Humor can't control pernicious disputes but for the more mundane disagreements, it diminishes the risk of a contentious issue deteriorating to violence. Much has been written about the anthropological study of violence within tribes because of its potential relevance to hominid evolution—humor may be an essential part of the story.

Another reason why humor may be linked to group size is because humor and laughter are candidate group-selected traits (Gervais and Wilson, 2005; Wilson and Sober, 1994). Humor is a form of complex communication—a trait only seen when animals aggregate with lesser related individuals. Laughter is preferentially shared by lesser related individuals and non-kin. Humor is not deceptive in nature—in fact, it is just the opposite. Although humor can be used to probe social issues or advance personal agendas, the bulk of information revealed by humor is shared by the community and therefore can be considered altruistic. Although humor perception appears to be quite uniform, greater variability is observed on the production side (greater variability in a trait could suggest a group selected trait through adaptive specialization). Clowns (or other funny people) could represent "humor specialists," evolved to reduce tense social situations through humorous injections.

Conclusion

Humor is a fascinating cognitive function. The relative ease in how we use it belies its considerable complexity. Humor appears to be a function of Homo sapiens' augmented social abilities and as an extension of language, could perhaps be the most complex cognitive function in the animal kingdom. We have reviewed the major structural and evolutionary theories of humor, in addition to a number of topics potentially relevant to deciphering the origins of humor—animal models, genetics, children's humor, humor in pathological conditions, neurobiology, humor in traditional societies and cognitive archeology. In our view, the origins of language, spirituality, hominid group size and animal teasing may have particular relevance to humor. A number of humankind's higher cognitive functions could well be inextricably rooted in humor's evolutionary history, thus making this subject worthy of further exploration.

Acknowledgements: The authors thank Drs. Jennifer Laforce and Christine Polimeni for having rated and discussed numerous accounts of humor in traditional societies.

References

Aiello, L.C. and Dunbar, R.I.M. (1993). Neocortex size, group size and the evolution of language. *Current Anthropology, 34*, 184–193.

Alexander, R.D. (1986). Ostracism and indirect reciprocity: the reproductive significance of humor. *Ethology and Sociobiology, 7*, 253–270.

Apte, M.L. (1985). *Humor and Laughter: An Anthropological Approach.* Ithaca: Cornell University Press.

Apter, M.J., and Smith, K.C.P. (1977). Humour and the Theory of Psychological Reversals. In A.J. Chapman and H.C. Foot, (Eds.), *It's a Funny Thing, Humour* (pp. 95–100) Oxford, England: Pergamon Press.

Banyas, C.A. (1999). Evolution and Phylogenetic history of the frontal lobes. In Miller, B.L., and Cummings, J.L. (Eds), *The Human Frontal Lobes: Functions and Disorders* (pp. 83–106). New York: The Guilford Press.

Barrett, L., Dunbar, R., and Lycett, J. (2002). *Human Evolutionary Psychology.* Princeton: Princeton University Press.

Bennett, M.P., Zeller, J.M., Rosenburg, L., and McCann, J. (2003). The effect of mirthful laughter on stress and natural killer cell activity. *Alternative Therapies in Health and Medicine, 2*, 38–45.

Black, D.W. (1982). Pathological laughter: a review of the literature. *Journal of Nervous and Mental Disease,* 170(2), 67–71.

Boyer, P. (2001). *Religion Explained: The Evolutionary Origins of Religious Thought.* New York: Basic Books.

Bremmer, J. (1997). Jokes, jokers and jokebooks in Ancient Greek culture. In J. Bremmer and H. Roodenburg, (Eds.), *A Cultural History of Humor* (pp. 11–28). Malden, MA: Blackwell Publishers.

Bremmer, J., and Roodenburg, H., (Eds.). (1997). *A Cultural History of Humor.* Malden, MA: Blackwell Publishers.

Butoskaya, M.L, and Kozintesv, A.G. (1996). A neglected form of quasi–aggression in apes: Possible relevance for the origins of humor. *Current Anthropology, 37*, 716717.

Caron, J.E. (2002). From ethology to aesthetics? Evolution as a theoretical paradigm for research on laughter, humor and other comic phenomena. *Humor, 15*, 245–281.

Chapman, A.J., (1976). Social aspects of humorous laughter. In A.J. Chapman and H.C. Foot (Eds), *Humor and Laughter: Theory, Research and Applications* (pp. 155185). London: John Wiley and Sons.

Cherkas, L., Hochberg, F., MacGregor, A. J., Snieder, H., and Spector, T.D. (2000). Happy families: A twin study of humour. *Twin Research, 3*, 17–22.

Chewings, C. (1936). *Back in the Stone Age: The Natives of Central Australia.* Sydney, Australia: Angus and Robertson. As seen in the eHRAF Collection of Ethnography: Web (15/10/2005), http://www.yale.edu/hraf/index.html.

Corcoran, R., Cahill, C. and Frith, C.D. (1997). The appreciation of visual jokes in people with schizophrenia: a study of "mentalizing" ability. *Schizophrenia Research, 24*, 319–327.

Dabby, R., Watemberg, N., Lampl, Y., Eilam, A., Rapaport, A., and Sadeh, M. (2004). Pathological laughter as a symptom of midbrain infarction. *Behavioral Neurology, 15*, 73–76.

Dagge, M., and Hartje, W. (1985). Influence of contextual complexity on the processing of cartoons by patients with unilateral lesions. *Cortex, 21*, 607–616.

Darwin, C. (1872/1920). *The Expression of the Emotion in Man and Animals.* New York: D. Appleton.

Dawkins, R. (2004). *The Ancestor's Tale*. London: Weidenfeld and Nicolson. De Waal, F. (1982). *Chimpanzee Politics: Power and Sex Among Apes*. New York: Harper and Row.

De Waal, F. (1996). *Good Natured: The Origins of Right and Wrong in Humans and Other Animals*. Cambridge: Harvard University Press.

Deacon, T.W. (1997). *The Symbolic Species*. New York: WW Norton and Co. Dunbar, R.I.M. (1993). The co-evolution of neo-cortical size, group size and language in humans. *Behavioral and Brain Sciences 16*, 681–775.

Edwards-Lee T.A. and Saul R.E. (1999). Neuropsychiatry of the right frontal lobe. In B.L. Miller and J.L. Cummings (Eds), *The Human Frontal Lobes: Functions and Disorder* (pp. 304–320). New York: The Guilford Press.

Farrant, A., Morris, R.G., Russell, T., Elwes, R., Akanuma, N., Alarcon, G., and Koutroumanidis, M. (2005). Social cognition in frontal lobe epilepsy. *Epilepsy and Behavior, 7*, 506–516.

Freud, S. (1905/1963). *Jokes and Their Relation to the Unconscious*. New York: W.W. Norton.

Fry, W. (1994). The biology of humor. *Humor, 7*, 111–126.

Fuster, J.M. (1997). *The Prefrontal Cortex: Anatomy, Physiology and Neuropsychology of the FrontalLobe* (3rd ed.). Philadelphia: Lippincott-Raven.

Gamble, J. (2001). Humor in apes. *Humor, 14*, 163–179.

Gardner, H., Ling, P.K., Flamm, L., and Silverman, J. (1975). Comprehension and appreciation of humorous material following brain damage. *Brain, 98*, 399–412.

Geary, D.C. (2005). *The Origin of Mind: Evolution of Brain, Cognition, and General Intelligence*. Washington, D.C.: American Psychological Association.

Gervais, M., and Wilson, D.S. (2005). The evolution and functions of laughter and humor: a synthetic approach. *The Quarterly Review of Biology, 80*, 395–430.

Goel, V., and Dolan, R.J. (2001). The functional anatomy of humor: Segregating cognitive and affective components. *Nature Neuroscience. 4*, 237–238.

Goodall, J. (1986). *The Chimpanzees of Gombe*. Cambridge, MA: Belknap Press.

Grady, C.L. (1999). Neuroimaging and activation of the frontal lobes. In B.L. Miller, and J.L. Cummings (Eds.), *The Human Frontal Lobes: Functions and Disorders* (pp. 196–232). New York: The Guilford Press.

Hauser, M.D., Chomsky, N., and Techumseh Fitch, W. (2002). The faculty of language: what is it, who has it, and how did it evolve? *Neuroscience, 248*, 1569–1579.

Hobbes, T. (1651/1981). *Leviathan*. London: Penguin Books.

Jenness, D. (1922). *The Life of Copper Eskimos*. Ottawa, Ont.: F.A. Acland. As seen in the eHRAF Collection of Ethnography: Web (02/04/2006), http://www.yale.edu/hraf/index.html.

Jung, W.E. (2003). The Inner Eye theory of laughter: Mindreader signals cooperator value. *Evolutionary Psychology, 1*, 214–253.

Kaplan, H.I., and Sadock, B.J. (Eds). (1985). *Comprehensive Textbook of Psychiatry* (4th ed.). Baltimore, Maryland: Williams and Wilkins.

Koestler, A. (1964). *The Act of Creation*. New York: Macmillan.

LaFollette, H., and Shanks, N. (1993). Belief and the basis of humor. *American Philosophical Quarterly, 30*, 329–339.

Lichtenstein, P., Ganiban, J., Neiderhiser, J.M., Pederson, N.L., Hansson, K., Cederblad, M., Elthammar, O., and Reiss, D. (2003). Remembered parental bonding in adult twins: genetic and environmental influences. *Behavior Genetics, 33*, 397–408.

Martin, R.A. (2001). Humor, laughter and physical health: methodological issues and research findings. *Psychological Bulletin, 127*, 504–519.

Mayr, E. (2001). *What Evolution Is*. New York: Basic Books.

McCullagh, S., Moore, M., Gawel, M., and Feinstein, A. (1999). Pathological laughing and crying in amyotrophic lateral sclerosis: an association with prefrontal cognitive dysfunction. *Journal of Neurological Sciences, 169(1–2)*, 43–48.

McGhee, P. E. (1983). The role of arousal and hemispheric lateralization in humor. In McGhee, P.E., and Goldstein, J.H. (Eds), *Handbook of Humor Research* (pp. 1337). New York: Springer-Verlag.

Mithen, S. (1996). *The Prehistory of Mind.* London, England: Thames and Hudson.

Mobbs, D., Greicius, M.D., Abdel-Azim, E., Menon, V., and Reiss, A.L. (2003). Humor modulates the mesolimbic reward centers. *Neuron, 40,* 1041–1048.

Moran, J.M., Wig, G.S., Adams, R.B. Jr., Janata, P., and Kelley, W.M. (2004). Neural correlates of humor detection and appreciation. *NeuroImage, 21,* 1055–1060.

O'Connell, J.F., and Allen, J. (1998). When did humans first arrive in greater Australia and why is it important to know? *Evolutionary Anthropology: Issues, News and Review, 6,* 132–146.

Okuda, D.T., Chyung, A.S., Chin, C.T., and Waubant E. (2005). Acute pathological laughter. *Movement Disorders, 20,* 1389–1390.

Panksepp, J., and Burgdorf, J. (2003). "Laughing" rats and the evolutionary antecedents of human joy? *Physiology and Behavior, 79,* 533–547.

Pearce, J.M. (2004). A note on gelastic epilepsy. *European Neurology, 52,* 172–174.

Polimeni, J., and Reiss, J.P. (2006). Humor perception deficits in schizophrenia. *Psychiatry Research, 141,* 229–32.

Povinelli, D.J. (2000). *Folk Physics for Apes: The Chimpanzee's Theory of How the World Works.* New York: Oxford University Press.

Provine, R.R. (2000). *Laughter: A Scientific Investigation.* New York: Viking.

Ramachandran, V.S. (1998). The neurology and evolution of humor, laughter, and smiling: the false alarm theory. *Medical Hypotheses, 51,* 351–354.

Rankin, A.M., and Philip, P.J. (1963). An epidemic of laughing in the Bukoba district of Tanganyika. *The Central African Journal of Medicine, 9,* 167–170.

Raskin, V. (1985). *Semantic Mechanisms of Humor.* Dordrecht: D. Reidel Pub. Co. Roberts, W.A. (1998). *Principles of Animal Cognition.* Boston: McGraw-Hill.

Rothbart, M.K. (1977). Psychological approaches to the study of humour. In A.J. Chapman and H.C. Foot (Eds.), *It's a Funny Thing, Humour* (pp. 87–94). Oxford, England: Pergamon Press.

Schiefenhövel, W. (1984). Der Witz als transkulturelles ästestisches Phänomen—Versuch einer biologischen Deutung. *Mitteilungen der Anthropologischen Gesellschaft in Wien (MAGW), 114,* 31–36.

Schultz, W. (2000). Multiple reward signals in the brain. *Nature Reviews-Neuroscience, 1,* 199–207.

Schulze, L. G. (1891). The Aborigines of the upper and middle Finke River: Their habits and customs, with introductory notes on the physical and natural history features of the country. *Transactions of the Royal Society of South Australia, 14,* 210–246. As seen on eHRAF Collection of Ethnography: Web (15/10/2005), http://www.yale.edu/hraf/index.html.

Shammi, P., and Stuss, D.T. (1999). Humor appreciation: A role of the right frontal lobe. *Brain, 122,* 657–666.

Shultz, T.R. (1976/1996). A cognitive–developmental analysis of humour. In A.J. Chapman and H.C. Foot (Eds.), *Humour and Laughter: Theory, Research and Applications* (pp. 11–36). London: John Wiley and Sons.

Simonet, P.R., Murphy, M., and Lance, A. (2001). Laughing dog: Vocalizations of domestic dogs during play encounters. *Animal Behavior Society Conference.* Corvallis, Oregon, 14–18 July 2001.

Striedter, G.F. (2005). *Principles of Brain Evolution.* Sunderland, MA: Sinauer Associates.

Suls, J.M. *(1972).* A two-Stage model for the appreciation of jokes and cartoons: an information processing analysis. In J.H. Goldstein and P.E. McGhee (Eds), *The Psychology of Humor: Theoretical Perspectives and Empirical Issues* (pp. 81100). New York: Academic Press.

Turnbull, C.M. (1965). *Wayward Servants: The Two Worlds of African Pygmies.* Garden City, New York: Natural History Press.

Turnbull, C.M. (1961/1968). *The Forest People.* New York: Simon and Schuster. Vaid, J. (1999). The evolution of humor: do those who laugh last? In D.H. Rosen and M.C. Luebbert, (Eds.), *Evolution of the Psyche* (pp. 123–138). Westport, Connecticut: Praeger Publishers.

Van Hooff, J.A.R.A.M. (1972). A comparative approach to the phylogeny of laugher and smiling. In R.A. Hinde, (Ed.), *Nonverbal Communication* (pp. 209–241). Cambridge: Cambridge University Press.

Veatch, T.C. (1998). A theory of humor. *Humor, 11,* 161–215.

Weisfeld, G. (1993). The adaptive value of humor and laughter. *Ethology and Sociobiology, 14,* 141–169.

Wild, B., Rodden, F.A., Grodd, W., and Ruch W. (2003). Neural correlates of laughter and humor. *Brain, 126,* 2121–2138.

Wilson, D.S., and Sober, E. (1994). Reintroducing group selection to the human behavioral sciences. *Behavioral and Brain Sciences, 17,* 585–654.

Wilson, E.O. (1975/2000). *Sociobiology.* Cambridge, MA: Belknap Press.

Wilson, G.D., Rust, J., and Kasriel, J. (1977). Genetic and family origins of humor preferences: a twin study. *Psychological Reports, 41,* 659–660.

Winner, E., Brownell, H., Happe, F., Blum, A., and Pincus, D. (1998). Distinguishing lies from jokes: Theory of mind deficits and discourse interpretation in right hemisphere brain-damaged patients. *Brain and Language, 62,* 89–106.

Ziv, A., and Gadish, O. (1990). The disinhibiting effects of humor: Aggressive and affective responses. *Humor, 3,* 247–257.

Chapter 2

TOWARD DEFINITION OF LAUGHTER ...
Laughing Dogs, Panting Chimpanzees, and Pleasure-
Driven Rats

Physiology and
Evolution of Laughter

by Ewa Wasilewska (2012)

This chapter has been the most difficult to research but also the most rewarding to write. As explained in the *Preface*, my interest in laughter has not evolved "naturally" from my anthropological training and work in archaeology and cultural anthropology of the Middle East and Central Asia. It was an outcome of an unexpected diagnosis of a brain disorder, NCSE (non-convulsive *status epilepticus*), which put me at a very high risk of SUDEP (Sudden Unexpected Death in Epilepsy). As medical and neurological sciences have been rather inconclusive in regard to my case, I have been "forced" to try to understand the mysteries of the brain on my own. After eliminating all possible causes for two long-lasting grand mal seizures in 2003 and countless number of non-convulsive ones, I have focused on my behavioral changes, which could in turn have affected the functioning of my brain (e.g., Bremmer 2002). The most obvious one was the emotional trauma I was going through at the time, which suddenly turned me into a "humorless" and "laughterless" person, so opposite to my usual overly "sunny and funny" personality. Since laughter has been often referred to as a "seizure-like activity," it was a logical step for me to explore it. The connection seemed to be even stronger because of a disorder, a rare one, called "gelastic epilepsy[1]" in which outbursts of energy, usually resulting in convulsive seizures or a brief loss of "consciousness," manifest themselves in the form of laughter (and, in some cases, crying). I have been in an unusual but advantageous position which has allowed me to approach this topic from both *emic* (native/insider) and *etic* (observer/outsider) points of view. With an exception of three grand mal seizures in which my existence was limited to convulsions and breathing with no consciousness whatsoever, I can watch all my seizures (on EEG, of course) and I am aware of rare temporal episodes of automatism in which my brain seems to be operating mostly at the subcortex (a highly functional automatism in my case) level, with memory impairment during and after. So, I definitely know how it "feels." The goal then became to understand why and how it happens, as well as why my brain is able to "control[2]" these seizures,

---

1   From Greek (gelos) meaning laughter. Gelotology is a scientific name for physiological study of laughter in spite of the fact that until 1990s, this study seems to be much less scientific than its "fancy" name suggests. For a brief summary on the research on gelastic epilepsy see, for example, Wild *et al.* 2003.

2   None of the pharmacological wonders of the 21ˢᵗ century alleviate my condition. Actually, almost all medications (including such benign non-prescriptive drugs like *Benadryl*) affecting the Central Nervous System have paradoxical effects on me causing episodes that otherwise

while other people's brains have no control over theirs. Is it possible that when I stopped laughing for prolonged periods of time, my outbursts of energy needed to find another outlet to be released, resulting in convulsive and/or confusing neurological episodes? I don't have an answer yet but in view of what I have learned about laughter, everything is possible.

Vocalizing Laughter

Studying laughing is not a laughing matter. Even today there are scholars who chuckle when you mention your interest in this topic. Many seem to believe that there is little we can learn either because of limitations in technology and methodology (too speculative), or because laughter and even humor appear to be of little value to science[3]. The general public, on the other hand, is often genuinely surprised that there is any need to study laughter and humor because we already "know everything" (O.K., "almost" everything). Thus, spending time and funds on learning "more" about them is yet another example of wasting both in pursue of "proving" obvious truths, no different from "humans are bipedal" and "Russians speak Russian." Consequently, whoever is willing to research these issues must be prepared for a fair amount of dismissive criticism and become the subject of jokes about himself or herself.[4]

One of the most obvious "truths" is that speech and laughter are uniquely human characteristics.[5] However, recent studies[6] indicate that this might not necessarily be true, and that much depends on how these two concepts are defined. If speech is an activity that allows a speaker to express himself/ herself (thoughts, feelings, ideas, etc.,) by using an intelligible vocalization, a similar phenomenon seems to be observable with other animals, but in a less developed/sophisticated form. As mentioned in the Introduction (Section 5), vocalized communication among some animals is confirmed, but due to its perceived range seemingly limited to survival needs only, the terms "speech" and "language" are avoided in its description. The history of the scholarly debate on whether animals have language or not, already over 150 years old, has been skillfully reviewed and presented by Gregory Radick in his book, *The Simian Tongue: The Long Debate about Animal Language*, (2007). While his personal views seem to be carefully hidden, those of the others' are discussed openly with the focus on Richard Lynch Garner[7] (1848–1920), an

---

could have been avoided. The only medication, which doesn't seem to do anything (neither does it stop my brain waves from spiking almost continuously, nor does it make me sick, but hopefully controls possible convulsions), is *Lamictal (lamotrigine)*. The only reason that I am taking it now is "just in case" it does something positive to my brain. I have been perfectly well without it at the "control time" of my choosing. I must add that a patient like me is a total nightmare for medical doctors—I want to be in control of my own brain and I am willing to take all risk associated with it. So far, it has served me well, but I won't recommend it for anyone …

3   Askenazy, who provided a very good summary regarding research on laughter by 1987, pointed out that "Laughter is not usually included in the curriculum of medical schools; therefore, it is often neglected by physicians" (1987: 317). This statement is also applicable to many, if not all, fields, whose contributions are necessary in order to understand laughter in its entirety.

4   Personally, I don't mind. As a blond woman of Polish origin raised in the Catholic faith of communistic Poland, I have heard probably the worst and/or funniest of them. Oh, I forgot to mention that I also live in Utah (and enjoy it tremendously).

5   It seems that Aristotle (384–322 B.C.) is the first documented scholar who saw humans as the only laughing "creatures."

6   Actually, the idea that animals have emotions and laughter is not so new, although it has been neglected for many years. Leavens briefly outlines the history of studies going back to Darwin (2009).

7   Garner's life and views are quite fascinating and controversial, but shouldn't reflect on his collection of data (recordings of primate calls), which has been questioned too. He was a racist (actually most scholars were at the time), believing that African languages and ape language are so primitive that they must be related. Reportedly, he wanted to learn this animal language as he hoped for establishing trade with apes. He had his favorite monkey, the Capuchin, as he believed it to be "the Caucasian" among apes with more civility and less aggression than others.

American scientist who studied animal communication in the wild (the French Congo). The debate over language-like ability of animals will not end any time soon. Animal calls are consistently denied the "honor" to be addressed by a more cognition-implied term of "language or language-like," in spite of a difference between single vocalized calls and combination calls, at least in some animals. While the former might be "just" an expression of basic needs, moods and motivations (see the subcortex, which is discussed below), the latter is much more complex and appears in different contexts with additional variables increasing the complexity of a message (e.g., Cleveland & Snowdon 1982; Robinson 1979 and 1984; Mitani & Marler 1989; Schassburger 1993; Crockford & Boesch 2003 and 2005; Radick 2007). This indicates that there must be some sort of a system of symbols that some (if not all) animals use in their communication. While traditionally it was believed that humans and their brains have "unique properties" that don't exist in other animals, recent research indicates that this statement is false (e.g., Roth & Dicker 2005). Human higher intelligence has been ascribed to mainly four factors: size of the brain, cortex, prefrontal cortex and degree of encephalization. However, none of them alone seems to be a true measurement of intelligence in mammals and others as humans are shown not to be always "the best" in different categories. According to Roth and Dicker, the best qualitative measurement of intelligence seems to be "[a] number of cortical neurons combined with a high conduction velocity of cortical fibers,[8]" (2005: 256) but "the

---

[8]   The higher a number of cortical neurons alone is not indicative of higher intelligence, as cetaceans and elephants are very close to humans in this number. What seems to be actually providing humans with an advantage is the thickness of neurons and an overall much higher neuron density. However, these two variables are presently not known in elephants and cetaceans (Roth and Dicker 2005). On the funny side, cats have smaller brains than dogs but the cell density of their brains is much higher. This at least provides "justification" for this very popular joke:
Pet Diaries: Dog vs. Cat

The Dog's Diary

8:00 am	Dog food! My favorite thing!
9:30 am	A car ride! My favorite thing!
9:40 am	A walk in the park! My favorite thing!
10:30 am	Got rubbed and petted! My favorite thing!
12:00 pm	Milk bones! My favorite thing!
1:00 pm	Played in the yard! My favorite thing!
3:00 pm	Wagged my tail! My favorite thing!
5:00 pm	Dinner! My favorite thing!
7:00 pm	Got to play ball! My favorite thing!
8:00 pm	Wow! Watched TV with the people! My favorite thing!
11:00 pm	Sleeping on the bed! My favorite thing!

The Cat's Diary

Day 983 of my captivity.

My captors continue to taunt me with bizarre little dangling objects. They dine lavishly on fresh meat, while the other inmates and I are fed some sort of dry nuggets. Although I make my contempt for the rations perfectly clear, I nevertheless must eat something in order to keep up my strength. The only thing that keeps me going is my dream of escape. In an attempt to disgust them, I once again vomit on the carpet. Today I decapitated a mouse and dropped its headless body at their feet. I had hoped this would strike fear into their hearts, since it clearly demonstrates my capabilities. However, they merely made condescending comments about what a "good little hunter" I am. Jerks!

There was some sort of assembly of their accomplices tonight. I was placed in solitary confinement for the duration of the event. However, I could hear the noises and smell the food. I overheard that my confinement was due to the power of "allergies." I must learn what this means, and how to use it to my advantage. Today I was almost successful in an attempt to assassinate one of my tormentors by weaving around his feet as he was walking. I must try this again tomorrow, but at the top of the stairs.

I am convinced that the other prisoners here are flunkies and snitches. The dog receives special privileges. He is regularly released, and seems to be more than willing to return. He is obviously retarded. The bird must be an informant. I observe him communicate with the guards regularly. I am certain that he reports my every move. My captors have arranged protective custody for him in an elevated cell, so he is safe. For now.

outstanding intelligence of humans results not so much from qualitative differences, but from a combination and improvement of these abilities" (2005: 256). So far, as to my knowledge, there is no research that relates the number of cortical neurons, or other seemingly intelligence-related elements, to the ability of "thinking/processing/expressing" information in symbolic terms. Consequently, I am somewhat puzzled that vocalized language-like communication is denied to animals other than *Homo sapiens*, and possibly Neanderthals[9], as based simply on a traditional view of the superiority of humans[10]. After all, the language-like communication doesn't have to have the same pattern of the human syntactical-grammatical language. The Wernicke's speech area is not unique to humans (e.g., Preuss 2000) and the Broca's area associated with the speech production[11] might or might not be necessary for animals (e.g., Preuss 2000; Gannon *et al.* 2000) since it could be "substituted" with some other "center" of neuron activation. This vocalized language-like capability is probably one of the means of animal communication[12] and is limited in its use but not necessarily because the potential is not there, but rather because there is no need to utilize it in the same way as humans do[13]. The so-called gestural flexibility hypothesis suggests the use of symbols in gestural communication in early *hominins* (e.g., Pollick and de Wall 2007). However, at this time we can only hypothesize about what has fostered a transition from limited cognitive vocalizations and/or gestural communication to the formation of a protolanguage eventually leading to the development of the human syntactical-grammatical language. One of such hypotheses focuses on gestural and vocal interactions (motherese ["baby talk"]) between a mother and an infant, which allowed *hominin* mothers to control the behavior of their children,[14] i.e., from prosody to language (e.g., Falk 2004[15]). Falk points out that, among other things, in most mothers of the controlled group studied by Nwokah and colleagues (1999; see also 1994), "speech and laugh began simultaneously and incorporated prosodic, affective, repetitive rhythmic features that typify vocal motherese" (Falk 2004: 498). This is possible because of *hominin* transition to bipedalism, which freed "the thorax of the mechanical demands of quadrupedal locomotion and loosening the coupling between breathing and vocalizing" (Provine 2000: 87), thus allowing for the development of speech and vocalized laughter (see below). However, prosodic as well as affective vocalizations such as human laughter and crying seem to involve the right hemisphere of the human brain, while speech vocalizations, as well as non-speech vocalizations, involve mostly left-hemisphere auditory processing (Sander & Scheich 2005). Vocalized species-specific communication is also processed mostly by the left hemisphere. Laughing and crying, strong emotional vocalizations, activate human amygdala, insula, and auditory cortex (Sander & Scheich 2001), that have been shown to "participate in the processing

---

9   Both have the same mutation of FOXP2, which is not found in other animals (see below for more explanation).

10   Consequences of recognition of the presence of language/language-like communication among animals go beyond science. For example, by keeping them in captivity, we are enslaving other species so, after all, the "Cat's Diary" above might not be so far fetched (pun intended).

11   There is an ongoing research in connecting Broca's area with the mutation of FOXP2 as a language or speech adaptation for humans (Corballis 2004).

12   Multimodal animal communication has been suspected and/or recorded among members of the *Hominoidea* superfamily, i.e., apes and humans (e.g., Corballis 2002, Byrne 2006; Pollick and de Waal 2007).

13   Last I checked, no other species besides humans have been interested in discussing politics or arguing over the meaning of life.

14   According to Falk, "Motherese has provided a rich source of information for this [prelinguistic evolution in early hominins] discussion, which is appropriate since it is the only available model for elucidating how human universally acquire spoken languages today, and therefore may have acquired them in the past" (2004: 503). This statement is up for debate (see below). Rejecting the possibility of using animal models for understanding speech and language evolution seems to me somewhat premature.

15   Since the strengths and weaknesses of this hypothesis are addressed in the Open Peer Commentary following the article, there is no need to discuss them here, as they are not instrumental for the topic of this chapter.

of emotional acoustic ... " (Sander & Scheich 2005: 1520). The amygdala appears to involve greater left-hemisphere processing of laughter (and crying) than the right hemisphere[16], and the left auditory cortex seems to be predominantly active (ibid)[17]. However, the right insula is much more involved in laughing (and crying) than the left one. As confusing as this short description might be, the results indicate (at least to me) that the role of the insula in processing both cognitive information and affect is somewhat more integrative in its function than it was previously believed. Thus, in my view, the difference in processing linguistic/conceptual information and laughter (and crying) is in the functioning of the insula, whose "subjectivity" contributes to the final outcome being either more cognitive or emotional or outright confusing[18]. However, both are processed as means of communication. Through studies of brain lesions and defects, it has been established that the right hemisphere plays a very im-

portant role in humor processing and comprehension (Wapner *et al.* 1981; Brownell *et al.* 1983, Bihrle *et al.* 1986; Shammi & Stuss 1999), so the integrative function of the right insula should not be overlooked.

There is no doubt that laughter is an intrinsic part of human physiology[19] and behavior whose affects and consequences cannot be avoided, nor can be ignored. Babies laugh when they are about four months old (e.g., Sroufe & Waters 1976), though recent research on smiling and laughter[20] among human newborn infants indicates that laughter may appear in infants as young as 17 days[21] (Kawakami *et al.* 2006). People whose sensory abilities are impaired and/or cognitive abilities limited due to different disorders laugh too (Eibl-Eibesfeldt 1989). Laughter is natural to humans but it is not foreign to animals either.[22] While this is not a "mystery" to many pet owners who can swear that they observed their animals "laughing,"[23] the

16   For the purpose of this chapter, differences between laughing and crying versus time reversed laughing and crying are omitted from the discussion. It is sufficient to say that the former are natural, while the latter are extraneous (although they may sound similar) to the brain.

17   The involvement of left cortical areas and amygdala (in addition to subcortical areas) in elicitation of laughter in both humans and monkeys was also confirmed by Meyer *et al.* (2007).

18   For the review of the research on insula and specific references see Craig 2010.

19   I was able to locate only one article that mentioned an absence of vocalized laughter in one patient. Its author, Max Levin, reported that by 1931 only two cases have been reported (1931). Consequently, whether there is such a disorder remains doubtful.

20   Laughter and smiling are two different activities although may occur together. Unfortunately, they are commonly confused leading to differentiation between different types of laughter (e.g., Kozintsev & Martin 2010). The true, "Duchenne smile" (named after Guillaume Duchenne, a French neurologist of the 19th century) involves both muscles of the mouth and of the eyes, but incomplete smiling has only one of those two. Tyra Banks' famous smizing (smiling with one's eyes) is an example of such an incomplete smiling.

21   There is no agreement regarding time when babies start laughing. Although the period of 4 months is most frequently referred to, earlier cases have been recorded and/or proposed (e.g., Gewirtz 1965 [after Askenazy 1987]; Izard 1977; Black 1984, Challamel *et al.* 1985).

22   It must be noted that many scholars, including those who identified laughter in other mammals, are often cautious referring to laughter in animals as laughter-like vocalizations. There is a considerable amount of discomfort among scientific community regarding animal emotions and our ability to learn about them. Furthermore, the general public, although at times more accepting of scientific breakthroughs regarding this topic (we love our pets!), is often caught in the maze of religious and moral values preferring to recognize humanity in animals but not animality in humans. Panksepp & Burgdorf briefly discuss these issues in their 2003 publication. For discussion of animal emotions see, for example, Bekoff 2007 and Bekoff & Byers, eds., 1998.

23   "Laughing" should not be confused with smiling, which is a form of facial expression and a different form of behavior although it often occurs at the same situations as laughing (as, for example, an expression of joy). As based on their study of infants Kawami *et al.* suggest,

truth is that, although their perception of "laughter" in their animals might be right, physically they could not have heard it (except for primates) and/or distinguished it from other sounds. Consequently, animals officially don't laugh until proven "guilty" of this "human" behavior.

However, research on primates (especially chimpanzees), rats, and dogs has already demonstrated that they all laugh. They laugh differently from how humans do, but they still laugh when reacting to such common physical stimuli of laughter such as tickling and rough-and-tumble play, or play in general. The closest relative to the human laughter was found in chimpanzees studied by Provine (2000, 2004). He was not the first one to notice that primates such as chimpanzees, gorillas, and orangutans make laugh-like sounds (e.g., Darwin 1872; Fossey 1983), but he was the first one who approached this topic scientifically, not anecdotally. He arrived at the conclusion that chimpanzee laughter is simply panting, the "pant–pant" response to a play. This panting–laughter is not vocalized in a human way because a chimpanzee's breathing pattern is different from that of a human. The human laughter is closely connected with speech since both are "produced exclusively during an outward breath" (Provine 2000: 81). So, we "speak" as we laugh, while chimpanzees produce only one sound during each exhalation and inhalation. While as humans we can imitate their laughter,[24] they cannot imitate ours. This observation led Provine to an even more important discovery known as the Bipedal Theory of Speech.[25] Provine postulates that speech in humans evolved as the result of bipedalism, which in turn freed the thorax from its supportive role in synchronizing locomotion and breathing cycles in quadrupeds by changing patterns of breathing.

"'Spontaneous smile' and 'Spontaneous Laugh' might be different behaviors from the beginning" (2006: 65).

24   In addition to voiced laughter (Provine's "ha ha ha," etc.,) humans also have a form of unvoiced laughter which "is noise-based, analogous to whispered speech or consonants like /s/ and /f/" (Owren & Bachorowski 2003: 189).

25   I prefer its more "affectionate" term used by the media: The "Walkie-Talkie" theory of speech.

This facilitated the development of vocalization. Bipedalism alone is not a sufficient factor for development/evolution of speech but it seems to be necessary, at least in humans, to "start" the process leading to both comprehensive speech and "modern" human laughter. When and why this event (bipedalism) took place is not very clear.[26] However, for example, Richmond & Jungers (2008) suggest that this key human adaptation can be dated to ca. 6 million years ago (within 1 million margin) and is confirmed for the first time (as of today) in *Orrorin tugenensis*, already of the *Hominin* lineage (like both chimpanzees and humans). The origin of capability for coherent speech is a tricky one, if not more than tricky. The 2001 discovery of FOXP2, the so-called "language gene[27]" (Lai *et al.* 2001), helped scholars to date this event to before 300,000 years ago, since the specific mutation of this gene is shared with Neanderthals[28] (Kraus *et al.* 2007), but not with chimpanzees and other primates.[29] Considering the divergence of ancestors of modern humans (*Hominina*) from their close relatives chimpanzees took place some time between 3 to 5 million years ago (depending on the scholar), this genetic mutation developed some time between this date and 300,000 years ago[30]. Thus, Provine's idea that first we walked and then we talked is somewhat confirmed by genetic studies. "Modern[31]" vocalized human laughter must have developed some time in between[32] and is different or sounds differently from laughter in other animals. However, the question remains how did we laugh, if at all, before the evolution of speech?

While we may never know the answer to "how," we can be pretty certain that we did. Though serious research on animal emotions is a relatively new field, reports regarding possibility of animal laughter, started to be more frequent in the last 15 years as more scientific, experiment-based studies[33] have been conducted (see, e.g., Bekoff & Byers, eds. 1998). There is little doubt[34] that rats (Panksepp & Burgdorf 2000; 2003; Burgdorf & Panksepp 2001; Panksepp 2005; 2007) and dogs (Simonet, Murphy & Lance 2001; Simonet, Versteeg & Storie 2005) are laughing animals. While rats make "chirping" laughing sounds (50 kHz ultrasonic vocalizations), dogs vocalize their laughter as "a breathy pronounced forced exhalation" (Simonet, Versteeg & Storie 2005), sounding as a series of short "h" sounds during laryngitis.[35]

Do other animals laugh too? If so, has their laughter, vocalized or some other form of non-vocalized or unvoiced "laughter," developed as an adaptive strategy to their specific environment? My grandmother used to tell me that laughing loudly[36] is not a proper behavior for a lady because it attracts attention

---

26   There are too many hypotheses to be even outlined here. Let's just say that evolutionary biologists and anthropologists are not the most agreeable bunch.

27   Actually as catchy as this name is, FOXP2 has little to do with language and grammar. However, this gene is essential for acquisition of language and vocal learning (e.g., White *et al.* 2006).

28   This means that FOXP2 must have been present in their common ancestor.

29   The human mutation of this gene differs in two respects.

30   According to Noonan *et al.* (2006) humans and Neanderthals shared a common ancestor ca. 706,000 years ago and split from each other ca. 370,000 years ago. Their research has been based on genetic studies and evidenced that we share with Neanderthals at least 99.5% of genetic make-up.

31   Distinctive "ha, ha; ho, ho; he, he" sounds.

32   For more on FOXP2 relevance for the study of laughter see section on "recognizing humor."

33   However, possibility not only of an animal laughter but its similarity to human laughter in apes has been considered already by Darwin (1872).

34   There are always skeptics who have a "bone to pick."

35   For a recorded sample of dog-laugh see http://www.petalk.org/DogLaughSpect.html (Simonet, Versteeg, Storie 2005).

36   This loud and uncontrollable laughter is associated with the hypothalamus (a part of the ancient brain system present in all mammalian brains).

of men. Is it possible that some animals may not vocalize or voice their laughter because it may attract predators the same way as my laughter were to attract "unsuitable" men so much feared by my grandma?[37]

There is no doubt that many animals, if not all, play.[38] However, even such a seemingly simple question "why do they play?" seems to be contentious among scholars (see, for example, Bekoff and Byers, eds. 1998). Thus, I found it really refreshing to have a straightforward statement that "Animals love to play because play is fun, and fun is its very powerful reward" (Bekoff[39] 2007: 94). If they play to have fun, how do they express this emotion if not through laughter-like behavior? Is there such a phenomenon as "silent" laughter? So, is the definition of laughter as the respiratory–vocal behavior revealing joyful emotions to others a sufficient definition of this phenomenon?

Why Do We Laugh?

The easiest, but also the most simplistic, answer is that we humans, as all other animals, laugh out of joy. However, laughter has been linked to other emotions too (e.g., Provine 2000; Owren & Bachorowski 2003). We laugh when angry, scared, embarrassed, and nervous, probably to mask our true feelings. We laugh to get attention, attract a potential sexual partner, and to show our submission or to establish authority. Thus, laughter as a vocalized signal has many different functions, in addition to its main association with joy and happiness. Since most of laughter is linked with pleasant emotions, this specific laughter is often referred to as mirthful laughter.

Animal laughter is frequently called "play sounds" or "play vocalizations" because these are the sounds exhibited during playing activities.[40] These sounds can be accompanied by facial displays, but not always, as they might have evolved independently and in humans they are incorporated into the full (acoustic and facial) expression of laughter. The most common and easily recognized stimulus for laughter is tickling. We all laugh when tickled as a result of signals sent by nerve fibers associated both with touch and pain. The tickling sensation is pleasant and laughter-producing for a limited period of time, but only when pressure is applied to the ticklish areas.[41] Prolonged tickling may induce "pain"[42] instead of laughter. Vettin and Todt's research indicates that laughter produced during tickling is different in interval duration and acoustic frequency from laughter elicited during conversations and by humorous material[43] (2004; 2005).

37   Although they certainly did not meet my grandmother, Panksepp & Burgdorf also suggest this possibility (2003).

38   "Even" turtles play (see Burghardt 1998).

39   Bekoff's book is a fascinating glimpse into emotional lives of animals, raising questions such as "do animals have morality?" that are often avoided or dismissed by the scientific community.

40   It must be noted that play sounds interpreted as laughter have been confirmed (as of today) only among primates, dogs, and rats. Thus, the term "animal laughter" used here is somewhat misleading.

41   "Heavy" tickle-inducing laughter is known as *gargalesis*. A lighter one is know as *knismesis*, the sensation of having an insect or spider crawling on one's skin (definitely doesn't induce laughter in me but might in others).

42   The most famous tickling-inducing pain is known as "Chinese tickling torture" allegedly used on nobility since it did not leave any traces and was not too difficult to recover from. In modern western world there are only a few documented cases of the use of such torture causing serious damage (i.e., madness in their subjects). Even rats don't like too much tickling (Panksepp & Burgdorf 2003).

43   It must be noted here that, although conversational laughter differs, acoustically speaking, from laughter induced by humorous material, it doesn't mean that it doesn't originate in the same part of the brain as "a stimulus-driven and emotionally valenced" (Duchenne laughter) laughter as Gervais and Wilson (2005) insist. The problem is (and has already been pointed out by Kozintsev and Martin 2010) that what Keltner & Bonnano (1997) described as non-Duchenne laughter is just a smile, not laughter, sometimes forced as we are "taught" to be polite. It might be accompanied by laughter-like sounds attempted by a conversationalist the same way as actors are faking it whenever necessary. Kozintsev and Martin expressed their disagreement with the "division" of laughter in much stronger words: "The underlying logic (which

They concur that "human laughter evolved from a play signal of non-human primates, as suggested in previous studies (van Hooff 1967; 1972; Preuschoft & van Hooff 1997)" (2005: 236), because acoustic features of play sounds/vocalizations are similar to human laughter in general, but especially to laughter elicited through tickling. Ross *et al.* have taken their research even further (2009). Through their experimental study, they were able to establish "a common evolutionary origin for tickling-induced laughter in humans and tickling-induced vocalizations in great apes" that goes back in time at least 10 to 16 million years ago "to the last common ancestor of human and modern great apes" (ibid[44]). However, this doesn't mean that there was no laughter before, rather, that it probably sounded differently as the vocalizations of the primordial acoustic laughter "were likely to be generally longer and slower than those of human and extant great apes, included a smaller number of more uniformity noisy calls with fewer changes in vibration regimes, and showed both alternating and more consistently egressive airflow" (ibid).

"Laughing rats" studied by Panksepp and colleagues, not only chirped/laughed happily when tickled, but also developed a social bond with their "ticklers," seeking the same touch and emotions as often as possible (Panksepp 2003, 2005, 2007; Panksepp & Burgdorf 2000, 2003). Bonding through tickling is clearly visible in humans, establishing simplest forms of communication between mothers and their infants, as well as between all who are seeking such a communication through socially acceptable non-verbal contact[45]. This socially acceptable contact refers to familiarity between a tickler and a tickled, i.e., some sort of social bond or need is already established.[46] Interestingly, Panksepp and Burgdorf observed the same need with young rats (2003) who responded fully to tickling only after being socially isolated for about two days, and had a chance to familiarize with a new environment (2000, 2003). Tickling oneself does not have the same effect i.e., it does not induce laughter due to its neurological self-discrimination

agrees with lay logic) is plain; the normal response to humorous stimuli is genuine laughter; these stimuli are pleasant; pleasure is expressed by "Duchenne laughter"; therefore laughter in response to humorous stimuli is genuine, whereas that in other contexts is non-genuine, like the laughter feigned by bereaved people (Keltner and Bonanno, 1997). And, because only a minority of cases of everyday laughter is related to humorous stimuli (Provine, 2000, p. 43), it follows that in most cases laughter is non-genuine. This absurd conclusion is a necessary sequel to the belief that the principal function of laughter is to convey positive emotion, and that the distinction between "Duchenne" and "non-Duchenne" expressions is more important than that between laughter and smiling" (2010: 82).

44   As based on different acoustic laughs they have created phylogenetic trees, which match already widely accepted trees based on genetic data (split, mutations, etc.).

45   So far no "tickle center/receptor" has been identified either in animals or in humans (Seldom 2004).

46   One does not tickle strangers to get acquainted with them. At least I hope so.

(Blakemore, Wolpert & Frith 1998). Thus, tickling can be considered to be one of the most ancient forms of social bonding and a source of pleasure[47] in all animals seeking or being exposed to social contacts (in and/or outside of their species).

Laughing animals, including humans, are observed as seeking the company of others who are making laughing sounds. Rats favored "chirping rats" over "chirpless" ones (Panksepp & Burgdorf 2003), while dogs immediately run to other dogs that happen to be "laughing" at the time. The dog laugh is so powerful that upon hearing it all other dogs attempt to play with the maker of this sound, whether a human or a dog (Simonet, Versteeg, Storie 2005).

Humans do the same. Though we all seek the company of those who laugh, women and men do it for different reasons. Provine's research indicates that women laugh more than men (2000). Men seek women who laugh at their jokes and women seek men who make them laugh. Laughter is elicited by humor, which, according to the sexual selection model, "evolved as a mating display to signal intelligence and genetic fitness (Miller, 1998, 2000, 2000a, 2000b)" (Li et al. 2009: 932). However, Li et al. suggest that humor is both an initiator and an enforcer/maintainer of already existing sexual/romantic attraction between interested parties, thus going beyond the original sexual interest by signaling mediating and cooperative potential[48] (2009).

The similar behavior might be exhibited by rats since Panksepp & Burgdorf noticed that "after puberty females tend to remain more playful than males" (2003: 537). Are they seeking sexual attention? Is their behavior related to sex differences in brain responding to humor? Azim et al. suggest that this is a distinct possibility (2005). Their research indicates that all things equal,[49] women actually activate more the left prefrontal cortex and the mesolimbic reward center (especially the nucleus accumbens [NAcc]) than men do[50]. This results in females processing humor in a more thoughtful, language-based, and executive manner than men. This is because executive functions include "coherence, potentially using working memory, mental shifting, verbal abstraction, self-directed attention, and irrelevance screening" (2005: 16500). And, after all this "work," they seem to enjoy humor more than men, possibly expecting fewer rewards.[51] Does this mean that female laughter is more "calculated" i.e., more programmed to attract the attention of the opposite sex, or that women are simply seeking the company of others who make the signaler feel safe and wanted[52]?

The reward, i.e., the laughing "company," seems to trigger the dopamine reward circuits in the brains of both rats and humans (Panksepp 2005). The direct connection between humor[53] and the "reward" center

---

47   Tickling elicits laughter when it is considered to be a pleasant sensation and during a humorous play. Although Harris and Alvarado (2005) postulate that tickling evokes a different type of laughter than humor, they have been unable to prove it and, at the same time, it seems they confused smiling with laughter to begin with. Kozintsev and Martin have already pointed out problems with their research and conclusions (2010).

48   This, of course, makes humor "funnier" when it is coming from or exchanged between parties already having the so-called sexual chemistry (see also Section 9).

49   It is interesting to note that this particular research did not demonstrate "significant difference in the number of cartoons found funny, the degree of funniness, or RT to stimuli" along gender lines (2005: 16500). This difference was also not recorded by Martin and Gray in an earlier research (1996). However, gender differences in rating three different types of humor—neutral, sexual, and aggressive—have been reported as a part of psychological/behavioral studies (for discussion see Gruner 1997: 107–130; and Section 9).

50   For more discussion of their article see Section 9.

51   Gender differences in the reward center responses have also been found during computer game-play (Hoeft et al. 2008).

52   For discussion see Section 9.

53   Positive and joyful reaction to humor is expressed by laughter.

of the brain[54] was established by Stanford University researchers (Mobbs *et al.* 2003). Sixteen participants were asked to view a number of carefully[55] selected cartoons when their brains were monitored with a technique known as fMRI (Functional Magnetic Resonance Imaging).[56] Then, the same exercise was repeated with half of the same cartoons from which the "funny" part was removed. The experiment demonstrated that funny cartoons activated the mesolimbic dopaminergic reward center of the brain i.e., "a network of subcortical structures, including VTA[57] [ventral tegmental area], NAcc, and the amygdala[58]" (Mobbs *et al.* 2003: 1043). The Stanford researchers have continued their inquiries into understanding the neural systems responsible for processing humor and the functioning of the brain's reward center. The research on cataplexy suggests that patients who experience this debilitating disorder[59] find humorous cartoons less funny than healthy subjects, probably because instinctively they have learned to suppress laughter, a common trigger for an attack. However, the NAcc and the hypothalamus' activity of patients suffering from cataplexy is greater when viewing the same cartoons than of healthy subjects. This suggested to the researchers an overdrive of the emotional circuitry that was compensated by decreased activity or complete shutdown of the hypothalamus (Reiss *et al.* 2008).[60] One may ask whether strong emotions, such as those caused by laughter , fear, or their "combination" can cause a temporary shutdown of the hypothalamus[61] also in non-cataplectic individuals.

There is no doubt that laughing is infectious (e.g., Martin and Gray 1996; Provine 2000) both on a neurological and social level.[62] Warren and her team (2006) have shown that people "lighten up" at the sound

54 The "reward" center releases dopamine (a neurohormone, a natural opiate) to "reward" certain behaviors such as sex, financial gain, use of drugs such as cocaine and methamphetamines, etc.

55 I assume that these cartoons were selected as representing "neutral humor" i.e., humor which is the least offensive (all humor is offensive in its nature) as not related to the most common sources of high degree offensiveness such as hate, gender, ethnicity, religion.

56 The fMRI is the most popular "tool" in measuring changes in an active part of the brain by using MR imaging.

57 It is interesting to note that, according to Reimers-Kipping *et al.*, 2010, changes in FOXP2 mostly affected brain regions connected via cortico-basal ganglia circuits i.e., those which are known to be associated with laughter and/or humor processing (such as the limbic sector/reward producing center).

58 The amygdala is believed to be associated with emotions such as fear or arousal, as well as hormonal secretions. It has been found that somehow its dysfunction is involved in various disorders such as depression or Parkinson's disease. It is a part of the brain's limbic system (the most ancient part of the brain dealing with basic instincts and emotions) that also includes the hippocampus, the thalamus, and the hypothalamus. VTA and NAcc are considered to be the main culprits in addictions as directly related to dopamine increases, pleasure and motivations. See also Sander & Scheich: 2001 & 2005.

59 Strong emotions such as fear and those accompanying laughter trigger cataplexy resulting in muscular weakness, even total collapse, but with hearing and awareness intact.

60 Although, or might be especially, because my knowledge of neurology is limited, I wonder whether increased activity of the hypothalamus and, consequently, of NAcc reflects the conflicting nature of the information to process, leading to the shutdown of the hypothalamus. There are two conflicting cognitive messages sent to the hypothalamus at the same time: a cognitive stimulus (funny cartoon) for a mirthful emotion and a message of fear to suppress the predictable outcome (laughter) of the mirthful emotion. The conflicting nature of both emotions causes the hypothalamus' overload so it starts decreasing its activity and, during a full cataleptic attack, goes to "fail-safe only" mode. It shuts down everything non-critical for the survival, keeping critical functions of the body working, including limited cognitive functions (awareness, hearing, partial vision, etc.). Like a computer, it shuts down outputs but keeps inputs open to return to a proper functioning from a "fail-safe only" mode.

61 Lesions on hypothalamus known as hypothalamic hamartoma are believed to be responsible for most cases of gelastic ("laughing") epilepsy, but not all (e.g., Panagariya 2007).

62 The contagious nature of laughter has been noticed already in antiquity when people were hired to applaud at dramatic performances. The 19th century witnessed the establishment of professional *claqueurs* (from *"claque"*—French for "clapping") in France, not only to applaud but also to laugh on cue. The laugh track on TV is a modern equivalent of the same.

of laughter i.e., the brain areas responsible for laughter and smile[63] become activated just by hearing it. It appears then that we are somehow "tuned" for laughter as well as other affective vocal communications. Warren *et al.* postulate "the enhanced motor response to perception of positive emotions provides a mechanism for mirroring [[64]] the positive emotional states of others during primate social interaction" (2006:13074). This mirroring of positive emotions is probably crucial for establishing social bonds among primates[65] and increasing their chances for survival. This survival mechanism probably exists among other species. Are rats one of them? Their "chirping" "may transmit moods of positive social solidarity, thereby promoting cooperative forms of social engagement" (Panksepp & Burgdorf 2003: 540) and prepare rats (and probably young humans) for future mature and productive socio–sexual behaviors (Panksepp 2007). Consequently, laughter might be hypothesized as facilitating creation of social bonds and relationships. This facilitation is done by laughter signaling a "message." However, as Owren & Bachorowski postulate, laughter, as well as other nonlinguistic vocalizations, does not have to signal any specific meaning and/ or include content[66] (2003). It can simply be used as an affect-inducer, i.e., the sound itself produces a desired affective (emotional) response (see above: Warren *et al.* 2006). Its direct effect might be drawing an attention to oneself for whatever purpose is intended (e.g., protection, sex) while its indirect effect might be an "attempt" to control affective responses in others (e.g., establishing position of authority, fear) which would give the inducer "leverage over those individuals' emotional states" (Owren & Bachorowski 2003: 187). Thus, laughter might also be used as a non-conscious strategy of influencing others. This also strengthens the argument that laughing is a social construct i.e., there is no such thing as solitary laughter. Although Simonet, Versteeg, Storie reported that dogs laugh even without a play-partner, they still play with something i.e., an animated object chased or tossed up (2005). This could be an equivalent of human "solitary" laugh when watching a funny movie or reading a funny story.

Where Does Laughter Come From?

Of course, we all know—it comes from our heart since we laugh when we are happy. In reality, laughter or its neural circuits are located in the most ancient parts of our brain, the subcortical brain system that developed in humans before the cerebral cortex.[67] The fact that at least some animals laugh too does not mean that *Animals Laughed Long Before Humans, Study Says* as the title of Lovgren's article suggests (2005). In all probability humans had laughed before they developed speech, but expressed or vocalized laughter differently. Were they "laughing humans" or just pleasure-expecting animals such as rats whose laughing ability was sort of denied to them by Dr. Brian Knutson of the National Institutes of Health in Bethesda, MD. In an interview for the *Science News* (Millus 2008) Dr. Knudson, who also observed chirping in rats when they played together, pointed out that since the "same"[68] chirping sound is made "before receiving

---

63   For the discussion of "smile," its origin, processing, recognition, and interpretation see, for example, Waller *et al.* 2007; Niedenthal *et al.* 2010.

64   Mirror neurons are visuomotor neurons that are active even with just a perception of action performed by others and, of course, during such action (Rizzolatti & Craighero 2004).

65   Warren *et al.* research was limited to primates only (2007).

66   This is referred to as "representational" approach to signaling—signals have to stand for something.

67   The cerebral cortex is a "visible" part of the brain, an outer layer responsible for thought and memory, etc.

68   Actually the "play chirping" is much higher than chirping produced in different behavioral contexts such as sex (Panksepp & Burgdorf 2003: 535). Should we draw a conclusion that sex is less rewarding than laughter-inducing activities?

morphine or having sex," the rat is probably expecting "something rewarding," not necessarily laughing. However, Wöhr and Schwarting's research indicates that the 50-kHz ultrasonic vocalizations are also a form of social communication (approach behavior) among rats (2007). The 50-kHz sounds, both flat and modulated, are an expression of rats' "happiness[69]" including being high on drugs (e.g., Burgdorf et al. 2001). In contrast, low frequency vocalizations are associated with the opposite "emotions/behavior" and can be alleviated by tranquilizers (anxiolytic drugs; e.g., Sanchez 2003). Juvenile rats seem to be more susceptible to ultrasonic vocalizations while older rats appear to keep loosing their interest in fun with aging (Wöhr and Schwarting 2007). The 50-kHz calls/laughter have also been noted when there is nothing to laugh and/or be happy about such as a separation of rat friends[70]. One may wonder whether they are sending each other a friendly call, "love you, miss you," laughing through tears? (Just kidding … or not?)

Understanding more of animal laughter is an important and valid research since it helps scientists to learn more about the brain's reward circuitry. However, such research is not an easy one because modern technology, including fMRI, is not adequate yet. As Panksepp and Burgdorf noticed:

> The existing imaging techniques only identify regions of interest for further analysis. […] Indeed, there is no unambiguous way to ascertain whether the activations that are obtained are directly reflective of the active processing of emotional feelings, as opposed to the active inhibition of mind–brain processes that accompany such experiences (2003: 534).

Continuous developments in genetics might become very helpful. Since laughter is a non-conscious and natural response to external and, at least in humans, internal (cognitive) stimuli, somewhere in the subcortical circuitry of mammalian brains, there must be (a) gene(s) that "caused" its emergence and operation. The discovery of the FOXP2 ("language") gene not only confirms this possibility, but may even aid us in future research on laughter[71]. Weiguo et al. (2005) engineered mice with copies of FOXP2 genes (one or both disrupted) in order to understand more about its role in vocalized communication with possible application for advancement in studies on autism and/or other speech/language disorders. The results are simply fascinating. The disruption of one copy of FOXP2 severely impaired mice ultrasonic vocalizations (USVs), while disruption of two copies "silenced" them completely. Thus, it appears quite reasonable to believe that the presence of FOXP2 makes vocalized communication possible across species. However, I believe that the most important discovery of this experiment is in its unrealized potential in understanding the physiology of laughter. The researchers noticed that disruption of FOXP2 "caused severe motor impairment" reflected by cerebellar abnormalities (especially in Purkinje neurons). The cerebellum plays a crucial role in coordination and motor control connecting through neural pathways with the cerebral motor cortex and spinocerebellar tracts. In simple terms, any problems with the cerebellum result in serious impairment of motor actions (e.g., movements, posture). Lesions limited to the cerebellum have

---

69   It seems to come from the same sources as for humans: tickling, mating, playing, eating well, and addictive drugs. Furthermore, "rat laughter" can also be caused by electrical self-stimulation of the brain (Burgdorf et al. 2007); something that might be similar to a "center" of laughter in humans.

70   For more on animal emotions, compassions, even altruism see, for example, de Waal's work (e.g., 1996; 2007).

71   The FOXP2-associated disorder is also linked to "anomalies in subcortical structures (including caudate and cerebellum [essential for proper processing of laughter]) (Watkins et al., 2002b) and abnormal patterns of cortical activation during language-based tasks (Liegeois et al., 2003)" (White et al., 2006: 10376–10377).

been discovered as a possible culprit in pathological laughter[72] and crying (PLC) disorder (Parvizi *et al.* 2001). However, lesions in other parts of the brain seem to be responsible for pathological laughter too as listed and charted by Wild *et al* (2003). While most laughter is connected with joy, whether through physical and/or cognitive stimuli, other laughter may not only be unwelcome, but even fatal. Pathological laughter is most commonly associated with pseudobulbar palsy, unilateral brain lesions, or gelastic epilepsy (Mendez, Nakawatase & Brown 1999).[73] These uncontrollable bursts of laughter (or crying as PLC) have no connection to any stimuli, nor are they appropriate responses to existing stimuli (nothing to laugh or cry about). They have been traditionally (e.g., Mendez, Nakawatase & Brown 1999) associated with "a loss of direct motor cortical inhibition of a laughter and crying [presumed] centre" (Parvizi *et al.* 2001: 1710). This might not be the case as Parvizi's and his team's study of a 51-year old man who experienced PLC after a stroke indicates. After careful examination of this patient, Parvizi *et al.* concluded that his lesions (all located in the white matter of the cerebellum) were disturbing communication between the cerebellum and telencephalic structures (2001). Since they suggested that cerebellar functions go beyond motor coordination to perform modulatory functions, the disabled circuitry (specifically in the area of cerebellum that alters laughing and crying) causes quite a messy motor display of these behaviors i.e., uncontrollable fits of laughter or crying. The cerebellum is to modulate laughing and crying "according to specific contexts" recognized "as a result of learning (i.e., pairing certain social contexts to certain profiles and levels of emotional response)"[74] (2001: 1715). These contexts then are either missing or unrecognizable due to the circuitry problem so their visible signals are completely haphazard. Progressive cerebellar ataxia is also responsible for *kuru*, one of the neurodegenerative diseases classified as prion diseases. One of its symptoms is inappropriate laughter (euphoria)[75] that may appear along relatively fast (on average of 17 months from its onset) deterioration of motor functions[76]. Consequently death from *kuru* is known as "laughing death." This disease has been traditionally associated with the practice of endocannibalism

---

72   Pathological laughter is also known under the term "pseudobulbar affect."

73   For a list and a short discussion of "laughing" disorders (pathological laughter) see, for example, Black 1982; Askenazy 1987; Provine 2000: 153–187; Wild *et al.* 2003.

74   If this is the case, the involvement of the cerebellum in suppressing laughter response to self-produced tickle sensation (Blakemore, Wolpert & Firth 1998) is not only related to motor coordination and "prediction" of consequences of the tickling movement, but might be more "conscious" choice made by the cerebellum—there is no-one to bond with or to induce affect on so there is no need for laughing behavior.

75   This is one of the possible connections with seizures that got me interested in the subject. According to Collinge *et al.* myoclonic jerking is very rare with this disease and clonus episodes when they occur are very brief (2008). Since the recent research by Mark *et al.* (2011) noted that epilepsy (among other coordination and consciousness disorders) may be connected with changes in the cerebellum, more specifically in the P/Q-type calcium channel blocking proper transmission of nerve signals. I wonder if the result/symptom might manifest either through (inappropriate?) laughter or epileptic convulsions/jerks.

76   The incubation period seems to be very long and is estimated between 34 and 56 years or even longer (Collinge *et al.* 2006; Collinge *et al.* 2008). Collinge *et al.* also noted that "many long incubation cases of *kuru* would have died of some other cause and would not have been detected" (2008: 3734) due to the low life expectancy in the area (Papua New Guinea).

(ritualized cannibalism[77] of the dead) reported among the Fore of Papua New Guinea[78]. The oral tradition indicates that *kuru* was present in the area in the 19th century, with cases noted in the 1920s and then reaching epidemic[79] proportion in 1950s and the early 1960s when it was monitored and investigated by medical doctors and scholars (e.g., The Institute of Human Biology, later known as Papua New Guinea Institute of Medical Research). The practice of cannibalism was outlawed by Australian authorities in the mid-1950s and *kuru* cases ceased because the main transmission route was eliminated. However, due to a long incubation period, the *kuru* deaths are still recorded (in older patients) and investigated (e.g., Collinge *et al.* 2008). This disease is an infectious one (transmissible spongiform encephalopathy) and can be carried between species as it was successfully transmitted to chimpanzees (Gajdusek *et al.* 1966; Collinge *et al.* 2008).

So, what do we know so far? The "centers" of laughter and/or humor are believed to be associated with frontal lobes, especially the right frontal lobe, which is responsible for the cognitive processing of humor. Shammi & Stuss (1999) postulate that humor appreciation is impaired if there is damage to the superior anterior region of the right frontal lobe. They believe this is the area where cognition and affect are integrated, allowing not only for understanding of a humorous situation, but appreciating it with physical response: laughter. There is also significant activity occurring in the occipital lobe that is associated with motion when laughing (Chaudhuri 2001).

An accidental "discovery" was made at UCLA Medical School when a 16-year-old girl (referred to as A.K.), who was undergoing brain stimulation to localize her seizures (NOT gelastic seizures) in preparation for a surgery, burst into uncontrollable and mirthful laughter (Fried *et al.* 1998). The area that was stimulated as a part of mapping her cerebral cortex, was on her left superior frontal gyrus[80] (a part of the frontal lobe) in the region of the supplementary motor area (SMA) that has long been suspected to be associated with initiation of speech and movement. The more intensely the area was stimulated, the more prominently the girl laughed, explaining *(post factum)* to the researchers that she did find them or anything else "funny." Once the stimulation stopped, they were no longer "funny[81]." During the laughter all hand and speech activities stopped. This is quite an important discovery, not only because stimulation of part of

---

77   The term "cannibalism" has a negative connotation, as the practice is considered to be "primitive and barbaric." Among the Fore it was just a way of disposing of the body after respectfully distributing it among the living, with women usually consuming the brain (the carrier of the prions) and other organs, while men were eating the flesh. Consequently, the kuru affected women the most at the time of the epidemic. Cannibalism is still being practiced in its symbolic form, for example, by Catholics (holy communion), and modern practices of organ and tissue transplantation is yet another form of cannibalism. Thus, modern scholars have proposed and used a new term, "transumption" (e.g., Collinge *et al.* 2006 & 2008).

78   Recent biochemical and physical evidence confirmed that cannibalism has been practiced world-wide for more than 500,000 years (both *Homo sapiens* and Neanderthals) and probably "resulted in a series of prion disease epidemics in human prehistory ... " (Collinge *et al.* 2008: 3728; referring to Mead *et al.* 2003). Consequently, humans developed genes protecting them from "brain-wasting prion diseases."

79   Laughter itself (so-called hysterical laughter) has been a cause and a symptom of other epidemic events, for example, in Tanzania (the Tanganyika laughter epidemic of 1962), (e.g., Rankin & Philip 1963; Bean 1967; Sebastian 2003; Hempelmann 2007). It has been classified as mass hysteria—or Mass Psychogenic Illness (MPI) together with similar events like meowing nuns, the 1983 West Bank fainting epidemic, etc. (e.g., Bartholomev 2001).

80   Significant activity in the left inferior temporal gyrus has been also noted by other researchers using fMRI to monitor humor and laughter (Mobbs *et al.* 2003; Moran *et al.* 2004). Arroyo *et al.* also reported that stimulation of the fusiform gyrus or the parahippocampal gyrus was responsible for outburst of mirthful laughter (1993). The left posterior middle temporal gyrus, the left inferior frontal gyrus and the left posterior inferior temporal gyrus, the right posterior middle temporal gyrus and the cerebellum have been shown to be activated when phonological and semantic jokes were processed by subjects in Goel and Dolan's studies (2001).

81   Wild *et al.* refer to other cases of brain stimulation, which were able to elicit brief episodes of smiling and/or laughing, as well as to attempts for animal brain stimulation (2003).

the left superior frontal gyrus triggered laughter, but also because it triggered feelings of joy (mirth) after laughter began.[82] Additionally, A.K. was able to come up with a "story", i.e., a stimulus context, to explain her laughter. So, it seems that the so-called "center of laughter" in this stimulation study is not really the center of laughter that regulates non-conscious activity in the subcortical brain system, but it actually is the center of a "happy" emotion, which is reflected by laughter. Interestingly, this response seems to be able to originate without any outside stimulus such as tickling, chasing, or cognitive humor.[83] Furthermore, it also indicates that there is "a close link between the motor, affective, and cognitive components of laughter" (Fried *et al.* 1998); i.e., the SMA controls their motor operations. This incident taught us that it is possible to directly internally stimulate the brain for mirth without using any external stimuli, cognitive or not. One can argue that the mechanical stimulation of this locus is an outside stimulus as well. There might be more than one area that is "capable" for eliciting laughter through stimulation but they can be located "too far to touch," i.e., in the subcortical system. Furthermore, the supplementary motor cortex was one of the brain structures activated when Iwase *et al.* (2002) researched the connection between brain responses and laughing and smiling induced by comic videos. The laughter/smile as involuntary movements activated SMA and putamen while voluntary movements (mimicking laughter/smile), stimulated the primary motor area (M1) and bilateral SMA. They further proposed, as based on their research and of others (Mendez, Nakawatase & Brown 1999; Parvizi *et al.* 2001[84]), "a new neuroanatomical model of emotional facial expression by combination of basal ganglia motor circuit and cerebro-ponto-cerebellar pathways" (Iwase *et al.* 2002: 767).

Wild *et al.* summarized the existing research on neural paths of laughter dividing them into the "involuntary" (pathological)/"emotional" laughter streaming through the "amygdala, thalamic/hypo- and subthalamic areas and the dorsal/tegmental brainstem," and the "voluntary" laughter originating "in the premotor/frontal opercular areas" and passing through the motor cortex and the pyramidal tract to the

---

82   Mendez, Nakawatase, & Brown (1999) reported that laughter in some seizures from the anterior cingulated gyrus is also associated with the feeling of mirth.

83   The patient in the studies by Parvizi *et al.* also reported that the feeling of joy or sadness was produced after "inappropriate" outbursts of laughing or crying but appropriate (i.e., joy after laughing and sadness after crying) to the behavior that was just displayed (2001).

84   Two opposite views on pathological laughter.

ventral brainstem." The laughter-coordinating center seems to be in the dorsal upper pons, while the perception of humor is processed through "the right frontal cortex, the medial ventral prefrontal cortex, the right and left posterior (middle and inferior) temporal regions and possibly the cerebellum … " (2003). Wild *et al.* suggest that true laughter is connected with ceasing of the cortical frontal inhibition; i.e., pathological laughter occurs when the inhibitory system is damaged (2003). Thus, their proposed model of natural laughter induced by humor starts with humor processing in frontal and temporal regions of the brain; once activated, facial and laughter reactions "mediated by dorsal brainstem regions" follow and are to be "inhibited by the ventral brainstem, probably via frontal motor/premotor areas" (Wild *et al.* 2003: 2134). Of course, much more research is needed, but the subcortical center/"location" of laughter seems to be undeniable, albeit the paths through which the "laughing signals" are sent require more of experimental neurological studies.

Recognizing Humor

For so many years animals were denied human emotions, from pain and sadness to laughter. Currently, when a number of emotions in other animals seem to be shared with humans, questions about their cognitive abilities can be raised, hopefully without being accused of humanizing or anthropomorphicizing other animals. Again, such research is more about searching for animality in humans, than humanity in animals. As demonstrated above, humans and other animals have the same, although differently vocalized and voiced, laughing responses to "primitive" stimuli such as tickling, rough-and-tumble play, and chasing. These are instinctive and spontaneous expressions of basic drives and urges (emotions and motivations) supported by subcortical brain systems. The subcortical brain region is present in all mammals. The subcortex is so essential for survival and adaptation because it contains areas that are basic to normal functioning. Any damage to this area has serious consequences, including death.[85] These basic functions of the subcortex are modulated to adjust to different circumstances within biological constraints of any given organism. Thus, once humans became bipedal and acquired the ability—or rather the option—to speak, etc.,[86] the subcortical brain systems may have been modulated to respond to new pleasurable activities such as verbal or visual humor, the same way as to the basic physical stimuli (e.g., tickling) directly connected with laughter. This cognitive humor is a sort of verbal, visual, or mental "tickling" (cognitive "tickling"), and is supposed to be one of the main characteristics distinguishing humans from other animals. In order to understand and then enjoy cognitive humor, one must have the areas of brain related to learning and understanding activated. Derks *et al.* (1997) observed electrical patterns on EEG (electroencephalograph) when their subjects laughed. They noted that an electrical wave (negative charge) moved through the cerebral cortex within less than 0.5 second after something funny was perceived and laughter resulted. The positive charge did not result in laughter so it is assumed that the subject did not find the stimulus funny. The "route" of electrical brainwave through various circuits of the brain such as the left side of the cortex (analyses of the structure and words of the joke), frontal lobe (emotional and social responses), the right hemisphere of the cortex (intellectual processing of the joke), motor sections (physical motions) and the sensory processing areas of the occipital lobe (visual signals), indicates the

---

85   Not so in the case of the cerebral cortex i.e., even an extensive damage may not cause death.

86   I.e., circumstances have changed leading to the emergence of new or additional cortico-cognitive abilities in humans reflected, among other things, by verbal joking.

complexity of laughter as a response to humor. It suggests that if one part of this "route" is damaged, the perception of humor and resulting response might also be impaired.[87] So, the brain is exercised through jokes, mental and visual stimuli, as well as through any other more serious "thinking" tasks.

The existence of cognitive humor among animals has been "denied" since their cognitive abilities seem to be either limited or non-existent. However, as William Cowper once said, "[A]bsence of proof is not proof of absence," so we may want to remain open-minded. As Panksepp commented, if there is rat humor "it will likely be heavily laced with slapstick" (2005: 63) but, in my view, still would have to be recognized as cognitive humor.

Once again, there is plenty of anecdotal evidence that "joking" stimuli exist in the animal kingdom. Provine, for example, provides some examples of "presumed intentional 'misnaming' and 'misusing'" objects by primates for a sheer purpose of amusement at the level of preschool children (2000: 94–97). Each animal lover probably has a story to tell in which his/her beloved pet played a joke on its owner or other animal companion. Sauvage, my big, white male cat, used to "amuse" himself and me with his well-thought-through antics. His favorite play involved my other cat, Squeak, who was a pretty tortie, but not a very smart one.[88] On occasions, without any apparent reasons, Sauvage would express a sudden interest in playing with younger Squeak, whom he mostly ignored in spite of her playful "invitations." He would lure Squeak to the kitchen making sure she was watching him opening a kitchen cabinet where I kept their food. Then, he would jump in, mess up some cans, jump out and wait patiently for Squeak to do the same. The moment Squeak was in, Sauvage would slam the door shut so she could not get out without my or his help. Freed of her presence, Sauvage would resume his dignified position on the couch waiting for me to find his poor victim. When terrified Squeak jumped out of the cabinet, Sauvage would joyfully "slap" her butt and go about his business. If cats laugh, I am sure that Sauvage laughed his head off at Squeak's vulnerability. One may also note that in this humorous situation Sauvage was an aggressor, so his laughter would have been related to joy in aggression.[89]

Sauvage's play with Squeak cannot be easily explained without giving him credit for designing and executing his plan. He showed the same cognitive skills over and over again in different situations. For example, he was not particularly happy about taking a prescribed medication every day, but he always "swallowed" his pill with the look of a martyr on his face. After each pill I checked his mouth to make sure I was not being fooled. Imagine my surprise three or four months later, when moving out to my new condo I found a very attractive "pyramid" of pills in the corner of my closet! Not only did Sauvage fool me, not only did he "carry" pill after pill to the same place for hiding, but also he must have selected this specific corner "knowing" that I rarely, if ever, check on my sleeping bags.

The above "Sauvage stories" are a perfect example of the anecdotal evidence[90] plentiful among animal lovers. Unfortunately, most scholars are rather humorless when it comes to their "selection" of the scien-

---

87   It seems that especially damage to the right frontal lobe (processing center) is responsible for restricting one's sense of humor, especially cognitive humor (chasing, etc., still can be perceived as funny). Shammi & Stuss (1999) consider the anterior region of the right frontal lobe to be the most crucial for understanding and appreciating cognitive humor.

88   Note that as a typical cat (animal) lover I automatically raise my cats to a human level by referring to them using human gender distinction. Since many people, including scholars, are "guilty" of the same sin, research on animal cognitive abilities, including humor, seems to be impeded by subjectivity.

89   Panksepp & Burgdorf recorded that, in some cases, rats chirped laughter sounds during aggressive encounters (2003: 538–539). Is it possible then that animals, like humans, also might find pleasure in aggressive actions and produce "evil laughter"?

90   ... although I personally witnessed them and have at least one independent witness.

tific evidence but … There is plenty of evidence that animals think and their minds evolve (so do ours). Geoff Clark, skillfully, briefly although somewhat pointedly[91] summarized them in his critique of Davies & Underdown's article in the Cambridge Archaeological Journal (2006):

> Humans are, after all, nothing more (or less) than highly intelligent, technologically sophisticated, socially complex animals. And we are only unique in the same way that any species is unique, by virtue of possessing a unique evolutionary heritage. Much of research has been done in recent years on aspects of animal behavioural complexity. Among other things, it shows that octopi have personalities, are capable of planning depth, deception and jealousy and that African grey parrots can not only count but also grasp the concept of zero. Self-recognition, empathy, and tool-making traditions are documented in both chimpanzees and dolphins. There is evidence for individual face-recognition and self-awareness amongst sheep. Courtship songs are documented in mice, and laughter in rats. With the emergence of these studies, we are gaining a fuller appreciation not only of the unsuspected complexity of animals and birds but also of their profound resemblances to ourselves (Siebert 2006). (Clark 2006: 350).

I agree with Clark, Panksepp, de Waal (e.g., 1996, 2007) and others that we, as humans, are not that unique and share commonalities in behaviors, affects and cognitive skills with other animals or they rather share them with us. Thus, if our moral sense/ethical standards are innate (e.g., de Waal 1996) so is propensity for religion (e.g., Dennet 2006), why not then humor? However, until a humor gene, or something else of this magnitude, is found and demonstrated to be shared with other animals, I am out of luck to prove cats' superiority in the field of humor over other animals. In my view, they definitely "get a joke" but their laughter, not discovered yet, might not be the social laughter of a dog or a rat since cats are known to be solitary; at the same time, cats are opportunistic in their nature.[92] They have never been truly domesticated, although all domestic cats can genetically trace their origin to their opportunistic ancestors around 9000 years ago (Driscoll *et al.* 2007), who decided to profit from human domestication of plants and of other animals in the Near East, somewhere in the Fertile Crescent, probably in Mesopotamia. With humans producing and storing food there was no need to waste both time and energy in search of a wild prey so cats just moved near a "free" food market with fresh meat and treats supplied daily. To add an insult to the injury, cats did not even bother to develop *neotenies* seen in other domestic animals i.e., they have not carried their juvenile characteristics into adulthood to adapt "better" to a new environment.[93] The only *neoteny* in domestic cats is continuing use of kitten vocal sounds such as "miau" when around humans[94] (Turner & Bateson 2000). So, as Gorman's title says, *Dogs may laugh, but only cats get the joke* (2006). And this joke is on us.

In the absence of the humor gene, we cannot be sure when humans actually started to use humor. Verbal humor is proposed to be dated at least before 35,000 years ago (Polimeni & Reiss 2006). The

---

91   Better him than me …

92   See feline self-healing through purring in the chapter on health benefits of laughter.

93   I guess cats must have realized a long time ago that they are cute enough to be loved for what they are. Dogs, on other hand, keep on trying to be more desirable (compare domesticated dogs to their wild ancestors—wolves).

94   I am not really sure that this is a *neoteny*. They might also have discovered that persistent vocal communication with not-so-smart humans is a sure way to get their attention and more freebies so when a part of a social group they adjust their communication skills (sort of like switching between languages in humans).

reasoning is pretty simple. Since Australian Aboriginals were recorded as having a sense of humor upon their first contact with researchers, and they seem to have been genetically isolated for 35,000 years, the use of humor must have existed before this date[95]. However, the oldest recorded joke is of the Sumerian origin and dates to ca. 1900 B.C.[96] (The University of Wolverhampton World's Ten Oldest Jokes, 2008). It reads "Something which has never occurred since time immemorial: a young woman did not fart in her husband's lap." If you don't like this sort of scatological (toilet) humor, you can enjoy a quip on a pharaoh: "How do you entertain a bored pharaoh? You sail a boatload of young women dressed only in fishing nets down the Nile and urge the pharaoh to go catch a fish" (ca. 1600 B.C.). The University of Wolverhampton's list of jokes clearly demonstrates that our sense of humor has not changed for thousands of years. We still laugh at three-type combination (a Rabbi, a Catholic priest, and a Mormon bishop …) jokes and like smart off-color remarks such as this one from Ptolemaic (the 4th to the 1st century B.C.) Egypt: "Man is even more eager to copulate than a donkey—his purse is what restrains him."

Of course, the above "oldest" jokes are not "the oldest jokes" but "just jokes" which survived in the archaeological record because they were written down and "recovered" by modern scholars. They were, in all probability, not even the most popular jokes—we just happen to know about them through accidental nature of archaeology.[97] Verbal humor must have been used a long time before writing was invented in ca. 3300–3200 B.C. (both Sumer and Egypt) and after the time when the FOXP2, "the language gene," became fully "appreciated." Consequently, we are back once again to a timeframe of hundreds of thousands years if not millions. However, the verbal humor is "easy" to date[98]; i.e., in order for it to exist, one must have a language and obviously, with the discovery of FOXP2, we can "narrow" down dates. Furthermore, the brain needs both more space[99] and more "connections" to process information associated with language that is a higher cognitive skill than Sauvage's alleged planning and executing. It requires, among other things, the ability to make abstract/symbolic associations and to preserve them in short-, long-term and working memories. The verbal humor probably requires even a more complex network: the symbolic nature of the language itself is transformed, in the verbal humor, into another set(s) of symbolic values. Thus, it seems that "getting a joke" might be as complicated and/or complex brain processing as learning high math.

Conclusions

Both laughter and humor seem to be innate in humans and possibly in many other animals, from the top of the evolutionary ladder to its bottom. While there is less and less resistance in recognizing similarities in acoustic vocalizations (both laughter and speech) between primates and humans, other species haven't received much attention yet with regard to their expression of various emotions as these emotions are often denied to them. However, in my view, there is no reason to doubt that animals besides humans are

---

95   One must, however, note that an independent development of verbal humor is also possible, although, in my view, highly unlikely.

96   This is actually an Old Babylonian "copy" so the joke itself is older, at least by a few hundred years. Sumer (more or less southern part of modern Iraq) is one of the so-called cradles of civilization dating back to at least ca. 3400 B.C. They invented the cuneiform script (used all over the ancient Near East for ca. 3000 years) in which this joke was recorded.

97   As archaeologists, we may know what we are excavating but have no idea what we are going to find.

98   Other forms of humor which also involve cognitive skills in addition to motor ones are even too speculative to discuss here with regard to their "dating."

99   Whether development of language with its all "consequences" requires a larger brain or not is still debatable (Polimeni & Reiss 2006).

capable of laughter as it is connected with the most ancient part of the brain, the subcortex, that is present in all mammals. If vocalized/voiced, this laughter might not have been noted yet due to frequencies of its acoustic. If non-vocalized, its discovery might only be possible through continuous mapping of the brain to understand paths through which emotions are being processed. Consequently, the definition of laughter might require future adjustments as we learn more about neurological circuits involved in processing laughter and humor. Since tickling induces laughter in humans, primates and rats, there is also the possibility that other laughter-inducing activities are shared by them. "Cognitive tickling," i.e., humor, might be one of them regardless of the presence of language or language-like vocalizations in animals. Humor is not limited to its verbal form so we cannot ignore the possibility that animals enjoy it too, whether as slapstick, chase, or playing pranks. If laughter and humor are inherent in human (and possibly other animals) nature as a part of our physiological/neurological make-up, do they have any other functions than emotional and/or cognitive forms of communication? The future research may answer this question as the evolutionary origin of both laughter and humor is definitely worth exploring further.

Bibliography

Arroyo, S., Lesser, R.P., Gordon, B., Uematsu, S., Hart, J., Schwerdt, P., *et al.* (1993) Mirth, Laughter, and Gelastic Seizures. *Brain,* 116: 757–80.

Askenazy, J.J.M. (1987) The Functions and Dysfunctions of Laughter. *Journal of General Psychology.* 114 (94): 317–334.

Azim, E., Mobbs, D., Jo, B., Menon, V., and Reiss, A.L. (2005) Sex Differences in Brain Activation Elicited by Humor. *Proceedings of the National Academy of Science of United States,* 102:16496–16501.

Bartholomew, R. E. (2001) *Little Green Men, Meowing Nuns and Head-Hunting Panics: A Study of Mass Psychogenic Illness and Social Delusion.* Jefferson, North Carolina: MacFarland and Company.

Bean, W.B. (1967) *Rare Diseases and Lesions. Their Contributions to Clinical Medicine.* Springfield, Illinois: Charles C. Thomas.

Bekoff, M. (2007) *The Emotional Lives of Animals.* Nocato, California: New World Library.

Bekoff, M., and Byers J. A. (1998) *Animal Play: Evolutionary, Comparative, and Ecological Perspectives.* Cambridge: Cambridge University Press.

Bihrle, A.M., Brownell H.H., Powelson J.A., and Gardner H. (1986) Comprehension of Humorous and Nonhumorous Materials by Left and Right Brain-damaged Patients. *Brain and Cognition,* 5: 399–411.

Black, D.W. (1982) Pathologic Laughter. A Review of the Literature. *The Journal of Nervous and Mental Disease,* 170: 67–71.

Black, D.W. (1984) Laughter. *Journal of American Medical Association.* 252: 2995–2998.

Blakemore, S.J., Wolpert D.M., and Frith, C.D. (1998) Central Cancellation of Self-Produced Tickle Sensation. *Nature Neuroscience* 1: 635–640.

Bremmer, J. D. (2002) *Does Stress Damage the Brain? Understanding Trauma-Related Disorders from a Mind-Body Perspective.* New York: W.W. Norton and Company.

Brownell, H.H., Michael, D., Powelson, J., and Gardner, H. (1983) Surprise But Not Coherence : Sensitivity to Verbal Humor in Right-hemisphere Patients. *Brain and Language,* 18: 20–27.

Burgdorf, J., and Panksepp, J. (2001) Tickling Induces Reward in Adolescent Rats. *Physiology and Behavior,* 72: 167–173.

Burgdorf, J., Knutson, B., Panksepp, J., and Ikemoto, S. (2001) Nucleus Accumbens Amphetamine Microinjections Unconditionally Elicit 50-kHz Ultrasonic Vocalizations in Rats. *Behavioral Neuroscience,* 115: 940–4.

Burgdorf, J., Wood, P.L., Kroes, R.A., Moskal, J.R., and Panksepp, J. (2007) Neurobiology of 50-kHz Ultrasonic Vocalizations in Rats: Electrode Mapping, Lesion and Pharmacological Studies. *Behavioral Brain Research,* 182: 274–283.

Burghardt, G. M. (1998) The Evolutionary Origins of Play Revisited: Lessons from Turtles. *Animal Play: Evolutionary, Comparative, and Ecological Perspectives*, M. Bekoff and J. Beyers eds. Cambridge: Cambridge University Press. pp 1–26.

Byrne, R.W. (2006) Parsing Behaviour. A Mundane Origin for an Extraordinary Ability? *The Roots of Human Sociality: Culture, Cognition, and Interaction*. S. Levinson and N. Enfield, eds. New York: Berg. pp 478–505.

Challamel, M.J., Lahlou, S., Revol, M., and Jouvet, M. (1985) Sleep and Smiling in Neonate. A New Approach. In *Sleep 84*. W.P. Koella, E. Ruther, and H. Schultz eds. New York: Gustav Fisher Verlag. pp 290–292.

Chaudhuri, T. (2001) A Serious Look at Laughter. *Serendip, Biology 103*, Web Paper 2. http://serendip.brynmawr.edu/exchange/node/2054.

Clark, Geoffrey A. (2006): Some Observations on 'The Neanderthals: A Social Synthesis' (Davies & Underdown *Cambridge Archaeological Journal* 16.2. (June) 2006, 145–64). In *Cambridge Archaeological Journal*. 16 (3). pp. 349–351.

Cleveland, J., and Snowdon, C.T. (1982) The Complex Vocal Repertoire of the Adult Cotton-top Tamarin *(Saguinus Oedipus Oedipus)*. *Zeitschrift für Tierzuchtung und Zuchtungsbiologie (Journal of Animal Breeding and Genetics)*, 58: 231–270.

Collinge, J., Whitfield, J., McKintosh, E., Frosh, A., Beck, J.; Mead, S., Hill, A.F., Brandner, S.; Thomas, D., and Alpers, M.P. (2006) Kuru in the 21st Century—An Acquired Human Prion Disease With Very Long Incubation Periods. *Lancet*, 367: 2068–2074.

Collinge, J., Whitfield, J., McKintosh, E., Frosh, A.; Mead, S., Hill, A.F., Brandner, S., Thomas, D., and Alpers, M.P. (2008) A Clinical Study of Kuru Patients With Long Incubation Periods at the End of the Epidemic in Papua New Guinea. *Philosophical Transactions of the Royal Society*, 363: 3725–3739.

Corballis, M.C. (2002) *From Hand to Mouth: The Origins of Language*. Princeton: Princeton University Press.

Corballis, M.C. (2004) FOXP2 And The Mirror System. *TRENDS in Cognitive Sciences*, 8 (3): 95–96.

Craig, A.D. (2010) Once an Island, Now the Focus of Attention. *Brain, Structure and Function Journal*, 214: 395–396.

Crockford, C., and Boesch, C. (2003) Context Specific Calls in Wild Chimpanzees, *Pan troglodytes verus*: Analysis of Barks. *Animal Behavior*, 66: 115–125.

Crockford, C., and Boesch, C. (2005) Call Combinations in Wild Chimpanzees. *Behaviour*, 142 (14): 397–421.

Darwin, C. (1872) *The Expression of Emotions in Man and Animals*. New York: D. Appleton and Co.

Davies, R. and Underdown, S. (2006) The Neanderthals: A Social Synthesis. *Cambridge Archaeological Journal*, 16 (2). pp. 145–164.

de Waal, F.B.M. (1996) *Good Natured—The Origins of Right and Wrong in Humans and Other Animals*. Cambridge, MA: Harvard University Press.

de Waal, F.B.M. (2007) With a Little Help from A Friend. *PLoS Biology* 5 (7) e190.doi:101371/journal.pbio.0050190.

Dennett, D. (2006) *Breaking the Spell: Religion as a Natural Phenomenon*. New York: Simon and Schuster.

Derks, P., Gillikin, L.S., Bartolome-Rull, D.S., and Bogart, E.H. (1997) Laughter and Electroencephalagraphic Activity. *Humor*, 10: 285–300.

Driscoll, C.A., Menotti-Raymond, M., Roca, A.L., Hupe K., Johnson, W.E., Geffen, E., Harley, E.H., Delibes, M., Pontier, D., Kitchener, A.C., Yamaguchi, N., O'Brien, S.J., and Macdonald, D.W. (2007) The Near East Origin of Cat Domestication. *Science*, 317: 519–523.

Eibl-Eibesfeldt, I. *Human Ethology*. New York: Aldine de Gruyer, 1989.

Falk, D. (2004) Prelinguistic Evolution in Early Hominins: Whence Motherese? *Behavioral and Brain Sciences*, 27: 491–541.

Fossey, D. (1983) *Gorillas in the Mist*. Boston: Houghton Mifflin.

Fried, I., Wilson, C.L., MacDonald, K.A., and Behnke, E.J. (1998) Electric Current Stimulates Laughter. *Nature*, 391: 650.

Gajdusek, D.C., Gibbs Jr., C.J., and Alpers, M. (1966) Experimental Transmission of a Kuru-like Syndrome to Chimpanzees. *Natur*, 209: 794–796.

Gannon, P.J., Kheck, N.M., and Hoff, P.R. (2000) Language Areas of the Hominoid Brain: A Dynamic Communicative Shift on the Upper East Side Planum. K. Gibson and D. Falk eds. *Evolutionary Anatomy of the Primate Cerebral Cortex.* 1st ed. New York: Cambridge University: 216–240.

Gewirtz, J.L. (1965) The Course of Infant Smiling in Four Children Rearing Environments in Israel. *Determinants of Infant Behaviour.*(3) B.M. Foss (ed.). London: Methuen.

Gorman, J. (2006) Dogs May Laugh, but Only Cats Get the Joke. *The New York Times,* September 5.

Gruner, C.R. (1997) *The Game of Humor.* Piscataway, New Jersey: Transaction Publishers.

Hempelmann, C.F. (2007) The Laughter of the 1962 Tanganyika Laughter Epidemic. *Humor. International Journal of Humor Research,* 20 (1): 49–71.

Hoeft, F., Watson, C.L., Kesler, S.R., Bettinger, K.E., and Reiss, A.L. (2008) Gender differences in the mesocorticolimbic system during computer game-play. *Journal of Psychiatric Research.* 42 (4). 253–258.

Hooff, J.A.R.A.M. Van (1967) The Facial Displays of the Catarrhine Monkeys and Apes. *Primate Ethology* (ed. Morris D.). Chicago, IL: Aldine. pp. 7–68.

Hooff, J.A.R.A.M. Van (1972) A Comparative Approach to the Phylogeny of Laughter and Smiling. Non-verbal Communication (Hinde, R.A., ed.). Cambridge: Cambridge University Press: 209–241.

Iwase, M., Ouchi, Y., Okada, H., Yokoyama, C., Nobezawa, S., Yoshikawa, E., Tsukada, H., Takeda, M., Yamashita, K., Takeda, M., Yamaguti, K., Kuratsune, H., Shimizu, A., Watanabe, Y. (2002) Neural Substrates of Human Facial Expression of Pleasant Emotion Induced by Comic Films: A PET Study. *Neuroimage* , 17(2): 758–768.

Izard, C.E. (1977) *Human Emotion.* New York: Plenum Press.

Kawakami, K., Takai-Kawakami, K., Tomonoga, M., Suzuli, J., Kusaka, T., and Okai, T. (2006) Origins of Smile and Laughter: A Preliminary Study. *Early Human Development* 82 : 61–66.

Krause, J., Lalueza-Fox, C., Orlando, L., Enard, W., Green, R.E., Burbano, H.A., Hublin, J.J., Hänni, C., Fortea, J., de la Rasilla, M., Bertranpetit, J., Rosas, A., and Pääbo, S. (2007) The Derived FOXP2 Variant of Modern Humans Was Shared with Neandertals. *Current Biology,* 17(21): 1908–1912.

Lai, C., Fisher, S.E., Hurst, J.A., Vargha-Khadem, F., and Monaco, A.P. (2001) A Novel Forkhead-Domain Gene is Mutated in a Severe Speech and Language Disorder. *Nature,* 413: 519–523.

Leavens, D.A. (2009) Animal Communication: Laughter is the Shortest Distance between Two Apes. *Current Biology,* 19 (13): 1106–1111.

Li, N.P., Griskevicius, V., Durante, K.M., Jonason, P.K., Pasisz, D.J., and Aumer, K. (2009) An Evolutionary Perspective on humor: Sexual Selection or terest dication? *Personality and Social Psychology Bulletin,* 35: 923–936.

Liegeois, F.J., Baldeweg, T., Connelly, A., Gadian, D.G., Mishkin, M., and Vargha-Kadem, F. (2003) Language fMRI Abnormalities Associated with FOXP1 Gene Mutation. *Nature Neuroscience,* 6: 1230–1237.

Lovgren, S. (2005). Animals Laughed Long Before Humans, Study Says. *National Geographic News* (March 31) http://www.nationalgeographic.com.nes/pf/57038415.html.

Mark, M., Maejima, T., Kuckelsberg, D., Yoo, J., Hyde, R., Shah, V., Gutierrez, D., Moreno, R., Kruse, W., Noebels, J., and Herlitze, S. (2011) Delayed Postnatal Loss of P/Q-Type Calcium Channels Recapitulates the Absence Epilepsy, Dyskinesia, and Ataxia Phenotypes of Genomic Cacna1A Mutations. *The Journal of Neuroscience,* 31: 4311–4326.

Martin, G.N., and Gray, C.D. (1996) The Effects of Audience Laughing on Men's and Women's Responses to Humor. *Journal of Social Psychology* 136: 221–231.

Mead, S., Stumpf, M.P.H., Whitfield, J., Beck, J.A., Poulter, M., Campbell, T., Uphill, J., Goldstein, D., Alpers, M.P., Fisher, E.M.C., and Collinge, J. (2003) Balancing Selection at the Prion Protein Gene Consistent with Prehistoric Kurulike Epidemics. *Science,* 300 (5619): 640–643.

Mendez, M.F., Nakawatase, T.V., and Brown, C.V. (1999) Involuntary Laughter and appropriate Hilarity. *Journal of Neuropsychiatry and Clinical Neurosciences* 11:253–258.

Meyer, M., Baumann, S., Wildgruber, D., and Alter, K. (2007) How The Brain Laughs. Comparative Evidence from Behavioral, Electrophysiological and Neuroimaging Studies in Human and Monkey. *Behavioural Brain Research,* 182: 245–260.

Miller, G.F. (1998) How Mate Choice Shaped Human Nature: A review of Sexual Selection and Human Evolution. *Handbook of Evolutionary Psychology: Ideas, issues, and applications.* C. Crawford and D. Krebs, eds. Mahwah, NJ: Lawrence Erlbaum. pp. 87–130.

Miller, G.F. (2000a) *The Mating Mind: How Sexual Choice Shaped the Evolution of Human Nature.* New York: Doubleday.

Miller, G.F. (2000b) Mental Traits as Fitness Indicators: Expanding Evolutionary Psychology's Adaptationism. *Evolutionary Perspectives on Human Reproductive Behavior.* D. LeCroy, and P. Moller, eds. New York: New York Academy of Sciences. pp. 62–74.

Miller, G.F. (2001) Aesthetic Fitness: How Sexual Selection Shaped Artistic Virtuosity as a Fitness Indicator and Aesthetic Preferences as Mate Choice Criteria. *Bulletin of Psychology and the Arts,* 2: 20–25.

Mitani, J.C. and Marler, P. (1989) A Phonological Analysis of Male Gibbon Singing Behavior. *Behaviour,* 106: 20–45.

Mobbs, D., Greicius, M.D., Abdel-Azim, E., Menon, V., and Reiss, A.L. (2003) Humor Modulates the Mesolimbic Reward Centers. *Neuron,* 40:1041–1048.

Moran, J.M., Wig, G.S., Adams Jr., R.B., Janata, P., and Kelley, W.M. (2004) Neural Correlates of Humor Detection and Appreciation. *Neuro Image,* 21:1055–1060.

Niedenthal, P.M., Mermillod, M., Maringer, M., and Hess, U. (2010) The Simulation of Smiles (SIMS) Model: Embodied Simulation and the Meaning of Facial Expression. *Behavioral and Brain Sciences,* 33: 417–480.

Noonan, J.P., Coop, G., Kudaravalli, S., Smith, D., Krause, J., Alessi, J., Chen, F., Platt, D., Pääbo, S., Pritchard, J.K., and Rubin, E.M. (2006) Sequencing and Analysis of Neanderthal Genomic DNA. *Science,* 314: 1113–1118.

Nwokah, E.E., Hsu, H.C., Dobrowolska, O., and Fogel, A. (1994) The Development of Laughter in Mother–Infant Communication: Timing parameters and temporal sequences. *Infant Behavior and Development,* 17: 23–35.

Nwokah, E.E., Hsu, H.C., Davies, P., and Fogel, A. (1999) The Integration of Laughter and Speech in Vocal Communication: A Dynamic Systems Perspective. *Journal of Speech, Language, and Hearing Research,* 42: 880–894.

Owren, M.J. and Bachorowski, J.A. (2003) Reconsidering the Evolution of Nonlinguistic Communication: The Case of Laughter. *Journal of Nonverbal Behavior,* 27 (3): 183–200.

Panagariya, A., Bhawna, S., Gautam, T., Hrisikesh, K., and Agarwal, V. (2007) Gelastic Epilepsy Associated with Lesions Other Than Hypothalamic Hamartoma. *Annals of Indian Academy of Neurology* 10 (2):105–108.

Panksepp, J. "Neuroscience: Feeling the Pain of Social Loss." *Science* 10, 302, 5643 (2003) 237–239.

Panksepp, J. (2005) Beyond a Joke: From Animal Laughter to Human Joy? *Science,* 308:62–63.

Panksepp, J. (2007) Neuroevolutionary Sources of Laughter and Social Joy: Modeling Primal Human Laughter in Laboratory Rats. *Behavioural Brain Research,* 182 (2): 231–244.

Panksepp, J., and Burgdorf, J. (2000) 50k-Hz Chirping (Laughter?) in Response to Conditioned and Unconditioned Tickle-Induced Reward in Rats: Effects of Social Housing and Genetic Variables. *Behavioral Brain Research* 115: 25–38.

Panksepp, J., and Burgdorf, J. (2003) 'Laughing Rats' and the Evolutionary Antecedents of Human Joy? *Physiology and Behavior,* 79: 533–547.

Panksepp, J., Knutson, B., and Burgdorf, J. (2002) The Role of Brain Emotional Systems in Addictions: A Neuro-Evolutionary Perspective and New 'Self-Report' Animal Model. *Addiction,* 97: 459–469.

Parvizi, J., Anderson, S.W., Martin, C.O., Damasio, H., and Damasio, A.R. (2001) Pathological Laughter and Crying: A Link to the Cerebellum. *Brain,* 124:1708–1719.

Polimeni, J. and Reiss, J.P. (2006) The First Joke: Exploring the Evolutionary Origins of Humor. *Evolutionary Psychology*, 4:347–366.

Pollick, A. S., and de Waal, F.B.M. (2007) Ape Gestures and Language Evolution. *Proceedings of the National Academy of Sciences of the United State of America*, 104 (19): 8184–8189.

Preuschoft, S., and Hooff, J.A.R.A.M. Van (1997) The Social Function of 'Smile" and 'Laughter': Variations Across Primate Species and Societies. *Non-verbal Communication:Where Nature Meets Culture*. Segerstrale, U., and P. Molnár, eds. Mahwah, NJ: Erlbaum. pp. 171–189.

Preuss, T.M. (2000) What's Human About the Human Brain? *The Cognitive Neurosciences*. M. S. Gazzaniga, ed. Cambridge, MA: MIT Press. pp. 1219–1234.

Provine, R. (2000) *Laughter: A Scientific Investigation*. New York: Penguin Books.

Radick, G. (2007) *The Simian Tongue: The Long Debate About Animal Language*. Chicago: University of Chicago Press.

Rankin, A.M. and Philip, P.J. (1963) An Epidemic of Laughing in the Bukoba District of Tanganyika. *Central African Journal of Medicine*, 9: 167–170.

Reimers-Kipping, S., Hevers, W., Pääbo, S., and Enard, W. (2010) Humanized FOXP2 Specifically Affects Cortico-Basal Ganglia Circuits. *Neuroscience*, 175: 75–84.

Reiss, A.L., Hoeft, F., Tenforde, A.S., Chen, W., Mobbs, D., and Mignot, E.J. (2008) Anomalous Hypothalamic Responses to Humor in Cataplexy. *PLoS ONE* 3(5): e2225.

Richmond, B.G., and Jungers, W.L. (2008) *Orrorin Tugenensis* Femoral Morphology and the Evolution of Hominin Bipedalism. *Science* 319 (5870): 1662–1665.

Robinson, J.G. (1979) An Analysis of The Organization of Vocal Communication in The Titi Monkey, *Callicebus moloch*. *Zeitschrift für Tierzuchtung und Zuchtungsbiologie (Journal of Animal Breeding and Genetics)*, 49: 381–405.

Robinson, J.G. (1984) Syntactic Structures in The Vocalizations of Wedge-capped Capuchin Monkeys, *Cebus olivaceus*. *Behaviour*, 90: 46–79.

Ross, M.D., Owren, M.J., and Zimmermann, E. (2009) Reconstructing the Evolution of Laughter in Great Apes and Humans. *Current Biology*, 19 (13): 1106–1111.

Roth, G., and Dicke, U. (2005) Evolution of the Brain and Intelligence. *TRENDS in Cognitive Sciences* 9(5): 250–257.

Sanchez, G. (2003) Stress-induced Vocalisation in Adult Animals. A Valid Model of Anxiety? *European Journal of Pharmacology*, 463: 133–143.

Sander, K., and Scheich, H. (2005) Left Auditory Cortex and Amygdala, but Right Insula Dominance for Human Laughing and Crying. *Journal of Cognitive Neuroscience*, 17 (10): 1519–1531.

Sander, K., and Scheich, H. (2001) Auditory Perception of Laughing and Crying Activates Human Amygdala Regardless of Attentional State. *Brain Research Cognitive Brain Research*, 12: 181–198.

Schassburger, R.M. (1993) *Vocal Communication in The Timber Wolf, Canis lupus, Linnaeus: Structure, Motivation and Ontogeny*. Berlin: Paul Parey Scientific Publishers.

Sebastian, S. (2003). Examining 1962's 'Laughter Epidemic'. *Chicago Tribune*. July 29. http://articles.chicagotribune.com/2003–07–29/features/0307290281_1_laughing-40th-anniversary-village.

Seldon, S.T. (2004) Tickle. *Journal of American Academy of Dermatology*, 50: 93–97.

Shammi ,P., and Stuss, D.T. (1999) Humor Appreciation: A Role of the Right Frontal Lobe. *Brain* 122: 657–66.

Shu, W., Cho, J.Y., Jiang, Y., Zhang, M., Weisz, D., Elder, G. A., Schmeidler, J., De Gasperi, R., Gama Sosa, M.A., Rabidou, D., Santucci, A.C., Perl, D., Morrisey, E. and Buxbaum, J.D. (2005) Altered Ultrasonic Vocalization in Mice with a Disruption in the Foxp2 Gene. *Proceedings of National Academy of Science* 102, 27 (2005): 9643–9648.

Siebert, C. (2006): The Animal Self. In *The New York Times Magazine* http://www.nytimes.com/2006/01/22/magazine/22animal.html?pagewanted=all.

Simonet, P.R., Murphy, M., and Lance, A. (2001) Laughing Dog: Vocalizations of Domestic Dogs During Play Encounters. Paper presented at the Meeting of the Animal Behavioral Society Conference, Corvallis, Oregon.

Simonet, P., Versteeg, D., and Storie, D. (2005) Dog-Laughter: Recorded Playback Reduces Stress Related Behavior in Shelter Dogs. *Proceedings of the 7th International Conference on Environmental Enrichment.*

Sroufe, L.A., and Waters, E. (1976) The Ontogenesis of Smiling and Laugher: A Perspective on the Organization of Development in Infancy. *Psychological Review,* 83:173–89.

Turner, D., and Bateson, P. (2000) *The Domestic Cat: The Biology of its Behaviour.* Cambridge: Cambridge University Press.

The University of Wolverhampton World's Ten Oldest Jokes. Dave's Quite Interesting Facts, 2008, http://uktv.co.uk/dave/item/aid/604717.

Vettin, J., and Todt, D. (2004) Laughter in Conversation: Features of Occurrence and Acoustic Structure. *Journal of Nonverbal Behavior,* 28: 93–115.

Vettin, J., and Todt, D. (2005) Human Laughter, Social Play, and Play Vocalizations of Non-Human Primates: An Evolutionary Approach. *Behaviour,* 142 (2): 217–240.

Waller, B.M., Bard, K.A., Vick, S.J., and Smith, M.C. (2007) Perceived Differences Between Chimpanzee (*Pan troglodytes*) and Human (*Homo sapiens*) Facial Expressions Are Related to Emotional Interpretation. *Journal of Comparative Psychology,* 121 (4): 398–404.

Wapner, W., Hamby, S., and Gardner, H. (1981) The Role of the Right Hemisphere in the Apprehension of Complex Linguistic Materials. *Brain and Language,* 14: 15–33.

Warren, J.E., Sauter, D.A., Eisner, F., Wiland, J., Dresner, M.A., Wise, R.J., Rosen, S., and Scott, S.K. (2006) Positive Emotions Preferentially Engage an Auditory-Motor "Mirror" System. *Journal of Neuroscience,* 26 (50): 13067–13075.

Watkins, K.E., Vargha-Khadem, F., Ashburner, J., Passingham, R.E., Connelly, A., Friston, K.J., Frackowiak, R.S., Mishkin, M., and Gadian, D.G. (2002) MRI Analysis of an Inherited Speech and Language Disorder: Structural Brain Abnormalities. *Brain,* 125: 465–478.

White, S.A., Fisher, S.E., Geschwind, D.H., Scharff, C., and Holy, T.E. (2006) Singing Mice, Songbirds, and More: Models for FOXP2 Function and Dysfunction in Human Speech and Language. *The Journal of Neuroscience.* 26 (41): 10376–10379.

Wild, B., Rodden, F.A., Grodd, W., and Ruch, W. (2003) Neural Correlates of Laughter and Humour. *Brain,* 126: 2121–2138.

Chapter 3

TOWARD LAUGHTER BENEFITS …
Le Chat Botté (Puss In Boots) Laughs the Best

Laughter: The Best Medicine?

by Ewa Wasilewska (2012)

G iven our present state of knowledge, laughter would deservedly be banned from the marketplace if it were a drug with unknown side effects" wrote Dr. Robert Provine, the world-renowned scientist on laughter in his fascinating and provoking book entitled "Laughter: A scientific investigation" (2000:207). Though this quote summarizes well what we don't know (yet) about laughter, it is also somewhat misleading: the marketplace is full of drugs whose side effects or even mechanics are barely understood, but whose effectiveness and benefits in the treatment and/or management of certain conditions are believed to outweigh the unknown factors. I am referring to brain medications developed to treat and/or control mental disorders (whose definition is quite fluid, often depending on health unrelated factors) such as depression, as well as brain disorders (for example, epilepsy). Sometimes, as for example, in the case of schizophrenia, some disorders fall under both categories. The rate of increase in mental disorders, especially depression, seems to be out of control. While in 2005 it was estimated that ca. 18.8 million of American adults (over 18) were affected by depressive disorders for which they sought help (Murray & Fortinbery 2005), the IMS[1] Health data from 2008 indicate that only two years later this number had increased to 30 million patients (Cohen 2008). Since these numbers refer only to documented cases, i.e., patients being treated with antidepressant prescriptions, one can say that over one-third (1/3) of the U.S. population is depressed.[2] The Centers for the Disease Control and Prevention report that "only" 1/10 of the U.S. adult population is afflicted with depression, i.e., a disorder that meets the criteria[3] of the Diagnostic and Statistical Manual of Mental Disorders, the 4th Edition. However, the same organization reported that the use of antidepressants went up by 400% in the last two decades in the U.S. and over one-third of Americans ages 12 and over have been

---

1   Intercontinental Marketing Services.

2   It is estimated that only 20% of the depressed population seeks treatment.

3   There are a total of nine criteria being used when defining depression, but for the purpose of the survey on which the data was based, only eight were included in the Patient Health Questionnaire as "The ninth criterion in the DSM-IV assesses suicidal or self-injurious ideation" and could not be properly evaluated through telephone intervention (Gonzales *et al.*, 2010). This survey was based on interviews of 235,067 adults (in 45 states, the District of Columbia [DC], Puerto Rico, and the U.S. Virgin Islands), who then were "diagnosed" as having depression if two or more criteria out of seven were met. The most depressed states in the U.S. are "southeastern states, where a greater prevalence of chronic conditions associated with depression has been observed (e.g., obesity and stroke)." (http://www.cdc.gov/Features/dsDepression.)

taking antidepressant medications. Furthermore, the National Health and Nutrition Examination Survey reported that "antidepressants were the third most common prescription drug taken by Americans of all ages from 2005 to 2008 and the most frequently used medication by people between the ages of 18 and 44" (Wood 2011). This means that the fastest-growing market for any medication is, in all probability, "the brain market[4]."

The effectiveness of the known and prescribed brain medications is continuously debated, especially because the exact "mechanics" of such drugs are not fully understood. The recent figures suggest that antidepressants work for only between 30% to 45% of the depressed patient population i.e., only the most severely depressed patients benefit from these drugs, while the rest of the population would be just as "happy" taking a placebo.[5] In view of such statistics one should not be surprised that Charles Barber's book, *Comfortably Numb: How Psychiatry is Medicating a Nation,* has become such a bestseller immediately after its publication in February 2008.[6] This nation of overmedicated individuals is more than just a social, economic and political problem. This is also a serious health risk since various brain medications appear to be linked to violence, suicide, brain tumors, etc.[7] However, these side effects did not ban them from the market, although regulatory warnings have been issued by various governments including the U.S. and Canada.

Thus, even if laughter were to become a "drug," it would not have been banned from the market because, in view of the recent research, its benefits would have been much more important than its risks[8]. The potential of laughter as a medicine to treat or alleviate different disorders is becoming more of a reality than ever before with increasing knowledge of its origin, mechanics, and functions. Jaak Panksepp of the Washington State University at Pullman[9] and one of the "discoverers" of laughter in rats, refers to this potential by stating that research on laughter may help us to " … even stumble on new molecules to alleviate depression as well as disorders of excessive exuberance [such as mania and attention deficit/hyperactivity disorder]" (2003)[10].

---

4   This includes both mental and other brain disorders as they are often treated by the same or similar medications.

5   Of course, there is always a question as to whether patients comply in taking medications.

6   While most reviews of this book have been positive and agreeable on many points, there are some critics of Barber's statistics and "exaggerations." For example, see Kramer 2008.

7   The effectiveness of anti-depressants and other similar medications is a hot subject among medical providers and scientists, and, obviously, outside of the scope of this book. For reader-friendly explanations of its main issues see Szalavitz 2012.

8   Actually humor/laughter therapy is already "prescribed" by numerous hospitals in the United States (e.g., University of Maryland Medical Center, Miami's Children Hospital, Rochester General Hospital), which provide patients with comedic material in the form of books, movies, comedy channels, even with clown rounds! This laughter therapy doesn't target any specific areas of the human body but rather focuses on providing relaxation (gelototherapy; e.g., Askenazy 1987).

9   Formerly a professor of psychobiology at Bowling Green State University in Ohio, where his research on rats was conducted.

10   Potential for using study of human and other animal laughter and/or humor for understanding better and consequently providing a better treatment for patients with so-called 'brain disorders' seems to be of a great extent. For example, it is known that children with autism and Down's syndrome laugh, but frequency of laughter and situations in which they laugh as well as their responses to humor, differ from children who are not inflicted with these disorders (e.g., Vasudevi, Williams & Vaughan: 2002). Or, is this really a disorder? Recent genetic research explores an option that such disorders like autism, ADHD, Asperger's and Tourette's Syndrome might be a result of human hybridization with Neanderthals as 1% to 4% of all human (except for populations who have not migrated out of Africa) genome is of the Neanderthal origin. Thus, these disorders are not necessarily disorders but species-specific cognitive and behavioral adaptations. Laughter and humor might be among these adaptations. However, at this point this is just a speculation.

Laughter as a Potential "Drug"

Almost each and every article, book, or website dealing with alternative medicine refer to benefits of laughter and humor, or at least to positive attitude, which is to help one will himself or herself out of sickness.[11] The idea that there is a mind–body connection is actually quite ancient[12] but it has been popularized by Norman Cousin (1979), who believed to cure himself from a very painful, degenerative disease (a form of painful arthritis known as *ankylosing spondylitis*) with mega-doses of vitamin C and comedy shows[13]. Among other things he reported, "ten minutes of solid belly laughter would give [him] two hours of pain-free sleep" (1989: 126). Others jumped on the proverbial "wagon," and in the blink of an eye, the general public has accepted health benefits of laughter and humor as a fact. The so-called laughter-clubs have been established all over the U.S. and abroad.[14] In almost no time laughter and humor have become associated with having positive attitude to life that was to conquer any sickness. However, the truth is not that simple.

Until very recently, hard scientific evidence in support of the benefits of laughter and/or humor in medicine and in the effectiveness of related therapeutic approaches has been lacking.[15] While laughter alone involves definitely two brain functions, i.e., motion and emotion ("basic instincts"), the third one, cognition, is connected with humor leading to laughter. As discussed in the previous chapter, laughter is an involuntary[16], respiratory–emotional behavior. Thus, potentially, laughter and humor influence and help to "exercise" our intellect/intelligence (cognition), mental stability (emotion), and physical parts related to

U of U   ANTHROPOLOGY OF HUMOR
RX# U0264984   DATE 04/25/2012

Dr. Ewa Wasilewska

TAKE ONE CAPSULE BY MOUTH AS NEEDED

LAUGHTER HO HA 40 MG CAPSULE

DR. SILLY GAL M.D.   QTY:120
Do not operate heavy machinery while laughing. Too much laughter can be harmful to your health or even fatal.

breathing (e.g., lungs), moving (e.g., limbs and abdominal areas), etc. In fact, laughter in humans involves almost the entire body, so no-one should be surprised that its benefits may extend even beyond the above.

---

11   This is actually quite annoying because almost everyone who has learned about my research into this topic seemed to be more "informed" about it than scholars specializing in laughter and humor. Some were almost shocked that such a topic even requires researching (sort of "and your name is Bond, James Bond" response).

12   Hippocrates' (ca. 460–377 B.C.) work on paleohumorology, although it has nothing to do with humor (in his work humor refers to fluids), was a precursor to mind–body connection through his search for the balance of a human body. The four humors represented four related personalities (blood—sanguinicus; phlegm—flegmaticus; black bile—melancholicus; yellow bile—cholericus). They have been further researched by the 2nd century A.D. Graeco–Roman doctor Galen (Claudius Galenus) who proposed that in sickness a body might be lacking sufficient amounts of a humor so through the use of medicine (father of pharmacology) a proper balance can be restored.

13   The Marx Brothers' movies and Candid Camera shows are reported to be his favorites.

14   If you are interested check http://www.worldlaughtertour.com for one near you.

15   Positive attitude (whatever it means since its definition is quite subjective) does not seem to have any curative physical powers that can be proven in a scientific way.

16   For the purpose of this chapter, an exact definition of laughter is not necessary as it was already explained in the previous one.

Reward Pathway

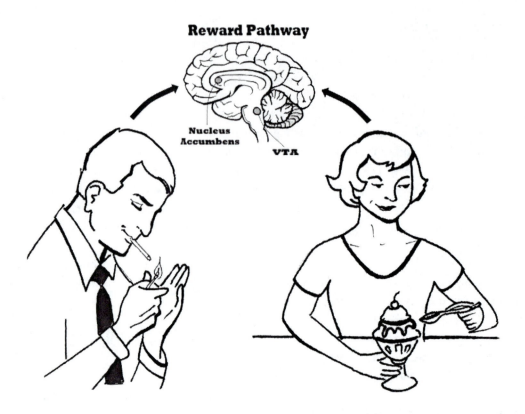

The Association for Applied and Therapeutic Humor (http://www.aath.org) posts a list[17] of "What everyone should know about humor and laughter" (http://www.laffingoutloud.com/pdf/aath.pdf) on the Internet, and provides access to its own library, which is designed to introduce the reader to this topic. This list is too extensive to be discussed here, and some claims need more research before definitive statements can be made. However, there is a general agreement that laughter and humor[18] may help in counteracting the effects of some mental disorders such as depression, by elevating the brain secretions (growth hormones) responsible for increasing "happy" moods and by "manipulating" the reward center of the brain into rewarding response. Lee Berk[19] and his team noted (American Physiological Society session at Experimental Biology 2006) that happy and mirthful laughter (watching a funny movie, for example) increased beta-endorphins[20] by 27% and human growth hormones by 87% (Natural News 2006). Furthermore, the benefits of the mirthful laughter during one single session lasted from 12 to 24 hours.[21] Even an anticipation of laughter improved the functioning of the immune system by suppressing

---

17   This list is based on research done by Dr. Ron Berk of the Johns Hopkins University and is periodically updated upon publications of new research. The 2008 update was done by Dr. Rod Martin, Dr. Don Baird and Dr. Bob Nozik.

18   This list divides health benefits between humor and laughter. However, since laughter is an expression of humor, I am not sure that such a division actually is necessary or correct.

19   Just a note: Dr. Lee Berk, a leading scholar on benefits of laughter and humor, has been encouraged and funded at the beginning of his research by Norman Cousins.

20   They ease up depression.

21   McGhee reported that the effects of a strengthened immune system lasts for "30 minutes for IgA, IgG, number of B cells, activation and number of T cells, activation and number of natural killer cells, and gamma interferon. The immunoenhancement effect was still present

the release of cortisol (stress hormone) by 39%, adrenaline (epinephrine) by 70% and dopac (a dopamine catabolite which contributes to the production of adrenaline) by 38% as reported by Lee Berk and his team[22] (American Physiological Society 2008). At the same time, "happy laughter" activates more T-cells, increases natural gamma interferon (disease-fighting protein), elevates levels of immunoglobulin A (IgA), G (IgG) and Complement 3 (protein) and produces natural killer (NK) cells (McGhee 1996, 1999; Berk *et al.* 2001). The increase in immunoglobulin A made by B cells in bone marrow and mucosae is noticeable, for example, in saliva that is believed to protect us from common respiratory diseases such as the cold or flu. So watching an hour of a funny video boosts our protection against common sicknesses. The increase in B cells that are responsible for making immunoglobulins, of which the most important seems to be immunoglobulin G (antibodies), boost all the other immune defenses such as T-cells, natural killer (NK) cells, and gamma interferon. The effectiveness of humor and laughter on the immune system has been also reported by other scholars focusing on various natural immune defenses such as NK cells (e.g., Lefcourt, Davidson-Katz & Kueneman 1990; Bennett *et al.* 2003[23]). Thus, laughing and enjoying humor appear to fight some deadly intruders such as tumors, viruses or other kinds of infections.

Laughing is known to decrease pain but this might be just a distraction i.e., it allows us to "forget" that we are in pain. Since laughter increases the heart rate and oxygen intake while lowering blood pressure, it seems to be quite beneficial in improving the functioning of the cardiovascular system. According to the research of cardiologists at the University of Maryland Medical Center led by Michael Miller (press releases, 2000, 2005), laughter increases blood flow by expanding the endothelium, i.e., an inner lining of blood vessels. By maintaining a healthy level of endothelial cells with humor and laughter, "treatments" of disorders like pathological vasoconstriction (narrowing blood vessels thus limiting blood and causing high blood pressure), blood clotting, atherosclerosis, inflammation etc., might be enhanced.[24]

The vascular benefits of humor in connection with a body movement may work as an aerobic exercise.[25] William F. Fry, professor emeritus at Stanford University and a precursor on laughter research and its physiological benefits[26] (for example, 1971, 1977, 1992, 1994; Fry & Stroft 1971; Fry & Savin 1988) stated: "Laughing 100 times amounts to the same exercise as riding a stationary bike for 15 minutes or using a rowing machine for 10 minutes."[27] Buchowski and his team (2007) measured energy expenditure (EE) and heart rate (HR) of 45 adult friends dyads when they watched funny and not-funny video clips in the controlled environment. They concluded that genuine voiced laughter increased 10–20% in both EE and HR. This translates to burning between 20 to 40 calories during 10–15 minutes of belly laughter.[28] Like any physical exercise, laughter increases endorphins that are essential in fighting stress and depression as

---

12 hours later for IgA, IgG, number of B cells, complement 3 and gamma interferon" (1999).

22   Berk, Lee, Stanley A. Tan & Dottie Berk: Cortisol and Cetecholamine Stress Hormone Decrease is Associated with the Behavior of Perceptual Anticipation of Mirthful Laughter. Paper presented at the 121st Annual Meeting of the American Physiological Society, Experimental Biology 2008.

23   Their research involved 33 healthy adult female subjects divided into humor and distraction groups. It measured immune system functioning (specifically release of the NK cells) in connection with "happy" laughter or self-reported stress.

24   I am not sure about the importance of their findings regarding an observation that people with heart diseases laugh less and are more angry/hostile. Common sense dictates that we are less cheerful when sick because there is not much to laugh about. It is difficult to laugh when one is depressed so one of the main points of benefits of laughter and humor is to be able to induce them to alleviate both physical and mental pain.

25   The term "internal jogging" is sometimes used for laughter (McGhee 1999).

26   For his brief biography see http://www.aath.org/gold/fry.html.

27   His most famous sayings have been recorded at http://www.laughterlinks.com/flash/quotes.swf.

28   So keep laughing 15 minutes a day and between 4 to 5 pounds of your weight will "laugh out" of your body in a year.

well as pain. The breathing patterns occurring especially with deep belly laughter might also be helpful with improving the respiratory system by providing additional ventilation and clearing impurities.[29]

In view of the above, one may think that finally science has caught up with common sense and there is no doubt that a good sense of humor is very beneficial for overall physical and mental health of an individual[30]. However, Boyle and Reid's research[31] on the effects of humor on health conducted on 504 subjects (2004), does not support the working hypothesis that those of us who have a better sense of humor also enjoy better health! Furthermore, Martin points out that data on longevity and sense of humor indicate that "humorless people" live longer (2006), but those with a good sense[32] of humor probably enjoy a better quality of life. These findings seem to be discouraging but one must remember that these results can be explained in numerous ways. Boyle and Reid (2004) pointed out that the responses they received were dependent on the samples used: whether subjects were in good health or not, whether they were students or not, etc. While validity of the Multidimensional Sense of Humor Scale (MSHS)[33] instrument is shown by their research; it must be also pointed out that the MSHS is not designed to measure specific physiological health beneficial changes, as discussed above. It only deals with psychological factors such as optimism, self-esteem, depression etc., leaving the perception of one's health to the subject's self-evaluation. Consequently, Boyle and Reid's results refer only to psychological benefits that are demonstrated by this research such as using humor as coping mechanism or lowering pain (2004). Regardless, this research seems to show that laughing more does not guarantee good health. However, due to its nature, it cannot be denied that laughing and humor may improve well-functioning of specific body systems. Martin's longevity data (2006) might be explained by the more optimistic and possibly careless nature of those with better sense of humor, which could shorten their lifespan. They may take more risks whether climbing the Himalayas, ignoring their health problems, or overindulging in bad habits. Both data can also be explained by differences in defining such concepts as laughter, humor, and sense of humor.[34] Laughing a lot does not mean that one has a great sense of humor. Laughing at funny videos does not translate to having a good sense of humor either. We must remember that most of our daily laughter comes not from observing funny cartoons, stand-up comics, or comedies, but from every day interactions with others. While Boyle and Reid's research (2004) focused on the sense of humor and its relation to health, their definition of sense of humor and health self-evaluation might not be the same as the one used by Sven Svebak of the Norwegian University of Science and Technology, whose research resulted in contradictory data. Svebak and his team demonstrated that actually people with a great sense of humor outlived those who don't have it by 35% (Elias 2007). His research was based on tracking lives of 54,000 Norwegians for seven years and took into consideration other variables which affect survival.

29   Belly laughter might be clearing lungs since it releases more air than it takes in.
30   The creator of Theory L (a cognitive-shirt theory), Robert Latta, focuses on relaxation as the evidence or rather a defining factor of humor (1999) that brings out these positive effects. However, he also believes that "'the audible aspect' gives laughter much of its power to bring relaxation, and thus it is not surprising that it has developed to the point it has in the course of evolution" (1999: 52). As convincing as his argument may appear, the audibility of human laughter might be one of the factors but certainly not the main one (see discussion in the previous chapter). Furthermore, if relaxation is to define humor, there should be then little doubt that even rats have it.
31   This appears to be the most comprehensive research on this topic in a diversified group ("community group, university students, and respondents with a medical condition") with control over multiple variables. While its main hypothesis has not been proven, it certainly raised new issues to be investigated further.
32   See footnote #91 of the Introduction.
33   Sheldon Cooper's "Humometer" (The Bing Bang Theory).
34   Some of these problems are addressed by Bennett & Lengaher 2006.

The results of monitoring 2,015 cancer patients suggest that people with a great sense of humor have 70% more chances of prolonging their lives.

Humor may increase intellectual performance as the research at Johns Hopkins University Medical School indicates.[35] Dr. Ron Berk is a leader in this field, having published numerous articles and books[36] on this topic and having shown the statistical validity of his experiments and the benefits of laughter in teaching and learning processes[37] (e.g., Berk & Nanda 2006; Berk, R. 2002).

Social benefits of humor and laughter in humor are incontestable. They increase self-esteem, creativity as well as attract others for company. This is even confirmed by the research on dogs. Simonet, Versteeg, and Storie noted that dog-laughter or playing the recording of its vocalizations "diffuses stress-related behavior and initiates pro-social behavior in shelter dogs, thus potentially reducing residencies at the shelter before adoption" (2005).

Recognizing that humans and animals experience the same emotions such as joy, pain, fear, or lust, and researching the same brain mechanisms underlying these emotions are of great importance. Understanding how these mechanisms work may lead to new revolutionary therapeutic approaches to treat mental disorders and other brain diseases without overmedicating and with fewer side effects than modern medications. The first step has already been made: we have recognized laughter for what it is, i.e., an ancient and involuntary response to various stimuli.[38] The next step is to find out if it is possible to consciously control it[39] or trigger it, if its benefits are potentially as rewarding as they seem to be. Some of the possible benefits emerging from the research on laughter and joy are mentioned, for example, by Panksepp and Burgdorf (2003). They include better treatments for ADHD (attention deficit hyperactivity disorders), drug addictions (Panksepp, Knutson & Burgdorf 2002[40]), and especially new treatments for depression. The last is so important because existing brain medications are designed to suppress feelings of unhappiness and other negative emotions. The "laughter"-based drugs could be designed to induce or to elevate positive emotions by increasing the sense of rewards that seems to be missing from the brains of those who are severely depressed.

---

35   Students taking the identical exam scored higher when instructions were provided in a humorous way.

36   A list of Dr. Ron Berk's publications can be found at http://www.ronberk.com/html/articles.html.

37   There are others researchers who have pointed out similar benefits of humor in education and at work (e.g., Morreall 1999; Liebertz 2005; Martin 2006). Just a note: I have been incorporating humor into this book in order to facilitate its comprehension and break up monotonous narrative. Hope it works!

38   Rats and humans are believed to be separated in their evolutionary process ca. 75 millions years ago.

39   Outside of humor, which induces "normal" laughter when a humorous situation is evaluated as funny and not offensive "enough."

40   This article is especially important because, using an evolutionary approach, its authors postulate that "certain drug addictions and social interactions utilize some of the same neural circuits" (2002: 465). Since then their premise has been supported by many other researchers (see Chapter 2). Thus, understanding this connection in less complex organisms, for example, rats, "may enable scientists to predict drug-related phenomena such as abuse potential, anatomical location of mediating neural substrates, and the psychological impact of withdrawal" (2002: 459).

I believe that laughter as a drug is not about having a positive attitude and/or willing oneself to health only. It is more about what part(s) of neural circuitry of laughter can be "manipulated" in order to enhance the overall functioning of our bodies or its parts, to repair broken circuits, and to induce positive moods and/or physical reactions to be held cumulatively when making positive behaviors without relying on the "medically" induced laughter. Can humor be used to replace addictions to different drugs, etc., providing the same reaction as they do in the reward center of the brain? If so, does it mean that we may become addicted to humor?[41]

In Lieu of Conclusions: *Le Chat Botté* Laughs The Best

In view of the above, it is reasonable to argue that nature/evolution has equipped humans (and possibly other animals) with a beneficial, simple, and effective strategy for self-healing: laughing. Over a period of time, acoustic and other characteristics of laughter could have changed and with or through the emergence of humor, this seizure-like activity could have been induced in a more "controllable" manner, turning them both into effective weapons to counteract and repair "technical difficulties" (disorders) of our bodies and minds. In my view, Polimeni and Reiss (2006) are quite correct in calling for more research on humor as an adaptive strategy within an evolutionary context, preferably both social and physical. After all, laughter neural circuits are located somewhere in the subcortex, the most ancient and vital part of our and other animals' brains, and they must be there for a reason. I find it hard to believe that laughter survived through thousands of generations just "because." In all probability, laughter has more than one function, all developing at different times under different evolutionary constraints. So, yes, Provine's statement that "laughter no more evolved to make us feel good or improve our health than walking evolved to promote cardiovascular fitness" (2000:189–190) is probably correct but … after all, walking actually promotes cardiovascular fitness, although it did not emerge for this reason; so why is it so difficult to believe that laughter may do the same (or something similar)? The multi-functionality of a human (and other animal) body and mind's units are not disputed by anyone: they exist for one or more than one reason.

Scholars who have been trying to understand the mystery behind cats' purring[42] raised the identical issue. While, so far, there is no hard evidence that purring[43] is the feline equivalent of laughter,[44] an analogy can be made. Feline purring has been already compared to smiling[45] as reported by Stuart (2009). However, I believe that Kelly Morgan actually meant "laughter" since the reasoning provided "People will smile when they're nervous, when they want something, when they're happy … " describes laughter, not smiling. Like human laughter, cats' purring begins in the brain and probably its original "terminal" is in

---

41 A few years ago, I would consider even asking such a question to be completely an overstretch of others' and my imagination. However, today, I seriously consider such a possibility since, for example, seizures are known to be one of multiple symptoms of drug withdrawals. Were my seizures then one of the withdrawal symptoms from humor/laughter addiction?

42 No, I am not a "crazy cat lady" although I am a lady and I love cats. Cats have been selected for the discussion here because I have been living with and observing them for almost thirty years (four cats total in this time span). Furthermore, I have been somewhat mystified (and "insulted") that both rats and dogs have been shown to laugh, while cats have been "ignored" by laughter researchers.

43 The term "purring" has been used for vocalizations of other mammals too but only "purring cats" and two species of genets (cute cat-like [feliform] mammals) meet a specialized definition of purring (e.g., Peters: 2002; Eklund *et al.* 2010).

44 I am not aware of any research connecting laughter with purring in cats.

45 Kelly Morgan, DVM, Clinical Instructor, Chicago Center for Veterinary Medicine of the University of Illinois at Urbana-Champaign College of Veterinary Medicine.

the feline subcortex (neural oscillator)[46]. The neurons from the oscillatory system (Remmers & Gautier 1972) then travel to the laryngeal and diaphragmatic muscles causing rhythmic vibrations separating vocal cords on inhalation and exhalation[47]. If we are to speculate that feline purring is an equivalent of human laughter, then we may also want to speculate about their ability to use more vocalizations when communicating with humans—a language-like interspecies communication. The high frequency *"miau" ("meow")* seems to be universal[48] in all cats, which have been raised with or around humans[49]. They seem to use it every time, with or without purring, when they demand attention from humans or are willing to "warn" them. Since they are capable of making other sounds, the choice of this persistent, even obnoxious, *"miau"* to communicate with humans might be somewhat conscious. It could have developed at the time when the closest relative of a modern domestic cat *(Felis catus)*, African/Middle Eastern wildcat *(Felis silvestric lybica)* began to live with or near humans ca. 9,000 to 10,000 years ago[50] (Driscoll *et al.* 2007; Driscoll *et al.* 2009). Purring is one of the means of feline communication and *"miau"* is a version of cry, which usually gets the attention from nurturing parents[51] (McComb *et al.* 2009). Consequently, this inter-mammalian communication "initiated" by felines might have its roots in the "observation" of humans reacting not only to their crying offspring but also "drooling" over kittens' cries which have similar acoustic[52].

As discussed above, cats are quite opportunistic animals and try to conserve their energy as much as possible (e.g., Turner & Bateson 2000; Lyons 2006). They are quite "lazy"—domestic cats sleep for an average 13 to 18 hours per day. Even wild cats spend most of their time "relaxing" on a tree or on the ground. While this "laziness" cannot be good for their bones, cats show remarkable ability not only not to break them but also heal them much faster than other animals.[53] The connection between this healing ability and purring has been made by Muggenthaler & Wright (2003) after Clinton Rubin's presentation at the Welcome Trust in 1999[54], when he suggested that anabolic frequencies between 20–50 Hz (at low dB) stimulate bone growth and strength so are important not only for maintaining healthy bones but

---

46   I must admit—I've got defeated when trying to understand neural pathways in cats. Even those who understand how they work, still don't know where purring originates (Schötz & Eklund 2011). I am just happy to "report" that not only do cats have a cerebral cortex, but also all the gyrus connections that are essential in humans to laugh and process humor; thus, I won't give up on "cat meows."

47   See vocalized laughter in humans and chimpanzees as discussed in the previous chapter. Since cats purr at the rate of 25 to 150–200 vibrations per second (Hz), it seems reasonable to assume that they make more than one sound per inhalation/exhalation. If this is correct, feline purring would be remarkably more similar to human laughter than to chimpanzees'. However, the *"miau"* vocalization is limited to exhalation only.

48   The ancient Egyptian term for a cat was *"miau."* Consequently, I am following the ancient Egyptian "spelling" (Polish and Italian too), with the reference to cats' "vocabulary." The word for this sound is of onomatopoeic origin in all languages that I am familiar with.

49   Adult cats don't *"miau"* with each other. This sound is only used when kittens need the attention of their mom-cat.

50   Discovery of farming and necessity for storing food by humans seem to have provided small cats with an option to acquire "fast/processed" food in contrast of "cooking from scratch."

51   The idea that cats *"miau"* because they need humans to do something for them is neither new, nor shocking. Many veterinarians and animal researchers have commented on it but McComb *et al.* were finally able to formulate it in scientific and convincing terms (2009).

52   A strongly suspected cat-lover under an Internet name of "burntbiscuits" posted the following comment in 2009 under Lyons' article: "Cats are born with the genetic inability to make the "n" sound in their voicebox. In fact when you think they are saying *"meow"* they are actually saying 'me-now.' Their proximity to an object helps the human understand the context of 'meow.' I.e. Next to the food bowl 'feed me-now,' next to the door 'me-now out/inside,' rolling on the floor in front of you 'pet/notice me-now,' etc. Thus, breaking the cat/human language barrier." Now, we only need to prove that cats invented the English language too!

53   "If you put a cat and a sack of broken bones in the same room the bones will heal," goes the old veterinarian joke as cited by Muggenthaler & Wright (2003) and Lyons (2006).

54   "Strain mediate augmentation of bone mass and morphology: Is it possible to harness the anabolic potential of mechanical stimuli without necessarily requiring exercise?" Since I was unable to locate Rubin's original paper I rely on its summary provided by Muggenthaler & Wright (2003).

also for healing. Sure enough: cats' purring frequencies are between 20 Hz and 150 Hz (e.g., Lyons 2006). Even more amazing is the fact that "all the [cat] species [used in the experiment][55] had frequencies, notably 25 Hz, 50 Hz, 100 Hz, 125 Hz, that correspond exactly with the best frequencies determined by the most research for bone growth, fracture healing, pain relief, relief of breathlessness, and inflammation" (Muggenthaler & Wright 2003). The 25 Hz frequency also works on humans helping their wounds to heal faster (Benjaminin L. Hart, DVM, Ph.D., a distinguished Professor Emeritus at the University of California, Davis School of Veterinary Medicine; After Stuart 2009). No wonder, then, that cats purr not only when they are happy, but also when they are under stress and in pain! They seem to "know" how to make the best use of their "nine lives."

We still don't know whether purring is a voluntary or involuntary action in cats, especially since not all cats seem to purr[56]. Felines which do not purr are those which roar[57] (lion, *Panthera leo*; tiger, *Panthera tigris*; jaguar, *Panthera onca*; leopard[58], *Panthera pardus*). Those, which don't roar, purr (the rest[59]). This simple division also seems to point out that big cats, which don't purr, must move more as they cover bigger territories than small (here: domestic) cats which are happy to move from one couch to another as the food is served to them.

Is it possible that, like with laughter, purring is involuntary but cats have "learned" how to induce it the same way as we induce laughter through humor or other stimuli[60]? If this is correct, cats might have "discovered" their natural survival mechanism ("an internal vibrational therapeutic system") in purring before we, as humans, are even ready to realize our similar potential in laughter and humor. So who is laughing (or purring or …) now?

The research on laughter and humor is a fascinating topic but not a field. Thus, it requires a much closer cooperation between various, seemingly unconnected, disciplines than we have today.[61] As demonstrated (hopefully) in the last two chapters laughter and humor are serious matters, studying which might not

---

55   Cheetah's frequencies are plus-minus 2Hz off from other cats'.

56   The above research was conducted on recorded purrs of cheetah, puma, serval, ocelot and domestic cats.

57   The original division on purring versus roaring cats was made by Richard Owen (1834/1835—after Enklund 2010). The reasons for this division and its classificatory value are subjects of an ongoing debate.

58   There is no clear agreement on classification of Snow and Clouded Leopards (e.g., Peters 2002; Eklund 2010).

59   There are 35 to 40 species of cats (Sunquist & Sunquist 2002; Wilson & Reeder: 2005). Domestic cats are divided into 60 or so breeds (Menotti-Raymond *et al.*: 2008).

60   Feline purring seems to be also individualized (Schötz & Eklund 2011).

61   For example, neurologists usually don't care too much about cultural aspects of humor and/laughter, veterinarians are not in the habit of talking with psychologists/psychiatrists (unless they need one for personal reasons), evolutionary biologists are not particularly fond of all the above, and medical doctors have usually no time to listen to their patients.

only improve quality of but also save many lives. My gratitude goes to all scholars who have been brave enough to approach these subjects with the attention they deserve. My journey into the mysteries of the brain, laughter and humor continues with the hope that at the end these scholars will laugh the best![62]

Bibliography

American Physiological Society. (April 10, 2008) Anticipating a Laugh Reduces Our Stress Hormones, Study Shows. *Science Daily*, http://www.sciencedaily.com/releases/2008/04/080407114617.htm.

Askenazy, J.J.M. (1987) The Functions and Dysfunctions of Laughter. *Journal of General Psychology,* 114 (4): 317–334.

Barber, C. (2008) *Comfortably Numb: How Psychiatry is Medicating a Nation.* New York: Pantheon.

Bennett, M.P, and Lengacher, C. (2006) Humor and Laughter May Influence Health: II. Complementary Therapies and Humor in a Clinical Population. *Oxford Journals, Evidence-based Complementary and Alternative Medicine* 3, 187–190.

Bennett, M.P., Zeller J.M., Rosenberg L., and McCann, J. (2003) The Effect of Mirthful Laughter on Stress and Natural Killer Cell Activity. *Alternative Therapies in Health and Medicine,* 9: 38–45.

Berk, L., Tan S.A., and Berk, D. (2008) Cortisol and Cetecholamine Stress Hormone Decrease is Associated with the Behavior of Perceptual Anticipation of Mirthful Laughter. Paper presented at the 121st Annual Meeting of the American Physiological Society, Experimental Biology.

Berk, L.S, Tan, S.A, Fry, W.F, Napier, B.J, Lee, J.W., Hubbard, R.W, Lewis, J.E. and Eby, W.C. (1989) Neuroendocrine and Stress Hormone Changes During Mirthful Laughter. *The American Journal of the Medical Sciences,* 298: 390–396.

Berk, L.S, Felten, D.L., Bittman, B.B., and Westengard, J. (2001) Modulation of Neuroimmune Parameters During the Eustress of Humor-Associated Mirthful Laughter. *Alternative Therapies in Health and Medicine* 7, (2): 62–76.

Berk, R.A., and Nanda, J.P. (2006) A Randomized Trial of Humor Effects on Test Anxiety and Test Performance. *Humor: International Journal of Humor Research,* 19:425–454.

Berk, R. (2002) *Humor as an Instructional Defibrillator: Evidence-Based Techniques in Teaching and Assessment.* Sterling, Virginia: Stylus Publishing.

Boyle, G.J., and Joss-Reid, J.M. (2004) Relationship of Humour to Health: A Psychometric investigation. *British Journal of Health Psychology,* 9 (1): 51–66.

Buchowski, M.S., Majchrzak, K.M., Blomquist, K., Chen, K.Y., Byrne, D.W., and Bachorowski, J.A. (2006) Energy Expenditure of Genuine Laughter. *International Journal of Obesity,* 31: 131–137.

Cohen, R. (April 19, 2008) One Side Effect of Surge in Antidepressant Use: Debate. *StarTribune.com,* www.startribune.com.

Cousins, N. (1979) *The Anatomy of an Illness as Perceived by the Patient.* New York: E.P. Dutton.

Cousins, N. (1989) *Head First: The Biology of Hope.* New York: Norton.

Driscoll, C.A., Menotti-Raymond, M., Roca, A.L., Hupe, K., Johnson, W.E., Geffen, E., Harley, E.H., Delibes, M., Pontier, D., Kitchener, A.C., Yamaguchi, N., O'Brien, S.J., and Macdonald, D.W. (2007) The Near East Origin of Cat Domestication. *Science,* 317: 519–523.

Driscoll, C.A., Clutton-Brock, J., Kitchener, A.C., and O'Brien, S.J. (2009) The Taming of the Domestic Cat. *Scientific American,* June: 68–75.

Eklund, R., Peters, G. and Duthie, E.D. (2010) An Acoustic Analysis of Puriing in the Cheetah *(Acinonyx jubatus)* and in the Domestic Cat *(Felis catus). Proceedings of Fonetik.* June. Lund University, Lund, Sweden. pp.17–22.

---

62   "He who laughs last, laughs best," as the old English proverb says. Or was it Friedrich Nietzsche (1844–1900), a German-Swiss philosopher and writer, who proclaimed, "He who laughs best today, will also laughs last?"

Elias, M. (March 11, 2007) A Laugh a Day May Help Keep Death Further Away. *USA Today.* (http://www.usatoday.com/news/health/2007–03–11-health-laughter_N.htm?csp=34.)

Fry, W.F. (1971) Laughter: Is It the Best Medicine? *Stanford M.D.,* 10: 16–20.

Fry, W.F. (1977) The Respiratory Components of Mirthful Laughter. *Journal of Biological Psychology,* 19: 39–50.

Fry, W.F. (1992) The Physiologic Effects of Humor, Mirth, and Laughter. *Journal of the American Medical Association,* 267 (13): 1857–1858.

Fry, W.F. (1994) The Biology of Humor. *Humor: International Journal of Humor Research* 7(2): 111–126.

Fry, W.F., and Savin, W.M. (1988) Mirthful Laughter and Blood Pressure. *Humor. International Journal of Humor Research* 1: 49–62.

Fry, W.F., and Stroft, P.E. (1971) Mirth and Oxygen Saturation of Peripheral Blood. *Psychotherapy and Psychosomatics,* 19: 76–84.

Gonzalez, O., Berry, J.T., McKnight-Eily, L.R., Strine, T., Edwards, V.J., Lu, H., and Croft, J.B. (2010) Current Depression Among Adults, United States, 2006 and 2008. *Morbidity and Mortality Weekly Report.* Centers for Disease Control and Prevention. (http://www.cdc.gov/mmwr/preview/mmwrhtml/mm5938a2.htm?s_cid=mm5938a2_e%0D%0A.)

Kramer, Peter D. (2008) Prozac Nation? The Returns Aren't In. *Slate* (February 11, 2008). (http://www.slate.com/id/2184073.)

Latta, R.L. (1999) *The Basic Humor Process. A Cognitive-Shift Theory and the Case Against Congruity.* Berlin, New York: Mouton de Gruyter.

Liebertz, C. (2005) A Health Laugh. Got problems? A Little Humor Will Help You Get Past Them—and Could Even Ward Off Illness. *Scientific American.* September 21.

Lefcourt, H.M., Davidson-Katz, K. and Kueneman, K. (1990) Humor And Immune-System Functioning. *Humor. International Journal of Humor Research,* 3(3): 305–321.

Lyons, L.A. (2006) Why Do Cats Purr? *Scientific American.* April 2. (http://www.scientificamerican.com/article.cfm?id=why-do-cats-purr.)

Martin, R. (2006) *Psychology of Humor: An Integrative Approach.* Burlington, MA., London: Elsevier Academic Press.

McComb, K., Taylor, A.M., Wilson, C., and Charlton, B.D. (2009) The Cry Embedded Within the Purr. *Current Biology,* 19 (13): R507-R508.

McGhee, P.E. (1999) *Health, Healing and the Amuse System.* Dubuque, Iowa: Kendall/Hunt Publishing Company.

McGhee, P.E. (1999) Humor and Health. *Holistic Online,* http://holisticonline.com/Humor_mcghee_article.htm.

Menott-Raymond, M., David, V.A., Pflueger, S.M., Lindblad-Toh, K., Wade, C.M., O'Brien, S.J., and Johnson, W.E. (2008) Patterns of Molecular Variation Among Cat Breeds. *Genomics,* 91: 1–11.

Morreall, J. (1991) Humor And Work. *Humor. International Journal of Humor Research.* 4 (4/4): 359–373.

Muggenthaler, E. Von, and Wright, B. (2003) Solving The Cat's Purr Mystery Using Accelerometers. *Brüel and Kjaer Magazine,* 1. (http://www.bksv.com/NewsEvents/BruelKjaerMagazine/OtherArticles/TheCatsPurrMystery.aspx.)

Murray, B., and Fortinbery, A. (January 15, 2005) Depression Facts and Statistics. *Uplift Program. (http://www.upliftprogram.com/depression_stats.html.)*

(July 17, 2006) Natural News Maybe Laughter Really Is the Best Medicine, And It's Prophylactic! Press release, http://www.naturalnews.com/z019675.html.

Panksepp, J. (2003) Neuroscience: Feeling the Pain of Social Loss. *Science,* 302: 237–239.

Panksepp, J., Knutson, B., and Burgdorf, J. (2002) The Role of Brain Emotional Systems in Addictions: A Neuro-Evolutionary Perspective and New 'Self-Report' Animal Model. *Addiction,* 97: 459–469.

Peters, G. (2002) Purring And Similar Vocalizations in Mammals. *Mammal Review,* 32 (4): 245–271.

Polimeni, J., and Reiss, J.P. (2006) The First Joke: Exploring the Evolutionary Origins of Humor. *Evolutionary Psychology,* 4: 347–366.

Provine, R. (2001) *Laughter: A Scientific Investigation.* New York: Penguin Books.

Reddy, V., Williams, E., and Vaughan, A. (2002) Sharing Humour And Laughter Autism and Down's Syndrome. *British Journal of Psychology,* 93: 219–242.

Remmers, J.E., and Gautier, H. (1972) Neural and Mechanical Mechanisms of Feline Purring. *Respiration Physiology,* 16 (3): 351–361.

Schötz, S. and Eklund, R. (2011) A Comparative Acoustic Analysis of Purring in Four Cats. *Proceedings of Fonetik.* Lund University, Lund, Sweden. pp. 9–12.

Simonet P., Versteeg, D., and Storie, D. (2005) Dog-Laughter: Recorded Playback Reduces Stress Related Behavior in Shelter Dogs. *Proceedings of the 7th International Conference on Environmental Enrichment.*

Stuart, A.(2009) Why Cats Purr. *WebMed.* (http://pets.edbmd.com/cats/features/why-cats-purr.)

Sundquist, M., and Sunquist, F. (2002) *Wild Cats of the World.* Chicago: University of Chicago Press.

Szalavitz, M. (2012) New Research on the Antidepressant-vs.-Placebo Debate. *Time Healthland.* (http://healthland.time.com/2012/01/18/new-research-on-the-antidepressant-versus-placebo-debate.)

Turner, D., and Bateson, P. (2000) *The Domestic Cat: The Biology of its Behaviour.* Cambridge: Cambridge University Press.

University of Maryland Medical Center, Baltimore, Press releases 2000 and 2005. (http://www.umm.edu/news/releases/laughter.htm.)

Wilson, D.E., and Reeder, DeeAnn, M. (eds.) (2005) *Mammal Species of the World. A Taxonomic and Geographic Reference.* Baltimore, Maryland: John Hopkins University Press.

Wood, J. (2011) Antidepressant Use Up 400 Percent in US. *PsychCentral.* (http://psychcentral.com/news/2011/10/25/antidepressant-use-up-400-percent-in-us/30677.html.)

Chapter 4

TOWARD AGRESSION AND OFFENSIVENESS ...
Sticks and Stones May Break My Bones But
Words Will Never Hurt Me

Offensiveness and Humor

by Ewa Wasilewska (2012)

T he field of ethics or moral philosophy in its practical application is supposed to provide us with at least a guidance, if not answers, to recognition and comprehension of what is considered to be right or wrong behavior. While most humans are capable of intuitively recognizing a proper behavior as based on the so-called Golden Rule of "doing to others what we would like them to do to us," and consequently avoid actions deemed harmful morally and/or physically, this single normative principle (or even a set of principles) is not often clear when applied to specific issues. Humor is one of those "disciplines" of high moral content where the Golden Rule is no longer golden but takes all shades of gray.

All humor is offensive as long as its joking matter involves human characters, human actions, and/or human emotions, regardless of its subject matter. There are winners and losers (e.g., Gruner: 1997), there is always a perception of violation and of normality required to be present at the same time and in connection with emotional attachment to the principles involved (e.g., Veatch, 1998); consequently, there is always a response to any humorous situation. This response or reaction to a humorous situation seems to qualify it on many levels as, for example, funny or not funny; neutral, aggressive, or sexual; hateful or benign; socially/morally/ideologically, etc., acceptable or not[1]. However, the response/reaction to humor is also dependent on other outside factors that are not a part of a joke *per se* but frame it up in a specific environment (both time and space) in such a way that a humorous situation is perceived as a statement reflecting not only personal but societal, ideological, and political values deemed to be present at the time[2]. Thus, humor is often a reflection of perception of reality regardless of factual evidence that this "reality" is incorrect, flawed, incomplete and by itself has its beginning in humorous or not-humorous stereotyping of its representative(s)[3]. The humor "receivers" make a moral judgment as to the degree of offensiveness (intended or not) by the humor "producer/presenter" and react accordingly. However, this judgment, as well as the reaction that follows, is not always a result of the humor content and it might be strongly influenced by one's disposition toward laughter. There are three general concepts of human

---

1   See Chapter 9 for discussion of humor appreciation.

2   In order to review main theories on disparagement humor see, for example, Ferguson & Ford 2008.

3   For example, intellectual abilities are not associated with color of hair (not all blondes are dumb, neither all brunettes are smart) or violence is not an intrinsic trait of the Islamic religion.

disposition[4] toward the ridicule: *gelotophobia*[5], *gelotophilia*[6], *and katagelasticism*[7], which only recently have been getting more attention from scholars (Proyer & Ruch 2010).

Gelotophobia is a pathological fear of being laughed at[8] and ridiculed, which has been observed in clinical practice, having a negative impact on gelotophobes who appear to share similar characteristics described as a general pattern:

> For example, they seem to have a biased view of their own self and on their abilities. In various studies, they were shown to underestimate their ability to create humorous productions, their self-estimates of their intellectual abilities are below their psychometric intelligence, and their self-rated virtuousness is lower than are peer-ratings of their virtuousness (Proyer & Ruch 2010: 51).

Consequently, their ability to produce as well as to enjoy humor is limited and, as one can easily suspect, their level of offensiveness is very high. While such a fear seems to be extreme and its causes are subject to an ongoing research, it has been already pointed out that *gelotophobia* might have more of a social impact than originally expected, influencing even elections in the U.S. (Lewis 2009) or parenting styles.[9] The research on *gelotophobia* has branched out to studies on *gelotophilia* and *katagelasticism,* demonstrating that some people, gelotophiles, tend to look for "situations in which they can make others laugh at them" (Proyer & Ruch 2012: 51), while others, katagelasticists, find a lot of pleasure at laughing at others whom they can actively seek. These three dispositions toward laughter may not seem too significant for the study of humor and laughter, as most people would probably fit within the range of normality with regard to fear or joy of laughter, but ... such dispositions almost certainly influence and even dictate the degree of permissibility (range) of humor offensiveness in social situations of which gelotophobes, gelotophiles, and katagelasticists have control. Thus, although individual perception of humor as based on one's moral set of values and emotional attachment to the subject of ridicule[10] may differ from person to person; moreover, its public display may or may not be permissible due to societal constraints or to values, disposition, as well as "sense of humor" of those in power[11] and/or those seeking power. Thus, non-pathological fear of

---

4   This statement refers to the extremes in the disposition toward laughter. Most people seem to be within the "normal range," which has not been well defined yet.

5   The fear of being laughed at.

6   The joy of being laughed at.

7   The joy of laughing at others.

8   Fear of being laughed at has been addressed by early humor theorists, Hobbes and Bergson. A thorough critique of their approaches based on superiority (Hobbes) and social correction (Bergson), has already been offered by Davies (2009) so there is no need to discuss it here any further.

9   After Proyer and Ruch (2010) who are leading researchers on this topic dedicating Vol. 52 of *Psychological Test and Assessment Modeling* to the issue of human dispositions toward laughter.

10   Thomas Veatch's theory of humor (1998) postulates that in order for humor to occur and be appreciated through laughter, two conditions must be present at the same time: a situation appears to be normal (N) but there is a violation (V) which violates a perception of normality. In simple terms, if things are normal (individual perception of normality), they are not funny. If they are not normal, then other emotions and understanding take over instead of humor-induced laughter. Only having both at the same time has a potential for humor. However, the potential for humor is not enough; one has to understand both normality and violation and must have an emotional attachment toward it (Veatch' Levels 1, 2, and 3). Thus, the subjective moral order is a deciding factor of what is perceived to be allowable/enjoyable to joke about or what is not. Consequently, what might be hilarious to some humor recipients, might be too painful and/or offensive to others.

11   See, for example, a discussion on sexist humor in Chapter 9 of this book.

laughter seems to vary in different societies and might be connected with not only what is allowable[12] but also what is perceived as "proper behavior.[13]" Davies postulates that shame and hierarchy are main elements that dictate the degree to which such a fear is experienced by members of any society (2009). In societies that are characterized by a "collective responsibility," any violation of social norms may result not only in personal shame, embarrassment, and disgrace, but also it may influence the standing of a group. This group might be just a family or a bigger entity based on ethnicity, religion, etc. The loss of a proverbial "face" is also the loss of "honor," a situation, which is perceived to be hard to repair. Ridiculing any elements of such a society might be understood as an attack on the society as a whole. This is due to the perception that others laugh at them because they regard them inferior as based on values, achievements in any fields, and/or perceived abilities and/or propensity to any particular behavior. Here then we are dealing with the concept of identity[14] being strongly developed but, at the same time, are always afraid of being judged as based on the actions of others. The fear of being laughed at associated with the perception of losing one's honor has a very high potential for offensiveness. The laughers are considered to be katagelasticists who are searching for an excuse to humiliate others, singling out specific groups. This could be the cause of the violent responses to the now infamous Danish cartoons[15], which were published by *Jyllands-Posten* (The Jutland Post, a daily newspaper) on September 30, 2005 in an article entitled "Muhammeds ansigt" ("The Face of Muhammad"), and were reprinted in more than fifty (50) countries. What the publishers considered to be not only an exercise in freedom of the press but also an effort to include Muslims in all aspects of the Danish culture, was perceived by many Muslims around the world as hate humor and as an attack on their religion. Publication of these twelve cartoons was accompanied by an explanation offered by a *Jyllands-Posten's* culture editor, Flemming Rose:

> The modern, secular society is rejected by some Muslims. They demand a special position, insisting on special consideration of their own religious feelings. It is incompatible with contemporary democracy and freedom of speech, where you must be ready to put up with insults, mockery and ridicule. It is certainly not always attractive and nice to look at, and it does not mean that religious feelings should be made fun of at any price, but that is of minor importance in the present context. […] we are on our way to a slippery slope where no-one can tell how the self-censorship will end. (Rose 2005)

Peaceful protests started immediately but due to the refusal of the publishers and the Danish government to apologize, quickly spread outside Denmark and eventually cost the lives of ca. three hundred (300)

---

12 What is "allowable" is classified by Davies as "fear of laughter in a hierarchical society" (2009). For example, leaders of communistic governments of countries of which I am personally familiar (e.g., Poland, Bulgaria, Soviet Union), who often were able to reach the highest levels of the governing apparatus, commonly considered any attempt on humorous situation aimed against them personally or against their government in general as an active attempt to overthrow their power. However, what they feared the most was laughter emerging from the ridicule of their qualifications (mostly lack of thereof) that put them in charge of the lives of others. Thus, common fear of intelligentsia who cleverly were able to outsmart them led to consistent attempts of eliminating it from any public scene.

13 All so-called *faux pas,* i.e., violations of cultural norms (etiquette, manners, customs, etc.) are objects of ridicule putting a subject in a position to be laughed at.

14 It must be noted here that the concept of identity refers to personal and institutional identities.

15 The so-called "cartoon wars" of 2005 and 2006 have been addressed by other authors (for example, Fischer 2009).

people (plus countless injuries) around the world[16]. Reprinting these cartoons in other western media as a part of the discussion of how far is too far only fueled worldwide protests[17]. What to the mostly Christian West were benign cartoons[18], for the Muslim world they symbolized intentional blasphemy, hate speech demeaning their culture, religion, and tradition. The West, in their view, crossed the line[19], as they should have known better than committing sacrilege[20]. While it is commonly believed that Islam opposes figural presentations (both humans and animals) in art and architecture, this is not exactly the truth especially with private and secular settings of different art forms[21]. The perceived ban on figural presentations is the result of the belief that only Allah can create living forms and any artistic vision of Allah's creation would not do them justice. The Qur'an condemns idolatry[22] and uses the term *"musawwir"* (an artist, a maker of forms) as one of Allah's epithets. However, this does not necessarily mean that figural presentations are actually forbidden (as to my knowledge, no direct reference to such a prohibition is present in the Qur'an), but they are definitely not to be worshipped. Specific condemnation of figural presentations can be found in some Hadiths[23] but, since they are not infallible and often contradictory, a case can be made that they are not only allowed but also "encouraged." Actually, in some "twisted" (perceived as a Western interpretation) way, one may even argue that violent reaction to images of Prophet Muhammad in Danish cartoons was against the teachings of Islam as it elevated the position of the Prophet beyond his role of Allah's messenger. There is no doubt, however, that militant attacks against innocent people are not supported by any teachings of the Qur'an. Regardless of any theological or scholarly arguments that can be

---

16   Based on reports from different countries. Most cited number is, however, over 139 deaths but these reports, allegedly, do not include human losses in Nigeria.

17   Six (6) out of these twelve (12) cartoons were reprinted by *Al Fagr*, an Egyptian newspaper on October 18, 2005, which condemned them but nothing violent has become of this re-publication (Fischer 2009).

18   After all, much worse things have been done to images of Jesus Christ and other icons of Christian tradition. However as Alston and Platt noted "Cartoons form excellent sources of material for analyses of acceptable targets ... Drawing for commercial purposes, the cartoonist must restrict his themes to those which he feels will be accepted by the public. He must therefore attempt to capture contemporary values and humor fads acceptable to the general readers of his magazine" (1969: 218).

19   One of my students in Spring 2012 class, Anna Rasmussen, described the "line" between humorous and offensive as follows " ... a flexible cord with which we are all attempting to play jump rope with. Humor occurs every time you jump without hitting the rope; offensiveness, every time you hit it. You can dance on the very edge; skim the cord; do fancy tricks—however, if you come in contact with the 'line' you lose and have crossed over into offensiveness."

20   For an explanation on joking in Islam and about Islam see Chapter 8.

21   For example, Behesht-i Zahra, near Teheran, Iran, is the resting place for ca. 200,000 soldiers, who died during the war with Iraq (1980–1988). Their graves are marked with boxed displays of their pictures, some memorabilia, as well as pictures of the Shi'a Imams and even Prophet Muhammad. If not for an explanation from a few mullahs and even one ayatollah, I would have never guessed that images that I interpreted as of a beautiful, young, female, of a movie-star quality were actually of Prophet Muhammad.

22   As idolatry involves the use of figural presentation, pictures and even photographs, might be considered to be its form.

23   See Chapter 9. The following are a few Hadiths referring to the subject figural presentations as widely cited by a variety of sources on the Internet. "Ibn Umar reported Allah's Messenger (may peace be upon him) having said: Those who paint pictures would be punished on the Day of Resurrection and it would be said to them: Breathe soul into what you have created." (*Sahih Muslim*)

"This hadith has been reported on the authority of Abu Mu'awiya though another chain of transmitters (and the words are): Verily the most grievously tormented people amongst the denizens [inhabitants] of Hell on the Day of Resurrection would be the painters of pictures ... ." (*Sahih Muslim*)

"Narrated [Muhammad's wife] Aisha: Allah's Apostle said, 'The painter of these pictures will be punished on the Day of Resurrection, and it will be said to them, Make alive what you have created.'" (*Bukhari*)

"Narrated Aisha: The Prophet entered upon me while there was a curtain having pictures (of animals) in the house. His face got red with anger, and then he got hold of the curtain and tore it into pieces. The Prophet said, 'Such people as paint these pictures will receive the severest punishment on the Day of Resurrection.'" (*Bukhari*)

"Umar said, 'We do not enter your churches because of the statues and pictures. Ibn Abbas used to pray in the church provided there were no statues in it.'" (*Bukhari*)

made for or against figural presentations in Islam or of Islamic figures, the truth is that perception is often stronger than reality. The Danish cartoons were then considered to be a direct attack on Islamic values under the "pretext" of "a joke is just a joke.[24]" On February 17, 2006, Flemming Rose addressed the issue again in his article for the Washington Post, *Why I Published These Cartoons*. The following are excerpts from this article as his justification goes straight to the core of the issue of humor offensiveness and censorship:

> … I commissioned the cartoons in response to several incidents of self-censorship in Europe caused by widening fears and feelings of intimidation in dealing with issues related to Islam. And I still believe that this is a topic that we Europeans must confront, challenging moderate Muslims to speak out. The idea wasn't to provoke gratuitously—and we certainly didn't intend to trigger violent demonstrations throughout the Muslim world. Our goal was simply to push back self-imposed limits on expression that seemed to be closing in tighter … .
>
> … So, over two weeks we witnessed a half-dozen cases of self-censorship, pitting freedom of speech against the fear of confronting issues about Islam …
>
> … Has Jyllands-Posten insulted and disrespected Islam? It certainly didn't intend to. But what does respect mean? When I visit a mosque, I show my respect by taking off my shoes. I follow the customs, just as I do in a church, synagogue or other holy place. But if a believer demands that I, as a nonbeliever, observe his taboos in the public domain, he is not asking for my respect, but for my submission. And that is incompatible with a secular democracy …
>
> … As a former correspondent in the Soviet Union, I am sensitive about calls for censorship on the grounds of insult. This is a popular trick of totalitarian movements: Label any critique or call for debate as an insult and punish the offenders. That is what happened to human rights activists and writers such as Andrei Sakharov, Vladimir Bukovsky, Alexander Solzhenitsyn, Natan Sharansky, Boris Pasternak. The regime accused them of anti-Soviet propaganda, just as some Muslims are labeling 12 cartoons in a Danish newspaper anti-Islamic …
>
> … The lesson from the Cold War is: If you give in to totalitarian impulses once, new demands follow. The West prevailed in the Cold War because we stood by our fundamental values and did not appease totalitarian tyrants … (Rose 2006)

His argument is clear and easily defendable from the perspective of democratic values as they are understood in Western societies. However, its logic and reasoning are not acceptable by radical Islamists. These views representing a conflict between democracy and totalitarianism, between secularity and religiosity, also reflect functional extremes of humor as social control and social conflict. *Jyllands-Posten* used humor to repair what it considered to be social inequality, while Islamic radicals used its arguably offensive content to instigate violence. The irony is that if not for the direct identification of these cartoons with Prophet Muhammad (*Muhammeds ansigt*), violence might not have resulted from their publication. They would have fallen under a category of political cartoons that are plentiful both in the West and in the Middle East. Some of them would not be even comprehensible outside of Denmark and at least one of them would be considered internationally funny ("Stop, stop, we have run out of virgins!") for different reasons. The most offensive of them "depicting the prophet with a bomb in his turban" has been

---

24   This would make Muslims to be gelotophobes. This is just a generalization of collective attitude as perceived by the West.

interpreted as the Western statement that "the prophet is a terrorist or that every Muslim is a terrorist" although Rose offers a more complex explanation of this image:

> I read it differently: Some individuals have taken the religion of Islam hostage by committing terrorist acts in the name of the prophet. They are the ones who have given the religion a bad name. The cartoon also plays into the fairy tale about Aladdin and the orange that fell into his turban and made his fortune. This suggests that the bomb comes from the outside world and is not an inherent characteristic of the prophet (2006).

I am a fairly intelligent person specializing in the Middle East and recently also in humor, but I have definitely missed points explained by Rose in the last two lines of the above paragraph. Thus, from my point of view, any expectation that others shouldn't is simply a wishful thinking. While publication of these cartoons has opened even more venues for dialogue in Denmark, thus turning the "negative" into positive, the same has not necessarily happened outside of her borders. The cartoons themselves and reaction to them have played well intro extremists' points of view that the West have no respect for Islam and that Muslims want to Islamicize the West. Thus, the madness continues as illustrated by several pictures on the Internet with the caption "I will see your jihad and raise you a crusade."

The Danish cartoons have also "started" the "cartoon wars" with Iran playing a central role. The so-called "cockroach cartoon controversy" of May 2006 in Iran, which resulted in hundreds of arrests and unknown numbers of deaths and injuries, was blamed on the West, although this was a local conflict. The Azeri (Turkic speaking minority in Iran) were offended by the publication of cartoons in *Iran* (a newspaper) that they felt had compared them to cockroaches, which "don't understand human [Persian] language." The riots followed inside Iran but this ethnic conflict was spun off into interference of the U.S. government in the internal affairs of Iran. The Holocaust Cartoon Contest was next as its exhibit opened up on August 14, 2006. It was in response to the Danish cartoons, claiming that the West is very choosy as to whom to offend as cartoonists avoid any topics sensitive to Judaism and Jews such as the Holocaust. Its existence was not denied but its tragedy was minimized. Comparisons of Israel to Nazi Germany were frequent, and images of Palestine as the new Auschwitz were not uncommon. Humor, once again, was used as a sword, an effective weapon in one of many battles of seemingly conflicting ideologies.

While many Westerners complain about the sensitivity of many Muslims, they forget that American society might be quick to react to any form of humor, which is perceived politically incorrect. It took only 24 hours to take down the billboard along the Manhattan highway (the West Side Highway near 130th Street) that advertised "wódka[25]" (vodka) of "Christmas quality" at "Hannukah pricing" (by Real Wódka Vodka). The billboard also featured two dogs, a bigger one wearing a *yarmulke* and a small one sporting a Santa hat. Stephen Colbert[26] was also quick to point out that one of the dogs is an Afghan so with one billboard, the company managed to offend both Jews and Muslims. Of course, Muslims didn't care whatsoever although Colbert's commentary on the whole situation was incredibly funny. In all probability, the majority of Jews[27] were not offended, at least not too much, as they are used to many jokes

---

25   "Wódka" was spelled in Polish. So, how about offending Poles as playing on a stereotype of perceived Polish anti-Semitism as most of the Nazi concentration camps, including Auschwitz, were located in Poland that, at the time, was under total control of Germans?

26   *The Colbert Report* on November 30, 2011, as a part of *Yahweh or NoWay* series.

27   Brian Gordon, a team leader of this campaign, is Jewish. Once again, a *post factum* explanation has been somewhat forced as most people, supposedly, wouldn't get a positive message: "As a Jew growing up, the only thing we could say was we had eight nights and Christmas

about their perceived frugality. However, politically correct Christians as well as the Anti-Defamation League,[28] supported by a few other complainers, believed that such an advertisement was "crude and offensive" (Harris 2011) reinforcing anti-Semitic[29] stereotypes. There was no similar uproar regarding another billboard by the same company, which advertised a black Russian (a drink). A black male model was wearing a Russian fur hat playing then to not so positive stereotypes, considering the recent history of black people in Russia[30]. "Movie Star Quality, Reality Star Pricing" featuring the same (I assume) Afghan dog could also be offensive implying much lower quality of reality shows so much beloved by TV viewers. How about "Escort Quality, Hooker Pricing" in a country in which prostitution is illegal? Whether *Wódka Vodka* ads should be classified as being shockvertising (shock advertising) is an issue for advertising specialists, but its relatively low degree of offensiveness (always in the eye of the beholder) makes it humorous to many people who are far away from being prejudiced. The billboard "wars" are also a good example of applicability of Veatch's theory of humor to potentially funny situations. While the above ads for inexpensive vodka can be concluded to be witty, the Heartland Institute's planned ad campaign[31] to express its disbelief in global warming and distrust for those who dare to differ was a total flop. Its premise to compare believers in global warming to serial killers "because what these murderers and madman have said differ very little from what spokespersons for the United Nations, journalists for the 'mainstream' media and liberal politicians say about global warming" (Nuwer 2012) was already too risky for any successful humor to occur as murder is socially and culturally unacceptable[32]. Furthermore, their choice of "notorious killers" such as Theodore Kaczynski, Fidel Castro, and Osama bin Laden—among others—would most certainly offend Polish, Cuban, and Muslim minorities in the U.S. Needless to say, the first billboard in Chicago[33] featuring Kaczynski proclaiming, "I still believe in global warming. Do you?" was removed in less than 24 hours. It was not an intervention of the Anti-Defamation league, but simply bad taste and negative reaction of corporate donors who called the shots[34]. The incongruity was not enough to elicit even one iota of humor, not only because it was forced, but also because an emotional attachment was extremely high—murderers can be activists, but activists don't have to be murderers.

---

had only one day, so we had eight days for the price of one," Gordon explained by phone from Los Angeles, where he said he was attending his niece's bat mitzvah" (Grinberg 2011).

28   "In a crude and offensive way of trying to make a point that their vodka is high quality and inexpensive, the billboards evoke a Jewish holiday to imply something that is cheap and of lesser value when compared to the higher value of a Christian holiday," ADL regional director Ron Meier said. It "reinforces anti-Semitic stereotypes" (after Flock 2011).

29   The term "anti-Semitic" is commonly used but this doesn't mean that it is correct. The term "Semitic" refers to a group of languages spoken in the Middle East for at least 5000 years (beginning of the written record). It includes such ancient languages as Akkadian, Assyrian, Babylonian Aramaic and modern ones such as Hebrew and Arabic. Consequently, the term "anti-Semitic" doesn't even refer to religion (Judaism) but covers both Hebrews and Arabs.

30   Racism in Russia is flourishing as never before. Daily incidents of beatings, robberies, and even killings are quite common (e.g., Jackson 2006; see comments too).

31   Leaders of both campaigns would have benefited from reading professional articles on humor and advertisement that focus on the relationship between humor mechanism and humor perception (e.g., Cho 1995).

32   This doesn't mean that there are no jokes about this topic as nothing is too sacred for humor. However, like with the "dead baby" jokes, rarely can they be considered to be funny and/or tasteful by the "mainstream" receivers.
Q.: Why did Jeffrey Dahmer keep testicles in the fridge?
A.: Sometimes you feel like a nut, sometimes you don't.

33   The most Polish populated city in the world, where the use of *Poglish*, a combination of English and Polish, impossible for non-bilingual people to understand (so-called language interference), is a testimony to the not-always-wanted fusion of different cultures.

34   The war of billboards on global warning issues continues in Chicago but nothing funny has emerged yet.

Corporate sponsors were also responsible for removing Don Imus from national TV. On April 7, 2007, in the conversation with Sid Rosenberg (a sport announcer), he referred to the Rutgers University women's basketball team as "nappy-headed hos" on his MSNBC hosted show *Imus in the Morning*. The reaction was immediate, although only a very few saw the show airing very early in the morning. It became a national scandal leading to peaceful demonstrations, hate mail, and numerous discussions on and off the topic, some helping the healing, others stirring a proverbial pot. Many people acted surprised but … given Imus' reputation as one of the most notorious shock jocks in the U.S., and given his numerous conversations with Sid Rosenberg disparaging athletes, women, etc., there was nothing to be surprised about. Rosenberg shocked the world more than once and reportedly was fired by Imus a few times. Probably the most shocking comment made by Rosenberg (denied by him later) was on June 21, 2001: "One time, a friend, he says to me, 'Listen, one of these days you're gonna see Venus and Serena Williams in Playboy.' I said, 'You've got a better shot at National Geographic'" (MMTV 2007). While Rosenberg's intentions are difficult to discern, as his job description does not require humor, Imus's is on the air because of his outrageous comments. There is no doubt that Imus' attempt at a humorous description was very offensive but was it racially motivated? Not only did he apologize profusely, but also met privately with the only hero of this whole racially divisive incident, Vivian Stringer (the Rutgers' coach) and her team. At the April 10, 2007 press conference, she showed the whole world how the most controversial, painful, and potentially violent social issues can be handled with grace, dignity, and class. She put to shame not only the offenders but also some of the offended who used the situation to advance their political and societal views, conveniently forgetting their own bigotries[35]. There were no winners in the controversy created by a spontaneous humor as pointed out by Nicolaus Mills, a professor of American Studies at Sarah Lawrence College[36]:

> Sadly, the Imus controversy, like the O. J. Simpson trial, has been more successful in widening the racial divisions in the country than in shedding light on them. On the one side, Jackson and Sharpton increased their personal prestige with a quick victory over a shock jock who made himself an easy target. But in winning as they did, they undermined any effort to reach a shared standard for acceptable and unacceptable speech. Both men showed that in addition to being unwilling to be honest about their own controversial pasts, they were unwilling to mount an all-out attack on a rap culture that long before Imus used the word "ho," popularized it. These days that culture, operating at the highest possible decibel level with a youthful fan base among both blacks and whites, continues to portray black women as "hos" and "bitches" and influences thinking in the black community far more than Imus ever could (Mills 2007).

Imus' and Rosenberg's comments have been widely categorized as hate speech, or rather hate humor, both protected by the First Amendment. The notable exception is the "Shouting fire in a crowded theatre" expression used by Oliver Wendell Holmes, Jr. in his opinion in the United States Supreme Court case Schenck v. United States in 1919. This ruling was overturned by Brandenburg v. Ohio in 1969. "Under it, advocacy of unlawful action might be proscribed only where it was 'directed to inciting or producing

---

35   For example, Jesse Jackson and Al Sharpton (Mills 2007).
36   He is also an author of *Like a Holy Crusade: Mississippi 1964—The Turning of the Civil Rights Movement in America*, (1993).

imminent danger that such action may in fact be provoked'" (Schwartz 1994: 237)[37]. The question then arises of whether hate humor or humor in general might incite or produce imminent danger. The Danish cartoons might fall under this law because the publishers of these cartoons must have been aware of possible consequences[38]. This is why American newspapers[39] refused to reprint them at the time. However, the White Aryan Resistance, a neo-Nazi racist group, has included a great deal of hate humor in their WAR publication since 1980 and on its website. The group is advancing the superiority of the Aryan race[40] over any other races, although there is no such beast as the Aryan race. The term "Aryan" in Sanskrit simply means a "noble/spiritual" person with regard to individual qualities. I am sure that neo-Nazis would be unpleasantly surprised to find out that the name "Iran" actually refers to the "land of Aryans," i.e., of the people speaking Indo–Iranian languages. These are the same groups that they hate (among the others). There is no need to outline their philosophy or narrate their humor because this has already been done by others (e.g., Oring 2003: 41–57). However, some of their cartoons and/or jokes clearly call for violence against groups, which they disparage. Captions such as "Let's Face it! Rampant black crime is bringing this nation to its knees … If you care about the future of yourself, your family, and your race … [A picture of a "good Aryan" smashing the head of a monstrous black person] … It's time to strike back!" (Oring 2003: fig. 5), seem to "instruct" others how to deal with "the problem." The Aryan humorous messages are actually statements about their identity, which they can openly celebrate and communicate to others. As Oring pointed out, the WAR humor is not a disguised aggression as this aggression is fully displayed (2003: 56–57). One might even doubt if it is offensive as the groups who would be offended are not even exposed to it; thus, its mere existence may not even qualify it as humor, but rather as a production of hateful pictures that are appealing to in-group members only.

However, Ari Shaffir, a Jewish–American stand-up comedian and actor has much wider appeal as his film shorts for National Lampoon[41] are watched by millions of viewers, especially college students. The type of humor that he offers to his audience varies, but his comedic shows often focus on a so-called scatological humor. His performances are already quite controversial, as one has to have a very specific sense of humor to enjoy "jokes about abducted children, diarrhea gone horribly awry, or an anal-sex miscue with a twist" (MacPherson 2012). Those who don't like it always have the choice to stand up and leave his routines, or turn off a TV or the computer. This choice, however, is denied to those who are a direct target of his "racial humor", i.e., "assaults" as the Amazing Racist effectively seeks minority groups to offend them verbally and through staged actions. He provokes people to respond violently to his "comedy" and then runs away laughing, protected by cameras and the First Amendment. One of his most famous or infamous shorts is entitled *Beaners*. He hires a group of illegal immigrants for an imaginary job and then drives them to the Immigration Office, insulting them all the time while driving his pick-up truck through every little and big hole he can find on the road. In another one Shaffir, dressed in a Ku Klux Klan robe, is trying to have it cleaned in the blackest neighborhood of Los Angeles, and then tries to get gas from African–American customers of a gas station saying "I'm late for a meeting and I have to burn something." In the episode aimed at Muslims, not only does he set up his stand in front of a mosque selling,

---

37   For discussion of the Supreme Court decisions and American democracy see, for example, Barnum 1993.

38   The so-called "Rushdie affair" of 1988 should have been a good predictor of what could happen (and it did).

39   Only a few student newspapers reprinted all or a few of them.

40   Following the "definition" of the Nazi origin.

41   His credits also include, for example, the HBO comedy series *Down and Dirty* with Jim Norton and appearances on TBS's *Minding the Store* and ESPN *Classic's Cheap Seats*.

among other things, T-shirts that read, "My parents went to Mecca and all I got was this terrible body odor", but he also walks to the mosque itself selling other similarly offending items, disrupting praying Muslims, and then literally touching women gathered in the women-only section of this prayer house. The offended people show tremendous restraint not to respond with violence, but the question often asked on the Internet is " how is it possible that he is still alive?" Honestly, I don't know. However, what is a concern to many is that if any of his victims responds by doing any harm to him, they will be charged with an assault with or without a deadly weapon. He, on the other hand, is allowed to physically lay hands on others under a banner of a "comedy show." Regardless of whether many of his victims signed or didn't sign a release form, his comedy acts seem to fall under the category of actions "inciting or producing imminent danger[42]," yet Shaffir's humor is still recognized as an artistic expression. The Amazing Racist's routines also interfere with his victims' ability to perform their jobs, affecting then their families and all others who depend on them. Furthermore, Shaffir's shorts are "advertised" by others, not necessary members of the White Aryan Resistance groups[43], as instructional videos:

> " ... an excellent idea of how to battle the brown tides coming across our border ... "
> " ... an amusing instructional video on how to rid your community and your country of invading Mesitizos ... "
> "I think we should take this idea and run with it ... " (Jackson 2005).

Ironically, the WAR website refers to those who don't appreciate and/or enjoy Shaffir's humor as "White haters have no sense of humor."

The Amazing Racist's type of comedy is an example of hate humor that may elicit more violence than laughter. It has the highest potential for offensiveness and unpredictability of reaction with regard to its consequences. The content of humor, its producer/presenter, the physical environment (time and space) and its targets are responsible for creating immediate and long-term responses/reactions to specific humorous situations. The Golden Rule of an ethical behavior is lost when non-humor related issues (e.g., politics, right to free speech, political correctness) come into play.

While Shaffir is able to get away with his behavior because he is a professional comedian, others cannot because they "should know better." President Barack Obama's National Security Advisor, General James Jones, learned this lesson the hard way[44]. In his opening remarks at the Washington Institute for Near East Policy event on April 24, 2010, he shared the following joke with the audience:

> A Taliban militant gets lost and is wandering around the desert looking for water. He finally arrives at a store run by a Jew and asks for water.

---

42   There are people on his shorts who actually chase him out, break cameras, try to break his windshield, throw tomatoes at him, etc. They are not actors, they are just people who act upon very strong emotions.

43   Of course, these groups strongly support Shaffir's sense of humor in spite of such concerns as, for example, this one: "I was watching the 'Amazing Racist' videos on your site, and they're hilarious. One question, though, what's the Amazing Racist's real name? I could swear he's a Jew; he certainly looks like one. At the beginning of the Chinese restaurant video he mentions his name, and it sounds like he says, "Maury Shapir" ... . Sounds like a Jew to me. Anyhow, unless those videos are staged, which I don't think they are, the guy's got balls." Another one, "Here's some more of those amazing racist videos [.] I found out it was going to be a reality show from national lampoon it was going to be called lost reality but I guess it was a bit too real and got the boot before it could even start. The guy on the video is a Jew named ari shaffer a kike comedian imagine that ... lol (http://www.resist.com/updates/2005/SEP_05/AryanUpdate_21SEP05.htm).

44   Of course, he profusely apologized for his lack of better judgment.

The Jewish vendor tells him he doesn't have any water but can gladly sell him a tie. The Taliban begins to curse and yell at the Jewish storeowner. The Jew, unmoved, offers the rude militant an idea: Beyond the hill, there is a restaurant; they can sell you water.

The Taliban keeps cursing and finally leaves toward the hill. An hour later he's back at the tie store. He walks in and tells the merchant: "Your brother tells me I need a tie to get into the restaurant."

This joke is neither new, nor original. While many people in the audience laughed[45], some felt offended as it was narrated by a top official of the American government. The media and the Anti-Defamation League almost "crucified" (pun intended) Jones for his "lack of sensitivity" while many others of both Jewish and non-Jewish affiliation basically said "lighten up." Was this joke out of place? This depends on the point of view. Technically speaking, this joke was shared with the in-group as the Washington Institute for Near East Policy is known for its pro-Israel position. Did Abraham Foxman, a national director of the Anti-Defamation League of B'nai B'rith[46], overreact in the name of "sensitivity" or "political correctness?"

"To make fun of Jews in terms of 'Jews won't help you in need, Jews want to sell to you?' Whoa!" Foxman says. "Where's the sensitivity? The irony of it is General Jones went to this forum to reach out to the Jewish community. Of all the jokes this is probably the worst one he could have picked" (Blakely 2010).

Two points only: humor is one of the most effective ways to "reach any community", especially within an in-group, and there are countless Jewish jokes that could have been a much worse choice[47]. The disturbing thing is that, reportedly, "one of our government's top intelligence experts said he believed the joke he told was a true story" (Kemmers 2010). While humorous *faux pas* can and should be forgiven, ignorance at the top level of international policy is not only laughable but also inexcusable.

On the other hand, due to the offensiveness of humor, humor might be one of a very few still permissible ways of communication in Western societies (and possibly others) through which the motives of a dominant group can be expressed as they can be dismissed under the banner "a joke is just a joke." Hodson, Rush, & MacInnis argue this point within much broader Social Dominance Theory (SDT[48]), stressing that "humor orientation can maximally facilitate dominance motives to the extent that advocating a good sense of humor holds positive social value," as "[c]avalier and dismissive humor orientations may therefore justify

---

45   Those who laughed included many Jews who they didn't feel offended or threatened by the joke causing any change in the American policy toward Israel. After all, the Washington Institute for Near East Policy, a think tank, was founded in 1985 with the assistance of many Jewish donors.

46   "Sons of the Covenant."

47   *Old man Moskowitz was getting along in years. He decided to retire and let his 3 sons run the company, which manufactured a wide variety of nails. The sons thought they could increase market share with some judicious billboard advertising. Only a week later the old man was taking his usual Sunday drive in the country when he saw the first billboard ad. There it was—a picture of Christ on the Cross—with the caption: "Nails for Every Purpose. Use Moskowitz Nails." The old man immediately met with his 3 sons to voice his concern. He explained that the backlash could be horrendous. The company could be ruined. The sons agreed to discontinue that ad. A week later the old man was again taking his usual Sunday drive when he saw the second billboard ad. There it was—a picture of the same cross, empty, with Christ crumpled on the ground below ... and the caption: "Next Time Use Moskowitz Nails."*

48   The same abbreviation is used for a self-determination theory whose autonomy motivation and control motivation's effects on hostility expressed in humor appreciation are discussed by Weinstein, Hodgins & Ostvik-White (2011).

maintenance of the status quo[49] by trivializing intergroup-based communications that can oppress others" (2010: 662). The cavalier and dismissive humor is not a hard-core, in-your-face, offensive or hateful humor, but rather it is funny, non-committal, "just a joke" humor. This is a type of humor that is easily dismissed as not causing harm to others. However, Hodson, Rush, & MacInnis' experimental studies (2010), suggest that cavalier humor beliefs (CHB) endorse hierarchy-enhancing and legitimizing myths, although they are not necessarily the evidence of prejudice. The effectiveness of humor in perpetuating such myths seems to be in the attitude itself since a joke is not really a serious endeavor and is being created and/or transmitted and/or retransmitted by those who are not considered to be prejudiced and/or dominant. Even when such humor is used to expose the others' bigotry and intolerance, etc., it can still perpetuate the same myths. Hodson, Rush & MacInnis refer to characters created by Sacha Cohen (Borat and Brüno) as "meta-bigots" who simultaneously represent and mock prejudices (2010: 678). *Borat: Cultural Learnings of America for Make Benefit Glorious Nation of Kazakhstan*[50], both the movie and extra scenes, which have never made it to the big screen, are not only examples of exposing bigotry and perpetuating it at the same time, but also reflect the role of humor as social control and/or conflict. The "audience" eagerly participating in the movie in which they were set up to expose their "true" feelings has been ridiculed for their prejudice (positive). However, the humorous means through which this self-exposure was achieved has been quite controversial, causing conflict with in- and out-audiences. Sacha Cohen, producers and distributors of the movie, have been sued for defamation, unlawful use of images, misrepresentation, etc. Reportedly, none of these lawsuits resulted in any penalties. The movie has been both criticized and prized, even in Kazakhstan, a victim country, where it was eventually banned. Unfortunately, in spite of its obvious comedic character, there are still too many people believing in an outrageous portrayal of Kazakhstan[51]. Thus, Borat, the movie, has managed to accomplish two main functions of humor: control and conflict at the same time.

None of the humorous situations presented above seem to be intended as political humor, but each and every one of them, including the Amazing Racist's racial discourse, has had socio-political repercussions. They were all allowed to happen because in most modern Western societies the humor "perpetrators" (?) are protected by the free speech and freedom of expression acts. However, although humor is encouraged and almost all of its forms are permutable under the law, other forces have replaced governmental control as socially corrective media. The issue is that these forces are neither perfect, nor objective: corporate sponsors, politically correct media, inspiring or expiring politicians, etc., are using their judgment[52] on what should be permissible in humor and, consequently, creating social censorship. In response, comedic media ridicule the establishment, which has the power to control them, and continue the humor based socio-political chaotic order of correctness. Humor is then a modern equivalent of the ancient Ouroboros, with no beginning and no end, but a continuum of human reactions.

"When humor goes, there goes civilization."
—Erma Louise Bombeck (1927–1996)
An American author and humorist.

---

49 The *status quo* here refers to the incongruity of the Western cultures defined by them as "the coexistence of blatant intergroup inequalities on the one hand and societal prescription of norms favoring equality on the other" (Hodson, Rush, & MacInnis 2010: 662).

50 This comedy or rather a mockumentary was directed by Larry Charles and distributed by 20th Century Fox in 2006.

51 As recently as March 2012, the fictitious Kazakh anthem from the movie was played at the H.H. The Amir of Kuwait International Shooting Grand Prix in Kuwait when honoring the Gold Winning medalist, Maria Dmitrienko from Kazakhstan. This international incident was blamed on mistakenly downloading the wrong song from the Internet. An apology was issued and awarding was re-staged but the damage was done, only proving how ignorance plays an important role in creating and/or perpetuating untruthful images.

52 Judgment that also depends on their disposition toward laughter.

Bibliography

Alston, J.P., and Platt, L.A. (1969) Religious Humor: A Longitudinal Content Analysis of Cartoons. *Sociological Analysis,* 30: 217–22.

Barnum, D.G. (1993) *The Supreme Court and American Democracy.* New York: St. Martin's Press.

Bergson, A. (1963 [1924]) Le Rire, Essay sur la Signification de Comique. *Oeuvres.* Paris: Presses Universitaires de la France. pp. 384–485.

Blakely, J. (April 26, 2010). Anti-Defamation League: National Security Adviser Jones Told "appropriate, Stereotypic" Joke About Jewish Merchant. *Political Punch.* ABC News. (http://abcnews.go.com/blogs/politics/2010/04/antidefamation-league-national-security-adviser-jones-told-inappropriate-stereotypic-joke-about-jewi.)

Cho, H. (1995) Humor Mechanisms, Perceived Humor And Their Relationship To Various Executional Types Advertising. *Advances in Consumer Research*, 22: 191–197.

Davies, C. (2009) Humor Theory And The Fear of Being Laughed At. *Humor. International Journal of Humor Research.* 22(1/2): 49–62.

Ferguson, M., Ferguson A., and Ford, T.E. (2008) Disparagement Humor: A Theoretical and Empirical Review of Psychoanalytic, Superiority, and Social Identity Theories. *Humor,* 21 (3): 283–312.

Fischer, M.M.J. (2009) Iran And The Boomeranging Cartoon Wars: Can Public Spheres at Risk Ally with Public Spheres Yet to Be Achieved? *Cultural Politics,* 5(1): 27–62.

Flock, E. (2011) Hanukkah Vodka ad pulled after protests from Jewish groups. *Washington Post.* November 23.

Grinberg, E.(2011) Vodka ad boasting 'Christmas quality' at 'Hanukkah pricing' to come down amid complaints. *CNN.* November 22.

Gruner, C.R. (1997) *The Game of Humor.* Transaction Publishers.

Harris, E.A. (2011) Billboard Called Anti-Semitic Is Quickly Pulled. *New York Times.* November 22.

Hobbes, T. (1999 [1640]) The Elements of Law Natural and Politic: Human Nature and De Corpore Politico with Three Lives. *Human Nature.* Gaskin, J.C.H., (ed.). Oxford: Oxford University Press.

Hodson, G., Rush J. and MacInnis, C.C. (2010): A Joke Is Just a Joke (Except When It Isn't) Cavalier Humor Beliefs Facilitate the Expression of Group Dominance Motives. *Journal of Personality and Social Psychology,* 99 (4): 660–682.

Jackson, C. (2005) The Racist humor of a Jewish Comedian from The Comedy Store in Los Angeles has inspired members of a neo-Nazi group to target undocumented Mexican worker. *Racist 'Humor' spires Hate.* Teaching Tolerance. July 20. (http://www.tolerance.org.)

Jackson, P. (2006) Living With Race Hate in Russia. *BBC News.* February 24. (http://news.bbc.co.uk/2/hi/4737468.stm.)

Lewis, P. (2009) *Partisan Gelotophobia and Preemptive Humor Strategies.* Paper presented at the 21st Annual Conference of the International Society for Humor Studies, Long Beach, CA. June.

Lynch, O.H. (2002) Humorous Communication: Finding a Place for Humor in Communication Research. *Communication Theory,* 12 (4): 423–445.

MacPherson, G. (2012) Ari Shaffir doesn't miss a chance to make his audience squirm. *StraightCom.* March 30. (http://www.straight.com/article-648926/vancouver/ari-shaffir-doesnt-miss-chance-make-his-audience-squirm.)

Mills, N. (2007) The Gotcha Game: Don Imus and His Critics. *Dissent Magazine. March 20.* (http://www.dissentmagazine.org/online.php?id=7.)

MMTV (2007) He's Back? Rosenberg alluded to previous racially insensitive remarks that first got him fired from Imus. *MediaMatters For America.* March 28. (http://mediamatters.org/mmtv/200703280001.)

Nuwer, R. (2012): Heartland Pulls Billboard on Global Warming. *New York Times.* May 4, (http://green.blogs.nytimes.com/2012/05/04/a-new-tactic-for-climate-skeptics.)

Oring, E. (2003) *Engaging Humor.* University of Illinois Press.

Proyer, R.T., and Ruch, W. (2010) Editorial: Dispositions Towards Ridicule and Being Laughed at: Current Research on Gelotophobia, Gelotophilia, and Katagelasticism. *Psychological Test and Assessment Modeling,* 52 (1): 49–59.

Remmer, J.K. (April 26, 2010) Did You Hear The One About The Jewish Merchant And The Taliban Fighter? *The Moderate Voice.* (http://themoderatevoice.com/70463/did-you-hear-the-one-about-the-jewish-merchant-and-the-taliban-fighter.)

Rose, F. (September 30, 2005) Muhammeds ansigt. *Jyllands-Posten.*

Rose, F. (February 17, 2006) Why I Published Those Cartoons. *Washington Post.*

Stephenson, R.M. (1951) Conflict and Control Functions of Humor. *American Journal Sociology,* 56 (6): 569–574.

Schwartz, B. (1994) Holmes Versus Hand: Clear and Present Danger or Advocacy of Unlawful Action? *The Supreme Court Review,* 209–245.

Veatch, T.C. (1998) A Theory of Humor. *Humor: the International Journal of Humor Research.* 11:161–215.

Weinstein, N., Hodgins, H.S., and Ostvik-White, E. (2011) Humor as Aggression: Effects of Motivation on Hostility Expressed in Humor Appreciation. *Journal of Personality and Social Psychology,* 100 (6): 1043–1055.

Chapter 5

TOWARD VERBAL EXPRESSIONS ...
You Talk Funny

Is It Ever Just a Joke?

by Martina Volfova[1] and Mercedes Douglass[2] (2012)

Introduction

Language plays a vital role in our social lives. We use language to greet people, to agree or disagree, to complain, to give compliments. We tell sad stories and funny ones. Through language, we are able to create and maintain meaningful social interactions, without which, our lives would be unrecognizably different. As Goodwin (1990) and Hanks (1996) assert, talk is "**social action**," and so is never simply about a subject. From a simple assertion like "the sky is blue" to a minister's proclamation, "I now pronounce you husband and wife," language does things (Austin 1962). Through language we accomplish goals, urge people to act, and propose certain definitions of reality. All of this is just as true for humor as it is for any other form of speech. Keating and Egbert (2004) remind us, "the production of humorous 'moves' in conversation is far from trivial and has important implications and consequences in the work of building relationships and social life" (2004:171).

The moment we craft a joke or pull one out of a joke book and say it aloud (or gesture it, or publish it), it takes on a social life. For example, Karp (1988) asserts that "humor and irony are subtle and powerful means of expression available to people whose communicative options are otherwise constrained by the social conditions in which they act" (36). Goldstein, in a similar vein, writes "humor is a vehicle for expressing sentiments that are difficult to communicate publicly or that point to areas of discontent in social life ... humor is one of the fugitive forms of insubordination" (2003:9). As we will see in the remainder of this chapter, humor serves a multitude of social functions of which making people laugh is just the beginning.

---

1 Martina is a former student and a teaching assistant of Dr. Ewa Wasilewska in her class on "Anthropology of Humor and Laughter" at the University of Utah. She is presently an MA candidate in linguistic anthropology at Northern Arizona University, Flagstaff, AZ. Her interests and research focus is on language revitalization and maintenance, construction and negotiation of self through language as well as cross-cultural collaboration and conflict resolution.

2 Mercedes is a doctoral student at the University of California, Los Angeles, CA. Her primary interests include the study of performance and situated interaction, and have culminated for her in research on humor, medical interactions, political oratory, and issues of local governance.

There are two ideologies (lay theories) of humor that we would like to debunk from the start. Not only do these theories contradict one another, they are self-serving (though not always in a bad way) in that they permit the teller or recipient of a joke to justify socially charged utterances by either diminishing their significance or overstating their relation to reality. Firstly, it is common to hear people argue that the value of humor is in its ability to bring the truth to light, a sentiment expressed here by the cartoon character, SpongeBob SquarePants (Funny pants 2005):

1. SpongeBob: Time for work, Squidward.
2. SpongeBob: Another day, another dollar. ((*laughs*))
3. Squidward: More like another nickel. ((Squidward's face is serious))
4. SpongeBob: ((*laughs*)) Good one, Squidward.

((*as Squidward and SpongeBob walk to work, SpongeBob is still laughing*))

5. SpongeBob: Another day, another nickel. ((*laughs*))
6. Squidward: It's not that funny. ((visibly annoyed))
7. SpongeBob: It's funny because it's true! ((*laughs*))

As this sequence subtly points out, however, the assertion that things are funny because they are "true" is overly simplistic. Squidward isn't actually arguing that he makes a nickel a day. Rather, his deadpan delivery denotes sarcasm. He exaggerates reality, at once comparing *and* contrasting it to an alternate reality, in an effort to critique what he perceives to be a low wage. At the most basic level, humorous utterances derive their funny factor from the "surprises" (i.e., contradictions, and incongruities) they set up, an argument Beeman (2000:103) explains below:

> Basic incongruity theory as an explanation of humor can be described in linguistic terms as follows: A communicative actor presents a message or other content material and contextualizes it within a cognitive "frame." The actor constructs the frame through narration, visual representation, or enactment. He or she then suddenly pulls this frame aside, revealing one or more additional cognitive frames which audience members are shown as possible contextualizations or reframings of the original content material. The tension between the original framing and the sudden reframing results in an emotional release recognizable as the enjoyment response we see as smiles, amusement, and laughter. This tension is the driving force that underlies humor, and the release of that tension—as Freud pointed out—is a fundamental human behavioral reflex.

Language and reality itself become humorous depending on how we frame them and contrast them to other phenomena and interpretations. From the simplest of puns to the bawdiest of jokes, we find things funny because in one way or another they contrast with expectation. More importantly, our ability to turn the juxtaposition of objects, people, and ideas into a pleasurable experience makes humor a useful tool in establishing, maintaining, and challenging social norms. As joke tellers, we highlight the differences between our words and actions—and those of others[1]— and what is considered to be expected or normal.

---

1 The "butt" of a joke is the person who is being targeted by or made fun of in a joke. In this example, the butt is the person being treated, albeit jokingly, in an overly friendly and pushy way.

Whether or not the receiver of a joke interprets the joke as funny depends on how the receiver interprets the joke teller's efforts and the contrasts that he or she highlights. Importantly, however, our perceptions of the joke may not correlate with our responses. We cannot assume that because people laugh, they truly appreciate a joke. Conversely, people may avoid laughing at jokes they actually find funny.

This brings us to the second lay theory we would like to address: the notion that a joke is *just* a joke. This notion can be used to imply the following:

a.   Humorous utterances are trivial and irrelevant to serious business.
b.   The joke I am telling is only meant to be funny; it has no deeper social meaning.

We argue that jokes are never simply funny utterances. Even language play, such as punning, accomplishes important social goals. By pitting words against one another in language play, interlocutors make claims about the appropriateness and silliness of certain words and sounds in particular contexts, thereby challenging, experimenting with, or reaffirming the linguistic standard and signaling certain speakers or types of speech as abnormal, funny, or inappropriate, for example.

A common, though not necessary, quality of jokes is that those who tell them assert some perspective on reality while at the same time sending the message that what they are conveying is not entirely truth—hence the claim, "it's just a joke." For example, the joke, "what has wheels and flies?" (answer: a dump truck) hinges on the joke recipients' understanding that the question isn't exactly what it appears to be. Like a con artist, the joke teller pulls a "bait and switch" in which he or she hopes the recipient will be lured by the verb form of the word "flies." What the recipient actually must "buy" when the punch line is revealed, however, is the noun form. Although jokes such as this help us think critically about language, they are fairly harmless, and few would be inclined to think that the joke teller believes a dump truck can fly. Other forms of humor come with greater risk.

Folks who are engaged in "risky" humor, such as jokes about ethnic stereotypes, dead babies, or suicidal bunnies, often assert that their depiction "is just a joke"[2] as a means of distancing themselves from what they are saying and the view of reality that it seems to assert (Basso 1979; Hill 2008). When a person tells a dead baby joke or posts a suicidal bunny picture on the bulletin board of his or her desk, the overt denotation may be that the person derives pleasure directly from the pain of helpless creatures. However, it is just as likely, perhaps more, that the person is attempting to convey some other message, for example: I do not think death should be a taboo subject; I try not to take life too seriously, or; joking about death takes the sting out of it. Years ago, I (Mercedes) met a man named Dave[3] who, among other severe injuries, was nearly blinded when a driver hit Dave's motorcycle and fled the scene of the crime. When I met Dave about a year after this event, he was still in physical therapy, and it was clear that the accident remained fresh in his mind. As he told me about the accident he pointed to a bumper sticker on his truck that read "It's all fun and games until somebody loses an eye." In popular culture, this expression is attributed to mothers warning their children not to play dangerous games. For Dave, however, this

---

2   A speaker may literally state "it's just a joke" in an effort to disassociate themselves from the joke's claims or they may assert that a humorous utterance is "just a joke" through gestures like winking or crossing their fingers behind their backs. However, the humorous frame itself may be assumed to convey this idea. In the example of Apache jokes about white American social behavior, the performer behaves as a white person under the assumption that his or her interlocutor perceives the behavior as a joke and not an attempt to get away with unacceptable behaviors.
3   Dave is a pseudonym.

admonishment is not just a warning but a reality; displaying the sticker proudly on his car was a way to assert his new identity as a differently abled person and confront the reality of what had happened to him with some levity.

The receivers of risky jokes, however, may not be willing to accept the connoted meanings that a joke teller hopes to convey. Basso's (1979) study describes a form of Western Apache joking that provides an apt example. The joker imitates behavior that the Apache attribute to white American culture and consider rude and offensive: i.e., excessive touching, probing into a person's emotional state by asking how they are feeling, calling acquaintances "friend," being bossy or pushy, and disrespecting a person's right to speak when ready and to make decisions without being coerced. If the joke is successful, the butt of the joke or some onlooker makes a remark about the social ineptness of whites, thereby validating the joke's success and calling an end to the joking frame (Basso 1979:57). Basso (1979:51–52) provides the following example from a man (J) joking with a clan brother (L) who has come to visit. At the end, J's wife (K) provides an assessment:

J: How you doing?
    How you feeling, L?
    You feelin' good?

  . . .

J: Come right in, my friend!
    Don't stay outside in the rain.
    Better you come in right now.
    Sit down!

  . . .

J: You hungry?
    You want some beer?
    Maybe you want wine?
    You want crackers?
    Bread?
    You want some sandwich?
    How 'bout it? You hungry?

      . . .

K: Whitemen are stupid!

Participants in Basso's study found this form of humor to be dangerous (Basso 1979:43) and best reserved for only the closest friends because the receiver of this imitative behavior could reject the joking frame (that is, reject the notion that it is "just a joke"). In this case, the imitation comes to feel too much like reality for the butt, and the failed joke becomes an offense (Basso 1979:75).

In this chapter, we seek to understand humor as a multifunctional tool for accomplishing a plethora of social goals. We explore the ways that people incorporate humor into their social lives, approaching our analysis from the premise that the study of humor should not be separated from the contexts in which it is created, decontextualized, and recontextualized[4] (Briggs 1988). Moreover, we argue that humor helps to create contexts in which speakers interact. To understand humor's multifunctional role in human relationships, we consider interconnections between humor and the following key concepts:

a) performance,
b) intersubjectivity, and
c) multivocality.

By highlighting the links between humor, performance, intersubjectivity, and multivocality[5], we seek to emphasize that humorous utterances have social lives and cannot be reduced to the validity, absurdity, or even hilarity of their claims. It is important to note that in our analysis of humor's social functions, we do not concentrate on the topic of aggressive humor that is intended to cause emotional harm to its hearers. This topic is addressed by other authors in this book. Rather, we address both failed and successful attempts at humor intended to make its interlocutors laugh.

Humor and Performance

In its normal, everyday meaning, performance refers to the completion of an action or the enactment of a role or task before some form of audience. Consider, for example, the following utterances: "Even though John performed well at his job, he did not get the promotion," or "we enjoyed the guitarist's performance in the concert last night." However, anthropologists—linguistic anthropologists, in particular—define performance somewhat differently. For linguistic anthropologists, a performer does not need to be a professional and performances do not have to be enacted on a literal stage. Rather, performance is a "mode of speaking" (Bauman 1975:290). A simple conversation around the water cooler at work can contain various instances of performance.

Bauman and Briggs (1990) define performance as "the enactment of the poetic function," and as "a specially marked, artful way of speaking that sets up or represents a special interpretive frame within which the act of speaking is to be understood" (73). Performers "mark" their speech with devices such as repetition, rhyme, changes in vocal quality, and the use of certain expressions (like parables, and proverbs) and other forms of verbal artistry. The process whereby speakers embellish their talk with these devices is called **entextualization**.

Speakers entextualize their speech for a variety of reasons. For example, through performance (and, hence, entextualization) speakers distinguish their discourse (in part or whole) from normal speech. As a result, their speech stands out, becoming memorable, repeatable and effective at achieving some communicative, social goal (Bauman and Briggs 1990:73, 79). Furthermore, using speech that is poetic, repetitive, and predictable assures that participants and viewers know what to expect, even if they don't know the precise words a person is going to say. This makes entextualized speech appealing for ritual

---

4   Decontextualization refers to the process by which text is removed from its original context. Importantly, what is decontextualized is, at the same time, recontextualized, or rather, placed into a new context (Bauman and Briggs 1990:74). When we tell a second-hand joke, we decontextualize it by removing the joke from the context in which we first saw or heard it, and recontextualize it by putting it to work in a new context.

5   We will explain and explore these terms in greater detail in the pages to come.

performances such as healing and diagnosis (Briggs 1996; Wilce 2008), political oratory (Silverstein 2003), and joke-telling all of which rely on audience participation and buy-in if they are to be truly effective.

One of the ways that speakers frame their discourse is by providing a "characterization" of the joke (for example, as silly, dirty, or a "good one"), and, or revealing the source of the joke (Sacks 1974). In so doing, a potential joke performer obtains his or her audience's approval to tell the joke and provides information about how to interpret the coming discourse. Moreover, the humorous frame, like all frames, is **metacommunicative** in that it gives interlocutors information about how they should respond (Bateson 1972:188). After all, humor is dependent on the participation of a receptive audience (Beeman 2000:103). The most expected response to the completion of a humorous utterance—and to laughter itself—is laughter (Jefferson 1979). However, before a joker can get to the punchline, his or her interlocutor often must participate in other ways.

Joke tellers involve their audiences in the joke-telling process through a variety of means. Reminiscing over past, humorous events involves the recycling of old material and involves various members of a group in the telling of a story (Norrick 2004). The collaborative, enjoyable nature of humorous reminiscing makes it an important part of a conversationalist's repertoire (Norrick 2004:81). When an interlocutor wants to propose the conarration of a story, he or she often says something akin to "do you remember ... ?" or "it was the funniest thing," thereby keying the frame of humorous remembrance and inviting those with knowledge of the events to participate in their telling.

This brings us to another strategy for involving interlocutors, familiar adjacency pairs that help to frame discourse as humorous. Adjacency pairs are "sequences" of dialogue in which a particular comment, question, or request is meant to be followed by a particular response or response type (Sidnell 2010:4). Adjacency pairs are common elements in conversation. "Thank you" followed by "you're welcome," or even "mhm," is a common adjacency pair. The typical joke usually begins with an adjacency pair. The expression "have you heard the one about___?" is a classic example. The moment an interlocutor hears this expression, he or she knows a joke is brewing. To complete this adjacency pair, the most appropriate response would be "no" or "yes, I have" (or some variation thereof). Of course, the joke teller is probably hoping the interlocutor will simply say "no," an indication to proceed with the joke. The following riddles begin with a "wh-" question. Unless the recipient wants to take a stab at the answer, the most common response would be, quite simply, "I don't know."

1. What has wheels and flies?	I don't	A garbage truck.
2. Why did the banana go out with the prune?	know.	Because he couldn't find a date.
3. Why did the Turtle cross the road?		To get to the shell station.

The traditional "knock, knock" joke contains two adjacency pairs that precede the punch line, for a total of five lines. The first pair is formulaic. The joker says "knock, knock" and the interlocutor responds "who's there?" In the second adjacency pair, the joker says a word, which the interlocutor must repeat and follow with "who."

1.   Joke teller: Knock knock!   First adjacency pair
2.   Interlocutor: Who's there?
3.   Joke teller: Little old lady ...   Second adjacency pair

4.   Interlocutor: Little old lady who?

5.   Stop yodeling and open the door!   Punchline

The following knock, knock joke plays with the expected formula, a process that results in repetition of the standard adjacency pairs:

1.   Knock, knock
2.   Who's there?
3.   Banana
4.   Banana who?
5.   Knock, knock
6.   Who's there?
7.   Banana
8.   Banana who?
9.   (the joke teller should repeat the "knock, knock" sequence until he/she gets bored or the recipient shows signs of annoyance or fatigue)
10.   Knock, knock
11.   Who's there?
12.   Orange
13.   Orange who?
14.   Orange you glad I didn't say banana?

Although interlocutors will eventually tire of the game, they initially find themselves compelled to keep responding when the joke teller calls out "knock, knock." This makes a point known all too well by conversation analysts: the "machinery," or organizing principles of conversation[6] drive us to respond to our interlocutors, and to do so according to conventions of conversation (Sacks 1974; Sidnell 2010). Because of our desire to participate in interactions with others and be good conversationalists, we may continue to play along with the joke teller. We have limits, however; we expect our interlocutors to be respectful of our time and to not repeat questions that have already been answered. In the punchline ("orange you glad I didn't say banana?"), the joker recognizes his or her interlocutor's dilemma (wanting it to be over, but wanting to be a good participant in the joke-telling).

Conversation analysts argue that we do not just respond randomly to what was said before. Rather, the social situations in which we interact with other people help to organize and structure what we say or don't say, giving conversation a predictable organization and flow (Sacks 1974; Sidnell 2010; Jefferson 1979). Although we may not know exactly what a person will say, we can predict the type of response we should expect. Thus, there is a distinction between the "possible completion" and the "actual completion" of a turn-at-talk (Sidnell 2010).

At the same time that jokes and other such utterances frame discourse as humorous, jokes must also be understood to be framed by the discourse that surrounds them. When we study only a performance itself,

---

6   Conversation analysis is an approach to transcribing and analyzing interaction that was initially developed by Harvey Sacks, Emmanuel Schegloff, and Gail Jackson. It is based on the notion that human interaction is orderly and proceeds according to certain principles and preferences. Conversation analysts assess the turn-by-turn development of talk in order to understand the impact and significance of interlocutors' words and actions on one another. Harvey Sacks coined the term "machinery" to describe the organizing principles of conversation. Fittingly, it conjures images of a factory in which the activation of a gear makes possible a chain reaction of movement in other parts.

we miss important details that affect how the performance is enacted, how it is perceived by audience members, and how the performance relates to other texts (Bauman 1996; Briggs 1988). Bauman (1996) points out that recontextualization of a text is "linked" to the processes under which it is decontextualized (301). Thus, the performer's orientation to the text (for example, as authoritative, flawed, or open to interpretation) will affect the ways he or she performs it. "There is a dynamic tension," Bauman (1996:302) argues, "between the ready-made, socially given element, that is, the persistent cultural entity that is available for recontextualization in performance, and the emergent element, the transformation of this entity in the performance process." Dynamic tension refers to a process whereby opposing forces exert pressure upon one another. On one hand, jokes and the situations we confront in the real world have an original context. At the moment of telling, however, we impress upon these texts and events a social context and significance that are particular to that context. The teller, audience, time of day, location of telling, etc., all play a part in the ways that an utterance is constructed and interpreted.

The following example, published in *Ways with Words* by Shirley Brice Heath (1983:63–65), exemplifies the importance of perceiving humorous performances in context. The narrative, told by an elderly black woman, named Miss Bee, was elicited by a group of black high school students who were collecting oral histories from local residents. Only half of the transcript provided by Heath is reproduced here; however, the pattern set up in the selected passage continues in the passage not reproduced here.

Miss Bee's narrative is not blatantly humorous. Were it not for her repeated chuckles, this story could be perceived as a serious recounting of historical facts. By following key moments in her narrative with laughter, however, she lets her audience know that the details she shares should be perceived as humorous. Accordingly, the interviewers don't laugh until Miss Bee laughs in line 3. Yet, the humor of the situation serves a social purpose that goes beyond simple entertainment. Heath (1983:65) notes that "varied repetitions" and "lilting chant-like quality" in Miss Bee's performance occur in reminiscences of others in the African–American, North Carolina community that she studied (which she renames "Trackton"). This style of recounting the past, Heath argues, helps to frame memories of the past as humorous while also conveying pride in and acceptance of the past—regardless, or even because of, its challenges. Miss Bee's laughter punctuates the fact that much has changed and been "accomplished" (Heath 1983:65). In line 7, one of the high school students interviewing Miss Bee proclaims "You gon' say dat?" after Miss Bee attests that she had grown up in a house in the middle of a cow pasture. Perhaps the interviewer suspects that Miss Bee has embellished her description for comedic effect, or perhaps the interviewer is expressing surprise upon learning of Miss Bee's humble past. Regardless, the interviewer demonstrates awareness that Miss Bee is framing the events of her childhood not only as humorous but also as having been so difficult or different from the current norm as to be unbelievable.

We can also see how Miss Bee structured her narrative to fit with its humorous frame. Notice that Miss Bee repeatedly begins her examples with 'n (and). This repetitive, parallel structure helps to draw her listeners' attention to the relationships between key details in her narrative, making them more memorable on one hand, and, on the other, setting up the tale's humorous aspects. Between the first round of laughter and the second, Miss Bee follows each "'n" with actions, i.e., raining, snowing, and seeing chickens through spaces in the floor boards, that one might not expect to occur in a house. In addition, after line 14, she switches her use of prepositions to draw attention to the fact that strange things didn't just occur "in de house" but also "under de house." By the time she states that the chickens would be under the house "eatin'," it is clear to all that she intended for these details to be understood as funny, and Miss Bee and the interviewers laugh in unison. Between lines 20 and 64, Miss Bee starts a new narrative. This

1.	Miss Bee:	In my chil'hood, I kin remember when we live in a li'l log	
2.		house, in de *pasture*—	
3.		|: 'mong de *cows*	(laughter)
4.	Interviewers:		(laughter)
5.	Miss Bee:	*cows* and *hogs*	(laughter)
6.			(laughter)
7.	Single	You gon' say dat?	
8.	interviewer:		\[
9.	Miss Bee:	'n de cows 'n hogs, in de pasture,: |	
10.		li'l log house, 'ere's two li'l windows to it,	
11.		|: 'n it *rained* in de house,	
12.		'n it *snowed* in de house	
13.		'n we could look down through de *crack*,	
14.		'n see de *chickens*,	
15.		*Under* de house: |	
16.		Eatin'	(laughter)
17.	Interviewers:		(laughter)
18.			\[
19.	Interviewers:	eatin'	
20.	Miss Bee:		(laughter) 'n-er-uh,
21.	Single		\[
22.	Interviewer:	All right	
23.	Miss Bee:	'n-er-uh, (long pause) I know my *mother* (clears throat)	
24.		|: had put (pause) paper, magazines	
25.		'n patched *up* de house for us to keep *warm*,	
26.		Plastered de house all over wid magazines, to keep us	
27.		Warm: |	
28.		'n-er-uh, (long pause), 'n 'member when	
29.		|: we worked in de *fiel'*, she worked in de fiel: |	
30.		did, for 'bout (pause) thirty-five cents a day.	
31.		'n den (clears throat) (pause) she had to carry her little baby	
32.		Out in de fiel' sittin' under de *shade* tree, while we workin'	
33.		inne *fiel'*.	
34.		'n-er-uh den we *move* from dere to a better house.	
35		'n in de *spring*, dey'd uh (pause) wash de bed ticks	
36		[mattress coverings]	
37		up off de *beds*, an' empty de straw out of 'em	

. . .

54.		'n we'd whitewash all 'round de house wid mud get out de	
55.		branch,	
56.		'n den we whitewash de trees out de yard: |	(pause)
57.		Dat's in de spring,	
58.		now everything's beautiful	(laughter)
59.			\[
60.	Interviewers:		(laughter)
61.			\[
62.	Miss Bee:	Whitewash de fireplaces	
63.			(laughter)
64.			\[
65.	Interviewers:		(laughter)

. . .

time each "'n" details a different chore that she and her family did around the house and out in the field. In keeping with her chosen frame for this narrative, Miss Bee wraps up this lengthy list of exhausting chores on a positive note, saying "now everything's beautiful" and with an invitation to laughter[7], which the interviewers take up in lines 60–65. "Now everything's beautiful" is a significant line when considering how sharply it contrasts with the difficult work involved and the critical nature of this work. Restuffing the beds with fresh straw, whitewashing the walls to keep them sanitary, and whitewashing the trees to prevent bug infestations and overexposure to the sun are not simply vane acts, they are important to a family's health and financial well-being. In a third part of the narrative (not reproduced here), Miss Bee uses the "'n" construction to list the challenges of traveling by foot. The audience learns how funny these details are when Miss Bee reveals that the "bossman" who owned the property they lived on had a car—highlighting that the technology was available to get them off their feet, but they were too poor to access it. If we perceive Miss Bee's narrative and her use of humor as social action, we see that Miss Bee's laughter and her framing of her childhood as humorous go hand in hand with a view of the past as enjoyable and worthwhile. Thus, while her joking frames aspects of her life as humorous, the surrounding serious text conversely helps to frame her humorous claims as matters of serious business.

Analysis of this transcript underscores an important point made by Briggs (1988): because effective performances often contain the "intermingling" of performance and non-performance styles, it can be difficult to determine clear boundaries between performance and other types of speech (17). Not only do we see that the humorous aspects of Miss Bee's performance blend with its more serious aspects, we see how changing times and the presence of a young audience impact Miss Bee's telling of events from her childhood. Briggs (1988:17–18) argues that analyses that focus solely on performances themselves, either removing them entirely from context or summing up the speech that precedes or follows them, lose an important sense of the performance's meanings and functions. Recognizing the embeddedness of performance in the discourse surrounding it permits researchers to perceive performers' attention to the conceptual and stylistic "fit" of their performances with the surrounding speech (Briggs 1988:18–19). Briggs' point is particularly relevant to the study of humor, a highly stylized form of speech that becomes so bracketed away from the context of its telling that we have entire books and web pages filled with them.

Bauman and Briggs' (1990) assertion that performance " ... sets up or represents a special interpretive frame within which the act of speaking is to be understood" (1990:73) is important to understanding how people convey messages through humor. We may be aware (consciously or unconsciously) of the ways that discourse is being framed (i.e., as playful, humorous, serious, romantic) without a speaker having to state the frame explicitly (Bateson 1972:186–187).

When people tell jokes or put on other humorous performances, they provide clues, sometimes very clear and overt, other times more subtle, that what we are hearing is meant to be interpreted as funny. In fact, the teller of a humorous anecdote may wait until the punchline to reveal that the events involved have a humorous resolution or significance. In other words, the performance of humor and of performance in general should be understood in some non-literal sense (Bauman 1975:292). According to Bauman (1975:292) "performance represents a transformation of the basic referential[8] ("serious," "normal" in Austin's terms) uses of language."

---

7 Miss Bee invites laughter through her own laughter, an indication that others should laugh too (Jefferson 1979).

8 Referential language is language with a literal frame. It refers directly to a specific topic, person, thing, or idea without resorting to implication, connotation, or poetic ornamentation, for example.

The following joke, made by President Barack Obama at the 2011 White House Correspondents' Association (WHCA) Dinner[9] provides a further example of how people use contrast to frame serious—or, at least, neutral—commentary as funny. Obama's time at the podium is preceded by a patriotic song by Rick Derringer, titled *Real American*. As the song plays, images of American icons[10] appear in front of an American flag on the large screens above the auditorium. Intermittently, Obama's birth certificate, proving his U.S. citizenship, appears in the middle of the flag, pulsing to the beat of an electric guitar. When the song ends, Obama has the following interchange with his audience of journalists, politicians, and celebrities:

1. Obama: alright everybody (.) please have a seat
2. Obama: my FEllow Americans
3. Audience: ((cheers, hoots, and claps))
4. Obama: maHAlo
5. Audience: ((laughs))
6. Obama: ((chuckles))

Obama begins this interchange with a serious comment. He addresses the audience as his "fellow Americans," placing emphasis on the word "fellow." In so doing, he aligns himself with the patriotic images and lyrics just seen and heard and asserts that he is a "real American"[11]. Obama's supporters in the audience hoot and cheer their support of the president's claim. However, when he responds saying *"mahalo,"* a way of expressing gratitude in Hawaiian, the audience laughs this time. They do not laugh because the word *"mahalo"* is inherently funny or even because he said it in a particularly funny way. Rather, the audience laughs in recognition of Obama's sudden change of frame and the political claims it makes. Prior to saying *"mahalo,"* Obama asserted his "real American-ness" with traditional symbols of American culture or pop culture icons representing American strength and victory. *Mahalo,* on the other hand, is a polite term with non-Christian, spiritual origins that represents a geographical region (Hawaii, the place of Obama's birth) that mainland Americans have historically exoticized and othered. By telling his audience *"mahalo"* right after calling them his "fellow" Americans, Obama sets up a humorous contrast that challenges notions of what it means to be a "real" American.

The complex relationship between humor and the truth or literalness of its claims becomes more meaningful when we consider potentially dangerous forms of humor. If a person from culture X imitates the manner of dress or style of communication of people from culture Y and successfully makes his audience laugh, we cannot say that the audience is laughing simply because the depiction is true. Rather, the joke teller has managed to represent people in culture Y in a way that sets up a humorous surprise, perhaps by simply emphasizing the contrast between the cultures. Basso (1979:44) refers to the process of "portraying (one's) characters so as to make them appear ludicrous and ridiculous" as "epitomization."

---

9   Speeches at the WHCA Dinner revolve primarily around politics, but are mostly comical and light-hearted. Speakers often "roast" other important guests and poke fun at themselves.

10   For example, a bald eagle, Mount Rushmore, cowboys on horseback, Rocky Balboa, Hulk Hogan, and the Karate Kid.

11   Throughout his candidacy and subsequent presidency, Obama has responded to critics who attempt to disassociate Obama and his supporters from an ethos of American-ness and love of country. Obama's critics also point to Obama's non-Western European name, African heritage, and alleged foreign birth as evidence that he is un-American and unfit for the presidency. Obama has proved repeatedly, however, that he was born in the United States.

In Basso's (1979) study, Apache jokers use the contrast and distortion principles[12] to demonstrate and exaggerate the differences between white and Apache people.

The following example from comedian, Russell Peters' show, *Red, White and Brown* shows how a joke performer can use comparison in addition to contrast and distortion when attempting to epitomize a subject and frame him or her as humorous. Peters, who is Indian–American, is known for his humorous depictions of people of various cultures.

1.	Peters:	Any Brazilians?[13]
2.		Are you Brazilian? ((looking at someone in the audience who is off camera))
3.		Brazilians speak Portuguese right so?
4.		So you speak Portuguese, though, right ((Peters points at the person))
5.	Audience member:	yeah
6.	Peters:	so if you speak Portuguese
7.		obviously you can understand Spanish then right?
8.		'cause they're very similar
9.		to each other aren't they?
10.		you ever hear somebody speaking Portuguese?
11.		doesn't it sound like
12.		Spanish being spoken by a deaf person?
13.		Portuguese just sounds like
14.		really badly pronounced Spanish doesn't it?
15.		Here's a Spanish guy counting to three.
		unos (sic), dos, tres ((Peters stands straighter, holds out his hand, and makes a very serious face; he enunciates clearly and speaks in a moderate tone of voice))
16.		Here's a Portuguese guy.
		UNOSH, DOSH, TRESH. ((Peters yells and his voice is monotone and nasal))
17.	Audience:	((laughs))
18.	Peters:	CUATRO, SHINCO
19.	Audience:	((laughs))
20.	Peters:	BAKAKA. ((nonsense sounds))
21.	Audience:	((continues laughing))
22.	Peters:	Here's a Spanish guy.
23.		Como estás ((again, Peters face and voice convey seriousness))
24.		Here's a Portuguese guy.
		COMO ESTASH. ((Again, Peters yells and his voice is monotone and nasal))

---

12 According to the contrast principle, the joker(s) juxtapose(s) two subjects by performing certain aspects associated with each subject (i.e., their behavior, manner of speech, social role). The aspects chosen should demonstrate how the subjects differ in socially meaningful ways. According to the distortion principle, the joker intensifies and calls attention to the differences between the subjects by modifying them in some way (Basso 1976:44–45).

13 Peters is asking if there are any Brazilian people in the Audience.

Peters frames Spanish as "serious-sounding" (see lines 15 and 23) and as a standard by which to compare Portuguese. He begins by asserting that Spanish and Portuguese are "very similar" in lines 5–7 and then proposes a humorous contrast between the two languages in line 10–14 when he argues that Portuguese speakers talk as though they can't actually hear or as though they are speaking Spanish "badly". He then exaggerates the vocal qualities of spoken Portuguese, making Portuguese sound more like Spanish than it actually does and overemphasizing the nasal sound of Portuguese to liken it to the ways that deaf people talk. In this way, he is able to set up a contrast that frames Portuguese and deaf speech as humorous, particularly when compared to spoken Spanish.

Much of what Peters says *derives* from truth. Spanish and Portuguese are quite similar (although not exactly mutually intelligible as he claims). Additionally, both Portuguese and deaf speech have nasal qualities, and Portuguese nasalizes many words that spoken Spanish does not. The manner in which he frames the speech of these three types of speakers, however, exaggerates and distorts reality and invites a humorous interpretation of them. It also invites potential offense over the manner in which he pokes fun at deaf people, a matter which he points out right after line 25. As this example and the example of Apache jokes about the Whiteman show, risky, potentially offensive humor exploits the boundaries of truth, making its interpretation dependent upon how the listener chooses to interpret the frame.

A final example will illustrate even further how risky humor exploits the boundaries of truth, and how humor, in general, opposes the literal frame. Racist jokes and other depictions of blacks, especially before the civil rights movement, often showed black people eating watermelon. However, watermelon-eating was not meant to be understood literally. It was a silent code for laziness, simplicity, and indulgence; furthermore, the properties of the watermelon itself (such as the red, fleshy interior, which was likened to the mouths of black people) could be compared to the physical properties of blacks—thereby dehumanizing them. Many young whites are unaware of stereotypes regarding blacks and watermelon and, thus, miss the racist, humorous frame and interpret them as harmless depictions of blacks just enjoying a snack. Yet, whether or not blacks indeed loved watermelon was not important to racist whites. How boring and potentially humanizing would such a claim be in a society that worked so hard to justify oppression and maintain social distance between blacks and whites.

Intersubjectivity and Meaning Making

Understanding processes through which we make sense of our interactions with others is crucial to perceiving humor as a social and interactional achievement. According to the 20th century philosopher, Edmund Husserl, the potential for humans operating in the natural world to attain shared understanding results from intersubjectivity (Duranti 2010). "For Husserl, intersubjectivity is the most basic quality of human existence, which is constitutive of the Subject and of the very notion of an objective world" (Duranti 2010:1). The word intersubjectivity is comprised of the prefix "inter," meaning "across" or "between," and the root word "subject." When we call people "subjects," we call attention to the fact that people are not created in a vacuum. Rather, people are *subject to* the conditions (i.e., political and social) that surround and mold them. In intersubjectivity, we see the meeting of subjects who have the *potential* to achieve some degree of shared understanding because of their common nature and any efforts they may make to communicate and empathize with one another (Duranti 2010:6–7).

Intersubjectivity is the meaning-filled space that exists between subjects when they interact—either directly or by way of objects and signs that imply the presence of another (Duranti 2010:10). We can think of intersubjectivity as occurring on a spectrum, with a high level of intersubjectivity, or full understanding on one end and a low level on the other. In the space between, we find partial and even assumed understanding between interactional participants (Sidnell 2010; Bailey 2006). High levels of understanding result, when interlocutors share the same language, cultural knowledge, or experiences necessary to interpret an utterance or an event in the same way. We use the term "full" intersubjectivity here, however, with the recognition that intersubjectivity can never *actually* be "complete" since the subjective experiences of individual interlocutors can never fully be shared with others (Bailey 2004:396). With partial intersubjectivity, only certain forms of knowledge or experience are shared by interlocutors. Finally, unless our interlocutors send clear signals to us that they do not understand what is happening, we tend to assume that there is shared understanding. Sometimes, people use this to their advantage. Take, for example, a second language learner who recognizes the humorous frame around an utterance and, consequently, laughs even though he or she does not understand the joke's punchline. By laughing, this person avoids the embarrassment of revealing his or her lack of cultural or linguistic knowledge and avoids disrupting the flow of conversation. Thus, although this language learner has only partial knowledge, he or she takes advantage of our conversational tendencies to give the impression of full understanding.

Full understanding does not only result when interlocutors share knowledge. It is also achieved interactionally (Sidnell 2010; Bailey 2004; Hanks 1996). "Everyday talk proceeds on a turn-by-turn basis, and interactions are built up incrementally, sequentially, and interactionally" Bailey (2004: 398) asserts. Therefore, even where intersubjectivity appears to be complete, understanding has actually been building over time and across many interactions and perhaps even generations, leading Garfinkel to describe intersubjectivity as an "operation" and not just the crossing of knowledge and experience (1967:30). Turn by turn, interlocutors negotiate and approximate common understandings of activities in which they are engaged. The incremental and interactional structuring of conversation provides participants with regular opportunities to repair or avoid potential misunderstanding. Repair includes a range of techniques used by all parties in interaction to resolve breakdowns in communication. Consider the following example:

1. A: He looked so familiar to me and then I remembered that I'd met him before.
2.   I'd met him at that big party.
3. B: What party?
4. A: That big party at Sara's house last summer.
5. B: Oh, that ...

In the first utterance, speaker A makes a reference to a big party where she met someone. Speaker B is not clear on what party speaker A is referring to, so she asks for clarification. Speaker A clarifies and speaker B follows up with "oh, that," letting speaker A know that she has understood the reference. Chick (1990) compares intra-cultural encounters (encounters between people who share cultural knowledge) to ballroom dancing with a familiar partner, where both dancers are expecting and anticipating each other's moves. The result is a smooth ballroom performance. By contrast, in cross-cultural settings, in particular, encounters can be compared to ballroom dancing between strangers—unable to anticipate each other's moves, they struggle to establish mutually agreeable sequences (Chick 1990).

When an attempt at humor is accompanied by partial subjectivity, the speaker's humorous utterance may be in danger of becoming failed humor. Bell and Atardo (2010) define failed humor as the inability to respond appropriately to humor, and, more specifically, as:

> … any instance of speech production in a communicative setting in which any of the participants fails to notice the (potential) perlocutionary intention to amuse (be funny, elicit mirth, etc., as per Raskin 1985), or fails to process the text/situation in such a way as to be able to access the information whereby one of the other participants considers the situation (to have been intended or be potentially interpretable as) funny (2010: 426).

Bailey (2004:403) uses the following example to demonstrate difficulties that can arise in cross-cultural settings. The interaction below occurred between a Korean immigrant shopkeeper in Los Angeles and his customer, an African–American man, who had recently returned from a trip to Chicago.

1.	Owner:	Is Chicago cold?
2.	Customer:	Uh! ((shakes head side to side)) Man I got off the plane
3.		and walked out the airport I said 'Oh shit'.
4.	Customer:	heh heh heh
5.	Owner:	((no smile or laughter)) I thought it's gonna be nice spring season over there.

Importantly, the interlocutors seem to understand each other's words at the denotative–referential level (the meaning of the utterance) as evidenced by the topic relevance of the Korean man's response to the customer's implication that the weather in Chicago was bad. However, in declining the invitation to laughter extended by the customer's own laugh (Jefferson 1979) the Korean man declines to engage in a culturally appropriate response to a highly affective account of events. In this case, a simple form of repair would not be possible here without sounding awkward.

The process of repair occurs frequently in daily interactions and, for the most part, goes largely unnoticed to the interlocutors. The moment we are unable to make simple repairs work to our desired ends, we become aware of ambiguities associated with our utterances. The classic "Who's on first?" baseball comedy routine by Bud Abbott and Lou Costello is an extreme example of this, as its humor relies on the inability to manage effective repairs to establish understanding:

1.	Abbott:	Strange as it may seem, they give ball players nowadays very peculiar names.
2.	Costello:	Funny names?
3.	Abbott:	Nicknames …
4.	Abbott:	Now, on the St. Louis team we have uh
5.		Who's on first, What's on second, I Don't Know is on third.
6.	Costello:	That's what I want to find out.
7.		I want you to tell me the names of the fellas on the St. Louis team.
1.	Abbott:	I'm telling you. Who's on first, What's on second, I Don't Know is on third …
8.	Costello:	You know the fellas' names?
9.	Abbott:	Yes.
10.	Costello:	Well, then who's playing first?

11.	Abbott:	Yes.
12.	Costello:	I mean the fellow's name on first base.
13.	Abbott:	Who.
14.	Costello:	The fellow playin' first base for St. Louis.
15.	Abbott:	Who.
16.	Costello:	The guy on first base.
17.	Abbott:	Who is on first.
18.	Costello:	Well, what are you askin' me for?
19.	Abbott:	I'm not asking you—I'm telling you. Who is on first.
20.	Costello:	I'm asking you—who's on first?
21.	Costello:	That's who's name?
22.	Abbott:	Yes …

The different versions of the routine range anywhere from one to ten minutes and were based on humorous confusion and attempted repair to avoid confusion about the nicknames of infielders "Who" (first base), "What" (second base) and "I Don't Know" (third base). The humor results in part from the ambiguity created by these nicknames and the acted out frustration these comedians express as they repeatedly attempt repairs in an effort to establish a higher degree of intersubjectivity.

According to Bell and Attardo (2010) humor fails when the recipient of a joke does not realize the utterance was intended to be humorous or lacks the knowledge necessary to perceive the humor. In an effort to understand these failures, the authors attempt to construct a typology of failed humor and identify different levels of potential failure, such as failure to understand the meanings of words, failure to understand the pragmatic forces of utterances such as irony and sarcasm, failure to recognize the humorous frame, mistaking a humorous situation for a serious one and serious one for humorous one, failure to understand incongruity of the joke and failure to join in the joking.

The following transcript of an interaction that took place between an Australian newscaster and the Dalai Lama demonstrates another example of failure. The newscaster decided to tell the Dalai Lama a joke about the Dalai Lama, however, the joke failed to deliver the desired effect. (The video of this failure in action is available on youtube.com.)

1.	Newscaster:	so the Dalai Lama walks into a pizza shop
2.	Dalai Lama:	(in Tibetan, asks for a translation, looks up to the translator)
3.	Interpreter:	pizza shop (speaks Tibetan)
4.	Newscaster:	pizza?
5.	Dalai Lama:	pizza, pizza shop (nodding his head)
6.	Newscaster:	yeah pizza shop
7.		and says
8.		can you make me one with everything
9.	Dalai Lama:	(puzzled look) hmm
10.	what's that?	(laughs slightly, looks up to a translator)
11.	Interpreter:	(speaks in Tibetan)
12.	Dalai Lama:	oh, yes (looks at A, waiting for more)
13.	Newscaster:	do you know what I mean? (laughs)

14.	Dalai Lama:	(puzzled, laughs slightly)
15.	Newscaster:	can you make me (joins palms in front of him)
16.		one
17.		with everything (makes circular motion with his hands)
18.		(laughs)
19.	Dalai Lama:	ahh (puzzled, speaks Tibetan)
20.		oh
21.	Newscaster:	oh (puts a hand over his eyes in embarrassment)
22.		I knew that wouldn't work
23.	Dalai Lama:	(Laughs out loud) (4sec)

In this example, the joke failed on at least two different levels. First, the most obvious failure occurred due to a language barrier between the newscaster and the Dalai Lama. While this is a relatively simple joke, the Dalai Lama had to ask an interpreter to translate certain parts of it for him on several occasions. Second, the joke failed because of the lack of cultural knowledge. Here the humor relies on the denotational ambiguity of the phrase "make me one with everything." In order to understand the punchline, one has to be familiar with the phrase "make me one [pizza] with everything," where everything denotes all the toppings appropriate for pizza, and "make me one with everything [the universe]," where everything denotes being one with the universe. Even though it is relatively common to hear such a phrase in a place where one orders food, it seems unlikely that the Dalai Lama would know this. The idea of "being one with the universe" or "one with everything" is also a mantra that Westerns commonly attribute to Buddhism. It seems unlikely that the Dalai Lama would have been familiar with either the phrase or the misconception associated with the phrase. Even though it is impossible for the average viewer to know how exactly the interpreter translated this phrase, from the Dalai Lama's reaction, clearly not understanding or recognizing the punchline, we can assume that the interpreter also lacked the bicultural knowledge necessary for identifying the denotational ambiguity and therefore getting the joke.

If we think of the earlier metaphor of ballroom dancing, the video *Italian Man Who Went to Malta* evokes a painful image of clumsy dancers, repeatedly stepping on each other's toes and tripping over one another at every step. In this video, an Italian man goes on vacation to Malta, where he runs into some communication difficulties as well as resistance from the Maltese due to his thick Italian accent and perhaps his temperament. The following is a transcript of the video, which is available on youtube.com:

1.	Italian man:	one a day I am gone to Malta
2.		to a big a hotel
3.		in the morning I go down a
4.		to eat a breakfast
5.		I tell a waitress I wanna
6.		two pieces [pisses] of toast
7.		she brings my only one piece[piss]
8.		I tell her I want two [to] piece [piss]
9.		she says go to the toilet
10.		I say you no understand
11.		I wanna two [to] piece [piss] on my plate

12.	she say you better not piss on the plate
13.	you son of a bitch
14.	I don't even know the lady
15.	and she is calling me son of a beach
16.	later
17.	I go to eat at a bigger restaurant
18.	the waitress brings me a spoon, and a knife but no fork [fuck]
19.	I tell her I wanna the fork [fuck]
20.	she tell me everybody want to fuck
21.	I tell her you no understand
22.	I wanna fork [fuck] on the table
23.	she say you better not fuck on the table
24.	you son of a bitch
25.	so I go back to my room in a hotel
26.	and there is not sheets [shits] on the bed
27.	call the manager and tell him
28.	I wanna sheet [shit]
29.	he tell me to go to the toilet
30.	I say you no understand
31.	I wanna sheet [shit] on my bed
32.	he said you better not shit on the bed
33.	you son of a bitch
34.	I go to the check out
35.	and the man at the desk say
36.	peace on you
37.	I said piss on you too
38.	you son of a bitch
39.	I'm going back to Italia

This video demonstrates the previously mentioned turn-by-turn structuring of talk, taking place across lines of social and linguistic difference. Each time, both parties display the interpretations of prior turns and attempt to build on them, based on their understanding of them. Clearly, turn-by-turn, there is a consistent breakdown in communication. These breakdowns are followed by weak, unsuccessful attempts by the Italian man to repair and manage them in order to accomplish his intended goals. His repeated repairs in the form of "you no understand …" are over and over met with a complete unwillingness to accommodate and repair from the Maltese. The repetition of the same type of communication breakdowns and the same unwillingness to repair and accommodate is precisely what makes this video humorous for the viewer. In some sense, this repeating pattern is structurally similar to the "knock, knock" jokes where the humor rests precisely on repetition of a pattern. The repetition of breakdowns makes the situation absurd and the repeated assumptions made paint an outrageous picture of the situation. In the last segment of the video, we can see that at last, after many frustrating encounters, the Italian man has lost his willingness and desire to repair these breakdowns. As he walks out of the hotel, he is told by the hotel receptionist "Peace on you," which, based on the previous interactions with the Maltese, he hears as "Piss on you," and to which he responds "Piss on you too, you son of a beach [bitch], I am going back to Italia."

The misfortunes of the Italian man who went to Malta highlight one other dimension of intersubjectivity: the intersubjectivity between the video creator and the video viewer. This video clearly points to a socio-cultural dimension and to historical power relations that many of the viewers might not be familiar with, but nevertheless, it is still humorous. On the surface, the misunderstandings between the Italian man and his Maltese hosts are humorous because they contrast benign words like "fork" and "sheet" with swear words that make his speech seem offensive. However, to have a deeper understanding, a deeper level of intersubjectivity, one must ask why the joke involves an Italian man, in particular. The Republic of Malta has two official languages, Maltese and English and a large portion of the population is competent in both. To a lot lesser degree, Italian is also spoken in Malta, however, both Italian and English are unpopular there, mainly due to the fact that both Britain and Italy ruled the islands in various points in history. Nevertheless, even if we, the viewers, are unaware of the specifics of the Italian–Maltese relations, a partial level of intersubjectivity permits us to find the joke humorous and overlook the social critique embedded within it. We may, for example, remember our own frustrations and misunderstandings while trying to communicate in a foreign language or with someone whose accent is unfamiliar to us. We might also recall our own experience attempting to communicate in a foreign language and being either misunderstood or not understood at all.

While it is relatively easy to teach a student when it is appropriate to apologize or thank someone (and which expression to use in doing so), teaching students how to appropriately initiate or respond to humorous utterances and situations is not as simple. As Bell & Attardo (2010) point out, "there is rarely an obligatory or preferred context for humor, as there is for most speech acts" (442). Furthermore, there is no way that a teacher could ever hope to convey all the cultural knowledge a student would need in order to understand the jokes he or she may come across. Instead, the authors suggest that helping students develop cross-cultural pragmatic awareness of humor is a better starting point. By teaching students when, where, and with whom humor is appropriate and raising learners' awareness of complexities of humor, instructors can address those areas of humor that are most amenable to instruction. The difficulty of teaching humor in second language classrooms demonstrates how profoundly linked humor is to cultural knowledge and to emergent, ongoing processes of relationship building. Quite often, humor emerges from the situations in which we find ourselves rather than a prepackaged joke that a speaker pulls out of a joke book at an opportune time.

What happens, then, when people who don't speak the same language must interact? Can intersubjectivity be achieved without the use of a common language? Is humor even possible in such a situation? My husband and I (Volfova) often made trips back to my home country, visiting my family in the Czech Republic. My husband was born and grew up in the suburbs of Detroit, Michigan, so his knowledge of the Czech language, while well-articulated, was limited to simple phrases such as *dobrý den* (hello), *nemluvím Česky* (I don't speak Czech), *nerozumím* (I don't understand), and *ne, děkuji nemám hlad* (no, thank you, I am not hungry). During these trips, I was a self-appointed translator for him, determined to translate as much as I could, hoping to include him in everything that was going on around us. I wanted him to not only get to know my friends and family, but I also wanted him to appreciate the witty Czech sense of humor and all the cultural nuances that come with it. I even attempted to translate some classic Czech films we were watching on television, making sure he understood the value of these national treasures.

Soon, however, after becoming a bit lax in my exhausting job as an interpreter and translator, I started to notice that my husband was interacting with my family without my help. Although their interactions drew from a limited vocabulary, my husband and my family nevertheless developed a creative and effective manner of communicating. They defied linguistic and cultural boundaries by deliberately committing to communication, committing to getting to know each other, regardless of the fact that they didn't share a common language. In doing so, they called upon skills that we put to work on a regular basis. As Duranti (2010:2) asserts, "people go in and out of social encounters, managing to maintain a joint focus of attention that entails *some* form of communication that does not rely on spoken or written language" (Duranti 2010:2). I witnessed my father, who doesn't speak English, giving my husband a tour of his woodworking shop one day and showing him Czech-made tools and items my father constructed over the years. My father used a variety of gestures to communicate ideas and show my husband how things worked. My husband would replicate these gestures, usually adding some English words, hoping that by chance, he could stumble upon a cognate or two to confirm that a degree of mutual understanding was being achieved. On another occasion, my stepmother and my husband successfully negotiated dinner plans together. The more time we spent with my family, the more comfortable they all became with each other. They gestured, they drew pictures, they intuited, and they laughed—a lot.

On our last visit, I observed a fascinating interaction. It was our last full day at my father's house when a number of family members, friends and neighbors gathered for a typical rural Czech occasion. My father had organized the slaughter of a small pig to replenish his annual provisions of meat. In the evening, after a full day's work, the usual activities wound down, and drinks began to flow. My husband, who had spent part of the day helping, joined everyone for drinks, while I finished packing upstairs. Hearing raucous laughter coming from the lower level, I decided to see what was going on. When I entered the room, everyone, including my husband, was laughing in unison. I soon understood what was happening. One of the Czechs would call out a Czech swear word or vulgar expression, and then everyone would laugh riotously as my husband gladly attempted to reproduce the lude words. His willingness to participate in this game seemed to win all the Czechs over and as they all laughed, they simultaneously kept his glass of Slivovice (strong plum brandy) full and new words coming. My husband did not know what exactly he was repeating, but from the context, he was able to figure out what was happening, appreciate the humor in this situation, and willingly engage in it.

This was all done with no malice, a fact that was clear not only to me, but all who participated in this activity. Laughter had become a form of communication, a fact that begs the question: How much intersubjectivity is necessary for successfully accomplishing interaction? As Bell and Attardo (2010) point out, appreciation of humorous situations may occur even without full comprehension. Despite the lack of higher degree of intersubjectivity due to the ever present lack of a common language, a degree of some intersubjectivity was achieved through being able to relate to a common human experience, and the situation provided for an excellent bonding opportunity between people who do not have a common language available to them. What this example illustrates is that there are other ways of achieving intersubjectivity besides through language and cultural knowledge. Laughter, gestures, and even silence are all ways of communicating and, as such, play an important role in the achievement of intersubjectivity and finding humor in interaction.

Multivocality

The work of Mikhail Bakhtin has been influential in many different fields of social science. Bakhtin's concept of heteroglossia describes the coexistence of distinct varieties of speech within a single linguistic code. "Authorial speech, the speeches of narrators, inserted genres, the speech of characters are merely those fundamental compositional unities with whose help heteroglossia (*raznorečie*) can enter the novel" (Bakhtin 1981:262) "and by the differing individual voices that flourish under such conditions" (1981:263). In his analysis of novel as a literary form, Bakhtin argued that the power in novel lies precisely in the coexistence of different types of speech—distinct voices. These distinct voices can be understood as the speech of the various characters and the speech of the narrator, for example, all coming to the reader, *via* the voice of the author. These distinct voices may be social dialects, generational forms of language, gendered speech and various jargons, for example. In the Bakhtinian sense, a person does not command only one voice, but a multitude of distinct voices, reflecting his or her life experiences, background, affiliations with others, occupation, etc. In every day interactions, these voices come together to create our personal narrative that encodes important information. For example, a doctor might use different ways of speaking with his patients, the nurses he works with, other doctors, his friends, his wife, his children, etc. Many voices of this sort coexist and interact to produce socially significant meanings whose interpretation relies on the participants' recognition of indexical references. In every day interactions, whether they are intended to be humorous or not, we take advantage of the power of indexical references in language and rely on the interlocutors' ability to recognize them.

The cartoon above illustrates how language carries with it socially significant meanings and highlights the role of context in the process of meaning making. The mismatching of a voice with a given context, or the inability to recognize the appropriateness of a certain voice in a given context, has the potential to result in socially significant consequences. It is clear that Dudley and Daisy are friends and in this relationship, have a certain way of talking to each other as friends. This way of talking might include words that other people, in other contexts, might find upsetting. Dudley shares with Daisy that he has used a word that got him in trouble. Daisy, aware of the fact that one has to carefully choose how one speaks and what words one uses, tries to convey this idea to Dudley, who seems to be oblivious to this socially important knowledge. In the process of explaining, Daisy uses a distinctly different voice than the voice they are accustomed using with each other and by doing so, transforms the situation anew. By using this voice, the two instantly fall into a teacher–student model of sort. Daisy in her teacher-like voice uses two metaphors, that of a painter and of a composer, to convey the importance of matching language with context, while Dudley momentarily fulfills the role of an enquiring student. However, Daisy's teacher-like voice gets quickly interrupted by Dudley's "no there fucking aren't" interjection. In response to this, Daisy immediately abandons her teacher-like voice and matches Dudley's voice, friend-to-friend. Daisy produces a response that still acknowledges the importance of voice and context while at the same time aligning herself with her friend's frustrations. By saying that "it's just some bullshit you have to follow," Daisy summarizes her teacher voice argument in a voice that is appropriate for the context of her friendship with Dudley.

Even though Bakhtin's concepts were originally applied to novelistic discourse, multivocality or heteroglossia has been studied in relation to many genres. In Sclafani's (2009) analysis of the November 2006 *South Park*[14] episode about Martha Stewart[15], the authors see the use of voice as an important part of the process of accomplishing humorous parody of this famous TV personality. Two distinct techniques involving voice index Ms. Stewart's branded image of a highly skilled, creative feminine homemaker on one hand and a distinctly upper class, savvy business executive on the other. The first image attempts to match the profile of her intended audience, while the other underlines the reality that Ms. Stewart could not have become what she is solely with her homemaker skills and creativity. As Sclafani points out, Stewart's image:

> … of the 'Good Woman' who is ingenious and successful in traditional homemaking enterprises like cooking, gardening, and craft making—was endangered by her indictment for insider trading and subsequent five-month prison sentence, which she served from October 2004 to March 2005 (2009: 616).

The conflict between the public and private image of Martha Stewart is what the creators of this particular *South Park* episode explored. To capture the duality of Martha Stewart's persona, a number of stylistic features indexing the two very different personalities can be observed. Most notable, as Sclafani points out, is the fact that Stewart's voice is clearly performed by a male.

> The use of a man's voice to perform an icon of upper-middle-class femininity is a particularly useful parodic strategy because it draws attention to the double-voiced nature of the skit. In doing so, it also highlights the paradox between Stewart's traditionally feminine gendered linguistic style and her identity as a high-powered business executive—a normatively masculine

---

14 *South Park* is an American animated sitcom created for Comedy Central television network by Trey Parker and Matt Stone. The series is intended for adult audiences, often featuring satirical portrayals of celebrities. There have been a number of controversies associated with the show. *South Park* debuted in 1997 and is so far the longest running show on Comedy Central television network.

15 Martha Stewart is an American celebrity widely known for her television show and magazine publishing, featuring exceptionally creative homemaker skills. In 2004 Stewart was found guilty of conspiracy, obstruction of justice and illegal stock trading. Stewart served a five month sentence in a federal prison.

role, which was often commented on when her legal troubles became widely publicized in 2003 (Sclafani 2009:621).

The creative manipulation of voices and linguistic style to achieve a parodic effect is what makes this skit humorous.

Similarly, Glick (2007) analyses British stand-up comedian Eddie Izzard's use of voices in dialogue with each other in his distinct style of comedy routines. The short segment Glick examines, *The Flags*, is a part of Izzard's an hour and a half long stand-up comedy show *Dressed to Kill,* filmed during his 1998 performance in San Francisco. In this segment, Izzard acts as a narrator while facilitating fictionalized dialogue between different nations and peoples who were involved in the European project of colonization, either as the colonizers or the colonized. The following is a transcript of the opening scene of Izzard's segment. Present in this short segment are three distinct voices, the voice of the narrator, the British colonizing voice and the voice of the Indian people (Glick 2007).

1.	Narrator voice:	so we built up empires
2.		we stole countries
3.		that's how you build up empires
4.		we stole countries with the cunning use of flags
5.		we sailed around the world
6.		and stuck a flag in them
7.	British voice:	I claim India for Britain!
8.	Narrator voice:	they go
9.	Indian voice:	you can't claim us, we live here
10.		five hundred million of us
11.		we don't need a bloody flag
12.		it's our country you bastard
13.	British voice:	no flag, no country,
14.		you can't have one

Izzard draws on historical facts as well as on distinct voices of people involved to create a fictionalized conversation, which only highlights the absurdity of the situation. Izzard's use of stylized voices highlights certain aspects of social inequality between the characters involved in the conversation. In addition Izzard uses the positionality of his body to enact imaginary, visually rich landscapes in particular times in history. In skillfully performing this politically charged material, Izzard never loses sight of his American audience and its familiarity with the subject at hand. The above transcript raises the question: What does Izzard mean by repeatedly using the personal pronoun "we?" Izzard not only acknowledges the British collective responsibility for colonizing, but also invites his American audience to align with him. After all, America is a product of colonialism. Keeping his audience in mind, Izzard makes the topics culturally relevant and familiar, while bringing in narratives of significant historical events that aided in shaping both the contemporary United States as well as Britain. Hanks tells us that "the work of verbal art exists as a form of mediation between the socially defined producer(s) and receiver(s), between the individualized qualities that it has as a unique work and the broader historical structure of which it is a part" (1996:187). These fictional conversations, taking place in a particular time and place come to play an important role in how

Izzard achieves humor. In his routine, Izzard "transposes the historical process of colonial occupation into a single conversation and thereby speaks in a kind of imaginary historical real-time" (Glick 2007:295). This offers both Izzard and his audiences the ability to contemplate the correlation between distinct entities such as working-class Brits and colonial East Indians in a way that brings their similarities and differences to life (Glick 2007). As if a map of the world were imprinted on the empty stage, Izzard uses his body and voice to move across this vast, imagined geographical space, transporting his audience with ease from Europe to India and North America, using humor to highlight the absurdity and tragedy of the situation.

Conclusion

In this essay, we have analyzed humorous language in light of the theoretical paradigms of performance, intersubjectivity, and voice. In so doing, we have stressed that humor is a vital, multifunctional aspect of human communication. Moreover, we have argued that humor must be understood in the context of the serious discourse within which it exists and which it comments upon. Finally, we have argued against two common ideologies of humor: a) that humor is a frivolous topic, and b) that utterances are funny because they are true.

As a form of performance, humor frames discourse and signals to hearers that the meaning of an utterance lies somewhere beyond its literal interpretation. Yet, the human capacity for intersubjectivity provides for shared understanding of the situations that humorous utterances comment upon. This shared understanding can be partial, full or even assumed, but because of our common human experience, it is always present to some degree as long as we are conscious and aware of our surroundings. This means that interlocutors need not even share a common language for humor to be possible.

Through humorous performances people accomplish a multitude of social goals: they negotiate relationships and identities, construct one another as moral actors, juxtapose people, things and ideas, make claims about reality, and question the status quo. A variety of qualities of humorous utterances makes humor ideally suited to these tasks. Firstly, humor is often highly entextualixed and thus memorable and repeatable, making it easy to transfer to a variety of contexts. Secondly, classic jokes with their prescribed response formats and humorous, collaborative reminiscences help to facilitate interaction and the achievement of greater levels of intersubjectivity. Next, humor often involves manipulation of the voice system, a strategy that permits interlocutors to negotiate the social significance of various actors, including the ideas and contexts associated with them. Finally, the contrasting frames that humor sets up provide a means of exploring multiple interpretations of reality and of imagining and even embodying alternative realities.

References

Austin, J. L.

   1962 How to Do Things with Words. Oxford: Oxford University Press.

Bailey, Benjamin

   2004 Misunderstanding. In A Companion Linguistic Anthropology. Alessandro Duranti ed. pp. 395–413. Malden: Blackwell Publishing.

Bakhtin, M.M.

   1981 The dialogic Imagination: Four Essays. Austin: University of Texas Press.

Basso, Keith H.

   1986 Wisdom Sits in Places: Landscape and Language Among Western Apaches. Albuquerque: University of New Mexico Press.

   1979 Portraits of "the Whiteman": Linguistic Play and Cultural Symbols among the Western Apache. Cambridge: Cambridge University Press.

Bauman, Richard

   1996 Transformations of the Word in the Production of Mexican Festival Drama. In Natural Histories of Discourse. Michael Silverstein and Greg Urban, eds. pp. 301–327. Chicago: The University of Chicago Press.

   1977 Verbal Art as Performance. Rowley, Mass.: Newbury House.

   1975 Verbal Art as Performance. American Anthropologist, New Series 77(2):209–311.

Bauman, Richard and Briggs, Charles L.

   1990 Poetics and Performance as Critical Perspectives on Language and Social Life. Annual Review of Anthropology 19:59–88.

Bauman, Richard and Sherzer, Joel

   1975 The Ethnography of Speaking. Annual Review of Anthropology 4:95–119.

Bateson, Gregory

   1972 Steps to an Ecology of Mind. Chicago: the University of Chicago Press.

Bell, Nancy, and Salvatore Attardo

   2010 Failed Humor: Issues in Non-native Speakers' Appreciation and Understanding of Humor. Intercultural Pragmatics 7–3: 423–447.

Best, Janice

   1994 The Chronotope and the Generation of meaning in novels and paintings. http://findarticles.com/p/articles/mi_m2220/is_n2_v36/ai_15435238.

Brice Heath, Shirley

   1983 Ways With Words: Language, Life, and Work in Communities and Classrooms. New York: Cambridge University Press.

Briggs, Charles L.

   1996 The Meaning of Nonsense, the Poetics of Embodiment, and the Production of Power in Warao Healing. In The Performance of Healing. Carol Laderman and Marina Roseman, eds. pp. 185–232. New York: Routledge.

   1988 Competence in Performance: The Creativity of Tradition in Mexicano Verbal Art. Philadelphia: University of Pennsylvania Press.

Chick, J. K.

   1990 The Interactional Accomplishment of Discrimination in South Africa. In Cultural Communication and Intercultural Contact. D. Carbaugh ed. pp. 225–252. Hillsdale, NJ: Lawrence Erlbaum.

YouTube

    2011 The Dalai Lama Walks into a Pizza Shop. YouTube, June 9. http://www.youtube.com/watch?v=xllrl80og8c

Duranti, Alessandro

    2010 Husserl, intersubjectivity and anthropology. Anthropological Theory 10(1–2):16–35.

    1997 Linguistic Anthropology. New York: Cambridge University Press.

Garfinkel, H.

    1967 Studies in Ethnomethodology. Englewood Cliffs, NJ: Prentice-Hall.

Glick, Douglas, J.

    2007 Some Performative Techniques of Stand-Up Comedy: An Exercise in the Textuality of Temporalization. Language & Communication 27: 291–306.

Goodwin, Marjorie H.

    1990 Talk as Social Action. *In* He-Said-She-Said: Talk as Social Organization among Children. pp. 1–17. Bloomington: Indiana University Press.

Goldstein, Donna M.

    2003 Laughter out of Place: Race, Class, Violence, and Sexuality in a Rio Shantytown.

    Berkeley: University of California Press.

Goffman, Erving

    1974 Frame Analysis: An Essay on the Organization of Experience. Cambridge: Harvard University Press.

Hanks, William F.

    1996 Language and Communicative Practices. Boulder: Westview Press.

Hill, Jane H.

    2008 The Everyday Language of White Racism. Malden: Blackwell Publishing.

    1995 The Voices of Don Gabriel: Responsibility and Self in A Modern Mexicano Narrative.

    In The Dialogic Emergence of Culture. Dennis Tedlock and Bruce Mannheim, eds. pp. 97–147. Urbana: University of Illinois Press.

Jefferson, Gail

    1979 A Technique for Inviting Laughter and its Subsequent Acceptance/declination. *In* Everyday language: Studies in ethnomethodology. George Psathas, ed. pp. 79–96. New York: Irvington.

Karp, Ivan

    198 Laughter at Marriage: Subversion in Performance. Journal of Folklore Research. 25(1/2): 35–52.

Keating, Elizabeth, and Egbert, Maria

    2004 Conversation as a Cultural Activity. *In* A Companion Linguistic Anthropology.

    Alessandro Duranti, ed. pp. 169–196. A. Malden: Blackwell Publishing.

Norrick, Neal R.

    2004 Humor, Tellability, and Conarration in Conversational Storytelling. Text 24(1):79–111.

Peters, Russell

    2008 Red, White and Brown. DVD. Paramount Pictures. Hollywood.

Sacks, Harvey

    1974 An Analysis of the Course of a Joke's Telling in Conversation. In *Explorations in the Ethnography of Speaking*. Richard Bauman and Joel Sherzer, eds. pp. 337–353. Cambridge: Cambridge University Press.

Sclafani, Jennifer

    2009 Martha Stewart Behaving Badly: Parody and the Symbolic Meaning of Style. Journal of Sociolinguistics, 13(5): 613–633.

Silverstein, Michael

    2003 Death and Life at Gettysburg. *In* Talking Politics: The Substance of Style from Abe to "W". M. Silverstein, ed. pp. 33–62. Chicago: Prickly Paradigm Press (distributed by University of Chicago).

SpongeBob SquarePants

    2005 Funny Pants. Nickelodeon, September 30. http://spongebob.nick.com/videos/clip/funny-pants-full-episode.html

Wilce, James M.

    2008 Scientizing Bangladeshi psychiatry: Parallelism, enregisterment, and the cure for a magic complex. Language in Society 37(1):91–114.

Videos

The Daily Show with Jon Stewart. "Quitter." *The Daily Show with Jon Stewart* video, 6:16. July 27, 2009. http://www.thedaily-show.com/watch/mon-july-27-2009/quitter.

Group, Composer or Performer. *Title*. Medium. Recording Company.

The Italian Man Who Went to Malta: http://www.youtube.com/watch?v=m1TnzCiUSI0.

Eddie Izzard: The Flag: http://www.youtube.com/watch?v=UTduy7Qkvk8.

The Dalai Lama Walks into a Pizza Shop: http://www.youtube.com/watch?v=xllrl80og8c.

Chapter 6

TOWARD CONFLICT RESOLUTION …
Thank You for Insulting …

Special Affinities and Conflict Resolution

West African Social Institutions and Mediation

by Mark Davidheiser (2005)

Introduction

Social scientists have identified a particular kind of interpersonal relationship in West Africa that has been variously labeled "joking kinships," "joking relationships," "special affinities," "*cousinage*," and "*plaisanterie*"[2]. Many West Africans are connected by overlapping networks of these relationships, which can include reciprocal obligations, behavioral taboos, and stereotyping by ethnicity, region of origin, and clan affiliation. Joking kinships have been proposed as grassroots institutions that reinforce positive inter-ethnic interaction and mitigate inter-group conflict[3]. This paper examines the role of joking relationships in micro-level conflict mediation among the Mandinka of southwestern Gambia and then considers the implications of this type of relationship to mediation and conflict transformation more broadly.

Quotes From Gambian Mediations

"Joking relations are essential to peacemaking, without them there would be no peace in this world. Even if you do not want to do so, you have to forgive because of joking kinship."

"It is obligatory for me to reconcile you and bring you back together. I appeal to you to please consider our relationship (joking partners) and agree on one thing."

Empirical and interview data on mediation were collected during 28 months in southwestern Gambia.[4] Mediators were interviewed individually and in stratified panels[5], and actual mediations were observed[6], and when possible recorded. The data indicate that Gambians tend to conceptualize conflict and mediation in a different manner from Americans. The Mandinka generally view mediation as a matter of persuading disputants to end their conflict and reconcile, rather than as a structured process of facilitated problem-solving and negotiation. Mediators rely heavily on social ties and persuasion in their work, and they use local values and social institutions to legitimize their interventions in disputes and to increase their leverage over the disputants.

Joking relationships are arguably the most effective institution used by mediators in that manner. Joking bonds are particularly intriguing because in some cases they were instrumental in the transformation of long-standing conflicts that had been resistant to prior intervention efforts. The role of joking kinship in Gambian mediations illuminates broad dissimilarities in Gambian and American modalities of conflict resolution. The field study did not aim to investigate joking relationships, but encountered them during the investigation of local mediation practices. The assertions made here are therefore indicative rather than conclusive. However, the project findings add further evidence that pervasive trends in American mediation are culture-specific. This raises both problems and possibilities for the further development and the export of theories and practice models.

Overview of Joking Relationships in The Gambia

Joking relationships are customary ties that link various groups and individuals. This social institution can be found in many parts of Sub-Saharan Africa. In The Gambia, such ties can exist between the members of different ethnic groups and of different patriclans, between the people of specific villages, between kinfolk such as cousins and grandparents and grandchildren, and between people whose lineage is connected with certain regions[7]. These relationships often signify a symbolic or fictional kinship, as exemplified below with the Jola and Serer.

The majority of Gambian ethnic groups practice this type of joking. The Mandinka, Fula, Wolof, Jola, Serahule, Serer, and Bambara (different ethnic groups) are linked through multiple crosscutting ties, including joking kinship. The Aku and the Manjago—two groups that migrated to The Gambia relatively recently—generally do not have institutionalized ties of this sort, however[8]. These relationships include mutual obligations and are most commonly manifested in semi-ritualized banter. The banter usually revolves around food, with individuals who share such ties teasing each other about their big bellies and love of eating. That is the most popular type of joke, but the ribbing can be extended to other topics as well. These relationships involve greater freedom of speech and behavior as one is allowed to interact with joking partners in a manner that would ordinarily be frowned upon or cause offense. Joking kin are not supposed to become angry at each other, and harming a joking partner is strongly prohibited.

There are different kinds of joking relationships in The Gambia. The distinction made by Diallo[9] between "major" and "minor" joking relations in the Ivory Coast is also applicable to The Gambia. In Mandinka, the trade language of southwestern Gambia, joking bonds are commonly known as *sanaweyaa* or *dangkutoo*. *Sanaweyaa* can refer specifically to joking ties between cousins, but is also used as a general name for joking relationships. *Dangkutoo* means to stop at something or to not go beyond a certain point, and it implies a more serious relationship. The mutual obligations of *dangkutoo* are stronger than those of *sanaweyaa* and include a strong threat of spiritual sanctions for offending or injuring one's joking partner.

Gambian oral histories include accounts of the origins of joking links. According to Diallo, in western Burkina Faso local histories depict joking relations as the product of a "blood pact" made after a conflict between "two legendary persons"[10]. Gambian Mandinka usually refers to legendary or past events of a more cooperative nature as the source of such ties.

For example, the *dangkutoo* between Jola and Serer is attributed to a time when their progenitors were traveling in a boat. A storm caused the vessel to split in two. Those in one portion of the boat floated away in one direction, landed in the forest, and became the Jola. The other group floated in another direction, ended up by a river, and evolved into the Serer ethnic group.

The descendants of the people of the Empire of Kaabu *(Kaabunka)* and the descendants of the inhabitants of the Kombo kingdom *(Kombonka)* also maintain a joking relationship[11]. This tie is associated with the rise of the Mandinka to socio-political supremacy in the Kombo region of coastal Gambia. The Kaabu Empire sent an army to help the Kombonka Mandinka overcome the Jola and the Bainunka and establish supremacy over southern coastal Gambia. The states became allies and the joking tie between their citizens was established[12].

The joking relations between the patronymic lineages of Fofanna and Jaiteh are said to have begun when their ancestors were traveling on a long journey without food. The student *(talibe)* Fofanna went into the bush and cut some meat from his leg and roasted it so that his teacher could eat. The teacher *(karamo),* Jaiteh ate it without realizing that it was from his student's body. They continued traveling, but Fofanna was bleeding and he became very weak. Jaiteh asked why he was so weak and Fofanna showed him his leg. Jaiteh healed the wound by laying his hands on it and praying. They then made an oath that their descendants would always support each other and never quarrel under the threat of misfortune[13]. In the personalized cosmology of the Mandinka, the historically rooted and supernatural dimensions of the joking relationship make them powerful tools for potential mediators.

Different Conceptualization of Conflict, Different Methods of Conflict Mediation

Using joking ties as an analytical lens illuminates variance in how Gambians and Americans perceive conflict and peacemaking. In societies with an agrarian base, views of conflict and conflict mitigation tend to vary from those in industrialized societies. In Northern countries, conflict is often seen as a natural component of society, and is sometimes recognized as potentially productive[14]. Legal anthropology has historically presented African societies and customary dispute resolution as harmony and reconciliation oriented[15]. This idea is rooted in functionalist theory and has been critiqued by Martin Chanock[16].

Chanock, a political scientist, argues that African customary law and the scholarly views of it are artificial constructs promulgated by anthropologists with the cooperation of African lawyers and elites. He asserts that the literature has reinforced a one-dimensional conceptualization of African dispute settlement. Chanock's critique is well taken—Africans can be vigorous and enthusiastic in their disputing. Large and small groups of Africans can be riven by conflict despite the presence of customary mechanisms for conflict mitigation and social norms that promote harmony. The application of African customary law can also result in settlements that favor particular parties and do not bring about reconciliation. However, recent studies, including this one, have confirmed the harmony and reconciliation orientation in many African societies[17]. While we should avoid over-simplification, we can acknowledge that there are differences between African and Northern perceptions of conflict, and that these play a role in conflict management.

This variance is related in part to communalistic versus individualistic social organization. In highly variable environments people use dense social networks as coping strategies to reduce their vulnerability to disaster[18]. The climactic conditions of the Sahel region of West Africa has been characterized as volatile with frequent periods of drought, floods, and other extreme conditions[19]. Groups and individuals whose crops fail and animals die often survive by calling upon others with whom they maintain relationships of reciprocity. In times of need, these relationships provide a source of shelter, food, seeds, animals, and so forth[20]. The development of societies that value harmonious relationships is therefore a "rational" socio-cultural adaptation to an unpredictable environment.

In Gambian villages interpersonal interaction is constant, economic interdependence is the norm, individuals are part of multiplex networks of social ties, and interpersonal harmony is highly valued[21]. Locals sometimes say, "Everyone in The Gambia is related to one another" and the complexity of social networks is truly amazing. Conflict can disrupt the webs of reciprocity that Gambians use to avail themselves of help in times of need.

Rural Gambians are primarily engaged in labor-intensive agro-pastoralism. In the local moral economy, maintaining good relations with others is vital to the production and distribution of farm products[22]. For example, cooperative work groups (kafos) assist farmers at key times in plowing fields and transplanting and harvesting crops. Such groups work for very little pay or for food and will not work for people on bad terms with the community.

Scholars have argued that in African societies spirituality is integrated into every aspect of life[23]. Perhaps it is natural then that Gambians share beliefs about supernatural sanctions related to disputing. In interviews conducted by this researcher, members of all three targeted ethno-linguistic groups expressed strong views about the dangers of disputing. Conflict is also potentially hazardous because disputants can go to marabous and/or animist shrines to ask for their intercession, thereby endangering the well being of their opponent(s). Mandinka often cite hadiths (sayings of the Prophet Mohammed) about how Muslims should be peaceful and should not dispute with each other. Gambians hold common beliefs about divine rewards for peaceful people and temporal punishment for those who dispute with others[24].

In general, there is widespread consensus among Gambians that conflict is negative and should be avoided. Interpersonal and communal harmony is highly valued in the cosmologies of rural Gambians. In such a context, the emphasis in conflict management is on reconciliation rather than problem-solving through negotiation and compromise.

Reconciliation Versus Problem-Solving Oriented Approaches to Mediation

The practice of law in the industrialized countries of the North is, in its ideal form, based on abstract principles and carried out in impersonal forums[25]. This paradigm extends to alternative dispute management (ADR) and mediation. A multiplicity of mediation models and praxis exist in Northern nations. However, certain pervasive trends that have long influenced the field can be identified.

One of the strongest conventions in American mediation is the notion of neutral third-party mediators who are expected to facilitate the identification of essential underlying issues and the negotiation of a "win–win outcome." Principled negotiation is one of the touchstones of this paradigm. Mediators are instructed to separate the people from the problem, uncover the essential interests of the parties, identify options for mutual gain, and use objective criteria to select the best option[26]. Other currents exist[27], but the tenets of rational problem-solving has long dominated the field[28].

Among the Mandinka, the approach to dispute mediation can be quite different. Local mediation, as with most African customary law, approaches conflict from a relational perspective rather than being issue-driven. In this perspective the focus is on reinforcing social solidarity, rather than addressing essential underlying issues[29.] The emphasis is often on maintaining and restoring good relations with others, and this can take precedence over negotiating agreements about substantive or concrete issues. One reason that mediation is popular and effective in The Gambia is that it is consistent with local cosmologies of conflict; mediation is integrated into the fabric of society and consistent with attendant beliefs and norms.

"Separating the people from the problem" is contrary to the Gambian world-view in which one's identity and status is of great significance. The identities of the disputants are of great concern to Mandinka mediators. For Gambians, social status is linked to behavioral roles and norms, and mediators operate very much within the framework of customary values. Mediators are usually not viewed as impersonal and neutral third parties; instead their status and relationships with the disputants are of primary importance[30]. Mediators tend to be more concerned with the relations between the parties than with the specific causes of the conflict. Negotiation over concrete or substantive issues is therefore not as much a part of the mediation process in The Gambia (and this is true for all the populations in this study) as in the USA.

Forgiveness Rather Than Principled Negotiation

As alluded to above, interview, panel, and empirical data were collected on how Gambians mediate. The foundation for the coding scheme applied to these data was generated from the literature and from the author's own experience as a volunteer mediator in a community mediation center. It quickly became apparent that Gambians employ activities not found in mainstream American literature and training, and inductively generated codes had to be added to the codebook. One such code represents the activity of mediators appealing for forgiveness.

Although most American models have no corresponding activity, the Mandinka often mentioned forgiveness. "Forgiving" often entails one or more of the disputants dropping their demands and agreeing to reconcile[31]. Mediation outcomes may or may not result in agreements about compensation, changes in behavior, or other arrangements, and such agreements may be very specific or extremely general.

Participants in mediations often make statements along the line of "if you forgive now then when you (or your child or animal) make a similar mistake people will be willing to forgive you" and speak of divine rewards for forbearance. "Sabari"—a word derived from the Arabic "sabarr" meaning patience—is a concept that is mentioned in the majority of the collected mediations. As with much of Islam, the term "sabarr" has been re-interpreted in the Gambian context with the local meaning connoting forbearance and forgiveness. Often, one of the first things that people say to disputants is "sabari," and mediators commonly urge the disputants to forgive each other. One mediator, a marabou from the family of a local Imam, was fond of quoting Arabic proverbs such as "Inna Allah ma es-sabarriin" (God is with the patient/forgiving ones), and "Es-sabr miftahul farajj" (patience/forbearance is the key to success). Mediators' use of the sabari construct exemplifies how the Mandinka do not privilege negotiation in conflict settlement.

In fact, in some cases mediators told disputants that they did not even want to hear their explanations or narratives about the conflict. The activity of disputants presenting their viewpoints about a conflict is a component of every model of mediation that the author is aware of. In some of the Gambian cases, however, the mediators told the disputants that they did not want to hear their narratives, or discuss the issues at all[32]. These mediators were concerned only with ending the dispute and bringing about reconciliation. This pattern is associated with specific factors,[33] but forgiveness was a common theme across the different sets of cases.

In the USA, mediators are often told to "trust the process"—the idea being that they have been trained in facilitation techniques that they apply using a unilinear staged model. The model is designed to allow the disputants to explain their viewpoints, exchange ideas about their needs and desires and generate options for a mutually beneficial settlement agreement. Gambian mediators are more likely to use persuasion to reconcile disputants, and may or may not work out an agreement relating to the issues[34].

In this approach, mediators rely on social norms to gain leverage over the disputants. Such leverage is often essential in getting disputants to reconcile, even in the absence of a compromise agreement. Mediators often highlight interpersonal ties when they begin mediating and when they call for the disputants to reconcile and/or forgive their opponent(s).

Personalized Approaches Versus Neutral Third Parties

American models of mediation generally include a setting the stage phase when mediators create an environment conducive to effective problem-solving[35]. This usually entails explaining the nature of the process, going over the ground rules of the mediation (such as not interrupting the other disputant), and so forth. Setting the stage activities were quite common in Gambian mediations, but were more contextual and personalized than procedural in nature.

In creating an appropriate atmosphere, most Gambian mediators discussed their connections with the disputants, going over the history of relations between their families and relatives and mentioning any other links that they might share. They cited friendships and other bonds between their ancestors or current members of their families. Mediators have a wealth of potential socially accepted relationships to choose from such as karamo–talibe (Islamic teacher–student) interactions, talibeeyaa or ties between individuals who study the Quran together, seey nyo yaa or neighborliness, Muslimeiyaa, the common bond between Muslims, hadameiyaa, fictional kinship based on the idea of common descent from Adam and Eve, or baadiiyaa another broad fictional kinship.

Mandinka can be very creative in constructing and inventing kinship and collective identities and can get quite general making statements like, "we are all of the same village, we are all of the same ethnic group, we are all Africans," etc. In the local political economy, such relationships imply mutual responsibilities. When the mediators appeal to disputants to forgive and reconcile, they can greatly strengthen the force of their appeal by invoking such ties.

One of the most powerful bonds is that of joking kinship. When mediators use joking kinships, they invoke an established history of relations. Such relationships provide a script for cooperative interaction with varying degrees of reciprocal obligation. Joking relations provide mediators with considerable leverage over disputants.

Joking relationships invoke religion as well as custom and tradition. In The Gambia, Islam has been intertwined with local practices and beliefs. Before Islam, the Mandinka practiced animism. Respect for elders and one's ancestors is still very strong, making the concept of ancestors swearing an oath binding their descendants very potent.

In addition, joking kinships have been incorporated into Islamic practice. One informant, a griot, related the joking kinship between his patronym, Camara Kunda and Seesay Kunda, to Islam by saying that their ancestors lived in Mecca and then moved to Mali and from there to The Gambia. Other informants asserted that mamariiyaa, or joking between grandparents and grandchildren, originated with the Prophet Mohammed (PBUH). They explained that Mohammed's grandchildren would disturb him by pulling on his shirt and playfully pushing him while he was praying. Eventually the angel Gabriel appeared to Mohammed and told him to better train his grandchildren. Mohammed then began "beating them gently" with a stick when they disturbed him, teaching the grandchildren about respect. These examples of Mandinka intertwining joking relations and Islam demonstrate the malleability of this institution, a feature that will be discussed further in a later section of this paper.

Mandinka social organization has historically been highly hierarchical with numerous behavioral constraints on its members. In the pre-colonial era, the caste system provided a social category that facilitated conflict mediation. The nyamoolooluu, or members of the artisan classes (griots, leatherworkers, and blacksmiths), were allowed greater behavioral latitude than nobles and peasants[36]. The mediation of disputes was a part of the conventional activities of the nyamoolooluu caste. They were highly effective mediators due to their ability to speak relatively freely, to criticize even powerful people without fear of retribution, and to browbeat people into reconciliation[37]. Islamicization and Northern influences have diminished the significance of caste relations in contemporary Gambia. The behavioral restrictions found in Mandinka society are still extensive, however.

Mediators' use of joking relations can open up liminal space in which the transcendence of ordinary boundaries and scripts becomes possible. The application of the mediators' leverage in this liminal space heightens possibilities for attitudinal shifts and conflict transformation. This phenomenon of mediators using a social institution associated with increased behavioral latitude and with spiritual sanctions to resolve disputes is reminiscent of the role of the nyamoolooluu in pre-colonial society. The institution of joking kinships may therefore be providing some continuity in a social function previously provided by the nyamoolooluu. In the Mandinka states of the past, peasants and rulers were expected to heed the advice of the nyamoolooluu; contemporary Gambians are expected to accede to the wishes of their joking partners.

The social capital of joking kinships is used quite deliberately by Gambians. A special affinity tie is the reason that a migrant from Kaabu, Fa Mamodou, joined the *sate keybaalu* (council of elders) of one village in the region. The other village elders are heads of the seven main clans or wards of the village. Fa Mamodou was included because of the *dangkutoo* that he, as a descendant of the Kaabunka, had with the Kombonka[38]. The *dangkutoo* relationship that stemmed from the Kaabu Empire sending military help to the Kombonka Mandinka is still respected. Fa Mamodou's *dangkutoo* with the Mandinka of the coastal region of The Gambia made him an especially effective mediator there, and he intervened in disputes all over the region. He claims a very high success rate and the position appears to be evolving into a hereditary one. Fa Mamodou has groomed his son to take over his position, and now that he is quite old he usually remains at home letting his son go in his place[39].

Relational Mediation and Intractable Conflict

Joking relationships are so effective in mediation that in some cases they have been instrumental in settling very challenging conflicts. Scholars have identified some types of disputes as especially resistant to conflict management efforts, and labeled them as "intractable conflicts."[40] These include conflicts over identity, values, and ideology[41]. In such cases conventional negotiation and mediation techniques are less likely to be successful since ideological differences are difficult to resolve using bargaining techniques developed from organizational theory to negotiate win–win outcomes. In these contexts forgiveness and tolerance may be essential in mitigating the conflict. Informal institutions with a great deal of legitimacy, social capital, and mobilizational potential offer great promise for tackling such disputes. Several examples from The Gambia illustrate how the influence of a mediator who has a relationship of special affinity with the disputants has great potential for transforming difficult conflicts.

One interviewee, a Camara, explained that his joking relationship with a husband allowed him to intervene in a marital dispute the man was having with his wives. The husband, from the Ceesay patriclan, was a very feared marabou and people were unwilling to mediate as is usually done when a marital conflict arises. The interviewee stated that he was only able to approach the marabou because of the *dangkutoo* between them and he used it to convince the marabou not to divorce his wife. He stated that when he used his *dangkutoo* relationship with the marabou it brought the marabou to tears, and he willingly took back his wives. Their reconciliation has been a lasting one as they are still together at present[42].

Another elder described a case in which he traveled upriver to a village where there were two brothers who had been disputing for approximately ten years before his arrival. Many people had tried to mediate between them, but none were successful. The elder was able to reconcile them using his *dangkutoo* relationship with them to make a strong appeal for their reconciliation, an appeal that they felt compelled to heed.

Land disputes constitute some of the most intense conflicts in the region. The Gambia is one of the most densely settled countries in West Africa[43], and the southwestern region is growing especially quickly[44]. The relative high fertility of the area and the availability of marine and forest resources have attracted many migrants and spurred a population boom. The construction of new tar roads linking the southwestern corner of the country with the urban areas to the north has also led to a spike in land sales. Informants cited multiple cases of land disputes that were successfully resolved. Villagers also used joking relations to defuse tensions in a very heated land dispute involving three villages in the area.

The presidential elections of 2001 presented great potential for communal mobilization and inter-ethnic conflict. Informants asserted that joking relationships were instrumental in minimizing violence and interpersonal conflict prevention, during this time of heightened tension when parochial communalistic feelings were highlighted. Collective identities were fore-grounded as various interest groups mobilized and jockeyed for power.

The incumbent president Al-Hajji Yahya Jammeh is a Jola who was strongly supported by minority populations such as the Manjago and Jola. The candidate and many leaders of the main opposition party were Mandinka, and public opinion identifies the party with that ethnic group. During the campaign and afterwards, people insulted each other using joking scripts, thereby dissipating some of the tension. No historical joking relations exist between the Mandinka and the Jola, however, some Gambians were adept at reframing inter-communal stress using the lens of joking ties. Interviewees explained that drawing upon this widely known social institution was useful in promoting integration and cooperation during this time of competition[45]. The kind of liminal space created by joking kinship combined with the forgiveness and reconciliation-oriented approach makes them effective even in cases resistant to other mediation attempts.

Constructing Joking Kinship

Social scientists know that custom, "tradition," and identities are dynamic and elastic[46]. The malleability of joking relationships is heightened by the fact that they vary by region, they are not codified, and they are extendable. This raises the possibility that joking relationships could be adapted for use in a range of conflict situations.

Gambians are adept at manipulating and reframing their identities. According to many informants, in the past, some members of the historically disadvantaged Jola minority group of The Gambia frequently re-invented themselves as Mandinka. In the wake of the coup of 1994, which brought a Jola president to power, these individuals have rediscovered their Jola identity and are reconstructing their identities accordingly.

The researcher has personally observed the impressive facility that Gambians have in shifting their identities. For example, some Mandinka claimed other ethnic identities based on family ties in certain contexts. Local identities are multi-faceted and dynamic and Gambians emphasize and de-emphasize various components of their identities (such as region of origin, caste, religion, clan affiliation, the identities of relatives and so forth) based on situational factors and the interactional context at hand.

As mentioned previously, Gambians also exhibit remarkable creativity in the crafting of social ties. In addition to joking kinship, Gambians may construct ties by drawing upon myriad potential factors such as extended family members growing up in the same compound, sharing the same name, friendships between relatives, religious ties, mentor relationships, ties built through the participation in ceremonies, narrow or broad common identities such as students of the same or similar Islamic teachers, inhabitants or descendants of inhabitants of the same area, members of the same ethnic group, common kinship of descent from Adam and Eve, and so forth. Fictional kinship abounds in local social relations, and the Mandinka are quite dexterous in linking themselves to others in a way that could theoretically make it possible for almost anyone to claim some sort of joking relation[47].

Diallo and Wilson-Fall[48] have illustrated the elasticity of joking kinships in their discussions of how Fulbe migrants use them to integrate themselves into the social and economic fabric of new areas. As mentioned previously, a common form of joking kinship is that between particular lineages. Patronymics may shift according to geographical area, a phenomenon described by Wilson-Fall as the "lateral correspondence of patronyms"[49]. Regional family names have corresponding counterparts in other locations and migrants can assume these when traveling.

In the Gambia these types of linkages can be both intra- and inter-ethnic. For example, the Fulbe Bah are also said to be "the same as" the Jola Badjie, meaning that they can theoretically avail themselves of each other's social networks. People from different parts of The Gambia also cite variations in joking ties. In some areas Badjie Kunda may joke with Sonko Kunda, while in other areas Badjie Kunda may joke with Jarjue Kunda, for example.

The variation of joking partners by region opens the door to potential manipulation of this institution by mediators or others[50]. There is no definitive or written list of these relationships so they can be invoked in many different situations and are difficult to challenge. Most mediators agreed that it is possible to build a joking relationship with disputants without having a firm historical basis for doing so. They explained that one can, for example, connect with the person on an individual level, reference other social ties, and use them in a similar manner to joking kinship.

In addition, according to a local saying in Islam, a lie is not a lie when it is for a good cause[51], thereby providing religious justification to those who might manipulate joking relations. Some mediators stated that they might invoke *dangkutoo* or *sanaweyaa* even if they were unsure of whether they actually had such a relationship with the disputants. For example, one mediator explained that he might start joking with disputants, even if he did not have an established joking kinship with them. If the disputant responded favorably, he would use that tie to encourage the disputant to end the dispute. If the disputant challenged it, he would say something like, "Well, you are acting like one of my joking partners."

In an observed case regarding a heated cross-ethnic land dispute between two villages, a partisan mediator was able to construct a fictional joking relationship that proved vital. A meeting between the parties had become very tense and seemed destined to result in an increase, rather than a decrease, in grievances. However, a nominally Mandinka mediator invoked a joking relationship common to the Jola ethnic group. Maternal uncles have a strong joking relationship with their nephews and nieces, and the mediator's mother was a Jola. On that basis, he claimed a joking relationship with the members of the Jola village. The Jola villagers responded positively to this and the resultant joking had an obvious calming effect. At that point, the tone of the meeting began to shift from quarreling to discussing possible agreements. We cannot be certain that the outcome would have been different had this imagined relationship not been created, but it is worth noting that the meeting was a success[52].

Although relationships such as joking kinship can be highly effective institutions for mediators to draw upon, there are limits to the efficacy of such ties. The author was impressed by the creativity of Gambian mediators in constructing social ties, but their inventiveness did not always result in successful outcomes. In one observed case, the mediator used his status as a respected elder and the head of his clan or ward and also invoked multiple social ties in a marital mediation, yet the mediation was unsuccessful. In a caucus with the husband, he constructed multiple ties between them saying that he had looked after the husband's father when he was undergoing circumcision, and that they were both soldiers and had a common bond. None of these strategies worked, however, and the elder went on to say that if they had had a historically robust *dangkutoo* relationship then his hand would have been greatly strengthened and the husband would have been likely to agree with him. Clearly, widely accepted ties with strong historical roots will generally be more effective than constructed relationships that are based on more tenuous links.

Therein lies the power of joking kinship—they are socially sanctioned[53] and historically rooted, they are associated with both Islamic and pre-Islamic beliefs, and they include an implicit threat if disregarded. However, joking relationships have their limitations. In the unsuccessful marital case above, for example, the elder who mediated explained that a very serious consideration kept the husband from agreeing to reconcile, despite the elder's strenuous efforts. Beliefs and behavior undergo continual processes of modification, adaptation, and re-negotiation; no custom or tradition is absolute[54]. Contextual factors can prevent disputants from agreeing even when their joking partners plead with them to do so. In other cases people even enter into disputes with their joking partners[55]. It should be clear that the utilization of joking kinship does not guarantee conflict cessation, although it greatly heightens that possibility in the Gambian context.

Many elders expressed a fear that young people are moving away from their historical heritage and may not respect customary institutions such as joking relationships. It is worth noting that there is considerable latent tension between youths and elders in The Gambia. Elders are fond of complaining about youths in regard to any number of topics. Young people themselves expressed a strong respect for joking kinship. Youths referred to elders as the source of knowledge about customary institutions, but stated that they believe this one to be legitimate and significant. Overall, youths appeared to be less likely to engage in the ritualized interaction common to these relationships, but that follows a general trend in which Mandinka become increasingly "traditional" as they age. Follow-up research on this topic is needed to clarify when, how, and how often Mandinka will use these ties as their society continues to change and adapt.

Implications for Mediation Studies and Praxis

The use of joking kinship in peacemaking raises several points relevant to dispute resolution more broadly. Implicit and explicit suggestions that conflict resolution practice models largely transcend cultural differences have been reviewed and debunked elsewhere[56]. Nevertheless, recently Senger reported that in his international travels he found the tenets of interest-based negotiation to hold up reasonably well[57]. However, these tenets were not compatible with the beliefs expressed by Gambian mediators or with much of their peacemaking behavior. Mandinka mediation preferences suggest that the paradigm of negotiated problem-solving is not a universally relevant framework, but is the product of a particular socio-cultural milieu.

The concerns dealt with by Mandinka mediators support alternative views of conflict management that incorporate affective and symbolic components of disputing and conciliation. There is currently a movement to shift the focus of the field from problem-solving to a more relational framework. Efforts in that direction include the transformative mediation approaches of Bush and Folger, John Paul Lederach, and Michelle LeBaron[58], and narrative mediation[59]. The investigation of other modes of mediation should continue.

In a similar vein, Gambian mediators' use of special affinity relations suggests that there is great promise in exploring new ideas in mediation. For example, prior to dispute intervention efforts, should anthropologists identify key actors who have relevant ties with the disputants? These actors could then be trained in mediation techniques and attempt an intervention on their own, or in collaboration with the diplomats and/or professionals who have dominated past efforts.

Can we incorporate informal institutions into mediation? Might it be possible to combine the affective power of Gambian-style mediation with the strengths of Northern models? Can we formulate hybrid methods combining the strengths of different approaches? Should Northern mediators construct, reinvent, or invoke shared identities and socially rooted scripts to aid in conflict transformation? Could liminal space be created during Northern mediations? It would be fascinating to see mediators trying creative ideas in their work such as incorporating prayer, sharing food, drawing on social institutions such as sports, and so forth.

The popularity of mediation in The Gambia has implications for organizations involved in international peacebuilding initiatives. Efforts to promote conflict mitigation in Southern countries are often led by individuals whose experience is based around Northern modes of disputing and peacemaking. The worldviews of these experts leads them to perceive such modes as appropriate and effective, although locals may find them awkward and/or alien[60]. Exporting Northern models piece-meal to other countries may therefore not constitute the most effective approach.

Instead, international and intercultural mediations should incorporate local mediation techniques, resources, and institutions in order to draw on social capital that may assist in dispute transformation. All mediators should be aware of societal influences in training and praxis. In some cases indigenous mediation styles may tend to be more personalized than formal or professional, and may rely more on persuasion than negotiation and "rational" problem-solving. The existence of local mediation techniques should be recognized and training programs should be adapted accordingly, in order to avoid adding to the colonial legacy of imposition of foreign models on African societies[61]. Training programs should consist of more collaborative efforts that aim to create hybrid procedures, and/or draw from the best aspects of different approaches[62].

Laura Nader has raised valid concerns about the influence of harmony models on ADR[63]. It is true that a focus on reconciliation can lead to the sidelining of significant disputant concerns and policymakers should keep this in consideration. On the other hand, we must also be careful about imposing hegemonic cultural norms and notions of "justice" on others. The notion of "justice" is socially constructed and deeply embedded in conceptual frameworks, and as such is subject to ideological and cultural influences.

It is worth noting that Gambian disputants frequently expressed satisfaction with mediation outcomes. Some individuals, even those who appear to be disadvantaged by a settlement, may consider a mediation to have succeeded if they are reconciled with their opponent(s). False consciousness or controlling processes notwithstanding, we should be wary of adopting the stance that we have a better understanding of what others need than they themselves do[64]. The fact that the hierarchy of goals of other societies may differ significantly from our own should not lead us to dismiss their concerns and ignore their perspective. If a farmer is willing to forgo compensation for damaged crops in favor of forgiveness, thereby shoring up ties with others who may offer vital assistance in the future, it seems patronizing to assume that is a product of harmony models imported from the North and bolstered by local elites.

In addition, nations such as The Gambia have a weak and limited legal–rational judicial system, where access to formal judicial forums is difficult and expensive, and unbiased treatment of disputants is by no means guarantee[65]. In such areas, mediation may provide a vital means for underprivileged disputants to seek redress and in some cases may actually empower them. The example of the marabou marital mediation discussed above demonstrates one of the positive aspects of joking kinship—they can have a leveling effect in which normal social hierarchies are de-emphasized and opportunities for conflict transformation are opened up.

In countries where courts may reinforce structural inequalities (consider, for example, the case of Islamic law in Northern Nigeria), ADR may actually offer a more empowering option for disadvantaged peoples. Although micro-level mediations may not immediately change the structural violence inherent in stratified societies, they can provide effective mechanisms for addressing concerns of both high and low status peoples. The use of historically rooted mechanisms for ADR presents potential benefits as well as challenges to those interested in equitable peacemaking[66].

Conclusion

The intention here is not to set up a strict dichotomy between Gambian and American mediation styles. A range of practices exists in both contexts. For example, in some cases Gambian mediators do deal with concrete issues and facilitate negotiations. When doing so, they may use techniques that are taught to American peacemakers, such as addressing less contentious issues first and highlighting areas of potential or actual agreement in order to create positive momentum. American mediation is an enormous and diversified field with a number of different currents. The growth of lawyers practicing mediation may be leading to an increase in directive mediation in the U.S. and the aforementioned alternative approaches are promoting a more relational praxis. In the American milieu, these trends exist in contradiction to one another. Overall, the mediation style of Gambians is simultaneously more directive and more reconciliation-oriented than the style of mediation used in most American training programs.

One of the goals of this paper is to discourage debating over what single method of mediation should be institutionalized and encourage an inclusive perspective on mediation with multiple options for potential consideration and use. Perhaps mediation approaches should vary on a case-by-case basis. For example, it is not always possible to work out a win–win solution, and third-party assisted negotiations will sometimes fail. Can the Gambian approach of forgiveness and reconciliation offer a model that could be used in such contexts? Perhaps mediation styles should also vary according to the worldviews of the participants, but we do not yet know to what extent this may be true. These questions require further exploration.

In summation, viewing mediation through the lens of joking relationships provides a fresh perspective on the challenge of conflict transformation. Those interested in enhancing mediation theory and praxis would do well to consider "alternative" approaches to alternative dispute resolution. The author anticipates continuing this line of inquiry and hopes to participate in the development of more diverse and robust repertoires of mediation. In a world characterized by increasingly destructive and dangerous conflicts such a development offers great promise.

Notes

1   For a more anthropological analysis of this topic, see Davidheiser, M. (2006). "Joking for Peace: Social Organization, Tradition, and Change in Conflict Prevention and Resolution." Cahiers d'Etudes Africaines. No. 183–184.

2   Colson 1953; Radcliffe-Brown 1940; Stevens 1978; Wilson-Fall 2000.

3   Moreau 1944; Radcliffe-Brown 1940.

4   The author is grateful to the United States Institute of Peace and the University of Florida's Center for African Studies for their financial support of this project.

5   Panels were stratified by the inductively and deductively significant variables of age-set, village, religion, sex, and ethnicity.

6   How mediation should be defined is a contentious issue in the literature. Following calls for inclusive theorizing and analysis (see for example Bercovitch 1996), mediation is conceptualized here in its most fundamental sense—as the intervention outside of the legal domain of one or more individuals into an interpersonal or inter-group dispute in order to manage or resolve a conflict (cf. Doob 1993). This investigation focused primarily on inter-personal mediations; cases between spouses, family members, neighbors, and farmers and herders were some of the common types.

7   The grandparent–grandchild relation is known as *mamariiyaa,* and the relationship between cousins is referred to as *sanaweyaaa.* One informant also stated that his caste, the griots or bards, has a joking kinship with the Dyula people of Mali, Cote de Ivoire, and Burkina Faso. The exact configurations of these ties may vary Among the Jola, a special affinity exists between maternal uncles and their nephews and nieces.

8   The Aku are descendants of the members of the Krio ethnic group of Sierra Leone. They migrated to The Gambia to work as officials in the colonial administration. They usually live in urban areas and are largely outside the complex matrix of networks that cut across rural Gambia. The Manjago migrated to The Gambia from Guinea-Bissau and the Casamance region of southern Senegal. Some Gambian Manjago do practice *mamariiyaa* or joking between grandparents and grandchildren.

This may be the result of cultural diffusion from the Mandinka who dominate rural southwestern Gambia. One respondent indicated that in Guinea-Bissau, Manjago from different regions such as Churr and Pulund might have a special affinity relationship. However, most Manjago stated that their customs do not include any joking relations.

9 Diallo 2002.

10 Diallo 2002:2.

11 The Kaabu Empire of the Mandinka existed in the 15th through 19th centuries and was located in parts of present-day Guinea-Bissau, Casamance, and upriver Gambia. The kingdoms of Kombo were located on the coastal southern-bank Gambia and a small part of northwestern Casamance.

12 Sonko-Godwin 1994.

13 Another informant recounted the same story in reference to the Touray and Camara relationship and a Fula informant referred to this story when explaining the origin of the tie between the patronyms Bah and Jallow. A similar account is also used to explain the kinship between the Bozo and the Dogon of Mali (Galvan 2003).

14 Abu-Nimer 1996; Fisher and Ury 1991; Duryea and Grundison 1993; Myers and Filner 1997.

15 e.g. Elias 1956; Gibbs 1973; Gluckman 1967; Maquet 1972.

16 Chanock 1985; cf. Nader 1991, 1997.

17 E.g. Darboe 1982; Hoffman 2000; Mengisteab 2002; Rugege 1995.

18 Blaikie et al. 1994.

19 Behnke and Scones 1992; Ellis and Swift 1988; Freudenberger 1995.

20 Bassett 1988; Guéye 1994.

21 Darboe 1982.

22 See James Scott's The Moral Economy of the Peasant (1976) for a thorough explanation of such systems.

23 E.g. Maquet 1972; Mazrui 1993.

24 Mediators told disputants that they would not receive the normal blessings from undertaking the *Hajj* or pilgrimage to Mecca if they had an ongoing interpersonal conflict when they went there, for example.

25 Holleman 1974, cited in Darboe 1982.

26 See Fisher and Ury (1991) for a highly influential presentation of this approach.

27 For example, two recent approaches—transformative and narrative mediation—offer a more relational and post-structuralist take on mediation (cf. Bush and Folger 1994, 1996; Winslade and Monk 2000). However, most American practice remains based on the problem-solving framework (Stempel 2002).

28 Scholars have used a variety of different labels to refer to the prevailing paradigm in which conflict is considered to be the product of objective issues or problems. Kressel and Pruitt (1989) label this as a "task-oriented" approach, Crocker, Osler, and Aall (1999) as "structuralist," and Picard as "content mediation" (2002). Students of Fisher and Ury refer to this as "interest-based negotiation" (Fisher and Ury 1991; Senger 2002). Proponents of transformative mediation often use the label "problem-solving model" when referring to the standard Northern approach (e.g. Bush and Folger 1994; 2001). Abu-Nimer 1996; Stempel 2002.

29 In the Mandinka world-view a win–win outcome may actually be conflict cessation and reconciliation. In some cases that is the main "issue" that the participants feel must be dealt with. Darboe 1982; Elias 1956.

30 In marital disputes, for example, wives often ask their husbands' friends to mediate.

31 Mandinka mediators often make statements such as: "No matter how angry you are and how difficult the situation is you must leave it."

32 Such cases were infrequent, comprising 10 out of 121 observed cases. Long-time intercultural mediator Richard Salem observed a similar pattern among the "mamas" engaged in dispute mediation in South Africa (personal communication 5/10/03). Also in Griots at War, Barbara Hoffman describes a mediation in Mali in which the mediators told the disputants

not to give their testimony (Hoffman 2000). The disputants gave their testimony anyway, something that also occurred in some of the Gambian cases.

33 For example, cases in which mediators told the disputants not to explain what happened in the dispute were usually ones where the mediators were of higher status than the disputants, or had a joking relationship or other strong bond with them.

34 Only 55% of 45 observed Mandinka cases included negotiation of substantive issues.

35 Burton 1986; Moore 1993; Myers and Filner 1997.

36 Janson 2002; Sonko-Godwin 1997.

37 Sidia Jatta personal communication 1999; Hoffman 2000.

38 Fa Mamodou's surname identifies him as a descendent of the *Nyanchoo* ruling class of the Kaabu empire (Faal 1999).

39 The service Fa Mamodou and his son provide is unpaid; it does bring them respect and happy disputants may give them gifts of appreciation, but they are essentially volunteer mediators.

40 cf. Kriesberg, Northrup, and Thorson 1989.

41 Burton 1990; Lederach 1995.

42 How to determine whether mediation was a success is a complex and thorny subject. Not only do scholars disagree on how to define success (cf. Bercovitch 1996), the whole notion of "success" is highly subjective and linked to ideological factors. Transformative mediators define success in a much different manner than problem-solving mediators, for example (Bush and Folger 1994, 2001). Here an emic definition of success is employed with statements by the disputants that they are pleased with the outcome of mediation used as indicators of a successful outcome.

43 Dibba 2003; Swiss Tropical Institute 2003.

44 Touray 2001.

45 As previously noted, joking kinship exists in many parts of Africa including Cote de Ivoire. A comparative analysis of the historical, ideological, social, material, and political variables that enabled the contribution of these ties to conflict mitigation in The Gambia, while they were either not used or did not have a significant effect in Cote de Ivoire would be a fascinating study.

46 Benedict Anderson (1991) presents a classic discussion of the constructed or "imagined" nature of identity (cf. Nagel 1994). See Hobsbawm and Ranger (1992) for a seminal presentation of the construction and re-invention of "tradition" and custom.

47 In fact, the author was drawn into joking relations with others through his Gambian patronymic.

48 Diallo 2002 and Wilson-Fall 2000.

49 Wilson-Fall 2000, p.56.

50 For example, a census worker pretended to have joking kinship with the inhabitants of villages where he had problems getting responses to his survey. This "imaginary" joking relation proved quite effective in his successful accomplishment of his task. O'Bannon's chapter in this volume provides further examples of the extendable nature of these relationships. See in particular his account of the Jola, Wolof, Serer encounter in Casamance.

51 Gambians describe this saying as a *hadith* or saying of the Prophet Mohammed (PBUH). According to Saudi Arabian scholars of Islam, this *hadith* refers only to exceptional situations, particularly to cases of war when a leader is killed or severely injured (Dr. Aida Bamia personal communication 12/5/03).

52 How to determine whether mediation was a success is a complex and thorny subject. Not only do scholars disagree on how to define success (cf. Bercovitch 1996), the whole notion of "success" is highly subjective and linked to ideological factors. Transformative mediators define success in a much different manner than problem-solving mediators, for example (Bush and Folger 1994, 2001). In this study, statements by made by disputants—in the absence of the other mediation participants—that they were pleased with the outcome of the mediation were taken as indicators of success.

53 In an observed peacemaking, the mediator—who had *dangkutoo* with the disputants—was told that he would have "had bad things happen to him" if he had not intervened. In another example of the widespread social acceptance of this institution, a police officer insisted upon mediating between his joking partners instead of taking up formal legal proceedings.

54 Boone 2003; Hobsbawm and Ranger 1992.

55 Disputes between joking partners appear to be fairly infrequent as most Gambians attempt to avoid such situations and act quickly to resolve them when they occur. During the study period a young man exhibited great concern when his joking partner became upset with him. Despite feeling that he was correct in that situation, he went to great lengths to humble him, appease his partner, and ensure that there would be no hard feelings between them. It is unlikely that conflicts between joking kin will become violent since spilling the blood of your joking partner is one of the strongest taboos of these relationships.

56 e.g. Abu-Nimer 1996; Avruch 1998; Cohen 1996; Merry 1987.

57 Senger 2002.

58 Bush and Folger 1994, 1996, John Paul Lederach 1995, and Michelle LeBaron 2000, 2002.

59 Alternative approaches to mediation have their own culturally-rooted components. For example, transformative mediation is sometimes presented as aiming to empower individuals by encouraging them to affect their own destiny and to resolve or transform their disputes (Bush and Folger 1996). These beliefs in individual responsibility, agency, and empowerment are profoundly Northern (cf. Brigg 2003). Cobb 1994; Winslade and Monk 2000.

60 This was in fact the response by panels of Gambian mediators after listening to the commonly used training guidelines encountered by the author during his training and his assisting in the training of prospective mediators.

61 See Myers and Filner 1997 for an example of general suggestions for cross-cultural mediation training.

62 For a strong proposal in this direction, see John Paul Lederach's elicitive approach to peace-building (1995).

63 Laura Nader 1991, 1997.

64 In terms of the field of socio-economic development and assistance, this attitude has led to many a failed project.

65 For example, a woman describing a mediation that took place after her child's garden was destroyed by cows said, "The reason we mediated it is because if you go to the government they will not do anything about it. They will twist and turn, and in the end nothing will come out of it."

Notes on Some Joking Relationships Between Hui and Han Villages in Henan

by Elisabeth Allès (2003)

"Speech, whether insulting or flattering, beneficial or injurious, carries life force above all; in all its uses it retains the constant quality of being language". (M. Griaule)[2]

A man, who is Han, arrives at a stall run by Hui (Chinese Muslims). The man suddenly makes some remarks which Huis considers to be insulting and bursts out laughing. The young daughter of the stallholder, who is only 17, is furious and dismayed. She knows that such remarks could set off a brawl involving several hundred people. Turning to her father, she is amazed to see him laughing as well. What's going on? She cannot understand the situation, she has never seen this man before, he is not a friend of the family. Then her father says, to reassure her: "Don't worry, it's normal, between his village and ours it's been like this for hundreds of years, they're harmless (meiyou nao) jokes (mawanr)".

This form of alliance, usually called a "parenté à plaisanteries" or "cathartic alliance", is not unknown to anthropologists; this type of relationship is well attested to in Western Africa[3] and other areas of the world[4], but does not appear in the literature on China. There is no reference to it either in the older or in more recent books on village life. These deal mainly with village and lineage organisation[5] or with situations of conflict between villages[6]. Where relationships between Chinese Muslims (the Hui) and the Han are concerned, studies have concentrated on the Hui identity, on the deep roots of Muslims in China, on the conflicts which have taken place over the centuries with the state and the Han/Hui?, as well as between the Hui themselves[7].

What we call here joking relationships do not concern relations between individuals connected by marriage, but rather the specific relations between members of different villages who do not necessarily know each other. This is why we use the term relationships rather than kinship, even though, as we shall see, the symbolism of relationship by marriage lies at the heart of the subject. This specific relationship is expressed through insulting, sometimes coarse words, or abnormal attitudes, without producing violent reactions. In a way, in the words of the English anthropologist, Alfred R. Radcliffe-Brown, "the relationship is one of permitted disrespect"[8].

It was in the year 2000, in the province of Henan, that for the first time in China we were told of these kaiwanxiao de guanxi (joking relationships) and were able to observe manifestations of them. In 2002 and

2003, we carried out a series of studies in two directions. On the one hand we sought other examples in areas which are homogeneously Han, or contain other minorities. We chose Hunan, more specifically a mountainous area where relations between villages have not always been easy, and Guangxi, where a number of minorities live. In neither case did we find anything resembling joking relationships. On the other hand, a further series of studies was carried out in Hui villages on their relationships with their Han neighbours in various regions (Hainan, Yunnan, Xinjiang) without further conclusive results[9]. The province of Henan and its northern section was therefore the main focus[10] of studies carried out in March and July 2003, in about ten villages.

There are virtually no writings on the history of these alliances. The local monographs we were able to consult, produced over the last twenty years, are completely silent on the subject[11]; a few traces are to be found on steles in ancestral temples, or in genealogies (jiapu). The main part is transmitted by word and gesture. On this subject we should like to point out that, because of their fascination with Chinese writing, Westerners have long neglected the role of speech in China[12]. Being undervalued, speech was unable to attain the nobility of writing and could not carry as powerful a meaning. In the last few years, linguists, anthropologists and historians have called into question this very Western vision of the contrast between the oral and the written, and have reassessed the place they assigned to speech[13].

I—Words, Gestures and Attitudes

First of all we must specify that the joking relationships observed or described by villagers (both Han and Hui) concern only men; women are completely excluded from them. They generally know of the existence of these kinds of relationships, they may be present, but they never actively participate. The terms we have found are always linked to the terminology of kinship[14]. What makes these terms insulting is the fact that they are used between people from two groups who are supposedly unable to have any links of kinship by alliance, because they are of different religions; in our day people talk of the difference of *"minzu"* (nationality)[15]. Besides these words connected to the terminology of kinship, there are others, probably spoken more spontaneously, which are called "dirty" *(zang)* by those who use them, and to which this researcher, being both female and foreign, could not gain access, either orally or in writing, all the more so as these expressions are generally in dialect. Sometimes the gesture is sufficiently evocative. One can imagine what these expressions are, coarseness being as popular in China as it is in the rest of the world. The only indication given is that they must not concern the interlocutor's mother or daughter. Educated circles cannot use them nor even provide any examples of them, retired professors (both Han and Hui) emphasise the lack of culture in peasant circles *(meiyou wenhua)* to explain these differences of language. The most common term is *gufu:* uncle (husband of the father's sister). For example:

A Han says to a Hui (or the other way round): *"jiao wo gufu!"* (Call me uncle), the Hui answers: *"bu jiao, weishenme jiao ni gufu!"* (No, why should I call you uncle).

Or else *"gufu, gufu lai le!"* (Uncle's coming!), *"gufu zai …* (name of the Hui or Han village)" (Your uncle is from …). In response the Hui or the Han will answer with an insult or make a significantly insulting gesture.

The other terms are *jiujiu:* uncle (the mother's brother)[16] or *lao gan die* (dry father)[17].

For example:

"Jiujiu ni qu nar?" (Where are you going, uncle?)[18], *"Xiao jiu le!"* (Little uncle!). Where the word *jiujiu* is concerned, some state that it is only used by the Hui to a Han, others only the opposite.

"Oh! *lao gan die!*" (Hey, dry father!) between two people who meet. This term is used by both Han and Hui.

As far as we know, the terms of address involved in joking relationships do not take into account the generations of individuals. That is to say that the terms *gufu*, *jiujiu* or *laogandie* are used equally by young and old, whatever the age of the interlocutor. These terms of address, which in ordinary circumstances are unremarkable, become insulting between a Han and a Hui, for they affirm the existence of an unacceptable and unimaginable kinship between the interested parties, either because one is Muslim and the other not, or because they belong to two different *minzu*. Moreover the term *gufu* marks a form of superiority, for it affirms that the speaker belongs to a generation older than that of his interlocutor. Pursuing the idea further, the use of a kinship term in this context suggests the idea of a conversion, since there can be kinship only between members of the same religion, and nobody will accept such an idea since religious belonging is transmitted within patrilineage.

We should also note that the words *gufu* and *jiujiu* designate people whose children could marry. This refers to marriage between first cousins, a match which one could consider as being preferential in China, at least until it was proscribed by the new marriage law passed in 1981. Where the relationship with the maternal uncle *(jiujiu)* is concerned, we have observed on many occasions the important role the latter plays for his nephew or niece, particularly his accompanying role in difficult situations, and his role in mediation. Among the Hui, for example, the maternal uncle is present at the moment of his niece's marriage; also, in areas where the Hui practise circumcision, the *jiujiu* will be close to his uterine nephew for the occasion. Among Hui and Han alike, the maternal uncle can intervene when a conflict arises between a father and his child. Moreover, it is not unusual in China for a joking relationship to be established between brother- and sister-in-law, which makes it possible to maintain a certain emotional distance and to divert potential conflicts within a family.

In joking relationships, the man who pronounces the insulting expressions will pass his hand across his face or the back of his neck, and then let his arm fall suddenly to his side in order to demonstrate clearly that he is not being serious. Sometimes the men jostle or thump each other, their bodies tangling in an imaginary struggle. These joking relationships can happen on any occasion, there is no favoured place or time. However it seems that these encounters are often linked to the bustle of market days. They are a way of being recognised or of starting a conversation in a joking mode. Finally, these occasions seem to have been more frequent before the 1960s.

Among the kinds of behaviour quoted, stories are told of lack of consideration, of abnormal behaviour which would be likened to theft in normal times. For example, a Hui relates: "We would go into a Han village and take grapes off a stall, eat them and laughing, leave without paying, there wasn't any fighting!". Or again "One day someone from (Han) village X came into one of the eating-houses in our Hui village and ate everything that took his fancy. When he'd finished, he stood up to leave, and the owner came over to settle up. It was then that the customer made himself recognised and began to laugh, there was a playful scuffle and he left.".

Reference to the idea of alliance prevents any violence or bloodshed, and imposes the obligation of hospitality as if it were a member of the family.

II—Legends and Foundation Narratives

The inhabitants of a particular area know exactly with which village they have joking relationships. Sometimes they may mention such relationships between other villages while often making mistakes[19]. Some say that these relationships really became important during the first half of the twentieth century and particularly during the period of "great Han chauvinism" *(dahan zhuyi)*[20]. However the origins of these relationships remain largely unknown to them. "This has been going on forever, for hundreds of years". A Hui says: "Even if we don't know why, we can't forget" *(wang bu liao)*. A young man adds: "The old know—we don't!".

Some old people, retired teachers or village cadres, recount, with local variations, the following legend: "All that began under the Tang dynasty. Some Hui soldiers came from far away, from Arabia *(Tianfang)*; they had come to support the Emperor of the Tang. After the victory, some remained and became mandarins *(dang guan)*. But they had come without women, they were sad, they were bored!". It is at this point that the versions diverge. In some, despite the misgivings of his entourage, one of the great mandarins of the time, a native of (Han) village X, decided to give his daughter to one of the Hui, who had become an officer. Ever since, all the Hui of China know that village[21], because it was the site of the first marriage between Han and Hui, and since that time there has been mutual joking. In other versions, the Emperor decided to give the most beautiful woman in the (Han) village X to one of them, who settled in the Hui village.

We should note that these legends fall within the framework of the foundation narratives of the Hui *minzu* (nationality): Arab and Persian Muslims, soldiers, scientists and merchants, came during the Tang (618–907) and Song (960–1277) dynasties and founded lines by marrying Han women; this was how the Hui *minzu* arose. Han mothers symbolise belonging to the Chinese world, while Hui fathers justify the existence of a foreign religion and the creation of a different *minzu*. General works on the history of the Hui in China always refer to this outline, although many of them subsequently emphasise the coming of large numbers of Muslims from Central and Western Asia during the Mongol Yuan dynasty (1277–1368)[22].

The best-known narrative on the subject relates, in substance[23], that during the revolt of An Lushan, the Emperor Xuanzong, in a difficult position, called on Hui soldiers[24], thus winning the battle. He then told them to stay in Chang'an[25], and three of them did so. But they had neither wives nor children with them, they were homesick and wanted to leave the capital. This worried the Emperor and his ministers suggested that the only way to keep them was to marry them off. But no Han father would have agreed to give his daughter to a Hui soldier. So the Emperor allowed the Hui soldiers to take their wives by force, which they did at the Lantern Festival. With the Emperor's permission, and on condition that they remained in Chang'an, they each took nine wives[26].

While the local legends all refer to a founding marriage, there are no marriages between the villages involved[27]. In explanation of this fact, the villagers specify: "it is impossible because the *minzu* is different, the customs are different".

Joking relationships involve only two villages at a time. However friendly relations can be maintained with other villages, without taking the form of this specific relationship. We observed that, in one case, a Hui village has a joking relationship with a Han village, as well as good relations with another Han village. With the latter, exchanges at New Year replace insults or jokes. One side (the Hui) give demonstrations of martial arts *(wushu)* in the Han village and the Han perform dances *yangge*[28] in the Hui village. This is no doubt an unusual situation because the two villages are practically on opposite sides of a road to each other. In this case, understanding is based on services rendered. We quote here the basic elements of the narrative engraved on a stele[29] in the ancestral temple of the Han village concerned: more than 500 years ago, the Chen family had been honoured by the Ming Emperor[30] and their ancestor was a high mandarin *(zuojun)*. One of his descendants was named magistrate of the area. At the time, the people of the Hui village came to buy and sell cattle and sheep. They had to cross the territory and had many problems with the customs post over taxes and levies. Thanks to the intervention of the magistrate, the difficulties were resolved, and thus began the friendship between the two villages.

On the Hui side, some of the village elders relate another version of the origins of this friendship, which is not, however, engraved on a stele. They explain that at the end of the Ming dynasty and at the beginning of the Qing (1644), the villages formed two *"she"* (groups of families) who together worked the fields near a river which now flows between the two villages. Friendship was forged in the difficulties of the time and that is why one speaks of *"sheqin"* (kinship by association) to describe this relationship. In the Hui village, the younger generations (those aged under about 50) adhere to the written version. This difference of interpretation is probably attributable to events which took place during the Republican period, which we will return to below, of which the older villagers have painful memories.

We should mention another example of cordial relations, which do not concern a whole village but a branch of a Han lineage which has become Hui[31]. It is said that it all began, long ago, with a friendship and a marriage. Two men farmed together an area situated at the edge of their respective village territories. They got along very well and had become good friends. One day the wind rose and a thunderstorm arrived. The two men took shelter in a ditch *(gou)* of red earth. They talked and agreed to marry their children to each other. One, the Han, had a son, and the other, the Hui, a daughter. Two boys were born of this union. Unfortunately at the end of the Ming dynasty and the beginning of the Qing (1644), disturbances came to the region, and the men were enrolled in the army[32]. There was no way of resisting. So the mother took her two sons and went to stay with her two brothers in her home village, which was Hui. This is how this branch became Hui and everyone remembers the "Red Earth Ditch" agreement which today symbolises the idea of marriage[33]. Every New Year, the Hui members meet with the Han branches of this lineage in the home village, where there are celebrations around the ancestral temple.

This narrative shows a situation which is the opposite of the traditionally accepted model of a Han woman marrying a Hui man. The woman is expected naturally to adopt her husband's religion. In Hui discourse, marriage between a Hui woman and a Han man is theoretically impossible unless he converts to Islam, which seems presumably unlikely. In fact it is a situation we have observed on many occasions in the towns of Eastern China.

Joking relationships also sometimes manifest themselves by mutual help between villages. In the middle of the nineteenth century, Hui villagers went to the edge of an allied Han village in order to wash in the river the sheepskins which were the craft supplement essential to the survival of the village[34]. The Han, for their part, could come and sell their produce in the Hui village. In the 1970s, the same village made a gift to its Han ally of a machine which would make it possible to increase its production of flour. At the end of the 1990s, the Hui village, having prospered, contributed financially to the repair of the main road and to the construction of a secondary school in the Han village, which has remained poor[35].

During our research, we observed the economic dimension of this distinctive relationship, whether this involves a business or other activity. We have just mentioned the use of the water of a river. In other places the Hui came, and still come, to the village to buy live cattle and sheep for their meat trade; the Hui are reputed for this profession. In other cases, it can be the presence of Hui who have opened a restaurant, or are carrying on other businesses in the market of a Han village.

III—Some Elements of Local History

It is also necessary to look at local history, which was particularly violent during the early twentieth century. However, we must first localise the area concerned according to joking relationships. We have been able to observe relationships of this kind between villages in several cantons along a road from Luoyang to the provincial capital, Zhengzhou. Many of these villages lie north of the Yellow River, and some south of it. Distances between allied villages average 10 to 20 kilometres by road and sometimes less across the fields. These villages are in some cases separated by other Han villages, with whom the Hui do not have good relations, as we shall see. According to our observations, the Han villages do not have this kind of relationship, and further to the east of the province, it does not seem that similar situations exist between Hui and Han.

If we take the construction of mosques as an indicator of relative prosperity, the Hui in this region built a good number of them in the nineteenth century. Some are very ancient, such as that in Bo'ai or those in the village of Xiguan, situated west of the city, which date back to the end of the Yuan dynasty or the beginning of the Ming (late fourteenth and early fifteenth century)[36]. It seems that at that time, each village had a mosque for men and one for women. However, owing to the long period of peace under the Qing dynasty and the increase in the population during the eighteenth century, the Muslim lineages which formed and increased in number, each founded their own mosque during the nineteenth century. The major Muslim revolts in the middle of the nineteenth century which involved the Hui in Shaanxi, Gansu and Yunnan, as well as the Uyghurs in Xinjiang, do not seem to have had any direct effect on this region of the central plain. However the revolt of the Nian[37] in Shandong had some repercussions, as did the repression of the revolt of the Taiping which took place a little further south. Moreover, the frequent rises in the water levels of the Yellow River caused serious flooding and food shortages were recurrent.

The Hui's relations with their Han neighbours declined seriously during the time of the warlords, and in the 1930s, with the Japanese invasion and occupation. Some Han in the region tell of how, as children, they had acquired the habit of throwing stones at any Hui who approached the road situated between the Han and Hui villages, which obliged the Hui to stoop in order to be able to pass. It was no doubt a way of expressing their resentment at the prosperity of certain Hui villages at the time, and perhaps also a reaction to the practice the Hui had of adopting Han children born out of wedlock, and particularly girls, whom the families in the neighbouring villages did not want and would abandon[38]. In any case, whatever the reasons, such incidents increased during the time of the warlords. Here are two examples which left a profound impression.

The first, which took place in the district of Bo'ai, recalls the pogroms in Russia or in Central Europe. A large number of peasant self-defence militias had been constituted in the early 1920s in reaction to the bands of looters who were plundering the region, at a time when the trade in arms and drugs was a highly profitable activity. These militias, organised as secret societies, subsequently opposed the warlords and fought against the exorbitant taxes the latter sought to impose. However, as is often the case, these groups finally turned to crime. In 1927, Henan became the centre of these groups organised in networks of villages which belonged to the Red Spears Society *(hongqianghui)*[39].

In Bo'ai, a local monograph[40] reports that a group of this society was created in 1925, and had more than 500 members in 1927[41]. In the same year, the Multicoloured Spears Society *(huaqianghui)* had more than one thousand[42]. According to the same source, in 1927, the Red Spears Society decided to oppose the Hui, and set up in a village near the Hui village of Daxinzhuang. Clashes *(xiedou)* became more and more numerous and took a tragic turn that year. It is not known how things began, but the village of

Daxinzhuang was attacked by groups from all the surrounding Han villages. The Hui of the district came to the rescue and violent battles lasted several weeks. It was the arrival of beifa[43] troops which put an end to the confrontation[44].

The second incident is more closely linked to the prevarication and the greed of the local Han authorities of the time. The Hui village of Sanpo, through its two activities of sheepskin production and farming, was reputed to have a comfortable income for the time. Many times over the local authorities had raised various taxes. But in April 1943, probably because the villagers refused to pay any more, troops organised by the local Guomindang district leader who was seeking to extort further funds from them, surrounded the village. There was a sudden attack and a terrible massacre: in a single night there were 110 dead, 400 houses set alight, the mosques burned and several hundred families plundered[45].

After 1949 relations between the Hui villages and neighbouring Han villages became more peaceful. Nevertheless, when collective work needed to be carried out, such as repairing the roads, the local cadres managed to assemble the Hui crews with those of their respective allied Han villages. They thus avoided any fighting breaking out. However, while some individuals remembered this alliance, it had somewhat lapsed during the previous thirty years. Some could remember as children having seen Han allies in their village, but nothing since. In the early 1990s, nobody spoke of it[46]. In fact, the steles erected date from 1999 and 2001.

Since the reforms, conflicts between Han villages[47] and between Hui and Han have begun again, in Henan as elsewhere. These are often clashes in the markets, usually minor. But in 1992, in the small town of Yuanyang, north of Zhengzhou (the provincial capital), a confrontation took on disquieting proportions. After a fight in the market and the profanation of the mosque, violent clashes lasted several days. There were several deaths, and the intervention of the army was needed to restore order. One could quote other examples of increased tension between Han and Hui in other regions[48], which are a general phenomenon and are not accompanied by joking relationships.

In this context, also marked by the difficulties encountered by the central government in the management of peripheral territories such as Tibet and Xinjiang, the authorities have relaunched the slogan of "unity of the nationalities" (minzu tuanjie)[49]. One can therefore understand the wish of local authorities, whether Han or Hui, to utilise everything which might calm things down. As in the Republican period, the Hui react quickly to anything which might appear to be insulting. In order to avoid a repetition of demonstrations similar to those against a book entitled Sexual Morals[50], the Chinese authorities respond quickly and favourably when the Hui demand the banning of a publication; this fits into the political framework of the status of minzu and of the protection of minorities[51].

Thus while the reforms have reawoken conflicts, they have at the same time made it possible for the members of each community to revive a part of their history and to re-establish old connections. But as is often the case in China, these memories are also instrumentalised by the authorities.

IV—Some Interpretations

We must now understand the internal motivations of these relationships, of which we had no knowledge until now. Before attempting any interpretation, and in the absence of any possible comparisons with other Chinese regions, we would like to take a detour via Africa, where descriptions of these sorts of relationships are ancient and numerous.

The Chinese examples observed do not present such an elaborate system (since they do not incorporate such wide-ranging services and obligations) as that which is described in the alliance between Dogon and Bozo known as *Mangou;* in particular the reversal of the ordinary rules of politeness at the moment of the end of mourning ceremonies, or the role played by conciliation. But there are a number of points in common. The first manifestation of this form of relationship takes the form, as in China, of insult. "The most appreciated insults are also those which would inevitably lead to a brawl, if one were not *Mangu*"[52].

M. Griaule[53] relates: "No restraint is observed, even on religious subjects (...) The Bozo accuses his partner's religious leader of having had himself licked by a great snake and of never washing[54]. The other retorts that the Bozo[55] are "evil creatures of the water", a veiled allusion to the fact that they are said to be water spirits who have become impure".

The origin narratives of this specific relationship refer, as in China, to a service rendered or a blood relationship. M. Griaule presents two narratives[56]: "The most common version relates a famine which broke out in ancient times, during which the Bozo and the Dogon died in large numbers. One day, a Bozo (or Dogon) chief seeing a Dogon (or Bozo) child about to die, cut a piece of flesh from his calf and, having roasted it, gave it to the unfortunate, who recovered". "Another narrative is more explicit and brings out an initial relationship between Bozo and Dogon. The spirit of water (...) which was female (...) gave birth to a daughter. Rising to the surface later, she saw some children of the same family, with the same mother and father as the Dogon, to whom she gave her daughter. "Your daughter is beautiful, they answered. You are the woman of the water and you are going back to it. We will keep your daughter". They called her Sorogonn, a word which means "those who can live as easily in the water as on the surface of the earth" and which is now given to the Bozo. They took the girl to a village in Mandé; she gave birth there at the same time as a Dogon woman and died soon after, while her husband was on a journey. The Dogon woman adopted the orphan which she breastfed like her own, and during a famine, she cut off part of her thigh to feed both children. Then the husband of the woman Sorogonn returned and said to the other woman: "You have been good to my child and I do not know how to repay you. Since my child has eaten your flesh, it will not be able to marry yours nor do harm to any of your race. We have become gara *(mangou)*". Even more explicit, D. Paulme relates[57] "The ancestor of the Peul and that of the blacksmiths came to this country together from Mecca. The blacksmith was married and had daughters. The Peul did not even have a wife. The blacksmith is said to have given him one of his daughters in marriage, assuring him that it was to be the last and only marriage between their two clans".

The partners in this relationship cannot do each other harm and owe each other assistance and hospitality[58]. "Blows are forbidden between *Mangu.* (...) blood must not flow in front of them *(Mangu)*"[59]. According to M. Griaule, "the breaking of such bans brings about an impurity which places the individual concerned in an irresolvable situation from the religious point of view, purification being almost impossible"[60].

This specific relationship is accompanied, in Africa as in China, by the ban on intermarriage. For the Han and the Hui, the friendly relations which exist between villages connected by joking relationships forbid and make impossible any matrimonial alliance, while it can exist between Han and Hui who are not members of these villages. Finally the economic character of the relationship constitutes another point. It translates in Africa into the exchange of services and obligatory presents[61], and in China by commercial links.

Thus from the observation of Chinese phenomena and the comparison with African experience, four main elements appear: the prohibition of intermarriage, insults, friendly relations, and the creation of peaceful areas.

The Prohibition of Intermarriage

Joking relationships are accompanied by the ban on marriage between members of the villages concerned. When a marriage occurs, writes Denise Paulme[62] who herself relies for her demonstration on the description of blood kinship by E.E. Evans-Pritchard[63], "there is what one can call a "blood service" rendered by the parents of the wife to the parents of the husband, by the female side to the male"[64]. D. Paulme suggests a mechanism analogous to that of the blood relationship: "the originating act of the alliance thus takes on the character of an exception, or even of an offence, which makes it all the more memorable; if it had been repeated with impunity, it would have lost all efficacy"[65]. For his part, Radcliffe-Brown develops the idea of a sanction act and considers that "The prohibition against interfaçage maintains this separation by preventing the creation of relations of kinésique between members of the two groups"[66]. He adds "The "friendship" appears in the prohibition, under supernatural sanction, against the shedding of the blood of a member of the allied people".

In the light of these analyses, one may consider that the ban on reproducing the founding event which was the marriage between a Hui man and a Han woman, distinguishes the specific relationship between the Han and Hui villages concerned by joking relationships. This may be a way of sanctioning the relationship of alliance or of friendship (to which we will return) which cannot be of the same nature as that which exists in the kinship relations between Hui or even, in specific conditions, with other Han.

Insults

Radcliffe-Brown, in his desire to build a general theory of what the joking relationship represents does not really address the meaning and the exact role of the insult. He situates the phenomenon more as an alternative to extreme respect[67]. M. Griaule's analysis refers to a specific situation, that of the Dogon. From Dogon mythology and cosmogony, he concludes that invective in this case is cathartic: it makes it possible both to relieve and to be relieved. It is a permanent means of purification[68]. He explains: "When the Bozo pronounced the formula (the oath), part of the force *(nyama)* which was in him passed in his words, breath and mist, entered the ear of the Dogon blacksmith, and by a complex circuit, reached his liver. This mechanism was in all ways comparable to that of the impregnation of women by the word, with the difference that, in the latter case, the end result is the womb"[69]. He continues "the *Mangou* can say anything, for each has a little of the other's *nyama* and it is to this part that each one speaks, that is to say to himself: therefore there are no repercussions. It is the part of *nyama* deposited in the other which is brought into action when there is meeting and insult".[70]

A comparison with the Chinese situation would require a lengthy study of widely different aspects, but from this description it seems useful to retain the idea that agreed insult is the way to control violence.

Friendship

Radcliffe-Brown expands particularly on the aspect of friendship, introducing a distinction between friendship and solidarity: he puts forward the idea of "a relation neither of solidarity nor of hostility but of "friendship" in which the separateness of the group is emphasised, but open conflict between the groups or the members on the two sides is avoided by establishing a relation in which they may insult each other without giving or taking offence"[71]. He emphasises the distinction to be made with relations of solidarity which impose complex systems of obligation.[72]

Where the situation between Han and Hui is concerned, the terms employed to express this relation are *biaoxiongdi* (first cousin on the mother's side) and *pengyou* (friend), *tamen shi hao pengyou* (they are good friends, real friends). The term *xiongdi* (brothers) which usually expresses relations of solidarity between individuals or between groups is not used at all in this kind of situation. Neither is it the kind of relationship which obliges blood relatives of the same generation and beyond to intervene in case of disagreement with neighbours. Acts of solidarity or mutual help in joking relationships are merely selective. Moreover they concern the group as a whole, whereas, on the contrary, insults are exchanged only between individuals. The reference to insult and to the notion of friendship brings us to our last point.

The Creation of Peaceful Areas

In Chinese history, situations of violence happen daily: if it is not the violence of arms, it is that of natural catastrophe, flood or famine. Tensions run high between the Han and the Hui. Although the Hui have participated in the same forms of popular organisation as the Han inside secret societies[73], this does not make possible the resolution of conflicts in daily life. In fact the specific form of relationship which is the joking relationship has made it possible through agreed insult to control violence and has undoubtedly facilitated the creation of pacified areas where the Hui could carry on their economic activities. Situated far enough away to allow an opening up of Hui villages, they constituted areas of mutual help and peace at the most critical moments.

Notes

1 To insult or abuse without it being of any consequence.

2 M. Griaule, 1948, "L'Alliance cathartique", *Africa,* vol. XVIII, p. 242.

3 See for example M. Mauss, 1927–28, "Parenté à plaisanteries", Annuaire de l'Ecole Pratique des Hautes Etudes; H. Labouret, 1929, "La parenté à plaisanteries en Afrique occidentale", *Africa,* T. 2, pp. 244–254; Evans-Pritchard Dr. E. E., 1933, "Zande Blood Brotherhood", *Africa,* vol. VI, n° 4, pp. 369–401; D. Paulme, 1939, "Parenté à plaisanteries et alliance par le sang en Afrique occidentale", *Africa,* vol. XII, pp. 433–444; Pedler F. J., 1940, "Joking Relationships in East Africa", vol. XIII, n° 2, pp. 170–173; Radcliffe-Brown A. R., 1940, "On Joking Relationships", *Africa,* vol. XIII, n° 3, pp. 195–210 (reprinted in *Structure and Function in Primitive Societies; Essays and Addresses* by the same author, London, 1952); M. Griaule, 1948, *op. cit.,* pp. 242–258.

4 Among them J. Y. Loude et V. Lièvre, 1984, *Solstice païen,* Paris, Presses de la Renaissance. Particularly the chapter entitled "Le jour du poing brandi. Insultes entre villages", pp. 210–218.

5 For example: Fei Xiaotong, 1947 (first edn. 1939), *Peasant Life in China: a Field Study and Country Life in the Yangtze Valley,* London, Kegan Paul; Yang Maochun, 2001, (first edn. 1945 in English), *Yige Zhongguo cunzhuang. Shandong Taitou. A Chinese Village, Taitou,* Shandong Province, Nanjing, Jiangsu renmin chubanshe; Faure David, 1986, *The Structure of Chinese Rural Society: Lineage and Village in the Eastern New Territories,* Hong Kong, H. K., Oxford, N. Y., Oxford University Press; Thireau Isabelle et Wang Hanheng, 2001, *Disputes au village chinois. Formes du juste et recompositions locales des espaces normatifs,* Paris, Maison des sciences de l'homme.

6 Bianco Lucien and Hue Chang Ming, 1995, "*Xiedou* et traditions: le retour des vendettas paysannes", *Perspectives chinoises,* n° 32, pp. 15–20.

7 Among works in Chinese: Bai Shouyi, 1952, *Huimin qiyi* (Hui Uprisings), Shanghai, Shenzhou guoguangshe, 4 vols; Ma Tong, 1983, *Zhongguo yisilan jiaopai yu menhuan shidu shilüe* (A history of Muslim religious movements and the *menhuan*

system in China), Ningxia, Ningxia renmin chubanshe. Among recent works in Western languages: Fletcher J., 1986, "Les voies (turuq) soufies en Chine", in A. Popovic et G. Veinstein (éds.), *Les Ordres mystiques dans l'islam, cheminements et situation actuelle*, Paris, Ehess, pp. 13–26; Gladney Dru C., 1991 (re-edited, 1996, 2000), *Muslim Chinese. Ethnic Nationalism in the People's Republic*, Cambridge and London, Council on East Asian Studies, Harvard University; F. Aubin, 1995, "Chine"; H. Chambert-Loir et C. Guillot, *Le culte des saints dans le monde musulman, Etudes thématiques*, n° 4, Paris, EFEO, pp. 367–388; J. Lipman, 1997, *Familiar Strangers: A History of Muslims in Northwest China*, University of Washington Press, Seattle-London; E. Allès, 2000, *Musulmans de Chine. Une anthropologie des Hui du Henan*, Paris, Ehess.

8   A. R. Radcliffe-Brown, 1940, op. cit, p. 196.

9   We asked the question as well to Muslim and non-Muslim families living in Hong Kong, originally from villages in the province of Guangdong, without receiving any positive answer either.

10 This was already the case with our study of women's mosques. E. Allès, 2000, *op. cit.*,ch. XII et XIII.

11 *Bo'ai xianzhi* (monograph of the xian of Bo'ai), 1994; *Yanshi xianzhi* (monograph of the xian of Yanshi), 1992; *Qiaozuo shijiaoqu zhi* (monograph of the environs of Qiaozuo), 1993; *Meng xianzhi* (monograph of the xian of Meng), 1991; *Henansheng Huizu difangzhi* (local monograph of the Hui of Henan), 1989; *Henansheng Huizu zhi* (monograph of the Hui of Henan), 1986; *Henansheng zhi* (monograph of Henan), 1994; *Guangcheng huizuqu zhi* (monograph of the Hui quarter of Guancheng), 1989; *Luoyangshi Chanhe huizuqu zhi* (monograph of the Hui quarter of Chanhe of the city of Luoyang), 1988. When we are able to gain access to earlier sources, we will of course have to consult the monographs of the Ming and Qing dynasties and those of the Republican period.

12 "They assumed on the one hand that Chinese writing was disconnected from speech, and on the other that the civilisations of the Far East were overwhelmingly graphic, and little interested in the oral", V. Alleton, in V. Alleton (ed.), 1997, *Paroles à dire, Paroles à écrire; Inde, Chine, Japon*, Paris, Ehess, p. 11.

13 V. Alleton (éd.), 1997, *op.cit.;* see also, J. Levi , 1995, "La voix et l'encre, la chaussure et la trace: langue, écriture et tradition romanesque en Chine", in Levi J., *La Chine romanesque. Fictions d'Orient et d'Occident*, Seuil, pp. 33–61.

14 Terms of kinship are widely used in China in order to signify a respectful proximity, without there being any real relationship for all that.

15 A neologism which arrived from Japan at the end of the nineteenth century, the word *minzu* is polysemic, meaning: nation, people, national, nationality; China today is made up of 56 *minzu*, of whom the most numerous are the Han (92%). On the history, use and ambiguities of the word, see J. Thoraval, 1990, "Le concept chinois de nation est-il "obscur"? A propos du débat sur la notion de "minzu" dans les années 1980", *Bulletin de sinologie*, n° 65, pp. 24–41; F. Dikötter, 1992, *The Discourse of Race in Modern China*, Stanford, Stanford University Press.

16 On the place and the role of the uterine uncle, see the general literature on the subject. For example J. Goody, 1959, "The Mother's Brother and the Sister's Son in West Africa", *Journal of the Royal Anthropological Institute*, n° 89, pp. 61–88.

17 *Die* is a familiar term for father, the addition of *gan* (dry, dried out) means that there is no blood relationship.

18 This is a common expression in China and also a way of saying hello.

19 Which makes necessary a systematic checking in each village.

20 This was during the Republican period (1911–1949). The Hui in this case use an expression used by the Chinese Communist Party at the same time.

21 Obviously, as soon as one leaves the area concerned, the name of the village in question is unknown.

22 The Mongols dominated the north of the country after the fall of Beijing in 1215.

23 We here summarise the legend collected in 1979 in Wuzhong in Ningxia. Li Shujiang, Luckert Karl W., 1994, *Mythology and Folklore of the Hui. A Muslim Chinese People*, Albany, State University of New York Press, pp. 240–241.

24 The text speaks of Huihe soldiers. This is the generally accepted version of the origins of the word Hui as lying in a deformation of the name of a people, the Huihe, from the northwest of China, who had been Islamised.

25 The imperial capital of the time, now Xi'an.

26 The compilers of these legends note that this is undoubtedly a reference to the nine wives which the Prophet had after the death of his first spouse. Li Shujiang, Luckert Karl W., *op. cit.*, p. 241 (note 4).

27 In the course of a conversation, reference was made to the case of a marriage, but it seems the people concerned had been already living in town for some time.

28 A popular dance in Northern China. Cf. F. Graezer, 1999, "The *Yangge* in Contemporary China. Popular Daily Activity and Neighbourhood Community Life", *China Perspectives*, No. 24, pp. 31–43.

29 The stele was inscribed in 2001.

30 The Ming dynasty reigned from 1368 to 1644.

31 This narrative is partly engraved on a stele set up in the village school, and is presented as the genealogy *(jiapu)* of the lineage concerned.

32 After the overthrow of the Ming by the Qing, the region, like many others in China, became the scene of serious fighting between troops who had remained faithful to the Ming dynasty, among them a certain number of Hui, and those of the Manchurian dynasty.

33 The reference to the colour red, symbol of marriage in China, reinforces the image.

34 Most Chinese villages have always combined crafts and trade with agriculture.

35 In the Han village, near the river, a stele was erected in 1999 which relates some aspects of this story.

36 The stele of the women's mosque in Xiguan gives as the date of construction the period of Yongle of the Ming (1403–1425).

37 A peasant movement organised as a secret society which, for over ten years (1851–1863), struggled against the corruption of the Qing mandarins and the disastrous effects of the Opium Wars. The Nian were famous for their highly mobile guerilla actions. E. Perry, 1992 (first edn. 1980), *Rebels and Revolutionaries in North China 1845–1945,* Stanford, Stanford University Press, pp. 96–151.

38 This information on adoption by the Hui was given to us by the Han women in the villages in question. Moreover, when one talks to Hui women in the mosques, even now, they ask, with a disapproving air, if abroad we still have the same habit as the Han of not burying children who have died at birth, and of throwing them anywhere without a burial.

39 On the Red Spears Society: R. Slawinski, "Les Piques Rouges et la révolution chinoise de 1925–1927", in J. Chesneaux, F. Davis, Nguyen Nguyet Ho (éds.), 1970, *Mouvements populaires et sociétés secrètes en Chine aux XIXe et XXe siècles,* Paris, F. Maspero, pp. 393–406; L. Bianco, 1970, "Sociétés secrètes et autodéfense paysanne (1921–1933)", in J. Chesneaux, F. Davis, Nguyen Nguyet Ho (éds.) *op. cit.,* pp. 407–420; E. J. Perry, 1992, *op. cit.,* pp. 152–207 and note 3 pp. 284–285; Tai Hsüan-chih, 1985, *The Red Spears,* 1916–1949, Ann Arbor, The University of Michigan Press.

40 *Bo'ai xianzhi,* 1994, pp. 18–19.

41 They are said to have numbered in the whole of the province of Henan at least 398,000 members. R. Slawinski, 1970, *op. cit.,* p. 401.

42 This is no doubt a generic term for the various societies which were created in the wake of the Red Spears; there were societies of yellow, green, white and black spears.

43 The nationalist troops of the Guomindang who were marching north in order to reunite the country.

44 E. Allès, 2000, *op. cit.,* pp. 167–168.

45 For a detailed history of these events and the song in memory of this massacre see E. Allès, 2000, *op. cit.,* pp. 79–81.

46 We did surveys in the region during this period and nobody at that time mentioned such relations, nor were we able to witness this type of exchange.

47 Cf. L. Bianco et Hua Chang Ming, 1995, *op. cit.*

48 Violence broke out in a village in Shandong in December 2000. A butcher who sold pork and other meat had placed or left in his window the sign *qingzhen* (pure and real) which means that the meat is *hallal.* The Hui demanded that the seller remove the sign, and the local authorities responded by arresting the Hui leaders, which set off serious confrontations resulting in five deaths among the Hui.

49 A slogan of the Cultural Revolution which is regularly re-used, especially since, in the last few years, relations between the Han and the other minorities, particularly in Tibet and in Xinjiang, have seriously deteriorated.

50 Dru Gladney, 1991, *op. cit.,* p. 2; L. Cherif-Chebbi, 1991, "Contre les Rushdie chinois. Le réveil des musulmans hui", Mémoire de DEA, IEP, Paris.

51 The most recent case of this sort took place in June 2003: the July issue of the famous literary magazine *Duzhe* was withdrawn from sale because of two metaphorical texts, one considered to be insulting to the Muslims and the other to the political authorities.

52 D. Paulme, 1939, *op. cit.,* p. 435. The author spells *mangu* with a simple "u", while M. Griaule spells it with an "ou".

53 M. Griaule, 1948, p. 247.

54 Allusion to the cult of Lébé.

55 The Bozo are Muslims.

56 M. Griaule, pp. 252–253. Simplified versions of these myths are also described by D. Paulme.

57 D. Paulme, 1939, p. 442.

58 M. Griaule recounts following case: two Dogon adolescents from the south of the subdivision of Bandiagara who had run away for adventure, had fetched up in Markala, on the Niger river. They were taken in by a Bozo family on seeing their hairstyle and clothing. Housed and fed, they did no work and seemed quite happy, even though they spoke none of the languages in the region and could communicate with their hosts only in the most rudimentary fashion. Their stay had lasted several weeks when we met them (in September 1946) and it seemed that the Bozo were simply counting on public rumour to alert the parents to their presence in Markala.

59 D. Paulme, 1939, p. 436.

60 M. Griaule, 1948, p. 243.

61 H. Labouret, 1929, pp. 252–253.

62 M. Griaule says himself that he takes no position on this question and therefore does not tackle it at all.

63 E. E. Evans-Pritchard, 1933, *op. cit.*

64 D. Paulme, 1939, p. 440.

65 D. Paulme, 1939, p. 443.

66 Radcliffe-Brown, 1952, *op. cit.,* p. 112.

67 Radcliffe-Brown, 1940, p. 197.

68 M. Griaule, 1948, p. 254.

69 M. Griaule, 1948, p. 252.

70 M. Griaule, 1948, p. 253.

71 Radcliffe-Brown, 1952, p. 111.

72 Radcliffe-Brown, 1952, p. 110.

73 In Henan, some Hui were members of Sun Yat-sen's organisation, the Tongmenghui. Cf Allès E., 2000. In Shanxi, there were numerous Hui groups belonging to the Society of the Elders and Ancients *(Gelaohui)* Park Sang Soo, *La révolution chinoise et les sociétés secrètes,* thèse de doctorat, Ehess.

References

Electronic reference

Elisabeth Allès, « Notes on some joking relationships between Hui and Han villages in Henan », *China perspectives* [Online], 49 | september-october 2003, Online since 17 January 2007. URL : http:// chinaperspectives.revues.org/649.

Chapter 7

TOWARD ETHNICITY ...
My Culture or Yours?

The Innocents Abroad, Updated

by P.J. O'Rourke (1988)
In *Holidays in Hell*. Grove Press: New York.

On Saturday, June 8, 1867, the steamship *Quaker City* left New York harbor. On board was a group of Americans making the world's first package tour. Also on board was Mark Twain making the world's first fun of package tourism.

In its day *The Innocents Abroad* itinerary was considered exhaustive. It included Paris, Marseilles, the Rock of Gibraltar, Lake Como, some Alps, the Czar, the pyramids and the Holy Land plus the glory that was Greece, the grandeur that was Rome and the pile of volcanic ash that was Pompeii.

When these prototypical tourists went home they could count themselves traveled. They had shivered with thoughts of lions in the Colosseum, "done" the Louvre, ogled Mont Blanc, stumbled through the ruins of the Parthenon by moonlight and pondered that eternal riddle—where'd its nose go?—of the Sphinx. They had seen the world.

But what if Mark Twain had to come back from the dead and escort 1980's tourists on a 1980's tour? Would it be the same? No. I'm afraid Mr. Twain would find there are worse things than innocents abroad in the world today.

In 1988 every country with a middle class to export has gotten into the traveling act. We Yanks, with our hula shirts and funny Kodaks, are no longer in the fore. The earth's travel destinations are jam-full of littering Venezuelans, peevish Swiss, smelly Norwegian backpackers yodeling in restaurant booths, Saudi Arabian businessmen getting their dresses caught in revolving doors and Bengali remittance men in their twenty-fifth year of graduate school pestering fat blonde Belgian *au pair* girls.

At least we American tourists understand English when it's spoken loudly and clearly enough. Australians don't. Once you've been on a plane full of drunken Australians doing wallaby imitations up and down the aisles, you'll never make fun of Americans visiting the Wailing Wall in short shorts again.

The Japanese don't wear short shorts (a good thing, considering their legs), but they do wear three-piece suits in the full range of tenement-hall paint colors, with fit to match. The trouser cuffs drag like bridal trains; the jacket collars have an ox yoke drape; and the vests leave six inches of polyester shirt snapping in the breeze. If the Japanese want to be taken seriously as world financial powers, they'd better quit using the same tailor as variety-show chimps.

The Japanese also travel in packs at a jog trot and get up at six A.M. and sing their company song under your hotel window. They are extraordinary shoplifters. They eschew the usual clothes and trinkets, but automobile plants, steel mills and electronics factories seem to be missing from everywhere they go. And Japs take snapshots of everything, not just everything famous but *everything*. Back in Tokyo there must be a billion color slides of street comers, turnpike off-ramps, pedestrian crosswalks, phone booths, fire hydrants, manhole covers and overhead electrical wires. What are the Japanese doing with these pictures? It's probably a question we should have asked before Pearl Harbor.

Worse than the Japanese, at least worse looking, are the Germans, especially at pool-side. The larger the German body, the smaller the German bathing suit and the louder the German voice issuing German demands and German orders to everybody who doesn't speak German. For this, and several other reasons, Germany is known as "the land where Israelis learned their manners."

And Germans in a pool cabana (or even Israelis at a discotheque) are nothing compared with French on a tropical shore. A middle-aged, heterosexual, college-educated male wearing a Mickey Mouse T-shirt and a string-bikini bottom and carrying a purse—what else could it be but a vacationing Frenchman? No tropical shore is too stupid for the French. They turn up on the coasts of Angola, Eritrea, Bangladesh and Sri Lanka. For one day they glory in l'*atmosphère très primitive* then spend two weeks in an ear-splitting snit because the natives won't make a *steak frite* out of the family water buffalo.

Also present in Angola, Eritrea and God-Knows-Where are the new breed of yuppie "experience travelers." You'll be pinned down by mortar fire in the middle of a genocide atrocity in the Sudan, and right through it all come six law partners and their wives, in Banana Republic bush jackets, taking an inflatable raft trip down the White Nile and having an "experience."

Mortar fire is to be preferred, of course, to British sports fans. Has anyone checked the passenger list on *The Spirit of Free Enterprise?* Were there any Liverpool United supporters on board? That channel ferry may have been tipped over for fun. (Fortunately the Brits have to be back at their place of unemployment on Monday so they never get further than Spain.)

Then there are the involuntary tourists. Back in 1867, what with the suppression of the slave trade and all, they probably thought they'd conquered the involuntary tourism problem. Alas, no. Witness the African exchange students—miserable, cold, shivering, grumpy and selling cheap wrist watches from the top of cardboard boxes worldwide. (Moscow's Patrice Lumumba University has a particularly disgruntled bunch.) And the Pakistani family with twelve children who've been camped out in every airport on the globe since 1970—will somebody please do something for these people? Their toddler has got my copy of the *Asian Wall Street Journal,* and I won't be responsible if he tries to stuff it down the barrel of the El Al security guard's Uzi again.

Where will Mr. Clemens take these folks? What is the 1980's equivalent of the Grand Tour? What are the travel "musts" of today?

All the famous old monuments are still there, of course, but they're surrounded by scaffolds and green nets and signs saying, "Il pardonne la restoration bitte please." I don't know two people who've ever seen the same famous old monument. I've seen Big Ben. A friend of mine has seen half of the Sistine Chapel ceiling. No one has seen Notre Dame Cathedral for years. It's probably been sold to a shopping mall developer in Phoenix.

We've all, however, seen Dr. Meuller's Sex Shop in the Frankfurt airport. Dr. Meuller's has cozy booths where, for one deutsche mark a minute, we modern tourists can watch things hardly thought of in 1867. And there's nothing on the outside of the booths to indicate whether you're in there viewing basically healthy Swedish nude volleyball films or videos of naked Dobermans cavorting in food. Dr. Meuller's is also a reliable way to meet your boss, old Sunday School teacher or ex-wife's new husband, one of whom is always walking by when you emerge.

Dr. Meuller's is definitely a "must" of modern travel, as is the Frankfurt airport itself. If Christ came back tomorrow, He'd have to change planes in Frankfurt. Modern air travel means less time spent in transit. That time is now spent in transit lounges.

What else? There are "local points of interest" available until the real monuments are restored. These are small piles of stones about which someone will tell you extravagant lies for five dollars. ("And here, please, the Tomb of the Infant Jesus.") And there are the great mini-bars of Europe—three paper cartons of anise-flavored soda pop, two bottles of beer with suspended vegetable matter, a triangular candy bar made of chocolate-covered edelweiss and a pack of Marlboros manufactured locally under license. (NB: Open that split of Mumm's ½-star in there, and $200 goes on your hotel bill faster than you can say "service non compris.")

In place of celebrated palaces, our era has celebrated parking spots, most of them in Rome. Romans will back a Fiat into the middle of your *linguine al pesto* if you're sitting too close to the restaurant window.

Instead of cathedrals, mosques and ancient temples, we have duty-free shops—at their best in Kuwait. I never knew there was so much stuff I didn't want. I assumed I wanted most stuff. But that was before I saw a $110,000 crêpe de chine Givenchy chador and a solid-gold camel saddle with twelve Rolex watches embedded in the seat.

The "sermons in stone" these days are all sung with cement. Cement is the granite, the marble, the porphyry of our time. Someday, no doubt, there will be "Elgin Cements" in the British Museum. Meanwhile, we tour the Warsaw Pact countries—cement everywhere, including, at the official level, quite a bit of cement in their heads.

Every modern tourist has seen *Mannix* dubbed in forty languages and the amazing watch adjustments of Newfoundland, Malaysia and Nepal (where time zones are, yes, half an hour off), and France in August when you can travel through the entire country without encountering a single pesky Frenchman or being bothered with anything that's open for business—though, somehow, the fresh dog crap is still a foot deep on the streets of Paris.

Astonishing toilets for humans are also a staple of up-to-date foreign adventure. Anyone who thinks international culture has become bland and uniform hasn't been to the bathroom, especially not in Yugoslavia where it's a hole in the floor with a scary old lady with a mop standing next to it. And, for astonishing toilet paper, there's India where there isn't any.

No present-day traveler, even an extra-odoriferous Central European one, can say he's done it all if he hasn't been on a smell tour of Asia. Maybe what seems pungent to the locals only becomes alarming when sniffed through a giant Western proboscis, but there are some odors in China that make a visit to Bhopal seem like a picnic downwind from the Arpege factory. Hark to the cry of the tourist in the East: "Is it dead or is it dinner?"

Nothing beats the Orient for grand vistas, however, particularly of go-go girls. True, they can't Boogaloo and have no interest in learning, but Thai exotic dancers are the one people left who prefer American-made to Japanese. And they come and sit on your lap between sets, something the girls at the Crazy Horse never do. Now, where'd my wallet go?

Many contemporary tourist attractions are not located in one special place the way tourist attractions used to be. Now they pop up everywhere—that villainous cab driver with the all-consonant last name, for instance. He's waiting outside hotels from Sun City to the Seward Peninsula. He can't speak five languages and can't understand another ten. Hey! Hey! Hey, you! This isn't the way to the Frankfurt airport! Nein! Non! Nyet! Ixnay!

American embassies, too, are all over the map and always breathtaking. In the middle of London, on beautiful Grosvenor Square, there's one that looks like a bronzed Oldsmobile dashboard. And rising from the slums of Manila is another that resembles the Margarine of the Future Pavilion at the 1959 Brussels World Fair. I assume this is all the work of one architect, and I assume he's on drugs. Each American embassy comes with two permanent features—a giant anti-American demonstration and a giant line for American visas. Most demonstrators spend half their time burning Old Glory and the other half waiting for green cards.

Other ubiquitous spectacles of our time include various panics—AIDS, PLO terror and owning U.S. dollars predominate at the moment—and postcards of the Pope kissing the ground. There's little ground left unkissed by this pontiff, though he might think twice about kissing anything in some of the places he visits. (Stay away from Haiti, San Francisco and Mykonos, J.P., please.)

Then there's the squalor. This hasn't changed since 1867, but tourists once tried to avoid it. Now they seek it out. Modern tourists have to see the squalor so they can tell everyone back home how it changed their perspective on life. Describing squalor, if done with sufficient indignation, makes friends and relatives morally obligated to listen to your boring vacation stories. (Squalor is conveniently available, at reasonable prices, in Latin America.)

No, the Grand Tour is no longer a stately procession of like-minded individuals through half a dozen of the world's major principalities. And it's probably just as well if Mark Twain doesn't come back from the dead. He'd have to lead a huge slew of multinational lunatics through hundreds of horrible countries with disgusting border formalities. And 1980s customs agents are the only thing worse than 1980's tourists. Damn it, give that back! You know perfectly well that it's legal to bring clean socks into Tanzania. Ow! Ouch! Where are you taking me!?

Of course you don't have to go to Africa to get that kind of treatment. You can have your possessions stolen right on the Piccadilly Line if you want. In fact, in 1987, you can experience most of the indignities and discomforts of travel in your own hometown, wherever you live. Americans flock in seething masses to any dim-wit local attraction—tall ships making a landing, short actors making a move, Andrew Wyeth making a nude Helga fracas—just as if they were actually going somewhere. The briefest commuter flight is filled with businessmen dragging mountainous garment bags and whole computers on board. They are worst pests than mainland Chinese taking Frigidaires home on the plane. And no modern business gal goes to lunch without a steamer trunk-size tote full of shoe changes, Sony Walkman tapes and tennis rackets. When she makes her way down a restaurant aisle, she'll crack the back of your head with this exactly the same way a Mexican will with a crate of chickens on a Yucatán bus ride.

The tourism ethic seems to have spread like one of the new sexual diseases. It now infects every aspect of daily life. People carry backpacks to work and out on dates. People dress like tourists at the office, the theater and church. People are as rude to their fellow countrymen as ever they are to foreigners.

Maybe the right thing to do is stay home in a comfy armchair and read about travel as it should be—in Samuel Clemens's *Huckleberry Finn*.

The 'Myth' of Jewish Humor

by Dan Ben-Amos (1973)
In *Western Folklore*[1]

T he current conception of Jewish humor originated, as many modern ideas have, with Sigmund Freud. He was the first to single out "self-criticism" as the unique quality of Jewish jokes. This attribute becomes immediately apparant in the relationship between the raconteur and the subject matter of his anecdotes. In Jewish jokes, Freud suggested, the narrator is also the butt of his story. In the context of a general discussion concerning the hostile aggressive nature of tendentious jokes *(tendenziösen Witz),* Freud commented cautiously:

> A particularly favorable occasion for tendentious jokes is presented when the intended rebellious criticism is directed against the subject himself, or, to put it more cautiously, against someone in whom the subject has a share—a collective person, that is (the subject's own nation, for instance). The occurrence of self-criticism as a determinant may explain how it is that a number of the most apt jokes ... have grown up on the soil of Jewish popular life. *They are stories created by Jews and directed against Jewish characteristics* [italics mine].
> Later on, Freud concludes that paragraph and comments:
> Incidentally, I do not know whether there are many other instances of a people making fun to such a degree of its own character.[2]

This casual remark, which first appeared in print in 1905, has become the cornerstone for most of the subsequent popular and scholarly conceptions of the essence of Jewish humor. Not only Freud's ardent disciples, but also literary critics, sociologists, and artists, have unquestioningly embraced "self-ridicule" as the qualitative earmark of Jewish humor. Before the publication of *Jokes and Their Relation to the Unconscious,* the actual existence of humor among the Jews was in question. As late as 1893 it appeared meaningful to combat the idea that the Jews lack humor which Ernest Renan and Thomas Carlyle had

---

1   This is a modified version of an Hebrew essay: "Jewish Humor—The Concept from a New Viewpoint," *Folklore Research Center Studies: Vol. 1,* eds. Dov Noy and Issachar Ben-Ami (Jerusalem, 1970), 25–34.

2   Sigmund Freud, *Jokes and Their Relation to the Unconscious,* Standard Edition, vol. 8, trans. James Strachey in collaboration with Anna Freud (London, 1960), 111–12. Original German ed.: *Der Witz und seine Beziechung zum Unbewussten* (Leipzig and Vienna, 1905).

respectively expressed.[3] However, ever since Freud's comments until today, his conception of Jewish wit is dominant and is accepted as common knowledge and an axiom of our culture. "Now everyone knows that the special quality of Jewish humor since long before the invention of the gramophone has been the ability to indulge in critical self-ridicule," writes a record reviewer.[4] Encyclopedists and folklorists alike have endorsed this idea.[5] If, on occasion, other even contradictory qualities shine through these jokes and anecdotes, the literary critic is fast to correct such an impression as false. For example, the following joke seemingly contradicts the notion of Jewish self-mockery:

> You tell a joke to a peasant and he laughs three times: when you tell it; when you explain it; and when he understands it.
>
> A landowner laughs only twice: when he hears the joke and when you explain it. For he can never understand it.
>
> An army officer laughs only once: when you tell the joke. He never lets you explain it—and that he is unable to understand it goes without saying.
>
> But when you start telling a joke to another Jew, he interrupts you: "Go on! That's an old one," and he shows you how much better he can tell it himself.[6]

Yet Irving Howe, a writer and a literary critic, comments upon it:

> Now offhand this anecdote seems merely to express an unattractive sense of group superiority: the Jew is more clever than anyone else. But take a second look at it and you see that it contains something more subtle and complex. The anonymous narrator is really poking fun at the weakness of his own people; their intellectual impatience and overconfidence. Though usually subtle, this persistent self-criticism of Jewish humor sometimes verges on self-denunciation.[7]

Later he sums up this idea in a more general manner:

> Though a joke usually involves a thrust at someone else, Jewish humor is often a thrust at the Jews themselves. The plight that is ridiculed is often that of the narrator, with whom the audience can so easily identify itself.[8]
>
> Martin Grotjahn, a psychoanalyst, follows suit:
>
> Aggression turned against the self seems to be an essential feature of the truly Jewish joke. It is as if the Jew tells his enemies: "You do not need to attack us. We can do that ourselves—and even better."[9]

---

3   Ernest Renan, *Histoire générale et système comparé des langues Sémitiques* (Paris, 1863), 1:11–12.

4   Isaiah Sheffer, "'You Don't Have to Be Jewish'," *Midstream* 13 (February 1967): 58.

5   Jacob P. Kohn and Ludwig Davidsohn, "Jewish Wit and Humor," *The Universal Jewish Encyclopedia* (New York, 1943), 10:545–47; Haim Schwarzbaum, *Studies in Jewish and World Folklore* (Berlin, 1968), 26–27, 92–93.

6   Irving Howe, "The Nature of Jewish Laughter," *The New American Mercury* 72 (1951): 211–12.

7   Ibid.

8   Ibid., 217.

9   *Beyond Laughter: Humor and the Subconscious* (New York, 1957), 12.

This conception of Jewish humor is so deeply rooted in modern thought that even a popular character like Portnoy, the hero of Philip Roth's best seller, who lives in the midst of a Jewish joke, could state, as a matter of course: "self deprecation is, after all, a classical form of Jewish humor."[10] Other writers hail this particular quality of Jewish humor as the one feature of culture which enabled the Jews to overcome the tribulations which continued to haunt them historically. Maurice Samuel has recently expressed this notion eloquently:

> There was nothing jolly and hilarious about the destitution that lay like a curse on millions of Jews in the Yiddish-speaking world; and it would be grotesque to speak of Sholom Aleichem's and Men-dele's *kaptsonim* (paupers) and *evyonim* (indigents) as "poor and happy." They were miserable, and knew it; but the question that haunts us historically is, why did they not disintegrate intellectually and morally? How were they able, under hideous oppression and corroding privation, under continuous starvation—the tail of a herring was a dish—to keep alive against a better day the spirit originally breathed into man? *The answer lies in the self-mockery by which they rose above their condition to see afar off the hope of the future* [my italics].[11]

Unlike fictional characters as Portnoy, scholars did not stop at mistaking Freud's interpretation for fact, but continued to advance hypotheses concerning the primary causes of this apparently unique type of humor. They did so without questioning for a minute the validity of Freud's insight, the very premise upon which their theories rest. The primary cause for "self-mockery" in Jewish humor was sought in two conditions: the allegedly unique nature of the Jewish psyche itself, and the social environment in which the Jewish people lived. According to Theodor Reik, the very behavior of the Jewish people distinguishes itself historically by oscillation between masochistic and paranoic tendencies.

> The masochistic attitude of ancient Israel was recognized at least in their relationship with God, whose punishment they took as deserved without complaint. They considered also the cruelty with which they were treated by their powerful neighbors as punishment for their sins, especially for deserting God. The paranoid attitude in the form of an idea of grandeur is obvious in the Jewish claim of being the "chosen people." There is even a subterranean tie between the masochistic and the paranoid attitude in the idea that God chastises those He loves. Such an exceptional position has been claimed by the Jewish people since ancient time.[12]

In other words, according to Reik, humor is but an expression of the general psychopathology of the Jewish people. As in their general behavioral pattern, so in their jokes the jews oscillate "between masochistic self-humiliation and paranoid superiority feeling."[13] Psychoanalytically, the "unattractive sense of group superiority" which bothers Howe is not explained away as a superficial impression. Rather, this trait is conceived as a logical and essential aspect of Jewish humor. Masochism and its verbal expression in self-mockery is compatible with paranoia and a sense of superiority as their polar opposite and mir-

---

10   Philip Roth, *Portnoy's Complaint* (New York, 1967), 265.
11   *In Praise of Yiddish* (New York, 1971), 210–11.
12   Theodor Reik, *Jewish Wit* (New York, 1962), 230–31.
13   Ibid., 233.

ror image. Crucial to Reik's explanation are the Freudian postulates of the "collective mind" and of the "inheritance of psychical dispositions." Freud himself reluctantly postulated "the existence of a collective mind, in which mental processes occur just as they do in the mind of an individual.[14] As Freud further stated he would have preferred to rely on a more empirically testable thesis, and resorted to the notion of "collective mind" only because of the lack of any other verifiable theories. Reik, on the other hand, embraces this hypothesis wholeheartedly and applies clinical observations to verbal behavior in social occasions, as joking is, without accounting for the different types of data under his scrutiny. No wonder that he titled the last chapter of *Jewish Wit* "Psychology and Psychopathology of Jewish Wit" assuming that the dynamics of social "collective" expressions are identical with those of individual fantasies.

The second fundamental postulate, that of "the inheritance of psychic dispositions," though untenable in terms of modern genetic theories, is more germane to Freud's thought and the ideas he developed in *Totem and Taboo*.[15] Although he hardly developed these ideas in his scientific writings, Freud entertained the application of Lamarkian principles to psychoanalysis in his correspondence with his students. He thought of demonstrating that the Lamarkian "'necessity'—[which] creates and transforms organs, is nothing but the power of unconscious ideas over one's own body."[16] Reik does not go that far. Although he assumes that the inheritance of psychic dispositions is a real process, in advancing his own ideas about Jewish humor, he actually does not argue that it is biologically based. Rather, the assumption of continuity in the social relations between Jews and other nations makes it logically possible for him to interpret nineteenth- and twentieth-century Jewish jokes on the basis of the psychic pattern which he inferentially observed among ancient Israel. Without hesitation Reik likens the position of the ancient Hebrews among their neighbors to that of the Jews among European nations, disregarding the equality in political independence and strength they enjoyed in the first case, and the social inferiority of a minority group from which they suffered in the second. This continuity, alleged in social relations, makes the inheritance of psychic dispositions both functional and possible. Historically, only religion manifested the oscillation between masochism and paranoia; currently, humor also represents the same pattern.

Other psychologists, sociologists, and folklorists have a more dynamic conception of history and Jewish society and its "collective mind." They realize the radical difference between the relationship ancient Israel had with its neighboring peoples and the position of the Jews in European society. Consequently, they consider Jewish humor, and its self-mocking feature in particular, a more recent phenomena and seek its direct cause in the socio-economic situation of European and American Jewry. This shift in perspective implies a crucial theoretical change. Jewish humor is not inherently Jewish any more; it is not an expression of the postulated "inheritance of psychic dispositions," but a reflection of certain given socio-economic environmental factors. Similar circumstances should produce the quality of self-ridicule in the humor of any other ethnic group. Thus, according to this social rather than psychological determinism, Jewish humor is not an expression of the genius of the Jewish people, but just a particular case of a general sociological principle.

Yet, what are the circumstances that are responsible for the self-mocking quality in the humor of the Jews? Two contradictory socio-economic situations have been singled out as possible primary causes for

14   Sigmund Freud, *Totem and Tabu and Other Works,* 13th standard ed. (London, 1955), 157.

15   See Derek Freeman, "Totem and Taboo: A Reappraisal," in *Man and His Culture: Psychoanalytical Anthropology after 'Totem and Taboo,'* ed. Warner Muenster-berger (London, 1969), 63–65.

16   Hilda C. Abraham and Ernst L. Freud, eds., *A Psycho-Analytical Dialogue: The Letters of Sigmund Freud and Karl Abraham 1907–1926,* tr. Bernard Marsh and Hilda C. Abraham (New York, 1965), 261.

this trait. Edmund Bergler, a psychoanalyst, suggested that life in the European ghettos and small towns bred self-ridicule in humor. "The seclusion, poverty, absence of opportunity and bitterness of life in the ghetto certainly favored psychic masochism; so did the persecution and the bias encountered outside the ghetto."[17] In contrast to Bergler, Sadan,[18] Landmann,[19] and Rosenberg and Shapiro[20] consider the primary cause of the self-hatred characteristic in Jewish humor, the actual emancipation of the Jews from the bonds of their own closed community, and their integration into the urban life of the majority. Accordingly, the cultural duality and the ambivalent identity of the assimilated, or at least educated, Jews is the source of self-mockery in humor. Sadan, an Israeli folklorist and literary critic, suggests that masochism is not at all an indigenous element of Jewish humor. Contradictory to Bergler's thesis, this trait is absent from the jokes of traditional European Jewry who populated the ghettos and *shtetles*. Sadan considers it specifically part of the folklore of the "transitional Jew." The type who emerged from the ghetto but did not shed its culture, who interacts among urbane intellectual society, of which he is not yet an integral part. Self-mockery in humor is a product of this twilight zone of cultures. Actually, it is a form of verbal instrument which functions in the very process of assimilation and integration into the new society. By laughing at traditional Jews, the transitional type would like to associate himself with the social majority. Somerset Maugham provides a literary example for the kind of Jews about whom Sadan's discussion revolves. In his story, "The Alien Corn," he describes a modern urbane Jew who specialized in mocking mimicry of traditional Jews in the social parties of London. Maugham adds a writer's remark to his portrayal of this character: "I was not quite sure of a sense of humour that made such cruel fun of his own race."[21]

Salcia Landmann furthers this argument and suggests that the socio-cultural transitional situation is not only the cause of Jewish humor, but its exclusive source. Before their emancipation, the Jews were actually a humorless people. Similarly, after they regained their political independence they lost their sense of humor. According to Landmann, the rise and fall of Jewish humor occurred between the eighteenth and the twentieth centuries. The stricture of these chronological boundaries allows Landmann to discuss "the death of Jewish humor" not only metaphorically but also literally. When she categorically states that "das neue Israel ist daher witzlos wie die Bibel,"[22] she is empirically wrong on both accounts; there was humor in biblical society and there is wit in modern Israel.[23] However, it was possible for her to err in this matter because she reifies an abstract concept such as sense of humor and conceives of it in terms of a particular repertoire of jokes. This enables her to establish a direct and exclusive interdependence between the socio-cultural environment and the quality of Jewish humor. Once these primary conditions disappeared, Jewish humor itself as a genus vanished.

In Western Europe and America the integration of the Jews into majority culture is not a finite process. For as long as Jewish society exists in these countries, it provides at least a secondary, if not primary,

---

17   Edmund Bergler, *Laughter and the Sense of Humor* (New York, 1956), 111.

18   "Additional Notes," in *Sehok Pynu (Our Mouth's Laughter): Anthology of Humour and Satire in Ancient and Modern Hebrew Literature*, ed. Ephraim Davidson (Tel-Aviv, 1951), 513–15.

19   *Der jüdische Witz: Soziologie und Sammlung* (Walter, 1962); and "On Jewish Humour," *The Jewish Journal of Sociology* 4 (1962): 193–204.

20   "Marginality and Jewish Humor," *Midstream* 4 (Spring 1958): 70–80.

21   W. Somerset Maugham, *Six Stories Written in the First Person Singular* (Garden City, New York, 1931), 195.

22   Landmann, *Der jüdische Witz* (Olten, 1962), 122.

23   See A. J. Baumgartner, *L'Humor dans l'ancien testament* (Lausanne, 1896); and Dov B. Lang "On the Biblical Comic," *Judaism* 11 (1962): 249–54; Jacob P. Kohn and Ludwig Davidsohn, "Jewish Wit and Humor," *The Universal Jewish Encyclopedia* (New York, 1943), 10:545–47. There are many anthologies of Israeli jokes. Standard collections in Hebrew are Dov Sadan, *Ka'arat Tsimukim* (Tel-Aviv, 1949), and *Ka'arat Egozim* (Tel-Aviv, 1952); E. Davidson, *Sehok le Israel* (Ramat Gan, 1958).

focus for ethnic identity. Hence, in the examination of Jewish humor in the United States, Rosenberg and Shapiro, two sociologists, suggests that the cause of self-hatred in Jewish humor is not the process of transition but "the psychological ambiguity of life in a marginal social position."[24] At present The American Jews find themselves caught in a social double-bind; "Where we previously hated ourselves for being Jews, we now frequently hate ourselves for *not* being Jews."[25] In other words, they define their ethnic identity in terms of dual polar comparisons: on the one hand they measure themselves in relationship to normative American culture, and on the other hand they set for themselves the standards of traditional Judaism. Since they resemble none of these, they consequently indulge in a self-derogatory humor.

Perhaps the only validation of the Jewish-masochism thesis is its mass acceptance by Jewish intellectuals, for the actual evidence derived from the jokes themselves does not support it. If Freud's suggestive remark is to be considered a convincing insight, it needs empirical substantiation which is based not upon literary presentations of humor, but on the folk joking process itself. Milton Barron came to a similar conclusion more than twenty years ago when he addressed himself to the problem of ethnic humor in general. At the summation of his research, he posed some unresolved problems, one of which was the question: "What basis is there to the suspicion that minority 'victims' may in some cases invent as well as communicate such self-derogatory jokes about themselves." The answer, he felt, could be found only "by empirical research in the field of *oral* communication."[26] As far as Jewish humor is concerned, such a study is still lacking.

Moreover, the various theories which attempt an explanation of the inward aggressiveness in Jewish humor have risen precisely because of the absence of such empirical examination. Essentially, they result from viewing the literary and social reality of Jewish jokes through Freudian perspectives.

Particularly significant in this case is the notion of "collectivity" in person and in thought which is crucial to Freud's conception of Jewish humor. As Abraham Kaplan noted, "the most serious shortcoming of collective terms is the continuous temptation they hold out to commit the sin of reification."[27] Jewish humor and the Jewish community fell victims to this lure. In the course of analysis, scholars slipped very easily into discussing these concepts as objective real entities rather than constructions of human minds and products of literary creativity. The textual basis for the whole idea of Jewish humor, as it developed in the twentieth century, is the personal recollections or the literary collections of jokes. The publication of such volumes in full force started in the early and mid-twenties in western Europe,[28] and later continued in the United States.[29] The editors of most of these anthologies were part of the growing Jewish educated elite who no longer lived within the confines of the traditional Jewish community. For them and their readers, these books represented the collective expression of Jewish humor, the accumulated wit of Jewish communities. Within the framework of this newly constructed whole, the narrators and the

---

24   Rosenberg and Shapiro, "Marginality," 72.

25   Ibid., 74.

26   Milton L. Barron, "A Content Analysis of Intergroup Humor," *American Sociological Review* 15 (1950): 94.

27   *The Conduct of Inquiry: Methodology for Behavioral Sciences* (San Francisco, 1964), 81.

28   For example: Immanuel Olsvanger, *Aus der Volksliteratur der Ostjüden, Schwänke, Erzälungen, Volklieder und Rätsel* (Basel, 1920); Chajim Block, *Ostjüdischer Humor* (Berlin, 1920): Heinrich Loewe, *Schelme und Narren mit jüdischen Kappen* (Berlin, 1920); Alexander Moszkowski, *Der jüdische Witz und seine Philosophie* (Berlin, 1923); Joshua Hana Rawnitzki, *Yidishe Witzn* (Berlin, 1922); Alter Druyanov, *Sefer na-bedihah ve-ha-hidud* (Book of Jokes and Wit) (Frankfort, 1922).

29   Jacob Richman, *Laughs from Jewish Lore* (New York, 1926); Samuel Felix Mendelsohn, *The Jew Laughs: Humorous Stories and Anecdotes* (Chicago, 1935); Rufus Learsi [Israel Goldberg], *The Book of Jewish Humor: Stories of Jewish Wit and Wisdom* (New York, 1947). For further references see Schwarzbaum, *Studies in Jewish and World Folklore* (Berlin, 1968), 26–27, 87–89, 92, 96, 403–5.

subjects of their jokes indeed do have an identical ethnic reference: both the storytellers and the *dramatis personae* of their anecdotes are Jewish. The ultimate conclusion that self-ridicule, and the psychic pattern which it reflects—masochism—are the essential attributes of this humor, is inevitable.

The allusion of self-mockery is even further enforced by the application of the notion of "collective person" to the entire community. The conception of a complex society as a single entity of a "Jew" "bestow(s) an ontological and total status on a typification that is humanly produced and that even as it is internalized, objectifies but a segment of the self."[30] No doubt, these distorted perspectives result from historical and social circumstances and even from analytical frameworks scholars have established. However, these have never affected the narrators of the jokes themselves. For them the Jewish society is a complex, heterogeneous social environment, in which each individual fulfills sexual and religious roles, belongs to distinct age groups and professional associations and defines himself in terms of economic classes. Like any other society, the Jewish community consists of a network of multiple interrelationships and affiliations. To view it as a collective person, as a holistic entity, larger in dimension than any individual, yet similar to one in quality, with which each member of the group identifies himself, means again committing "the sin of reification" to which collective terms are susceptible.

Finally, the attribution of self-ridicule as a quality of humor is conceptually incongruous. While humor is an abstract notion, self-mockery is a property of verbal action. National humor is an idea; self-ridicule is a behavioral pattern. Hence, the attribution of the latter to the former is an ascription of a realistic quality for an abstract concept.

Hence, in order to examine empirically the idea that Jewish humor involves self-criticism, and that masochism is its distinctive quality, it is necessary not to analyze the jokes in their accumulated form in literary anthologies, abstracted from their contextual setting, but to observe them as they are told during the communicative events of joking within the Jewish community. Furthermore, the view of Jewish society should be changed from an image of a united whole to a realistic picture of a complex and segmented group, which stratified according to social and economic classes and in which individuals identify each other in terms of social roles and subgroup affiliations. For the thesis of the masochism of Jewish humor to be valid, there should be a direct relationship of social identification between the narrator and the subject of his joke. A matchmaker has to mock matchmakers, a *mohel* has to ridicule *mohels,* and a mother-in-law should laugh at mothers-in-law and not at any other figures in the community. In short, for self-mockery to be a quality of Jewish humor, it first and foremost should be a factor in the actual joking process of the Jews.

Ideally, such an examination of this problem should be done within the framework of communicative events which are culturally designated for joke-telling, without interrupting the conventional behavior of the participants on these occasions. Practically, this is rarely possible. The very presence of a folklorist and his tape recorder introduces some artificiality into the behavior of the narrators. The joke tellers might censor their stories and exclude off-colored anecdotes as not fit for recording. In other cases, they might compete for the tape recorder "attention." Furthermore, although there are some ways of reducing the effect of the intruder's presence in the collecting situation, it is hardly possible for a folklorist to be present in all the communicative events of the society in which people exchange jokes spontaneously.[31]

---

30   Peter L. Berger and Thomas Luckmann, *The Social Construction of Reality* (Garden City, N.Y., 1966), 91.

31   One of my informants explained to me the length of jokes in his repertoire: "Before, when I used to work in the restaurant, I used to exchange jokes with the customers. A person would come and sit at a table, and I'd start telling him a story and he would reply with another

Consequently, the data upon which we would like to test Freud's hypothesis about Jewish humor was recorded in an artificial diad in which the folklorists and the narrators were the principal people present. These jokes were collected by Richard M. Dorson in 1954–1959 from Jewish students and young faculty members, second generation immigrants to the United States,[32] and by myself, in 1963, from four Jewish narrators from Indianapolis, two of whom were rabbis. The number of jokes is relatively small. Dorson's collection includes ninety-two, and mine about one hundred and fifty anecdotes recorded, all in all, from nine Jewish narrators. (Dorson's collection included also a few jokes which are told by non-Jewish informants, which reflect the collector's and his informants' conception of what Jewish jokes are.)

In spite of the small quantity of jokes and narrators in this sample, and in spite of the artificiality of the recording situations, these data enable us to examine, at least on a preliminary basis, the relationships between the narrators and their tales, and to check whether or not self-criticism and ridicule are indeed the essential features, or even distinctive qualities of Jewish humor, and whether or not they are symptomatic of psychic masochism. To do this requires the establishment of a correlation between the narrator's social position and his joke, and when this is done the Freudian theory about Jewish humor immediately collapses. It becomes apparent that within the communicative event of joke-telling in the Jewish society, there is no social identification between the ridiculer and the ridiculed. The narrator is not the butt of his story, and self-degradation could not possibly be a classical form of Jewish humor. Rather, joking serves as a vehicle for verbal aggression toward those from whom the narrator distinguishes himself unequivocally. To be sure, this does not mean that the narrators are not familiar with jokes which are told about the social groups with which they identify themselves. However, since the process of joke-telling involves selection from a larger repertoire that the narrators make, either consciously or unconsciously, the very fact that they do not tell jokes in which they mock their own characteristics, confirms the absence of self-ridicule from Jewish humor.

Perhaps the best example of the use of jokes as a means for social differentiation is dialect stories. This is a narrative genre that develops among immigrant groups. Although in most cases the narrative situation itself is funny, the narrators add comic effect by speaking the new language with the intonation and vocal system of the old language. In the United States, these jokes are common among several immigrant groups as well as among Jews.[33] However, Jewish writers and even comedians expressed particular sensitivity to this humor. Nathan Ausubel argued that "'Jewish dialect' jokes are not Jewish at all, but the confections of anti-Semites who delight in ridiculing and slandering Jews."[34] After the Second World War such jokes were so easily associated with political anti-Semitism that Jewish comedians had to retire from radio appearances under public pressure, or at least, to impose self-censorship. The Jewish comedian Sam Levenson, has stated clearly: " … in my own work I have deliberately expurgated dialect stories."[35] As it appears from these and other similar statements, the issue was directly related to self-ridicule as a distinctive mark of

---

anecdote, and we had time to tell long stories. Nowadays, the only opportunity we have to tell jokes is in conventions of Jewish organizations, usually while people are standing at the urine stalls in the men's room."

32   Richard M. Dorson, "Jewish-American Dialect Stories on Tape," *Studies in Biblical and Jewish Folklore*, eds. Raphael Patai, Francis L. Utley, and Dov Noy (Bloomington, 1960), 111–74; "More Jewish Dialect Stories," *Midwest Folklore* 10 (1960): 133–46.

33   Richard M. Dorson, "Dialect Stories of the Upper Peninsula: A New Form of American Folklore," *Journal of American Folklore* 61 (1948): 113–50.

34   Nathan Ausubel, *A Treasury of Jewish Folklore* (New York, 1948), 265.

35   "The Dialect Comedian Should Vanish," *Commentary* 14 (1952): 168. See also Henry Popkin, "The Vanishing Jew of Our Popular Culture: The Little Man Who Is No Longer There," *Commentary* 14 (1952): 46–55.

Jewish humor. Whereas in any other context, the same writers would have probably subscribed to the idea that self-mockery is an earmark of Jewish humor, they violently objected to any ridicule of a trait to which Jews, as any other immigrants, are very sensitive, namely speech. Such jokes represent not self-criticism but the very epitome of anti-Semitism. Yet Dorson's collection and my own research indicate without any doubt that dialect stories are not necessarily "confession of anti-Semites." Jews themselves tell such jokes, yet surely not all of them do so. Within the Jewish community it is possible to distinguish a clear social or age differentiation which correlates with the narration of dialect stories. The two groups are distinct from each other in terms of their relation to immigration to the United States. First generation immigrants, who speak English with an accent and Yiddish intonation, of course do not tell dialect jokes. These stories are part of the repertoire only of second generation immigrants, whose own English is normative and who at the same time heard at home the accented speech of their parents. Only they tell jokes changing the W's into V's, the suffix ING into INK and introducing other phonetic and intonational alterations. This was the pattern of joke-telling among three of the narrators I recorded, all of them middle-aged second generation immigrants. The fourth raconteur arrived in the United States as a ten-year-old child and preferred to tell most of his stories either completely or partially in Yiddish. Dorson's informants were younger and all of them were born in this country to immigrant parents. In the course of his collecting, Dorson encountered a situation which illustrates the generational difference in the usage of dialect. He reports:

> By chance, a fine example of the contrast between dialect and non-dialect storytelling developed in my recording of undergraduate Herschel Stroyman jointly with his father Bernard, an Indianapolis lawyer born in Russia and educated in Israel and at Harvard. The senior Stroyman told traditional Jewish jests, but possessing some accent to begin with, he could not, and made no attempt to flavor them with dialect. However, his son Hershel, speaking flawlessly when introducing his situations, would then break into highly exaggerated nasal speech, far beyond his father's natural accent, to caricature the Jewish immigrant.[36]

This generational distribution of dialect joking in the Jewish community indicates that these stories are neither anti-Semitic nor are they a case of self-mockery. By introducing accent into their anecdotes, the narrators do not laugh at themselves altogether, but rather ridicule a social group within the Jewish community from which they would like to differentiate themselves. These jokes serve the second generation in a dual capacity: they constitute a verbal means of social differentiation from the parental group and affiliation with the peer society of American-born youth.

The jokes that rabbis and laity tell about each other can serve as another example for reciprocal and self-criticism in Jewish humor. The American rabbi is in a rather ambiguous position. He depends upon the community he guides. They could hire and fire him. He has to provide them with religious leadership which they tolerate but hardly admire. His authoritative position has been drastically weakened in the light of the pursuit of material values which led the children of immigrants into the land of the middle class. Traditional Judaism, which he was led to believe was at the core of the community life, turned out

---

36   Dorson, "Jewish Dialect Stories on Tape," 114. For a recent discussion of Jewish dialect stories and their function in the American Jewish community, see Naomi and Eli Katz, "Tradition and Adaptation in American Jewish Humor," *Journal of American Folklore* 84 (1971): 215–220.

to be at most an excuse for social gathering and entertainment.[37] As a result of this frustration, the rabbi is actually bitter and hostile toward the members of his own community, and he continuously criticizes them, at least in his jokes, for neglect of traditional values.

A rabbi told me the following story:

> The story is told in this regard of the priest and the rabbi who … and a minister, who are walking down the street and they saw a new family moving into a new house in the suburb. And so they said: "Mmmm, a new family. I wonder what religion, who is going to get them, which church." So they said, "Well, the shades are up, let us take a look and see if we can recognize by the house, you know, whose it is."
>
> So the Catholic looks into the house, peeps in, then says: "Oh, no, it is not one of my flock."
>
> So the minister looks in and says, "Well, I don't see any Bible that I can recognize, it is not one of my flock."
>
> The rabbi says, "Well, let me take a look." The rabbi takes a look and then says, "Oh yes, it is one of my flock." They say, "What is it, you see a Jewish star or a *menorah* or something like that?"
>
> "No," he says, "Wall to wall carpet."

In a version of the same joke, a student told Dorson the distinction between Catholics, Protestants, and Jews is done from the point of view of the Negro maid. Naturally, she does not mention the Star of David and the *menorah* as Jewish symbols in contrast to the wall to wall carpet.[38] This contrast between conspicuous consumption and traditional observance expresses the particular antagonism the rabbis feel toward their congregation.

In other jokes, rabbis may be more explicit in their criticism of the leaders of the community for their ignorance of traditional Jewish knowledge. The same rabbi told me the following joke:

> There is a very pleasant one [joke] about the rabbi that came into a classroom with the committee, the school committee—this deals with the general *amuratzes* (ignorance) of American laity, you know, vis-a-vis the Judaic culture—and they are listening to a child. The rabbi wants to impress one of the children that's not paying too much attention, a naughty boy, and he wants to catch his attention yet not criticize him. So he says to him: "David, who broke the Ten Commandments? Who broke the tablets?" And David, who was not paying attention to the discussion jumped up and said: "I didn't!" So he got red in the face and he went on with the class. And as they walked out of the room, the chairman of the school committee turned around to the rabbi and he says: "Rabbi, I don't know," he says, "I think you are naive."
>
> He says: "What do you mean?"
>
> He said: "When you confronted David with the charge about who broke the tablets?" He said: "Yeah?"
>
> He said: "Well, did you see how he turned color when he answered that he didn't?" he said, "I really think he did, I think he's guilty."

37   See Jerome E. Carlin and Saul H. Mendlovitz, "The American Rabbi: A Religious Specialist Responds to Loss of Authority," in *The Jews: Social Patterns of an American Group*, ed. Marshall Sklare (New York, 1958), 377–414.

38   Dorson, "More Jewish Dialect Stories," 137.

Whereas the rabbis mock the community leaders for their ignorance, the latter cannot ridicule their religious authorities for their erudition. After all, learning is an aspired achievement in the Jewish community and is part of the fundamental traditional values. Hence, they choose other targets related to the rabbi, as the following story illustrates:

> … This rabbi has so many quarrels with his congregation that he finally had to conduct prayers in his own house. And it was the custom to lean out the window and see anybody coming along who looked Jewish and you'd invite him up to say prayers with you, and no good religious Jew would refuse because it was considered a sin to refuse to make up the *minyan*—to help to make up the *minyan* or the quorum.
>
> So finally one night this rabbi's got nine people in the house including himself, he needs the tenth man. And he tells his wife to look out the window and call up somebody. And his wife is an ugly old crone. Teeth missing, just snaggled tooth, hair stringing all over her face. A beak on her. Just terrible. And he had met her through a marriage agency because he wasn't too much interested in love and he had to get fixed up with a wife. No rabbi is complete without a wife. So he tells her O.K. He had the wife, so he tells her O.K., look out the window, and call up somebody to make up the *minyan*.
>
> So she looks out the window, just this horrible looking creature, and she sees someone coming along with a beard and she yells, "You hoo! Mistuh! You hoo!" And the man looks up. She says, "You vanta be the tenth?" *[loud, croaky]*.
>
> And the guy looks up and he sees this ugly face, and he goes, "Ptooh. Not even the first."[39]

The relationship between the teller and his narratives is consistent in these tales. Rabbis criticize the laity for pursuit of material goods and neglect of traditional Jewish values, whereas the members of the congregation ridicule the personal characteristics and familial situation of the rabbis. These themes occur repeatedly in jokes as they are told by the respective types of raconteurs. The reverse relationship in which the leaders of the community laugh at their own ignorance in Jewish matters, and the rabbis mock their own personal features, does not appear in the material available to us as a possibility of joke-telling in Jewish society.

There is only one kind of tale in which the repertoire of rabbis and laity overlaps. These are the stories which revolve around a situation in which the rabbi is in conflict with functionaries of other religions. Ed Cray accurately termed the Jewish hero of these stories "The Rabbi Trickster."[40] The narrative situation in these jokes consists of inter-ethnic conflict in which the rabbi is a representative of the Jewish people, and hence the intra-community antagonism gives way before the more general group identity. The conflict in most of these jokes is mostly verbal and the rabbi has the last word. This is hardly a case of masochistic humor. The following tale can illustrate this type of joke:

> This is the one in the service where they're coming back on the train. There are several of them—I don't know why it is they always pick on priests. But it always seems to be a priest and a rabbi arguing. This time the men are coming back from overseas. They both live in New

---

39 Ibid., 145–46.
40 *Journal of American Folklore* 77 (1964): 331–345.

York, and they're coming from the Pacific, and they get on the train the first day, and the meals on a troop train are pretty much the same. For breakfast it's bacon and eggs, and for lunch it's pork chops or pork sausages, for supper it's ham. The first day, of course, the rabbi doesn't eat anything at all. The priest asks him, "what's the matter? He says, "I can't eat this because it's against my religion; I'm not allowed to eat swine's flesh."

And the second day, of course, he gets quite hungry, and it's an extremely hot day. This troop train is rather typical, moving along at about twelve miles an hour—and the rabbi's getting hungry, but holds out.

The third day, however, they're getting along in the Colorado mountains, and he's very famished. And the priest says, "Come on, have some of my ham," and sure enough he does and boy, he likes it and he eats it up. And he goes around to all the soldiers there and anybody who's got leftover ham; and he eats, and he eats, and he eats.

"Boy is this good, boy oh boy, is this good!!"

Finally they get to New York, they get to the station, and the rabbi rushes out, and this beautiful, gorgeous woman comes up to him, hugs him, kisses him, throws her arms around him.

"Jake, it's wonderful to have you home. Let's go home immediately."

He says, "Wait a second, Sarah, I want you to meet my good friend, Father O'Reilly. Come on over here, Pat."

Pat comes over, and he—the rabbi—says, "Father O'Reilly, I want you to meet my wife Sarah."

"How do you do, Father."

"Say, Father, where's your wife?" he says.

"Oh, no, no, I'm, I'm, I'm not allowed to have a wife. You see it's, it's against my religion." *[softly]*

"Oh," says the rabbi, "You ought to try it, it's better than ham!" *[enthusiastically]*[41]

When a rabbi told me another version of this tale, he developed the episodes in such a way that the hero of the joke does not actually eat the forbidden meat.

The two examples of correlations between the narrator's social position and his narrative theme, clearly demonstrate that joking in Jewish society does not involve mocking of self either directly or indirectly. Rather, invariably the object of ridicule is a group with which the raconteur disassociates himself. Joke-telling is a verbal expression which manifests social differentiation. The fact that Jews tell jokes about each other demonstrates not so much self-hatred as perhaps the internal segmentation of their society. The recurrent themes of these anecdotes are indicative of areas of tension within the Jewish society itself, rather than the relations with outside groups. Apparently the proverbial social cohesion of Jewish family and society generates a great deal of internal friction and reciprocal criticism, much of which is expressed through humor.

There remains the question of Somerset Maugham's literary observations about a Jew who specialized in mocking traditional Jews by mimicry of their speech and gesture. In the light of the previous discussion, Maugham's impressions that this behavior was an example of "self hatred to ones race," appears to be erroneous. This Jewish party jester did not display hatred for his own characteristics, but his ability

---

41   Dorson, "Jewish-American Dialect Stories on Tape," 145–46.

to disassociate himself from his traditional past. For him, mocking was a proclamation of social distance rather than affinity, of sadism, if you like, rather than masochism. The message he signaled to his London partygoer friends was a call for acceptance into their own circles, exhibiting his own difference from other Jews. Maugham however, being a stranger to Jewish society, did not interpret the message adequately. Since he categorized all Jews together as a single group, he remained insensitive to the more subtle aspects of such behavior, and interpreted it as self-hatred. As we demonstrated, this was hardly the case.

Like every negative conclusion of research, there is, of course, always the theoretical possibility that future studies will discover a Jew who mocks himself. After all, masochism is not a psychopathology from which Jews are exempt. Yet this conceivable situation hardly confirms the notion that self-mockery is the distinctive quality of cultural and historical changes that occur in the humor of the Jews. Theoretically, it is quite possible that self-ridicule was the main trait of Jewish jokes in east and central Europe and that it disappeared from their society as they crossed the Atlantic to the United States. However, the single European-born informant whom I recorded, who often told his jokes in Yiddish about life in the *shtetle*, actually concurred with the principles outlined above.

In conclusion, the ethnography of Jewish humor toward which this study is but a preliminary step, has not only to examine the relationship between the narrator and the subject matter of his jokes, but also to map the direction of mockery within the network of the community itself. Since every narrator identifies himself with fewer groups than he disassociates himself from, it is necessary not only to examine against whom he directs his humorous remarks, but also whom does he avoid criticising. Only such an examination could adequately describe the dynamics of humor in the Jewish community and provide the empirical basis for a generalization concerning the nature of Jewish humor.[42]

University of Pennsylvania

Erratum

The editors wish to point out an inadvertent omission in Hartmut Breitkreuz's note on John Braine's proverbs *(WF* 31 [1972]: 130–31). Proverb six in Mr. Breitkreuz's list should read: "No one ever comes back from *Capua.*"

---

42   A theoretical framework and methodological model for such a study could be Dell Hymes' "Introduction toward Ethnographies of Communication," *The Ethnograpy of Communication,* eds. John J. Gumperz and Dell Hymes, special publication of American Anthropologist 66, no. 6, pt. 2 (1964), 1–34 and "Models of the Interaction of Language and Social Life," in *Directions in Sociolinguistics: The Ethnography of Communication,* eds. John J. Gumperz and Dell Hymes (New York, 1972), 35–71.

A Student's View of Negro Humor: The Power of Stereotypes

by John Simpson (2012)[1]

D r. Ewa Wasilewska has asked me to contribute this essay because of my unusual student perspective on this subject. While I have no claim on uniqueness, it became apparent to me as I took her class on "Anthropology of Humor and Laughter" that my life experiences were in marked contrast to those of most other students. I have lived through some of the transitions from Negro humor to Black humor that the younger generations regard as part of history. The first part of this essay is a simple narrative of the evolution of my relationship to Negro humor, and how it changed as my relationship to the Black community changed. This is followed by a historical account of the development of Negro humor within the Black and White communities respectively, and its transformation into racial humor. Finally, I will address the relevance of Negro humor as a way to negotiate shifting social relationships between Blacks and Whites, and as an expression of our universal human experience. I use the story of Brer Rabbit and the Tar Baby in different forms and in different contexts to illustrate the changing nature of Negro humor.[1]

I have taken the road less traveled and I have experienced social relations, politics, religions, and culture from the point of view of a minority individual. My most meaningful insights came in my quarter-century marriage to a Black woman. My origins are rather ordinary, growing up in 1950's as a White middle class Protestant in a small city in central New Hampshire. There was one family of Blacks that intermittently resided among us. My grandmother had lived for most of her adult life in a larger city with a Navy base and a much larger Black population. My mother had spent the years of World War II as an Army wife stationed in Virginia and Texas. I remember being amazed at how fast my Black classmate could run and how high he could jump. My grandmother informed me that Blacks were naturally athletic. I don't believe I was raised with any prejudice, but there was an apparent recognition of diversity, and stereotypes were perpetuated. Even among ourselves, the process of differentiation and ranking was evident. Certainly, religious and cultural backgrounds were identified, but more value seemed to have been placed on economic status.

My knowledge about Black people came mainly through the television, magazines, and the newspaper. One of the first programs I remember watching was "The Little Rascals," which had originally been

---

1   John is a former student of Dr. Ewa Wasilewska in several courses, including "Anthropology of Humor and Laughter" at the University of Utah.

produced as "Our Gang" in the 1930's.[2] Interestingly enough, the cast was integrated, and stories portrayed the kids going to school together, hanging out, and getting into trouble. This show perpetuated and amplified racial stereotypes, as it was slapstick comedy where the characters exaggerated and overacted their roles. The camaraderie and egalitarianism of the children were genuine and have given these programs enduring qualities. Another source of Negro humor during my formative years was the character of Rochester on the Jack Benny program.[3] Eddie Anderson played to prevailing stereotypes as a deferential employee, and yet he was a counterfoil to some of the Benny character's eccentricities, such as his fabled miserliness. Old cartoons were another way in which images of Black people reached our homes in New Hampshire. Vintage shorts from the 1930's and 1940's often portrayed Blacks with large lips, tooth-filled grins, wide eyes, and nappy hair, singing and dancing in rhythm. A major cultural event of my early years was going to the local theater and immersing myself in the full-color wide-screen Disney production of "Song of the South."[4] The congenial old Negro storyteller Uncle Remus made a hit of the song "Zip A Dee Doo Dah[5]," where "Mister Blue Bird's on my shoulder; It's the truth, it's actual, Everything is satisfatch'll … ." (Disney. 1946). I cannot dissociate the retelling of Brer Rabbit's encounter with the Tar Baby from a decidedly racial context. The dummy is Black and wears an old coat and hat. He stares blankly into space with two button eyes; his nose is the bowl of a corn-cob pipe. Uncle Remus is telling the story in dialect to a young White boy. The characters of the Rabbit, the Fox, and the Bear also speak in dialect. The story takes place in rural Georgia. Brer Fox is constantly vexed and outwitted by Brer Rabbit. He creates the Tar Baby to entrap the Rabbit, and so end his misery once and for all. In passing the black dummy, the Rabbit greets it. Receiving no response, the Rabbit becomes incensed at its insolence and smacks it. One hand, then both hands, then both feet, and finally his head get all stuck in the tar. The Fox has finally won his prey. Or so he thinks. The Rabbit tricks him though. Exclaiming that the very worse fate that could befall him is to be flung into the briar patch, worse than being roasted, hanged, drowned, or skinned alive even, the Fox unwittingly obliges, and the Rabbit is once again free. I found this movie thoroughly enjoyable and entertaining. Media portrayals of the warm, congenial, non-threatening servant role of Blacks also appeared on boxes of food products that sat on our kitchen shelves such as Aunt Jemima pancake mix, Uncle Ben's rice, and Cream O' Wheat cereal.

Against this lingering image of positive and non-threatening Blacks was the more potent current of the Civil Rights movement. Blacks and sympathetic Whites were pressing for the repeal of laws of discrimination and enforcement of the 1954 Supreme Court decision banning segregation in public schools. I remember watching the National Guard shielding the eight Black Little Rock high school students in 1957 from the angry mobs of White tormentors. I remember seeing pictures of the burning Greyhound bus in

---

2 "Our Gang" comedies were film shorts produced by Hal Roach between 1922 and 1944. The focus of the stories were antagonisms between the central group of poor kids with bullies, rich kids, and adult authority figures. The most well-known characters were Alfalfa, Spanky, and Darla (who were White) and Buckwheat, Stymie, and Farina (who were Black).

3 Jack Benny began as a vaudeville entertainer in the 1920's. He became a star on radio in the 1930's and 1940's and transitioned successfully into television in the 1950's and 1960's. Eddie Anderson became popular on Benny's radio programs and continued in the TV show. The format featured an ensemble of cast, skits, and guest stars.

4 This full-length film was based on Joel Chandler Harris's *Uncle Remus: His Songs and His Sayings*, originally published in 1880. The film was noteworthy in that it successfully combined live action with animation. It was originally released in 1946. It was re-released in 1956. There will be more discussion of this film below. *Song of the South*. Walt Disney Productions. Directed by Wilfred Jackson and Harve Foster. 1946.

5 "Zip A Dee Doo Dah". Written by Allie Wrubel and Ray Gilbert. Performed by James Baskett as Uncle Remus. Walt Disney Productions. 1945.

Alabama in 1961, set on fire by White protestors who did not want interstate commerce to be integrated, nor to share bus stations, restaurants, bathrooms, and water fountains with Black people.

In the Spring of 1962, I was nearing the end of 8th grade. I volunteered to compete in the annual Junior High School Prize Speaking Competition. We could choose a selection from a folder of prepared scripts, or upon approval, provide one of our own. I picked "Aunt Sylvia's Geography Lesson."[6] I was intrigued by the theatrical challenge of presenting two distinct female characters, rather than by the content of the script. The scene involves a young White girl returning home from school, bursting with enthusiasm for the knowledge she has acquired about the earth's astronomical relationship to the sun. She is attempting to share this information with the family's Black cook as she is preparing dinner in the kitchen. In retrospect, it is astonishing that such a piece of racist and anachronistic material was being presented as part of a public school program in 1962. It was alright with the teachers; it was alright with the parents; it was alright with my friends; and it must have been alright with me. I don't know if it was alright with my Black classmate and his family, though. As I memorized the lines and tried to develop the characters, I searched for references that would be helpful. Aunt Sylvia was described as "old" and "portly" and spoke with a deep dialect. I had a mental image of Aunt Jemima in a calico dress and apron with a bandana tied around her head, acting like a large lady from some of those old movies. I imagined Little Susie to be a Shirley Temple type, with a broad Southern drawl. I gave Aunt Sylvia a broad, deep, slow speech, and tried to develop for Susie a chirpy little falsetto voice. As Susie begins to describe what the earth looks like, Sylvia produces a watermelon from underneath one of the floorboards in the kitchen. She cautions Susie not to tell her father, "Marster" Coleman, about it, because he would think she had stolen it. Susie goes on to explain the earth's shape, rotation, and revolution in relationship to the sun and moon, all the while Sylvia is protesting with her own primitive and unscientific beliefs and faith in God:

Sylvia: Tole you what, Miss Sukey, you can't fool a Coleman nigger, n'on deedy, you'd be in a heap better bisness hef you'd go an tell dat yarn to a Mcwilliams' nigger, or mo like to dat Afican nigger on de ovver side dat watermillion. I aint no ignunt, oncibilized heathen dat doan know nuffin.

Susie: But Aunt Sylvia, can't you understand it? Haven't you got any understanding?

(Elocutionist's. 1889)

Of course the point is that Aunt Sylvia is ignorant, and this misrepresentation is humorous. The scene comes to a climax when Susie breaks down in frustration. Sylvia relents, knowing it is not good for Mr. Coleman's daughter to be upset with her. The situation is resolved emotionally, physically, and philosophically:

Sylvia: De lors a-massey sake alibe! Jis look at dat hoe-cake! Dat's what comes o' ignunt ole niggers talkin' bout white folks' consarns.

(Elocutionist's. 1889)

---

6   From *The Elocutionist's Annual*, Number 17. "The Latest and Best Selections for Reading or Recitation." Compiled by Mrs. J. W. Shoemaker. Philadelphia. The Penn Publishing Company. 1889. The original text appeared in 1889 as an exercise in public speaking. It is apparently a representation of relationships between Blacks and Whites that had existed in slavery. Sylvia refers to herself and other Blacks as "niggers" being owned by their masters and very fearful of being caught misbehaving. I have reason to believe that the word "nigger" in my 1962 version was changed to "colored people" or "Negro" as less offensive terms to describe a still unbalanced relationship.

Here, Aunt Sylvia is expressing the negative consequences of Blacks stepping outside their well-defined place that, in altering their relationship with White people by acquiring knowledge, will only cause trouble. It was not my intention to perpetuate racial stereotypes or advocate for discrimination and segregation. I naively saw this piece as a form of entertainment that presented certain artistic challenges that, if earned a prize, would give me status and recognition. Unfortunately, I did not win any prizes, and did not create a successful theatrical experience. I am not ashamed of what I did, nor do I regret doing it at all. I simply didn't know any better. I gave no thought to the implications of the content of the material, and the effect it might have on people I did not even know.

As the 60's rolled on, I acquired broader educational experiences, which involved developing skills in critical thinking and coming into contact with people of more diverse backgrounds. There were more voices contributing to the conversations, and more experiences to be understood. The Vietnam War took on increasing significance for us young men.[7] In 1965, I had the opportunity to listen to an informed and cogently presented argument against the War, which ultimately changed my perception of and my relationship with mainstream America. The murders of three civil rights workers in Philadelphia, Mississippi, in 1964 and of two men in Selma, Alabama, in 1965, brought home the high stakes involved in mobilizing for social change. This also made me realize to what lengths White supremacists would go to preserve the *status quo*.[8] Martin Luther King Jr. in 1965 united the Civil Rights struggle with the Anti-War movement, underscoring the linkage between political and economic interests, and the media.[9] He made a powerful connection between racism and imperialism.[10] The nature of the conversation was changing. So too was the character of Negro humor. Even the word "Negro" began to take on the connotations of the old stereotype: slow, subservient, and non-threatening. The word "Black," on the other hand, had a keener edge to it; definitive, dynamic, and confrontational. This is a good example of the power of language—a simple word—to convey deep and emotional meaning. In the early part of the 20th century, the term "colored" was used by both Whites and Blacks. As more progressive social relations were desired by elements of both communities, the term "Negro" came into usage before the Second World War. The dynamics of the Civil Rights movement in the 1960's required a new perspective; this one instituted by the Blacks themselves, to substitute the label "Black." The connotations of each term carried with them meanings of status, attributes, and identity. "Black" is a term of self-ascribed identity; it is a form of empowerment. It conveys a sense of liberation as in "Black Power," and is a term in opposition to "White." In our era of political correctness, most public discussion uses the term "African–American." Images of Blacks in movies and television began to show individuals who had more class, were better educated, were well-dressed, and were more equally paired with their White counterparts. Sidney Poitier set the tone for the new generation, in such movies as "Guess Who's Coming to Dinner?"[11] and "In the Heat of the Night."[12] Comedians such as Dick Gregory and Godfrey Cambridge challenged the *status quo* in nightclub

---

7 The United States became involved in the war in Vietnam ostensibly to prevent the Communist takeover of the entire country. The war was significantly escalated in 1964. The compulsory military draft was enacted for men between 18 and 24 years of age. College students enjoyed deferments. Growing unpopularity and public protests emerged around 1965 and continued to the conclusion of the war in 1975.

8 James Chaney (Black), Andrew Goodman and Michael Schwerner (White) were murdered in Mississippi for their attempts to register Black voters. See *New York Times,* August 7, 1964 and *Look Magazine* June 29, 1965. Rev. James Reeb and Viola Liuzzo (both White) were murdered in Alabama supporting the march for justice. See *New York Times* March 28, 1965.

9 *New York Times* July 3, 1965.

10 "Beyond Vietnam." Riverside Church, New York City. *New York Times* April 4, 1967.

11 Produced and directed by Stanley Kramer. Columbia Pictures. 1967. The theme of interracial marriage confronts racism.

12 Directed by Norman Jewison. Produced by Walter Mirisch. United Artists. 1967. Racism and law enforcement in the South.

acts, openly criticized Whites, and joked about what it was like to be a Black in America. Bill Cosby played an educated and sophisticated character in the TV program "I Spy" from 1965–1968.[13] Nipsey Russell was a regular on a number of game-shows, "To Tell the Truth"[14] and "Matchgame"[15] to name a couple, and was known for his humorous four-line poems.

My own journey took me from the liberal milieu of the Ivy League Northeast into the still conservative, racially segregated South in the Fall of 1966. The social concept of integration still had not taken hold in North Carolina. Although demographically Blacks made up a sizable percentage of the overall population,[16] there were numerous contexts in which Black were still missing. Blacks were found only in certain neighborhoods as employees of White homeowners. Blacks were not found in certain occupations, as members of the university faculties, or of the local country clubs. Except for the athletes, there were few Black men in the student body of Duke University. The only Black women I encountered on campus were the dormitory maids and the kitchen workers. In the neighborhoods where the Blacks resided there were few Whites, and Blacks could be found almost exclusively as cooks and waiters and in the Black churches. In many realms, this sizable population was all but invisible. And where Blacks coexisted with Whites, there was little interaction. Each group knew its place in relationship to the other and the boundaries were not openly challenged. The meaningful exchanges were rare, but memorable. Hitchhiking back from the coast late one Sunday afternoon, a car full of Black people stopped to give me a ride. I welcomed the lift, but felt very self-conscious: I was road weary and far from clean, and they, men and women both, were dressed in their Sunday best. They invited me to come along to their church. I accepted the ride, but under the circumstances declined the religious service. During another trip to the coast, I partook in the landing of the local fishing fleet. All Blacks, they beached their dories and sold their catch to the locals who had gathered there. One of the best dinners I have ever eaten.

In the Fall of 1967, I found myself in San Francisco in the heart of the Haight Ashbury.[17] Although it was a little too late for the Summer of Love, there was still a lot of energy around willing to transform, not just the society, but the whole world. Political activity focused on ending the Vietnam War and relieving the pressure of the local police force. Cosmic consciousness was a pathway to self-fulfillment, and drug use and psychedelic music were the cornerstones of the alternative culture. The young, mostly White, unpredictable and outrageous hippies had invaded a mixed, mostly working class, neighborhood. The incongruities created some interesting relationships. For a period of time, I shared a flat in a 3-unit Victorian house, which was owned by a middle-aged Black woman, with two Jewish women and a Black man. A long-term relationship with one of these women produced two children and provided me with a valuable education in a different culture. I chose an unconventional pathway for myself. As a result of the choices I made regarding my personal appearance, my politics, and my lifestyle, I found myself marginalized from and by mainstream America. I experienced ridicule, discrimination, physical violence, and harassment by the police. I felt that prejudice. And yet, I could undo that any time I wanted to; Black people had no such choice. I eventually found employment in the Post Office which, at least in San Francisco, had a long

---

13   Sheldon Leonard, executive producer. Three F Productions. 1965–1968.

14   1970–1978. "To Tell the Truth" Produced by Mark Goodson and Bill Todman.

15   1974–1975. "Matchgame." Produced by Mark Goodson and Bill Todman.

16   North Carolina. 1960 U.S. Census. 24.5% Black. Durham, NC—36.1% Black.

17   The Haight-Ashbury is a neighborhood of San Francisco that became a focal point of the emerging alternative culture known as the "Hippies." The spontaneous, celebratory experience fueled by psychedelic drugs and music in 1965 was known as "The Summer of Love." By September 1967, much of that spirit was gone.

tradition of equal opportunity. A good number of my co-workers were Black and so were several of my supervisors. I listened to what they talked about, how they talked to each other, and to the rest of us, and what they found funny. In 1977, the television program "Roots" aired.[18] It gave me an opportunity to understand generations of discrimination and segregation. I also examined my own family's role in the slave trade, and the maintenance of the institution. And I reflected on my own upbringing and understood that if I was part of the problem, I could also be part of the solution. In 1982 I met the Black woman who was to become my wife. She immersed me into her world. I had to abandon all my preconceptions and prejudices, and to trust in her guidance through unfamiliar territory. The transformation in lifestyle and cultural experience was almost diametrically opposed to everything I was familiar with. From a semi-suburban and nearly all-White neighborhood in San Francisco, I took up residence in a nearly all-Black working class neighborhood in East Oakland. Her family was now my family; her friends were now my friends; her music became my music, and I learned what she thought was funny. But more importantly, I acquired her vision of the world of prejudice and treachery, of discernment and trust, and that integrity transcended all color lines. Though that wasn't part of the plan, I understood what it meant to be working poor; to be disadvantaged meant that people with money controlled your life and it didn't matter if you were White or Black. She has a wonderful sense of humor and an infectious laugh. For her, there is no sense bemoaning your fate, you have to get busy and make things better. She reminded me that the images of lynchings[19] and of Emmit Till[20] are very real parts of Black Americans' cultural memory, but harboring hatred or fear serves no purpose. She and I are now leading separate lives, but as I have embarked on my courses of study, the insights she has given me about being Black in America have proven to be very valuable in understanding social relationships in culture. These insights have provided meaning to experiences not lived and otherwise not known. I sometimes think about my own upbringing, one of privilege, opportunity, and relative calm, and contrast it with those of people from different backgrounds and social contexts, including my children's Jewish immigrant ancestors' and my former wife's predecessors' who were sharecroppers in Mississippi.

This review of my own evolving relationship with Negro humor provides a lens through which to view its history. The term "Negro humor" is being used to describe a genre of entertainment that developed in America in the early 19th century and persisted through the first half of the 20th century. It represents a medium that defined and facilitated the social relationships between Blacks and Whites. The origins of Negro humor go back to West Africa, the homeland of most enslaved Blacks. Before their cultures were decimated by trafficking in human populations by Europeans and their agents beginning around 1500, great civilizations of Ghana, Mali, Songhay, Benin, and Ife were connected with trading networks, agricultural, and nomadic pastoral societies (Schechter 1970: 15, Abrahams 1983: 3). In varying degrees of complexities, these cultural groups depended on oral traditions to maintain cohesiveness, retain histories,

18   "Roots" 1977. Written by Alex Haley. Produced by Stan Margulies. A family history of an African–American from capture in West Africa and enslavement in the South to the present day Haley.

19   Lynchings occurred mainly in the South, from the end of the Civil War up into the 1930's. I had not seen any images or descriptions of lynching until I began poking around in bookstores and libraries in San Francisco in the late 1960's. The reality of this horrific brutality must be acknowledged. This is indiscriminate terrorism inflicted on Black populations outside any accountability to the law. See www.withoutsanctuary.org and the book, *Without Sanctuary: Lynching Photography in America*, by James Allen. Published by Twin Palms, Santa Fe NM, 2000 for some very compelling and disturbing visual evidence.

20   Emmit Till, aged 14, was brutally murdered in Mississippi in 1955 by two Whites for allegedly insulting a White woman. His death became a catalyst for the Civil Rights movement. I knew nothing of this incident until informed of it in the early 1980's. *Jet Magazine*, September 15, 1955, published pictures, at the insistence of his mother, which created a public national outcry for justice.

and to establish community identities. These spoken words also served to teach values, establish social relationships, and to diffuse tensions. Dependent on a skillful use of language, these stories utilized humor as a teaching tool and memory device. Storytelling was a formal element in organized society, serving both political and religious functions. A class of specialists evolved, known as *griots*, which developed extensive genealogies and reputations valued by the richest and most powerful rulers (Schechter 1970: 15). Because they existed outside the caste systems of the most stratified societies, and because they were itinerant, the *griots* often engaged in much appreciated burlesque and even ridicule of the king. Such temporary inversion of values[21] served to relieve social pressure and anxiety, and provided the community an opportunity to test its potential. Joking relationships have been an integral part of some African societies as a means to mediate interpersonal conflict. Carefully defined interactions allow for criticisms and insults to be exchanged and laughter expressed to diffuse potentially damaging situations and to restore harmonious, productive relationships (Davidheiser 2005). Another means to redirect negative energy involved the verbal contest of "Dozens." Opponents would trade insults directed at each other's family members ending in the ultimate affront that could not be topped (Hughes 1966: 119). At the community level, stories were told by the elders to instruct the youth and remind their parents of values and codes of behavior that were integral to the well-being of the cultural group. Often these tales would be allegories using animals and settings that were familiar to the listeners and were thus easy to remember. The origins of the Uncle Remus stories written by Joel Chandler Harris in the late 19th century (on which the Disney movie of 1946 was based) are in fact West African folk tales. Brer Rabbit and Brer Fox probably had indigenous counterparts of jackal, tortoise, and spider. Roger D. Abrahams (1983) has collected stories from African sources and provides this version of "Why the Hare Runs Away" from the Ewe people of present day Nigeria. The animals were in a quandary about what to do about the drought. They decided to cut off the tips of their ears, extracted the fat, and sold it to buy a hoe. All agreed except the hare. The animals successfully excavated a well. When the animals were gone, the hare surreptitiously took water. The animals were suspicious and created a trap for the hare. They covered a dummy with birdlime. When the hare came again to the well, he greeted the dummy. When the dummy did not respond, the hare slapped it and kicked it. He became stuck in the birdlime and his culpability was revealed. The animals whipped the hare and let him escape. Fearful, the hare never comes out in the open any more (Abrahams 1983: 74). The ability of a less powerful character to overcome challenging obstacles and more powerful adversaries using wit and craftiness was a popular theme throughout many of the stories. The Trickster and the ritual clown have also had important roles to play in the cultural traditions of West Africans. The Trickster, often in the form of a jackal or a hare, used duplicity and selfishness to bring about something useful for humans, engendering mockery and laughter in the process. Important lessons for correct behavior were taught in this way. The ritual clown provides an antithesis to order and proper relationships in religious ceremony, contrasting the sacred with the profane, providing not only a mirror but a window, in a hilarious and enjoyable manner (Apte 1985: 222, 229).

The enslavement of Black Africans tore tens of millions from their homelands and cultures, transporting them in chains to a foreign country, where they were subjected to total control by their White owners.[22] They were forced to adopt Christianity, Christian names, and the English language, to forsake

---

21   See Section 6 and Chapter 6 for the discussion of joking relationships.

22   *African Americans: A Concise History.* Darlene Clark Hine, William C. Hine, and Stanley Harrald. Pearson Education Inc. Upper Saddle River NJ. 2009. pp 24–43.

all that they had known as African, under the threat and use of physical violence. The slaves realized they could transform the appearance of their indigenous traditions to suit the Whites and still retain the essences of their beliefs and practices. In this way they found power and spirit to endure the harshness of their inhumane existences. Long hours in the fields under constant supervision, meager provisions for sustenance, being bought and sold as so much property, families split apart at the whim of the owner, sexual predation, and the threat of the whip, or amputation, for misbehavior, provided little opportunity for the slave to hope for a better life, or to think of himself in a dignified way. And yet, through covert expressions of faith and power, and frequent use of humor, the enslaved Blacks nourished their resilient souls and found strength in creating and maintaining bonds of understanding amongst themselves. Christian hymns and Bible stories were reinterpreted as protest songs and messages of overcoming, often using coded language to fool any White observers (Schechter 1970:26).[23] Songs sung in the fields were accompanied by hand clapping and foot stomping reminiscent of tribal gatherings, to engender solidarity and communicate messages of warning or information. The "Dozens" competitions were directed by field slaves toward house servants to relieve tension and prevent open conflict (Schechter 1970: 13). The folk tales of spider and jackal assumed the identities of animals found in the South, the rabbit and the fox. The theme of the ultimate triumph of the underdog was especially potent.

Minstrelsy, as a form of theatrical entertainment, originated in the late 18th century. White actors began using caricatures of Blacks in publicly performed skits and plays. As these characters gained popularity, their roles were enlarged, and their features and behavior became more exaggerated. "From the pathos and humor of the Negroes, their superstitions and their religious fervor, their plaintive and their hilarious melodies, their peculiarities of manner, dress, and speech, the white minstrel built his performance" (Wittke 1968: 7). Burnt cork was applied to the face, white circles were painted around the eyes, and the lips were grossly enlarged. A frizzy fright wig was added for effect. A colorful costume accompanied a distinctive style of speech, which portrayed a general lack of education and an innate lack of intelligence. The characters were lazy and irresponsible and had a predilection for indulging in watermelons and chicken. Thomas Dartmouth Rice brought his character "Jim Crow" onto the stage in Louisville around 1830. Jim Crow was the indelible image of racial segregation in the South well into the 20th century. His song and the dance step became very popular:

> "First on de heel tap, den on de toe.
> Ebery time I wheel about I jump Jim Crow.
> Wheel about and turn about and do jis so,
> An every time I wheel about I jump Jim Crow."

> (Wittke 1968: 26)

Full-fledged minstrel shows appeared in 1843 with The Virginia Minstrels in New York City and Christy's Minstrels in Buffalo (Wittke 1968: 41). A standard form emerged in which a semi-circular line of singers and musicians formed on stage after an introductory dance number. Bracketed by end men, one with a tambourine (Tambo) and the other with castanets (Bones) they were led through their routines by

---

23 Songs about the Israelites in bondage either in Egypt or in Babylon were synonymous with the enslaved condition of the Blacks, giving them hope for their own freedom, either by escape or by emancipation. For example, see "Wade in the Water" and "Steal Away" from the website of the city Owen Sound, Ontario ,Canada, Owen Sound's Black History. www.osblackhistory.com. Owen Sound was a destination of The Underground Railway, a system enabling slaves to escape to safety.

the interlocutor (Schechter 1970: 45). Their responses in malapropisms and mispronunciations were a great source of humor for the White audiences. The minstrel shows became hugely popular. Productions were greatly expanded to include musical numbers and variety acts, touring across the United States and even to Europe. Murphy and Mike's Minstrels played for 10 days at the Salt Lake Theatre in 1869 (Wittke 1968: 71). This is a sample of one musical ditty:

> "Ring, ring de banjo
>   and pound de tamborine;
> Massa gib us holiday—
>   We're de gayest darkies seen."

(Minstrel 1969: 107)

Stephen C. Foster composed a number of pieces for minstrel shows that have become standards of American music, such as "The Old Folks at Home"[24] and "Camptown Races." "Dixie," the anthem of the Confederacy, first appeared in a minstrel show in 1859 (Wittke 1968: 168).

That the minstrel shows originated, became popular, and persisted through the most challenging time for race relations in America deserves some study. Besides merely being a form of entertainment for a wide spectrum of the White population, the minstrel show helped to define Whites' relationship to Blacks. The issue of slavery and abolition was becoming a divisive social concern by the 1840's. The humorous portrayal of Blacks as inferior and subservient ameliorated the moral and legal implications of human enslavement. Creating stereotypes of the Black people served a more important and sinister purpose for the White people than just for simple amusement. It allowed the Whites to justify the deliberate and institutionalized enslavement of one human population by another (Apte 1985: 140). The process of differentiation was employed to manage this psychological and emotional conundrum. Not only were Blacks different from Whites, but they were innately inferior to Whites. The White creators of Black characters extracted characteristics of Black appearance, behavior, and expression, exaggerated them, and made them universally applicable to all Blacks. Making the Black person an object of humor resolved the moral violation of slavery and racial discrimination, and served to perpetuate this asymmetrical social relationship into the middle of the 20th century. Portraying the enslaved Blacks as happy and content with their status created the impression that slavery was actually a beneficial institution. Ascribing malevolent and impure qualities to the Blacks ensured a defensive separation of the races (Apte 1985: 114).

By 1880, the popularity of the minstrel show was fading. The question of slavery had been settled by the Civil War.[25] Reconstruction had come and gone. As the South entered into a new phase of legal segregation and discrimination, the threat of violence hung over the heads of the now free Blacks. The nature of life in the rural South was changing as more Blacks headed for the cities and destinations North. Black actors appeared in stage shows, often in blackface. Burlesque and vaudeville became new forms of entertainment. Productions became more elaborate and expensive and, with the development of the railroad, more mobile. Though the burnt cork was eventually discarded, the roles that Black actors could assume were still determined by the inferior status of Blacks in America. Subservient, submissive, and ignorant, these characterizations presented no threat to the White audiences who viewed them. During

---

24   We learned to sing this song in the thick Negro dialect in my fifth grade elementary school class.
25   Emancipation Declaration. 1863. Termination of hostilities. 1865.

this period time from 1880 to 1902, Joel Chandler Harris published several volumes of Uncle Remus tales. He claimed to have authentically reproduced stories told to him by elderly former slaves in rural Georgia and to have transcribed them with the genuine sound of their speech. He has been criticized for representing the favorable attitudes of his informants toward slavery and of the dense dialect of his storyteller.[26] He himself was critical of the " … intolerable misrepresentations of the minstrel stage." (Harris 1880: viii) They stand as an expression of an indigenous folklore, and also of the continuing imbalance between the Black population and the Whites. "The Wonderful Tar-Baby Story" is coupled with "How Mr. Rabbit was too sharp for Mr. Fox" to present the successful outcome of Rabbit's predicament. Brer Fox was preparing a trap for Brer Rabbit. He " … went ter wuk en got 'im some tar, en mix it wid some turkentime, en fix up a contrapshun wat he call a Tar-Baby … ." Trying to get the dummy to talk to him, Rabbit gets all stuck up in the tar. Fox appears and derides the Rabbit, "Den Brer Fox, he sa'ntered fort', lookin' des ez innercent ez one er yo' mammy's mockin' birds." (Harris 1880: 7, 10) Using a little reverse psychology, Brer Rabbit pleads with Brer Fox, "'I don't keer w'at you do wid me, Brer Fox,' sezee, 'so you don't fling me in dat brier-patch.'" (Harris 1880: 18) Of course that is exactly what the Fox does, and the Rabbit makes his escape.

New forms of media opened up new opportunities to perform different types of Negro humor. Cinema brought the entertainment acts to the screen and in doing so spelled the demise of live performances in local theaters. Al Jolson was featured in blackface as a minstrel performer in the first full-length talking film, "The Jazz Singer" in 1927. The character of Stepin Fechit made a star of the actor Lincoln Perry, but continued to perpetuate the stereotype of the docile, uneducated Black. He characterized his role as "The Laziest Man in the World." He appeared in many films in the 1920's and 1930's. I have recounted the impact of the appearance of the integrated cast in the Our Gang comedies. The "Amos 'n' Andy Show" debuted on the radio in 1925 (Schechter 1970: 103). White actors played Black characters. Their characterizations were still based on stereotypes. White audiences laughed at their ineptness and lack of sophistication. In the transition to television in the 1950's, Black actors assumed the roles played to the same stereotypical images. Moms Mabley, Pigmeat Markham, and Redd Foxx developed as nightclub comedians. Playing to Black audiences in what was known as the Chittlin' Circuit,[27] they became popular for telling it like it was, often with sexual content and provocative language. In these environments they could relate to the common experiences on inequality and discrimination. Humor has healing power. Langston Hughes observed that among Blacks, humor serves as a mitigator of pain and strength to continue living. "When you see me laughing, I'm laughing to keep from cryin'," he quotes, "but the laughter of these songs, implicit or overt, as often as not, absorbs the tears." (Hughes 1966: 97) Humor and deferential behavior ensured another tomorrow. Humor has healing power to mitigate inequality and domination. "White people in the South may never fully know the extent to which Negroes defended themselves and protected their jobs—and in

---

26 See Alice Walker "Uncle Remus: No Friend of Mine" in Southern Exposure. Spring 1981, vol. 9, no. 2, pp. 29–31.
    "Joel Chandler Harris and the Invention of Uncle Remus. The Dummy in the Window" *Living by theWord: Selected Writings.* Mariner Books. 1989. Walker was born and raised in Eatonton, GA, the hometown of Harris. Offering her perspective a hundred years later, she takes issue with the Brer Rabbit stories she was told by her family as to those put down on paper by Harris, and takes issue with Harris's role in social relations and literature.
27 The Chittlin' Circuit was a network of clubs and theaters mainly in the South and the East where Black entertainers could perform, mainly to Black audiences. It parodied the established Borscht Belt in the Northeast that provided venues for Jewish performers. Segregation laws were very strict. Few Black performers played before White audiences, and where they did were required to use service entrances, could not mingle with audience members, and could not stay in White hotels or eat in White restaurants. Chittlin's refers to a dish prepared from pork chitterlings, or small intestines, known well in Black dining.

many cases their lives—by perfecting an air of ignorance and agreement." (Hughes 1966: 253). I referred earlier to my personal experience of viewing Disney's "Song of the South" in 1956. Created in 1946, it reflects the persistent image of the pleasant and uneducated Black in relation to the well-spoken and well-dressed White people. The dialect of Uncle Remus has been lightened a bit, but the stereotype is still very clear. The film has suffered under contemporary scrutiny of political correctness, but it stands as a representation of perceptions and expressions of its time. The Tar Baby Story is presented very similarly in content to the original Harris version, though a little moralizing is provided for our edification. "To be sho'," Uncle Remus addresses the White Boy Johnny, "Jes' like Brer Rabbit when he took 'n' stuck his foot inna somthin' he don't know nothin' about an ain't had no business mixin up with in the firs' place … Brer Rabbit bein' little 'n' without much strength is supposed to use his head 'stead of his foots." (Disney, 1946) Interestingly, Disney had no problem showing the White boy and the little White girl skipping through the forest with the Black boy. The character of the Black as a congenial and non-threatening servant to White interests that was created for the film media in the early part of the 20th century, was carried through to television audiences into the 1960's. That image was very standard, one-dimensional, and rarely challenged. Other attributes of criminality, laziness, and lack of intelligence derived from these standard characterizations. That was the way it was, and many felt no harm was being done. After all, this was entertainment; we laughed because we thought it was funny. In a racially divided society, only a couple of generations removed from slavery, Negro humor maintained what many believed were the proper relationships between the Blacks and the Whites.

The Civil Rights movement that began in the mid 1950's and the effect of social integration in the 1960's changed Blacks' social relation to Whites, and changed the nature and tone of Negro humor as well. Black performers shunned the stereotypes and criticized their demeaning effects. The examples of Sidney Poitier, Bill Cosby, Dick Gregory, and Godfrey Cambridge have already been mentioned. They spoke boldly about the effects of racism and discrimination. They dressed well and spoke eloquently.

Comedians today still address the cultural divide that exists between the races. The television program "In Living Color" (1990–1994) showcased the talents of Keenan Ivory Wayans, his brother Damon, Jamie Foxx and many others. Chris Rock and Dave Chapelle appear in movies and on cable tv. There are still wide gaps in understanding of life experienced in contemporary America. The opportunity exists now to listen to these voices of different perspectives, and to appreciate through humor how we see ourselves and each other. It is important to know through historical perspectives where we stand in relationship to what came before. It is with this mind that musician, political activist, and scholar Julius Lester retold the Uncle Remus stories for our time, the end of the 20th century and the beginning of the 21st; the age of globalization and technological communication. He understood the heritage of these tales from ancestral West African communities. He also understood, and felt, the distraction of the heavy dialect and politics of Harris's renditions. And yet, he desired to make these stories a part of our contemporary culture, to be shared and passed on to future generations. The narrative remains the same, Rabbit gets stuck in tar because he is offended, and he convinces Fox to send him to his worst imagined fate. But Lester has streamlined the wording, "He snatched him off the Tar Baby and wound up his arm like he was trying to throw a fast ball past Hank Aaron and chunked that rabbit across the road and smack dab in the middle of the briar patch." (Lester 1987: 16)

The creation and maintenance of stereotypes has a four-fold effect. Stereotypes are created out of a perception of difference. Attributes may be real or imagined, yet they reflect perceptions shared within a group. Thus, stereotypes are a manifestation of group identity. Stereotypes in and of themselves are not valued and may function as neutral markers of differentiation. However, in the United States, built on the institution of the enslavement of Black Africans, racial stereotypes reinforced the dominant status of the White population in relationship to the subjugated Black population. The four-fold effect of the perpetuation of these stereotypes defined the relationship of White people to Blacks, and of Black people to Whites. It also defined what Black people thought of themselves, and what White people thought of themselves. The stereotypes were different of course for each application as they reflected inter-group dynamics, and they also varied from person to person as they reflected individual thought processes and experiences. That said, each form of social interaction utilizes stereotypes that are congruent with each individual's worldview and that group's social identity. Group identity is based on ascribed status, shared cultural traits and values, internal cohesion and interaction, and self awareness (Apte 1985: 111). Two identities are at play simultaneously: Self-identity (this is who we think we are) and The Other identity (this is who we think you are). The Whites, being the dominant population, established the rules. The Blacks, being enslaved, at least had to outwardly accept those rules. They had different perceptions of themselves and of White people, but could rarely overtly express them. Stereotypes were constructed on attributes, either real or imagined. These attributes include common origin, common culture or customs, religion, race or physical characteristics, language, consciousness of kind, common values or ethos, separate institutions, and minority status. One can see how these attributes helped to construct stereotypes in each of the four applications. Depending on the quality of the interactions of the social groups, these attributes may become exaggerated or transformed into something that has no basis in reality at all. They are examples of faulty reasoning processes that short-circuit critical thinking. They become emotionally loaded, misrepresent information, and interestingly enough, persist even after knowledge proves them to be wrong (Apte 1985: 114). The human mind is engineered to organize and classify. It is most adept at processing information gathered about other humans. We as social creatures are most productive in group activities. We construct groups based on perceived common attributes and perceived common goals. We ascribe values and relatedness based on the groups we form and belong to and create emotional bonds through cooperative labor and shared successes. We have built loyalty through positive social interaction and created a group identity. We believe we are like each other and think of ourselves as kin. Those who are not part of our group are not like us. They have not shared in our work and accomplishments. They are different; they don't even look like us; they have different values. Social hierarchies develop through imbalances of power, asymmetrical relationships, and conscious manipulation of group identity. Values are placed on perceived attributes and stereotypes are created to maintain these structures of power. As Pascal Boyer points out: "Racial stereotypes are among the representations that people create to interpret their own intuition that members of other groups represent a real danger and threaten their own coalitional advantages." (Boyer 2001: 290) Social conflict is, in the mind of Mahadev Apte (1985: 144), not always openly expressed but exists where there is a differential status of population groups. This enforced inequality expresses itself in negative assaults by the superior group on the inferior group. Humor is often considered a means to relieve tension to resolve conflict; " ... fun is made of the perceived behavior, customs, personality, or any other traits of a group or its members by virtue of their specific sociocultural identity." (Apte 1985: 108) However, humor sometimes becomes an aggressive tool of social control. Whether conscious or unconscious some forms of Negro humor used by Whites were expressions of hostility and fear. For the Whites, the humor based on the caricatures of Black people created a sense of emotionally distancing themselves from the realities of slavery, enhanced their feelings of superiority, and provided a rationalization and justification for their treatment of Blacks. The Blacks as a group knew they were not as the White people perceived them, but were generally powerless to change those perceptions. The humor they created channeled their hostility and aggression through emotional outlets, and shared amongst themselves their own perceptions of White people. They maintained their own personal dignity and strengthened their group solidarity knowing that in some very important ways, White people had no power over them.

I have benefited from living part of my life as a part of the Black community and learning how to see the world from their point of view. I have understood how subtle and often unintentional discrimination and prejudice can be expressed. I have felt the pain of being on the outside and without, at being laughed at and taunted, and finding no humor in these humiliating situations. I have also come to appreciate how laughter and humor can help to sustain the oppressed through the most inhumane conditions, to provide the spirit to carry on to another day, and to provide positive expression for a troubled heart.

The enslavement of Black Africans is a tremendous part of our American history and we have yet to come to adequate terms with it. The rise of Negro humor during this period was a strategy for Blacks and Whites to define who they were to each other. Amongst the Blacks, their humor was a means to maintain some essences of their African culture, to provide power and strength to deal with adversity, and as a weapon to use against their White oppressors. For the Whites, Negro humor was a way to create distance between themselves and the Blacks, to ameliorate the harsh realities of slavery and racial discrimination, and to provide justification for the perpetuation of domination and subjugation. Negro humor has evolved as the nature of American society has evolved. Efforts to achieve equality, integration, and harmony have always been met by resistance and pushback. Racial humor now can be a way to educate each other, and provide means of understanding, bridging the gaps of experience, and create genuine bonds of humanity.

Bibliography

Abrahams, Roger D. (1983): *African Folktales: Traditional Stories of the Black World*. Pantheon Books. New York.

Apte, Mahadev L. (1985): *Humor and Laughter: An Anthropological Approach*. Cornell University Press. Ithaca.

Boyer, Pascal (2001): *Religion Explained: The Evolutionary Origins of Religious Thought*. Basic Books. New York City.

Davidheiser, Mark (2005): Special Affinities and Conflict Resolution: West African Social Institutions and Mediation. In *Beyond Intractability*. Eds. Guy Burgess and Heidi Burgess. Conflict Information Consortium, University of Colorado, Boulder. Posted: December 2005. (http://www.beyondintractability.org/bi-essay/joking-kinship.)

Disney (1946): *Song of the South*. Wilfred Jackson and Harve Foster, directors. Walt Disney Productions. Buena Vista Film Distribution Co. 1999. Original release 1946.

The Elocutionist's Annual. (1889): *The Elocutionist's Annual*, Number 17. The Latest and Best Selections for Reading or Recitation. Compiled by Mrs. J.W.Shoemaker. The Penn Publishing Company. Philadelphia. (http://books.google.com/books.)

Harris, Joel Chandler (1880): *Uncle Remus: His Songs and His Sayings*. Appleton-Century-Crofts. New York.

Hughes, Langston, ed. (1966): *The Book of Negro Humor in America*. Dodd, Mead & Company. New York City.

Lester, Julius (1987): *The Tales of Uncle Remus: The Adventures of Brer Rabbit*. Dial Books. New York.

Minstrel Gags and End Men's Jokes (1969): Literature House. Upper Saddle River NJ. (c. 1875.)

Schechter, William (1970): *The History of Negro Humor in America*. Fleet Press Corporation. New York City.

Wittke, Carl (1968): *Tambo and Bones: A History of the American Minstrel Stage*. Greenwood Press. New York City. (Duke University Press. 1930).

Chapter 8

TOWARD RELIGION ...
My Religion, Not Yours

Humor in Religion

by Mahadev Apte (1985)

F ew aspects of human behavior have been studied as extensively as religion. Religion seems highly influential in shaping cultural values and in molding and maintaining social organization in human societies everywhere. It is a ubiquitous form of human behavior and is reflected in culturally complex elaborations. Religion resembles humor and language in being omnipresent, pervasive, and yet unobtrusive at the level of individual consciousness in the way in which it affects the rest of human behavior. Anthropological studies show that humor has been intimately connected with religion in many cultures. The concept of religion used in this chapter follows its broad-based interpretation in anthropological research (Malefijt 1968b; A. F. C. Wallace 1966), including the major components briefly described below.

Conceptualization. A primary concept of religion is that of the supernatural, which may include beings, objects, and spirits—in short, all metaphysical forces over which human beings exert little or no control. In addition, religion includes notions of the universe and incorporates ideas of morality and ethics that lead to distinctions between good and evil, benevolent and malevolent, and sacred and profane. These conceptualizations are closely interrelated and structurally interdependent.

Behavior. Any behavior that attempts to control or appease supernatural forces so as to affect human life positively from birth through death and beyond is considered religious. Such behavior is generally institutionalized and includes prayers, rituals, and rites. The primary purpose of such behavior is the well-being of a society and of individuals, from both the materialistic and the spiritualistic perspectives.

Actors and institutions. Certain individuals and institutions are primarily responsible for the propagation and sustenance of religious systems. Such individuals may claim to have special powers, enabling them to play a vital role in practicing and directing religious behavior of members of a culture and to act as links between them and the supernatural forces in the universe. Priests, shamans, saints, ritual clowns, and other religious leaders constitute a special group that develops religious instructions through customs, ceremonies, and rituals. I use the term "institution" to mean organized activity: it is patterned, recurrent, and involves aggregates of people.

Texts. Scriptures, mythologies, and other oral and/or written accumulated bodies of knowledge that explain the origin and the nature of the universe constitute religious texts. They also explain acts of creation and destruction of organisms, objects, and the life of human beings. Such a body of knowledge may also expound on the socially acquired moral and ethical codes and on their justification. All religions in the world have such accumulated knowledge.

After the joking relationship, humor in religion has received the most extensive attention from anthropologists. Clowning and other comical performances have been reported as part of religious ceremonies in ethnographic accounts of cultures from various parts of the world. Both ethnographic and ethnological studies of humor in religion exist, concentrating on the American–Indians, and date from the last quarter of the nineteenth century to the present. The primary reason for the existence of such extensive anthropological materials may be that humor has been a major feature of both rituals and mythologies of American–Indian religions.

In their ethnographic and theoretical studies of African societies, British social anthropologists noted what they considered to be unusual acts that formed part of African religions. Rituals with clowning and other incongruous acts in North India and Sri Lanka have also been described. Rites involving comical and amusing acts as part of the popular Christian rituals in Europe during the medieval period have been analyzed, and accounts of such activities in some parts of Western Europe even in modern time are available. Humorous aspects of rituals have also been explored from a cross-cultural perspective. The humorous and incongruous acts and the rites and rituals of which they are part have been labeled "Rites of Reversal" (Norbeck 1974), "Rituals of Conflict" (Norbeck 1963), "Rituals of Rebellion" (Gluckman 1963), "Institutionalized Licence" (Van den Berghe 1963), and "Licenced Rebellion" (D. B. Miller 1973). These labels suggest that one reason for the anthropological interest in the humorous aspects of religion in preliterate societies may have been the "exotic" nature of the rites, since they often involved scatological and sexual acts that appeared to be a strange combination of the "sacred" and the "profane" to the Western mind.

Interest in humor in religion from the perspective of play has also been growing. I discussed in an earlier chapter the complexity of the concept of play, the broad domain it covers, and the extensive research into its relevance for human existence. Because play has been viewed as the opposite of work, acts that seem antithetical to the seriousness and sacredness of religious rituals have been interpreted as playful acts contrasting with and reemphasizing symbolically the important ethical values of religion. The concept of play in this context includes sports and other games occurring at ceremonial occasions in many preliterate societies. Because play and humor have a close but complex interconnection, interest in "rites of reversal" within the framework of play has also been beneficial to studies of humor in religion. The notion that even the supernatural elements engage in play affecting the universe and human destiny has been significant in Hinduism and other religions.

In analyzing humor in religion, I shall focus on discerning its general attributes and the nature of its linkages to the institution of religion with respect to social–structural factors, behavioral patterns, and ideologies and values in a cross-cultural perspective. My objective is to formulate some hypotheses based on analyses of the interconnections between humor and religion. I shall also briefly evaluate theories of humor in religion. The dichotomy between religious behavior and the religious conceptual system is crucial to my overall discussion; religious behavior includes rituals and their characteristics, while the conceptual system subsumes mythologies and other religious texts. In this chapter I shall discuss only ritual humor. Humor in mythology and folklore, especially the widespread trickster theme, will be analyzed in a later chapter.

Ceremonial Bases of Humor

Rituals, rites, and ceremonials are conventional activities involving interaction with supernatural forces. Ceremonies constitute ways of appeasing nature and of coming to terms with it for the continued well-being of individuals and social groups. Anthropologists generally classify such activities into two broad categories: calendrical rituals and life cycle rituals.

Calendrical rituals are associated with seasonal changes, especially the transition from a winter to a summer solstice or the start and completion of agricultural cycles. Depending on geographical location and climate, a particular season can be a time for much religious activity. Calendrical rituals also include other important events, such as birth and death anniversaries of mythical heroes, saints, and saviors. Such ceremonial occasions seem to occur more frequently in societies that have well-established scriptures, which usually indicate important events in the life of prophets and other mythical and epic heroes.

Life cycle rituals, commonly known as "rites of passage" (Van Gennep 1909/1960), are religious activities associated with important events in the human life cycle—birth, puberty, entry into adulthood, marriage, pregnancy, childbirth, old age, and finally death. Such rituals signify the transition from one life stage to another and the accompanying change in social status. They are important because of the widespread belief that individuals who are in a transitional or liminal stage, that is, in between clearly identified life stages, are likely to be more affected by supernatural spirits and thus need to be protected. Rites of passage acquire significance also because certain rights and privileges publicly accrue to individuals in specific life states. Initiation rites in many societies, for example, mark the transition to manhood, and the new status permits young men to participate in activities from which they were formerly excluded.

Although calendrical rituals are generally more group oriented than rites of passage, both can and do involve group participation. Initiation and puberty rites in many African societies, for instance, involve large-scale group activities when they are performed for several individuals simultaneously. Religious ceremonies serve as occasions for changes of pace and for change of routine. They provide diversions from work, opportunities for entertainment and fun, a change in diet, and a relaxation of social norms. Rituals, then, signify the importance of religion to members of a culture, mark important social and calendrical occasions, and note the ensuing special status accorded to some individuals. Dramatization is the most effective and significant technique used within the framework of rituals. It takes many forms. Its most essential ingredients are action, play, cultural symbols, masks, costumes, tools and other paraphernalia, and special means of communication. Drama is both entertaining and educational. Humor plays a significant role in dramatization and is often the primary mode of entertainment, especially in preliterate societies.

Ritual Humor: General Attributes and Techniques Used

Numerous ethnographic accounts of rituals in different cultures suggest that the following properties are typical of ritual humor: an absence of social control; behavior contrary to established cultural norms; extensive sexual and scatological elements; a burlesque of rituals, people in authority, and foreigners; and an appearance of disorder and chaos.

The Suspension of Social Control

Much ritual humor appears to be rooted in the suspension of social control over verbal and nonverbal behavior and appearance. Individuals who engage in ritual humor have considerable freedom to depart from conventional behavior and to parody activities that are strongly disapproved in normal everyday social interaction or are even taboo. The removal of social control during rituals results in both unstructured and structured humor stimuli. The unstructured nature of humor is evident in the spontaneous and often unpredictable behavior of entertainers, who may engage in whatever suits their fancy, impulsively switching from one activity to another. They chase spectators, play practical jokes on members of the audience and on each other, engage in banter and horseplay, simulate sexual behavior, drink and eat all kinds of nonedible objects, wear absurd-looking costumes or no clothes at all, jump, dance, exaggeratedly imitate others, perform numerous types of antics, and generally frolic.

On the other hand, behavior as a part of ritual humor can be considered structured in the sense that it may be the exact reverse of behavior commensurate with social roles and customs. Alternatively, humor creation may be highly routinized in that the same stimuli may be used regularly year after year, and actions and their sequences, costumes, and props may become standardized. The same skits and short dramas may be presented routinely, with the same individuals playing the same roles. Although the dichotomy between the structured and the unstructured development of ritual humor is theoretically relevant, the two aspects are not totally separate in reality. Even when behavior is highly conventionalized, individual innovation often occurs. There is much improvisation and variation among individual entertainers, who display fervor and originality in humor.

Contrary Behavior

The reversal of established or common behavioral patterns associated with sex, social roles, and social status is characteristic of ritual humor. In every society people essentially follow the established cultural ways of eating, dressing, sleeping, playing, talking, and carrying out other routine tasks. Interpersonal interaction in social situations is also governed by cultural norms, as is behavior appropriate to specific roles. During rituals humorists often do the opposite. Anthropological literature commonly refers to such conduct as contrary behavior, inverse behavior, or reversal. Reversal occurs not only in behavior but also in physical appearances and in other aspects. Contrary behavior can occur collectively or individually. Ethnographic data indicate that such behavior is manifested primarily in three ways: by sexual inversion, by status inversion, and by routine behavioral inversion.

Transvestism is one of the most common modes of sexual inversion within ceremonial contexts. One sex simulates not only the appearance but also the overall behavioral patterns of members of the other sex and is achieved by the use of clothing, ornaments, body decoration, and even artificial sexual organs. Body motions as well as stylistic acts characteristic of the sexes are imitated. Much humor associated with ritual transvestism is generated by the incongruity between physical features and costumes characteristic of one sex and exaggeration of behavior associated with the other. Such transvestism is widespread in African societies during initiation ceremonies for boys and girls. Among the Masai of Central Africa, for example, young men wear the dress of married women during periods of recovery from circumcision (Huntingford 1953:116). Among the Nupe of Nigeria, transvestite boys comically imitate the walk, gestures, and manners of dancing women (Nadel 1954:82, 218). The inversion of sex roles also occurs in the context of other rituals and ceremonials. In the Zinacantecan communities of Highland Chiapas in Mexico, men masquerade as grandmothers during the Christmas and New Year festivals, wearing outfits normally worn by women, but behave like men and "express most dramatically how incongruous and inappropriate masculine behavior is for those who wear women's clothing" (Bricker 1973:15). Feminine conduct seems to be a common theme of clowns in spiritual and seasonal rituals among many American–Indian tribes (Parsons and Beals 1934; Steward 1931).

The inversion of social status in manifested by the ridicule of people in authority. In everyday social interaction, persons of high status have power and authority. This pattern is reversed during ceremonies. Individuals with status often become the butt of caricature, pantomime, parody, and burlesque and are ridiculed especially if they have overused their authority and power. Such spoofs are often carried out by people with low social status and without authority and power. At the other extreme are people of high social status who behave in a manner totally incongruent with their position by acting like common people. Both, then, manifest status inversion. During the potlatch ceremonies among the Kwakiutl Indians, skits are presented in which the host and his family are made to look foolish for the amusement of participants, and this is done with the host family's full participation (Codere 1956:339); the family just demonstrated high status by giving the potlatch. During the spring festival of *Holi* in North India, women of low castes chase and pretend to beat up elderly Brahmin men, especially those who are otherwise considered to be village leaders. Young men shout obscenities at old men and on occasion may make them the victims of practical jokes. The elders are not supposed to retaliate but are merely expected to protect themselves by running away or by taking shelter (Marriott 1966/1968; D. B. Miller 1973).

Contrary behavior not related to social status and sex roles also occurs as part of rituals. Such behavior is merely the reverse of everyday routine acts of speaking, walking, sitting, and so forth. Among the American–Indians of the plains and southwestern United States, for instance, clowns speak in terms that are contrary to their actual meaning. The Arapaho clowns pretend not to notice carrying a heavy load but groan under the weight of a light object (Kroeber 1902–1907:192, as quoted in Makarius 1970:63).

Sexual and Scatological Elements

Ritual humor is characterized by verbal and nonverbal activities of a sexual and scatological nature, perhaps because of the absence of social control. Obscene singing by participants and verbal repartee among clowns or between clowns and the audience with references to sexual organs and activities often form part of the ceremonials. Ba-Thonga men, for example, sing obscene songs and insult women, who retaliate by uttering obscenities at the men's expense during the selection of a new site for a village (Evans-Pritchard 1929). During the Christmas Day celebrations among the Abron of Ivory Coast, male performers insult the crowd by uttering obscenities, which are greeted with much laughter (Alland 1975:138). Obscene banter and joke telling occur during the carnival in the regions of Rhineland and Bavaria in Germany (Van den Berghe 1963).

Nonverbal obscene and scatological behavior as part of ritual humor is also widespread. Ritual clowns among the Hopi, Zuni, Arapaho, and Mayo Indians wear large artificial penes made of wooden sticks or knives (Crumrine 1969:7; Steward 1931:193). A lump of wood is bound to a boy's penis during the initiation ceremony among the A-Kamba in Africa and "in this condition he marches amid roars of laughter" (Evans-Pritchard 1929:318). Obscene horseplay, the touching and grabbing of sexual organs, the chasing of women and young girls, and pretended phallic advances toward them are common practices on the part of clowns at rituals among the Yakut, Yuki, Ponca, and other American–Indian tribes. Simulated sexual intercourse with each other or suggestive play with an artificial phallus and simulated masturbation are also part of ritual obscenity among these clowns.

The scatological aspects of ritual humor are just as varied. Ritual clowns of the Pueblo Indians "simulated eating and drinking the excreta they would pretend to catch in their wooden machete from the body of passing burro or horse or man or woman, even of one kneeling in prayer" (Parsons and Beals 1934:491). The drenching of other clowns or even spectators with urine or with urine mixed with feces or mud is widespread in ritual humor recorded among American–Indians and villagers in North India. Simulated defecation is a common scatological act of clowns and occurs in various contexts.

Burlesque

Humor development within the context of rituals also draws on caricature, burlesque, and the parody of social institutions, of the ritual themselves, and of foreigners and authority figures. This practice seems quite widespread, as the following examples illustrate. There is much cross-cultural variation, however. Humor development of this kind may be carried out individually by a person of either sex, regardless of age or social status, or collectively by a whole group. The social status of people who burlesque the various targets may have significance in some societies and not in others. On the other hand, among many American–Indian tribes, such acts may be carried out only by ritual clowns. The question of the performer's identity will be discussed later in this chapter.

Occasionally it is difficult to identify the target of burlesque during the rituals. The reason is that the object of ridicule depends on the focus within the context of rituals, which may shift periodically. Furthermore, the burlesque of the ritual itself cannot be considered apart from the identity of the performers; because the performers of rituals may themselves be persons of authority, humor of this kind caricatures not only the rituals per se but also the authority figures. Sometimes nonperformers of social prominence are ridiculed, and at other times outsiders become the target. The main point, however, is that rituals provide immunity to individuals who want to ridicule persons in authority within their own society.

Among the Yaqui Indians in Arizona, the traditional clowns known as *pascolas* and *fariseos* burlesque serious things in public ceremonies. While a marriage ceremony is being solemnly affirmed, the pascolas just a few feet away carry out an absurd burlesque of it that is charged with obscenity. During the Easter ritual, the masked pascolas leap and shiver and scrape imaginary filth from their legs whenever the name of Mary or God is mentioned. The clowns interfere with the members of the ceremonial societies, dangling toy monkeys before their faces in the middle of their prayers and sacred chants (Spicer 1940). Zinacantecan ritual clowns mock ceremonies, ritual curing prayers, and dances by introducing sexual and obscene connotations (Bricker 1973:31, 37). They also mock prayers of religious officials by exaggerated actions, crossing themselves with their rattles and praying loudly and ludicrously. The ritual clowns disguised as grandfathers exchange stick horses, mimicking the exchange of ceremonial flags between religious officials.

Among the Kiwai Papuans, characters called Imigi perform clowning acts during the great secret ceremony associated with the cult of the dead. The Imigi make obscene gestures at women, run helter-skelter, and also pretend to attack the spirits. All of this activity is considered very amusing by the audience (Landtman 1927:394, as quoted in Charles 1945:28). Women conduct play potlatching among the Kwakiutl Indians of the northwest coast, during which ridiculously small and valueless objects are distributed and participants are given funny names. Objects that are given away are often not owned by the donors. The customary giving of speeches is lampooned by the making of ridiculous claims. In general, then, play potlatches mock the whole potlatch ritual (Codere 1956).

Such mockery of the sacred elements and rituals is not of recent origin. During the holiday known as the "Feast of Fools," which flourished in parts of Europe during the medieval period, serious-minded commoners and priests who were ordinarily pious painted their faces, "strutted about in the robes of their superiors," and in general "mocked the stately rituals of the church and court" (Cox 1969/1972:1). Sometimes an ass was introduced into church during this festival while the Prose of the Ass was chanted. On such occasions a solemn mass was punctuated with brays and howls. In general, the composition of satirical verse, the performance of topical plays, and the preaching of burlesque sermons formed an important part of the Feast of Fools activities (Welsford 1935:200–203). The ceremony was condemned and criticized by the higher officials of the church. Nonetheless, it survived until the sixteenth century and gradually died out during the Reformation and Counter Reformation.

The burlesquing of foreigners appears to be a major stimulus of ritual humor, especially among American–Indians. Steward (1931:197) described it as one of the major themes of humor and provided many examples from previous ethnographic accounts of rituals among the Hopi and other tribes of the southwestern United States and among the Kwakiutl, Winnebago, and Iroquois. During the rituals, the appearance, costumes, and customs of the white man were spoofed. Occasionally, individual tribes caricatured other neighboring Indian tribes in similar fashion; the Yoruk and Maidu Indians seem to do so. Such humor probably helped develop community solidarity, because the whole community could empathize with the performer. No community member was the butt, and the caricaturing helped express collective fear, envy, contempt, or feeling of superiority with respect to the outsiders.

Disorder and Chaos

Although the burlesque of rituals, authority figures, and foreigners is a major aspect of ritual humor, other ceremonial activities, such as dancing, food preparation, sports and games, and processions are also imitated. Such imitations, however, must be out of tune with the activities being burlesqued before humor can develop. When clowns in American–Indian rituals imitate dancers, for example, they are always one step behind and pretend to miss the rhythm. In sports and games, the clowns fumble and break the rules. While the ritual ceremonies are going on, they dart in and out of processions, interrupt verbal incantations with their loud remarks and comments, perform all sorts of disruptive antics, and generally try to undermine any organized activity. In other words, the creation of disorder in the middle of order to give the appearance of incongruity is a chief goal of people who develop ritual humor.

Verbal obscenities, insults, ridicule, practical jokes, the exaggerated imitation of events, actions, and persons, and uninhibited behavior culminating in simulation of sexual and scatological acts appear to be the primary techniques used in ritual humor. Audio and visual aids and modalities are equally important in humor development because of the emphasis on imitating appearance and nonverbal behavior in addition to verbal communication. Costumes, masks, and other paraphernalia are generally used. The ethnographic accounts suggest that, on the whole, visual and action-oriented stimuli are just as important as verbal in ritual humor.

Ritual Humorists: Identity and Social Status

There is much cross-cultural variation regarding the choice of ritual humorists on the basis of such factors as their position within the context of ceremonials and their overall social status in the society at large. Cultures range from those in which any person of whatever social background and status can participate in humor-generating activities to those in which only a specially designated and socially high-ranking group of individuals can do so. Similarly, a single individual, or one or more groups of persons each identified on the basis of some specific sociocultural attributes, may be humorists. In some cultures, such groups may consist of specialists whose primary role is humor development, and they may act in an organized manner. In other cultures, engaging in humor may be a mass activity, so that a "free-for-all" situation exists. A major reason for the cross-cultural differences in the choice of ritual humorists is that such selection is structurally interconnected with the rest of the cultural system. It depends on and is affected by such sociocultural factors as the type of ritual involved and its significance for participants and for the community at large, the fundamental religious ideology underlying the ritual(s), the nature of social organization, ecological factors, and attitudes toward ritual humor in terms of the techniques used and the humor's effects.

The dichotomy between calendrical rituals and rites of passage is significant in determining who will engage in humor. It appears that, in rituals of the latter type, humor-generating activities are generally undertaken by relatives or friends of the individuals going through the ritual or by people who are connected with the ceremony itself in some way. Some examples follow. During funeral rites in such East African tribes as the Plateau Tonga, Kaguru, Luguru and others, only the funeral partner who is also the joking partner of the deceased in the utani relationship [...] is supposed to joke and ridicule the deceased. Such a funeral relationship may exist either with one or more members of a clan that has the utani relationship with the deceased's clan (Beidelman 1966; Christensen 1963; Colson 1953:53–54)· During the final phase of Tiwi funeral rites in Australia attended by the relatives of the deceased and members of other clans, mock fighting between all actual and potential spouses takes place. There is a great deal of shouting, with squeals of laughter, because tickling is also part of the fighting activity (Goodale 1971:287–88).

During wedding ceremonies in some cultures, women of either the bride's or the groom's side have the prerogative to engage in humor, and they do so mostly by burlesquing sexual activity, by singing obscene songs that may make fun of the bridegroom, or by parodying local social events. Such is the case in North India (E. O. Henry 1975; Jacobson 1977) and among the Magars in Nepal (Hitchcock 1966) and the Gimi of New Guinea (Gillison 1977). In many African tribes mock battles take place between members of the bride's kinsmen and those of the bridegroom (Norbeck 1963:1264). Puberty rites of boys and girls are also occasions for specific groups or individuals to engage in humor. Among the Gusii of East Africa, only mothers and other female relatives perform obscene and lewd acting and dancing, using artificial phalli during the girls' puberty rites (B. B. Whiting 1963:189). On the other hand, boys put on women's clothes and burlesque women's behavior during their initiation ceremonies in some African tribes (Norbeck 1963:1257–58).

Sometimes beliefs concerning life seem to influence the choice of the person who will engage in humor. In some African societies, calendrical rites at the start of the agricultural cycle involve licentious behavior, obscene joking, and nude dancing by women. The same thing occurs when a new site for a village is to be chosen. Perhaps women perform these activities because of their association with fertility, because the goal is a bountiful harvest or rapid growth of a new village. Among the American–Indian tribes of the Southwest, however, only male sacred clowns are associated with fertility rites (Steward 1931:199).

Social status and specific roles appear to determine which individuals will develop humor and which will be the target in the context of some ritual. It appears that in certain rituals the normally subordinate segments of society ignore behavioral constraints and take the lead in humor development. Generally, women constitute such a group in patrilineal societies; young men and women in societies with a geron-tocracy; and several groups with menial occupations and low socioeconomic status in highly stratified societies. These groups ignore societal norms and poke fun at their superiors during some rituals, and hence these are rites of reversal. Membership in secret societies, fraternities, or similar organizations often brings with it the privilege of humor development at specific rituals, as has been recorded for many American–Indian tribes. Among the Plains Indians, only members of secret societies participate in contrary behavior at rituals that provide many humor stimuli. Among the Yaqui, Hopi, and other Indians of the southwestern United States, there are clown societies, and only members seem to develop humor during rituals.

Perhaps no category of individuals occupies so distinct a position in developing humor among the American–Indian tribes of North and Central America as the ceremonial buffoons (Steward 1931), sacred fools (Beck and Walters 1977), sacred clowns (Parsons and Beals 1934), and ritual clowns (Crumrine 1969; Honigmann 1942; Makarius 1970). Although clowning has been noted to occur in many societies (Charles 1945), American–Indian ritual clowns and their activities constitute perhaps the most institu-tionalized development of ritual humor in any culture area of the world. The ritual clowning complex was a highly developed phenomenon among the Indians in much of North and Central America except the east coast (Steward 1931). Much cross-cultural variation concerning the form and substantive aspects of ritual clowning existed in areas where it was well developed, but some generalizations can be made.

Ritual clowns among the American–Indians seem to have two major attributes: they belong to spe-cific types of associations, fraternities, secret societies, and cults; and they are associated with various supernatural spirits and special powers. These attributes are reflected in the kind of humor in which ritual clowns engage and in the objects and techniques they use. Among the Yaqui, Hopi, and other southwestern Indians there are phallic clown societies. Ritual clowns belong to medicine societies in some Indian tribes, while in others they are members of military and secret societies or are associated with fertility cults. Clowns among the Zuni, Acoma, Hopi, Navaho, Apache, Iroquois, Cheyenne, Pa-pago, and other Indian tribes are believed to have powers to ensure success in war and hunting. They are also believed able to cure sickness through magical healing (Makarius 1970:47ff.). Among some Indian groups it is believed that ritual clowns practice black magic (Makarius 1970:55).

It should be obvious, then, that ritual clowns occupy a unique position in many American–Indian cul-tures. They are laughed at, but they are also respected. They are loved for the humor they provide but are also feared. People regard them with awe and associate them with supernatural origins and power. They are allowed considerable liberty in their interactions with religious authorities and with other participants in rituals. While the nature and degree of the clowns' distinctness varies across cultures, they generally seem to have a unique identity both in the context of rituals and in society at large. In addition to provid-ing entertainment and humor, they serve other functions that I shall discuss shortly.

The Relevance of Humor to Rituals

Determining the relevance of humor to rituals is a complex task, since relevance may be manifested by the linkages between the two through form, techniques, content, performers, underlying myths, and so on. The type and nature of these linkages as well as the degree of relevance vary cross-culturally. Theoretically, the range of variation may include cultures in which humor is extraneous to rituals and those in which humor cannot be separated at all from rituals formally, conceptually, or in any other way. In reality, ritual humor in most cultures seems to fall somewhere in the middle in the sense that some of it is well integrated into the rituals, while some is marginally linked. For the purposes of my discussion, two types of linkages are considered significant in judging the relevance of humor to rituals: conceptual integration and functional integration.

Conceptual Integration

Humor can be relevant to rituals because of its integration into myths and into the religious ideologies that constitute the bases of rituals. Individuals who engage in humor within the context of rituals often assume an identity with supernatural spirits or mythological characters. In the myths of some American–Indian tribes, the spirits and other mythological figures are not only supernatural but antinatural in the sense that their appearance and behavior are contrary to nature and customs (Ray 1945:87). The assumed identity of both supernatural and antinatural spirits allows the humorists to simulate anatomical deformations and extraordinary verbal and nonverbal behaviors, including contrary behavior. Such appearances and behavior appear to be the major humor stimuli during rituals. During the winter, guardian spirit dances among many southeastern Plateau Indians such as the Flathead, Spokane, and Kalispel, for example, the ritual involves assumed identification with the bluejay character of mythological times. This identification permits the individuals to appear in unusual costumes and to behave in a contrary fashion. The audience is specifically directed *not* to laugh at the antics (Ray 1945:80), which suggests that they are indeed comic. Among the Plains Cree and Northern Paiute Indians, buffoons imitating antinatural spirits wear costumes that produce the effect of a great hump on the back. Other distorted anatomical features include elongated noses, faces made grotesque with paint, and lumps on the legs and belly (Ray 1945:85, 103, 107). An association of anatomical deformation and antinatural spirits such as monsters also occurs in Balinese puppet theater, where clowns appear with pot bellies, enormous mouths, and very short legs as they amuse the spectators (Charles 1945:27).

The association between supernatural or antinatural elements and mythological characters on the one hand and ritual clowns or buffoons on the other is further reflected in the identification of the American–Indian clowns with mythological figures including tricksters […]. The ceremonial clowns among the Acoma Indians represent Koshari, the original clown (Stirling 1942:65, as quoted in Makarius 1970:45), or trickster. The clowns among the Iroquois are traditionally related to a legendary hero called False Face. They wear masks with twisted noses symbolic of the contest between False Face and the Great Spirit, during which False Face's nose struck the mountain he was supposed to push (Speck 1949:69–70, as quoted in Makarius 1970:45–46). In several other Indian tribes, either similar associations between clowns and mythological trickster figures occur or the clowns are supposed to have originated from tricksters (Makarius 1970:45–46). The trickster's antics are a part of the mythological oral tradition in many American–Indian groups. The buffoons are treated as the trickster's descendants and are obligated to imitate him in their antics.

Although the nature and degree of the clowns' power vary cross-culturally, power in most cases is perceived to derive from the violation of rules and prohibitions. The clowns' magical and healing powers are often attributed to their breach of taboo, and a parallel is found in the case of the mythological trickster figure. Sexual and scatological humor based on sexual, oral, and anal behavior and humor based on ridiculing sacred decrees, mocking religious rituals, and symbolically defiling sacred objects result from the breaking of taboos. The numerous breaches of taboo committed by ritual clowns have been noted in anthropological literature, and Makarius (1970:53) even suggests that violation of taboo is the clowns' raison d'être.

In many instances of the representation of supernatural spirits, the role-playing must be comical and witty because the character from mythology is so perceived (Ray 1945:89–90). Among the Dakota Indians the clowns, who are members of the Heyoka society, are assumed to be threatened by thunder and lightning if they do not perform the contrary ceremony. Thus they are clowns "by the direct necessity, by the imperative demands of a vision" (Steward 1931:202). Among some Indian tribes individuals cannot be clowns unless they have had a vision or a dream. Among the Dakota Indians a person can become a ritual clown by having in a dream a vision of the god Iktomi or of one of the beasts associated with him. Iktomi can be considered an ideal representative of the pure trickster (Makarius 1970:45). The clowns among the Arapaho Indians belong to a "Fools' Lodge," the founder of which is Nihaca, the trickster (Makarius 1970:46, n. 2). The clowns among the Plains Indians perform contrary speech and action only as a result of a vision, usually of thunder or lightening. Thus religious sanction is the basis of ritual humor in many American–Indian groups.

Humor itself is often ritualized and is thus integrated into the religious system. Among the Dakota Indians, the Heyoka ritual is antinatural, as it is among the Ponca Indians. In other words, antinaturalness is an essential aspect of religious conceptualization as well as of ritual humor. In some American–Indian tribes, the ritualization of antinaturalness is highly institutionalized by the establishment of "contrary" societies, whose members regularly engage in antinatural rituals. Such societies exist among the Mandan, Hidatsa, Arapaho, Atsina, and Blackfoot Indians and have been adopted as part of the contrary ceremonies by other Indian tribes such as the Cheyenne (Ray 1945:104). The Cheyenne even developed a cult called the Contraries, while among the Arikari Indians the cult of Foolish People existed. The Mandan and Hidatsa Indians had such names as Crazy Dog or Real Dog for these societies.

The primary activities of the members of such societies are dancing and contrary behavior within the context of rituals. The dancers have considerable freedom and are permitted to engage in all manner of mischief; they act in foolish and extravagant ways that are reflected in contrary actions and speech and in animal imitations, for example, the howling of dogs. Among the Hidatsa, one form of unnatural behavior is the ceremonial practice of randomly embracing women regardless of closeness of kinship. Sacred objects are shown no respect, and proprieties are disregarded. Contrary behavior includes such activities as shooting arrows backward over the shoulder, interpreting instructions in reverse, and use of reverse speech, all of which are humor-generating stimuli. The most antinatural behavior among several tribes includes the trick of withdrawing meat from boiling water as part of the ceremony (Ray 1945:91ff.).

The Functional Relevance of Ritual Humorists

Humor is integrated into the overall structure of rituals in still other ways. Clowns are connected with ceremonies in numerous capacities and assist the organizers in successfully performing them. The degree of the clowns' involvement in rituals and ceremonies in capacities other than as humorists, however, varies across cultures.

As members of various societies, clowns among different American–Indian tribes undertake curing, fertility, or military functions (Steward 1931:198). In general, clowns may act as messengers, wood cutters, and water carriers; may urge people to attend church during Lent and Easter ceremonies; may maintain law and order; and may punish antisocial behavior (Bricker 1973; Crumrine 1969; Parsons and Beals 1934:507). Ritual clowns are disciplinarians of children among some tribes and are also used as bogeymen. As if their masks, appearance, and impersonations of supernatural beings were not sufficiently scary, the clowns often threaten to whip the children and frighten them in other ways (Norbeck 1961:309). Ritual clowns also have alternating duties as priests (Crumrine 1969; Makarius 1970), fulfilling many sacred duties and on occasion acting as priests. Among the Zuni Indians, for instance, the Koyemshi, that is, the ritual clowns, perform several rites, especially the rain and fertility ceremonies.

Ritual clowns among some American–Indian groups function as medicine men. Since they are presumed to have supernatural powers, they are often credited with healing. Body wastes such as urine and excrement of both humans and animals, or dirty water that the clowns pretend is urine and use in their scatological antics, are presumed to have magical power. These substances are sprinkled on the spectators or are drunk and spat upon individuals (Makarius 1970:47–51; Ray 1945:85). Among some American–Indian groups, the ritual clowns rarely do anything except engage in humor and thus are not fully integrated into rituals either conceptually or functionally. Such seems to be the case among the Hopi Indians (Parsons and Beals 1934:494).

Ritual Humor as Perceived by the Indigenous Population

Two issues have not been discussed by anthropologists analyzing ritual humor: first, how to determine whether or not the indigenous participants in and spectators at ceremonials consider the clowns' behavior humorous, and second, what kinds of evidence should be adequate for such a determination. Without some explicit statements regarding these matters, the ethnographers' views regarding the occurrence of ritual humor remain etic, that is, observer oriented and formed from outside the cultural system. In regard to the second issue, another problem arises, namely, the extent of indigenous opinions. When it comes to determining what is humorous, there is much intracultural variation. All generalizations therefore need to be viewed as tendencies rather than as absolute statements. If we keep this caveat in mind, various observations can be considered to provide evidence of the humorousness of clowns' acts; observed evidence would include spectators' frequent laughter at the clowns' behavior, ceremony officials' specific prohibition of laughter (Ray 1945:80; Seligman and Seligman 1950:356; Steward 1931:200), and so on. Occasionally, ethnographers have commented on the negative responses of spectators and participants to clowns' acts (Crumrine 1969:4, 12), in which case the acts constitute ritual humor only from the anthropologists' perspective. Similarly, broad generalizations without adequate evidence need to be treated as anthropologists' own views rather than as factual statements. Norbeck's (1961:207) generalization that ritual reversals among the American–Indians are perceived by the people to be funny but that similar behavior in African cultures is not necessarily so, for example, should be considered as his own opinion rather than as a factual generalization.

Theoretical Considerations

The widespread occurrence and diversity of ritual humor has led to a plethora of interpretations, theories, and explanations that are psychological, sociological, cyclical, historical, or symbolic in orientation. Among them, psychological and sociological theories seem prominent and have a functional focus. Some explanations are multifarious because the researchers who propose them feel that all aspects of ritual humor cannot be satisfactorily explained within a single theoretical framework. Some of the theories are particularistic, addressing ritual humor within the context of rituals, while others are universal, viewing ritual humor within the framework of presumed universal psychological attributes of humans.

A common thread that runs through psychological theories is the emphasis on conflict resolution and on release from tension. Theories differ, however, regarding the nature of the tension, its causes, and its release. Some theories draw on the Freudian theoretical framework, while others refer to the context of the rituals themselves. Jacob Levine (1961), for instance, claims that tension exists due to intrapsychic struggle between impulse and defense: on the one hand, there are infantile, instinctual impulses of aggression and sexuality in an individual, and on the other, these are inhibited because of the censuring function of the superego, which causes guilt and anxiety leading to tension. Ritual humor makes possible the dissipation or release of such tension. Unfortunately, this explanation can be applied equally well to sexual and aggressive humor in secular social situations, and thus it fails to explain the significance of humor in the context of rituals satisfactorily. The same is true of other theoretical explanations.

Honigmann (1942) and Spicer (1954) also explain the role of ritual humor as the reduction of tension, but they see the occurrence of tension within the context of rituals. Honigmann claims that tension arises from feelings of frustration, powerlessness, and insecurity, which develop because opportunities for understanding the mystical experience of the ritual are lacking. Spicer argues that tension occurs primarily because of the extremely intense and complex interaction during rituals. Both writers see ritual humor as functioning to reduce tension: it produces social release, according to Honigmann, and comic relief, according to Spicer.

Particularistic psychological theories such as Spicer's appear plausible, because the occurrence of ritual humor is explained by the very nature of the rituals themselves. Spicer claims that increasing tension results from the intense and extended ceremonialism and also from the complex and highly charged social interaction. The tension needs to be dissipated for the continuation of the rituals. Spicer's theory seems possible in view of the fact that human beings are rarely, if ever, able to sustain any emotional state, or intense concentration, whether grief, anger, sorrow, mirth, or hilarity, for extended periods of time except when pathological conditions exist. In this context we should recall Darwin's comment (1872/1965:197) that only imbeciles have a perpetual smile on their faces or laugh frequently; most normal individuals smile and laugh only when appropriate stimuli are present. Ritual humor is necessary to allow participants to relieve their intense concentration and seriousness. Accounts of some ceremonies (Gossen 1976; Howard 1962) indicate precisely this transition from seriousness to light moods in ceremonies.

The nature of tension may vary, depending on the rituals involved. Gluckman (1963), for instance, states that, during the boys' circumcision ceremony among the Wiko people in Africa, tension occurs partly because aggression and sexual pleasure are banned in the village during the rites and also perhaps because circumcision symbolically signifies the separation of boys from their mothers as they enter the men's world. The tension is released by obscene humor, horseplay, mock fighting, and other similar activities in which adult men and women participate and symbolically display the sexual organs of the opposite sex.

Psychological theories that attempt to explain ritual humor in universalistic terms by alluding to human psychic tendencies emphasize neurosis, repression, and other psychopathological conditions. This is a rather negativistic perspective on human societies. In reality a culture is rarely a perfect functioning whole, just as it is rarely, if ever, in total anomie. Furthermore, the "innocent release of aggression" by way of catharsis becomes a catch-all concept for explaining ritual humor, if universalistic psychological theories of aggression dissipation are to be accepted. But such explanations are provided for other types of humor as well, including ethnic humor.

While Honigmann and Levine see the psychological function of ritual clowning as operating at both in individual and the societal levels, other researchers emphasize that it is primarily a "safety valve" mechanism for the whole community, reinforcing the existing social order (Gluckman 1954, 1959; D. B. Miller 1973; Parsons and Beals 1934). The sexual and scatological nature of ritual humor and its emphasis on reversal of everyday social relations and social status are seen as catharses of repressed biological and psychological tendencies in all human beings. Norbeck's (1974:50–54) premise that inverse rituals serve as "a channeling device that both permits and controls" appears similar to the views of other writers though not couched in a psychological framework.

According to one theory (Crumrine 1969), both the conflict and its resolution are executed by ritual clowns. They blur the existing structural distinctions in society and culture, which creates perceptual conflict, leading to heightened participant arousal and focus on resolving the conflict. When the Mayo ritual clowns are baptized and become men, they shed their clowning role. Participants and spectators going through this experience perceive traditional social relations and cultural values in greater depth. Thus clowns ritually mediate between numerous oppositions within the structure of Mayo culture and society. Crumrine calls his theory cultural–cognitive and uses a dialectical approach.

The sociological theories by and large emphasize social criticism and social control as the primary function of ritual humor. They differ, however, regarding the nature of social criticism. Codere (1956), for instance, claims that ritual humor in the play potlatch among the Kwakiutl Indians criticizes the "stuffed rigidities of potlatch" and also the emphasis on rank order and competition that permeates society. Bricker (1973), on the other hand, states that the social criticism of ritual humor is directed toward people who deviate from established sexual and social norms. In her opinion, ritual humor also emphasizes morality and thus also ridicules excessive sexuality. Some theories (Spicer 1954; Steward 1931) see the social function of ritual humor as primarily highlighting key values and conflicts in the sociocultural system and in group activities. Why humor should do so in the ritual context, however, and not in any other social situations remains unexplained. Universal psychological and sociological theories emphasize a functional linkage between ritual humor on the one hand and tension reduction and maintenance of social order on the other. Because statistical relationships for such theories cannot be easily established, they can be evaluated only on the basis of their internal logic and feasibility. One problem is their failure to explain why rituals are selected as the mechanism for catharsis to relieve tension and antisocial feelings. Unless cultures in which ritual humor is said to serve these functions share certain distinguishing traits, such theories are *post facto* explanations.

According to the cyclical theory proposed by Van den Berghe (1963), societies can be "viewed as going through a normative cycle consisting of a long 'normal' phase and a short 'licentious' phase" (p. 415). The two phases stand "reciprocally in the same antithetical relationship as the norms stressed in each phase" (p. 415).

Some schools of anthropological theory emphasize cultural contact and the subsequent diffusion of cultural traits as the primary reason for cultural and linguistic similarities among different societies (Harris 1968:376ff.). Diffusion is regarded as the principal reason for the existence of ritual humor among many American–Indian tribes by writers who propose historical explanations (Bricker 1973:167ff.; Parsons and Beals 1934; Ray 1945). The question of historical origins and diffusion with respect to ritual humor among American–Indians is interesting in part because of its occurrence during the Easter ceremonies, which postdate the Spanish influence. Bricker (1973:216–18) believes that the syncretism between the American–Indian and Spanish traditions occurred after the Spanish conquest. The Spaniards noted the similarities between their own tradition of humor and that of ritual humor in many areas of Middle America, which was primarily due to the Aztec influence. They therefore encouraged the Indians to incorporate Spanish customs in their social satire. Bricker sees the unity of the tradition of ritual humor as resulting not only from cultural diffusion during the pre-Columbian period but also from contact with Spanish culture.

Researchers who propose historical explanations emphasize that intercultural variation in the ritual clowning complex among the American–Indians, and even the Spanish influence, is unevenly reflected in its many aspects. These historical explanations lack answers to such questions as why and how the institution of ritual humor, especially clowning, originated in the first place. It appears from the sources listed in Bricker (1973:191–94) that the Aztec nobles maintained jesters to amuse them and that ritual humor took place during the fiesta in honor of Quetzalcóatl.

Makarius (1970) suggested that mythological tricksters and ritual clowns both essentially express "a general, basic, contradictory human experience that gives rise to dramatic situations" (p. 53). On the one hand, the clowns are humorists and breakers of social and ritual taboos and on the other hand serve as healers and guardians of traditions and ritual sanctity. The contradictory aspect is reflected even in the ambivalent behavior of the spectators, who respond with laughter but at the same time fear the clowns' magical power. Theories of ritual humor that concentrate on clowns and their activities seem to emphasize two sets of factors: the freedom accorded to ritual clowns and the emphasis on taboo breaking, and the so-called anomalous position of ritual clowns due to their roles, which straddle the Durkheimian dichotomy of the Sacred and the Profane. Makarius emphasizes the breaking of taboo as a major factor in her symbolic theory, expressed in terms of "collective social psyche." In explaining the actions of the Koyemshi sacred clowns among the Zuni Indians, she states that "the violation of taboo which they symbolize, namely incest, is that which persistently haunts the mind of the tribal people, giving rise to frantic imaginary elaborations" (1970:58).

Makarius sees the basic contradictory characteristic of ritual clowns as a conflict between the individual and society, because only individuals break taboos, and while such violation is good for the group, the violator is not rewarded but ridiculed. In order for Makarius's theory to apply, clowns have to act individually. She claims (p. 54) that they do indeed do so in many American–Indian groups; the clowns give individualistic performances even when they are in group. Many of the ethnographic data, however, indicate that ritual humor is collective activity, a characteristic that separates it from forms occurring on other social occasions. Humorous episodes and acts developed by ritual clowns generally need team effort. Even when ritual clowns are engaged in their own idiosyncratic form of humor, each is performing simultaneously with others who are similarly engaged. Such group participation has several consequences: first, it helps eliminate self-consciousness, which on such occasions is already reduced because of the masks or other costumes; second, it provides mutual reinforcement; and third, it encourages healthy competition that makes the clown innovative and creative in impromptu ways, an aspect that to some extent explains the daredevil activities in which ritual clowns engage in many American–Indian groups.

Zucker (1967) combines the symbolic and psychological perspectives in his theory of ritual clowns, calling his approach theological. According to his theory, self-contradiction is the most significant feature of the ritual clown, who expresses the absurdity and paradox of human existence. The clown produces a peculiar mixture of laughter and indignation in the audience. He accepts the "twofold role of breaking all taboos and receiving all the punishment for it" (p. 312). The audience has the opportunity "to experience vicariously the assault on order and to witness simultaneously the reduction to nothingness of the transgressor!"(p. 312).

In general, the following caveats need to be noted with regard to theoretical explanations of ritual humor. First, ritual humor appears by nature diverse, as are the ceremonies in which it occurs. Therefore, unitary theories explaining it beyond the constraints of individual cultures are likely to be low-level abstractions and as a result somewhat trivial. Such theories cannot be viable unless they demonstrate that such humor universally shows features associated with the universally shared features of rituals. In other words, intercultural and intracultural variations need to be taken into account.

Second, theories that explain humor in functional terms need to show its relevance to an integration into rituals. If humor is extraneous to rituals, then little significance can be attached to its occurrence in that context except with respect to its entertainment value. On the other hand, if humor appears to be highly integrated into rituals, then we need to explain why and how it is so integrated. Comparative studies therefore need to be undertaken, first, to determine the degree to which humor is integrated into rituals, using criteria similar to those that I discussed in a previous section, and second, to learn what cultural factors are responsible for it.

Third, indigenous explanations for the occurrence of humor should be sought. Although many theories of ritual humor have been proposed by scholars and have been discussed above, none has presented any indigenous views. Such explanations would provide insight into what people think about humor occurring within the context of their religious ceremonies and would suggest how they perceive its relevance to and significance for various other aspects of culture.

Fourth, general theories proposing functional explanations should take into account that humor either may serve several functions or may simply be an epiphenomenon with purely entertainment value.

The existing theories of ritual humor appear to be based on the questionable assumption that ritual humor is qualitatively different from humor in other forms of social interaction. Much ritual humor, however, like other types of humor, appears to be based on incongruity and exaggeration. Thus such humor highlights the existing nature of sociocultural systems because of "association by opposition." It emphasizes reversal of existing social reality or simply its absence. It stresses either reversal of existing structure or total freedom from it. This aspect cannot be cognitively perceived, however, without drawing attention to the existence of both social reality and social structure. In other words, humor is experienced because of an association by opposition with the existing social order, cultural norms, statuses, roles, and so forth. It is also noteworthy that ceremonies, especially in preliterate societies, merely provide a context for the engagement in humor, because on these occasions most members of the community come together. Ceremonies therefore provide a suitable setting for public entertainment by way of humor. Humor may not be an essential ingredient of rituals; they do exist without it in many societies, and even in those societies in which ritual humor occurs, it is not always present.

I would like to suggest that ritual humor *per se* is not fundamentally different from humor in other social interactions. Rather the rituals provide a special framework intensifying the degree, mode of exaggeration, and incongruity of humor. Rituals enable humorists to behave outrageously and to have immunity from public ridicule and punishment for such behavior. Individuals who engage in humor temporarily transcend their usual social roles and take on another role for which they are not held responsible. Rituals thus permit transformation of personalities, either individually or collectively and in direct or indirect ways. The direct ways result in extreme behavior and breach of etiquette, while the indirect ways result in freedom to express mirthful laughter at acts ordinarily considered so outrageous as to arouse shame and anxiety.

Theoretical Propositions

The discussion so far permits us to formulate the following theoretical propositions concerning ritual humor.

The degree to which humor is integrated in rituals seems to vary not only across cultures but from ritual to ritual within individual cultures.

Social relationships and membership in specific groups are important criteria in the selection of ritual humorists. Thus at rites of passage, relatives and close friends of individuals going through the rituals engage in humor. At other types of ceremonies, members of secret societies, cults, or other similar organizations predominate as ritual clowns.

Ritual clowns play an important role in ceremonials because they not only act as humorists but also carry out other important tasks.

The security of the group and of the ritual context enables ritual clowns to engage in all kinds of outrageous and ludicrous acts.

The chief purpose of ritual humor appears to be community entertainment; religious ceremonies are the main events for large group interaction, especially in preliterate societies.

Ritual humor is not qualitatively different from humor in other social interaction. Rather, the rituals provide a special context whereby humorists and participants are both temporarily freed from social sanction for whatever acts they wish to simulate.

Notes

1. Bricker (1973), Charles (1945), Codere (1956), Crumrine (1969), Hieb (1972), Honigman (1942), Howard (1962), J. Levine (1961), Makarius (1970), Norbeck (1961, 1963, 1974), Parsons and Beals (1934), Radin (1914), Ray (1945), Titiev (1975). See Steward (1931) for a good summary of clowns and their antics as reported in many early ethnographic studies of American Indian tribes.
2. For Africe, see Beidelman (1966), Evans-Pritchard (1929), Gluckman (1963), Nadel (1946, 1947, 1954); Norbeck (1963) has the most extensive survey of ethnographic materials on ritual humor

in Africa. For North India and Sri Lanka, see Amarasingham (1973), Marriot (1966/1968), D. B. miller (1973). For Europe, see Cox (1969/1972), Norbeck (1974), Van den Berghe (1963), Welsford (1935). For cross-cultural studies of ritual humor, see Norbeck (1961, 1963, 1974), and Van de Berghe (1963).

3. For additional examples, see Gorer (1935:36), Herkovits (1938:26), Krige (1937:105), Norbeck (1963), B. B. Whiting (1963:189).

4. For additional examples, see Grinnell (1923:2, 204–10, as quoted in Steward 1931:203), Harrington (1921:156), and Kroeber (1902–1907:192, as quoted in Makarius 1970:63), Norbeck (1963:1269), Parsons and Beals (1934:503), Ray (1945:93), Seligman and Seligman (1950:356).

5. For other examples, see E. O. Henry (1975), Marriott (1966/1968), D. B. Miller (1973), Parsons and Beals (1934:493), Sharman (1969:106).

6. For other examples, see Fewkes (1900:128–29, as quoted in Steward 1931:193), Hitchcock (1966:47), D. B. Miller (1973: 18), F. F. Williams (1930:251).

7. For examples, see Alland (1975:138), Crumrine (1969:7), Marriott (1966/1968:204), Nadel (1946:396), Steward (1931: 193–94).

8. For other examples of scatological aspects of ritual humor, see Crumrine (1969:7), Marriott (1966/1968:203).

9. For other examples, see Bourke (1891:5), Chambers (1909[2]:266–70), Crumrine (1969:7), Parsons (1936, as quoted in Makarius 1970:53).

10. For more examples, see Evans-Pritchard (1929:313), Goody (1957:91), Herskovits (1937/1971:211), Horowitz (1967:76–77), Kennedy (1970:41), B. B. Whiting (1963:623).

11. For examples, see E. O. Henry (1975), Jacobsen (1977), Marriott (1966/1968), D. B. Miller (1973), Steward (1931).

12. For other examples, see Steward (1931:199–200).

13. The following research deals with different theories of ritual humor. Psychological and social psychological: Charles (1945) Crumrine (1969), Gluckman (1954, 1959, 1963), Honigmann (1942), J. Levin (1961), Spicer (1954). Sociological: Bricker (1973), Codere (1956), Norbeck (1974). Cyclical: Van de Berghe (1963). Symbolic: Makarius (1970). Theological: Zucker (1967). Historical: Bricker (1973), Parsons and Beals (1934), Ray (1945). Some scholars have proposed several theories each of which belongs to a different type mentioned above. Parsons and Beals, for instance, propose both psychological and historical theories of ritual humor.

References

Alland, A., Jr. 1975. When the Spider Danced: Ethnography of the Abron of the Ivory Coast. Garden City, N.Y.: Anchor.

Beck, P., and A. L. Walters. 1977. The Sacred: Ways of Knowledge, Sources of Life. Tsaile, AZ., Navajo Nation: Navajo Community College.

Beidelman, T. O. 1966. *Utani*: Some Kaguru Notions of Death, Secuality, and Affinity. Southwestern Journal of Anthropology 22:354–80.

Bricker, V. R. 1973. Ritual Humor in Highland Chiapas. Austin: University of Texas Press.

Charles, L. H. 1945. The Clown's Function. Journal of American Folklore 58:25–34.

Christensen, J. B. 1963. Utani: Joking, Sexual License, and Social Obligations among the Luguru. American Anthropologist 65:1315–27.

Codere, H. 1956. The Amiable Side of Kwakiutl Life: The Potlatch and the Play Potlatch. American Anthropologist 58:334–51.

Colson, E. 1953. Clans and the Joking-Relationship among the Plateau Tonga of Northern Rhodesia. Kroeber Anthropological Society Papers 10:45–60.

Cox, H. 1972. The Feast of Fools. Perennial Library. New York: Harper & Row. (Originally published in 1969.)

Crumrine, N. R. 1969. Capakoba, the Mayo Easter Ceremonial Impersonator: Explanatons of Ritual Clowning. Journal for the Scientific Study of Religion 8:1–22.

Darwin, C. 1965. The Expression of the Emotion in Man and Animals. Chicago: university of Chicago Press. (Originally Published in 1872.)

Evans-Pritchard, E. E. 1929. Some Collective Expressions of Obscenity in Africa. Journal of the Royal Anthropological Institute of Great Britain and Ireland 59:311–31.

Gillison, G. 1977. Fertility Rites and Sorcery in a New Guinea Village. National Geographic 152(1):124–46.

Gluckman, M. 1954. Rituals of Rebellion in South-East Africa. Manchester, England: Manchester University Press.

———. 1959. Custom and Conflict in Africa. Glencoe, Ill.: Free Press.

———. 1963. The Role of the Sexes in Wiko Circumcision Ceremonies. In Social Structure, Meyer Fortes, ed. New York: Russell & Russell.

Goodale, J. C. 1971. Tiwi Wives: A Study of the Women of Melville Island, N. Australia. Seattle: University of Washington Press.

Gossen, G. H. 1976. Verbal Dueling in Chamula. In Speech Play, Barbara Kirshenblatt-Gomblett, ed. Philadelphia: University of Pennsylvania Press. Pp.121–46

Harris, M. 1968. The Rise of Anthropological Theory. New York: Cromwell.

Henry, E. O. 1975. North Indian Wedding Songs: An Analysis of Functions and Meanings. Journal of South Asian Literature 11:61–93.

Hitchcock, J. T. 1966. The Magars of Banyan Hill. New York: holt, Reinhart, & Winston.

Honigmann, J. J. 1942. AnInterpretation of the Social-Psychological Functions of the Ritual Clown. Character and Personality 10:220–26.

Howard, J. H. 1962. Peyote Jokes. Jornal of American Folklore 75:10–14.

Huntingford, G. W. B. 1953. TheSouthern Nilo-Hamites. East Central Africa, pt.8. London: International African Institute, Ethnographic Survey of Africa.

Jacobsen, D. W. 1977. Purdah in India: Life behind the Veil. National Geographic 152(2):270–86.

Kroeber, A. L. 1902–1907. The Arapaho. Bulletin 18. New york: American Museum of Natural History.

Landtman, G. 1927. The Kiwai Papuans of British New Guinea. London: Macmillan.

Levin, Jacob. 1961. Regression in Primative Clownin. Psychoanalytic Quarterly 30:72–83.

Makarius, L. 1970. Ritual Clowns and Symbolic Behaviour. Diogenes 69:44–73.

Malefijt, A. M. deW. 1968a. Dutch Joking Patterns. Transactions of the New York Academy of Sciences, ser. 2, 30:1181–86.

Marriott, M. 1968. The Feast of Love. In Krishna: Myths, Rites, and Attitudes, Milton Singer, ed. Chicago: University of Chicago Press. Pp. 200–12. (Originally published 1966.)

Miller, D. B. 1973. Holi-Dulhendi: Licensed Rebellion in a North Indian Village. South Asia 3:15–22.

Nadel, S. F. 1954. Nupe Religio. London: Routledge & Kegan Paul

Norbeck, E. 1961. Religion in Primative Society. New York: Harper.

———. 1963. African Rituals of Conflict. American Anthropologist 65:1254–79.

————. 1974. Religion in Human Life: Anthropological Views. New York: Holt, Rinehart, & Winston.

Parsons, E. C., and R. L. Beals. 1934. The Sacred Clowns of the Pueblo and Mayo-Yaqui Indians. American Anthropologist 36:491–514

Ray, V. F. 1945. The Contrary Behavior Pattern in American Ceremonialism. Southwestern Journal of Anthropology 1:75–113.

Seligman, C. G., and B. Z. Seligman. 1950. Pagan Tribes of the Nilotic Sudan. New York: Humanities Press.

Speck, F. G. 1949. Midwinter Rites of the Cayuga Long House. Philadelphia: University of Pennsylvania Press.

Spicer, E. H. 1940. Pascua, A Yaqui Village in Arizona. Chicago: University of Chicago Press.

————. 1954. Potam, A Yaqui Village in Sonora. Memoir 77. Menasha: American Anthropological Association.

Steward, J. 1931. The Ceremonial Buffoon of the American Indian. Papers of the Michigan Academy of Science, Arts, and Letters 14:187–207.

Stirling, M. W. 1942. Origin myths of Acoma and Other Records. Bulletin 135. Washington, D. C.: Bureau of American Ethnology.

Van den Berghe, P. L. 1963. Institutionalized Licence and Normative Stability. Cahiers d'etudes africanes 3:413–23.

Van Gennep, A. 1960. The Rites of Passage. Chicago: University of Chicago Press. (Originally published in French in 1909.)

Wallace, A. F. C. 1966. Religion: An Anthropological View. New York: Random House.

Welsford, E. 1935. The Fool: His Social and Literary History. New York: Farrar & Rinehart.

Whiting, B. B., ed. 1963. Six Cultures: Studies of Child Rearing. New York: Wiley.

Zucker, W. M. 1967. The Clown as the Lord of Disorder. Theology Today 24:306–17.

The Qur'ān and Humor

by Georges Tamer[1] (2006)

At first, speaking of humor in relation to the Qur'ān sounds perplexing. Religion in general, after all, seems to be a totally serious matter. The holy books of the monotheistic religions, in particular, are predominantly considered devoid of humor, preaching repentance and atonement for one's sins. However, this is only one side of the coin: upon further examination, Scriptures, as well as religious traditions related to them, do not in fact appear humorless. The reason for this lies in the essence of religion. Religion needs both God and man. While it is true that there is no religion without God, it is equally true that a religion only with God is unthinkable. The core of each of the monotheistic traditions is the encounter between God and man. These resemble the two poles of a magnet, which, together and in mutual reaction, create the tension that propels the development of religious ideas. Religions therefore bear not only divine but also human components, including a sense of humor and the ability to laugh, which are features particular to human beings, as philosophy has long acknowledged.[2] Due to the essential human nature of religion, humor is necessarily constituent of it.

In the Hebrew Bible's Psalms, which are solemn poetic prayers, for example, we can easily observe humor in the form of mockery and scoffing. In Psalm 2, the Lord is described as laughing at opponents and holding them in derision. Similar subjects are mentioned in several Psalms.[3] Elsewhere, Sarah laughs at the angelic message that she, as aged as she is, will become pregnant, an incident also mentioned in the Qur'ān.[4] Even in Job's narrative, dealing with the enigmatic question of why the righteous should undeservedly suffer, God's challenging questions to the suffering Job toward the end of the story (chapters 40–41) betray a touch of humor. The Gospels do not say that Jesus joked or laughed—however, nor do they say that he never did. Luke mentions Jesus' warning to those who are laughing now that they will mourn and weep.[5] Although this statement should not be understood as a general dismissal of laughter,

---

1   I wish to thank Prof. Sebastian Knowles (Ohio State University) for his valuable stylistic comments.
2   See Aristotle, De partibus animalibus III,10,673a. For an overview, see John Morreall (ed.), *The Philosophy of Laughter and Humor* (Albany 1987).
3   E.g., Ps 37:13; 59:9.
4   Gen 17:17; 18:12, 13,15. I will return to Sarah's laughter later in the present study.
5   Luke 6:25.

but only as applicable to the hostile context in which Jesus preached until he was crucified, it could have stimulated Church Fathers to admonish Christians against humorous entertainment.[6] Nevertheless, the history of the churches in East and West includes, not marginally, the development of phenomena attached to humor, such as the saints called Fools for Christ, the Carnival, and the joyful celebration of liturgical feasts. Several passages in the books of the New Testament tell Christians to rejoice and be happy about redemption through Christ.[7]

Unlike the Gospels, which can be considered memoirs of disciples and early followers about their experiences with Jesus of Nazareth, the Qur'ān is held in Islam to be God's direct speech, transmitted to Muhammad in Arabic through the intermediation of the Angel Gabriel (Jibril). Humor in the Qur'ān, therefore, is to be considered God's humor. Would God's speech contain humor? How could humor be connected to the serious image of God in the Qur'ān? Does humor fit in a book arguing most earnestly for belief in God, changing one's way of life, and struggling for the new faith?

Furthermore, and perhaps due to an image of Islam as totally different from other religions, studies on the relation of Islam and humor are far fewer than those on the relation of humor to Judaism or Christianity.[8] In his monograph *Humor in Early Islam,* Franz Rosenthal presents humorous materials ascribed to the legendary figure Ash ab from Medina and thereby makes a good case for reconciling Islam with humor.[9] In a pioneering article, Mustansir Mir tries to show "that the Qur'ān does possess an element of humor."[10] Based on his interpretation of a number of passages, he argues that "Qur'ānic humor is, mainly, either humor of situation or humor of character."[11] Pointing out that some of the Qur'ānic humor gets lost in the translation, Mir concludes at the end of his notes that further scholarly work is needed to dig it out.

Although the present author agrees with Mir's basic argument that humor is not alien to the Qur'ān,[12] many of the cases presented in his article do not really reflect Qur'ānic humor. This particularly applies

---

6   John Chrysostom (ca. 354–407) claimed that Jesus never laughed (Homiliae in Hebr XV,8). He said that laughter, as well as jocose speech is not "an acknowledged sin, but it loads to acknowledged sin" (quoted in John Moreall, *Taking Laughter Seriously* [New York 1983], p. 86). He wondered how Christians could laugh, when they should be keeping in mind the suffering of Christ and continuously praying. Kari Josef Kuschel makes an attempt at a critical theology of laughter in: Lachen Gottes und der Menschen Kunst (Freiburg 1994).

7   See, e.g., Luke 13:7; John 4:36. Philippians 2:18; 3:1; 4:4; 1 Peter 1:8; 4:13.

8   General works on the relation between religion and humor usually focus on Western traditions and exclude Islam from consideration. See Peter L. Berger, *Redeeming Laughter: The Comic Dimension of Human Experience* (Berlin 1997); Ingvild Sælid Gilhus, *Laughing Gods, Weeping Virgins: Laughter in the History of Religion* (London, New York 1997). An exception is John Morreall, *Comedy, Tragedy, and Religion* (New York 1999), in which Islam, as well as Asian traditions, is included in the discussion. For works of popular Christian theology, see Elton Trueblood, *The Humor of Christ* (New York 1964); Harvey Cox, *The Feast of Fools: A Theological Essay on Festivity and Fantasy* (Cambridge 1969); Cal Samra, *The Joyful Christ. The, Healing Power of Humor* (New York 1986); Conrad Hyers, *And God Created Laughter: The Bible of Divine Comedy* (Atlanta 1987); Earl F. Palmer. *The Humor of Jesus. Sources of Laughter in the Bible* (Vancouver 2001). For humor in the Hebrew Bible, see Athalya Brenner and Yehuda T. Radday (eds.), *On Humour and the Comic in the Hebrew Bible* (Journal for the Study of the Old Testament: Supplement Series 92, Bible and Literature Series 23: Sheffield 1990); J. William Whedbee, *The Bible and the Comic Vision* (Cambridge 1998). On humor in Jewish and Christian traditions, see Jakob Jonsson. *Humour and Irony in the New Testament: Illuminated by Parallels in Talmud and Midrash* (Beihefte der Zeit-sehrift für Religions—und Geistesgeschichte 28, Leiden 1985).

9   Franz Rosenthal. *Humor in Early Islam* (Leiden 1956). For an approach considering humor in contemporary Muslim societies, see Sabra Webber, art. "Humor and Religion: Humor and Islam", in. Lindsay Jones (ed.), *Encyclopedia of Religion. Second edition:* vol. VI, (Detroit 2005), pp. 4210–4218.

10   Mustansir Mir, "Humor in the Qur'ān", in; *The Muslim World* 81 (1991). pp. 179–193, here. 193.

11   Ibid., p. 186.

12   Cf. Ulrich Marzolph, art. "Humor", in: Jane Dammen McAuliffe (ed.). *Encyclopaedia of the Qur'ān*, 5 Vols. (Leiden, Boston 2001–6). vol II. pp. 464f.

to two major instances most extensively discussed in his mentioned article: the episode of Moses with the wooden staff and the story of Moses with Khidr.[13] Both stories lack any sense of humor or irony. Moses' long-winded description of the benefits of his staff might appear funny to some readers simply because it exceeds in detail what is required by God's question, "What is that Moses, you have in your right hand?"[14] However, Moses' answer does not seem to reflect a humorous attitude. Humor also seems to be absent in the story of Moses and Khidr, which instead reflects serious astonishment about extremely strange events.[15]

Nevertheless, the Qur'ān definitely contains humorous situations and statements that can easily be connected to psychological phenomena with which humor is usually associated,[16] as I will show in this study. My essay consists of two parts. In the first part, I discuss humorous statements and situations in the Qur'ān. Since the physical indications of humor, a smile and laughter, are distinctive, both will be included in the discussion. Similar phenomena, such as scoff (sukhr), mockery, and ridicule (huz'), which are deeply related to humor in the Qur'ān, will also be considered. In the second part of the study, I present Arabic jocular literature in which Qur'ānic verses have been assimilated in jokes and anecdotes.

I. Humor and Related Phenomena in the Qur'ān

The Qur'ān contains a number of statements and situations that reflect humor and related phenomena, such as laughter and mockery. They can be arranged in different categories which illustrate various aspects of humor.

The Seriousness of the Qur'ān

Let us start our search for what is humorous and funny in the Qur'ān with what is instead serious.[17] A reflexive statement occurring presumably in an early Meccan passage (Q 86:13–14), according to the Suras chronology suggested by Theodor Nöldeke,[18] describes the announcement made in the previous part of Sura 86 as decisive speech that is no joke (al-hazl).[19] This statement follows immediately after an oath (vv. 11–12), which should eliminate any doubt the audience could have regarding the announced eschatological events. The truth of the Qur'ān is self-affirmed through the declaration that its purpose is not to amuse—which could imply that a joke does not contain the truth. This self-characterization is structurally similar to the Qur'ānic statement that God did not create the world playfully.[20] The reaction of the unfaithful when they hear of the Judgment drawing closer, presented in another passage from the same period, directly opposes the seriousness of God's statements. They marvel (ta'jabūn) and laugh

---

13   Mustansir Mir. "Humor in the Qur'ān" (see note 9), pp 182ff., 187ff.
14   Q 20.10–21, here: 17.
15   Q 18:65–82.
16   See in general Jeffrey H. Goldstein and Paul E. McGhee (eds.), *The Psychology of Humor: Theoretical Perspectives and Empirical Issues* (New York 1972); Mahadev I., Apte. *Humor and Laughter: An Anthropological Approach:* (Ithaca, London 1985).
17   Cf. Charles Pellat. "Seriousness and Humor in Early Islam", in; *Islamic Studies* 2 (1963), pp. 353–362.
18   Theodor Nöldeke and Friedrich Schwally. *Geschichte des Qur'āns. Erster Teil: Über den Ursprung des Qur'āns* (Leipzig 1909; reprint Hildesheim 2005).
19   Cf. Nicolai Sinai. "Qur'ānic Self-referentiality as a strategy of self-authorization". in: Stefan Wild (ed.), *Self-Referentiality in the Qur'ān* (Wiesbaden 2006). pp. 103–134, here: 110.
20   Q 21:16–17.

(tadhakūn), doubting the truth of the speech *(al-hadīth)* instead of crying *(tabkūn)*.[21] While seriousness is a characteristic of God's words, laughter is discredited here as a signal of disbelief. In this early stage of the Qur'ān, which is mainly occupied with eschatological punishments against unbelievers, it seems that God has nothing to do with humor.

God as Creator of Laughter

God's absolute power is emphasized in an early Meccan passage that begins with a reference to someone who, it is said, turned away, gave a little, and then held back all.[22] According to the majority of the exegetes, the passage recalls the story of al-Walīd b. al-Mughīra, who followed Muhammad but then, after strong denunciation by the Meccans, decided to turn away from the prophet and instead give money for someone who had promised to replace him in hell—in case Muhammad was right. But he did not pay in full.[23] Anyway, the behavior of this person contradicts the knowledge he should have obtained from "the scrolls of Moses and Abraham" *(suhuf Mūsā wa-Ibrāhīm)* (vv. 36–37), an expression that could be understood as an allusion to the Old Testament. The Qur'ān wields rhetorical questions against this person's conduct, arguing, for example, that during the Last Judgment everybody will be responsible for his or her own life. Furthermore, as stated in the aforementioned scrolls, along with all other things, people ultimately return to the Lord; and it is the Lord who causes them to laugh and to cry, to die and to live, and who created the pair, the male and the female, from an emitted sperm (vv. 43–46). The aim of the entire passage is to present the central theological theme that everything in human life and history is under God's control. The comprehensive spheres of God's power appear in the form of three parallel pairs, in the first of which God makes people laugh and cry, behaviors that indicate the correlative emotions of joy and sorrow. It remains unspecified whether the statement refers to a worldly or an eschatological state of affairs.[24] At any rate, as an expression of joy, the laughter mentioned in this passage differs from the aforementioned jeering laughter of the unbelievers when they hear about the coming Judgment.[25]

Humor of Superiority

Laughter appears in another passage, which is considered early Meccan, as a physical expression of superiority. Within the framework of the description of the eschatological status of both the believers and the unbelievers, the Qur'ān retrospectively relates from the standpoint of the fulfilled Judgment how humor is integrated into the discourse of political power:

> The sinners used to laugh at the believers; when they passed by them, they used to wink at one another, and when they returned to their people, they returned jeering, and when they saw them, they said, "These men are astray!" Yet they were not sent as watchers over them. So

---

21   Q 53:57–62.

22   Q 53:33–55

23   Cf. al-Tabarī. *Jāmiʿ al-bayān fī tafsīr al-Qur'ān*. 12 vols. (Būlāq 1328–9/1910–1), vol. XI: juzʾ XXVII, pp. 41f.

24   The issue of human freedom vs. God's determination of human actions in relation to Q 53.43 is briefly discussed in Ludwig Ammann, *Vorbild und Vernunft: Die Regelung von Lacken und Scherzen im mittelaltertichen Islam* (Arabistische Texte und Studien 5, Hildesheim, Zürich, New York 1943). pp. 21–23.

25   Cf. Q 53.60. Cf. Josef van Ess. "Lachen von oben und Lachen von unten. Das Lachen Gottes und der Witz des Menschen im Islam", in: *Religionen unterwegs* 11 (2005), pp. 14–23.

today the believers, upon couches, are laughing at the unbelievers, watching to see whether the unbelievers have been rewarded for what they have done.[26]

The passage consists of two parts. The first part depicts the present situation of the believers as if it were the past. From an eschatological standpoint, the time of their oppression is past history. The attitude of the unbelievers toward the believers is both aggressive and derisive. Humor here combines laughter and mockery. It is sinful, and as such turns out to be subject to eschatological punishment. In the second part, the believers are those who laugh. The evoked present time of the Hereafter has replaced the real present time of oppression. The conditions are reversed: it is the believers' turn to laugh at the unbelievers passing by. A cheerful scene is sketched in the last two verses of the Sura: the believers are sitting, relaxed on couches, observing the extent to which those who had earlier mocked them are getting their reward for their previous actions. The attitude of the believers implies that they are not feeling sympathy with the unbelievers, but rather *Schadenfreude* and satisfaction. Their vengeance thus contains a bit of humor and mockery.[27]

As an expression of their triumph, the believers laugh, presenting an aspect of humor connected to the feeling of superiority. In their current situation, this eschatological humor conveys the promised power they will wield over their enemies. Although the date of the final scene cannot be defined, due to its eschatological nature, the present tense of the verbs, as well as the use of the adverbial *al-yawm*, "today", serves as warrant that the power, expressed in terms of humorous behavior, will be their own. The community of believers plagued in the present time should be comforted by the vision of eschatological humor guaranteed them in the future.

Similar eschatological humor, in the form of *Schadenfreude* at the prospect of coming punishment, is presented in a passage dealing in some detail with the torture that the sinful will suffer. According to Sura 44, the sinful will be fed from the bitter Zaqqūm tree.[28] Those who are in charge of pouring boiling water over the head of the sinful will also feed him—most likely from the tree—saying: "Taste; you are truly the mighty, the noble!" (v. 49). They mock him with disingenuous praise, which stands in stark contrast with his humiliation. The scene resembles a caricature. The actors in hell, presumably angels, scoff at the sinful while torturing him, creating, therefore, a case of humorous incongruity. The vivid scene should not only give the oppressed believers hope of vengeance, it should also amuse them and let them laugh at their enemy, whose eternal suffering will eclipse the believers' temporal discomforts.

The apparent message of these early Qur'ānic statements is simple: the powerful who enjoy a pleasant playful life will certainly be punished. Conversely, those who struggle toward God will be rewarded with everlasting joy. Both sides will experience radical change. However, it is remarkable that the Qur'ān does not condemn joyful life as such, but specifically that which is related to sin. Such a life is bound to earn punishment.[29] The prophet, who feels the duty to call the unbelievers to follow God's commandments, is told to let them "plunge and play" (*yakhūdū iva-yal'abū*) until they encounter the day they are promised.[30]

---

26   Q 83.29–36. Cf. 52:18 for a similar description of rejoicing (*fākihīn*) God-fearing people in gardens dwelling in bliss.

27   Fakhr al-Dīn al-Rāzī, *Mafatih al-ghayb*, 8 vols. (Cairo 1307–8/1889–90), vol. VIII, p. 358 delivers a similar interpretation of the passage.

28   Q 44.43–50. For further references, see Salwa M.S Awa, art. "Zaqqūm". in: *Encyclopaedia of the Qur'ān* (see note 11), vol. V, pp. 571f.

29   Q 80:38–39; 84:6–15.

30   Q 70.42.

Connected to joyful life, humor does not seem to he pursued by the believers; for them, all that matters is the Hereafter, preserved for them and their allies.

Mocking the Judgment

Corresponding to the mocking of God's prophets and messengers by those who refuse their messages, the Qur'ān relates a case of mockery that is specifically directed toward the religious teaching of the Last Judgment. Undoubtedly, the Last Judgment is the most powerful metaphysical idea with which the Qur'ān—herein not really different from the Bible—could threaten opponents. Accordingly, they will be punished severely when the Last Hour comes. For their part, the unbelievers respond with pointed mockery not only to express their disbelief in the Judgment but also to ridicule Muhammad's proclamation:

> The unbelievers say: "Shall we show you a man who will tell you that even when you are all scattered to pieces in disintegration, you will be raised in a new creation?"[31]

The unbelievers argue as if they believed in resurrection—but in fact they do not. In asking ironically whether Muhammad has invented a falsehood against God or has gone mad,[32] they accuse him of having done so. The way they deal with the issue is playful and provides an obvious case of incongruity. We can also observe that mocking the prophetic announcements of God's signs is generally connected in the Qur'ān to arrogance; it deserves, thus, humiliating torture.[33] Furthermore, the Qur'ān mentions another disbelieving attitude, which could be related to mockery, towards the Final Judgment. It is that of challenging Muhammad to let it happen instantaneously if it is truly going to happen.[34] Mockery is used in this context as a powerful technique replacing any other form of logical argumentation.

The unbelievers make usually fun of eschatological themes; thus, it seems, according to the Qur'ānic *Weltanschauung,* only a logical result to associate this earthly world with play and amusement.[35] Indeed, Qur'ānic statements like the above provide the foundation for an ascetic rejection of laughter and joking in Islam.[36] However, the statement "God does not love those who exult" (Q 28:76) which is primarily used to support arguments against humor and laughter later in Islam should be understood in its immediate context where it specifically applies to those who exult due to material richness.

Satanic Humor

The type of humor expressed against God's prophets and messengers seems to be connected to an original Satanic attitude towards both God and Adam. According to different Qur'ānic accounts, God commanded the angels to prostrate themselves before the newly created Adam. Satan (*Iblīs*) refused to fulfill this command. According to one passage, he justifies his behavior with the question: "Shall I prostrate myself before one you have created from clay?"[37] In other passages, he explains that he considers himself better

---

31 Q 34:7.

32 Q 34:8.

33 Q 45:8–10.

34 Q 42:18.

35 Q 6:32; 62:11.

36 Cf. Ludwig Ammann, *Vorbild and Vernunft* (see note 23). pp. 74ff.

37 Q 17.61. Cf. 15:33.

than Adam since he is created from fire.[38] No doubt, his explanation reflects his arrogance. But it also seems to reflect a form of humor caused by his consciousness of his superiority against Adam as well as his surprise regarding God's command to the angels to prostrate themselves before a creature who is inferior to them. Convinced of his superiority to Adam, whom he was asked to honor, Satan might have pointed towards him with an evil satirical smile referring to Adam's inferior status and demonstrating his abhorrence at being forced to honor him. Satan's humor in the Qur'ān is connected to arrogance and it is sinful.

Abraham's Humor

In several Qur'ānic accounts, Abraham *(Ibrāhīm)* renounces the idols of his people after he discovers monotheism.[39] However, two passages tell the story pointing out Abraham's sense of humor.

We read in Q 37:85–89 how Abraham argues with his father and his people declaring his aversion against idolatry and inviting them to worship the one God. As the people turn away from him, he turns towards their gods saying: "Will you not eat? Why do you not speak?"[40] As they did not respond, he started hitting them with his right hand (v. 93).

Let us add to the sketched scenery some further details which are implied without being explicitly mentioned. In a sudden movement, Abraham handed food over to the idols, inviting them to eat. Taking into consideration his already articulated rejection of the idols, the passage suggests that Abraham definitely knew that they were unable to eat. For him, they were already lifeless statues. It is unlikely that he wanted to assure himself of their life. On the contrary, with this deed he was mocking the gods demonstrating in a humorous surprising way their inanimate nature. As they did not react to his offer, he continued to scoff at them with ironical questions.

Abraham's sense of humor is also demonstrated in the course of his serious debate with his people while he was urging them to dispel polytheism and worship God. A touch of humor is obvious in his question to them: "Do you worship what you hew?" (Q 37:95). The question indicates ironically how absurd Abraham considers the deification of idols by those who produce them, while they actually should rather worship God who created mankind (v. 96). The people then threw Abraham into the fire but he was rescued by God. Another passage,[41] presumably of later date, adds the following detail to the story. Abraham destroyed the idols except their biggest. As the people discovered what happened and knew who did it, they brought him to a public tribunal to ask him if he was the blasphemous culprit (vv. 58–62). He answered: "No, but this, their chief, did it; so ask them if they can speak."[42]

What in Abraham's answer appears to be a lie is in fact a humorous statement mocking not only the idols, but also his idolatrous people urging them to an absurdity: to communicate with their idols and expect them to respond—which could never happen. Abraham surprises the people and shocks them with his suggestion. His humor is striking; it causes them to turn to themselves and think about their gods and discover that they cannot speak (vv. 64–65).

---

38   Q 7:12; 38:76.
39   Q 6:74–84, 19:41–50); 21:51–73: 26:69–86; 29:16–27. 37:83–98: 43:26–27: 60:4. Cf. Reaven Firestone, art "Abraham", in: *Encyclopaedia of the Qur'ān* (see note 11), vol. I, pp. 5ff.
40   Q 37:91–92.
41   Q 21:51–73.
42   Q 21.63.

Abraham in the Qur'ān is, among the prophets, unique in his humor which is based on feeling himself superior to his people due to his faith in God. Usually, prophets and God's messengers are, in the Qur'ān, subjects of mockery and laughter by their powerful opponents. On many an occasion Muhammad is told that all former prophets had to suffer under the scoffing of God's enemies.[43] The same is reported to have happened to Muhammad himself.[44] His wondering about the divine signs he saw is contrasted in one passage with the impudent mockery of his opponents.[45] But just as in all similar cases reported in the Qur'ān, God promises Muhammad to reverse the situation asking him to be patient.[46] It should be pointed out that one aspect of the stories of the prophets in the Qur'ān is the humor of the prophets' adversaries, who make fun of the prophets as long as their messages are not widely recognized. Therefore, one could say that the Qur'ānic account of God's communication with mankind bears within its manifold wrinkles a certain form of humor which is assimilated in the articulated opposition to God.

Women and Humor

In Q 11:69–73 the Qur'ān tells how the angels visited Abraham bringing him the good news of the birth of a son. Sarah, Abraham's wife, who was listening, laughed out loud, wondering and disbelieving that this could happen. She explains her doubt with the following words:

Woe is me! Shall I bear a child while I am an old woman, and this, my husband, is an old man too? This is truly amazing![47]

A very old woman, long beyond the age of natural pregnancy, Sarah was shocked by the news. She expresses her shock with laughter which could also be understood as an expression of mockery against herself and her old husband. She was not able to believe that the announcement could be fulfilled. Presumably with a gesture of humor she points at herself and her old husband to express her doubt in a clear unmistakable way.[48]

Another case of a woman with a sense of humor is presented in the Qur'ānic story of Joseph in Sura 12.[49] His master's wife tried to seduce him, but failed (vv. 23–25). The event was known to women in the city who started to gossip about her, making her love for him and her failed seduction into a subject of rumors and chitchat (v. 30). As she heard of their gossip, she invited them to her house to show them Joseph's beauty so that they would pardon her for desiring him. She devised a tricky plan that betrays a clear sense of humor:[50]

(...) she sent to them, and made ready for them a repast, then she gave to each one of them a knife. "Come forth, attend to them," she said [to Joseph]. And when they saw him. they so

43   Q 11.25–27.38; 21.41, 36:30; 43.6–7, 46–47.

44   Q 21:36.

45   Q 37:12–14.

46   Q 21:36–41; 23:110–111. 40:83–84.

47   Q 11.72.

48   Cf. Ludwig Ammann, *Vorbild und Vernunft* (see note 23), pp. 19–21.

49   Cf. Mustansir Mir, "Irony in the Qur'ān: A Study of the *Story* of Joseph", in: Issa J. Boullata (ed.), *Literary Structures of Religious Meaning in the Qur'ān* (Richmond 2000), pp. 173–187.

50   Q 12:31 (translation by Arthur J. Arberry *The Karan Interpreted* [London 1953]). A variant reading of the Arabic word *muttaka'an* ("repast") is *mutkan* which could mean *al-utrujj*, which is a citrus fruit. See al-Tabarī. *Jāmi al bayān* (see note 22), vol. VII: juz' XII. p. 119.

admired him that they cut their hands, saying, "God save us! This is no mortal; he is no other but a noble angel."

The hostess wanted to convince the gossiping women of Joseph's beauty. However, she did not show him to them in a simple "normal" situation. She created a subterfuge which caused a heightened atmosphere and enabled her also to take vengeance against them for their gossips at the same time. She shocked them with his appearance as they were in a situation requiring a high level of concentration. She might have expected their distracted reaction—she knew but too well how beautiful the young man was—and she might have been full of humor expecting their reaction. We could assume that she felt *Schadenfreude* and was able to make fun of the ladies, as they cut their hands.

Mutual Humor: Solomon and the Ant

In Q 27:17–19 we read that when Solomon and his big army reached the valley of ants, an ant said to its companions: "O ants, enter your dwellings, lest Solomon and his troops crush you, without noticing it" (v. 18). Solomon, who, according to the Qur'ān, could understand the language of the animals, "smiled, laughing at its saying (*fa-tabassama dāḥikan min qawlihā)"*and turned to thank God for his grace (v. 19). In recognizing an extremely serious danger, the ant makes an interesting humorous remark, suggesting that Solomon and his soldiers would smash them without even noticing it. The brief remark betrays genuine humor which is caused by contrasting implicitly the hugeness of the army with the smallness of the ants. The humorous character of this statement is more striking because it is made in a deadly serious situation. On the other hand, Solomon, who understood the humor combined with the warning, countered also with humor. He smiled, laughing at its saying and indicated in his following prayer that he was totally aware of his power. Therefore, the story unveils two different forms of humor: that which occurs in hazardous situations and that which is raised by the relinquishing consciousness of one's own power with which in the context no one could compete.[51]

Theological Humor: God's Daughters

One of the several aspects of humor is to play with conventions and manipulate their application in a way that creates shock and laughter.[52] This aspect of humor can be observed in statements ascribed to the Meccan period of the Qur'ān. They deal with the Qur'ānic rejection of the polytheistic belief of God having daughters. The names of the three "daughters of God" al-Lāt, al-'Uzzā and Manāt are mentioned in Q 53;19–20.[53] They are considered as those of idols or goddesses worshipped in Mecca and elsewhere in the Hijāz before Islam. Arguing against this conviction, the Qur'ān alludes to the custom of the pre-Islamic Arab idolaters to dispose of unwanted female infants while still alive (*wa'd*).[54] Three passages deal with this issue. They criticize the habit of the Arabs, but the social critique is, in fact, impeded in the theological

---

51   On Solomon's laughter and the debate among classical Muslim scholars whether it is appropriate for a prophet to laugh Cf. Ludwig Ammann, *Vorbild und Vernunft* (see note 23), pp. 9f.; idem, art. "Laughter", in: *Encyclopaedia of the Qur'ān* (see note 11). vol. 111. pp. 146ff.

52   Cf. Anton C. Zijderveld, *Humor and Gesellschaft: Eine Soziologie des Humors und des Lachens* (Graz, Wien, Köln 1976). pp. 22ff.

53   Cf. Shahab Ahmed, art. "Satanic Verses", in: *Encyclopaedia of the Qur'ān* (see note 11). vol. IV, p. 531.

54   Cf. Q 81:8–9; Donna Lee Bowen, art. "Infanticide", in. *Encyclopaedia of the Qur'ān* (see note 11). vol. II. pp. 511f.

argument against the false belief of the pagans. The way the argument is developed is clearly humorous. In the presumably earliest of the three passages, the pagans are asked:[55]

> Do you have the male and He has the female? That indeed is an unjust division!

The Qur'ān does not denounce directly the false teaching of the opponents, but it wonders ironically how they would ascribe to God what they usually do not keep. The broken norm reveals that the unbelievers have diverted from their habitual customs, treating God unequally. Furthermore, what is more surprising is that the Qur'ān, with the rhetorical question, seems to adopt the standpoint of the unbelievers, allowing God, for a moment, to share with human beings the characteristic of having children. The Qur'ān delivers here a clear case of violation of its own most important theological principles. Finally, the Qur'ān makes fun of the division suggested by the unbelievers, describing it as "unjust division" (qisma dīzā).

Another passage exaggerates the reaction an Arab pagan would usually have at the birth of a daughter:[56]

> And they assign to God daughters; glory he to Him! And they have their desire; and when any of them is given the good tidings of a girl, his face turns permanently black and he chokes inwardly, as he hides himself from the people because of the evil of the good tidings that have been given unto him, whether he shall preserve it in humiliation, or trample it into the dust. Ah, evil is that they judge!

The passage draws obviously a caricature describing the external and internal reactions which used to happen to the "standard" pagan Arab when he suddenly knew that for him a daughter was born. As realistic as it is, the description, including the physiognomy, psychology, and social behavior of the person, intentionally exaggerates in order to make the reaction of the Arabs to the birth of daughters as ludicrous as possible. The humorous description is intended here as a technique to criticize the Arabs for not accepting daughters. However, the humorous critique of this social practice takes place in the course of the serious theological argument against the wrong belief that God has daughters. But the Qur'ān does not argue in a dialectical–logical way. It, rather, through the satirical description of the opponents, shows the absurdity of their conviction. Qur'ānic humor is integrated here in a theological debate with social reformative dimensions. The Arabs' belief in God's daughters and their killing of their own daughters are both, at the same time, reviled in the way of humorous polemics.

The third passage goes further challenging the polytheists to show their knowledge about God. Here he is the speaker:[57]

> So ask them for a pronouncement—Has your Lord daughters, and they sons? Or did We create the angels females, while they were witnesses? It is out of their perversion that they say, "God has begotten". They are truly liars, Has He chosen daughters above sons? What ails you then,

---

55 Q 53:21–22.
56 Q 16:57–59.
57 Q 37:149–157.

how you judge? What, and will you not remember? Or have you a clear authority? Bring your Book, if you speak truly!

The prophet is commanded to ask the pagans how they would ascribe to God what they do not accept for themselves. God is making fun of them, by inviting the prophet to do the same. The imperative *fastaftihim,* addressing the prophet to challenge his opponents asking them what should embarrass them, is used ironically, to give the impression that the prophet's opponents would have the right answer.[58] But this can clearly not be the case. Again the Qur'ān is arguing against its principles, mocking the opponents in a deeply humorous way, showing their knowledge about divine issues as defective. God continues to challenge the pagans with the following question: "Or did We create the angels females, while they were witnesses?" Of course, those who claim for God daughters were not present as he created the angels; of course, he has not preferred daughters over sons, as the last question in the passage indicates.[59] Raising ironical questions, the Qur'ān challenges the unbelievers showing that they do not know what they are talking about. The way the Qur'ān deals with this issue is certainly humorous, contrasting God's superiority with the ignorance of the unbelievers.

God's Mockery

In Mecca, Muhammad was obviously not able to stop those who scoffed at him or to respond to them adequately in a way that could hurt them, just as they hurt him. God comforts him in that stage of his mission with the assurance that He will defend him from the scoffers who set another god against God. How this could happen is not further explained; it is merely anticipated that they will know.[60] The tables were turned in Medina. There, Muhammad gained power and became a leader of a religious and political community, which was able soon to undertake military expeditions to expand and enforce its power. In connection with these political developments, the Qur'ānic discourse on humor seems to show distinctive changes regarding the confrontation with the pagans, the relations to the Jews, and the internal affairs of the Muslim community.

The second Sura *al-Baqara,* "The Cow", is widely considered as the first Medinan Sura. One passage in the Sura reflects a problem with which Muhammad and his community in the new context were confronted. Some of the people in Medina pretended to accept Muhammad's teachings while they were in fact only mocking, remaining faithful to their devils.[61] Their mockery can easily be connected to their power which enabled them to play this double role.[62] The Qur'ān states God's reaction to their attitude as follows:[63]

God mocks them and gives them the latitude to wander aimlessly in their intransigence.

---

58   In addition to Q 37.149 cf. 37:11.

59   Similarly developed questions are in God's dramatic speech to Job aforementioned.

60   Q 15:95–96. The majority of the commentators mention that live person who excelled in scoffing Muhammad und have been brought to death, each one of them through some harm. However, the commentators do not agree on their names. According to Jalāl al-Dīn al-Mahallī and Jalāl al-Dīn al-Suyūtī, Tafsir al-Jatalayan (Būlāq 1343; 1923–4). p. 220, they were al-Walid b. al-Mughīra, al- Ās b. Wā il, 'Udayy b. Qays, al-Aswad b. al-Muttalib and al-Aswad b. Abd Yaghùth Cf. al-Tabarī. *Jamī albayān* (see note 22). vol. VII: juz' XIV, pp. 47ff., Fakhr al-Din al-Rāzī. *Mafatih al-ghayb* (see note 26). vol. V. p. 282.

61   Q 2:14.

62   Cf. Camilla Adang. art. "Hypocrites and Hypocracy". in: *Encyclopaedia of the Qur'ān* (see note 11), vol. II, pp. 468ff.

63   Q 2:15.

For the first and only time in the Qur'ān, it is said that God mocks the enemies of the Muslim community. The statement in the present tense *yastahzi'u* does not express a wish or a curse which should be fulfilled in the future, but makes clear that God mocks the hypocrites in the present time of the community as well as in general. It implies that God's power, which immensely exceeds the power of the mocking enemies, is not only going to be manifested in the Hereafter, but also in the present world as well. His mocking of the liars takes the shape of paradoxical dealing with them. This is subsequently described in three different parables which all betray a touch of humor. Let us consider them closely:

1. The Qur'ān describes those who do not believe wholeheartedly as follows:[64]
   Those are the people who have bought error at the price of guidance; but their trade made no profit and they have not found the right way.
   The metaphor, which is taken from the world of commerce, a world with which Muhammad himself as well as many of his city-men were but very much familiar with, presents obviously a case of violating commercial rules. We could imagine that such an example should have caused among the audience a kind of *Schadenfreude* against their adversaries who were so stupid that they traded with loss.

2. Furthermore, the situation of those people is compared to those who kindled a fire, and when it lit all around them, God made them blind, so that they were no longer able to see.[65]
   Here we have a story which demonstrates a situation well known to the inhabitants of the desert who used to burn fire in order to get light and warmth in dark cold nights. Everything went well for the people mentioned in the story until God suddenly interfered. He did not extinguish their fire, which would be generally expected, but surprisingly and much more severely blinded them in a blink of an eye. God's action is shocking; it creates not only angst, but to the same extent, *Schadenfreude* which is to be increased by the paradoxical situation of the enemies: their fire is still illuminated, but they cannot benefit from the light they kindled. The humor lies in the juxtaposition of the external light of fire and the internal darkness of blindness.

3. The third parable presents a much more drastic situation. Those who pretend to believe, without doing that in reality, resemble those who:
   (…) in the midst of a cloudburst from the sky accompanied by darkness, thunder and lightning put their fingers in their ears to guard against thunderbolts for fear of death: and God is encompassing the unbelievers. The lightning almost takes away their sight; when it flashes they walk in it, but when it darkens they stand still. Had God willed, He would have taken away their hearing and their sight. God is truly almighty.[66]

---

64   Q 2:16.
65   Q 2:17–18.
66   Q 2:19–20: translation by Majid Fakhry. *An Interpretation of the Qur'ān: English Translation of the Meanings: A Bilingual Edition* (New York 2000), modified.

The described scenery includes several humorous elements. First, let us consider those scared people, who in the midst of a heavy thunderstorm try to avoid death by closing their ears. Their instinctive behavior is comical because it is merely an automatic reaction caused by deadly-fear without being able to diminish its reasons and change the situation for the better. Closing the ears so that the sound of thunder cannot be heard does not save one from death by lightning. It only grants the illusion of being safe.

Another element of humor in the passage lies in a further paradox: it is so dark that they are dependent on the lightning to see their way. This means that they are totally contingent on that which could kill them at any moment. Their highly paradoxical situation is humorously amusing to the believers who feel relieved. They are safe from such terrible situations because of their faith. With the humorous description, the parable provides them with an anticipated occasion of vengeance: their enemies will be punished deservedly.

A third aspect of humor is expressed in the manipulation those people are subjected to by the lightning. They walk when it shows them the way and stop when it does not. As in a thriller, these people are forced to embrace fear, totally at the mercy of the lightning in order to proceed. But that which they need is actually the danger from which they must flee: the moments of light are simultaneously moments of jeopardy. Paradoxically enough, they can feel safe when it is dark; but darkness means for them the inability to move out of the endangered area.

The whole situation generally demonstrates a humorous way which God applies to treating the hypocrites who think themselves powerful enough to cheat Muhammad and his community. According to the Qur'ān, God is able to make them deaf, dumb and blind: they are absolutely under His all-embracing power. But He chooses here to leave their senses intact, so that they can be frightened longer and more intensively with that which they can see and hear. Their punishment lasts as long as they continue to exist in this situation. God's mockery is humorously horrible.

A later passage describes the comical way in which the hypocrites react to the invitation to come to Muhammad so that he may seek forgiveness for them. They jiggle their heads (*lawwaw ru'ūsahum*) and turn away arrogantly mocking the offer.[67] However, regarding the coming punishment, Muhammad is told in another passage to challenge the hypocrites to keep mocking him as well as God and His signs.[68] In presumably one of the latest instances, even the possibility that God would on Muhammad's intercession forgive the hypocrites is abolished, because they basically disbelieved in God and His messenger.[69] The mocking of the believers qualifies them, instead, to earn God's mockery which is combined with painful torture.[70]

Anti-Jewish Humor

Not only those who pretend to be Muslims without being faithful are subject to humor in the Qur'ān. A parable addressing the Jews goes as follows:[71]

---

67   Q 63:5.I adopt Mir's translation of *lawwa* as "jiggle": Mustansir Mir, "Humor in the Qur'ān" (see note 9), p. 192. Cf. Q 47:20 where the hypocrites, "who are sick-hearted" look at Muhammad like someone "who swoons of death" when they hear lighting mentioned.

68   Q 9:64–65.

69   Q 9:80.

70   Q 9:79.

71   Q 62–5 (translation by Arthur J. Arberry, *The Koran Interpreted* [see note 49]).

The likeness of those who have been loaded with the Torah then they have not carried it, is as the likeness of an ass carrying books.

The Qur'ān is criticizing here the Jews who fail to follow the teachings of the Torah; it has been given to them, but they did not carry its burden. Like an ass which carries books, without being able to know what it carries or to benefit from it, they do not learn from the Torah what is written there about Muhammad and they do not recognize him as a prophet.

The example is extremely humorous with important implications. The donkey is for the Arabs the best example of ignorance and inability of understanding. It is considered to be a dumb animal; it is presented here as loaded with nothing else but books. When contrasted with the fact that books were at that time highly estimated as the main source of knowledge, the stupidity of the donkey becomes more emphasized. Nothing is more ignorant than a donkey that carries knowledge, without being able to recognize the value or the contents of its load. In this parable, knowledge and ignorance are extremely close to each other; in the light of knowledge ignorance becomes more obvious. And this is, indeed, the aim of this humorous parable: to show clearly the stupidity of the Jews, who did not understand the statements in the Torah anticipating Muhammad's appearance. In this sense, the parable could have in the inter-religious context of Medina the function of a relief valve; it could have given expression to Muhammad's anger at the Jews who not only did not follow him, but also tried to hinder his mission. On the other side, the parable contains an element of humorous aggression. It could, thus, be considered a part of the verbal attack against the Jews who have been accused of attempting to murder Muhammad. Comparing them to an ass means the absolute denial of their ability to understand the Torah. They are cut off from the possibility to gain knowledge from the book they adhere to, which consequently means that they become cut off from the pre-Muhammadan history of monotheism. This humorous polemic could be connected to the militarily subduing of the Jews by Muhammad and his community in Medina.

Non-humorous Internal Affairs

It is important to notice that the Qur'ān, while speaking of God's mockery against the hypocrites, does not invite the believers to mock their opponents. On the contrary, they are told:[72]

He has sent down upon you in the Book that when you hear God's signs (or: verses, *āyāt*) being disbelieved and made mock of, do not sit with them until they plunge into some other talk, or else you will surely be like them. God will gather the hypocrites and the unbelievers all in hell.

The believers are urged to avoid meetings in which God's signs are subject to disbelief and mockery. They should not be listening to others denying and making fun of God's revelations, so that they would not be influenced by that and perhaps start doing the same. The command aims at preventing the believers from imitating the unbelievers in making fun of God's signs. This purpose is further pursued through the final statement on God's gathering the hypocrites and the unbelievers in hell. Nevertheless, the intensity of the warning shows that the Qur'ān is aware of the dynamic nature of mockery which could easily be spread to embrace a larger group of communicants. Accordingly, mockery is an attractive danger,

---

72   Q 4.140 (Arberry's translation [see note 49], modified).

especially if its subject is the Divine. But mockery as such is not forbidden in the aforementioned verse; what is forbidden is a particular form of mockery addressed to God's signs.

In another passage, however, the believers are addressed with the following words:[73]

> O believers, let not any people scoff at another people who may be better than they; neither let women scoff at women who may be better than themselves. And find not fault with one another, neither revile one another by nicknames. An evil name is ungodliness after belief. And whoso repents not, those—they are the evildoers.

The verses state clearly that it is forbidden for Muslims to mock each other. Pointing out particularly the women in the community might be an indication of their inclination to make fun of each other in the social milieu of Muhammad. The reason given for the prohibition of mockery within the community is in both cases the same; the scoffed may be better than the scoffers. This explanation reveals an important aspect of the phenomenon of scoff and mockery, namely that its subject is the shortcomings of others and that it is deeply connected to the consciousness of superiority over others. The Qur'ānic argumentation deals with this psychological phenomenon in an extremely interesting way. The Qur'ān does not invite the believer, male or female, to be humble and consider all other believers better than he or she is, but it presents a psychological strategy based on the fact that human beings, no matter how fully we may seem to know them, still keep elements which remain hidden from other people and are only known to God. That is the reason why the scoffer ultimately cannot be certain whether the scoffed person is really inferior to him or her and whether this person consequently deserves to be mocked. It is actually an act of keeping balance between the people who, regarding their insufficient knowledge of each other have always to respect each other, avoiding mocking one another. Men and women are, in this sense, equal in their inability to possess perfect knowledge about each other which would enable them to feel themselves superior to others and mock them. Absolute knowledge is only God's; He is superior to everything in the world. Mockery remains, according to the Qur'ān, His business.

In times of war. especially when victory is not certain yet, there is not much space for humor and laughter. After an expedition which took place in the summer and was not attended by many Muslims who wanted to avoid the heat,[74] the Qur'ān makes the following statement:[75]

> Those who stayed behind rejoiced at tarrying behind the Messenger of God, and hated to struggle with their wealth and their lives in the way of God. They said, "Do not go forth in the heat." Say: "The fire of hell is hotter, if only they would understand!" Let them laugh little, and weep much, as a reward for what they have been earning.

Muhammad is called upon to tell those who were happy for not having participated in the battle because they feared the heat, that the fire of hell is exceedingly hotter than the summer heat. In response to their joy and laughter they are starkly threatened with a painful punishment. The clear message to them

---

73   Q 49.11 (Arberry's translation [see note 49]).

74   It is regarded to be the expedition of Tabūk which took place in 9/630, Cf. Mohammad A. al-Hakhit, art. "Tabūk", in *Encyclopaedia of Islam: New Edition*. vol. X (Leiden 2000, p. 50).

75   Q9.81–82.

is that their current laughter weighs but little compared to their longer lasting weeping in the Hereafter. God's command, let them laugh little and weep much, bears obvious mockery based on God's powerful attitude towards them. It is just like somebody who, full of irony, tells those whom he absolutely has under his control to laugh, knowing for sure that their laughter is merely temporary and that it will certainly be followed by a much larger extent of weeping out of pain. The antithesis of laughing and weeping reflects how much power those people have. As long as they are powerful, they are able to laugh. God's statement presents a form of humor which is connected to His absolute power.

To sum up: The Qur'ān contains statements and situations which reflect various aspects of humor in a broad sense. In most cases, humor in the Qur'ān is connected to power and serves as expression of superiority or aggression; in this case, it can be related to sarcasm. For that reason it is not allowed for the believers to apply it to each other in order to keep the unity of the community intact. On the contrary, humorous expressions are assimilated in inter-religious polemics as well as against the pagans. Taking into account the fact that humor is always addressed to deficits and shortcomings of other people, it remains in the end God's issue to mock the adversaries. As a speaker in the Qur'ān, God even argues in a serious theological debate in a humorous way to reject the idea that he would have daughters. The God of the Qur'ān not only allows humor; He also, in a simple human manner, applies it in His dealing with human beings. Thus, humor appears as a means of communication to convey important ideas in a powerful way from a superior standpoint.

II. The Qur'ān in Jocular Literature

Several works of classical Arabic literature contain a large amount of jocular texts which are arranged according to their topics. Just as humorous situations and statements are not lacking in the Qur'ān, this Scripture is also one of the topics listed in these books. It does not belong to the popular topics of the collected jokes and funny stories in which sexual humor and ridiculed groups such as the Bedouins are almost always favorites. However, the collected texts resulted from a much broader oral tradition which reflects the variety of themes that were omnipresent in the everyday life of medieval Islamic society. Taking into consideration the wide presence of the Qur'ān in the life of Muslims as well as the social, religious, and moral restrictions connected to its revered status, we could observe that the Qur'ān contributed to the development of a certain kind of Arabic jocular literature which deals with religious topics and could, thus, be considered as reflecting a certain type of humor which could be considered Islamic since it deals with specifically Islamic themes.[76]

In which sense, in which specific cases of everyday life and to what extent, is the Qur'ān involved in jokes and funny anecdotes? In order to answer these questions and furthermore to attempt to describe significant features of Islamic humor, I am going to discuss some jokes and anecdotes which deal with the Qur'ān.[77]

---

76   Cf. Ulrich Marzolph. "The Qur'ān and Jocular Literature", in: Arabica 47 (2000). pp. 478–487. especially 486 l.

77   I will be using materials collected in Ulrich Marzolph, Arabia ridens. Die humoristische Kurzprosa der frühen adab-Literatur im internationalen Traditionsgeflecht, 2 vols. (Frankfurter Wissenschaftliche Beiträge. Kulturwissenschaftliche Reihe 21: Frankfurt am Main 1992). The given numbers left to the backslash refer to the items, the numbers right to it refer to the pages in the second volume of Marzolph's book. Cf. also his contribution in the present volume.

In one story, a sponger recites Qur'ānic verses containing numbers in order to cadge from his partner the same number of bites. To get the first bite he recited "Your God is surely one" (Q 37:4). He snatched the second and the third bites with a verse recalling God sending two messengers to a city and a third one to reinforce them (Q 36:14). The sponger's partner gave finally up as he recited Q 8:65 with the numbers twenty, one hundred, two hundred, and a thousand. Self-confident, the sponger said that he could go even further to one hundred thousand and more, recalling Q 37:147.[78] The sponger in the story did not show any disrespect of the Qur'ān, but he dealt with verses playfully, taking them out of the context to support his greed. Obviously, his partner was powerless against this tricky way to obtain food: how could he have rejected arguments supported by the Qur'ān? Contrary to this sponger who was obviously knowledgeable in the Qur'ān, another one knew only one Qur'ānic verse that specifically contains the demand to bring lunch (Q 18:62).[79]

A different form of humor is expressed in the way a false prophet uses a Qur'ānic verse in order to justify his pretending of prophecy, or a faulty physician to justify his medical mistake. The authority of the Scripture is used in such cases to credit a behavior the acceptability which it does not actually have.[80] This is done on purpose with full awareness of the situation. This cannot be claimed for the stupid man who used not to feed his donkey, but to recite above its nosebag the verse "Say: He is God, One" (Q 112:1). As the donkey starved, the man was angry at the verse and said:

By God, I never would have thought that the verse "Say: He is God. One" kills donkeys! By God, I am sure it is even more lethal for humans, so I will not recite it again as long as I live![81]

The joke does not make fun of the central Islamic doctrine of God's Oneness, but of the stupidity of the donkey's owner. Nevertheless, his comic behavior gains more intensity through the striking contrast created by connecting the sublime theoretical idea of God's Oneness to the banal act of feeding a donkey. We find similar naïveté in the soothsayer who said that God had taken the ring which had been stolen and was found hidden in a Qur'ān.[82] In both stories central theological doctrines are dealt with humorously, however, without reflecting any blasphemous attitude against God or the Qur'ān.

Furthermore, we find stories about lax playful treatment of the Qur'ānic text, such as adding parts from different verses to each other or replacing words in verses through new words which create new statements which serve the purpose of the protagonist.[83] Thus, the mother of the person whose balance of good deeds will be found light on the Day of Judgment becomes "whore" (zāniya) instead of "pit" (hāwiya) which stands for hell in Q 101:8–9.[84] The eschatological meaning of the text becomes changed in this manner abruptly to a curse. Another anecdote presents a witness in the court who recites, instead of the Qur'ān, meaningless rhymed sentences which the judge held for Qur'ānic verses and granted the witness credibility.[85] After an attack by the Kurds one recites Q 9:97 replacing the Bedouins criticized

---

78   Ibid.. 766/180: cf. 1035/229 for dividing food according to certain verses.
79   Ibid., 755/178.
80   Ibid., 246/64; 250/65.
81   Ibid., 674/162. A longer version of the anecdote is in idem, "The Qur'ān and Jocular Literature" (see note 75), p. 478.
82   Idem, *Arabia ridens* (see note 76), 611/150.
83   Ibid., 898/203; 1239/266.
84   Ibid., 940/211f.
85   Ibid., 903/204.

there through the enemies.[86] In a similar way, the Imam who mentioned falsely the Turks instead of the Byzantines in his recitation of Q 30:2 and was made aware of his mistake said that they were but the same.[87]

Another category of humorous dealing with the Qur'ān is that which contains anecdotes in which the meaning of Qur'ānic statements is altered or applied to a totally alien context, without changing the verbal text of the Scripture. Following the statement in Q 3:161. "who defrauds shall bring the fruits of his fraud on the Day of Resurrection", a thief used to steal only perfume bottles because they are light to carry on that day.[88] In the same way an obsessed man who was tormented by children and fled into a house identified his situation with the eschatological situation described in Q 57:13:

> And a wall shall be set up between them, having a door in the inward whereof is mercy, and against the outward thereof is chastisement.[89]

Furthermore, a cadger who, without being invited, joined poets who were invited to a banquet justified his deed saying that he belonged to the perverse who follow the poets according to Q 26:224.[90]

Some anecdotes make fun of the way Qur'ānic verses are applied inappropriately to deal with certain situations. A man to whom it is recommended to recite verse Q 55:33 in order to defend himself against dogs is told to also take a staff because not all dogs know the Qur'ān.[91] The Arabs are declared stupid because they asked God to rain down upon them stones out of heaven, according to Q 8:32.[92] In a joke, Moses is mocked because he delivers a long answer with unnecessary details to God's question what he was holding in his hand.[93] No doubt, Qur'ānic verses are here the object of humorous interpretation which is directed to a prophet, but, at the same time, challenges the integrity of the Qur'ānic text.

In another anecdote, a man reciting from Q 59:9, "(…) those who made their dwelling in the abode (…) prefer others above themselves, even though poverty be their portion", wants to urge his companion to give him his coat as a gift. Refusing to do that, the coal owner argues ingeniously in the same way known in the Qur'ānic science of the occasions of revelation (asbāb al-nuzūl) that this verse was revealed in Arabia, where the weather is hot, not in Syria, where it is cold.[94] Furthermore, we read about Qur'ānic verses used in a dispute between an ugly woman and a man who made fun of her physical appearance.[95] Some other anecdotes tell how verses are used by female slaves who competed with each other about the right to sleep with their lord that night.[96]

---

86   Ibid.. 999/222. Q 9:97: "The Bedouins are more stubborn in unbelief and hypocrisy, and apter not to know the bounds of what God has sent down on His Messenger; and God is All-knowing, All-wise." (Arberry's translation [see note 49]).
87   Ulrich Marzolph. *Arabia ridens* (see note 76). 1215/26l. Q 30:2: "The Byzantines have been vanquished." (Arberry's translation [see note 49]).
88   Ulrich Marzolph. *Arabia ridens* (see note 76), 8/2.
89   Ibid., 355/89; cf. 18/5.
90   Ibid., 757/178.
91   Ibid., 778/182. Q 55:33. "O tribe of jinn and of men. If you are able to pass through the confines of heaven and earth, pass through them! You shall not pass through except with an authority." (Arberry's translation [see note 49]).
92   Ulrich Marzolph, *Arabia ridens* (see note 76), 48/13.
93   Ibid., 1048/231; cf. Q 20:17–18.
94   Ibid., 595/147.
95   Ibid., 1103/241.
96   Ibid., 406/101:823/190.

Liturgical Qur'ān recitation is connected in several stories to sudden reactions that cause a state of humor. As the Imam halted at reciting the sentence "We have sent Noah" (Q 7:59; 71:1) and repeated it several times because he forgot the following verse, one of the audience exclaimed: "So send someone else finally and release us!"[97] A Bedouin said boldly to another Imam, who had just recited "What do you think? If God destroys me and those with me, or has mercy on us, then who will protect the unbelievers from a painful chastisement?" (Q 67:28), that he should perish alone.[98] In both cases the protagonists consider the Imam as directly involved in the actions indicated in the verses. For them, not God, but the Imam spoke through the Qur'ān. Contrary to them, a thief was horrified as he heard verses he applied to himself: he felt himself threatened and returned the stolen object immediately.[99] And a Bedouin whose name was *Mujrim,* which means "criminal", fled out of the mosque as he heard Q 77:18, where the criminals (*mujrimūn*) are heavily threatened with terrible punishments in the Hereafter.[100]

Finally, Qur'ānic verses used on an occasion reflecting social conflict grant the event humorous character. A poor man carried a rich man on his shoulders across a river. As he was carried, the rich recited: "Glory be to Him, who has subjected this to us" (Q 43:13). Just as they reached the middle of the river, the poor man threw him down in the water and recited:

And say, "O my Lord, harbor me in a blessed harbor, for You are the best of harborers" (Q 23:29).[101]

Both the boasting of the rich and the vengeance of the poor take a humorous shape because they are asserted through Qur'ānic verses that are applied to a comical situation in order to express power and triumph.

The anecdotes presented show that the Qur'ān was not only integrated in humorous situations, but also contributed to create humor in situations which would not have been humorous, if the Qur'ān had not been involved in them. Neither the protagonists nor the compilers of the anecdotes felt any restrictions to have the Qur'ān involved in funny, playful situations. Its presence there gives shape to a particular form of humor which can be called Islamic. However, we should keep in mind that these anecdotes do not include anything against the Qur'ān, its divine origin and the prophet who proclaimed it. Qur'ānic verses could be used for humorous purposes, and for that reason, they were altered or parodied. The Qur'ān can shape humor, but it is not allowed to be made an object of humor. This restriction equally applies to making fun of God, Muhammad and other prophets. These themes are in Islam taboo for humorists.

---

97 Ibid., 462/116.
98 Ibid., 907/205.
99 Ibid., 1048/232.
100 Ibid., 1115/243.
101 Ibid., 1179/253f.

Chapter 9

TOWARD GENDER, SEXUALITY AND SEXUAL INEQUALITY …
"Sex and the City"

Liberated Jokes: Sexual Humor in All-female Groups

by Janet Bing (2007)

Abstract

Females have formerly been under-represented in jokes. Many scholars have claimed that joke making is primarily a male activity, particularly in the domain of sexual jokes. In this paper, I discuss sexual jokes that women share with each other both in all-female groups and by e-mail. After reviewing some widely held assumptions about women and jokes, I explore liberated women's jokes, including their structure, use of stereotypes, and subversive ideas. Finally, I discuss why humor theory is incomplete without the inclusion of a female perspective and suggest that women should tell more jokes.

Keywords: Feminism; joke telling; sexual humor; stereotypes; women and language; women's sense of humor.

1. Introduction

When Apollo Mission Astronaut Neil Armstrong first walked on the moon, he not only gave his famous "one small step for man, one giant leap for mankind" statement, but followed it with several remarks to the other astronauts and Mission Control, including the remark, "Good luck, Mr. Gorsky." Over the years many people questioned Armstrong as to what the "Good luck Mr. Gorsky" statement meant, but Armstrong always just smiled. However, in 1995 after Mr. Gorsky had died, Neil Armstrong felt he could answer the question. When he was a kid, he was playing baseball with a friend in the backyard. His friend hit a fly ball, which landed just below his neighbor's bedroom windows. His neighbors were Mr. and Mrs. Gorsky. As he leaned down to pick up the ball, young Armstrong heard Mrs. Gorsky shouting at Mr. Gorsky, "Oral sex! You want oral sex?! You'll get oral sex when the kid next door walks on the moon!"

This story, reputed to be true, is a fairly standard narrative joke and follows one pattern of sexual humor identified by Raskin (1985) in his discussion of sexual jokes. Like all but two of the many examples of sexual jokes Raskin discusses, the story begins with a non-sexual script and switches to a sexual script. This particular joke works for a number of reasons, and has never failed to get a laugh from both men and women when I have told it.

However, there are many types of sexual jokes that generally are not told in mixed company. Many of these can be found in published collections such as Legman (1968, 1975). Because academic humor theorists have historically been predominately male,[2] the sexual jokes collected, published and analyzed have generally been those told in all-male groups. Until recently, the assumption has been that all-female groups do not create and share sexual jokes. This is not the case.

I have collected a number of sexual jokes from friends, colleagues, relatives, students and former students, jokes that women share with each other, often by e-mail, but sometimes at social occasions. In this paper, I am going to compare some of these "liberated" jokes to the typical sexual jokes found in mainstream collections. Traditional sexual jokes, such as the Neil Armstrong joke, are funny partly because they violate taboos against talking in public about sex. "Liberated sexual jokes" are funny because they violate taboos against talking about sexism.

After briefly reviewing some traditional assumptions about women and jokes, I discuss some of the differences between mainstream jokes (which tend to be from a male perspective) and liberated women's jokes, in terms of their structure, their use of stereotypes, and the subversive nature of some of the jokes discussed. Finally, I return to the issue of why humor theory is incomplete without the inclusion of a female perspective and I suggest that women should be encouraged to tell more jokes.

2. Who Tells Jokes?

I belong to several groups of friends who frequently exchange jokes by e-mail and, less frequently, tell each other jokes in social situations. Much to my surprise, the *New York Times* announced in May, 2005 that "the joke died recently after a long illness, of, oh, 30 years" (St. John 2005). According to St. John and his sources, standup comics no longer tell jokes onstage, and:

> ... out in the real world, the joke hung on for a while, lurking in backwaters of male camaraderie like bachelor parties and trading floors and in monthly installments of Playboy's "Party Jokes" page. Then jokes practically vanished. (St. John 2005: 11)

Among the possible reasons the article cites are the atomic bomb, short attention spans, the Internet, political correctness and the feminism of American culture. However, announcements about the death of the joke, like those that periodically report the demise of feminism, may be premature. Garrison Keillor's Prairie Home Companion radio program continues to have an annual joke show. Christie Davies (2004b: 6), a leading humor scholar, does not report the death of the joke, and even claims that rather than being extinct, jokes are increasing: "Indeed the modern technology of the Internet and email and ever-cheapening international phone calls has multiplied the volume of jokes and increased the speed of their circulation."

3. Women and Jokes

In addition to reporting the death of jokes, St. John also suggests in the same *Times* article that women cannot tell jokes. He quotes a former president of the International Society of Humor Studies, John Morreall, who summarizes some standard assumptions about women and jokes and who claims that women have been ahead of the trend because they prefer not to tell traditional jokes:

> Telling old-style jokes, he [Morreall] said, was a masculine pursuit because it allowed men to communicate with one another without actually revealing anything about themselves. Historically women's humor was based on personal experience, and conveyed a sense of the teller's likes and dislikes, foibles and capacity for self-deprecation. ... A very common quip was, "Women can't tell jokes" ... Mr. Morreall said. "I found that women can't *remember* jokes. That's because they don't give a damn. Their humor is observational humor about the people around that they care about. Women virtually never do that old-style stuff." (St. John 2005: 2)

Morreall may be basing his opinions partly on existing scholarship. In 1975, Robin Lakoff was apparently serious when she wrote:

> It is axiomatic in middle-class American society that first, women can't tell jokes—they are bound to ruin the punchline, they mix up the order of things and so on. Moreover, they don't "get" jokes. In short, women have no sense of humor. (Lakoff 1975: 56)

Hay (2000) also discusses a number of writers, beginning with Freud, who have reported that women do not tell jokes (except self-disparaging ones) and generally do not have a sense of humor. Kotthoff (2000) reports that in informal dinner conversations, women used more self-deprecating humor and men told more standardized jokes, used more disparaging humor, and did more sexual teasing. Both Coates (1996) and Kotthoff (2000) present data that support Morreall's conclusion that women prefer making spontaneous joking comments to telling traditional jokes. As Attardo (1994: 298) notes, for people in general, "canned jokes cannot occur as frequently as conversational jokes." It is quite possible that most women are still more comfortable with conversational humor and personal anecdotes than with joke telling, since, as (Norrick 2003: 1344) observes, "joke telling counts as a performance," but this does not necessarily entail that women do not enjoy "that old-style stuff." Nardini (2000) discusses the performance of jokes in an Italian ladies' club, where both formal and informal jokes are told. She notes (2000: 96) that none of these jokes could have been told in public, that is, in the presence of men. Evidence is growing to refute the opinion that "women have no sense of humor."

However, until recently, collections of jokes or academic writing on humor have supported the view that women do not create jokes, since the majority of published jokes and humorous stories are by men.[3] As part of an attempt to collect and write humorous stories about and for women, I confirmed Kramerae's (1981) earlier conclusion that in published collections of jokes, women exist only as the standard stereotypes: dumb blondes, nagging wives, Jewish mothers, angry feminists, mothers-in-law, and sex objects. Jokes, of course, depend on common stereotypes, and most stereotypes about women are negative in the fictional world of jokes. Compared to the numerous male-dominated collections of wit and humor there are very few on women's humor, such as Stillman and Beatts (1976), Kaufman and

Blakely (1980), Savanna (1991), and Barreca (1996). When I examined web-based joke pages and the joke books available in my local library and bookstores, I found far more humorous anecdotes by, for, and about men than women.[4]

4. Women and Dirty Jokes

Although the idea that women do not tell jokes and do not have a sense of humor has sometimes been challenged, most humor scholars still contend that "respectable" women generally do not tell dirty jokes. Mulkay (1988) quotes Legman (1968: 217) who asserts:

> One fact strikingly evident in any collection of modern sexual folklore, whether jokes, limericks, ballads, printed 'novelties,' or whatnot, is that this material has all been created by men, and that there is no place in it for women except as the butt.

Legman is correct in noting that most dirty jokes are "grossly anti-woman." He also claims (1975: 35) that a woman who tells dirty jokes is "effectively denying her own sex as a woman." In 1976, Gary Fine wrote that although society is changing, "In Anglo-American culture … sexual humor has been primarily a male prerogative, usually found at such times when females are not present." More recently, in response to an article about lesbian jokes (Bing and Heller 2003), Christie Davies (2004a) is surprised that lesbians invent sexual jokes. Referring to lesbian jokes he says (317), "It is then all the more interesting that in the absence of male interest, some lesbians should have taken to what was traditionally an allmale pastime, namely the inventing of jokes about sexual behavior."

A few researchers have questioned the prevailing assumptions about women and jokes, including sexual jokes. A study by Wilson (1979) found that women subjects gave slightly higher ratings for sexual jokes than men did and notes (125) that "there is little previous evidence of sex differences in the appreciation of sexual humour." He suggests "The studies showing less amusement of sexual humour among women employed chauvinist, professional wit—produced mainly by men for masculine amusement." Using jokes that were not hostile to women, Lundell (1993: 308), too, found "that women do like sexual jokes even more than men depending on the type and content of the joke as well as who tells it." Mulkay (1988) noted that some humor has been influenced by the women's movement. Feminists "have sought to address and make fun of the basic assumptions of men's views of women, which are linked to the basic assumptions of men's sexual humor."

Until quite recently, few researchers have published information about jokes told in all-female groups by young women (Preston 1994), lesbians (Bing and Heller 2003) older women (Mitchell 1978), women of Italian descent (Nardini 2000), women of ill repute (Johnson 1973), or feminists (Green 1977; Barreca 1991; Crawford 1995; Bing 2004). Yet, humor theorists continue to base their analyses primarily on jokes written by men because they find plentiful evidence in well-established sources.

Naturally, male scholars have had limited access to women's sexual humor or the jokes told in all-female groups. The sexual jokes that women share with each other are not necessarily those used publicly by the relatively small numbers of female joke writers and comediennes. In addition to factors that have discouraged women from other types of public discourse, one reason for the apparent public absence of female-initiated jokes is the role that jokes, particularly sexual jokes, have traditionally played in identifying women as sexually available or promiscuous. Quoting Freud, Peter Farb (1974) notes that a woman who laughs at a dirty joke is signaling a willingness to accept a man's sexual approach:

> A woman who agrees to listen to such a joke (or even sometimes tells one of her own) indicates that she is ready to accept such an approach. And once she has shown her willingness, it is very difficult for her later to revert to a pose in which she is shocked by the man's physical behavior. (Farb 1974: 96)

Legman (1975: 25) notes the "aphrodisiacal" effects of dirty jokes and claims that the telling of dirty jokes in mixed company often ends "by accompanying one of the ladies home at the end of the session and attempting to have sexual intercourse with her." (34) Walle's (1976) study of the role of humor, including sexual humor, as a preliminary step to a sexual pick-up provides further empirical evidence for this claim. As Freud, Legman, Farb and Walle suggest, women who wish to reject a male's advances, may do so by pretending to not understand a sexual joke or finding some excuse not to respond. Barreca (1991: 50) discusses the belief that only "Bad Girls" initiate humor of any kind, and she quotes the conclusion of anthropologist Matadev Apte that throughout the world, women who tell any type of jokes are regarded as sexually promiscuous. If they initiate sexual humor they appear even more promiscuous, since it takes a certain "fallen knowledge" to make, or even understand, such jokes. As in many other situations, women are in a double bind. If they don't tell or laugh at sexual jokes, even those directed against them, they have no sense of humor. If they do, they are available. Most males do not operate under such restrictions.

I questioned several undergraduate students and younger instructors by e-mail about whether young women perceive the situation to have changed. Jennifer, a witty student in her early twenties, responded by e-mail:

> When I pretend not to understand the joke (and I'm really good at playing dumb), the joke becomes centered around my sexual inexperience—when I don't laugh, I get laughed at. But when the boys would say something dirty and I would laugh, the "severity" of the jokes would escalate—either that or they would become more directed towards me. I definitely believe that a female with a sense of humor (and by that I mean laughing at sexual jokes) is judged as more sexual—sexually "open" at the very least, and most likely sexually available. A woman who tells dirty jokes, in the company of men, is seen as sexually assertive or even easy—I would definitely agree that once this type of "reputation" is established it is very difficult to be seen in any other way (i.e. shocked by a man's behavior.) ... I think that men telling sexual jokes in the presence of women has become a way of testing the waters—probing them for some insight into their sexual availability.

Jennifer is aware of the double bind for women in situations where sexual jokes are being told. An outspoken young instructor whom I queried agreed with Jennifer and concluded, "I've told jokes for years, as you know. But it's cost me." Crawford (2003: 1414) observes that jokes are one means of social interaction, and males and females use humor in gendered ways "thereby performing gender and re-producing the gender system." For example, when women pretend not to understand sexual jokes or laugh politely at sexist jokes, they are following the social expectations of the dominant culture and are "performing gender" in the socially expected way (Butler 1990; West and Zimmerman 1987). However, when they hear or tell jokes that do not meet conventional expectations, they are acting out of role, and dismissed as less than respectable, or even worse, "liberated women."

5. Whose Experience Counts?

Because I am a feminist, I often do not share the experience, the presuppositions, or the assumptions of my male academic colleagues.[5] Unlike most male scholars, my "communities of practice" (Eckert and McConnell-Ginet 1992) include many all-female groups and this has made it possible for me to collect jokes from a liberated woman's perspective. Thus, I bring a different value system and different personal experience to the issue of women and jokes than that of many male researchers. Although I have read repeatedly that women do not tell jokes, particularly sexual jokes, I continue to observe women of different ages telling jokes in a variety of settings: birthday parties, dinner parties, class reunions, restaurants, homes, and even the supermarket. In addition, friends, relatives, colleagues, students and former students continue to send me jokes by e-mail. As Davies (2004) notes, the Internet and e-mail have increased the volume of jokes being circulated. Many of my female friends are feminists and some are senior citizens, so age and the fact that some of these people know that I collect jokes may make my experience atypical, but I doubt that because I rarely initiate the joke-telling at parties and am seldom the sole recipient of the joke e-mails.

Feminist scholarship is often labeled political, and it is. However, feminist, critical and postmodern scholars such as Foucault (1972), Harding (1991), and Crawford (2000) argue that scholarship is *never* value-free and they agree with Banks (1993: 5) that all scholarship is political and "contains important human interests and normative assumptions that should be identified, discussed, and examined." Banks proposes that it is useful for all scholars and writers to recognize the positions and frames from which they present their data, interpretations, and analyses, whatever their biases, for these biases are usually consistent with their training and personal experience.

It might surprise some men to learn that many of the jokes I have collected are about sex. Barreca (1991) also reports that women she knows share jokes about sex:

> Sharing sexual stories and jokes has long been an underground activity for women, a private set of experiences monitored as fiercely as our weight and kept just about as secret. These stories could never make it to the light of day. (Barreca 1991: 151)

Is there any academic value in exploring the perspectives of putative minorities such as women? I believe there is. One goal of feminist scholars is to change the status quo in all academic fields by recognizing and including the perspectives and contributions of females.

6. Sexual Humor

In his chapter on sexual humor, Raskin (1985: Ch. 5) identifies several types of sexual humor, all of which involve a standard opposition of a non-sex-related script with a sex-related script. All involve sexual/

nonsexual oppositions, either specified or unspecified. Except for two of Raskin's examples, all the sexual jokes he quotes begin with a non-sexual script and end with a sexual script, as in the following joke:

(1) Early morning in a Russian forest. The door of a small hut opens and two men crawl out followed by a bear. The loud female voice sounds from inside: "You two, get out! And you, in a fur coat, you stay!" (Raskin 1985: 159)

If Raskin's examples are representative, the majority of sexual jokes follow a standard pattern in which the script opposition involves a switch from a non-sexual to a sexual script. Why is this joke funny? As Raskin notes, one of the reasons is the switch to a topic of forbidden sex, in this case, the introduction of bestiality in the punch line.

In addition to jokes where a non-sexual script is replaced by a sexual script, Raskin lists another type of opposition illustrated by the following example:

(2) A man objects to the price a prostitute has charged him, and at-tempts to have intercourse with her violently in and around her navel, shouting, "At these prices, I am going to make my own god-damn hole!" (Raskin 1985: 55)

In this joke, as Raskin explains (161), there is a possible/impossible contrast and "the hearer is re-minded of the non-sexual world while being immersed in the sexual world." In fact, the non-sexual world is not really evoked in this joke, and the "impossible" contrast is not clear to me, since the joke suggests a traditional pornographic fantasy of sex and pain being inflicted on a subservient woman. Interestingly enough, although Raskin notes the possibility of beginning with a sexual script and switching to a non-sexual one, the following joke is the only one of his many examples that does so:

(3) The parents of the bride put up their daughter and her bridegroom in their living room for their wedding night. After midnight, dying of curiosity, they creep up to the door and stand there listening. They hear tense, hoarse whispers: "Just a little to the right! Now! No, it won't get in. To the left. No. Wait. Stop. Could you raise the right leg just a little bit? Good. That's better. Now that's a different matter … " Completely satisfied that everything is going as it was supposed to, the parents retire to their bedroom. In the morning, however, they discover the living room window open and the piano missing. (Raskin 1985: 163)

In every other sexual joke discussed by Raskin, including ethnic and political jokes that are also sexual, the sexual frame is not abandoned, even when a non-sexual element is introduced.

Although switching from a sexual to non-sexual script seems to be rare in sexual jokes that men tell, such a switch occurs in many of the jokes my women friends tell and share with each other. For example, I have received the following joke, "MAKE ME FEEL LIKE A WOMAN" from various female friends through e-mail:

(4) On a recent transatlantic flight, a plane passes through a severe storm. The turbulence is awful, and things go from bad to worse when one wing is struck by lightning. One woman in particular loses it. Screaming, she stands up in the front of the plane. "I'm too young to die," she wails. Then she yells, "Well, if I'm going to die, I want my last minutes on Earth to be memorable! Is there

ANYONE on this plane who can make me feel like a WOMAN?"
For a moment there is silence. Everyone has forgotten their own peril. They all stare, riveted, at the desperate woman in the front of the plane. Then a man stands up in the rear of the plane. He is gorgeous, tall, and very well built. He starts to walk slowly up the aisle, unbuttoning his shirt
... one button at a time.
... No one moves.
... He removes his shirt.
... Muscles ripple across his chest.
... he whispers:
... *"Here, iron this."*

The tense situation, the plea, "Make me feel like a woman,"[6] the gorgeous, tall, and very well built man unbuttoning his shirt, and the muscles rippling across the man's chest all build up the tension of the sexual script. The incongruity of the switch from a sexual script to a typical domestic script in the punch line is the basis for the humor.[7] For a male listener or reader the humor of the joke may simply result from the buildup of tension in a sexual script and the release when the non-sexual script is introduced in the punch line, very much as in the newlyweds and the piano joke in (3). However, for some women, the introduction of a domestic script is almost as taboo a subject as certain sexual topics. For many heterosexual women, raising the topic of the unequal distribution of domestic responsibilities can be difficult, unless, of course, done in the context of a joke.

The following story (received from Anita Fellman, Jan. 2004) follows a similar pattern:

(5) A woman was sitting at a bar enjoying an after-work cocktail with her girlfriends when an exceptionally tall, handsome, extremely sexy middle-aged man entered. He was so striking that the woman could not take her eyes off him. The young-at-heart man noticed her overly attentive stare and walked directly toward her. (As all men will.)
Before she could offer her apologies for so rudely staring, he leaned over and whispered to her, "I'll do anything, absolutely anything, that you want me to do, no matter how kinky, for $20.00 ... on one condition." (There are always conditions.) Flabbergasted, the woman asked what the condition was. The man replied, "You have to tell me what you want me to do in just three words." (Controlling huh?) The woman considered his proposition for a moment, then selected a $20 bill from her purse, which she pressed into the man's hand along with her address.
She looked deeply into his eyes, and slowly, and meaningfully said ...
"Clean my house."

Unlike the airplane story in (4), which evokes a typical domestic script in which a woman does the housework, the joke in (5) evokes an atypical domestic script where housework might be done by a male rather than a female. In liberated jokes, it is the inferior status of women rather than the sex that is the focus of the punch line, as in comedian Pam Stone's comment (Barreca 1996: 1):

(6) I had a girlfriend who told me she was in the hospital for female problems. I said, "Get real! What does that mean?"

She says, "You know female problems."
I said, "What? You can't parallel park? You can't get credit?"

In Stone's joke, the phrase "female problems" evokes the standard stereotypes and raises mildly taboo sex-related topics such as menstruation, PMS, and menopause. It is then followed by the self-deprecating line "You can't parallel park" quickly followed by the punch line, which is somewhat dated, since only older women in the U.S. now remember the time when they could get credit only if their husbands or fathers would sign for them. A more up-to-date punch line for this joke might be a current female problem such as "You can't get elected to Congress?"

Women's sexual jokes often reflect concerns other than sex, as in the following joke from Crawford (1995):

(7) Joe used to spend many evenings at this neighborhood bar with his friends, having a beer and socializing. Then, inexplicably, he was absent for over a year. One evening, a beautiful woman came into the bar, sat down, and said, 'Hello everybody. Do you remember me? I used to be Joe, but I had a sex change operation, and now I'm Debbie.' His/her friends were astounded. They gathered around to hear the story.
'What was it like? Did you have to take hormones? Did you have to learn how to dress and walk like a woman? And wear high heels?'
'Yes, but that's okay, I liked it actually.'
'But … the operation! You know … Wasn't it horrible? I mean, when they cut … '
'Yes, I know what you mean. No, that part wasn't too bad, it was all done by medical experts.'
'Well, then, what was the *worst part* about becoming a woman?' Joe/Debbie replied slowly and thoughtfully, 'I guess it was when I woke up from the operation and found out that they'd cut my paycheck by forty percent.'   (Crawford 1995: 157)

This joke is also somewhat dated, since women's earnings are currently around seventy-five percent of men's in the United States. Not everyone finds liberated women's sexual jokes funny because many people, including many women, are unfamiliar with the scripts that jokes like this presuppose. Despite the efforts of feminists to make people aware of social inequities, many people in the U.S. are not bothered by the fact that women earn less than men for identical or comparable jobs, do a disproportionate share of housework, child and elder care, are not well-represented in the government, and do not have equal rights under the U.S. Constitution. Although men's jokes (and much e-mail spam) often refer to the size of sexual organs, many women today are more interested in the privileges that go along with a penis rather than the penis itself. As Hollander and Barreca (2003) note:

Penis-envy we don't have, although we wouldn't mind some of the benefits awarded to those members: full access to the power structure, political influence, a decent credit line, and the ability to walk into a garage without the mechanic grinning and thinking "Oh, good, now I can put that wing on my house" because we have a question about the transmission. (Hollander and Barreca 2003: 23)

Liberated women's jokes provide more than a laugh. They remind other women that although the situation of women has improved, there still remain some serious inequities. As Emerson (1973) and Attardo (1994: 328) note, a non-bona fide text can be used to introduce or convey a serious meaning.

7. The Stupid and the Canny

Until quite recently it was not wise for a woman to display her intelligence or compete too successfully with a potential mate. This may be changing. In addition to switching from sexual to non-sexual frames, liberated women's jokes now switch the underlying assumption about the relative intelligence of males and females. In mainstream jokes, women, particularly blondes, are dumb. As Davies (1998) has shown, many ethnic jokes deal with what he calls "the stupid and the canny." Davies makes a convincing case that dominant groups do not project their anxieties on other ethnic groups that are completely foreign to them, but rather on groups that are similar and familiar to the dominant group, but are also somewhat marginalized. For example, Canadians make stupidity jokes about the Newfoundlanders, Mexicans about the Yucatecos, British about the Irish, Russians about the Ukrainians, etc. This might help explain the popularity of blond(e) jokes among males. Since women are still marginalized and treated as inferior in many societies, it is natural for them to be stereotyped in jokes as stupid rather than canny.

However, increasingly, women are sharing jokes in which it is the women rather than the men who are the canny ones. As Lundell (1993: 313) notes, finding humor in jokes "is a function of getting one's stereotypes confirmed." In a study of how college men and women responded to different jokes, Lundell (1993: 311) reports that females found the following joke funnier than males did:

(8) Some people had heard that their neighbor's daughter was going to drive around Europe with her boyfriend during the summer, so they asked the father:
"Aren't you worried about your daughter driving around in Europe with her boyfriend?"
"Not at all," said the father. "They have safety belts."

Note that in this joke, as in the jokes discussed above, the implied sexual script is replaced with a non-sexual script. For some people the putative naïveté of the father might be the source of some humor, but it is also possible that the lack of the traditional double standard might be what makes females like the joke more than males.

I have received via e-mail another example of what I would call a liberated woman's joke:

(9) A couple goes on vacation to a fishing resort in northern Minnesota. The husband likes to fish at the crack of dawn. The wife likes to read. One morning the husband returns after several hours of fishing and decides to take a nap. Although not familiar with the lake, the wife decides to take the boat out. She motors out a short distance, anchors, and continues to read her book. Along comes a game warden in his boat. He pulls up alongside the woman and says, "Good morning, Ma'am. What are you doing?"
"Reading a book," she replies, thinking *"Isn't it obvious?"*
"You're in a restricted fishing area," he informs her.
"I'm sorry officer, but I'm not fishing, I'm reading."

"Yes, but you have all the equipment. For all I know you could start at any moment. I'll have to take you in and write you up."

"If you do that, I'll have to charge you with sexual assault," says the woman.

"But I haven't even touched you," says the game warden.

"That's true, but you have all the equipment. For all I know you could start at any moment."

In this joke, which is a variation of an older, all-male joke found in Humes (1975), the wife is in a relatively powerless situation. Not only is the officious game warden male, but he also is a representative of a governing system controlled by and favoring males. By being canny, the wife has bested not only this individual man, but by implication, a social system that feminists argue has traditionally kept women at a disadvantage. There are many e-mail jokes in which women are assumed to be more intelligent than men, including a number of genie jokes in which men who wish to become twice as intelligent find themselves turned into women or the one in which the man says, "I wish that no matter where I go, beautiful women will want and need me" and finds himself turned into a tampon.[8] As women tell and hear more liberated jokes, perhaps they will also become less fearful of public displays of their own competence and intelligence.

8. Role Reversal

Although women have long been underrepresented in mainstream jokes, there is a long tradition of women who create jokes, cartoons, and humorous stories by switching the sex of characters in different situations.

In 1915 Alice Duer Miller (quoted in Kaufman and Blakely 1980: 90) wrote the following:

(10) Why We Oppose Votes for Men
   1. Because men's place is in the army.
   2. Because no really manly man wants to settle any question otherwise than by fighting about it.
   3. Because if men should adopt peaceable methods women will no longer look up to them.
   4. Because men will lose their charm if they step out of their natural sphere and interest themselves in other matters than feats of arms, uniforms and drums.
   5. Because men are too emotional to vote. Their conduct at baseball games and political conventions shows this, while their innate tendency to appeal to force renders them particularly unfit for the task of government.

Gloria Steinem (1983) uses role reversal in her humorous piece, "If Men Could Menstruate" where she notes "Clearly menstruation would become an enviable, boastworthy, masculine event. Men would brag about how long and how much." Judith Stone (1990: 82) used role reversal in "If Santa were a woman," observing that if Santa were a woman, "She and her husband would be in couples therapy, because she'd empathize with his discomfort at being the dependent clause."

In a cartoon by Marian Henley (*Hysteria,* Summer 1993) a male robbery victim is filing a complaint to two policewomen. The text is:

(11) *Man: I've been ROBBED! Some &#* took my WALLET! Cop 1: Well, what did you EXPECT? Cop 2: You're dressed so EXPENSIVELY! Cop 1: I'm afraid you wouldn't have much of a case ... Cop 2: It'd be YOUR word against THEIRS!*

Man: WHAT?!

Cop 2: How could you prove that you weren't willing? Man: WILLING?!

Cop 1: Nice men keep their wallet covered in public. They spend money MODESTLY ...

Cop 2: ... and don't call attention to their FINANCIAL CHARMS! Cop 1: Otherwise, people get the wrong idea!

Cop 2: If someone takes your money, it's YOUR fault, not THEIRS! Man: This ...

THIS IS CRAZY! Cop 1: No, this is role-reversal!

Cop 2: I mean, if you arouse somebody financially, you've GOT to follow through ...

Rape has always been a taboo subject, one that makes rape victims afraid to speak out for fear that someone will blame them, and one reason that this joke is funny is that this taboo subject is introduced. Mary Crawford (1995, 2000: 230–232) discusses this "much-repeated feminist classic," that "applies the blame-the-victim logic often used about rape victims to robbery victims." As she notes, this joke "acknowledges men's ability to define reality in ways that meet their needs," and subverts that ability by exposing its social construction. This is a particularly good example of liberated women's humor that effectively challenges the status quo, but can still be appreciated by both females and males.

9. Stereotypes

When I examined a number of joke collections, I was struck not only by the misogyny of many of the jokes, but also by the fact that almost all the characters in the jokes were male. The situation is analogous to the prior use of the generic male pronouns such as *he, his,* and *him.* Feminist scholars, including Bem and Bem (1973), Martyna (1983), and Cameron (1995) have shown that rather than including females, so-called generic pronouns simply make women invisible. The absence of women in jokes also suggests that only males count. Feminists have often used role reversal to create humor, but such reversals can be difficult because most stereotypes of women are predominately negative, as discussed in *Bitches, Bimbos, and Ballbreakers: The Guerrilla Girls' Illustrated Guide to Female Stereotypes* (Guerrilla Girls 2003). Because so many jokes rely on negative stereotypes, switching the sex of a joke's characters can be difficult and often involves changing a number of other things as well.

Sometimes, switching the sex of the characters ruins the joke. For example, consider the well-known joke from Raskin (1985: 100):

(12) "Is the doctor at home?" the patient asked in his bronchial whisper. "No," the doctor's young and pretty wife whispered in reply. "Come right in."

Raskin chose this joke for a ten-page analysis (1985: 117–127) because of its "typicality and average-ness" (117). However, the humor in this joke depends on several factors that Raskin does not specify. Stereotypically, doctors are male, which is why the well-known feminist riddle about the doctor works so well.[9] In addition, the doctor's pretty young wife must be stereotyped as sexually available for any male, even a sick one, when her husband is away. This is like the male fantasy propagated on MTV, where unattractive male performers are surrounded by adoring beautiful young women eager for sex. Needless to say, if the sexes of the characters are switched, it is also necessary to change stereotypes. Raskin's joke in (12) could be written as (13):

(13) Although the FEDEX delivery woman was suffering from a bad cold, she made one last delivery for the day. "Is your wife at home?" she asked in her bronchial whisper of the man who answered the door. "No," the traveling salesman whispered in reply. "Come right in."

In one sense, the wife in Raskin's original joke is not completely typical, since it is the wife and not the male visitor who is active and looking for sex. More typically, females in jokes are passive. As Mulkay (1988: 136) notes, "In the world of the dirty joke, women often become no more than objects designed to cater for the needs of men," as in the following example taken from Legman (1968: 239):

(14) WIFE: a gadget you screw on the bed to get the housework done.
Mulkay suggests that males could also be represented as objects, as in his proposed alternative:

(15) HUSBAND: a gadget you screw on the bed to obtain a fur coat/to feed the kids/to stop getting hit/to protect your friends.

In my opinion, neither joke is funny, but there are a number of jokes with exclusively male characters that I do find funny. I sometimes attempt to rewrite the jokes to include women, and switching female characters to male can reveal attitudes about sexuality that are not originally obvious. For example, I received the following joke by e-mail from a friend:

(16) There was a boy who worked in the produce section of the market. A man came in and asked to buy half a head of lettuce. The boy told him that they only sold whole heads of lettuce, but the man replied that he did not need a whole head, but only a half head. The boy said he would go ask his manager about the matter. The boy walked into the back room and said,
"There's some asshole out there who wants to buy only a half a head of lettuce." As he was finishing saying this he turned around to find the man standing right behind him, so he added, " … and this gentleman wants to buy the other half."
The manager okayed the deal and the man went on his way. Later the manager called on the boy and said, "You almost got yourself in a lot of trouble earlier, but I must say I was impressed with the way you got yourself out of it. You think on your feet and we like that around here. Where are you from son?" The boy replied, "Minnesota sir."
"Oh really? Why did you leave Minnesota?" asked the manager. The boy replied, "They're all just whores and hockey players up there."
"Is that right?" said the manager, "My wife is from Minnesota!" The boy replied, "No kidding … what team did she play for?"

Changing all of the characters to females in this joke requires quite a few other changes, including changes to the final punch line:

(17) Female manager: "Where are you from, Hon?"

The girl replied, "San Francisco, Ma am."

"Oh really? Why did you leave San Francisco" asked the manager. The girl replied, "All the men there are either hairdressers or hung like hamsters."

"Is that right?" said the manager, "My husband is from San Francisco!"

The girl replied, "No kidding … What does he charge for

highlights?"[10]

Merely changing the quick-witted produce boy to a quick-witted girl and changing the manager and customer into females, the joke, as originally written, would no longer be funny since calling a woman's husband a "stud" is not an insult. In order to inadvertently insult the manager, the produce clerk in (16) needs to evoke the stereotypes of an under-endowed male or a homosexual.

It is relatively easy to switch the sex of characters in jokes when the subject is not about sex, or when the joke is about old people. For example, it was easy to switch the roles in the following joke, sent to me by a niece. In the original version the driver was male:

(18) As a senior citizen was driving down the freeway, her car phone rang.

Answering, she heard her husband's voice urgently warning her, "Bertha, I just heard on the news that there's a car going the wrong way on Interstate 77. Please be careful!"

"You don't know the half of it," replied Bertha. "It's not just one car. It's hundreds of them!"

Because this joke evokes stereotypes of bad women drivers and clueless old people, it was easy to make the protagonist a woman. All that was necessary was to replace the "Hell," with the milder "You don't know the half of it."

Although stereotypes about women in jokes are often negative, women can still use them to create jokes from a feminist perspective. The Guerrilla Girls make fun of female stereotypes by exaggerating them in their own ethnic doll collection, which includes, among others, Latisha, the Welfare Queen, Sallie Mae, White Trailer Trash, and Lauren, a Jewish American Princess. Similarly, the humor of Jill Connor Browne's Sweet Potato Queens is aimed at female and ethnic stereotypes such as the thin girls who compete in beauty contests. Unlike other beauty queens, the Sweet Potato Queens proudly ride their floats in green sequined gowns, stuffed at the top and the butt "with enough batting to make fifteen good-sized teddy bears" (Browne 1999: 10). These architectural wonders are based on the secret philosophy that:

[for] white males it is impossible to have tits that are too big, and for black males, you cannot get the butt big enough. At the same time, if your tits are big enough, white guys don't care how big your butt is: and if your butt's big enough, black guys don't care what's happening around front. (Browne 1999: 10–11)

Even jokes with negative stereotypes can carry a feminist message. Two friends who are Jewish feminists sent me the following joke:

(19) The first Jewish woman President is elected and calls her mother: "Ma, I've won the election, you've got to come to the Inauguration!"

"I don't know, what would I wear?"

"Don't worry. Christian Dior is designing a dress just for you." "But I only eat kosher food."

"Ma, the Rabbinical Assembly is sending a kosher caterer for the entire White House."

"But how will I get there?"

"I'll send Air Force One to pick you up."

"But where will I sleep?"

"You will sleep in the Lincoln Room and I'm having a mikvah (ritual bath) built just for you."

"OK, OK, if it makes you happy, I'll come." The great day comes and Mama is seated between Trent Lott and John Warner on the West Front of the Capitol. Mama nudges Senator Lott and says: "See that girl up there with her hand on the Bible?"

Senator Lott says, "Yes."

"Well, her brother is a doctor."

Like the joke comparing rape to robbery, this joke contains a covert message. It suggests that women as well as men perpetuate a system that celebrates the achievements of male children, but discourages the aspirations of females. Like many of the jokes discussed above, this liberated joke is about sexism rather than sex.

10. The Effects of Including a Female Perspective

Feminist scholars continue to speculate about why so many men insist that women don't tell jokes or funny stories. Crawford (1995) notes the interesting paradox in the widely accepted stereotype of women as humorless:

> If we accept the argument that humor is a subordinate mode of discourse that rarely disrupts social hierarchies, there seems to be no reason for the culture to represent women as lacking a sense of humor ... Racist stereotypes of African–American people traditionally portrayed them as smiling and laughing, joking, and telling tales—as exaggeratedly comic. Why then, the cultural representation of women as humorless? (Crawford 1995: 153)

There are a number of possible explanations for the belief that women don't create and tell jokes. One explanation is that most people, including men, prefer not to be laughed at. As Molly Ivins (in Barreca 1996) has observed:

> A surprising number of men are alarmed by the thought of a witty woman. They think of women's wit as sarcastic, cutting, "ball busting." Margaret Atwood, the Canadian novelist, once asked a group of women at a university why they felt threatened by men. The women said they were afraid of being beaten, raped or killed by men. She then asked a group of men why they felt threatened by women. They said they were afraid women would laugh at them. (Barreca 1996: 18)

Crawford (1995: 153) suggests that "women's humor poses more of a threat than the humor of other subordinated groups because of the social proximity of women and men." Jokes allow women to introduce and develop topics that would otherwise be taboo or difficult to introduce in a more serious mode either at home or in public. Even though both women and men now work in full-time jobs, some women still find it difficult to discuss issues of sharing childcare and domestic responsibilities with their partners, and jokes make it possible to do so in a less threatening way. Many people, including young women, assume that Western women now have the same rights, opportunities and privileges as men. When feminists publicly raise issues of pay inequities and the lack of protection for women under the U.S. Constitution, they are often dismissed as "angry feminists" and ignored. However, jokes such as the one about the male robbery victim (11) and the one about the Jewish woman president (18) can raise such issues in a non-threatening way, and as Emerson (1973) notes, a joking reference sometimes can open the possibility for a more serious discussion.

In her cartoons, Nicole Hollander's humor often takes advantage of the different world views of males and females. One of her cartoons available on T-shirts and calendars described in Crawford (1995: 155) has two panels. The first panel, titled "What men hope women are saying when they go to the washroom together," shows two women bragging about the skill of their lovers. The second panel, "What they are really saying," shows this conversation: "Do you think cake is better than sex?" The other woman responds: "What kind of cake?" (Hollander quoted in Crawford (1995: 155). Hollander (quoted in Barreca 1991: 198) agrees that "men are frightened by women's humor ... because they think that when women are alone they are making fun of men." Hollander adds, "but they think we're making fun of their equipment when in fact there are so many more interesting things to make fun of—such as their value systems. Or the way they act when they're sick."

Women humorists are providing alternatives to traditional assumptions about appropriate gender roles. Some are even revising fairy tales, as in this rather mean-spirited version:

(20) Once upon a time, a beautiful, independent, self-assured princess happened upon a frog in a pond. The frog said to the princess, "I was once a handsome prince until an evil witch put a spell on me. One kiss from you and I will turn back into a prince and then we can marry, move into the castle with my mom and you can prepare my meals, clean my clothes, bear my children and forever feel happy doing so."
That night, while the princess dined on frog legs, she kept laughing and saying, "I don't think so."

Whether or not they do so in mixed company, women create and share jokes among themselves. Women are speaking up in a number of previously male-dominated fields, including the field of humor, and are even beginning to go public with jokes about sex. As Regina Barreca ("Who's laughing now?" [n.d.]) notes:

To see the way wit functions for all of us—men and women alike—is to see a map of our culture: to focus on things we've seen but not necessarily processed or analyzed; explaining what we've sensed but not yet bothered to define. Humor may have been ignored or challenged, but it has always been a secretly potent, delightfully dangerous, wonderfully seductive and, most importantly, powerful way to make a statement, to tell our stories, to make sure *everyone's* voice is heard.

When both men and women accept the myth that women have no sense of humor, everyone loses. Scholars of humor who propose various theories about jokes might find it useful to learn about jokes that women tell each other, rather than assuming that such jokes do not exist. The sexual jokes told by liberated women are different from traditional sexual jokes. The social functions of liberated sexual jokes share some of the functions of mainstream jokes as discussed in Attardo (1994: 323–324). Certainly these jokes create group cohesiveness and establish common ground between feminists. In some cases, they may provide an outlet for disgruntled subordinates (Coser 1960). They may sometimes achieve what Attardo (1994: 325) calls decommitment, which can include either "probing," that is, checking the value system of someone else or "salvaging," saving an uncomfortable situation by noting, "It was only a joke."

Because liberated sexual jokes are more about sexism than about sex, they do not function to control the sexual behavior of other women, and they challenge rather than reinforce social norms. Like teasing (Mulkay 1988: 79) these subversive jokes introduce disagreement in situations where overt criticism might be difficult. Just as jokes allow patients in hospitals to introduce uncomfortable and taboo subjects about death, staff competence, and indignities to patients (Emerson 1973: 269), liberated women's jokes allow feminists to introduce uncomfortable subjects about societies that systematically keep females at a disadvantage. As Mulkay (1988: 220–221) notes, serious discourse "generates a language of domination and opposition rather than, let us say, a language of collaboration and accepted diversity," and in serious discourse alternative versions of events are continually denied. By contrast, liberated jokes suggest that existing social norms can be challenged and undermined. To date, humor theorists have paid relatively little attention to subversive humor and to how possible covert messages can be transmitted through jokes.

Clearly, women have the most to gain if they dispel the myth of the humorless female. Girls and women used to be told that it was unladylike to speak in public and that females have no aptitude for mathematics. Currently, experts inform women that they cannot tell or remember jokes, and some women apparently accept this. Like other skills, creating and telling jokes requires a bit of effort and practice, but women can learn a lot from creating jokes. Using jokes, women can refer to uncomfortable issues without being stereotyped as angry feminists and subsequently dismissed or ignored as extremists.

With jokes women can exploit new stereotypes, such as the stereotype that men will not ask directions. (Why did the children of Israel wander around the desert for 40 years? Even in Biblical times men wouldn't ask for directions.) Women can use existing stereotypes in creative new ways and undermine old stereotypes. They can become visible in jokes by rewriting old jokes to include girls and women. Although this is not always easy, it is usually revealing.

As the jokes discussed in this paper show, witty women are already using humor to remind others about financial and domestic inequities. In the future women may use their wit to note other concerns, such as inadequate maternity leave, childcare, healthcare, and transportation. Jokes exist in a fictional universe where anything is possible, and this allows people to introduce alternatives to current ways of thinking. Jokes can suggest both problems and possibilities, as in the cartoon where a newscaster reads: "Our stories tonight: world peace and universal equality for women have been achieved! But first, our top story: Hell has frozen over."

Old Dominion University

Notes

Correspondence address: jbing@odu.edu

1. I would like to thank Anita Fellman, Denni Chiavarini, Carolyn Rhodes, Janet Katz, Mary Ann Tetreaut, Bobbi Myers and many other friends, students and former students for providing an endless supply of good jokes. I would also like to thank Charles Ruhl, Lane Dare, and Carolyn Rhodes for suggestions on earlier versions of this paper.

2. For example, the editorial board of the journal, *Humor,* is currently mostly male, with three significant exceptions, and of the 23 consulting editors, only 4 are female. In 2000 only one member of the editorial board was female, and two of the consulting editors were female. Such an imbalance might give the impression that women have little interest in humor.

3. In light of the traditional absence of women in other domains, it is not surprising that women should be poorly represented in any form of public discourse. Before feminists began actively searching for works by women in history, literature, music, art, and the sciences, it was generally assumed that women had contributed little in a number of male-dominated fields. Because of the work of feminist scholars, the omission of women in many traditionally male areas continues to be challenged. As Kesselman et al. (2003: 10) discuss in their introduction to "What is Women's Studies?" women scholars "initially endeavored to address the absence of women in the literature of varied academic areas by uncovering women's achievements … It quickly became apparent, however that the central concepts of many academic disciplines excluded women or assumed women's inferiority to men. Even the language used to describe these concepts and ideas is often laden with assumptions about female inferiority." The following (admittedly dated) quotation from Legman (1975) is an example. In the context of telling dirty jokes, Legman states:

   > Aside from the obvious advantage in turning off a would-be 'wolf' or seducer, it seems clear that a woman's telling a man repulsive sex-jokes of this kind, whether privately or publicly, is intended further as a sort of turnabout rape, in which it is she who outrages and humiliates the man—her own secret assessment of what sexual intercourse amounts to, from the woman's position. She is also effectively denying her own sex as a woman. For in telling such stories, the woman openly telegraphs her demand to be accepted as a 'liberated woman' or imitation man and not as a woman at all … women who are anxious to compete with men and to achieve male status (pants, wage-slavery, sterilization, and all the glorious rest of it) cannot afford to, and never do take into account the real and natural differences between the sexes … That is why they invariably lose, unless they have chosen obviously inferior, crippled or 'castrated' males to compete with and dominate, as they generally do. (Legman 1975: 35–36)

4. Of the 80 books in the Norfolk Public Library listed under the subject, "wit and humor," two-thirds of the authors (53) are male, one-fifth (17) female, and 10 (such as "Children's Press Choice") cannot be determined. Of the 17 books authored by females, 11 of those are written for children and juveniles. Even in books written or edited by women, men predominate. The book by Sylvia Simmons, *How to be the Life of the Podium,* contains an index of 303 people who can be quoted in speeches. Of these, 294 are male and 24 are female. Women are seriously under-represented in a book of stories by James Humes, *Podium Humor: A Raconteur's Treasury of Witty and Humorous Stories,* which was published in 1975. Following Humes' introduction about the use of humor in public speaking, he lists 644 humorous stories, and

with the exception of a six-page section called "Tea Party," the vast majority of stories are about males and the characters in the jokes are almost always male. In the first 200 jokes, women are simply missing; the few stories where they are included almost always involve sex or marriage or disparaging "humorous" quotations about women such as:

> You remember what Sam Johnson said—a woman speaking is like a dog walking on his hind legs. You don't expect her to do it well; you're just lucky if she can do it at all. (Humes 1975: 265)

5. In their discussion of culturally-based academic styles, Stewart and Bennett (1991: 41–44) note that Americans tend to value inductive analytical styles of thinking and devalue the relational styles of thinking characteristic of many women and of some non-Western societies such as China. As Stewart and Bennett say (42), relational thinking "involves a high degree of sensitivity to context, relationships, and status and exists in cultures where the social order approaches a *gemeinschaft* pattern." These two patterns of thinking value subjectivity differently:

> One of the major differences between analytical and relational styles is how subjectivity is treated. The analytical style separates subjective experience from the inductive process that leads to an objective reality. The relational style of thinking rests heavily on experience and fails to separate the experiencing person from objective facts, figures, or concepts. (Stewart and Bennett 1991: 43)

As Stewart and Bennett note, Western objectivity is not a universal value.

6. In an unpublished paper, the philosopher, Judith Andre (n.d.), argues that in many contexts the words *man* and *woman* are not parallel. The word *woman* has sexual connotations that neither the word *man* nor the word *lady* share, as illustrated by the following sentences:

> You became a man today.
> You became a woman today.
> You became a lady today.

7. Following Raskin (1975), the following are formal statements of the implied scripts. The symbol "+" means that an attribute is present, the symbol ">" stands for "in the past" and "=" for "in the present."

(i) FEMALE FANTASY LOVER SCRIPT Subject: [+Human] [+Adult] [+Female]

Object [+Human] [+Male] [+Adult] [+Attractive]

Activity: Have intercourse

= Responds to requests for sex positively

= Has no other restraints or interests except sex

Place: = Any place

Time: = Any time female desires

(ii) TYPICAL HOUSEWORK SCRIPT

Subject: [+Human] [+Female]

Activity: Do a variety of household chores

= Iron clothes

= Clean house = cook

= Raise children, etc.

Place: in the home

Time: whenever male requests

8. Here is another type of sexual joke in which women rather than men are canny.

(i) A man is driving down a deserted stretch of highway, when he notices a sign out of the corner of his eye. It reads SISTERS OF MERCY HOUSE OF PROSTITUTION—10 MILES. He thinks it was just a figment of his imagination and drives on without a second thought. Soon, he sees another sign which says SISTERS OF MERCY HOUSE OF PROSTITUTION—5 MILES and realizes that these signs are for real. When he drives past a third sign saying SISTERS OF MERCY HOUSE OF PROSTITUTION NEXT RIGHT, his curiosity gets the best of him and he pulls into the drive.

> On the far side of the parking lot is a somber stone building with a small sign next to the door reading SISTERS OF MERCY. He climbs the steps and rings the bell. The door is answered by a nun in a long black habit who asks, "What may we do for you, my son?"

> He answers, "I saw your signs along the highway, and was interested in possibly doing business."

> "Very well, my son. Please follow me."

> He is led through many winding passages and is soon quite disoriented. The nun stops at a closed door, and tells the man, "Please knock on this door." He does as he is told and this door is answered by another nun in a long habit and holding a tin cup. This nun instructs, "Please place $50 in the cup, then go through the large wooden door at the end of this hallway." He gets $50 out of his wallet and places it in the second nun's cup. He trots eagerly down the hall and slips through the door, pulling it shut behind him. As the door locks behind him, he finds himself back in the parking lot, facing another small sign:

> GO IN PEACE, YOU HAVE JUST BEEN SCREWED BY THE SISTERS OF MERCY.

This joke merits analysis for many reasons, most of them beyond the scope of this paper. However, it does show women as canny. It is also another example that begins with a sexual script and switches to a non-sexual script, as do jokes (3) through (7).

9. A father and son are involved in a serious traffic accident and both are sent by ambulance to the nearest hospital. The father is taken to one operating room and the son to another. One surgeon gets right to work on the father, but when the son is wheeled into the other operating room, the surgeon there takes one look at the patient and says, with strong feeling, "I cannot operate on this patient; someone else will have to do it." Why did the surgeon refuse?

10. I would like to thank a former student, Michael Joyner, for this version.

References

Andre, Judith
   n.d.   Ladies and men. Unpublished manuscript.
Attardo, Salvatore
   1994   *Linguistic Theories of Humor.* Berlin/New York: Mouton de Gruyter.
Banks, James A.
   1993   The canon debate, knowledge construction, and multicultural education.
          Educational Researcher (June-July), 4–14.
Barreca, Regina
   1991   *They Used to Call Me Snow White … But I Drifted.* New York: Penguin.

1996   *The Penguin Book of Women's Humor.* New York: Penguin Books.

n.d.   Who's laughing now? Humor and community. http://www.gina.com. (Accessed on 4 February 2004).

Bem, Sandra L., and Daryl J. Bem

1973   Does sex-biased job advertising "aid and abet" sex discrimination? *Journal of Applied Social Psychology* 3, 6–18.

Bing, Janet

2004   Is feminist humor an oxymoron? *Women and Language* XXVII (1), 22–33.

Bing, Janet, and Dana Heller

2003   How many lesbians does it take to screw in a light bulb? *Humor, International Journal of Humor Research* 16 (2), 157–182.

Browne, Jill Conner

1999   *The Sweet Potato Queens' Book of Love.* New York: Three Rivers Press and
http://www.sweetpotatoqueens.com/spq.

Butler, Judith

1990   *Gender Trouble: Feminism and the Subversion of Identity.* New York: Routledge.

Cameron, Deborah

1995   *Verbal Hygiene.* London. Routledge.

Coates, Jennifer

1996   *Women Talk: Conversation between Women Friends.* Oxford: Blackwell.

Crawford, Mary

1995   *Talking Difference: On Gender and Language.* London: Sage.

2000   Only joking: Humor and sexuality. In Travis, Cheryl and White, Jacquelyn (eds.) *Sexuality, Society, and Feminism.* Washington, DC: American Psychological Association, 213–236.

2003   Gender and humor in social context. *Journal of Pragmatics* 35, 1413–1430.

Davies, Christie

1998   *Jokes and their Relation to Society.* Berlin and New York: Mouton de Gruyter.

2004a   Response to Bing and Heller. *Humor* 17 (3), 311–322.

2004b   *The Right to Joke: Research Report 37, The Social Affairs Unit.* Great Britain: St. Edmunsbury Press.

Eckert, Penelope, and Sally McConnell-Ginet

1992   Think practically and look locally: Language and gender as community-based practice. *Annual Review of Anthropology* 21, 461–490.

Emerson, Joan P.

1973   Negotiating the serious import of humor. In Birenbaum, A. and Sagarin, E. (eds.), *People in Places: The Sociology of the Familiar,* London: Nelson, 269–280.

Farb, Peter

1974   *Word Play: What Happens When People Talk.* New York: Bantam. Fine, Gary

1976   Obscene joking across cultures. *Journal of Communication* 26, 134–140.

Foucault, Michel

1972   *The Archaeology of Knowledge.* New York: Pantheon.

Green, Rayna

1977   Magnolias grow in dirt: The bawdy lore of Southern women. *Southern Exposure* 4, 29–33.

Guerrilla Girls
  2003   *Bitches, Bimbos, and Ballbreakers: The Guerrilla Girls Illustrated Guide to Female Stereotypes.* New York: Penguin Books.

Harding, Sandra G.
  1991   *Whose Science? Whose Knowledge?: Thinking from Women's Lives.* Ithaca, NY: Cornell University Press.

Hay, Jennifer
  2000   Functions of humor in the conversations of men and women. *Journal of Pragmatics* 32, 709–742.

Henley, Marian
  1993   Cartoon. *Hysteria,* Summer 1993.

Hollander, Nicole, and Regina Barreca
  2003   *The ABC of Vice.* Hartford, CT: Bibliopola Press.

Humes, James C.
  1975   *Podium Humor: A Raconteur's Treasury of Witty and Humorous Stories.* New York: Harper and Row.

Johnson, Robbie Davie
  1973   Folklore and women: A social interaction analysis of a Texas madam. *Journal of American Folklore* 86, 211–224.

Kaufman, Gloria, and Mary Kay Blakely
  1980   *Pulling Our Own Strings.* Bloomington: Indiana University Press.

Kesselman, Amy, Lily McNair, and Nancy Schniedewind
  2003   *Women: Images and Realities: A Multicultural Anthology.* New York: McGraw-Hill.

Kotthof, Helga
  2000   Gender and joking: On the complexities of women's image politics in humorous narratives. *Journal of Pragmatics* 32, 55–80.

Lakof, Robin
  1975   *Language and Woman's Place.* New York et al.: Harper & Row.

Legman, Gershon
  1968   *Rationale of the Dirty Joke: An Analysis of Sexual Humor.* New York: Grove Press.
  1975   *No Laughing Matter: Rationale of the Dirty Joke.* New York: Breaking Point. Lundell, Torborg
  1993   An experiential exploration of why men and women laugh. Humor 6 (3), 299–317.

Martyna, Wendy
  1983   Beyond the he/man approach: The case for nonsexist language. In Thorne, Barrie, Cherise Kramerae, and Nancy Henley (eds.), *Language, Gender and Society.* Cambridge, MA: Newbury House.

Mitchell, Carol Ann
  1978   Hostility and aggression towards males in female joke telling. *Frontiers* 3 (3), 19–23.

Mulkay, Michael
  1988   *On Humor: Its Nature and Its Place in Modern Society.* Oxford and New York: Blackwell.

Nardini, Gloria
  2000   When husbands die: Joke telling in an Italian ladies' club in Chicago. *Pragmatics* 10 (1), 87–97.

Norrick, Neal
  2003   Issues in conversational joking. *Journal of Pragmatics* 35, 1333–1359.

Preston, Cathy Lynn
    1994   "Cinderella as a dirty joke: Gender, multivocality, and the polysemic text." *Western Folklore* 53, 27–49.

Raskin, Victor
    1985   *Semantic Mechanisms of Humor.* Dordrecht/Boston/Lancaster: D. Reidel.

Savanna, Susan (ed.)
    1991   *More Jokes for Women.* Cincinnati, OH: Shenandoah Press.

Stillman, Deanne, and Anne Beatts
    1976   *Titters: The First Collection of Humor by Women.* New York/London: Macmillan/Collier Macmillan.

St. John, Warren
    2005   Seriously, the joke is dead. *New York Times,* Sunday, May 22, Section 9, 11–12.

Steinem, Gloria
    1983   If men could menstruate. In *Outrageous Acts and Everyday Rebellions.* New York: Henry Holt, 337–340.

Stewart, Edward C., and Milton J. Bennett
    1991   *American Cultural Patterns.* Yarmouth, ME: Intercultural Press.

Stone, Judith
    1990   If Santa were a woman. *Self,* 82.

Wilson, Christopher P.
    1979   *Jokes: Form, Content, Use and Function.* London: Academic Press.

Walle, Alf H.
    1976   Getting picked up without being put down: jokes and the bar rush. *Journal of the Folklore Institute* 13, 201–217.

West, Candace, and Don Zimmerman.
    1987   Doing gender. *Gender and Society* I, 125–151.

Image Credits

Stephen Colbert, Source: http://commons.wikimedia.org/wiki/File:Stephen_Colbert_4_by_David_Shankbone.jpg. Copyright © 2007 by David Shankbone. Cleared via Creative Commons Attribution-Share Alike 3.0 Unported license.

Security Checking, Source: http://commons.wikimedia.org/wiki/File:Chinglish.jpg. Cleared via Creative Commons Attribution-Share Alike 3.0 Unported license.

Caution Sign, Source: http://commons.wikimedia.org/wiki/File:CautionSign.jpg. Cleared via Creative Commons Attribution-Share Alike 3.0 Unported license.

Mechanic Sign, Source: http://commons.wikimedia.org/wiki/File:AuTech1HoustonTX.JPG. Copyright in the Public Domain.

Mark Twain, Copyright in the Public Domain.

Jerry Seinfeld, Source: http://www.flickr.com/photos/42274165@N00/210977776. Copyright © 1997 by Alan Light. Cleared via Creative Commons Attribution 2.0 Generic license.

Jason Alexander, Source: http://www.lasvegasvegas.com/viewer/v/2009+WSOP/Jason+Alexander+plays+Annie+Duke_s+charity+event+at+the+2009+WSOP.jpg.html. Photo by flipchip / LasVegasVegas.com. Cleared via Creative Commons Attribution-Share Alike 3.0 Unported license.

Julia Louis-Dreyfus, Source: http://www.flickr.com/photos/alan-light/251547225/. Copyright © 1994 by Alan Light. Cleared via Creative Commons Attribution 2.0 Generic license.

Michael Richards, Source: http://www.flickr.com/photos/alan-light/211287685/. Copyright © 1993 by Alan Light. Cleared via Creative Commons Attribution 2.0 Generic license.

Jim Parsons, Source: http://commons.wikimedia.org/wiki/File:Jim_Parsons.png. Cleared via Creative Commons Attribution-Share Alike 3.0 Unported license.

Larry David, Source: http://commons.wikimedia.org/wiki/File:Larry_David_at_the_2009_Tribeca_Film_Festival_2.jpg. Copyright © 2009 by David Shankbone. Cleared via Creative Commons Attribution 3.0 Unported license.

Big Minstrel Jubilee, Copyright in the Public Domain.

Richard & Pringle's, Copyright in the Public Domain.

Evolution, Source: http://www.flickr.com/photos/58462991@N00/149334529/. Cleared via Creative Commons Attribution 2.0 Generic license.

Tyra Banks, Source: http://commons.wikimedia.org/wiki/File:Tyra_Banks_2012_Shankbone.JPG. Copyright © 2012 by David Shankbone. Cleared via Creative Commons Attribution 3.0 Unported license.

"I'm Laughing at You," Source: http://commons.wikimedia.org/wiki/File:MyLOLcat.png. Cleared via Creative Commons Attribution-Share Alike 3.0 Unported license.

Text Credits

Joseph Polimeni and Jeffrey Reiss, "The First Joke: Exploring the Evolutionary Origins of Humor," Evolutionary Psychology, vol. 4, pp. 347-366. Copyright © 2006 by Evolutionary Psychology. Reprinted with permission.

Mark Davidheiser, "Special Affinities and Conflict Resolution: West African Social Institutions and Mediation," Beyond Intractability, ed. Guy Burgess and Heidi Burgess. Copyright © 2005 by The Beyond Intractability Project, The Conflict Information Consortium, University of Colorado. Reprinted with permission.

Elisabeth Allès, "Notes On Some Joking Relationships Between Hui and Han Villages in Henan," China Perspectives, vol. 49, trans. Michael Black, pp. 1-13. Copyright © 2003 by French Centre for Research on Contemporary China. Reprinted with permission.

P. J. O'Rourke, "The Innocents Abroad, Updated," Holidays in Hell, pp. 5-11. Copyright © 2000 by Grove / Atlantic Press. Reprinted with permission.

Dan Ben-Amos, "The 'Myth' of Jewish Humor," Western Folklore, vol. 32, no. 2, pp. 112-131. Copyright © 1973 by Western States Folklore Society. Reprinted with permission.

Mahadev L. Apte, "Humor in Religion," Humor and Laughter: An Anthropological Approach, pp. 151-176, 271-272. Copyright © 1985 by Mahadev Apte. Reprinted with permission.

Georges Tamer, "The Qur'an and Humor," Humor in der arabischen Kultur / Humor in Arabic Culture, pp. 3-28. Copyright © 2009 by Walter de Gruyter Inc. Reprinted with permission.

Janet Bing, "Liberated Jokes: Sexual Humor in All-female Groups," Humor: International Journal of Humor Research, vol. 20, no. 4, pp. 337-366. Copyright © 2007 by Walter de Gruyter Inc. Reprinted with permission.

CPSIA information can be obtained at www.ICGtesting.com
Printed in the USA
LVOW09s0052241115

463955LV00005B/69/P